2 EDITION

MARKETING research

Contemporary Approach

2 EDITION

MARKETING research

Contemporary Approach

DR. P. NARAYANA REDDY, Ph.D.
Prof. & Head, School of Management Studies, CBIT, Osmania University, Hyderabad

DR. G.V.R.K. ACHARYULU, Ph.D.
Faculty Member, School of Management Studies, University of Hyderabad, Hyderabad

EXCEL BOOKS

ISBN: 978-81-7446-957-1

First Edition: New Delhi, 2008
Second Edition: New Delhi, 2011

EXCEL BOOKS
A-45, Naraina, Phase I,
New Delhi - 110 028

INDIA SALES OFFICES
2/8, Ansari Road, Darya Ganj, New Delhi-110002
21/65, Anand Nagar, Vakola, Santacruz (East), Mumbai-400055
106/2, 2nd floor, Ramnivas, 6th 'C' Cross, Gandhinagar, Bangalore-560009
2-2-1167/2H, Near Railway Bridge, Tilaknagar, Nallakunta, Hyderabad-500044
S-3/21-23, Shastri Market, Near "B" Block Circle, Indira Nagar, Lucknow-226016

AFRICA SALES OFFICES
31 Field Street, Durban-4000, South Africa
71 Burg Street, Cape Town-8000, South Africa
211 Pietermaritz Street, Pietermaritzburg, South Africa
43 Biccard Street, Braamfontein, Johannesburg-2000, South Africa

Published by Anurag Jain for Excel Books, A-45, Naraina, Phase-I, New Delhi - 110 028
and printed by him at Excel Printers, C-205, Naraina, Phase-I, New Delhi - 110 028

BRIEF CONTENTS

DETAILED CONTENTS

PREFACE TO THE SECOND EDITION

Consumers in the changing marketing environment are giving marketing organizations a run for their objectives. This results in making sincere and serious efforts not only in understanding the new dimensions of marketing but to offer the best solution. Marketers who really face these challenges have to take them as opportunities rather than problems. The World Trade Organisation has helped in free movement of goods and services across the world. This has led to more dynamism in developing countries like India. In view of these challenges, the traditional marketing practices are completely obsolete and have forced the marketers to come out with altogether new solutions and practices. Here comes the role of marketing research.

Marketing research goes deeper and deeper into the marketing in understanding the consumers at micro level and sub-micro level in bringing out the marketing intelligence and latent information about the consumer and also at the macro level to assess the market trends. Now, the time has come to realize the importance of marketing research in the changed environment more vigorously and systematically. Recognizing this trend, we presented the first edition on marketing research. The response to it was extremely favorable. As authors, we are very happy to know that our efforts have given some fruits in the form of better understanding of the subject by the readers, particularly students and faculty across the country. The response encouraged us to venture to revise thoroughly and enlarge the contents of the previous edition better with latest developments by putting more efforts in refining this book.

Therefore, we have attempted to further enhance the utility of the book by widening its coverage and also with improved contents wherever necessary.

P. NARAYANA REDDY
G.V.R.K. ACHARYULU

PREFACE TO THE FIRST EDITION

Consumers in the post-liberalized environment are throwing a real challenge to the marketers to understand their requirements and offer them the best. Marketers who really face this challenge have to take these as opportunities rather than problems. The World Trade Organisation has helped in free movement of goods and services across the world. This has led to more dynamism in developing countries like India. The consumers are exposed to the national and international market environment. Besides, they are well aware and economically strong too. Similarly, the markets are also becoming very volatile. This new situation naturally leads them to expect the marketers to offer innovative goods and services and also to understand their requirements in a better way. Hitherto, traditional marketing practices followed by the marketers have become obsolete and forcing them to come out with new and innovative marketing practices. Here comes the role of marketing research. It is the marketing research which goes deeper and deeper into the market in understanding the consumers at micro level and sub-micro level in bringing out the latent information about the consumer and also at macro level to assess the market trends.

It is the marketing research which tries to understand the nature of the problems faced by the marketers and tries to find and offer the best alternative solution. In fact, it generates scientific information on all issues related to marketing. This, in turn, will become the basis for developing the right decision making system in the organizations. This facilitates the decision makers to make suitable decisions to remain ahead of the competitors in the market. In spite of the sincere efforts on the part of decision makers at the organization level in India, many companies are not able to see the success. This is just because they could not recognize the importance of marketing research. This shows that the marketing research is still in its initial stage in the Indian environment. However, the new breed of management executives in the country are becoming more and more professional in taking the scientific marketing research inferences in their decision making. This is certainly a good sign. Therefore, it is felt that there is a need to have a customized textbook on the subject of marketing research.

This book basically covers the entire scope of marketing research, in general, as per the needs of the management and commerce students of various universities across the country. The special features of this book are—extensive coverage of practical cases, model questionnaires, examples of data analysis, and practical case for analysis and interpretation. At the end, a glossary of related terms has been provided as a ready reckoner for the students.

P. NARAYANA REDDY
G.V.R.K. ACHARYULU

ACKNOWLEDGEMENTS

We are deeply indebted to the authors and researchers of various marketing research books and studies who have done enough work in this field in generating useful information which, in turn, helped us to write this small volume.

We express our sincere thanks to our respective heads of institutions for their support. We are very much thankful to our colleagues and students who helped us in various forms to come out with this revised text.

We sincerely thank our publisher, Excel Books, New Delhi, for encouraging us and bringing out this book in a record time.

We thank our family members for their help and encouragement. Finally, we appreciate the management and commerce students and various faculty members across the country who read this book and provided their feedback to make this book more refined in accordance with the latest changes and wider context in future.

ABOUT THE AUTHORS

Dr. P. Narayana Reddy is Professor and Head, School of Management Studies, CBIT, Hyderabad. He has received his Master's Degree in Commerce from S.V. University, Tirupati. He was awarded the PhD by S.K. University, Anantapur (AP). He has 25 years of teaching and research experience including nine years as lecturer and reader in the Dept. of Commerce, Goa University, from 1988 to 1996. He has published more than 45 research papers in various journals of repute and around 50 articles in other popular dailies. He has presented more than 25 papers in national and international conferences and seminars. He has also organized more than 15 workshops and seminars. He has authored 10 books including *Entrepreneurship: Text and Cases*, *Research Methodology and Statistical Tools*, etc. He is the Executive Editor of the *EB Journal of Management and Research*. He is on the Executive Board of Association of Indian Management Schools (AIMS). He conducts Personality Development Programmes regularly. He is also an advisor to half a dozen B-Schools. He has been the Member of the Board of Studies, Department of Business Management, Osmania University, Hyderabad.

Dr. G.V.R.K. Acharyulu is presently working as an Associate Professor at the School of Management Studies, University of Hyderabad. He has 10 years of teaching experience in management subjects and 10 years of industry experience. He did his MTech from REC-Warangal and MBA from Osmania University. He was awarded the PhD on Supply Chain Management by Osmania University, Hyderabad. He has published 10 research papers including two in international journals and presented several papers at various national and international seminars and conferences. He has also presented a research paper on Logistics and Supply Chain Management at the International Conference held in Brisbane, Australia, in 2004.

CHAPTER ONE

MEANING AND IMPORTANCE OF MARKETING RESEARCH

INTRODUCTION

It is the human instinct that endeavors to imagine the future from the present situation and find some relationship between present and the future. In other words, research is finding the way into the future. In this process, human beings try to find passage into the future. The Advanced Learner's Dictionary of Current English lays down the meaning of research as "a careful investigation or inquiry especially through search for new facts in any branch of knowledge." It is a systematized effort to gain knowledge. In other words, research refers to a critical and exhaustive investigation or experimentation having it as aim of revision of accepted conclusions in the light of newly discovered facts. Research may, in effect, turn to build up of new theories to take place of those no longer suitable to the data of the empirical world. In other words, research is a systematic endeavor to see beyond our level of knowledge, the truth and reality that are difficult to perceive. The Encyclopedia of Social Science defined research as "the manipulation of things, concepts or symbols for the purpose of generalizing to extend, correct or verify knowledge, whether that knowledge aids in construction of theory or in the practice of an art."

OBJECTIVES OF RESEARCH

The purpose of research is to discover new solutions to the problems through the application of scientific procedures. The objectives of any research are broadly studied under two headings, they are:

1. ***Academic in nature:*** By manipulating the things, a researcher tries to find new propositions or new concepts that result in generalizations and discovery of truth and intimate knowledge which by recording and reporting supplies or adds knowledge to the academicians.

2. ***Utilitarian:*** A research tries to render the society by offering solutions to the problems it faced. These solutions are normally based on the principles or theories.

Specifically, the objectives of research are as follows:

1. ***To gain knowledge:*** Man always tries to gain knowledge over the environment in which he/she is living. It is the instinct of human beings to gain knowledge and control over the environment.

2. ***To innovate new concepts and theories:*** The objective of the research is to find new concepts and theories that explain the existing ones or add to the existing ones. In this process, the researcher endeavours to establish new insights that lead to new theories.

3. ***To understand, analyze and explore the phenomena:*** The exploration to facilitate the new dimensions of the existing and emerging problems. Research facilitates the environment to familiarize the human beings that lead to comfortable life.

4. *To know the cause-effect relationship:* A research tries to establish what cause is and what are effect and its relationships. This type of effort leads to satisfaction for the mankind.
5. *For the improvement and benefit of society:* A research always aims to facilitate the society in order to enjoy the benefits of its observations and findings. Knowing more and more things which are generally unknown will lead to purposeful efforts.

❖ Classification of Research

Research can be classified into two major categories: (i) basic research, and (ii) applied research. Basic research is sometimes called fundamental research, theoretical research or pure research. It aims at expanding the frontiers of knowledge and does not directly involve pragmatic problems. The essence of basic research is that it addresses itself to more fundamental questions and not to the problems with immediate commercial potential.

Applied research, which is also called decisional research, on the other hand, proceeds with a certain problem, and it specifies alternate solutions and the possible outcomes of each alternative. Unlike basic research, it is prompted by commercial considerations. Applied research can be divided into two categories: (i) problem-solving research, and (ii) problem-oriented research. Problem-solving research, as the name implies, is concerned with a particular issue or a problem, and is usually proprietary in character, that is, such a research is undertaken within a firm or by an outside consultant on its behalf. Problem-oriented research is concerned with a class of issues or problems in which several firms may be interested.

This type of research is usually concerned with conceptual aspects, but is oriented towards applied problems. Marketing research does not qualify as basic research, as it does not address itself to basic or fundamental questions. On the contrary, it tackles, problems which seem to have immediate commercial potential.

BUSINESS RESEARCH

Business research is a systematic inquiry that provides information to guide managerial decisions. In other words, it is a process of planning, acquiring, analyzing, and disseminating relevant data, information, and insights to decision-makers in ways that mobilize the organization to take appropriate actions, that results in maximized business performance. A variety of different types of research projects are grouped under the label "business research".

In the recent past, so much attention has been placed on measuring and enhancing Return on Investment (ROI). At its most simplistic, when we measure ROI, we calculate the financial return for all expenditures. Increasingly, organizational managers want to know what strategies and tactics capture the highest return. In the last few years, as technology has improved our measurement and tracking capabilities, managers have realized that they need a better understanding of employee, stockholder, and customer behavior in order to influence the desired metrics. Business research plays an important role in this new measurement environment in choosing better strategies and tactics.

❖ Importance of Business Research

Several factors stimulate people to conduct an inquiry of a management dilemma, the problem or opportunity that requires a management decision.

1. ***Increased role of information technology:*** The explosive growth of company's websites, e-commerce, and electronic publications brings extensive amounts of new information but its quality and its credibility are suspicious.

2. ***Active role of stakeholders:*** Customers, workers, shareholders, and the general public demand to be included in company decision-making; armed with extensive information, they are more sensitive to their own self-interests than ever before and more resistant to an organization's stimuli.

3. ***Cut throat competition:*** Competition, both global and domestic, is growing and often coming from unexpected sources; many organizations refocus on primary competencies, while they seek to improve operations by reducing costs and converting customers to advocates.

4. ***Increased government's intervention:*** Government continues to show concern with all aspects of society, becoming increasingly aggressive in protecting its various policies by posing restrictions on the use of managerial and business research tools.

5. ***More complex decisions:*** Managers have more variables to consider in every decision, increasing the manager's need for more and better information and for greater insights from that information.

6. ***Development of management as a group of discipline:*** The quality of theories and models to explain tactical and strategic results in human resources, marketing, operations, and finance is improving and equipping managers with more knowledge and is developing as a discipline.

7. ***Greater computing power and speed:***

   (i) *Lower-cost data collection:* Computers and telecommunications lowered the costs of data collection, drastically changing knowledge about consumers at both store and household levels; employees at the position, team, and department levels; suppliers and distributors at the transaction, division, and company levels; and machines at the part, process, and production-run levels.

   (ii) *Better visualization tools:* High speed downloads of images allow researchers to help people visualize complex concepts, which enriches measurement capabilities.

   (iii) *Powerful computations:* Sophisticated techniques of quantitative analysis are emerging to take advantage of increasingly powerful computing capabilities.

   (iv) *More integration of data:* Computer advances permit businesses to create and manage a data warehouse, an electronic storehouse where vast arrays of collected, integrated data are ready for mining.

   (v) *High speed access to information:* The power and ease of use of today's computers offer us the capability to analyze more data more quickly to deal with complex managerial problems. Yet the quantity of collected raw data overwhelms users, necessitating a means to manage it. Early efforts to provide a flow of information to managers used a Management Information System (MIS). As time passed, the challenge of database management from an MIS perspective included removing obstacles like resistance to use, reluctance of managers to disclose fully their information needs and decision criteria, costs of single-user report generation, system design time, slow adaptation to changing organization structures, and decision relevance (standard versus tailored reports).

   (vi) *Advanced analytical tools for enhanced insights:* Organizations increasingly practice data mining, applying mathematical models to extract meaningful knowledge from volumes of data contained within internal databases. Enormous quantities of research data are reduced to relatively straightforward equations with statistical models. Expert systems, an outgrowth of artificial intelligence and data mining entered the 21st century as important tools for research.

(vii) *Customized reporting:* While routine MIS reports are useful for well-structured problems and those amenable to a standardized set of procedures, data must be more than timely and standardized; reporting must be customized to be truly meaningful to the user.

8. ***New perspectives on established research methodologies:*** Older tools and methodologies once limited to exploratory research are gaining wider acceptance in dealing with a broader range of managerial problems.

   To do well in such an environment, you need to understand how to identify quality information and to recognize the solid, reliable business research on which your high-risk decisions as a manager can be based. You also need to know how to conduct such research. Developing these skills requires understanding the scientific method as it applies to the decision-making environment. This book addresses your needs as information collector, processor, evaluator, and user.

WHAT IS GOOD RESEARCH?

Good research generates dependable data that are derived by professionally conducted practices and that can be used reliably for decision-making. In contrast, poor research is carelessly planned and conducted, resulting in data that a manager can't use to reduce his or her decision-making risks. Good research follows the standards of the scientific method; systematic, empirically based procedures for generating replicable research.

Several defining characteristics of the Business Research and the managerial dimensions of each are listed and discussed below:

1. ***Purpose clearly defined:*** The purpose of the business research, the problem involved or the decision to be made, should be clearly defined and sharply delineated in terms as unambiguous as possible. Getting this in writing is valuable even in instances where the same person serves as researcher and decision-maker. The statement of the decision problem should include its scope, its limitations, and the precise meanings of all words and terms significant to the research. Failure of the researcher to do this adequately may raise legitimate doubts in the minds of research report readers as to whether the researcher has sufficient understanding of the problem to make a sound proposal attacking it. This characteristic is comparable to developing a strategic plan for achieving an objective before developing a tactical plan or an action map.
2. ***Research process detailed:*** The research procedures used should be described in sufficient detail to permit another researcher to repeat the research. Except when secrecy is imposed, research reports should reveal with candor the sources of data and the means by which they were obtained. Omission of significant procedural details makes it difficult or impossible to estimate the validity and reliability of the data and justifiably weakens the confidence of the reader in the research itself as well as any recommendations based on the research. This characteristic is comparable to developing a tactical plan.
3. ***Research design thoroughly planned:*** The procedural design of the research should be carefully planned to yield results that are as objective as possible. When a sampling of the population is involved, the report should include evidence concerning the degree of representativeness of the sample. A survey of opinions or recollections ought not to be used when more reliable evidence is

available from documentary sources or by direct observation. Bibliographic searches should be as thorough and complete as possible. Experiments should have satisfactory controls. Direct observations should be recorded in writing as soon as possible after the event. Efforts should be made to minimize the influence of personal bias in selecting and recording data. This characteristic is comparable to developing detailed action plans for each tactic.

4. ***High ethical standards applied:*** Researchers often work independently and have significant latitude in designing and executing research projects. A research design that includes safeguards against causing mental or physical harm to participants and makes data integrity a first priority should be highly valued. Ethical issues in research reflect important moral concerns about the practice of responsible behavior in society. Researchers frequently find themselves precariously balancing the rights of their subjects against the scientific dictates of their chosen method. When this occurs, they have a responsibility to guard the welfare of the participants in the studies and also the organizations to which they belong, their clients, their colleagues, and themselves. Careful consideration must be given to those research situations in which there is a possibility of physical or psychological harm, exploitation, invasion of privacy, and/or loss of dignity. The research need must be weighed against the potential for adverse effects. Typically, you can redesign a study, but sometimes you cannot. The researcher should be prepared on this dilemma.

5. ***Limitations frankly revealed:*** The researcher should report, with complete frankness, flaws in procedural design and estimate their effect on the findings. There are very few perfect research designs. Some of the imperfections may have little effect on the validity and reliability of the data; others may invalidate them entirely. A competent researcher should be sensitive to the effects of imperfect design. The researcher's experience in analyzing data should provide a basis for estimating the influence of design flaws. As a decision-maker, you should question the value of research where no limitations are reported.

6. ***Analysis adequate for decision-maker's needs:*** Analysis of the data should be extensive enough to reveal its significance, what managers call "insights." The methods of analysis used should be appropriate. The extent to which this criterion is met is frequently a good measure of the competence of the researcher. Adequate analysis of the data is the most difficult phase of research for the novice. The validity and reliability of data should be checked carefully. The data should be classified in ways that assist the researcher in reaching pertinent conclusions and clearly reveal the findings that have led to those conclusions. When statistical methods are used, the probability of error should be estimated and the criteria of statistical significance applied.

7. ***Findings presented unambiguously:*** Some evidence of the competence and integrity of the researcher may be found in the report itself. For example, language that is restrained, clear, and precise; assertions that are carefully drawn and hedged with appropriate reservations; and an apparent effort to achieve maximum objectivity tend to leave a favorable impression of the researcher with the decision-maker. Generalizations that outrun the evidence on which they are based, exaggerations, and unnecessary verbiage tend to leave an unfavorable impression. Such reports are not valuable to managers wading through the minefields of organizational decision-making. Presentation of data should be comprehensive, easily understood by the decision-maker, and organized so that the decision-maker can readily locate critical findings.

8. ***Conclusions justified:*** Conclusions should be limited to those for which the data provide an adequate basis. Researchers are often tempted to broaden the basis of induction by including personal experiences and their interpretations-data not subject to the controls under which the research data were gathered. Equally undesirable is the all-too-frequent practice of drawing conclusions

from a study of a limited population and applying them universally. Researchers also may be tempted to rely too heavily on data collected in a prior study and use it in the interpretation of a new study. Such practice sometimes occurs among research specialists who confine their work to clients in a small industry. These actions tend to decrease the objectivity of the research and weaken readers' confidence in the findings. Good researchers always specify the conditions under which their conclusions seem to be valid.

9. ***Researcher's experience reflected:*** Greater confidence in the research is warranted if the researcher is experienced, has a good reputation in research, and is a person of integrity. Where it possible for the reader of a research report to obtain sufficient information about the researcher, this criterion perhaps would be one of the best bases for judging the degree of confidence, a piece of research warrants and the value of any decision based upon it. For this reason, the research report should contain information about the qualifications of the researcher.

Good business research has an inherent value only to the extent that it helps management make better decisions that help achieve organizational goals. Interesting information about consumers, employees, competitors, or the environment might be pleasant to have, but its value is limited if the information cannot be applied to a critical decision. If a study does not help management select, more effective, more efficient, less risky, or more profitable alternatives than otherwise would be the case, its use should be questioned. Alternatively, management may have insufficient resources (time, money, or skill) to conduct an appropriate study or may face a low level of risk associated with the decision at hand. In these situations, it is valid to avoid business research and its associated costs in time and money. Business research finds its justification in the contribution it makes to the decision-maker's task and to the bottom line.

MARKETING RESEARCH

The market is changing so rapidly that many products and services that successfully met consumer tastes and needs a few years ago are obsolete today. Proactive marketers must constantly monitor environmental change particularly customer buying habits and motives, and provide the force necessary to organize resources in the right direction. The modern day consumers are different and dynamic. Their preferences and expectations from the market are ever changing. The traditional marketing practices are no longer useful now. Not only the consumer has changed but the market is flooded with variety of goods and services, competition is intense, everyday new products are being introduced. In this changed marketing environment, no traditional marketing practices will work. That is why; every market is keen on understanding the consumer through various modern market research techniques.

❖ Definition of Marketing Research

Marketing research is the systematic, objective and exhaustive search for and the study of facts relevant to any problem in the field of marketing.

According to Majundar, marketing research is defined as *"the objective and formal process of systematically obtaining, analyzing and interpreting data for actionable decision-making in marketing".*

According to Wentz, *"marketing research is the gathering and analysis of information to assist management in making marketing decisions. These decisions involve the manipulation of the firm's pricing, production, distribution and product variables".*

Naresh Malhotra defined marketing research as *"the systematic and objective identification, collection, analysis, dissemination, and use of information for the purpose of assisting management in decision-making related to the identification and solution of problems (and opportunities) in marketing"*.

According to Parasuraman *et. al.*, *"marketing research is a set of techniques and principles for systematically collecting, recording, analyzing, and interpreting data that can aid decision-makers involved in marketing goods, services, or ideas"*.

Green and Tull defined marketing research as "*the systematic and objective search for an analysis of information relevant to the identification and solution of any problem in the field of marketing*".

According to Philip Kotler, marketing research is "*the systematic design, collection, analysis and reporting of data, and finding a solution relevant to specific marketing situation facing the company*".

According to American Marketing Association, "*marketing research is the systematic gathering, recording and analysis of data about problems relating to the marketing of goods and services. Marketing research is the function that links the consumer, customer and public to the marketer through information – information used to identify and define marketing opportunities and problems; generate, refine and evaluate marketing actions; monitor marketing performance; and improve understanding of marketing as a process*".

Marketing research is a systematic and objective study of problems pertaining to the marketing of goods and services. *Systematic* refers to the requirement that the research project should be well organized and planned: the research design must be detailed in advance, and the nature of the data to be gathered and the mode of analysis to be employed must be anticipated. *Objective* implies that marketing research strives to be unbiased and unemotional in performing its responsibilities. Marketing research has to be objective in providing meaningful information for decision-making. It is not restricted to any particular area of marketing, but is applicable to all its phases and aspects. Further, marketing research is the function which links the consumer, customer, and public to the marketer through information, that is, the information used to identify and define marketing opportunities and problems; generate, refine and evaluate marketing actions; monitor marketing performance; and improve understanding of market as a process. Marketing research specifies the information required to address these issues; designs the method for collecting information; manages and implements the data collection process; analyses the results; communicates the findings and their implications.

The above definitions of marketing research clearly suggest the following:

1. Marketing research, while it generates information to address the issues related to marketing follows scientific and acceptable procedures.
2. The marketing research that is conducted will address the problems and opportunities related to the marketing field with a clear objective. This clearly indicates that it will serve its purpose impartially.
3. Marketing research passes through various stages from the identification of the problem to the stage of solving the same.
4. Marketing research provides the researched observations to decision-makers so as to enable them to take right decisions.
5. Marketing research generate, refine and evaluate marketing actions.
6. Marketing research integrates all the actors involved in the marketing through information i.e., consumers, intermediaries, society and decision-makers.
7. Marketing research helps to understand marketing as a process.

❖ Role of Marketing Research

The role of marketing research is to help managers to better understand the environment in which they operate in order to improve the quality of the strategic marketing decisions they make. An increasing number of firms routinely use marketing research to generate relevant information for developing effective strategies, particularly in the early stages of strategy formulation. This is driven by the fact that increasing numbers of firms are embracing the marketing concept-the philosophy of customer orientation urging firms to uncover customer needs first and then coordinate all their activities to satisfy those needs. As an essential link between marketing decision-makers and the markets in which they operate, marketing research can and should play an important role in all three stages of planning and decision-making viz., identifying marketing opportunities and constraints, developing and implementing marketing strategies, and evaluating the effectiveness of marketing plans.

Concisely defined, "marketing research is a set of techniques and principles for systematically collecting, recording, analyzing, and interpreting data that can aid decision-makers involved in marketing goods, services, or ideas".

Basic Marketing Research Principles

Three principles serve as the foundation for useful marketing research. These principles serve as guide lines for generating information useful to managers. These principles are simple and perhaps even intuitive. Nevertheless, they are crucial to the proper and successful application of marketing research.

1. ***Attend to the timeliness and relevance of research:*** Marketing research can lead to erroneous decisions if not done on time. Thus, the timeliness and relevance of the data generated from the studies are questionable.
2. ***Define research objectives carefully and clearly:*** Careful and clear definition of research objectives is a key requirement for accurate and beneficial marketing research outcome.
3. ***Conduct research to support future decisions:*** Conducting marketing research when potential users have already made up their minds is not a productive use of scarce resources. Apparently management undertook the research merely to see whether the results would support a decision that had already been made.

The principles are as crucial to the effectiveness of marketing research as are quantitative tools and techniques. Finally, marketing research by itself cannot be expected to provide sound marketing decisions. It can, however, serve as a resource for decision-makers. It can take the form of basic research, which creates new knowledge, or applied research, which solves a specific problem.

❖ Nature of Marketing Research

1. ***Marketing research is an input to decision-making:*** Marketing research supplies the gathered data by converting it into information to the decision-makers as input. Decision-makers always need sufficient information as input to take the right decisions. It is the marketing research which facilitates the decision-makers with full information.
2. ***Marketing research is a continuous process:*** Marketing research is a part of marketing information system. Marketing information system is a continuous process where it generates and disseminates required information to the needed place in the organization. As a part of marketing information system, marketing research generates special and specific information from the field on a continuous basis.

3. ***Marketing research is interdisciplinary in nature:*** Marketing research is emerging as an independent discipline. It does not have its own fundamentals independent of other disciplines. It is using social sciences in drawing research methods and research methodology on one side and on the other side, it uses mathematical and statistical tools and integrates these things with management principles. In other words, marketing research draws data from economics, sociology, psychology, physics, chemistry, etc. to conduct research activities. That is why it is an emerging field.

4. ***Marketing research is descriptive:*** Marketing research tries to describe the situation, the background of any marketing problem. It helps the organization to understand fundamentally the underlying marketing problems.

5. ***Marketing research is exploratory:*** Marketing research explores the possibilities of various decision-making options to confirm or rule out the existing or proposed proposition.

6. ***Marketing research is evaluatory:*** Marketing research tries to compare various marketing strategies for the purpose of selecting the best option.

7. ***Marketing research is predictive:*** Marketing research prepares the organization for the future both in terms of risks and opportunities. Market research forecasts the future demand and market trends.

8. ***Marketing research gives meaning to data:*** Marketing research not only gathers the data but also gives the meaning to the data. In other words, marketing research tries to convert the raw data that is collected from different sources through various research instruments into information.

9. ***Marketing research is gathering information:*** The main job is to generate data from internal as well as external sources. Without data and information, there is no research. Marketing research always tries to gather data from different sources. Again this depends upon the type of problems and situation that is arising in the marketing field at any given point of time.

10. ***Marketing research is a team work:*** Marketing research is performed by a team of executives carrying out different functional activities. An integrated effort is needed from all the marketing research staff doing different jobs.

11. ***Marketing research is a profession:*** A profession refers to any occupation by which a person earns his livelihood. A profession is an occupation for which specialized skills and training are required and the use of these skills is not meant for self satisfaction, but these are used for the larger interests of the society. In marketing research, knowledge of various techniques of gathering, analyzing and interpreting of data is necessary; an individual can acquire this knowledge for entry into this profession; marketing research representative bodies exist; researchers have to adhere to certain code of conduct or ethics and for performing marketing research studies, the researcher gets reasonable remuneration or compensation.

❖ Objectives of Marketing Research

Marketing of a product implies anticipation of demand. No decision-maker can say that his/her forecast will be accurate or exact. Therefore, the main aims and obectives of marketing research are generally directed towards understanding this phenomenon.

1. To define the potential market for a particular product and to determine general marketing conditions and product distribution techniques.
2. To estimate the potential buying power of the consumers.
3. To assess the competitive strength of the product and consequences of planned marketing policies.

4. To recommend the most suitable distribution methods for the product and the market.
5. To estimate future sales of the product.
6. To know customers acceptance.
7. Evolve methods of collecting relevant and reliable information.
8. Specification of the relationship between various marketing factors, e.g., advertisement and sales relationship.
9. To post-mortem what had already taken place.
10. Provide solutions to marketing problems.
11. Risk reduction and discovery of opportunities.
12. It facilitates to reduce the marketing cost at every stage in the marketing process.
13. It helps the organizations to design suitable marketing strategies.

❖ Importance of Marketing Research

1. *Gap Filling:* The present day marketing environment clearly indicates the increased distance between the producers and the ultimate consumers. Due to increased distance between the producers and consumers, the producers fail to get the right information with the existing source of information. The marketing research fills the gap and provides right information to the producers and also to the consumers.

2. *Effective Competition Tool:* Modern marketing is consumer driven. Without considering the competitors, there is no scope to survive in the market. It is the marketing research that tries to understand the nature of competition and provide information to the organisation to develop suitable strategies to meet the competitors and survive. Marketing research is vital to maintain and improve company's overall competitiveness. Many organizations continually collect and evaluate environmental information to identify future market opportunities and threats.

3. *Strategic Information Tool:* Marketing research can helping answering the basic questions the marketers face. An increasing number of firms routinely use marketing research to generate relevant information for developing effective strategies.

4. *Decision-making Tool:* By emphasizing the need to gain a good understanding of customers, the marketing concept also stresses the importance of conducting marketing research in the early stages. Many firms have had major new product failures because they neglected to research market opportunities and constraints before deciding to introduce the products.

5. *Updating the Organisation:* In the changed environment, it is the marketing research that tries to understand the changes that are coming up in the marketing and helps the organization to bring the necessary changes in the organization to come up to the expectations of the changed environment.

6. *Marketing Orientation:* Marketing research tries to understand the market and the consumer thoroughly. The information generated by the research will act as panacea to the organization to bring market oriented approach at organization level.

7. *Impact Assessment Tool:* Impact of new developments in the science and technology field will be assessed by the marketing research and it will facilitate the decision-makers to take suitable steps keeping the impact of it in mind.

8. ***Marketing Mix:*** Good marketing research will identify whether or not the marketing mix is effective enough to maximize the benefits to the firm (in terms of sales, profits, customer satisfaction and value) from available opportunities.
9. ***Marketing Strategies:*** To benefit fully from the opportunities uncovered in the market place a firm must develop an effective marketing strategy with effective marketing mix. Extensive marketing research helps in developing suitable elements of marketing mix strategies.
10. ***Control Technique:*** Marketing research facilitates the organizations to generate feedback of information from the market place to plan the activities and suggest corrective action to control the same.

❖ Marketing Research and the Economy

1. ***Production:*** Marketing research evaluates the market and identifies the goods and services that have demand in the market. This information will facilitate the producers to produce required goods and services. This information also helps the producers to prepare and arrange the required inputs like investment, raw materials and other resources to meet the production requirement. In other words, marketing research helps the producers to plan production systematically.
2. ***Distribution:*** The marketing research not only identifies the required goods and services, but also facilitates producers to place the product at a convenient places so that the consumers will get the goods and services as and when and wherever they want to buy. In other words, systematic distribution system will be facilitated with the help of marketing research.
3. ***Employment:*** The impact of systematic production and distribution naturally generates employment opportunities to the people.
4. ***National income:*** Marketing research indirectly facilitates the economy by increased income through increased production and uniform distribution system and thus, more employment opportunities.
5. ***Reduce Recession:*** Marketing research estimates the demand for goods and services in the market accurately. This assessment will arrest production of unnecessary products and also production beyond demand. In other words, marketing research facilitates the economy by stopping production of goods and services beyond the amount required. Production more than the demand will naturally lead to recession.
6. ***Avoid Crisis:*** The other side of the problem is shortage. Without marketing research, producers may not have right information about the markets and its requirements. Producer may adopt pessimistic approach that will lead to shortage of goods and services in the economy. This situation leads to crisis. So it is the marketing research which will try to avoid the crisis situation in the economy.

❖ Functions of Marketing Research

Marketing research is a valuable tool to assist the marketing managers or take marketing decisions. While doing so, it performs the following major functions:

1. ***Marketing research is descriptive:*** Marketing research describes the situation, the background of any marketing problem. It helps us to understand in a preliminary manner, the underlying marketing problems.

2. ***Marketing research is exploratory:*** It explores the various decision alternatives, and examines them either to confirm/rule out them.
3. ***Marketing research is evaluatory:*** Marketing research compares two or more marketing strategies, for the selection of the best amongst them.
4. ***Marketing research is predictive:*** Marketing research prepares us for the future both in terms of risks and opportunities. Marketing research forecasts the future demand and market trends.
5. ***Marketing research is an essential input:*** Marketing research facilitates cost effectiveness in taking decisions.

Marketing research makes the total gamut of marketing activity more effective, it results into a right product mix with fair pricing, good distribution and effective promotion. In conclusion, the functions of marketing research are essentially what marketing research is capable of doing for modern business.

❖ Scope of Marketing Research

The scope of marketing research is nothing but the scope of the marketing itself. Wherever there is a problem in the scope of marketing, the role of marketing research originates. That means the marketing research will follow the marketing activities as a shade. Marketing research can be used in answering nearly every marketing related question. It can serve a diagnostic as well as a prognostic function in problem solving. Virtually all organizations carry out some marketing activity, regardless of whether or not it is formally termed marketing research. It means, the operation of marketing research activities starts before the installation of an enterprise and continues till it operates. Marketing research has wide scope and covers all aspects of marketing.

1. ***Consumer research:*** The research will help the decisions makers to have a better understanding of the consumers so as to enable to take suitable decisions. This encompasses knowledge of the demographic characteristics of the existing and potential consumers, to identify the consumers needs and product expectations, identify the factors influencing purchase intentions and ascertaining the levels of consumer satisfaction.
2. ***Market measurement:*** Assess market potential, market segmentation strategies, estimation of demand for a product, market share estimation.
3. ***Market research:*** Market research is related to markets and activities within the market. This research is to know about, size of the present market, potential market, assessing the market trends, ascertain the strength and weaknesses of competitors, study seasonal variation of a product, estimate size of the market, need analysis to find out where the product fits in the market.
4. ***Product research:*** One of the major areas of marketing research is to manage the current products and new products. In product management, marketing research is helpful in evaluating the performance of company's products in terms of sales, profits, market segments and market-testing of new products.
5. ***Price research:*** The research related to pricing is concerned with developing suitable pricing methods and policies. In fact establishing of price policies are complicated problems which require a thorough probing of various factors. The areas of price research includes:

   (i) Determining the price expectations of consumers in the different market segments,

   (ii) Comparing the price strategies of the competitors,

   (iii) Testing the alternative price strategies,

(iv) Evaluating the consumer reactions and responses to the company prices, and

(v) Competitor's reaction to companies' pricing strategies.

6. ***Promotion research:*** Promotional research is concerned with advertising, publicity, special sales promotional programmes and also personal selling.

7. ***Advertising Research:*** Advertising is an important arena where active research is required to be carried out extensively. The main purpose of research in this area is related to decide what type of advertising is suitable, what type of messages are to be included, inserted in the advertising, to evaluate the effectiveness of the advertising, identify the suitability of advertising layout and copy, etc.

8. ***Distribution research:*** Distribution research is concerned with the distribution aspects of marketing covering the distribution channel and physical holding and movement of finished products. It tries to find out best distributional channels, identify factors which influence the selected channels, distributional patterns, role of intermediaries, etc. *Physical distribution research*: Tries to find out what types of transportation system and mode of transport system, warehousing suitability, and inventory practices are suitable to the product, the company is set to distribute in the market.

9. ***Sales research:*** Sales research attempts to answer questions relating to the sales of company's products. The purpose is to find out the sales potential and appraise sales performance of company's products. The broad areas of sales research include: Determining and appraising sales methods, sales territories, sales performance, performance of sales personnel, Determining sales quotas and other standards of performance for different market segments and sales personnel; and Determining the mode of compensating sales personnel.

10. ***Competition research:*** The scope of marketing research is to understand the competitors and their product strategy, distribution strategy, promotional strategy, price strategies and price and non-price competition strategies. It also reveals the competitive position of the company as well as competitors activities. It is of paramount importance to measure the share of the market owned by a company's product by assessing its own strength and weaknesses. The company can also conduct an intensive study of competitors marketing practices and policies. The competitor's action and its impact on the company's marketing situation require a thorough probe to take appropriate decision by the companies.

11. ***Corporate research:*** Marketing Research is used to analyse corporate's effectiveness. Some examples are:

    (i) Assessing the image of the company.

    (ii) Knowledge of the company's activities.

12. ***Syndicated research:*** This is compiled by agencies on a regular basis and sold to organisations on subscription basis.

13. ***Customer satisfaction:*** The measurement of customer satisfaction and its link to product/service attributes is the vehicle for developing a market-driven quality approach. This approach requires a sequential research design that uses the results from each research phase to build and enhance the value of subsequent efforts. During this process, it is imperative to study lost customers, and determine why they left. This issue must be addressed early in the system design. The steps involved in customer satisfaction are:

    (i) Define goals and how information will be used.

    (ii) Discover what is really important to customers and employees.

(iii) Measure critical needs.

(iv) Act on the information.

(v) Measure performance over time.

(vi) Issues in questionnaire design and scaling in satisfaction research.

EMERGING APPLICATION OF MARKETING RESEARCH

❖ Database Marketing

A database is a customer list to which has been added information about the characteristics and the transactions of these customers. Businesses use it to cultivate customers – as they seek new customers.

Need of Database

A database provides the means for research to support decisions. It enables profiling of customers by searching for prospects who are similar to existing customers. It provides the means for implementation of profitable programs of repeat business and cross-selling. It assists in marketing, planning and forecasting. Further a database can:

1. Match products or services to customers' wants and needs.
2. Help to select new lists or use new media that fit the profile of existing customers.
3. Maximize personalization of all offers to each customer.
4. Provide for ongoing interaction with customers and prospects.
5. Pinpoint ideal timing and frequency for promotions.
6. Measure response and be accountable for results.
7. Help create the offers most likely to elicit responses from customers.
8. Help achieve a Unique Selling Proposition (USP), targeted to appeal to your customers.
9. Integrate direct-response communication with other forms of advertising.
10. Demonstrate that customers are valuable assets.

Types of Database

1. Active customers
2. Inactive customers
3. Inquiries

Benefits of Database Marketing

1. ***Customers are easier to retain than acquire:*** The first reason is that it takes five times the energy and budget to get new customer as it does to keep an existing one. Also, a disproportionately small number of your customers generate a very large proportion of your income.
2. ***Determine their "Lifetime Value":*** Building a lasting relationship becomes the obvious way to a prosperous and profitable future.

3. *Developing relationships with customers:* Understanding your customers' tastes and preferences on an individual basis is the foundation for relationship marketing. Relationship marketing combines elements of general advertising, sales promotion, public relations and direct marketing to create more and more effective ways of reaching consumers. It centers on developing a continuous relationship with consumers across a family of related products and services.

❖ Relationship Marketing

The relationship marketing process incorporates three key elements:

1. Identifying and building a database of current and potential consumers, which records and cross-references a wide range of demographics, lifestyle and purchase information.
2. Delivering differential messages to these people through established and new media channels based on the consumers' characteristics and preferences.
3. Tracking each relationship to monitor the cost of acquiring the consumer and the lifetime value of his or her purchases.

TYPES OF MARKETING RESEARCH

The various types of marketing research are basically in three forms:

1. *Basic research:* The sole purpose of basic research is to discover some new information to acquire knowledge for the sake of knowledge. It extends the boundaries of knowledge.
2. *Applied research:* It is the application of basic principles and other existing knowledge to the solution of operational problems e.g., to identify causes of declining sales or poor morale of sales people.
3. *Designated fact gathering research:* This research involves mere gathering of some predetermined data. Here the researcher can start from data collection stage. The type of research determines which activities are to be performed by the researcher. Marketing research can be classified in any of this research procedure depending upon the nature and purpose of the investigation.

The types of marketing research can be further classified into the following categories:

1. *Ad hoc research:* Ad hoc research is always conducted for some specific purpose. As and when the marketing manager faces a problem, he has to find the solution to over come the problem. So he immediately appoints a research cell or a committee to study the problem and offer a specific solution. Once, the committee finds a solution it looses its existence. This means, once the purpose of the research is over, the committee automatically ceases to exist.

2. *Continuous research:* In some organizations, particularly, large corporations there will be a separate research department which carries out research activities on behalf of the organization continuously. This type of research is called continuous research. In many organizations, they may not wait for the problems to surface. By the time the problem emerges, the research organization is able to anticipate the problems and offer solutions. In the globalised environment, continuous search is an essential prerequisite for the success of the organization. Continuous studies are made to decide about the market place and product performance.

3. *Exploratory research:* Exploratory research is often conducted because a problem has not been clearly defined as yet, or its real scope is as yet unclear. It allows the researcher to familiarize with

the problem or concept to be studied, and perhaps generate hypotheses to be tested. It is the initial research, before more conclusive research is undertaken. Exploratory research helps determine the best research design, data collection method and selection of subjects, and sometimes it even concludes that the problem does not exist. Another common reason for conducting exploratory research is to test concepts before they are put in the marketplace, always a very costly endeavor. In concept testing, consumers are provided either with a written concept or a prototype for a new, revised or repositioned product, service or strategy. Exploratory research can be quite informal, relying on secondary research such as reviewing available literature and/or data, or qualitative approaches such as informal discussions with consumers, employees, management or competitors, and more formal approaches through in-depth interviews, focus groups, projective methods, case studies or pilot studies. The results of exploratory research are not usually useful for decision-making by themselves, but they can provide significant insight into a given situation.

4. *Conclusive research:* Conclusive research is meant to provide information that is useful in reaching conclusions or decision-making. It tends to be quantitative in nature, that is to say in the form of numbers that can be quantified and summarized. It relies on both secondary data, particularly existing databases that are reanalyzed to shed light on a different problem than the original one for which they were constituted, and primary research, or data specifically gathered for the current study. The purpose of conclusive research is to provide a reliable or representative picture of the population through the use of a valid research instrument. In the case of formal research, it will also test hypothesis. Conclusive research can be sub-divided into two major categories: (i) Descriptive or statistical research, and (ii) Causal research.

   (i) *Descriptive research:* One part of the conclusive research is descriptive in nature. Majority of the issues that are to be studied by the research organizations are descriptive in nature. Under descriptive research, the issues are described rather than offering specific solution to the problem. This is more like exploration than solution for the problem. Descriptive research does not aim at directing solutions, instead, it addresses the more general issues than specific.

   (ii) *Causal research:* If the objective is to determine which variable might be causing certain behaviour, i.e. whether there is a cause and effect relationship between variables, causal research must be undertaken. In order to determine causality, it is important to hold the variable that is assumed to cause the change in the other variable(s) constant and then measure the changes in the other variable(s). This type of research is very complex and the researcher can never be completely certain that there are not other factors influencing the causal relationship, especially when dealing with people's attitudes and motivations. There are often much deeper psychological considerations that even the respondent may not be aware of. There are two research methods for exploring the cause and effect relationship between variables: (a) Experimentation and (b) Simulation.

5. *Observation Research:* Observation is a primary method of collecting data by human, mechanical, electrical or electronic means. The researcher may or may not have direct contact or communication with the people whose behaviour is being recorded. Observation techniques can be part of qualitative research as well as quantitative research techniques. There are six different ways of classifying observation methods:

   (i) Participant and non-participant observation,

   (ii) Obtrusive and unobtrusive (or physical trace) observation,

   (iii) Observation in natural or contrived settings,

(iv) Disguised and non-disguised observation,

(v) Structured and unstructured observation, and

(vi) Direct and indirect observation.

DIFFERENCE BETWEEN MARKET RESEARCH AND MARKETING RESEARCH

Generally market research and marketing research are confused to be the same. But there is a clear distinction between the both. The difference between market research and marketing research lies on at least two substantive grounds. In the first place, they differ in scope and measurement.

Market research is narrow in its scope and remains confined to a particular market itself and the consumers which constitute that particular market. Market research involves researching a specific industry or market. The market research is accurate for describing research into markets i.e., their size, composition, structure, geographical distribution, incomes, etc. For example, researching the automobile industry to discover the number of competitors and their market share. Market research concentrates on quantitative dimensions.

Marketing research is a broad and comprehensive term and is related to research on any problem in marketing area. Marketing research analyses a given marketing opportunity or problem, defines the research and data collection methods required to deal with the problem or take advantage of the opportunity, through to the implementation of the project. It is a more systematic method which aims to discover the root cause for a specific problem within an organisation and put forward solutions to that problem.

Marketing research emphasizes creativity; it concentrates on qualitative aspect as well. Market research is a haphazard attempt to collect and analyse the data, where as marketing research is a systematic process.

CHARACTERISTICS OF GOOD MARKETING RESEARCH

Research basically attempts to trace the cause for the situation and find better and innovative solutions to the problems faced by the decision-makers at marketing department level. A good marketing research indicates the following features.

1. *Use of scientific methods:* The marketing research tries to utilise scientific methods in its activities. As a result, the inferences of the research will be available for verification. Scientific research facilitates to apply the marketing research to collect, analyse, and interpret data. The scientific method is based on certain criteria. Freight has suggested five criteria for scientific activities: (a) Objectivity, (b) Reliability, (c) Definiteness and preciousness, (d) Coherence or systematic structure, (e) Comprehensiveness or scope of knowledge.

2. *Must offer solutions:* Marketing research must represent itself in an innovative way in identifying more solutions to the problems in hand. It must be able to offer better solutions and must also be able to prevent and minimize the problems. It must also offer predictable outcomes.

3. *Cost and benefits:* Marketing research must be able to provide better solutions at low cost. The cost benefit analysis of various types of marketing research will determine which type of research project should be used to conduct the research for the benefits of marketing management. The expected value of the research is evaluated in the context of the decision-making theory, and the

degree of market research is decided accordingly. The research must be able to maintain better balance between the value of information and cost involved in it. Finally, the company must be able to earn better offers with minimum effort.

4. *Applicability of models and data:* The marketing research must adapt various methods in drawing conclusions as well as advanced techniques to re-verify the earlier inferences if necessary. A good marketing research must be able to apply various quantitative and statistical models and tools to quantify the data to arrive at critical decisions which facilitate the companies.

5. *Offer better alternatives:* The marketing research must be able to find not just one course of action but multiple courses of action to solve the problems in the marketing area. The validity of better alternatives is evaluated before its application to marketing decisions. When the marketing manager chooses alternatives, he can rarely be certain of the consequences of each alternative. Good marketing research comes to his rescue and offers better alternatives.

6. *Better specialist services:* Depending up on the type of problems and the challenge, the marketing research must accomodate specialists in carrying out the activities to have unbiased results. Sound marketing research utilizes the services of specialists in the field of marketing. Marketing specialists are able to offer better selling techniques and also offer better suggestions to over come the problems with financial and other inputs to the organization.

MARKETING RESEARCH, MARKETING INFORMATION SYSTEM AND DECISION SUPPORT SYSTEM

1. Marketing research is the systematic and objective identification, collection, analysis, and dissemination of information for use in marketing decision-making. That means, marketing research tries to find solutions and or cause for the problem as and when there is a problem. In other words, marketing research is basically adhoc in nature.

2. Marketing Information System (MIS) on the other hand is a formalized set of procedures for generating analyzing, storing and distributing information generated through marketing research and sources such as internal records ad marketing intelligence to marketing decision-makers on an ongoing basis. This means MIS is a permanent activity in the organization. At the same time, there is little scope for manipulation.

3. Decision Support Systems (DSS) are information system that enable decision-makers to interact directly with both databases and analysis models. This comprises of hardware, communications network, data base, model base, software base and the decision-maker. The MIS is centralized in nature whereas the DSS is more decentralized. Thus, DSS facilitates to overcome the limitations of MIS.

❖ Opportunities in Marketing Research

As the focus of the marketing research slowly gets shifted from adhoc to a permanent activity in the business organizations, more and more career opportunities are created. Both within and out side the organizations. Career oppurtunities within the organizations are coming up as the external suppliers of information may not be more focused besides being costly. Outside the organizations, particularly more independent organisations are coming up to provide information to organizations resulting in innovative employment opportunities at different level. In the recent past, more and more international organizations have surfaced the global business scene and interesting career opportunities are coming up. This is certainly a new development. A very interesting development is demand for marketing methodologists. Basically, marketing methodologists are people who have a balanced and in-depth knowledge of the fields of statistics, psychometrics, marketing and buyer behaviour and apply that knowledge to describe and infer causal relationships from marketing data. These methodologists have to have specialized knowledge in one or other fields. These specialists may come from social sciences, engineering, political science anthropology, etc. This means, the course work may have interrelated subjects to enter into the feild of marketing methodologists. The existing unqualified and in experienced marketing researchers lead to more professional career opportunities in the modern days.

❖ Limitations of Marketing Research

1. Marketing research does not have abilities to tackle all the problems of marketing although its scope is similar to marketing.
2. Marketing research has not yet emerged as an exact science. For that matter, marketing itself is an inexact science. Therefore, what it offers may not really represent the problem to solve.
3. Marketing research is yet to integrate itself into the organization where the decision-maker treats marketing research as a regularly activity.
4. Marketing research comes into picture whenever the decision-makers find it difficult to take right decision, otherwise recognizing the marketing research is limited.
5. Staff carrying out the marketing research do not have enough training to do the research in more technical and complex situations.
6. There is no proper coordination and cooperation between the management of the organization and the management of the marketing research. This results in perceptual differences between them and leads to nowhere in solving the problems of the marketing.
7. In the fast changing marketing environment, the data collected through research will soon become historic in nature and the research findings may not be relevant.
8. Marketing research can only provide a base for predicting future events, it can't guarantee with certainty their shape or happening. Utmost it can reduce the uncertainty.

❖ Challenges to Marketing Research

Basically in any research, there are three important players involved. One is the organisation interested in research findings. Second, is the individual or a group, involved in conducting the research and finally, the public, who play as a respondent to the research. If any one of the players adopt unethical practices in their respective job, the research and its findings will automatically lead to wrong indications because the decision-making system is based on the research inferences. Therefore, it is a real challenge to the marketing research to maintain its identity and keep intact with its originality is the issue. This obviously leads to a basic question how ethical are the players in marketing research in doing their job.

MARKETING INFORMATION SYSTEM AND MARKETING RESEARCH

Information is defined as meaningful data, which is needed by the managers for taking correct and accurate decisions. Information is recorded experience that is useful for decision-making. In other words, it consists of that recorded experience which will reduce the level of uncertainty in making a decision. The emphasis in marketing is on the identification and satisfaction of customer needs. In order to determine customer needs and to implement marketing strategies and programs aimed at satisfying these needs, marketing managers need information. They need information about customers, competitors, and other forces in the market place. As the firms become national and international in scope, the need for information on large and more distant markets has increased. As competition has become intense, managers need information on the effectiveness of their marketing strategies and also need to know the strategies that their competitors are adopting. As the environment is changing more rapidly, marketing managers need more timely information.

The task of marketing research is to provide information to management that is useful for decision-making which must have the following characteristics:

1. *Relevant:* This refers to the pertinence and applicability of information to the decision and is the single most important characteristic.
2. *Accurate:* This refers to the degree to which information reflects reality. Accuracy should be judged as a relative criterion in terms of the specific decision at hand.
3. *Current:* This is the degree to which information reflects events in the relevant time period, past and present.
4. *Sufficient:* Information must be complete and/or detailed enough to allow a decision to be made.

Decision-making requires marketing research to provide sound information. If the management is clear that no additional information is likely to change its decision, it is obvious that the value of information is negligible. On the other hand, decisions cry out for information, which is not available at any price. Unless the information collected does not lead the manager to change or modify his decision, the information has no value. Information is useful in cases (i) Where one is unsure of what is to be done? (ii) Where extreme values, say, huge profits or losses are involved. By collecting the information, the management is reducing the chance of making a wrong decision. A question is, how much information should be collected in a given situation? As the collection of information involves a cost, it is necessary to ensure that the benefit from information is more than the cost involved in its collection.

Marketing information system: This is a continuing and interacting structure of people, equipment, and procedures designed to gather, sort, analyse, evaluate, and distribute needed, timely, and accurate information to marketing decision-makers.

Assessing information needs: Organisations are supposed to assess the information needs in view of the changes occurring inside and outside the organisation.

❖ Developing Information

1. *Internal records:* Information gathered from sources within the company to evaluate marketing performance and to detect marketing problems and opportunities.
2. *Marketing intelligence:* Everyday information about developments in the marketing environment that helps managers prepare and adjust marketing plans. Marketing intelligence is a strategic spin on marketing research. Marketing intelligence is a form that generates the data from the external sources and also linking and cross-analyzing existing database information and transformed for use in strategic planning and problem solving. Philip Kotler has defined Marketing Intelligence System as the set of sources and procedures by which executives obtain everyday information about development in the commercial environment. Components of marketing intelligence are focusing

on information and use of the information as a source of strategic advantage, not only to just to gather data but also to make use of the same to take right decisions. Marketing intelligence is needed because:

(i) Producers have little direct contact with the consumers,

(ii) Distribution channels need to have little knowledge about the customer's attitude, preference and changing tastes, understand competition, without spying on them,

(iii) Management goals involve sales targets and market share achievement,

(iv) Managers are often called upon to plan for new markets and product categories about which little is known,

(v) The future is uncertain, yet businesses do need to anticipate the future.

3. *Marketing research:* The function that links the consumer, customer, and public to the marketer through information – information used to identify and define marketing opportunities and problems; to generate, refine, and evaluate marketing actions; to monitor marketing performance; and to improve understanding of the marketing process.

4. *Information analysis:* Information gathered by the company through the three important sources should be analyzed further to solve the problems or to take better decisions.

5. *Distribution of information:* Marketing information has no value unless it is used by the managers in taking the decisions. Therefore, the analyzed information has to be distributed properly through right channels to the right place to take the decisions.

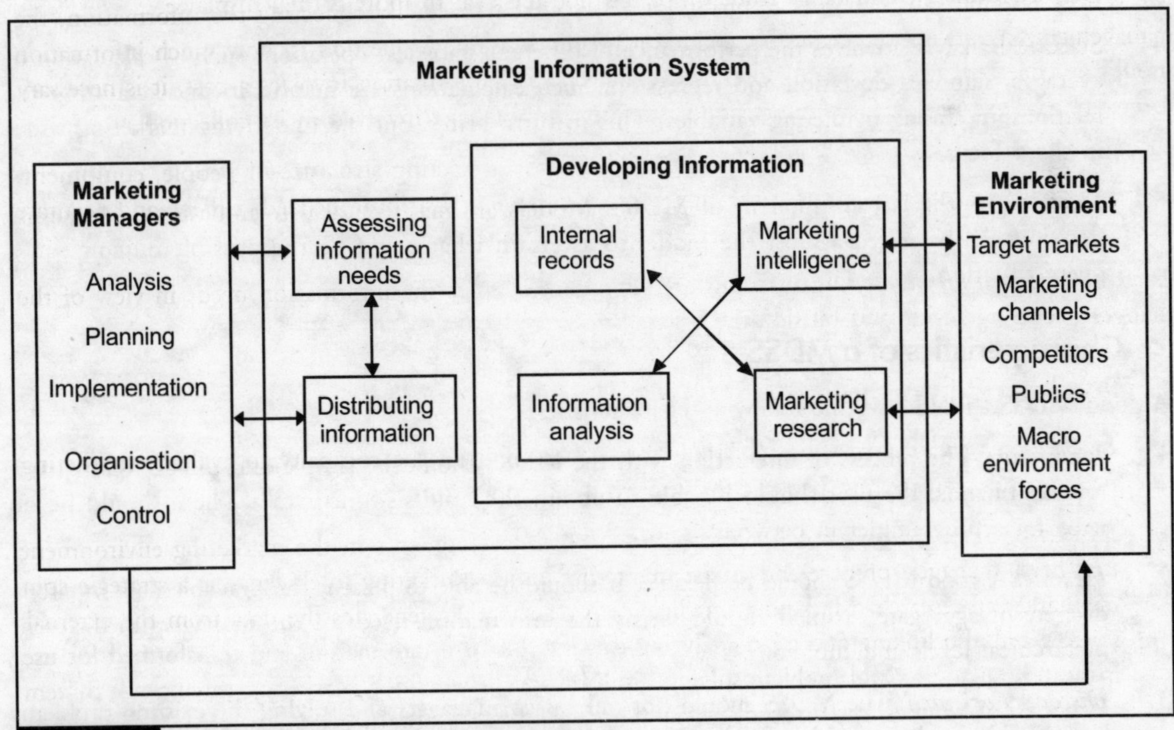

FIGURE 1.1 Marketing Decisions and Communications

MARKETING DECISION SUPPORT SYSTEM (MDSS)

Marketing manager receives lot of data from simple internal records such as sales report from the field sales force, consumer panel data, scanner data, demographic data, and internal cost and budget data. These data may also have various levels of detail and aggregation, often they use different reporting periods and incompatible languages. Data may also come about competitors' brands, their distribution systems, pricing and promotion strategies, etc. In other words, managers are exposed to data explosion. But the manager does not need these data as it is also volume. Manager needs only relevant data and that too in meaningful form. The manager generally needs (a) routine comparison of current performance against past trends on each of the key measure of effectiveness, (b) periodic exception reports to assess which sales territories or accounts have not matched previous years' purchases, and (c) special analysis to evaluate the sales impact of particular marketing programmes and to predict what would happen if changes were made. In addition, different divisions would like to be linked to enable product managers, sales planners, market researchers, financial analysts, and production schedulers to share information.

❖ Components of a Marketing Decision Support System

1. Data sources are a major component of MDSS. These sources can be both internal and external. These data may relate to consumer sales, buyer profiles, sales of retail outlets, evaluation of advertising campaigns, major economic, social and demographic trends, etc.
2. Database management involves identifying relevant data from a variety of sources, deciding on the extent of data and keeping the data in an easily available form.
3. Display formats could range from simple ad hoc retrieval to more formal displays.
4. Statistical analysis involves the performance of different statistical operations such as calculation of averages, standard deviation and regression. Such calculations are helpful in understanding the relationship among marketing variables. This in turn, brings out the underlying marketing issues in sharp focus.
5. Modeling is the last component of MDSS. Models are mathematical formulations. Marketing decision can be tested against the model to ascertain what could be the possible outcome in a given situation.

❖ Characteristics of a MDSS

A good MDSS should have the following characteristics:

1. *Interactive:* The process of interaction with the MDSS should be simple and direct. With just a few commands, the user should be able to obtain the results immediately. There should be no need for a programmer in between.
2. *Flexible:* A good MDSS should be flexible. It should be able to present the available data in either discrete or aggregate form. It should satisfy the information needs of the managers in different hierarchical levels and functions.
3. *Discovery oriented:* The MDSS should not only assist managers and solving the existing problems but should also help them to probe for trends and ask new questions. The managers should be able to discover new patterns and be able to act on them using the MDSS.

4. *User friendly:* The MDSS should be user friendly. It should be easy for the managers to learn and use the system. It should not take hours just to figure out what is going on. Most MDSS packages are menu driven and are easy to operate.

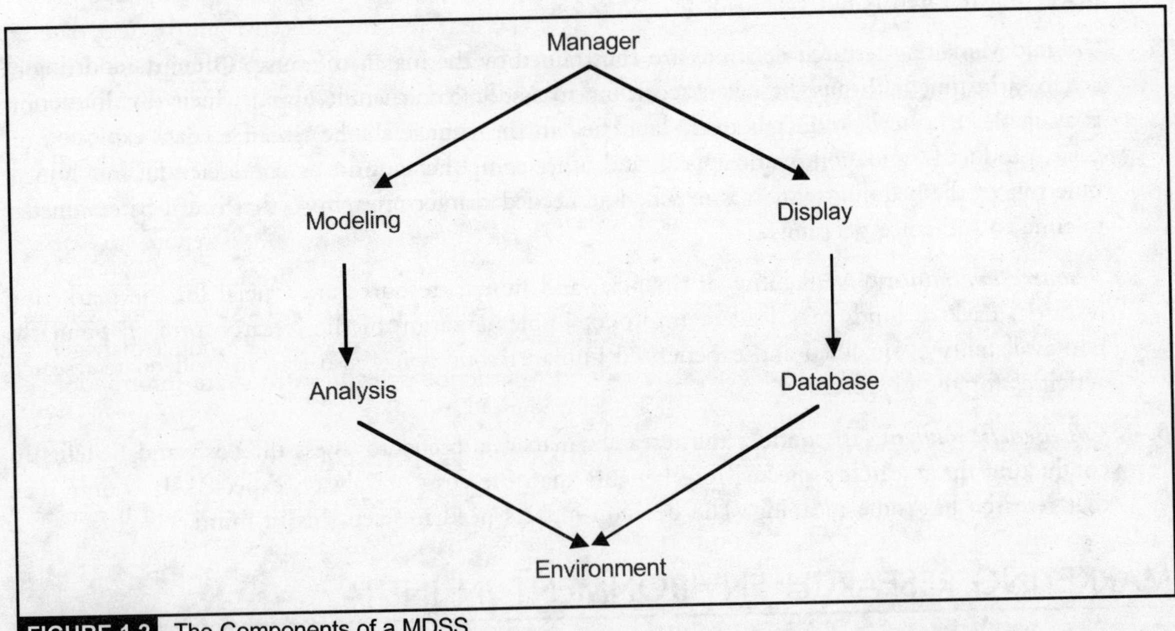

FIGURE 1.2 The Components of a MDSS

TABLE 1.1 MIS vs MDSS

MIS	MDSS
1. Structured problems	Unstructured problems
2. Use of reports	Use of models
3. Rigid structure	User-friendly interaction
4. Information displaying restricted	Adaptability
5. Can improve decision-making by clarifying raw data	Can improve decision-making by using What if Analysis.

DECISION TO MAKE USE OF MARKETING RESEARCH

Marketing research is not immediate or an obvious path to finding solutions to all managerial problems. A manager who is faced with a particular problem should not instinctly resort to conducting marketing research to find a solution to the problem. A manager should consider several factors before ordering marketing research. Sometimes it is best not to conduct marketing research. Hence, the primary decision to be made is whether or not marketing research is called for in a particular situation. The factors that influence this initial decision include the following:

1. *Relevance:* Research should not be conducted to satisfy curiosity or confirm the wisdom of previous decisions. Relevance comes through support of strategic and tactical planning activities, that is, by anticipating the kinds of information that will be required. This information is the backbone of the ongoing information system. As new circumstances arise and decision alternatives become more specific, research projects may be undertaken. Throughout the planning of these projects, the focus must be constantly on decisions.

2. ***Nature of information sought:*** The decision to conduct the marketing research depends on the nature of the information required by the marketing manager. If the information required for decision-making already exists within the organization in the form of results of a study contents, marketing research is not called for.

3. ***Timing:*** Marketing research decisions are constrained by the march of events. Often these decisions are fixed in time and must be taken according to a specified schedule, using whatever information is available. If a new product is to be launched in the winter, all the research based decisions on price, product formulation, name appeal, and other components must be conducted far in advance. One role of the planning system is to schedule needed market research so that it can be conducted in time to influence decisions.

4. ***Resource availability:*** Availability of financial and human resource are crucial for the marketing research. Lack of funds may lead to improper implementation of the research project. Similarly, non-availability of qualified and experienced human resource may also lead to inadequate research activities for the organization.

5. ***Cost-Benefit analysis:*** To conduct the research, managers prefer to assess the costs and benefits in conducting the research project. More benefits than the costs are always expected. It is only then that research has some meaning. The decision-makers need to keep this in mind.

MARKETING RESEARCH ENVIRONMENT IN INDIA

The India, marketing environment is dramatically fast changing over a period of last ten years. On one side, there is the forced environment outside the economy to go for change. Again this is due to the globalised economic environment. On the other side, there is a consistent effort on the part of the policy makers' and the industry and business to go for changing the marketing environment. They willingly want to participate in the liberalized environment and reap the advantages of the opportunities available because of the dawn of market oriented economic policies sweeping across the world. As a result, the Indian market environment is moving from the subsistence environment to dynamic environment, from local oriented to external oriented. In other words, the Indian marketing environment is undergoing transformation. The following features further substantiate the point.

1. ***Economic liberalisation:*** Indian economy has been liberalized since 1991 onwards. The liberalized economy is offering many opportunities and thronging many challenges too. This gave spurt to many foreign companies to enter into the Indian markets and become competitive to the domestic players. According to UN Conference on Trade and Development (UNCTAD), India has become the fourth largest recipient in the Asian region. The result is quite interesting to observe that the consumer is the ultimate beneficiary.

2. ***Technology accessibility to common man:*** Since the economy is liberalized, the Indian companies access foreign technologies to become competitive. As expected, the Indian industry is a strong force not only in India but also in the world. Thus, technology is accessed by common man.

3. ***Disposable income:*** India has a very good human resource and their earnings are also commensurate with the quality of labour. According to ECA, the worlds largest membership organization for international human resources professionals survey, Indian employees are set to receive the highest salary hike in 2007, with companies forecasting an annual hike of 12 per cent, resulting in real wages increase of seven per cent once inflation has been taken into consideration. As a result, they have sufficient disposable income.

4. ***Increased competition:*** As the world players are active in the Indian market, there is intense competition among the players. They find it difficult to market the product in Indian markets through the conventional marketing strategies any more. Profit margins are wafer thin, very frequently, new and innovative products are forced into the market. Marketers are forced to adopt innovative strategies to win the consumers.

5. ***Changed consumer:*** Indian consumer is not the traditional innocent consumer. The Indian consumers are quality conscious, demanding better bargaining and price conscious too. At the same time, Indian consumer is having enough purchasing power. According to Technopak estimate, there will be 1.8 million very affluent households and 6 million consumers in such households with annual income of ₹ 40 lakhs or more by the end of 2007.

6. ***Consumerism:*** There is a lot of resistance on the part of consumer not to accept the low standard product and expose the substandard products in the market. This poses a real challenge to the marketer to reassess the marketing strategies better than ever.

7. ***International market players:*** Indian consumers are now splurging on a very wide range of goods and services that include entertainment, electronics, cloths and accessories, jewellery, watches and pens, automobiles, household furniture and furnishings, and gourmet food and other products and services. Almost all major international players in almost all sectors are operating and some are in beeline to India from different parts of the world.

8. ***Wide choice before the consumer:*** Indian consumers today, are having a wide choice compared to earlier decades. Consumer is in a position to chose and reject the goods and services. To satisfy the Indian consumers, not only the Indian marketing agencies, but international marketing research groups too are active. In relation to advertising, with the increasing clutter in the media space, ad firms are forced to devise new ways to communicate effectively.

9. ***Retail boom:*** The retail boom gathered momentum last year. Reliance entered the market with its fresh Reliance Fresh stores; The Bharati Group threw its hat into the ring with its tie up with global giant, Wal-Mart; The Tatas started their foray with Croma; The Electronic store, and the Birlas have expressed their intentions to get in as well. Future group has stepped up its efforts on Big Bazaar and Pantaloons and their likes and other big international players – Tesco, Carrefour and Watson are also evaluating this market. All this means some thing for consumers, marketing, brands, media and communication agencies in India. In view of these changes, brand builders are forced to adopt market research as the best tool to come out with new marketing strategies in India.

10. ***Second biggest growing economy:*** After China, India has become the biggest fast growing economy. It is predicted that in the next few decades, Indian will emerge as a strong economic power in the world. At present GDP growth at constant prices is over 9.2 per cent. Expert's view that India will continue to record high growth rates. According to World Bank report, Indian will move from its present status (gross per capita income, $875) of a low-income country to the next level of a lower-middle income ($3,465) country by 2008.

In view of the above changes, businesses and industries are forced to recognize and depend on the marketing research as the rescue instrument not only to face the challenges but also to survive and sustain the existing marketing activities. Indian business community is now not bothering about simply surviving and sustaining, they are now looking for new market opportunities available elsewhere in the world. Hitherto the neglected discipline marketing research is slowly emerging as the centre for marketing activity not only to understand the marketing environment and identify the emerging marketing needs and wants of the consumers but also to explore the best opportunities for the Indian industries across the world.

USERS OF MARKETING RESEARCH

Marketing Research is generally used by two type of clients. They are internal and external clients. External clients are company vendors and franchisees. Internal clients are almost all the departments within the organization. Although research is conducted to generate information, managers do not readily use the information to solve their problems. The factors that influence a manager's decision to use research information are:

1. Research quality
2. Conformity to prior expectations
3. Clarity of presentation
4. Political acceptability within the firm and
5. Challenge to the status quo.

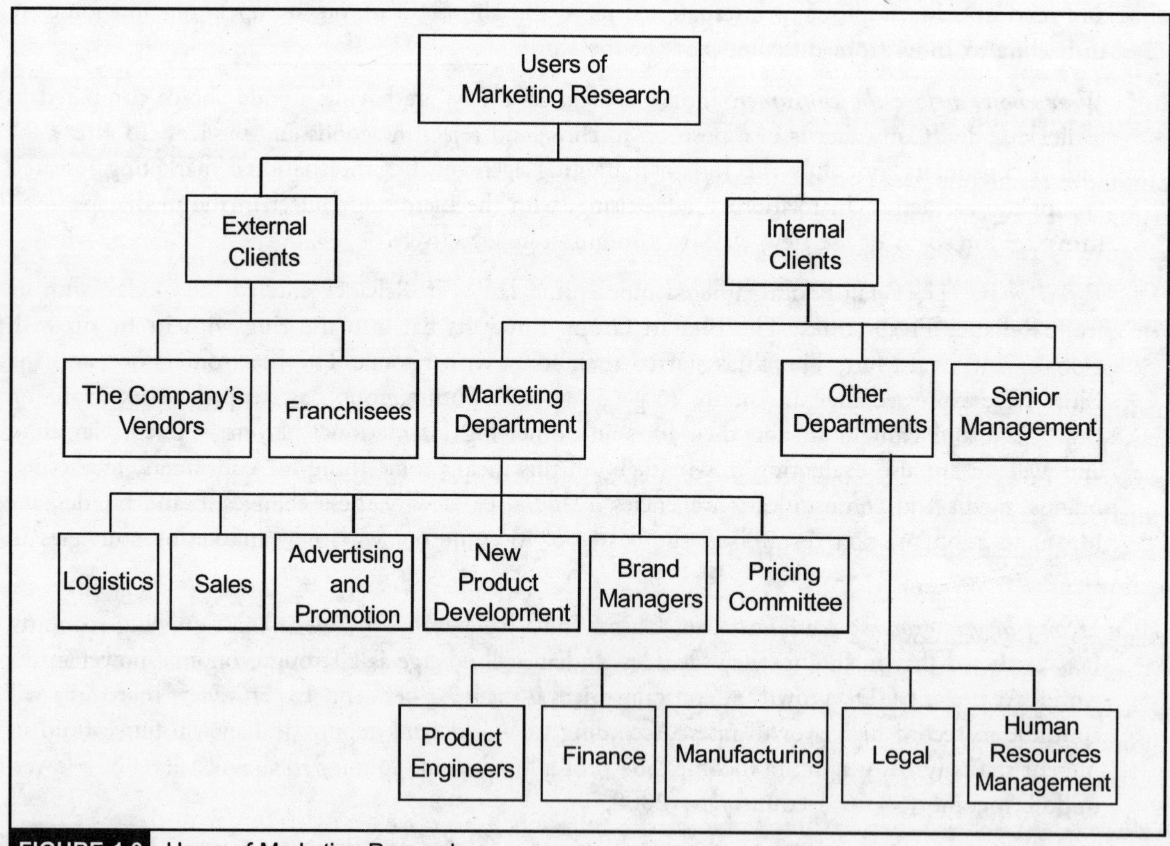

FIGURE 1.3 Users of Marketing Research

RESEARCH AND SCIENTIFIC METHOD

Research design must have a scientific base to achieve the desired objectives. A research design is the specification of methods and procedures for acquiring the information needed. The method and procedures should be scientific. Therefore, one should understand the scientific methods and their application to marketing research before deciding the research design.

The basic qualities of any scientific method are rationality and objectivity. No method known to man can entirely eliminate uncertainty. But scientific method, more than any other procedure, can minimize those elements of uncertainty which result from lack of information. By doing so, it reduces the danger of making a wrong choice between alternative courses of action. When the marketing research uses the research techniques, they apply methods of science to the art of marketing research. Application of scientific methods to marketing research has helped the researchers to arrive at correct conclusions. Suitable suggestions and recommendations can be provided to the marketing management with the application of scientific methods.

There are however certain difficulties in the application of scientific methods to marketing research. The researchers in marketing areas tend to reduce their objectivity. They are also influenced by other factors. There is a lack of precision in marketing research. The reliability and validity may be influenced by different factors affecting the market and the marketing mix. A time lag that influences the findings and their relevances to marketing problems may not be correct. The complexities of human actions and reactions do not make marketing research a very precise and comprehensive science. However, scientific methods are used to make marketing research more useful and lead to relevant conclusions. The emphasis in marketing research is to use scientific methods.

❖ Quantitative Research and Qualitative Research

Quantitative research is based on the measurement of quantity or amount. It is applicable to phenomena that can be expressed in terms of quantity. Qualitative research on the other hand, is concerned with qualitative phenomenon, i.e., phenomena relating to or involving quality or kind. For instance, when the researcher is interested in investigating the reasons for human behaviour, we quite often talk of motivation research, an important type of qualitative research. This type of research aims at discovering the underlying motives and desires, using in-depth interviews for the purpose.

Quantitative research is numeric oriented, requires significant attention to the measurement of market phenomena and often involves statistical analysis. For example, a bank might ask its customers to rate its overall services; as excellent, good, poor or very poor. This will provide quantitative information that can be analysed statistically. The main rule about quantitative research is that every respondent is asked the same series of questions. The approach is very structured and normally involves large numbers of interviews/questionnaires.

Perhaps the most common quantitative technique is the 'market research survey'. These are basically projects that involve the collection of data from multiple cases - such as consumers or a set of products. Quantitative surveys can be conducted by using post (self-completion), face-to-face (in-street or in-home), telephone, email or web techniques. The questionnaire is one of the more common tools for collecting data from a survey, but it is only one of a wide ranging set of data collection aids.

Qualitative research is especially important in the behaviour sciences where the aim is to discover the underlying motives of human behaviour. Through such research, one can analyse the various factors which motivate people to behave in a particular manner or which make people like or dislike a particular thing. Typical differences between qualitative and quantitative research is presented in the following Table 1.2.

TABLE 1.2 Qualitative vs. Quantitative Research

	Qualitative Research	Quantitative Research
1. Types of questions	Probing	Limited probing
2. Sample size	Small	Large
3. Amount of information from each respondent	Substantial	Varies
4. Requirements for administration	Interviewer with special skills	Interviewer with fewer special skills
5. Type of analysis	Subjective, interpretive	Statistical, summation
6. Hardware	Tape recorders, projection devices, video recorders, pictures, discussion guides	Questionnaires, computers, printouts
7. Degree of explicability	Low	High
8. Researcher training	Psychology, sociology, social psychology, consumer behavior, marketing, marketing research	Statistics, decision models, decision-marketing, marketing research
9. Type of research	Exploratory	Descriptive or causal

Qualitative research provides an understanding of how or why things are as they are. For example, a Market Researcher may stop a consumer who has purchased a particular type of bread and ask him or her why that type of bread was chosen. Unlike quantitative research, there are no fixed set of questions but, instead, a topic guide (or discussion guide) is used to explore various issues in-depth. The discussion between the interviewer (or moderator) and the respondent is largely determined by the respondents' own thoughts and feelings.

As with quantitative techniques, there are also various types of qualitative methodologies. Research of this sort is mostly done face-to-face. One of the best-known techniques is market research group discussions (or focus groups). These are usually made up of 6 to 8 targeted respondents, a research moderator whose role is to ask the required questions, draw out answers, and encourage discussion, and an observation area usually behind one way mirrors, and video and/or audio taping facilities.

TABLE 1.3 Applications of Qualitative and Quantitative Research

Topic Area	Settings Best for Qualitative Research	Settings Best for Quantitative Research
Advertising	A Company, marketer of Harpic cleaning products wants to come up with ideas for creatively communicating through a television commercial.	Two different commercials for Harpic cleaner have been developed; management wants to know which of the two will be more effective in favorably influencing target customers' preferences for Harpic
Product Planning and Promotion	The brand manager in charge of Kitchen Aid small appliances wishes to develop an understanding of how, when, where and why consumers use kitchen appliances.	The brand manager wants to conduct a large-scale segmentation study to identify heavy users of kitchen appliances.
Personal Selling	Sales of Ford Explorer have been dropping steadily; the sales manager wants to identify possible reasons for this decline.	From discussions with several dealers, the sales manager suspects that customer satisfaction with Ford Explorer is low and wants to confirm by using a customer satisfaction questionnaire.
Services Marketing	The administrators of Bhagyanagar Memorial Hospital, Hyderabad, want to develop a feel	The administrators want to ascertain patients' rating of specific attributes of such

Contd...

	for the nature and the extent of apprehension experienced by patients when they are in the hospital.	things as patient care, food service, and medical treatment.
Politics	Environmental researcher wants to understand the environmental concerns of Indian citizens before unveiling his Energy Plan to the public.	He wants to determine the support for oil exploration in the Godavari Basin, and possibly in waters off the beaches Bay of Bengal of (% of Indians in favor of it).

STATISTICS AND RESEARCH

Statistics is indispensable in research work. Most of the advancement in knowledge has been taken place because of experiments conducted with the help of statistical methods. It is impossible to understand the meaning and implications of most of the research findings in various disciplines of knowledge without having at least a peaking acquaintance with the subject, statistics. The following examples show the importance of statistics in various research situations:

1. Experiments about crop yields and different types of fertilizers and different types of soils.
2. Growth of animals under different diets and environments.
3. Statistical methods are very crucial in analyzing data in medicine and health for effective decision-making.
4. Clinical research trials require lots of data to be analyzed using statistics to identify patterns for developing new drugs.
5. Business research in the areas of marketing, production, finance, banking, operations, accounting, personnel and research and development uses statistical data for analyzing various problem situations to find out better solutions for effective decision-making.
6. Statistical methods are applicable to conduct research in all diversified fields such as economics, trade, commerce, agriculture, bio-sciences, physical sciences, education, astronomy, insurance, accountancy and auditing, sociology, psychology, meteorology and so on.

CLASSIFICATIONS OF RESEARCH – AN OVERVIEW

Research types or methods can be classified in several ways based upon different criteria. The following is a summary of some of the classifications of various research types.

Based upon the Relation with the Real World

1. *Basic research:* Research that seeks to resolve basic and fundamental problems regardless of whether or not the researcher seeks direct impact on everyday life.
2. *Applied research:* Research that seeks to resolve actual everyday life problems.
3. *Action research:* Research that seeks to resolve real life issues by influencing change and help, take action towards resolving the problem.

Based upon the Kind of Evidence or Source Data

1. *Primary research:* Research that relies on newly collected and innovatively generated, first-hand data.

2. *Secondary research:* Research that relies upon existing references and data previously collected, second-hand data.

Based upon Purpose of Research (Kinds of Inferences) or Chronological Standpoint

1. *Exploratory research:* Research that seeks to make an initial investigation of a problem.
2. *Descriptive research:* Research that seeks to describe a problem and recognize what is happening or has occurred about the problem.
3. *Explanatory research:* Research that seeks to explain the causes of a particular problem and answer why a phenomenon or a problem has occurred the way it did.

Based upon the Role of the Hypothesis of the Study (Purpose)

1. *Formulative research:* Research that seeks to build up theory or knowledge about a particular phenomenon or problem.
2. *Verification research:* Research that seeks to verify, test, confirm, corroborate, prove, substantiate, authenticate a theory or assumption about a particular phenomenon or problem, or refuse, contradict, and disprove such a theory or assumption

Based upon Type of Relationship between the Variables of the Study

1. *Experimental research:* Research that seeks to establish a causal relationship between variables. This type of research is sometimes called true experimental research.
2. *Quasi-experimental research:* Research that seeks to establish a less-than-causal relationship between variables. This type is sought after when experimental research is not possible.
3. *Correlational research:* Research that seeks to establish the existence of a relationship, connection, or association among variables that is not a causal relationship, but good enough for the purpose of the study.

Based upon Status of Evidence (in existence or not) and upon Possible Degree of Controlling the Conditions under which the Collection of data are to Take Place

1. *Historical research:* A research type used when the evidence data is in existence but simply needs to be located and evaluated.
2. *Descriptive research:* A research type used when the evidence data needs to be generated and collected (it is not in existence yet) and when controlling the conditions surrounding the generation of evidence is not possible.
3. *Experimental research:* A research type used when the evidence data needs to be generated and collected (it is not in existence yet) and when controlling the conditions surrounding the generation of evidence is possible including the ability of the researcher to assign subjects at random to groups under study.
4. *Quasi-experimental research:* A research type used when the evidence data needs to be generated and collected (it is not in existence yet) and when controlling the conditions surrounding the generation of evidence is possible but when the researcher cannot assign subjects at random to groups under study.

Based upon the Nature of the Research Question

1. *Descriptive research:* Research that seeks to investigate and examine a problem.
2. *Relational research:* A correlational research that seeks to explore the relationships between variables.
3. *Causal research:* An experimental research that seeks to explore the causal relationship between variables.

Based upon True Control of Events Surrounding the Collection of Data

1. Experimental research (includes true experiments of all kinds)
2. Non-experimental research (includes historical, descriptive, correlational, and quasi-experimental research types)

Based upon Research Context or Strategy

1. *Case study research:* Research that focuses upon one case study for gathering data.
2. *Survey research:* Research that focuses upon a group of subjects for gathering data.
3. *Experimental research:* Research that focuses upon conducting an experiment for gathering data.

Based upon Units of Analysis

1. *Individual:* Research that focuses upon individuals for the collection of data.
2. *Groups:* Research that focuses upon groups of individuals for the collection of data.
3. *Organizational:* Research that focuses upon organizations for the collection of data.
4. *Artifacts:* Research that focuses upon "physical things" for the collection of data.
5. *Phenomena:* Research that focuses upon "non-physical things" for the collection of data.

Based upon the Time Dimension

1. *Cross-sectional research:* Research conducted and data collected at one point in time (usually exploratory and descriptive).
2. *Longitudinal research:* Research conducted and data collected over an extended period of time. Trend studies focus on studying changes of general population over time. Cohort studies focus on studying changes of relatively specific subpopulations over time. Panel studies focus on studying the same set of people over time.

Based upon the Type of Data Collected in the Study

1. *Quantitative research:* Research that relies upon quantitative-type data (usually statistical-type study).
2. *Qualitative research:* Research that relies upon qualitative-type data.

Based upon the Data Collection Techniques Used

1. *Observational research:* Research that includes naturalistic, participant, or physical traces observational techniques.

2. *Survey research:* Research that includes questionnaires or interviews.
3. *Archival research:* Research that includes using existing documents.
4. *Experimental research:* Research that includes the use of experiments of any type.

❖ Limitations of Research

In India, research based decision-making has just made a beginning. There are still a number of gaps in understanding between the researchers and its users.

It may be made clear that research is there to help in decision-making and is not a substitute of decision-making. Some of the limitations are given below:

1. Research can provide a number of facts, but it doesn't provide actionable results.
2. Some problems just cannot be researched, e.g., a precise estimate of sales directly attributable to advertising.
3. It cannot provide the answer to any problem but can only provide a set of guidelines. Thus, management will have to consider research findings in the light of other factors such as production, finance and personnel, in arriving at the decision.
4. Managers normally do not include research in the overall problem or total decision-making. Partial decisions on specific issues and without proper timing and budget may not help in satisfactory solutions.
5. Managers rely more on intuition and judgement rather than on research.

POTENTIAL RESEARCH CONSTRAINTS

❖ In Asia

1. Vietnam and Cambodia have extremely high phone rates. In Vietnam, it is not uncommon to have 10 families in one building sharing one phone line.
2. In-person interviews are preferred, as they allow the researcher to show proper respect for the respondents.
3. In Thailand, only 212 per cent of the population lives in urban areas, and two thirds of that population is located in one city, Bangkok.
4. Face-to-face interviews are most common due to lack of telephones and the cultural unacceptability of giving strangers information over the telephone.
5. High cellular, as opposed to hard-line, penetration may cause low response rates in traditional telephone surveys.
6. Professionals, such as IT decision-makers, have a higher response rate than in the United States because they are not yet over surveyed.
7. A questionnaire to be administered in Singapore must have an English version as well as equivalent Malay, Hokkien, Mandarin, Tamil and Cantonese versions.

❖ In India

1. Due to lack of strong research infrastructure, the available research methods are limited.
2. Response rates for in-person interviews approach is up to 60 per cent for upscale markets and as high as 80 per cent in other population segments.
3. Due to lack of focus group facilities, hotel rooms with closed circuit television monitoring are often used.
4. Telephone and mail surveys are rarely used due to inadequate telephone penetration (1 per cent of households) and low literacy rates.
5. Resources such as customer databases, checkout scanners, and other automated equipment are almost non-existent.

REVIEW QUESTIONS

1. What are the objectives of research?
2. Explain various types of research.
3. What is Marketing Information System?
4. What is marketing research? What are the advantages of marketing research?
5. Differentiate between marketing information system and marketing research.
6. What is the importance of marketing research for industry and society?
7. What are the characteristics of good marketing research?
8. Who are the users of marketing research?
9. What is marketing research? Discuss the scope of marketing research.
10. What are the various research methods in marketing?
11. Discuss the limitations of marketing research.
12. Discuss the importance of statistics in research environment with examples.
13. Explain the marketing research environment in India.
14. What are the differences between qualitative research and quantitative research?

Case Study KFC

KFC, the world's largest chicken restaurant brand, is targeting 100 quick service restaurants in India by 2010 – end. The $ 12-billion brand, which is owned by leading global restaurant company Yum! Brands, Inc. that also owns other brands like Pizza Hut and Taco Bell, is present with 34 outlets across nine cities in the country.

The restaurant plans to close 2008 with a total of 50 stores. The business model of KFC is primarily a franchise one and the aggregate investment involved in this expansion will be ₹ 200-300 crore (estimate). KFC has recently inaugurated a quick-service restaurant in Kolkata which also happens to be the first in India to be manned entirely by hearing-impaired employees.

According to sources, over the next one to one – and – a - half years, expansion will mainly be in the metros and cities where KFC already has a presence. The company would be subsequently looking into tier-II and tier-III cities. In this business, a lot depends on the back end, including the supply chain and vendors. The company needs to have the infrastructure in place, before it moves into these smaller cities.

While growth will be primarily franchise-driven, about 20% of the new restaurants will be company-owned. The new outlets will come up both in malls as well as in high-street locations. This apart, KFC will also be aggressively expanding its menu in India by rolling out some 10-15 products over the next two to three years. Keeping Indian tastes and preferences in mind, it will have offerings suited to the India palate, low cost items as well as significant variety of vegetarian products. However, the brand does not want to compromise on its global image and will continue to uphold that. The restaurant wants to have 80% of offerings as international while rest will be especially for the Indian market.

The company was in a spot of bother with the outbreak of "bird-flu" in some parts of the country. The company retorted to this by asking for a certificate of safety from their vendors. However, the company stopped serving chicken during the ban.

Questions

1. Would the quick-service restaurants be successful in India? How can you use marketing research to help the company succeed in its project of quick-service restaurants?
2. What tactics and strategies would you adopt to retort to bird-flu or other contingencies like this? How can marketing research be helpful in this regard?

CHAPTER TWO

MARKETING RESEARCH PROCESS

INTRODUCTION

Research process is the main content of marketing research. It defines marketing research and describes the skills required to identify the problem, the decision alternatives, and the client's needs, which are critical components of a research activities. The marketing research is expected to understand the market information needs of decision-makers, and on the other hand, expected to follow the proper processes and procedures for obtaining that information.

RESEARCH PROCESS

Marketing research process involves a number of inter-related activities which overlap and do not rigidly follow a particular sequence. A researcher is often required to think a few steps ahead, because various steps in research process are inter-woven into each other and each step will have some influence over the other steps. In marketing research, even though our focus is on one particular step, other inter-related steps of operations are also being looked into simultaneously. As we complete one activity or operation, our focus naturally shifts from it to the subsequent one, i.e. the focus is not concentrated exclusively on one single activity or operation at any particular point of time. The research process provides systematic, planned approach to the research project and ensures that all aspects of the research project are consistent with each other. The steps involved in the research process are as follows:

1. ***Identifying Need for Marketing Research:*** The marketing research process begins with the recognition of a marketing problem or opportunity. Often, considerable analysis of historical data or secondary information basically provides the background of the problem or opportunity. While deciding about the need for the research, one has to consider the use of the research findings, availability of resources, management attitude towards the research and expected benefits against the cost involved in conducting the research. Albert Einstein went so far as to say that "the formulation of a problem is often more essential than its solution!" Sometimes, exploratory research is required to help in the formulation of the research problem. As changes occur in the firm's external environment; marketing managers are faced with the questions, "Should we change the existing marketing mix"? And if so, How? Marketing research may be used to evaluate products and services, promotion, distribution, and pricing alternatives. In the process of evaluation of various marketing activities, marketing managers may get the clue to arrive at a tentative problem situation. In addition, it may be used to find and evaluate new opportunities, in a process called opportunity identification. This stage will facilitate the researchers to come to the conclusion not only to recognize the problem situation but also need to proceed further to conduct the research. In abstract, this background leads to correctly defining the problem. In defining the problem rightly, Carl Mcdaniel

and Roger Gates, in their book on Marketing Research Essentials stated eight important steps. They are:

(i) Recognise the problem or opportunity,

(ii) Find out why the information is being sought,

(iii) Understand the decision-making environment (the industry, company, product, target market,

(iv) Use the symptoms to help clarify the problem,

(v) Translate the management problem into a marketing research problem,

(vi) Determine whether the information already exists,

(vii) Determine whether the question really can be answered, and

(viii) State the research objectives.

2. *Clarity of Research Objectives:* While deciding to conduct the research, one has to have clarity about the objective of the research. The clarity on objectives facilitates the research to move in the right direction. In other words, accurate definition of purpose of research requires:

(i) Identifying a number of specific issues to be covered, and

(ii) Deciding which of those issues is worth pursuing further.

The culmination of the problem identification process is a statement of the research objectives. These objectives are stated in terms of the precise information necessary to address the marketing research problem/opportunity. Well formulated objectives serve as a road map in pursuing the research project. They also serve as a standard that later will enable manager to evaluate the quality and value of the work by asking were the objectives met, and do the recommendations flow logically from the objectives and the research findings. Research objectives must be as specific and unambiguous as possible. After an introduction which describes the broader context within which the research should be situated, it is important to state the objectives or purpose pursued by the research itself. Often, this is a fairly broad or general statement as well. The purpose of the research is given as: "*The following study is an attempt to provide a more meaningful and defensible measure of public opinion*". This is a fairly vague statement and should have been followed up with a much more precise research question (in question format) or problem statement (a re-wording of the research question into a statement format). At this point of time, it is important to inform the reader about the breadth or scope of the study, other limitations may have to be imposed on the study due to cost or time constraints or accessibility to respondents. This type of limitation should not be confused with methodological limitations, which are addressed as part of the methodology of the study.

All research is based on a set of assumptions or factors that are presumed to be true and valid. For instance, it is generally assumed that respondents will reply honestly and accurately as far as they are able to do so. By stating these assumptions upfront, the researcher reduces potential criticism of the research, but without them, the research itself would not be possible. If you thought that respondents would lie, why would you bother doing the research?

In formal research, the researcher will provide an educated guess regarding the outcome of the study, called hypothesis. That means researcher states a research objective in the form of a hypothesis.

A hypothesis is a conjectural statement about a relationship between two or more variables that can be tested with empirical data; it is considered to be plausible, given the available information. The research will test the hypotheses, to prove valid/correct, invalid/incorrect. Sometimes, researcher will also state that a hypothesis tested positive (valid) or negative (incorrect). It does not matter whether researcher correctly predicts the outcome of the research or not, since rejecting a hypothesis does not mean that the research itself is poor, but rather that your research has results that are different from what the related literature led to believe should have been expected.

3. *Identifying Data Needs:* After deciding about the purpose of the research, the next step is to decide about the nature of data that is to be collected. Generally objectives of research indicate what type of data is required. Researcher should have clarity about the kinds of data that is needed. If there is mismatch between the purpose of research and data needs, the very purpose of the research will be a futile exercise.

4. *Identification of Data Sources:* Once the data needs are identified, the next step is to identify sources of data. Some times secondary data may be sufficient to accomplish the research. In some other situations, primary data may be required. However, in most of the cases, there is a need to collect both secondary as well as primary data. However, purpose of the research and urgency of the outcome may decide which source of data is needed.

5. *Research Design:* Research design is the plan to be followed to answer the marketing research objectives. Research design is a plan for addressing the research objectives or hypotheses. In essence, the researcher develops a structure or framework to answer a specific research problem/opportunity. The researcher has to decide which type of research design will be suitable to conduct research. There are broadly two types of research designs before the researchers. They are:

   (i) Exploratory research design

   (ii) Causal research design.

   The research design selection is again dependent upon the type of research. The purpose of the research will influence to a greater extent. There is a no single best research design. Instead, different designs offer an array of choices, each with certain advantages and disadvantages. Ultimately, trade-offs are typically involved. A common trade off is between research costs and the quality of the decision-making information provided. The design of the research project is a creative plan to obtain the necessary information in the best way possible. The correct design will save time and money and will result in valid and reliable information. The marketing research professional is expected to be an expert in this area, having the technical knowledge to design research projects that will provide a wide variety of marketing information to key decision-makers.

6. *Choosing a Basic Method of Research:* Again there is a need to decide about what type of probability method is to be decided or what type of non-probability sampling method is needed. Again this is dependent and influenced by the type of research conducted.

   A research design, either descriptive or causal, is chosen based on a project's objectives. The next step is to select a means of gathering data. There are three basic research methods:

   (i) *Survey research:* In survey research, investigator interacts with the respondents to gather data required for the research. This is often descriptive in nature but can be causal.

   (ii) *Observation research:* In this research, investigator observes the actions of the respondent without any direct interaction. Observation research is typically descriptive.

(iii) *Experiment research:* In this research, investigator changes one or more variables and observes the effect of these changes on another variable. Experiment research is almost always causal.

7. ***Selecting the Sampling Procedure:*** A sample is a subset from a larger population. Although the basic nature of the sample is specified in the research design, selecting the sampling procedure is a separate step in the research process. Several questions must be answered before a sampling procedure is selected. First, the population or universe of interest must be defined. This is the group from which the sample will be drawn. It should include all the people whose opinions, behaviours, preferences, attitudes, and so on will yield information needed to answer the research problem. After the population has been defined, the next question is whether to use a probability sample or a non-probability sample.

8. ***Collecting the Data:*** Most interviewer-based data collection is done by marketing research field services. Field service firms, found throughout the country, specialize in collecting data through personal and telephone interviewing on a subcontract basis. A typical research study involves data collection in several cities and requires working with a comparable number of field service firms.

9. ***Analysing the Data:*** After the data have been collected, the next step in the research process is data analysis. The purpose of this analysis is to interpret and draw conclusions from the mass of collected data. The marketing researcher may use a variety of techniques, beginning with simple frequency analysis and culminating in complex multivariate techniques.

10. ***Writing and Presenting the Report:*** After data analysis is completed; the researcher must prepare the report and communicate the conclusions and recommendations to management. This is a key step in the process because a marketing researcher who writes project conclusions must convince the manager that the results are credible and justified by the data collected. The researcher usually will be required to present both written and oral reports on a project. The nature of the audience must be kept in mind when these reports are being prepared and presented.

11. ***Follow up:*** After a company has spent a considerable amount of effort and money on marketing research and the preparation of a report, it is important that the findings be used. Management should determine whether the recommendations were followed and, if not, why not.

RESEARCH DESIGN AND SCIENTIFIC METHOD

Research design must have a scientific base to achieve the desired objectives. A research design is the specification of methods and procedures for acquiring the information needed. The method and procedures should be scientific. Therefore, one should understand the scientific methods and their application to marketing research before deciding the research design.

The basic qualities of any scientific methods are rationality and objectivity. No method known to man can entirely eliminate uncertainty. But scientific method, more than any other procedure, can minimize those elements of uncertainty which result from lack of information. By doing so, it reduces the danger of making a wrong choice between alternative courses of action. When the marketing research uses the research techniques, they apply methods of science to the art of marketing research. Application of scientific methods to marketing research has helped the researchers to arrive at correct consequences. Suitable suggestions and recommendations can be provided to the marketing management with the application of scientific methods.

The above methods are applied to marketing research, but there are certain difficulties in the application of scientific methods to marketing research. The researchers in marketing areas tend to reduce their objectivity. They are also influenced by other factors. There is a lack of precision in marketing research. The reliability and validity may be influenced by different factors affecting the market and the marketing mix. A time lag that influences the findings and their relevance to marketing problems may not be correct. The complexities of human actions and reactions do not make marketing research a very precise and comprehensive science. However, scientific methods are used to make marketing research more useful, and lead to relevant conclusions. The emphasis in marketing research is to use scientific methods.

According to Green and Tull, "*A research design is the specification of methods and procedures for acquiring the information needed. It is overall operational pattern or frame work of the project that stipulates what information is to be collected from which sources by what procedures.*" Research design is more or less a blue print of research. It basically consists of three elements viz., Plan, Structure and Strategy. The plan is an outline of research scheme on which the researcher is to work. The structure of research is a more specific outline or the scheme. Strategy shows how the method is carried out, specifying the methods to be used in the collection and analysis of data. Research design is a framework or blueprint for conducting the marketing research project. It specifies the details of the procedures necessary for obtaining the information needed to structure and/or solve marketing research problems.

Design is an outline of a research project's workings. It is a statement of not only the essential elements of a study, but those that provide the basic guidelines for the details of the project. It comprises a series of prior decisions that can be taken together to provide a master plan for executing a research project.

Concepts Relating to Research Design

1. ***Dependent and independent variable:*** A concept, which can take on different quantitative values, is called a variable, for example, weight, height, income, etc. Phenomena, which can take on quantitatively different values even in decimal points, are called 'continuous variables'. Age is continuous variable but number of children is a non-continuous variable. If one variable depends upon or is a consequence of another variable, it is termed as a dependent variable, and the variable that is antecedent to the dependent variable is termed an independent variable. For example, if height depends on age, then height is dependent variable and age is independent variable.

2. ***Extraneous variable:*** Independent variables that are not related to the purpose of the study, but may effect the dependent variable are termed as extraneous variables. Suppose the researcher wants to test the hypothesis that there is relationship between children's gains in social studies achievement and their self-concepts. In this case, self-concept is an independent variable and social studies achievement is a dependent variable. Intelligence may as well affect the social studies achievement, but since it is not related to the purpose of the study undertaken by the researcher, it will be termed as an extraneous variable.

3. ***Control:*** One important characteristic of a good research design is to minimise the effect of extraneous variable(s). The technical term 'control' is used when researchers design the study minimising the effects of extraneous independent variables. In experimental searches, the term 'control' is used to refer to the restrain on experimental conditions.

4. ***Research hypothesis:*** When a prediction or hypothesised relationship is to be tested by scientific methods, it is termed as research hypothesis. It is a predictive statement that relates an independent variable to a dependent variable.

5. ***Experimental and non-experimental hypothesis-testing research:*** In this case, the purpose of research is to test a research hypothesis. It can be of the experimental design or of the non-experimental design. Research in which the independent variable is manipulated is termed 'experimental

hypothesis-testing research' and a research in which an independent is not manipulated is called 'non-experimental hypothesis-testing research'.

6. ***Experimental and control group:*** In the research, when a group is exposed to usual conditions, it is termed a 'control group', but when a group is exposed to some special conditions, it is termed as 'experimental group'.
7. ***Treatment:*** The different conditions under which experimental and control groups are put are usually referred to as 'treatments'.
8. ***Experiment:*** The process of examining the truth of a statistical hypothesis, relating to some research problem, is known as an 'experiment'. For example, an experiment can be conducted to examine the usefulness of a certain newly developed drug. Experiments can be of two types viz., absolute experiment and comparative experiment.
9. ***Experimental unit(s):*** The pre-determined plots or the blocks, where different treatments are used, are known as experimental units. Such experimental units must be selected (defined) very carefully.

Benefits of Research Design

1. A researcher realises the objectives of the study with the help of research design which helps to bridge between what has been established and what is to be done.
2. Research design facilitates the researcher to understand and decide what data are needed to achieve the objectives.
3. A written design helps the researcher exactly in clear terms, what is to be done and why.
4. Design helps the researcher to keep the computations and thinking on the path to solutions and recommendations.
5. Design guides the researcher how to conduct the research.

TYPES OF RESEARCH DESIGN

Appropriate research design is very important in the research process. Depending on the research environment and the problem statement, the following diagram will help to select an appropriate research design.

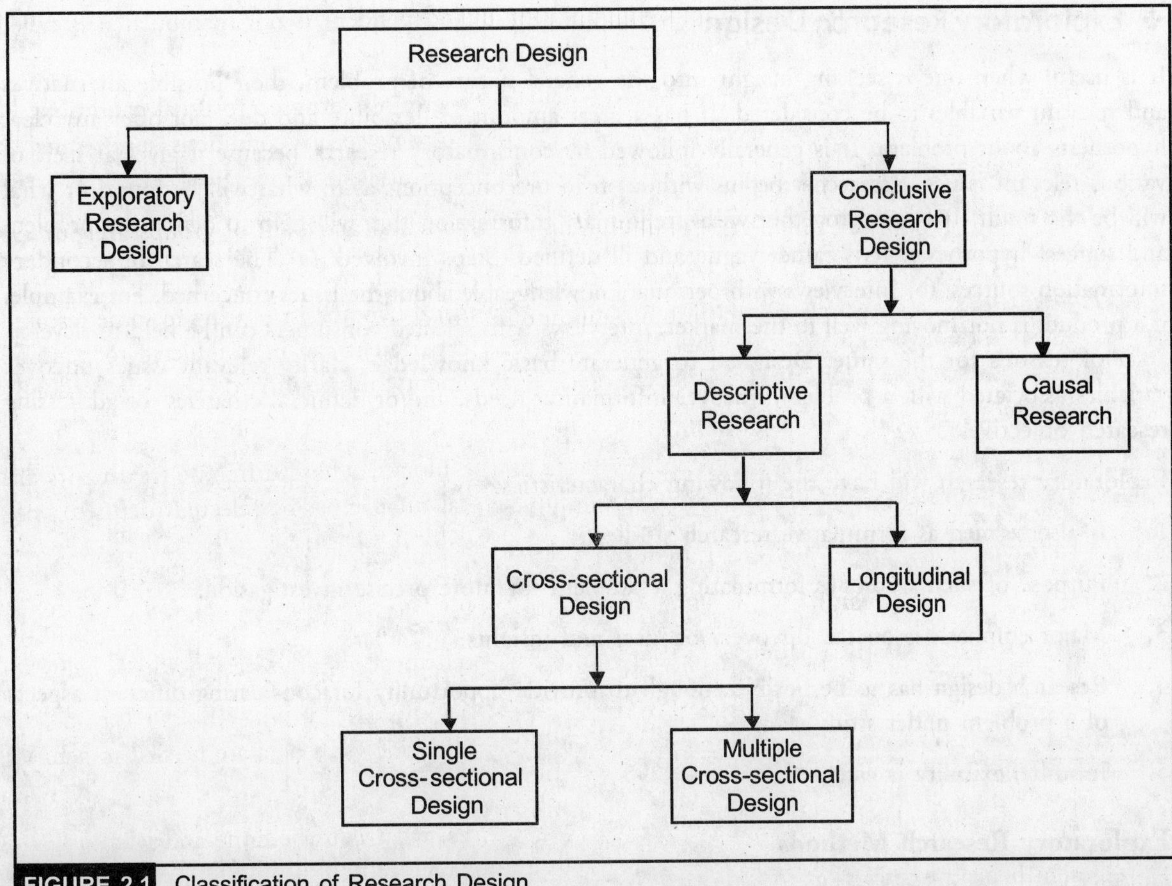

FIGURE 2.1 Classification of Research Design

The research process tends to become circular over a period of time. Exploratory research may define hypotheses, which are then tested by conclusive research, but a by product of the conclusive research may be suggestion of a new opportunity or a new difficulty. The following figure (Figure 2.2) suggests the process.

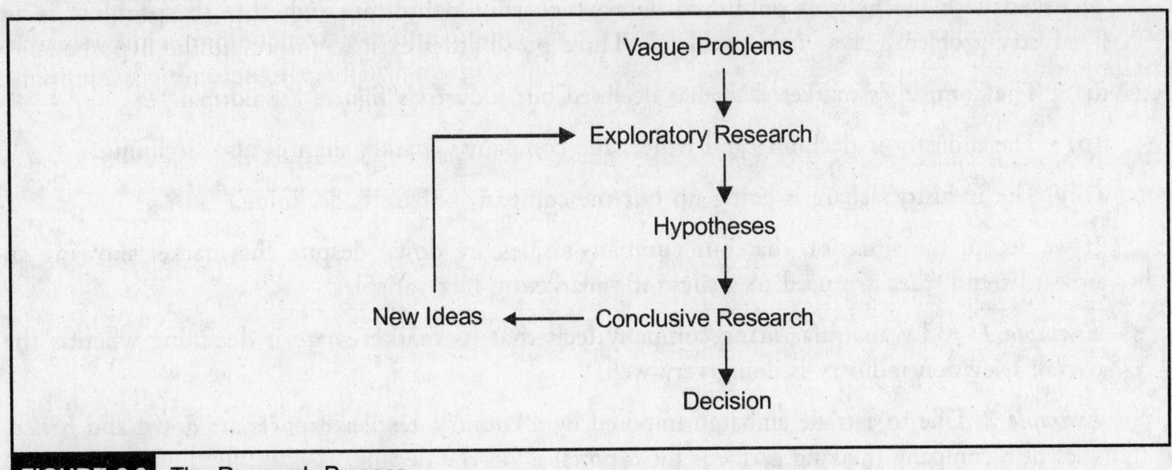

FIGURE 2.2 The Research Process

Different types of research designs have emerged on account of the different perspectives from which a research study can be viewed.

❖ Exploratory Research Design

It is useful when one is seeking insight into the general nature of problem, their possible alternatives and relevant variables to be considered. It has a great amount of flexibility and does not offer any clear hypothesis about problem. It is generally followed by confirmatory research because it gives a "feel" of various relevant issues. Researcher begins without firm preconceptions as to what will be found or what will be the result. It is used together with preliminary information that will help to define the problem and suggest hypotheses. It is rather vague and ill defined. Steps involved: (a) The search of secondary information sources, (b) Interviews with personal knowledgeable about the issues concerned. For example, if a product is not moving well in the market, interviews with selected consumers can be held to develop a set of reasons for the same. Designed to generate basic knowledge, clarify relevant issues uncover variables associated with a problem, uncover information needs, and/or define alternatives for addressing research objectives.

Exploratory research will have the following characteristics:

1. It also termed as formulative research studies.
2. Purpose of such studies is formulating a problem for more precise investigation.
3. Major emphasis is on the discovery of ideas and insights.
4. Research design has to be flexible enough to provide opportunity for considering different aspects of a problem under study.
5. Inbuilt flexibility is essential.

Exploratory Research Methods

The quickest and the cheapest way to formulate a hypothesis in exploratory research is by using any of the four methods:

1. *Literature Search:* This refers to "referring to a literature to develop a new hypothesis". The literature referred are: trade journals, professional journals, market research finding publications, statistical publications, etc. Example, Suppose a problem is "Why are sales down?" This can quickly be analyzed with the help of published data which should indicate "whether the problem is an "industry problem" or a "firm problem". Three possibilities exist to formulate the hypothesis.

   (i) The company's market share has declined but industry's figures are normal.

   (ii) The industry is declining and hence, the company's market share is also declining.

   (iii) The industry's share is going up but the company's share is declining.

   If we accept the situation that our company's sales are down despite the market showing an upward trend, then we need to analyse the marketing mix variables.

   Example 1: A TV manufacturing company feels that its market share is declining whereas the overall television industry is doing very well.

   Example 2: Due to a trade embargo imposed by a country, textiles exports are down and hence, sales of a company (making garment for exports) is on the decline.

   The above information may be used to pinpoint the reason for declining sales.

2. *Experience Survey:* In experience surveys, it is desirable to talk to persons who are well informed in the area being investigated. These people may be company executives or persons outside the

organisation. Here, no questionnaire is required. The approach adopted in an experience survey should be highly unstructured, so that the respondent can give divergent views. Since the idea of using experience survey is to undertake problem formulation, and not conclusion, probability sample need not be used. Those who cannot speak freely should be excluded from the sample.

Example 1:

(i) A group of housewives may be approached for their choice for a "ready to cook product".

(ii) A publisher might want to find out the reason for poor circulation of newspaper introduced recently. He might meet

(a) Newspaper sellers

(b) Public reading rooms

(c) General public

(d) Business community, etc.

These are experienced persons whose knowledge researcher can use.

3. *Focus Group:* Another widely used technique in exploratory research is the focus group. In a focus group, a small number of individuals are brought together to study and talk about some topic of interest. The discussion is co-ordinated by a moderator. The group usually is of 8-12 persons. While selecting these persons, care has to be taken to see that they should have a common background and have similar experiences in buying. This is required because there should not be a conflict among the group members on the common issues that are being discussed. During the discussion, future buying attitudes, present buying opinion, etc., are gathered.

Most of the companies conducting the focus groups, first screen the candidates to determine who will compose the particular group. Firms also take care to avoid groups, in which some of the participants have their friends and relatives, because this leads to a biased discussion. Normally, a number of such groups are constituted and the final conclusion of various groups are taken for formulating the hypothesis. Therefore, a key factor in focus group is to have similar groups. Normally, there are 4-5 groups. Some of them may even have 6-8 groups. The guiding criteria is to see whether the latter groups are generating additional ideas or repeating the same with respect to the subject under study. When this shows a diminishing return from the group, the discussion is stopped. The typical focus group discussion lasts for 1-30 hours to 2 hours. The moderator under the focus group has a key role. His job is to guide the group to proceed in the right direction.

USES	TYPES
1. (i) Formulate Problem more Precisely	1. Literary Search
(ii) Develop Hypothesis	
2. (i) Establish Priority for Research	2. Experience Survey
(ii) Eliminate impractical ideas	
(iii) Clarify Concept	
3. Gather information about practical problems regarding the carrying out of research on particular conceptual statement	3. Focus Group
4. Increase the Analysts familiarity	4. Analysis of selected cases

4. *Analysis of Selected Cases:* Analysing a selected case sometimes gives an insight into the problem which is being researched. Case histories of companies which have undergone a similar situation

may be available. These case studies are well suited to carry out exploratory research. However, the result of investigation of case histories are always considered suggestive, rather than conclusive. In case of preference to "ready to eat food", many case histories may be available in the form of previous studies made by competitors. We must carefully examine the already published case studies with regard to other variables such as price, advertisement, changes in the taste, etc.

❖ Conclusive Research Design

Research designed to assist the decision-maker in determining, evaluating and selecting the best course of action to take in a given situation. It is intended to verify insights and aid decision-makers in selecting a specific course of action. The primary purpose of conclusive research, also known as confirmatory research, is to help decision-makers choose the best course of action in a situation. It is especially useful when a decision-maker already has in mind one or more alternatives and is specifically looking for information pertinent to evaluating them. Since data requirements are clearly specified in a situation calling for conclusive research, and since such research is intended as an aid in the final stages of the decision-making process, conclusive research is typically more formal and rigorous than exploratory research. There are two basic forms of conclusive research: casual research and descriptive research. The distinction between the two is based on the primary purpose of a conclusive research project and the nature of the inferences one can draw from it.

Causal Research

It is used to obtain evidence of cause-and-effect (causal) relationships. Marketing managers continually make decisions based on assumed causal relationships. These assumptions may not be justifiable, and the validity of the causal relationships should be examined via formal research. Causal research is appropriate for the following purposes:

1. To understand which variables are the cause (independent variables) and which variables are the effect (dependent variables) of a phenomenon.
2. To determine the nature of the relationship between the causal variables and the effect to be predicted.

Like descriptive research, causal research requires a planned and structured design. Although descriptive research can determine the degree of association between variables, it is not appropriate for examining causal relationships. Such an examination requires a causal design, in which the causal, or independent, variables are manipulated in a relatively controlled environment. A relatively controlled environment is one in which the other variables that may affect the dependent variable are controlled or checked as much as possible. The effect of this manipulation on one or more dependent variables is then measured to infer causality. The main method of causal research is experimentation. Designed to provide information on potential cause-and-effect relationships. Most practical in marketing to talk about associations or impact of one variable on another.

Causal Design

A casual design investigates the cause and effect relationship between two or more variables. It helps in eliminating factors that are not relevant. It is based on reasoning along well tested lines. The three basic principles based on logic for casual research as stated by John Stuart Mill are:

1. ***Method of agreement:*** "When two or more cases of given phenomenon have one and only condition in common, then that condition may be regarded as the cause (effect) of the phenomenon." This method is called the method of agreement.

For example, there are two situations and three conditions (C, E, Z).

If we find observation Z in every case, where we find condition C, we may conclude that C and Z are causally related. E is to be eliminated. The effect is shown under:

Situation 1: C ⟶ Z

Situation 2: E ⟶ Z

Therefore C ⟶ Z are causally related.

2. ***Method of negative agreement:*** This states that when condition C is found not to associate with observation, without Z, we may conclude that negative relationship exists between C and Z. This means, that the method of negative agreement is exactly opposite to method of agreement.

3. ***Method of concomitant variation:*** It is also known as method of difference. In the following example, the first observation shows that C could cause Z and the second shows that other possible factors could not cause Z.

Situation 1: A ⟶ B ⟶ C Produce ⟶ Z

Situation 2: A ⟶ B ⟶ without C Produce No-Z

Therefore ⟶ C ⟶ Produces ⟶ Z

Descriptive Research

It provides an accurate position of a particular aspect of market environment. The purpose of this is to gather quantified measurements of specific type of reactions. It describes market structure and is survey method based. It's structure is concerned with answering questions like "what is the situation like"? It is used to find out the demographic and psychographic characteristics of consumers, consumer's attitude towards different brands in market, marked share and competitive position of a company, etc., It is used as a confirmatory study to prove or disprove certain conjectures developed during explanatory phase of research. The data collected is inform of direct and indirect questions and will depend upon:

1. Nature of research question
2. Tune frame of study
3. Funds available
4. Kinds of respondents.

Descriptive Research (who, what, where, how)

Designed to provide further insight into the research problem by describing the variables of interest. Can be used for profiling, defining, segmentation, estimating, predicting, and examining associative relationships.

Cross-sectional Designs

It studies the effect of different levels of treatments on several groups at the same time. It can be represented below. An example would be different kind of incentives (X_1 to X_4) given for the same product in various territories (O_1 to O_4). This would help in understanding the effect of varying the incentive on the sales performance across territories

Treatment 1: X_1 O_1

Treatment 2: X_2 O_2

Treatment 3: X_3 O_3

Treatment 4: X_4 O_4

1. *Single Cross-sectional Design:* Only one sample of respondents is drawn from the target population, and information is obtained from this sample only once. These designs are also called sample survey research designs.

2. *Multiple Cross-sectional Designs:* There are two or more samples of respondents and information from each sample is obtained only once. Often, information from different samples is obtained at different times over long intervals. Multiple cross-sectional designs allow comparisons at the aggregate level but not at the individual respondent level. As a different sample is taken each time a survey is conducted, there is no way to compare the measures on an individual respondent across surveys. One type of multiple cross-sectional design of special interest is cohort analysis.

Longitudinal Design

Longitudinal designs (also known as Time series designs) are an extension of the pretest-posttest design. They provide repetitive measurements of the same kind of events at various points in time. Changes that take place during those intervals are registered. This type of design is very useful in monitoring studies, where its performance feedback may signal problems. We instead will be speaking in terms of using this design for causal measurement.

Time series and trend designs: In a time series design, data is collected from the sample or population at successive intervals. The trend data relate to matched samples drawn from the same population at successive intervals. It can be of many types. A simple design can be represented as below:

$$X - O$$

Where X indicates the exposure of a group to an experimental treatment and O indicates the observation or measurement taken on the subject or group after an experimental treatment. Another method also involves a control group. This can be represented as below:

$$X - O_1\ O_2\ O_3\ O_4\ O_5\ O_6$$

Where 'O' represents measurement of the control group. This is termed as multiple time-series design.

Combinational Design

This design combines both the time-series and cross-sectional designs. This design is generally seen while measuring advertising effectiveness in a panel. An advertisement is run and the respondents are asked if they have seen it earlier. Those who have seen it earlier constitute the test group and those who have not constitute the control group. The purchase made before and after the advertisement by the test and the control group marks the advertising effectiveness. So many research designs have been listed. The one that is ultimately selected should help in solving the problem. It should help in arriving at the desired conclusions.

Experimental Research

In this category, the researcher plays an active role by manipulating the Independent Variable (IV) in the form of delivery of a treatment or intervention. Experimental research is conducted to examine cause and effect. Two types of design fall into this category. The following three elements must be present in a study for it to be considered an experimental design, Random assignment of subjects to the control/ comparison group or the experimental group, Manipulation of the IV by the researcher Control of the research setting and situation by the researcher.

Quasi-experimental Research

Because of the ethical nature of conducting studies with human subjects, often an experimental design is not feasible. The quasi-experimental design must include: Manipulation of the IV (Indirect Variable) by the researcher. However, in quasi-experimental design there is a non-equivalent comparison group. It is called a comparison group, instead of control group because members of the group were not randomly assigned to experimental or control conditions. Thus, there is no assurance that subject characteristics are equally and randomly distributed between groups, and this introduces a potential source of error. Control of the research setting and situation.

INTERRELATION BETWEEN EXPLORATORY, DESCRIPTIVE, AND CAUSAL RESEARCH

We have described exploratory, descriptive, and causal research as major classifications of research designs, but the distinctions among these classifications are not absolute. A given marketing research project may involve more than one type of research design and thus, serve several purposes. Which combination of research designs should be employed depends on the nature of the problem. We offer the following general guidelines for choosing research designs:

1. When little is known about the problem situation, it is desirable to begin with exploratory research. Exploratory research is appropriate when the problem needs to be defined more precisely, alternative courses of action identified, research questions or hypotheses developed, and key variables isolated and classified as dependent or independent.

2. Exploratory research is the initial step in the overall research design framework. It should, in most instances, be followed by descriptive or causal research. For example, hypotheses developed via exploratory research should be statistically tested using descriptive or causal research. Exploratory research in the form of secondary data analysis and focus groups was conducted to identify the social causes that American businesses should be concerned about. Then a descriptive cross-sectional survey was undertaken to quantity the relative salience of these causes.

3. It is not necessary to begin every research design with exploratory research. It depends upon the precision with which the problem has been defined and the researcher's degree of certainty about the approach to the problem. A research design could well begin with descriptive or causal research. To illustrate, a consumer satisfaction survey that is conducted annual need not begin with or include an exploratory phase each year.

4. Although exploratory research is generally the initial step, it need not be. Exploratory research may follow descriptive or causal research. For example, descriptive or causal research results in findings that are hard for managers to interpret. Exploratory research may provide more insights to help understand these findings.

TABLE 2.1 A Comparison of Basic Research Designs

	Exploratory	Descriptive	Causal
Objective	Discovery of ideas	Describes market characteristics	Determines cause and effect
Characteristics	Flexible, versatile. Front end research	Prior formulation of hypothesis. Planned, structured design.	Manipulates Independent variables. Control of other variables
Methods	Secondary data	Surveys	Experiments

TABLE 2.2 Differences between Exploratory and Conclusive Research

Research Project Components	Exploratory Research	Conclusive Research
Research purpose	General: to generate insights about a situation	Specific: to verify insights and aid in selecting a course of action
Data needs	Vague	Clear
Data sources	Ill defined	Well defined
Data collection form	Open-ended, rough	Usually structured
Sample	Relatively small; subjectively selected to maximize generalization of insights	Relatively large; objectively selected to permit generalization of findings
Data collection	Flexible; no set procedure	Rigid: well-laid-out procedure
Data analysis	Informal; typical non-quantitative	Formal; typically quantitative
Inferences	More tentative than final recommendations	More final than tentative

APPLICATION OF MARKETING RESEARCH TECHNIQUES

1. *Advertising tracking:* Periodic or continuous in-market research to monitor a brand's performance using measures such as brand awareness, brand preference, and product usage.
2. *Advertising research:* Used to predict copy testing or track the efficacy of advertisements for any medium, measured by the ad's ability to get attention, communicate the message, build the brand's image, and motivate the consumer to purchase the product or service.
3. *Brand equity research:* How favorably do consumers view the brand?
4. *Brand name testing:* What do consumers feel about the names of the products?
5. *Commercial eye tracking research:* Examine advertisements, package designs, websites, etc., by analyzing visual behavior of the consumer.
6. *Concept testing:* To test the acceptance of a concept by target consumers.
7. *Coolhunting:* To make observations and predictions in changes of new or existing cultural trends in areas such as fashion, music, films, television, youth culture and lifestyle.
8. *Buyer decision processes research:* To determine what motivates people to buy and what decision-making process they use.
9. *Copy testing:* Predicts in-market performance of an ad before it airs by analyzing audience levels of attention, brand linkage, motivation, entertainment, and communication, as well as breaking down the ad's flow of attention and flow of emotion.
10. *Customer satisfaction studies:* Exit interviews or surveys that determine a customer's level of satisfaction with the quality of the transaction.

11. ***Demand estimation:*** To determine the approximate level of demand for the product.
12. ***Distribution channel audits:*** To assess distributors' and retailers' attitudes toward a product, brand, or company.
13. ***Internet strategic intelligence:*** Searching for customer opinions in the Internet: chats, forums, web pages, blogs... where people express freely about their experiences with products, becoming strong "opinion formers."
14. ***Marketing effectiveness and analytics:*** Building models and measuring results to determine the effectiveness of individual marketing activities.
15. ***Mystery shopping:*** An employee or representative of the market research firm anonymously contacts a salesperson and indicates he or she is shopping for a product. The shopper then records the entire experience. This method is often used for quality control or for researching competitors' products.
16. ***Positioning research:*** How does the target market see the brand relative to competitors? What does the brand stand for?
17. ***Price elasticity testing:*** To determine how sensitive customers are to price changes.
18. ***Sales forecasting:*** To determine the expected level of sales given the level of demand. With respect to other factors like Advertising expenditure, sales promotion, etc.
19. ***Segmentation research:*** To determine the demographic, psychographic, and behavioural characteristics of potential buyers.
20. ***Online panel:*** A group of individuals who accepted to respond to marketing research online.
21. ***Store audit:*** To measure the sales of a product or product line at a statistically selected store sample in order to determine market share, or to determine whether a retail store provides adequate service.
22. ***Test marketing:*** A small-scale product launch used to determine the likely acceptance of the product when it is introduced into a wider market.
23. ***Viral Marketing research:*** Refers to marketing research designed to estimate the probability that specific communications will be transmitted throughout an individuals social network.
24. ***Social Networking Potential (SNP):*** Are combined with estimates of selling effectiveness to estimate ROI on specific combinations of messages and media.

REVIEW QUESTIONS

1. Define research design and discuss various research designs.
2. Explain the differences between exploratory and conclusive research designs.
3. Define and discuss the issues of research reliability and validity and explain the typical methods used to address these issues.
4. What is research process? Discuss the steps in research process.
5. Discuss the importance of research process.
6. How to define a problem?
7. Explain the applications of marketing research design in various fields.

Case Study 1 SI's Fading Jeans and Market Share

The Situation

As of 2006, SI's is a leading global apparel company, with sales in more than 110 countries. It has been a long standing company with over 150 years of being in the clothing business. While one may think this long history can only result in good things, SI's heritage has been its worst enemy. Philip Marineau, the president and chief executives officer for SI's Strauss & Co., had to work to revamp SI's antique image and make the brand appealing to younger generation in efforts to boost its declining sales. In the last five years, Marineau saw worldwide sales drop 40 per cent, losing market share to competitors like the Gap, and trendier ones such as Calvin Klien, Tommy Hilfiger, and Diesel. Another problem for Marineau came from store brand jeans, such as JCPenney's Arizona brand jeans or the Gap's in-house brand, which have changed their image and launched an assault on big brand names like SI's. These store brand jeans, along with other store label jeans, now target the teenage market with "cutting edge" advertising. American trade publication Brand Strategy estimated that the brand has lost about 50 per cent of the younger consumer market share worldwide between 1999 and 2005.

To compete with these brands and maintain leadership, SI's market leader, is considering introducing their own line of private-label jeans to capture a larger portion of the teenage market. Philip Marineau wonders. "How powerful is a national brand like SI's compared to an in-house brand like Gap or a store brand like JCpenney's Arizona jeans?"

The Marketing Research Decision

1. If you were Philip Marineau, what type of research would you want to conduct to help arrive at an answer?
2. Please explain how you would implement the type of research you have recommended.

Case Study 2 Sanku Autos

Sanku Autos has been in business since 1967. It has always been a successful, professional organization. Since the locality has an economy based mainly upon agriculture, their traditional customer has been the aspiring Indian consumer, usually business or professional people.

Recently they have noticed that their local market has changed considerably. Sanku has become a center for tourism and recreation for Indians from Banglore and Hyderabad, as well as Delhi and Calcutta. There are many beach clubs, hotels, apartments, and holiday condos.

Mr. Gopi, the sales manager at Sanku, feels that the company may have a problem. They do not know who their customer is and hence, cannot target advertising.

You are the Account Representative for Mita Marketing Research Associates. Advise Mr. Gopi on an appropriate method of marketing research, and describe any advantages and disadvantages of such a method.

Case Study 3 Gokul Housing

Gokul Housing, Inc. (GHI), is a local nonprofit organization located in Matruchaya Tirumalgiri. GHI provides assistance to homeless and very low-income individuals and families in finding emergency shelter, food, employment, transitional housing and affordable apartment housing. These services are provided through the following four basic GHI programs.:

1. The Drop-In Shelter: An emergency drop—in shelter for men located at AOC Gate.
2. The Hospitality House: A day shelter for homeless and very low income men and women.
3. The Gokul Housing Program: Provides transitional living arrangements for families and single men for six months or more depending on the needs of the individual/family and the unit.
4. The Housing Opportunity Program: Helps families in obtaining a lease.

As part of its planning, the board of directors of GHI was interested in determining ways to improve the organization's services. Their original thought was to conduct a survey of organization's paid staff, volunteers, and guests (the homeless staying at GHI or using its facilities or services), to determine which programs of GHI they found particularly useful, which should be revised, and what other programs or services might be of more assistance to guests.

However, the analysis of GHI's internal statistics and other published data indicated the need for GHI to narrow its focus. Specifically, internal information indicated the number of agencies serving the male homeless population was decreasing. Moreover, GHI was currently the only Madison shelter that served the male homeless population, and this community appeared to be undeserved.

In fact, the number of homeless men staying at GHI's Drop—In Shelter had increased 89 per cent, from 60% three years ago to 1,146 the past year. This was partly due to the closing of other male shelters in the last three years. Finally, the GHI shelter was filled beyond its capacity of 66 men per night. During the winter, there were frequently more than 90 men staying at the Drop-In Shelter on any given night, with many of them sleeping on the hallway floor.

Given this information, the board of directors decided to use the organization's limited resources to focus first on the Drop—In Shelter. More specifically, the board asked for an evaluation of GHI's current facilities and the services for the homeless as well as a determination of what future services and facilities it should try to provide.

Questions

1. What is the research problem?
2. How should the research be structured?
3. What kind of research design would be appropriate for this purpose?
4. What information would you collect for this research problem?

Case Study 4 Bhavatti Ltd.

Bhavatti Ltd. is a large Indian cement company. It has plants in almost all parts of the country. It is an established company and enjoys very high level of brand awareness among cement customers. However, its brands do not command highest levels of price premier in the market. Cement, being a logistics heavy commodity, tends to have its market boundaries within a given radius from the plant location. Cement plants tend to get located near the lime deposits (raw material) to save on the transportation costs. Competition is generally among the multiple plants, national cement brands and a few small regional companies. Cement demand originates basically from the following sectors:

1. Infrastructure Projects
2. Large Industrial Projects
3. Large Housing Projects
4. Private Individual Houses

All of the above sectors vary along their respective demand levels, brand salience and other buying considerations. Price sensitivities and competition intensities do also change significantly from one sector to another.

Bhavatti Ltd. is thinking of putting up a new plant in the North Indian state of Bharatkhand. Bharatkhand has very little deposit of lime. Therefore, the raw materials for this plant have to be brought from outside. Marketing factors are expected to be more important here. Bhavatti Ltd. wants to take the decision of starting the new plant systematically. Therefore, they would first like to collect proper market based data before the decision.

Question

1. Prepare a marketing research proposal for helping Bhavatti Ltd.

CHAPTER THREE

DATA COLLECTION METHODS

INTRODUCTION

The procedures and devices used to obtain primary data vary depending on the sampling and measurement requirements. Data collection is a key part of the research plan and often represents the biggest cost of primary research. Data collection methods need to be mastered by the professional marketing researcher. The purpose of marketing research is to aid the decision-making process in marketing, all decisions will be based on correct and accurate data supplied by the marketing research department. For marketing decisions to be effective, it is necessary that the research should be more focused and restricted to the crucial information which is being sought.

Common information sought by the marketing researchers:

1. *Product Management*
   (i) Analysis of existing products in terms of product usage and consumption pattern.
   (ii) Product Life Cycle and management.
   (iii) Product differentiation and consumer satisfaction with product and service.
   (iv) Feedback on the acceptance of new product.
   (v) Advertising and promotion of new products.
2. *Pricing*
   (i) Past trends and current price structures.
   (ii) Consumers and price sensitivity.
   (iii) Effects of price change.
3. *Distribution*
   (i) Effectiveness of distribution outlets in terms of sales and types of outlets.
   (ii) Feedback from distribution network.
4. *Market*
   (i) Total size of the market along with consumer profiles and requirements.
   (ii) Market segmentation including targeting, growing trends indicates growth or decline.

5. *Marketing strategy*
   (i) Composition of the market which includes major competitors – their market share
   (ii) Brand management
   (iii) Distribution management.
6. *Promotion*
   (i) Online and offline promotional activities.
   (ii) Events planning and creative development.
   (iii) Media data and promotion planning.
   (iv) Sales planning activities.

DATA SOURCES

One of the most important components of marketing research is collection of data required to solve a defined research problem. Data are basically of two type's viz., secondary data and primary data. Depending upon the nature of research, the importance will be given to the type of data. The general tendency of the researcher is to organize a survey and collect the data from the field. The most important point to be considered before this is to search for the secondary sources and gather data already available. This gives a logical perspective to problem solving. Only then the actual data is required to be collected from the primary source. Hence, it is imperative to know the advantages and disadvantages of Secondary and Primary data.

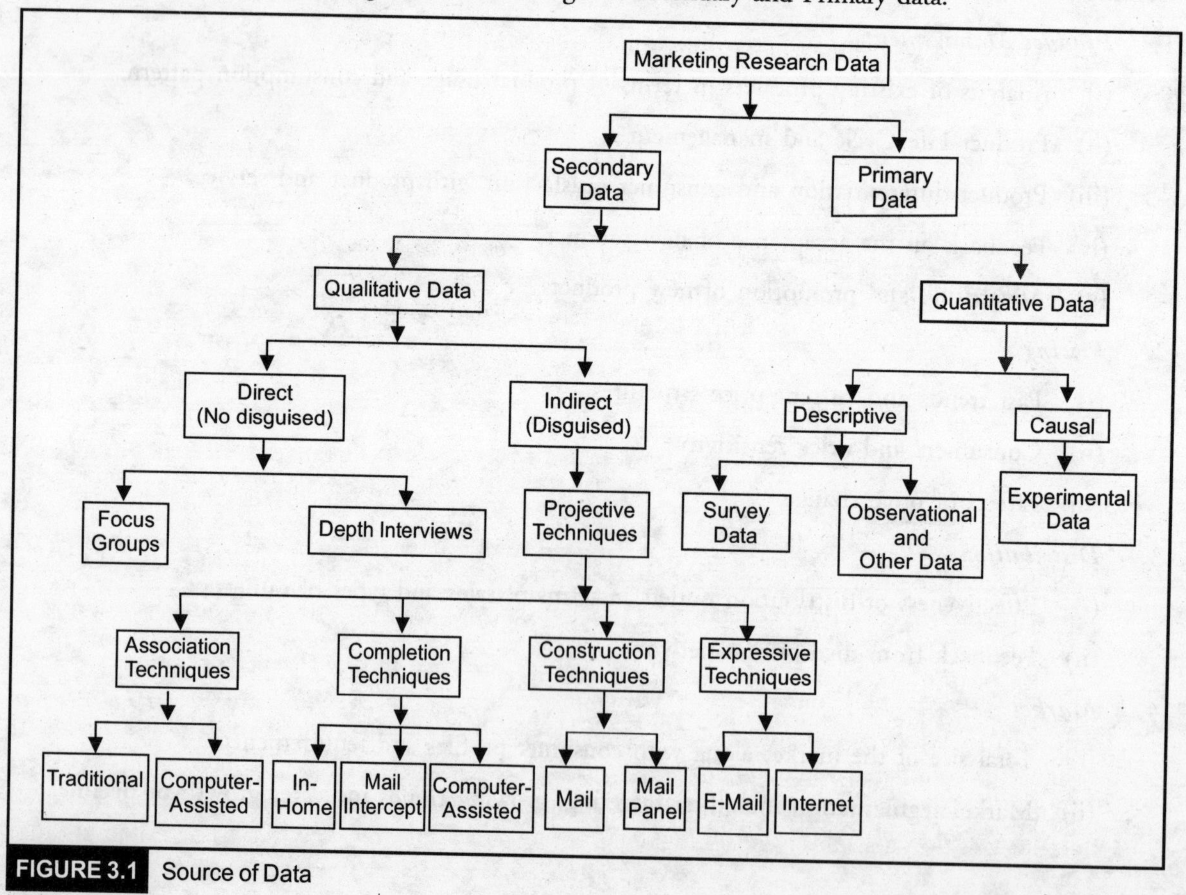

FIGURE 3.1 Source of Data

❖ Secondary Data

Secondary data is defined as the data that has been collected by individuals or agencies for purposes other than those of the particular research study. For example, if a government department has conducted a survey of, say, school going children, then a uniform manufacturer might use this data for his research purpose. As mentioned earlier, it is ideal to undertake a marketing research study after a prior search of secondary sources (also termed desk research). The reasons for this are summed up below. Many a time secondary data may itself be sufficient to draw conclusions and solve the problem. Primary data collection may not be required.

Advantages of Secondary Data

1. Secondary data is economical than collecting primary data. A thorough examination of secondary sources can yield a great deal more information than through a primary data collection exercise which needs to be critically evaluated.
2. Searching secondary sources is much less time consuming than primary data collection.
3. Secondary sources of information may at times consider a large sample and hence, can yield more accurate data than that primary research. This is especially true for census information or syndicated reports by government departments which are generally large scale. This is likely to yield far more accurate results than custom designed surveys that are based on relatively small sample sizes.
4. Secondary data can play a substantial role in the exploratory phase of the research when the main objective is to define the research problem and to generate hypotheses. The assembly and analysis of secondary data helps in better understanding of the marketing problem. This also gives an idea about the course of action and missing links in the primary research.
5. Secondary sources are very useful to structure the sample and define the problem.
6. Secondary data is the only resource in the case of historical documents.
7. Large-scale trends can be predicted only with secondary data.
8. Wide range of availability.
9. It serves as a source of comparative data.

Disadvantages of Secondary Data

Even though the secondary data offers a lot of advantages; it also has its own shortcomings. This corresponds to both the source and the quality of the data. The main disadvantages are as follows:

1. The researcher has to be careful while using the units defined in the data. It is better to study the definitions used prior to accepting the same for research purpose. Hence, while considering secondary data on the size of family, these definitions need to be kept in mind. It should be noted that definitions may change over time and if this is not evaluated, the conclusion derived may be wrong.
2. The errors of measurements are not generally published in secondary sources and hence, this should be considered while looking at data from secondary sources. The solution is to try to speak to the individuals involved in the collection of the data to obtain some guidance on the level of accuracy of the data. This is especially crucial if the stake is high in terms of commercial implications.

3. The data has to be validated for source biases as it may have been prepared to appear exaggerated or otherwise. Hence, it is better to go through details of the purpose for which the data had been collected.
4. The reliability of published data may vary over time. Hence, the data needs to be checked for time validity.
5. Many a time, the data collected may be outdated and hence it needs to be refreshed again. This may otherwise hinder the analysis. All these drawbacks do exist, but still secondary data has its own merits. It is ideal to use multiple sources of secondary data.

Sources of Secondary Data

Secondary data can be collected from two sources: internal sources and external sources.

Internal Sources of Secondary Data

Lot of data is available within the organization regarding day-to-day operations. These data can be utilized wherever required. These include:

1. *Sales data:* Sales orders are received, invoiced and delivered. Cost of the goods supplied is also recorded. Sales across different territories are recorded via the reports received from the field. Most of these reports can be used for making marketing decisions. These resources are helpful to answer questions pertaining to research objective, the population of interest and the time period selected, can be reworked as per requirement, cost of data and its worth and the data accuracy. Lot of information is generally available pertaining to sales by territory, sales by customer type, geographical area, etc. This data can be used to identify the most profitable products, tracking sales trends, analysis on discounts given, scattering pattern of sales orders, effect of seasonality on sales, etc.
2. *Financial data:* This relates to data on various costs involved in procurement of raw materials, production of goods, distribution of goods, conversion costs, labor costs, transportation cost, storage cost, etc. With such data, the efficiency of operation can be determined. It helps in assessing the cost of production of a new product, analysis the cost of free capacity, etc.
3. *Transportation data:* A good record of the data relating to transport operations determine which route to use, which transporter to use, cost of effective routing patterns, etc. This helps in determining whether it would be sensible to have your own vehicle or hire a vehicle. This enables decision towards a trade off analysis towards a better profitability.
4. *Human resource data:* Enormous information could be collected from an organizational perspective from the human resource department. Data on employee turnover, absenteeism, strength of employees could be obtained. This would help in man power planning for the present and future, succession planning, training and development for better productivity, etc.
5. *Storage data:* This may help in calculating the direct product profitability by calculating the rate of stock turn; stock handling costs, assessing the efficiency of certain marketing operations and the efficiency of the marketing system as a whole.

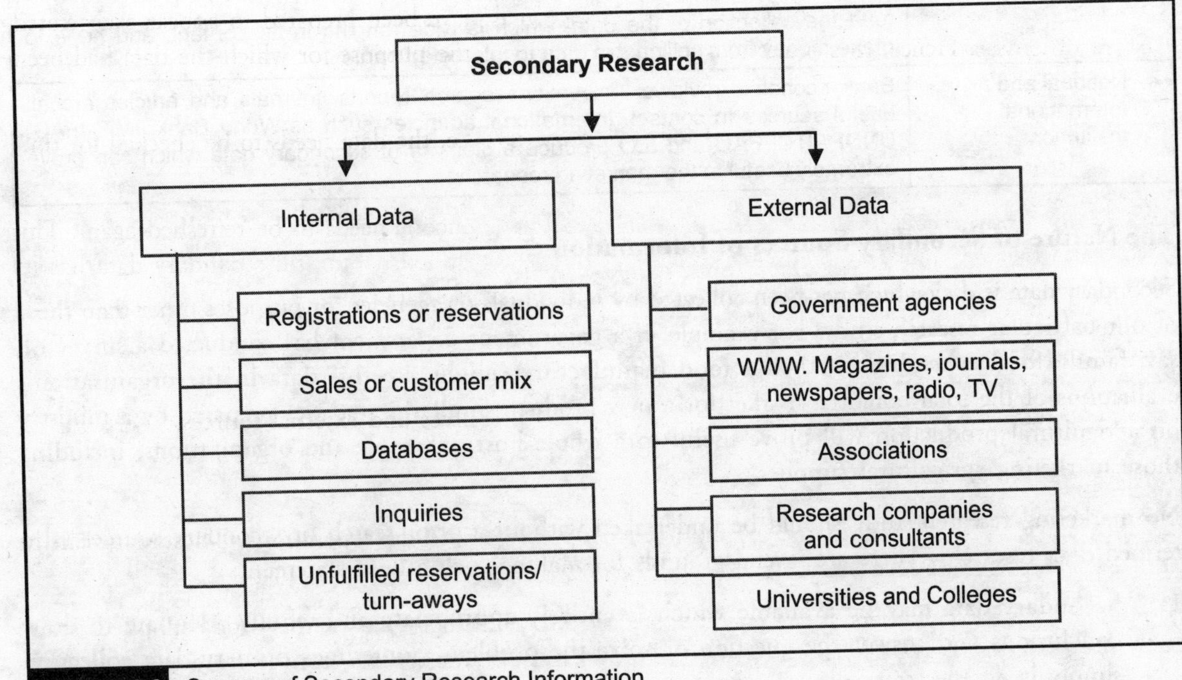

FIGURE 3.2 Sources of Secondary Research Information

External Sources of Secondary Data

Lot of secondary data is now available further to the discovery of World Wide Web and lot of institutions looking at such analysis. Large number of organizations provide marketing information including national and local government agencies, quasi-government agencies, trade associations, universities, research institutes, financial institutions, specialist suppliers of secondary marketing data and professional marketing research enterprises. The main sources of external secondary sources are: (1) Government (federal, state and local), (2) Trade associations, (3) Commercial services, (4) National and International Institutions.

TABLE 3.1 External Sources of Secondary Data

Sources of External Secondary Data	Description
1. Government Statistics	These may include all or some of the following: ● Population census ● Social surveys, family expenditure surveys ● Import/export statistics ● Production statistics ● Agricultural statistics.
2. Trade Associations	Trade associations differ widely in the extent of their data collection and information dissemination activities. However, it is worth checking with them to determine what they do publish. At the very least one would normally expect that they would produce a trade directory and, perhaps, a yearbook.
3. Commercial Services	Published market research reports and other publications are available from a wide range of organisations which charge for their information. Typically, marketing people are interested in media statistics and consumer information which has been obtained from large scale consumer or farmer panels. The commercial organisation

Contd...

	fund the collection of the data, which is wide ranging in its content, and hope to make money from selling this data to interested parties.
4. National and International Institutions	Bank economic reviews, university research reports, journals and articles are all useful sources to contact. International agencies such as World Bank, IMF, IFAD, UNDP, ITC, FAO and ILO produce a plethora of secondary data which can prove extremely useful to the marketing researcher.

The Nature of Secondary Sources of Information

Secondary data is data which has been collected by individuals or agencies for purposes other than those of our particular research study. For example, if a government department has conducted a survey of, say, family food expenditures, then a food manufacturer might use this data in the organisation's evaluations of the total potential market for a new product. Similarly, statistics prepared by a ministry on agricultural production will prove useful to a whole host of people and organisations, including those marketing agricultural supplies.

No marketing research study should be undertaken without a prior search of secondary sources (also termed desk research). There are several grounds for making such a bold statement:

1. Secondary data may be available which is entirely appropriate and wholly adequate to draw conclusions and answer the question or solve the problem. Sometimes primary data collection simply is not necessary.
2. It is far cheaper to collect secondary data than to obtain primary data. For the same level of research budget a thorough examination of secondary sources can yield a great deal more information than can be had through a primary data collection exercise.
3. The time involved in searching secondary sources is much less than that needed to complete primary data collection.
4. Secondary sources of information can yield more accurate data than that obtained through primary research. This is not always true but where a government or international agency has undertaken a large scale survey, or even a census, this is likely to yield far more accurate results than custom designed and executed surveys when these are based on relatively small sample sizes.
5. It should not be forgotten that secondary data can play a substantial role in the exploratory phase of the research when the task at hand is to define the research problem and to generate hypotheses. The assembly and analysis of secondary data almost invariably improves the researcher's understanding of the marketing problem, the various lines of inquiry that could or should be followed and the alternative courses of action which might be pursued.
6. Secondary sources help to define the population. Secondary data can be extremely useful both in defining the population and in structuring the sample to be taken. For instance, government statistics on a country's agriculture will help decide how to stratify a sample and, once sample estimates have been calculated, these can be used to project those estimates to the population.

The Problems of Secondary Data

Whilst the benefits of secondary sources are considerable, their shortcomings have to be acknowledged. There is a need to evaluate the quality of both the source of the data and the data itself. The main problems may be categorised as follows:

TABLE 3.2 Problems of Secondary Data

1. Definitions	The researcher has to be careful, when making use of secondary data, of the definitions used by those responsible for its preparation. Suppose, for example, researchers are interested in rural communities and their average family size. If published statistics are consulted then a check must be done on how terms such as "family size" have been defined. They may refer only to the nucleus family or include the extended family. Even apparently simple terms such as 'farm size' need careful handling. Such figures may refer to any one of the following: the land an individual owns, the land an individual owns plus any additional land he/she rents, the land an individual owns minus any land he/she rents out, all of his land or only that part of it which he actually cultivates. It should be noted that definitions may change over time and where this is not recognised erroneous conclusions may be drawn. Geographical areas may have their boundaries redefined, units of measurement and grades may change and imported goods can be reclassified from time to time for purposes of levying customs and excise duties.
2. Measurement error	When a researcher conducts fieldwork she/he is possibly able to estimate inaccuracies in measurement through the standard deviation and standard error, but these are sometimes not published in secondary sources. The only solution is to try to speak to the individuals involved in the collection of the data to obtain some guidance on the level of accuracy of the data. The problem is sometimes not so much 'error' but differences in levels of accuracy required by decision-makers. When the research has to do with large investments in, say, food manufacturing, management will want to set very tight margins of error in making market demand estimates. In other cases, having a high level of accuracy is not so critical. For instance, if a food manufacturer is merely assessing the prospects for one more flavour for a snack food already produced by the company then there is no need for highly accurate estimates in order to make the investment decision.
3. Source bias	Researchers have to be aware of vested interests when they consult secondary sources. Those responsible for their compilation may have reasons for wishing to present a more optimistic or pessimistic set of results for their organisation. It is not unknown, for example, for officials responsible for estimating food shortages to exaggerate figures before sending aid requests to potential donors. Similarly, and with equal frequency, commercial organisations have been known to inflate estimates of their market shares.
4. Reliability	The reliability of published statistics may vary over time. It is not uncommon, for example, for the systems of collecting data to have changed over time but without any indication of this to the reader of published statistics. Geographical or administrative boundaries may be changed by government, or the basis for stratifying a sample may have altered. Other aspects of research methodology that affect the reliability of secondary data is the sample size, response rate, questionnaire design and modes of analysis.
5. Time scale	Most censuses take place at 10 year intervals, so data from this and other published sources may be out-of-date at the time the researcher wants to make use of the statistics. The time period during which secondary data was first compiled may have a substantial effect upon the nature of the data. For instance, the significant increase in the price obtained for Ugandan coffee in the mid-90's could be interpreted as evidence of the effectiveness of the rehabilitation programme that set out to restore coffee estates which had fallen into a state of disrepair. However, more knowledgeable coffee market experts would interpret the rise in Ugandan coffee prices in the context of large scale destruction of the Brazilian coffee crop, due to heavy frosts, in 1994, Brazil being the largest coffee producer in the world.

❖ Primary vs. Secondary Data

Primary sources are the raw material of the research process, they represent the records of research or events as first described. Secondary sources are based on primary sources. These sources analyze, describe, and synthesize the primary or original source. Usage of primary source and secondary source should be complementary. Savvy entrepreneurs will do secondary research first and then conduct primary research. For example, the owner of a video-rental shop would want to know all about a neighbourhood before opening a new store there. Using information gleaned from secondary sources, the owner can find all kinds of demographic data, including detailed income data and spending patterns. They can then send out a questionnaire to a sampling of households to find out what kinds of movies people like to rent. That primary-research technique will help when it comes to stocking the store with the latest film releases.

Secondary research lays the groundwork and primary research helps fill in the gaps. By using both types of market research, business owners get a well rounded view of their market and have the information they need to make important business decisions. The selection of methods depends upon various factors like:

1. Scope of the study.
2. Objectives of the study.
3. Time availability for the study.
4. Degree of accuracy needed.
5. Study environment, respondents.
6. Budget estimated.

❖ Primary Data

Primary data collection begins when a researcher is not able to find the data required for his research purpose from the secondary sources. Market researchers are interested in a variety of primary data about demographic/socioeconomic characteristics, attitudes/opinions/interests, awareness/knowledge, intentions, motivation, and behavior. There are two basic means of obtaining primary data depending on the nature of the problem and the availability of time and money.

Collection of Primary Data and Methods of Collection

Primary data is data collected for the first time. It is original and collected for a specific purpose, or to solve a specific problem. It is expensive, and time consuming, but is more focused than secondary research. There are many ways to collect primary data. Observation, questionnaire, interview, focus groups, projective techniques, product tests, diaries, omnibus studies, clinics, surveys, case study, etc., are the prime methods.

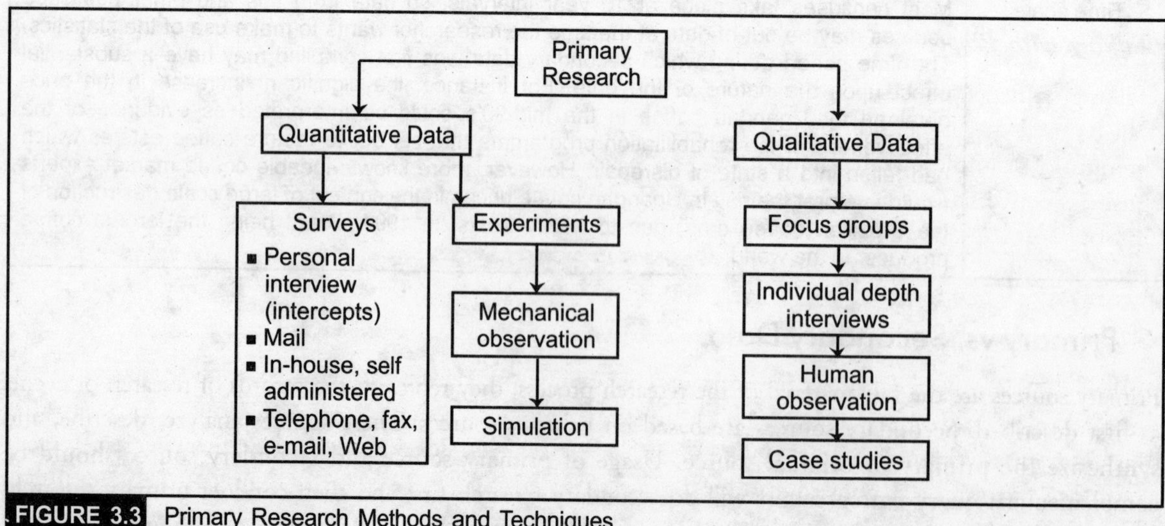

FIGURE 3.3 Primary Research Methods and Techniques

Primary data can be classified basically as qualitative and quantitative data. The same is explained in the following sections.

QUALITATIVE RESEARCH TECHNIQUES

Although qualitative research can be used as part of formal research, it is most commonly encountered when conducting exploratory research. Qualitative research techniques are part of primary research.

The characteristics of Qualitative research include:

1. The data is usually gathered using less structured research instruments.
2. The findings are more in-depth since they make greater use of open-ended questions.
3. The results provide much more detail on behaviour, attitudes and motivation.
4. The research is more intensive and more flexible, allowing the researcher to probe since s/he has greater latitude to do so.
5. The results are based on smaller sample sizes and are often not representative of the population.
6. The research can usually not be replicated or repeated, given its low reliability; and
7. The analysis of the results is much more subjective.

❖ Research Methods for Data Collection

There are many ways to get information. The most common research methods are:

Literature Search

It involves reviewing all readily available materials. These materials can include internal company information, relevant trade publications, newspapers, magazines, annual reports, company literature, on-line data bases, and any other published materials. It is a very inexpensive method of gathering information, although it often does not yield timely information. Literature searches over the web are the fastest, while library literature searches can take between one and eight weeks.

Talking with People

Talking with people is a good way to get information during the initial stages of a research project. It can be used to gather information that is not publicly available, or that is too new to be found in the literature. Examples might include meetings with prospects, customers, suppliers, and other types of business conversations at trade shows, seminars, and association meetings. Although often valuable, the information has questionable validity because it is highly subjective and might not be representative of the population.

The Pilot Study

When data is collected from a limited number of subjects selected from the population targeted by the research project, we refer to it as a pilot study. A pilot study can also take the form of a trial run. For instance, an advertising campaign is tested in a specific market before it goes nation-wide, to study the response by potential consumers. In a pilot study, the rigorous standards used to obtain precise, quantitative estimates from large, representative samples are often relaxed, since the objective is to gain insight into how subjects will respond prior to administering the full survey instrument. Although a pilot study constitutes primary research, it tends to be used in the context of a qualitative analysis. There are four major qualitative research techniques that can be used as part of a pilot study. These are:

1. *The Depth Interview:* When it is important to explore a subject in detail or probe for latent attitudes and feelings, the in-depth interview may be the appropriate technique to use. Depth interviews are usually conducted in person, although telephone depth interviewing is slowly gaining greater acceptance.

   With the approval of the respondent, the interview is audio-taped, and may even be video-taped, in order to facilitate record keeping. Although it is a good idea to prepare an interview guide ahead of time to be sure to cover all aspects of the topic, the interviewer has significant freedom to encourage the interviewee to elaborate or explain answers. It is even possible to digress from the topic outline, if it is thought to be fruitful.

   Interviewers must be very experienced or skilled, since it is critical that s/he and the respondent establish some kind of rapport, and that s/he can adapt quickly to the personality and mood of the person being interviewed. This will elicit more truthful answers. In order to receive full cooperation from the respondent, the interviewer must be knowledgeable about the topic, and able to relate to the respondent on his/her own terms, using the vocabulary normally used within the sector being studied. But the interviewer must also know when it is necessary to probe deeper, get the interviewee to elaborate, or broaden the topic of discussion.

   Since an interview can last anywhere from 20 to 120 minutes, it is possible to obtain a very detailed picture about the issues being researched. Even without considering the potential from interviewer bias, analyzing the information obtained requires great skill and may be quite subjective. Quantifying and extrapolating the information may also prove to be difficult.

2. *The Focus Group:* A focus group is used as a preliminary research technique to explore people's ideas and attitudes. It is often used to test new approaches (such as products or advertising), and to discover customer concerns. A group of 6 to 20 people meet in a conference-room-like setting with a trained moderator. The room usually contains a one-way mirror for viewing, including audio and video capabilities. The moderator leads the group's discussion and keeps the focus on the areas you want to explore. Their disadvantage is that the sample is small and may not be representative of the population in general.

   In the applied social sciences, focus group discussions or group depth interviews are among the most widely used research tools. General features of Focused Group are:

   (i) A focus group takes advantage of the interaction between a small group of people. Participants will respond to and build on what others in the group have said. It is believed that this synergistic approach generates more insightful information, and encourages discussion participants to give more candid answers. Focus groups are further characterized by the presence of a moderator and the use of a discussion guide. The moderator should stimulate discussion among group members rather than interview individual members, that is to say every participant should be encouraged to express his/her views on each topic as well as respond to the views expressed by the other participants. In order to put focus group participants at ease, the moderator will often start out by assuring everyone that there are no right or wrong answers, and that his/her feelings cannot be hurt by any views that are expressed since s/he does not work for the organization for whom the research is being conducted.

   (ii) Although the moderator's role is relatively passive, it is critical in keeping the discussion relevant. Some participants will try to dominate the discussion or talk about aspects that are of little interest to the research at hand. The type of data that needs to be obtained from the participants will determine the extent to which the session needs to be structured and therefore just how directive the moderator must be.

(iii) Although focus group sessions can be held in many different settings, and have been known to be conducted via conference call, they are most often conducted in special facilities that permit audio recording and/or video taping, and are equipped with a one-way mirror. This observation of research process as it happens can be invaluable when trying to interpret the results. The many disparate views that are expressed in the course of the 1 to 2 hour discussion make it at times difficult to capture all observations on each topic. Rather than simply summarizing comments, possible avenues for further research or hypotheses for testing should be brought out.

(iv) Focus groups are normally made up of anywhere between 6 and 12 people with common characteristics. These must be in relation to what is being studied, and can consist of demographic characteristics as well as a certain knowledge base or familiarity with a given topic. For instance, when studying perceptions about a certain destination, it may be important to have a group that has visited it before, while another group would be composed of non-visitors. It must, however, be recognized that focus group discussions will only attract a certain type of participant, for the most part extroverts.

(v) It is common practice to provide a monetary incentive to focus group participants depending on the length of the discussion and the socio-demographic characteristics of the participants being recruited. Usually several focus groups are required to provide the complete diversity of views, and thus this is a fairly expensive option among the research techniques. This incentive makes it easier to recruit participants, but can also lead to 'professional' respondents. These are people who participate in too many focus groups, and thus learn to anticipate the flow of the discussion. Some researchers believe that these types of respondents no longer represent the population.

3. ***Panels:*** When it is important to collect information on trends, whether with respect to consumer preferences and purchasing behaviour or changes in business climate and opportunities, researchers may decide to set up a panel of individuals which can be questioned or surveyed over an extended period of time.

The most common uses for panels are:

(i) Trend monitoring and future assessment,

(ii) Test marketing and impact assessment, and

(iii) Priority setting for planning and development.

There are some clear advantages to using panels. These include the fact that recall problems are usually minimized, and that it is even possible to study the attitudes and motivation of non-respondents. However, it must also be recognized that maintaining panels is a constant effort. Since there is a tendency for certain people to drop out (those that are too busy, professionals, senior executives, etc.), this can lead to serious bias in the type of respondent that remains on the panel. Participants can also become too sensitized to the study objectives, and thus anticipate the responses they should be giving. Although there are essentially three different types of panels.

(i) Consumer Panels

(ii) Nominal Group Technique

(iii) Delphi Method

When researchers are interested in detailed information about purchasing behaviour or insight into certain leisure activities, they will often resort to panels of consumers. A panel will allow the researcher to track behaviour using the same sample over time. This type of longitudinal research provides more reliable results on changes that occur as a result of life cycle, social or professional status, attitudes and opinions. By working with the same panel members, intentions can be checked against action, one of the more problematic challenges that researchers face when studying planned purchases or intentions to engage in certain behaviour (e.g. going on trips, visiting certain sites, participating in sports, etc.).

But looking at trends is not the only use for panels. They can also provide invaluable insight into product acceptance prior to the launch of a new product or service, or a change in packaging, for instance. Panels, whether formally established or tracked informally through common behaviour (e.g., membership in a club, purchase of a specific product, use of a fidelity card, etc.), can also be used to study the reaction to potential or actual events, the use of promotional materials, or the search for information.

Compared to the depth interview and the focus group, a panel is less likely to exaggerate the frequency of a behaviour or purchase decision, or their brand loyalty. Although panels only require sample once, maintaining the panel can be both time-consuming and relatively costly as attrition and hence finding replacements can be quite high. In order to allow researchers to obtain more detailed follow-up information from panel members, they are usually paid for their services. At the same time, this can introduce a bias into the panel, since the financial incentive will be more or less important depending on the panelists economic status. Possibly one of the more interesting advantages of panels is that they can provide significant insight into non-response as well as non-participation or decisions not to purchase a given product.

4. ***In-depth Interview:*** Personal interviews are a way to get in-depth and comprehensive information. They involve one person interviewing another person for personal or detailed information. Personal interviews are very expensive because of the one-to-one nature of the interview (₹100 per interview). Typically, an interviewer will ask questions from a written questionnaire and record the answers verbatim. Sometimes, the questionnaire is simply a list of topics that the research wants to discuss with an industry expert. Personal interviews (because of their expense) are generally used only when subjects are not likely to respond to other survey methods.

   (i) *Telephone surveys:* These are the fastest method of gathering information from a relatively large sample (100-400 respondents). The interviewer follows a prepared script that is essentially the same as a written questionnaire. However, unlike a mail survey, the telephone survey allows the opportunity for some opinion probing. Telephone surveys generally last less than ten minutes. Typical costs are between four and six thousand dollars, and they can be completed in two to four weeks.

   (ii) *Mail surveys:* These are a cost-effective method of gathering information. They are ideal for large sample sizes, or when the sample comes from a wide geographic area. They cost a little less than telephone interviews, however, they take over twice as long to complete (eight to twelve weeks). Because there is no interviewer, there is no possibility of interviewer bias. The main disadvantage is the inability to probe respondents for more detailed information.

(iii) *Email and internet surveys:* These are relatively new and little is known about the effect of sampling bias in internet surveys. While it is clearly the most cost-effective and fastest method of distributing a survey, the demographic profile of the internet user does not represent the general population, although this is changing. Before doing an email or internet survey, carefully consider the effect that this bias might have on the results.

❖ Projective Techniques

The technique of inferring a subject's attitudes or values based on his or her description of vague objects requiring interpretation. Projective techniques are borrowed from the field of psychology. They will generate highly subjective qualitative data. There are many examples of such approaches including: Inkblot tests – look for images in a series of inkblots, Cartoons – complete the 'bubbles' on a cartoon series. Sentence or story completion Word association – depends on very quick (subconscious) responses to words. Psychodrama – Imagine that you are a product and describe what it is like to be operated, warn, or used. Projective techniques consist of the following:

1. ***Word association tests:*** In word association test the subject is presented with a list of words, one at a time, and asked to respond with first that comes to the respondents mind. Both verbal and non-verbal responses are recorded. Word associations are frequently used to test potential brand names and company images among public interpreting word association tests is difficult, and the marketing researcher should make sure to avoid subjective interpretations when there is considerable agreement in the free-association process, the researcher assumes that the test has revealed the consumers inner feelings about the subject.

2. ***Sentence completion test:*** A projective technique in which respondents are required to complete a number of partial sentences with the first word or phrase that comes to mind. The sentence completion method is also based on the principles of free association.

   For example:

   People who smoke are ___________

   A man who smokes filter cigarette is______

   Imported cigarette is most liked by_______

   Women in politics are_______

   When comparing to word association tests the answers given to sentence completion tests tends to be more extensive. The intent of sentence completion questions are more apparent.

3. ***Product tests:*** Product tests are often completed as part of the 'test' marketing process. Products are displayed in a mall of shopping center. Potential customers are asked to visit the store and their purchase behavior is observed. Observers will contemplate how the product is handled, how the packing is read, how much time the consumer spends with the product, and so on.

4. ***Diaries:*** Diaries are used by a number of specially recruited consumers. They are asked to complete a diary that lists and records their purchasing behavior over a period of time (weeks, months, or years). It demands a substantial commitment on the part of the respondent. However, by collecting a series of diaries with a number of entries, the researcher has a reasonable picture of purchasing behavior.

5. ***Omnibus studies:*** An omnibus study is where an organization puts across a single or a few questions on a 'hybrid' interview (either face-to-face or by telephone). The organization will be one of many

that simply want a straightforward answer to a simple question. An omnibus survey could include questions from companies in sectors as diverse as health care and tobacco. This type of research is far cheaper, and commit less time and effort than conducting own research.

6. *Clinics:* The Clinic methodology constitutes a hybrid approach of both qualitative and quantitative, primarily for testing product or service concepts. A significant number of respondents are screened and recruited to a central facility (this may be a focus group facility or it may be a hotel conference room). Concepts are presented to the large audience of respondents; videos may be shown; product prototypes may be passed around; client technical people may make parts of the presentation. Each respondent is provided with a wireless remote answer device and, during the session, they are asked specific questions and reply in real-time through their wireless devices. Results can, as appropriate, be fed back instantaneously and are used at the end of the presentation phase to develop a list of those respondents who have answered in a certain way, and these are asked to stay for a focus group. Thus, the focus group might have people who liked a new product concept but were only prepared to pay little for it, or people who did not like some or all aspects of the product or offer. The result is a set of quantitative data from the broader audience, and qualitative insight from the highly focused focus group. The process can be undertaken quickly across multiple countries and the results made available within a few weeks.

QUANTITATIVE RESEARCH TECHNIQUES

Quantitative research is most common encountered as part of formal or conclusive research, but is also sometimes used when conducting exploratory research. Quantitative research techniques are part of primary research.

Quantitative research differs from qualitative research in the following ways:

1. The data is usually gathered using more structured research instruments,
2. The results provide less detail on behaviour, attitudes and motivation,
3. The results are based on larger sample sizes that are representative of the population,
4. The research can usually be replicated or repeated, given it high reliability; and
5. The analysis of the results is more objective.

The most common quantitative research techniques are:

1. Observation technique
2. Experimentation
3. Survey technique

❖ Observation Research

Observation is one of the methods of collecting data. It is used to get both past and current information. Instead of asking questions from people, as a survey does, observation depends on watching what people do. Specifically, observation research can be defined as the systematic process of recording patterns of occurrences or behaviours without questioning or normally communicating with the people involved. Instead of asking respondents about their current behaviour, we may observe it and record our observations. Although it is not possible to observe past behaviour, we may observe the results of such behaviour. In a way, secondary data reflect the results of the past behaviour of people as also of past occurrences. In marketing research, the observational methods are not used frequently. All the same, as it is used especially in marketing experimentation, a brief discussion is provided here. The major application of observation as an information collection method may be classified into categories of the audit, coincidental recording devices, and a general classification, direct observation.

TABLE 3.3 Observation Situations

Situations	Example
People watching people	Observers stationed in supermarkets watch consumers select frozen Mexican dinners, with the purpose of seeing how much comparison shopping people do at the point of purchase
People watching phenomena	Observers stationed at an intersection count vehicles moving in various directions to establish the need for a traffic light.
Machines watching people	Movie or video cameras record consumers selecting frozen Mexican dinners.
Machines watching phenomena	Traffic-counting machines monitor the flow of vehicles at an intersection.

Nature of Observation Research

Conditions for use:

1. Information must be observable or inferable from observation.
2. Behaviour must be repetitive frequent, or predictable.
3. Behaviour must be of relatively short duration.

Methods of Observation Research

There are several methods of observation of which anyone or a combination of some of them can be used by the observer. Thus, there are structured or unstructured methods, disguised or undisguised methods, or observations made in a natural setting or laboratory setting, direct-indirect observation, or human-mechanical observation. These are briefly discussed below:

1. ***Structured-unstructured observation:*** Structured observation is used when the research problem has been formulated precisely and the observers have been told specifically what is to be observed. They may be given a simple from of record their observations. Unstructured observation implies that observers are free to observe whatever they think is relevant and important. While structured observations are subject to this limitation. The extent of the bias may vary to the extent an observation is unstructured.
2. ***Disguised-undisguised observation:*** In the case of disguised observation, the subjects do not know that they are being observed. In some cases, disguised observation may be made by the observer by posing as one of the shoppers who are being observed. This type of observation is often preferred because it is feared that people may behave differently when they know they are being observed. It may be difficult to completely disguise an observation, though this apart, it poses an ethical question of its desirability when those who are being observed are kept in the dark.
3. ***Natural and laboratory setting:*** Another way to classify observations in on the setting, i.e. natural or laboratory. Observations in the field studies are their natural setting and are, therefore, undertaken in extremely realistic conditions. Sometimes, an experimental manipulation may be introduced in a field study. Observation in a laboratory setting, on the other hand, enables the observer to control extraneous variables which influence the behaviour of people. Observational studies in

laboratory setting have certain advantages over field studies. They enable the collection of data. Promptly and economically and in addition, permit the use of more objective measurements.

4. ***Direct-indirect observation:*** Direct observation of people and how they behave in situations of interest is a commonly used method of collecting information. Supermarkets and store managers continually rely on observation of traffic flows and length of waiting lines to determine proper location of various lines of products and the number and the location of the sales people and cash registers. In the case of direct observation, the event or the behaviour of a person as it occurs. In contrast, indirect observation implies that some of part behaviour is observed. In other words, the behaviour itself is not observed, rather its effects are observed. An observer engaged in indirect observation generally looks for physical traces of behaviour or occurrence of an event suppose, he is interested in knowing about the liquor consumption of a household, he would look for empty liquor bottles in the garbage. Similarly, the observer may seek the permission of the housewife to see the pantry. He may carry a pantry audit to ascertain the consumption of certain types of products. It may be noted that the success of an indirect observation largely depends on how best the observer is able to identify physical traces of the problem under study. Direct observation is far more common than indirect observation. Direct observations of purchases obviously have some limitations. Though perhaps more serious to the subjective than the objective. Thus, the selections of acts of records will depend on the behavioral of model of the observer. Direct observation discloses what rather than why. Motivation must be inferred. Inferences are often difficult to substantiate a result of lack of control over important variables.

5. ***Human-mechanical observation:*** Another way of classifying observations is whether they are made manually or by machines. Most of the studies in marketing research are based on human observation wherein trained observers are required to observe and faithfully record their observations. In some cases, mechanical devices such as eye cameras and audiometers are used for observation. One of the major advantages of electrical/mechanical devices is that their recordings are free from subjective bias. As against this advantage, such observations may be less valid than human observations. This is because observers power of integration can lead to a more valid evaluation of the observation.

6. ***Participation observation:*** As the name implies, it is a form of observation in which the observer actually participates in the activities of the group, he or she wishes to study. Examples are an anthropologist who lives with native tribes, a sociologist studying poverty who moves to a low income neighborhood. This form of observation is rarely used in marketing research, as by their nature marketing activities do not usually lend themselves well to such a technique. Participant observation studies both industrial and retail; salespeople have been made, however, one of the factors influencing the sale of a brand product is how readily it is kept in stock. An interested manufacturer may send some observers to a samples of stores to find out how frequently the product is out of stock.

   (i) In order to ascertain what prices are charged by competitors, a manufacturer may depute some observers to go round the stores.

   (ii) Today, certain mechanical devices are used for observation, for example, eye-camera, the pupil metric camera and the motion-picture camera.

Advantages of Observation

1. Avoid problems associated with willingness and ability of respondents to answer questions.
2. Some forms of data are gathered more quickly and accurately by observation.

3. Direct observation technique enables a researcher to record behaviour as it occurs. In contrast, other techniques record the data mostly retrospectively on the basis of the respondent's report after the event.
4. Observation is that it can be used regardless of whether the respondent is willing to report or not.
5. Observation is that it can be used even when it pertains to those who are unable to respond such as infants and animals.

Disadvantages of Observation

1. Firstly only the current behaviour of a person or a group of persons can be observed, the researcher does not learn about motives, attitudes, intentions, or feelings.
2. One is not unable to observe the past behaviour nor can one observe a person's future behaviour because the act of observation takes place in the present.
3. Observation does not help us in gauging a person's attitude or opinion on a certain subject nor his knowledge of the same.
4. The observational method is very slow and as such, when a large number of person's are to be contacted; it becomes unsuitable because of the long period required for this purpose.

Difficulties in Observation

1. ***Inadequacies of our sense organs:*** This is "operate in a highly variable, erratic and selective manner". Several studies, conducted by psychologists, show that the perception of a man depends on several factors such as his freshness, interest, and freedom from interruption. The more favourable the conditions, the more receptive the person will be to outside impressions. Further, an object that is large or clear and sounds that are repetitive are likely to receive greater attention of the person.
2. ***Interdependence of observation and inference:*** All perceptions, after the first week of life, is compounded of the stored experience. Anything that impinges on our senses conveys a meaning to us largely to the extent that we relate it to what we are already know. Observation and inference are inseparable. This means that whatever an observer sees he tries to explain or interprets it to on the basis of his past experience. Thus, the observer inference problem is the main difficulty in as much as the observer can draw wrong inferences from observations.
3. ***Effects of interaction between the observer and observed:*** The third set of difficulties crops ups because of the effects of interaction between the observer and observed. This may have two distinct dangers. First, persons being observed may become self-conscious of the observation and this may influence their normal behaviour. Second, observation may get distorted merely because one more person—the observer—is present and people are conscious of this presence.
4. ***Ambiguity:*** Although it has been suggested that, where practical to do so, information obtained by communication should be verified by observation, the implication should not be drawn that observation is free of ambiguity. In making observation we select, organize, and interpret visual stimuli into a picture that is as meaningful and as a coherent to us as we make it. Which stimuli are selected and how they are organized and interpreted are highly dependent on both the backgrounds and frames of reference of the observer. The trained observer will invariably 'see' more that relates to this or her specially in an ambiguous situation than the untrained observer.

❖ Experimental Research

Experimental research is also called "experimentation". It is a research process in which one or more variables are manipulated under conditions that permit the collection of data that show the effects, if any such variables in unconfused fashion. The other meaning of experimentation is, it is a process of manipulating one variable in a controlled environment while holding all other variables constant in order to establish a casual relationship. This indicates that the distinction between experimental and non-experimental research may be a matter of degree rather than of kind. Experiments must create artificial situations so that they can obtain the particular data needed and can measure the data accurately. Experiments are artificial in the sense that situations are usually created for testing purposes. Artificiality in general is the essence of the experimental method. This facilitates the researchers to have more control over the factors they are studying. If the researcher can control the factors present in a given situation, they can comfortably obtain more conclusive evidence of cause and effect relationships between any two observation and record accurately the effect on one factor when another is deliberately changed. This permits researchers to prove or disprove hypotheses that they could otherwise only partially test. It is for this reason that experiments have been the basis for the advancement of knowledge in most scientific fields. Experiments can be used in marketing when the researcher has established a hypothesis. Also the researcher must be in a position to control conditions pertinent to testing the hypothesis. Both these conditions must be fulfilled before the experiment can actually be started.

All experiments involve three basic components:

1. The variable manipulated in an experiment is referred to as the independent variable or test unit.
2. The actual alteration is called the treatment.
3. The actual variables chosen to measure the subject's response are known as dependent variables.

Experimental Design

"What people say they will do is not necessarily the way they will react in a given actual estimate of particular market situation". Best solution is to subject the respondents to some form of actual market situation. There are two methods out of number of methods which researchers prefer to use. These are:

1. ***Before-After without control group design:*** A company selects a test city for research. Sales before a price is measured (01). Then the price is increased (X) and the sales is measured again (02). The increase or decrease in sales is the effect of price increase.

   01 X 02

   Effect of X = 02-01

2. ***Before-After with control group design:*** A company selects two test cities comparable in terms of market characteristics. In one city, it increases the price and in the other it maintains the old price. The effect is measured as:

   Test city 01 X 02

   Control city 03 04

   Effect of X = (02-01) – (04-03)

   During testing period there can be other changes taking place in the market which is taken care by the control group. The major drawback here is in finding cities representative of total market and in controlling the external factors. It can be taken care by conducting experiments in laboratories which simulate real-life situations. The more closely the investigation can be defined (i.e. clear the objectives) the better will be the chance of success. It is best not to deal with the subject too wide.

Uses of Experimentations

Experimentation covers the entire range of marketing activities; some of the areas where experiments are predominantly used are mentioned below:

1. *Product Design:* Basic character, colour, shape and size are frequently studied by the experiments. Which product a consumer would buy most under what typically changed conditions of quality, shape, size, colour.
2. *Package Design:* A vast number of experiments have been conducted to study package designs in relation to product sales. Use of materials like glass; paper or plastic should be used to increase the product sales can be experimented in marketing research.
3. *Pricing Policies:* The price elasticity of demand can be better tested with the help of experiments. For example, magazine sellers frequently experiment by offering subscriptions at varying prices to different buyers on the mailing lists. It is visualized in the case of retailers also who test the effect of old prices.
4. *Promotion Policies:* The promotional policies have been very widely explored through experimentation as compared to other areas of marketing. Experiments are conducted to test advertising effectiveness, media effectiveness, appeals, and frequency of repeating the ad, the effect of colour, etc.
5. *Distribution Policies:* Distribution can be done through distribution channel management, physical distribution management, and distribution system management. This also uses experimentation as a technique of research.

TABLE 3.4 Threats to Internal Validity

Source of Bias	Means of Control
External Events over Time	
During the experiment, an external event other than the treatment may cause a difference between the pre-measurement and post-measurement.	Avoid the seriously flawed, "Experimental Group Only" design in favor of a genuine experimental and Control group design.
Internal Processes over Time	
Changes within subjects during the experiment, apart from external events, may cause a difference between pre and post-measurement.	Task and measure both experimental and control groups in the same way, at the same time, and over the same time period.
Pre-measurement Sensitization	
The pre-measurement may cause subjects to be more or less sensitive to the treatment than they would otherwise be.	Randomly assign subjects to treatments and use a post measure only design or the four-group, six-measure design.
Measurement Instability	
The measurement instrument or person doing the measurement may change in the interval between pre-measurement and post-measurement.	Use the same, standardized measurement instruments and procedures and the same human observers over treatment and control groups.
Systematic Selection	
Subjects aren't randomly assigned to the treatment or control group, so prior to the treatment, there are systematic differences between groups.	Randomly assign subjects to treatment groups and when that's impossible, match or assign subjects to treatments as closely to random as possible.

Contd...

Experimental Attrition	
Subjects assigned to some treatment groups withdraw at a higher rate than those in others or in the control group.	Strive to make the treatment and control groups' tasks and conditions equally difficult or demanding.
Regression to the Mean	
Some subjects have extreme premature scores merely by chance, so when they're tested again, the second measure will, on average, be less extreme.	Include the whole groups on pre and post-measures, rather than post measuring only those with extreme premature scores.

Field Settings vs Laboratory Settings

The settings in the process of experimentation mainly consists of two general classes: (a) Field settings and (b) Laboratory settings.

Field experiments are those occurring in the real world with subjects who are typically unaware of their participation. In this type of experiment, experimental variables will be taken to the field. Laboratory experiments are those, which occur, in artificial settings where subjects are aware that they are participating in some scientific work. Experiments in the marketing field, is where the consumer are brought to the office of the research conducting agency and the consumers are exposed to an experimental variable. Of these two the lab experiments are used maximum.

TABLE 3.5 Laboratory Experiment – Pros and Cons

Advantages	Disadvantages
Relatively small number of subjects can be recruited more readily and sampled more precisely than large numbers.	Relatively small number of subjects demands greater sampling precision and limits the reliability of generalizations to the population.
Laboratory setting provides greater control of the environment and potential confounds.	Artificiality of the laboratory setting creates a threat to external validity of results.
Subjects can be randomly *assigned* to treatment and control conditions.	Special facilities and perhaps special equipment are required.
Subjects can be given instructions and questioned to be sure they understand.	Subjects are required to come to the facility and must be compensated for time and travel.
Measures can be made to be sure experimental treatment(s) have been properly administered and experienced by subjects.	Disruption of the subjects' daily routine may cause changes in moods, emotions, or psychological states.
Controlled conditions allow the experimenter to use more elaborate, complex experimental designs.	Knowledge their behavior is being measured or tested may sensitize subjects to experimental conditions and treatments.

TABLE 3.6 Field Experiment – Pros and Cons

Advantages	Disadvantages
A larger number of subjects provides greater reliability of the generalized results.	Random selection or assignment to treatment and control groups may be impossible.
The "real world" circumstances mean subjects may not even know they are participating in an experiment to measure their behaviour.	The "real world" circumstances make it difficult to control potential confounds and threats to validity.
It's usually unnecessary for subjects to travel to a special location to participate.	Subjects can't be given instructions and questioned to be sure they understand.

Contd...

Subjects need not disrupt their daily lives or activities in order to participate, so their actions may better reflect everyday behaviour.	Take measures can't be used to be sure the experimental treatment(s) has been properly experienced by subjects.
The experiment often need not be completed in a matter of hours and may extend over days, weeks, or months.	Unexpected external events may jeopardize the experimental results or even the completion of the experiment.

Lab Research is conducted in a structured environment whereas field research is carried out in a natural setting.

The advantages and disadvantages of lab research are follows.

❖ Advantages

1. They enable the experimenter to complete the study in a condensed time span and thus, speed up the testing process.
2. They enable the standards or conditions, under which experiment is conducted, to be rigidly controlled.
3. They allow constant observations.

❖ Disadvantages

1. Number of units is limited; hence these cannot be used for marketing problems where participant's number is generally large
2. Lab experiments involve the use of costly equipment, which increase the total cost.
3. Lab experiments require continuous supervision and control.

External Factors that Influence Experiments

The following factors may influence experiments in different forms:

1. *History:* The history is exemplified by changes in current events external to the experiment but which still may have affected its outcomes.
2. *Maturity:* Workers mental level might have gone up owing to continuous working on the same job and machines, which affect the experimental outcomes.
3. *Repetitive tests:* When certain people are tested a number of times, they get familiar with these tests and their performance improves every time they are tested. Also the consciousness and awareness of the group increases under repetitive testing.
4. *Mortality:* Some of the original participants may drop out and change the outcome of the experiment. The substituted new units may not respond in the fashion original participants were responding.

Limitations of Experimentation

1. *Weak theoretical base:* Most research conducted at present are of theoretical or descriptive nature. The information required to formulate a hypothesis in such situations is not easily available, this is just because enough theoretical base is not available.

2. *Expensive:* The cost involved in the experimental research is more than in descriptive research, so it is expensive.
3. *Administrative procedures:* Close supervision and administration of the experiments are needed to carry out research effectively which is generally difficult for most of the organizations.
4. *Time consuming:* It takes a longer time to complete a marketing research experiment. Not only it takes long time but people change their preferences and opinions over a period of time. This results in difference between what is concluded and what the reality is.

❖ Survey Technique

All organizations, whether multinational corporations or domestic organizations need information. The organizations and institutions live and work with an unquestionable thirst for data. Much of the data organizations require concerns people and their operations. Some of this information about people is obvious and can be learned merely by casual observations. Some, but not much of it, and often not nearly enough. Organizations and institutions need answers to important questions. Those answers must be accurate, reliable, and valid. Survey research is one way and often the most effective and dependable to obtain that information.

The survey technique involves the collection of primary data about subjects, usually by selecting a representative sample of the population or universe under study, through the use of a questionnaire. It is a very popular since many different types of information can be collected, including attitudinal, motivational, behavioural and perceptive aspects. It allows for standardization and uniformity both in the questions asked and in the method of approaching subjects, making it far easier to compare and contrast answers by respondent group. It also ensures higher reliability than some other techniques. If properly designed and implemented, surveys can be an efficient and accurate means of determining information about a given population.

Need for Survey

Surveys are often conducted simply because it's the only way to get the information needed. Even when the information is available through other means, survey research may be an easier, quicker, less expensive, or more accurate way to get the required information. Individuals or organizations usually sponsor surveys for one of three basic reasons:

1. They want to influence or persuade some audience.
2. They want to create or modify a product or service they provide for a particular public.
3. They want to understand or predict human behavior or conditions because it's the focus of their academic or professional work.

Data Collection Options

Surveys certainly aren't the only means of acquiring data about people's attitudes, opinions, preferences, experiences, and the like. While survey research is the most common method for obtaining such primary data, there are other methods that are sometimes used either independently or in conjunction with surveys. They include quantitative methods such as behavioural laboratory or field experiments and systematic observation methods, as well as verbal methods, sometimes called qualitative techniques such as focus groups or depth interviews.

Potential Survey areas

A survey could be designed to measure the peoples

Attitudes: Knowledge, feelings, and expectations regarding the activity

Images: The mental picture they have developed of the programme or employer.

Decisions: When decisions are the topic of research, the focus isn't so much on the results of decisions in the past as on the decision process itself. Often people's choices require them to evaluate alternative courses of action. Their choices depend in pat on their information sources and the evaluative criteria they use for judgment. Those seeking survey information are often keenly interested in these aspects of the decision process that people use to choose actions.

Needs: Most behavior is directed toward the satisfaction of one or more human needs. Thus, the answer to the question of why is often obtained by measuring the relationship between actions and needs, desires, preferences, motives, and goals. People generally act with intent. This doesn't imply that they know, consciously, what personal motives and needs lie beneath the surface of their actions. Consequently, it can be a difficult job to dig out the needs that underpin behaviour and the motives that prompt action. The picture may be complicated further by the fact that (a) many different actions can serve the same motive or provide satisfaction for the same need and (b) several needs or motives may be served by one action or behavior pattern. To cope with these problems, the researcher must be willing to recognize the difficulties and to understand the nature of needs, desires, preferences, motives, and goals.

Behaviour: The measurement of behavior involves four related concepts-what the respondents did or did not do, where the action takes place, the timing of the behavior, and the frequency or persistence of behavior. In other words, it often means assessing "what, where, when, and how often." When research is used to establish which actions were taken by respondents, the alternative courses of action can be listed in categories to be sure the responses are comparable. Simple multiple choice items can then be used, with either a single or a multiple response permitted.

Affiliations: Social contact and interaction are often the focus of survey research or bear heavily on other issues that are relevant to the survey. So the family setting, memberships, social contacts, reference groups, and communications of respondents are frequently measured or assessed within the survey research process.

Demographics: Demographic factors often used in survey research include such variables as age, sex, marital status, family status, family life cycle stage, education, employment, occupation, income, and residential location and type, among others. Such data are often valuable to sponsors because (a) demographic groups often differ significantly on the issues of importance and (b) demographics can be used to identify segments, groups, audiences, or constituencies of people who are both identifiable and behave in similar ways.

Value of survey information: The importance of survey information depends on three main factors: (a) the cost of making an error, (b) the degree of uncertainty surrounding the decisions or actions, and (c) the amount of uncertainty the survey may reduce.

Survey Limitations

Despite the positive features of this type of research inquiry, survey research methods do have some intractable disadvantages and limitations. Apart from the most serious shortcoming, the limitations on assessment of causality cited earlier, survey research has other limitations that must be considered: (a) Threat and Sensitive Questions, (b) Cost, Expertise, and Error.

Even if no errors or omissions are discovered and the survey project goes precisely as planned, the results won't be definitive. They won't dictate decisions or contain the ultimate answers. Instead, survey results should be treated as another body of evidence or set of indications.

Types of Survey Techniques

There are three basic types of surveys:

1. *The Telephone Survey:* The use of the telephone has been found to be one of the most inexpensive, quick and efficient ways of surveying respondents. The ubiquity of telephone ownership as well as the use of unlisted numbers are factors that must, however, be considered as part of the sampling frame, where the number of households with phones approaches 100%. Telephone surveys also allow for random sampling, allowing for the extrapolation of characteristics from the sample to the population as a whole.

   There tends to be less interviewer bias than in interview surveys, especially if the interviewers are trained and supervised to ensure consistent interview administration. The absence of face-to-face contact can also be an advantage since respondents may be somewhat more inclined to provide sensitive information. Further, some people are reluctant to be approached by strangers, whether at their home or in a more public location, which can be overcome by the more impersonal use of the telephone.

   On the other hand, telephone surveys are also known to have a number of limitations. The length of the survey has to be kept relatively short to less than 15 minutes as longer interviews can result in refusal to participate or premature termination of the call. The questions themselves must also be kept quite short and the response options simple, since there can be no visual aids such as a cue card.

   The increasing use of voice mail and answering machines has made phone surveys more difficult and more costly to undertake. Calls that go answered receive a busy signal or reach a machine, require callbacks. Usually, eligible respondents will be contacted a pre-determined number of times, before they are abandoned in favour of someone else. The potential for response bias must be considered, however, when discussing the results of a study that relied on the telephone. The sample for a telephone survey can be chosen by selecting respondents from the telephone directory, for example, by calling every 100th name, through Random-Digit Dialing (RDD) where the last four digits of a telephone number are chosen randomly for each telephone exchange or prefix (i.e. first three numbers), or the use of a table of random numbers.

2. *The Self-Administered Survey:* Any survey technique that requires the respondent to complete the questionnaire him/herself is referred to as a self-administered survey. The most common ways of distributing these surveys are through the use of mail, fax, newspapers/magazines, and increasingly the internet, or through the place of purchase of a good or service (hotel, restaurant, and store). They can also be distributed in person, for instance as part of an intercept survey. Depending on the method of survey administration, there is a number of sampling frame considerations, such as who can or cannot be reached by fax or internet, or whether there is a sample bias.

   A considerable advantage of the self-administered survey is the potential anonymity of the respondent, which can lead to more truthful or valid responses. Also, the questionnaire can be filled out at the convenience of the respondent. Since there is no interviewer, interviewer error or bias is eliminated. The cost of reaching a geographically dispersed sample is more reasonable for most forms of self-administered surveys than for personal or telephone surveys, although mail surveys are not necessarily cheap.

In most forms of self-administered surveys, there is no control over who actually fills out the questionnaire. Also, the respondent may very well read part or all of the questionnaire before filling it out, thus, potentially biasing his/her responses. However, one of the most important disadvantages of self-administered surveys is their low response rate.

Depending upon the method of administration chosen, a combination of the following can help in improving the response rate:

(i) A well written covering letter of appeal, personalized to the extent possible, that stresses why the study is important and why the particular respondent should fill in the questionnaire.

(ii) If respondents are interested in the topic and/or the sponsoring organization, they are more likely to participate in the survey; these aspects should be stressed in the covering letter.

(iii) Ensuring confidentiality and/or anonymity, and providing the name and contact number of the lead researcher and/or research sponsor should the respondent wish to verify the legitimacy of the survey or have specific questions.

(iv) Providing a due date that is reasonable but not too far off and sending or phoning at least one reminder (sometimes with another survey, in case the original one has been misplaced).

(v) Follow-up with non-respondents.

(vi) Providing a postage paid envelope or reply card.

(vii) Providing an incentive, particularly monetary, even if only a token.

(viii) A well designed, visually appealing questionnaire.

(ix) A shorter questionnaire, where the wording of questions has been carefully considered. For instance, it might start with questions of interest to the respondent, while all questions and instructions are clear and straight forward.

(x) An envelope that is eye-catching, personalized and does not resemble junk mail.

(xi) Advance notification, either by phone or mail, of the survey and its intent.

3. ***The In-Person Interview Survey:*** Face-to-face interviews are a direct communication, primary research collection technique. If relatively unstructured but in-depth, they tend to be considered as part of qualitative research. When administered as an intercept survey or door-to-door, they are usually part of quantitative research.

The opportunity for feedback to the respondent is a distinct advantage in personal interviews. Not only is there the opportunity to reassure the respondent should s/he be reluctant to participate, but the interviewer can also clarify certain instructions or questions. The interviewer also has the opportunity to probe answers by asking the respondent to clarify or expand on a specific response. The interviewer can also supplement answers by recording his/her own observations, for instance there is no need to ask the respondent's gender or the time of day/place where the interview took place.

The length of interview or its complexity can both be much greater than in other survey techniques. At the same time, the researcher is assured that the responses are actually provided by the person intended, and that no questions are skipped. Referred to as item non-response, it is far less likely to occur in personal interviews than in telephone or self-administered surveys. Another distinct advantage of this technique is that props or visual aid can be used. It is not uncommon, for instance, to provide a written response alternatives. Also, new products or concepts can be demonstrated as part of the interview.

Personal interviews provide significant scope for interviewer error or bias. Whether it is the tone of voice, the way a question is rephrased when clarified or even the gender and appearance of the interviewer, all have been shown to potentially influence the respondent's answer. It is therefore, important that interviewers are well trained and that a certain amount of control is exercised over them to ensure proper handling of the interview process. This makes the interview survey one of the most costly survey methods.

Although the response rate for interviews tends to be higher than for other types of surveys, the refusal rate for intercept survey is higher than for door-to-door surveys. Whereas the demographic characteristics of respondents tend to be relatively consistent in a geographically restricted area covered by door-to-door surveys, intercept surveys may provide access to a much more diversified group of respondents from different geographic areas. However, that does not mean that the respondents in intercept surveys are necessarily representative of the general population. This can be controlled to a certain extent by setting quota sampling. However, intercept surveys are convenience samples and reliability levels can therefore not be calculated. Door-to-door interviews introduce different types of bias, since some people may be away from home while others may be reluctant to talk to strangers. They can also exclude respondents who live in multiple-dwelling units, or where there is security systems limiting access.

TABLE 3.7 Strengths and Weaknesses of Selected Data Collection Methods in Terms of Quality of Data Produced

Methods	Strengths	Weaknesses
Mall-intercept interview	Interviewer can show, explain, and probe.	Many distractions are inherent in the mall environment; respondent may be in a hurry, not in proper frame of mind to answer survey questions; there is respond more chance for interviewer bias; non-probability sampling problems arise.
Central-location telephone interview	Supervisor can monitor the interviewing processing easily, excellent samples can be obtained; interviewer can explain and probe.	Respondent may be distracted by things going on at their location; problems arise in long interviews and interviews with many open-ended questions. Many refuse to participate.
Self-administered questionnaire	Interviewer and associated biases are eliminated; respondent can complete the questionnaire when convenient; respondent can look up information and work at own pace.	There is no interviewer to show, explain, or probe; sample may be poor because of non-response; who actually completes the questionnaire cannot be controlled.
Mail survey	Same strengths as for self-administered method.	Same weaknesses as for self-administered questionnaire; sample quality is better with mail panel.
Online survey	Administration is inexpensive; data can be gathered quickly; questions can be readily personalized; response rates are high.	Users may not be representative of whole population; privacy concerns may arise; unrestricted sample provides skewed results; possibility of errors; downloading problems especially for the hard-to-reach.

TABLE 3.8 Comparison of Survey Methods

Criteria	Personal Survey	Mail Survey	Telephone Survey
1. Probable response rate	Fair	Poor	Good
2. Time required	Slow	Slow	Fast
3. Cost	High	Low	Low
4. Control of sample	Good	Poor	Excellent
5. Supervision of field work	Fair	None	Excellent
6. Quantity of information	Good	Limited	Limited
7. Quality of information	Good	Fair	Excellent
8. Versatility	Excellent	Fair	Good

REVIEW QUESTIONS

1. Distinguish between qualitative and quantitative research.
2. Describe the advantages and disadvantages of commonly used qualitative research techniques.
3. Describe the pros and cons of direct questioning, observation and in-market experiments.
4. Demonstrate how to construct an observational research project?
5. Discuss how to set up and conduct an in-market experiment?
6. Discuss the pros and cons of using surveys to obtain market information.
7. Explain the advantages and disadvantages of the three basic methods of direct questioning as well as combination methods (e.g., Phone-mail, phone-disk, etc.).
8. Describe the uses and the advantages and disadvantages of diary panels, store audits, electronic data generators in marketing research.
9. Describe the basic approaches and methods for merging data from different sources.

Case Study 1 Sony India

Sony, a multinational corporation based in Tokyo, Japan, stepped into India in early 1995, in the post liberalisation period. Within a couple of months in the same year, it set up its manufacturing unit. The company makes its presence felt in India through Sony Entertainment Television, Sony Music and Sony India. While the first two are comfortably placed in their niche markets, it is the third which is expected to bring in all those exciting Sony digital products.

Although the government has cleared its plans to manufacture its various products, it has not been smooth sailing for Sony India. Sony India is facing some major problems, one of which is the emergence of a grey market for its brands. While it is targeting its sales around ₹ 1,050 crores by the turn of the century, it has to have a better understanding of India's economic, social and political environment.

Sony India would like to develop itself as its parent company developed its business units in United States (New York), Europe (Cologne), and Asia (Singapore). Since it is a multinational company manufacturing multi-products, it has a challenging task.

Questions

1. Do you think research can play an important role in the development of Sony India?
2. If Sony India takes recourse to research, should it set up "in-house" research or hire the services of marketing research agencies?
3. If the choice is in favour of marketing research agency, what factors should it consider while selecting a particular agency?

Case Study 2 Omnipharm, Inc.

Your client, Omnipharm, Inc., is a leading European multinational pharmaceutical company with an excellent reputation in the area of cardiovascular drugs. They launched a new product, XPRESS, for the treatment of Hypertension, about three months ago. They are extremely excited about this product because it is in a new chemical class, and will have several major advantages over existing competition. Unfortunately, one of Omnipharm's major competitors, PharmAdvance, has just launched a product in direct competition, called PRESSOR. It is in the same new chemical class as XPRESS, and has a very similar profile in terms of efficacy and side effects.

Omnipharm is extremely concerned about this competitor, as it has the potential to negatively affect product sales despite the fact that Omnipharm was first in the market. In addition, they feel that PharmAdvance's promotional activities may adversely affect the image of XPRESS because of the additional noise created in the market. Finally, they are worried about the impact of PRESSOR on future launches of XPRESS. As a result, the General Manager has asked that market research be undertaken immediately to measure several key parameters for both products: product awareness; willingness to adopt by GPs and Cardiologists; product perceptions of (i.e., product benefits, advantages over traditional treatment); and the possible effect of PRESSOR on product image of XPRESS.

Omnipharm has a sizable market research budget set aside for this purpose. The General Manager, who has extensive experience in marketing, is encouraging the use of Internet as much as possible for all aspects of marketing, including its use in research. However, while the market research department at Omnipharm is extremely conversant with all research methodologies, they are somewhat skeptical about the use of the Internet for this research. Omnipharm has asked your agency to focus on 7 countries where XPRESS has been launched on the parameters mentioned above. They want feedback from both GPs and Cardiologists. Their time frame is 6 weeks, and they feel that the data must be collected as quickly as possible; however, they have also told you that the quality of the data you are collecting is of utmost importance. They want a well-defended proposal in which you support what your agency is recommending.

Questions

1. Would there be any advantages for Omnipharm to use Internet market research? Please list those you think are most important given their situation.
2. What disadvantages might arise for Omnipharm if they were to use Internet market research? Again, list those you consider most important.
3. What three key questions should you ask your internal client to help you decide on the appropriate methodology to recommend?
4. Would you recommend Internet market research as an appropriate choice for Omnipharm? Provide a strong rationale for your answer. If not, what would you recommend instead?

Case Study 3

"Yes, our specialization is in marketing research. During the last ten years of our operations, we have carried out more than four hundred market research assignments for large, medium and small scale enterprises covering consumer as well as industrial products. As to a readership survey, we carried out a small assignment for 'Gujarat Mitra' a fortnightly in Gujarat some five years back. However, we have the necessary expertise and experience to carry out an "All India Readership Survey" asserted by Mr. Keki Devar, Chief Executive of National Market Research Bureau during his discussions with Mr. R. K. Deshpande, Marketing manager of Audit Bureau of circulation. The latter was lately receiving many requests to initiate an All India Readership Survey by a large number of magazines, advertising agencies and also some of the business organizations. Due to the high cost involved in such a project, it was felt that all those who would be benefited by such an exercise, must pool their resources to meet the costs.

The readership survey would have been of extreme use to different organizations for various purposes as discussed below:

1. The magazines periodicals, etc. would know about the performance of readers to different types of literature, viz., fiction, poetry stories, etc., and would be in a position to offer through their magazines what their readers wanted.

2. To advertising agencies, it would have helped in proper selection of different media based on their effectiveness for preparing advertising plans for their clients.

3. To marketers, it would have provided data about readership, circulation, etc., that would help in selecting the media and filling the advertising plan with in the budget.

4. To media owners, it would give the feedback on their effectiveness that could be used to plan a pricing policy.

Thus, it was felt that an exercise of this nature would be of use to all. M/S National Marketing Research Bureau was asked to submit a detailed proposal covering objectives, methodology, coverage, time period, cost, etc.

Questions

1. Prepare a proposal for readership survey.
2. Discuss how the findings will be of use to different organizations in decision-making.

Case Study 4 Product Testing on the Internet

P&C is offering a number of different products and / or product versions over the Internet that you can't buy your local retail store. But a consumer can go to the P&C Web site (wwp.gcom) and under 'Services and offers' a consumer can click on Try and. Buy'. Then, for a number of products, P&C will offer you a free sample, a cents-off coupon, or the ability to purchase the actual product online. If the purchasers of a new item offered on the Web site give it great reviews, then P&C will consider making the product available in retail Stores.

Although P&C only began testing products online in 1998, the company already is doing 40 present or its 6,000 product tests and related research projects online. One successful new product that was launched as a result of online testing is C Whitestrips, a home tooth-bleaching kit. Despite its ₹ 100 retail price, P&C was able to sell 144,000 whitening kits 'online over an eight-month period, thereby providing evidence that the public would not balk at the product's rather steep price When the product was finally introduced nationally into retail stores, consumers spent almost ₹ 50 million on kits in the first three months.

Question

What personality traits do you believe many of the consumers who buy and try products found on the P&G Web site might share in common?

Case Study 5 Ramraj

Ramraj, owner of a company having chain of restaurants catering to business segment in South India wants to start one in South Mumbai. Before starting, in addition to location, viability, he wants to conduct a market research of the executives/employees of various corporates, in the South Mumbai area to know about their eating habits, preferences, entertaining lifestyle, etc.

You have been hired to conduct the marketing research to get the following answers:

1. What is the marketing problem?
2. Given the profile of the target market, what should be your structure of research design?
3. Draw a sequence of questions you would use in getting the information relevant to the problem.
4. What could be the secondary source of information for the research study?

CHAPTER FOUR

MEASUREMENT AND SCALING

INTRODUCTION

Entire process of carrying out research is to find answers to questions and dilemma's faced by the marketing personnel. Researchers observe, experience and interact with the environment. These things have to be converted into more meaningful information. This conversion is possible with the help of measurement. Unless the researcher systematically processes the gathered data into meaningful form, the entire effort of carrying out the research is aimless. That is why, researchers take the aid of measurement and scaling into their fold. Measurement is basically symbolic representation of real life situation. Measurement can be defined as a way of obtaining symbols to represent the properties of persons, objects, events, or states, which symbols have the same relevant relationship to each other as do the things represented. Measurement is the assignment of numbers to responses based on a set of guidelines. In other words, measurement is the assignment of numbers to objects to represent amounts or degrees of a property possessed by all the objects. If a characteristic or property or behaviour act is to be represented by numbers, there must exist a one-to-one correspondence between the number system used and the relations between various quantities (degrees) of that which is being measured. Three important characteristics or features of the real number series itself are:

1. ***Order:*** Numbers are ordered
2. ***Distance:*** Differences between numbers are ordered
3. ***Origin:*** The series has a unique origin which is indicated by the number zero.

In measurement numbers are assigned to objects (people) in such a way that the relations between the numbers reflect the relations between the objects (people) with respect to the characteristic involved. The end result is establishment of a scale of measurement, which allows the investigator to make comparisons of amounts and changes in the property being measured. In general the researcher observes empirical events, uses numbers to represent these events and a set of mapping rules. The marketing managers generally interested in research would want to know about three things. These are:

1. State of mind variables (attitudes of the consumers),
2. State of being variables (socioeconomic background of the consumers), and
3. Behavioural variables (intentions of the consumers and their behaviour).

Measurement in the form of assigning numbers to responses have the important benefits:

1. It is possible to summarise quantified data from a large sample more efficiently and economically than the non-quantified data.

2. It is possible to manipulate quantified data by using a variety of mathematical techniques.
3. The results of the data analyses can provide rich insights that may go undiscovered if we merely examine unquantified data.

MEASUREMENT

A measurement scale can be defined as a plan that is used to assign numbers to characteristics of objects. In marketing research there are several types of measurement scales available, the appropriate one to use depends on the researcher's assumptions about how the numerals resemble the real world observations. The levels of measurement are nominal, ordinal, interval and ratio scales.

TABLE 4.1 Types of Measurement Scales

Scale	Basic Empirical Operations	Typical	Typical Statistical	
			Descriptive	Inferential
Nominal	Determination of equality	Classification: Male-female, purchaser non-purchaser, social class	Percentage, mode	Chi-square, binomial test
Ordinal	Determination of greater or less	Rankings: Preference data, market position, attitude measures, many psychological measures	Median	Mann-Whitney U, Friedman, Two way ANOVA, Rank-order correction
Interval	Determination of equality of intervals	Index numbers, attitude measures, level of knowledge about brands	Mean, Range, Standard deviation	Product moment, correlation, t-test, Factor analysis, ANOVA
Ratio	Determination of equality of ratios	Sales, units produced, number of customers, costs		Coefficient of variance

TABLE 4.2 Purpose of Scale

Scale	Purpose
Nominal Scale	Measures in terms of name of designations or discrete units or categories. Example: Gender, Color of home, religion, type of business.
Ordinal Scale	Measures in terms of such values as more or less, larger or smaller, but without specifying the size of the intervals. Example: Rating scales, ranking scales, Likert-type scales.
Interval Scale	Measures in terms of equal intervals or degrees of difference but without a zero point. Ratios do not apply. Example: Temperature, GPA
Ratio Scale	Measures in terms of equal intervals and an absolute zero point of origin. Ratios apply. Example: Height, delay time, weight.

❖ Levels of Measurement

Most texts on marketing research explain the four levels of measurement: nominal, ordinal, interval and ratio and so the treatment given to them here will be brief. However, it is an important topic since the type of scale used in taking measurements directly impinges on the statistical techniques which can legitimately be used in the analysis.

Nominal Scale

The lowest measurement level you can use, from a statistical point of view, is a nominal scale. A nominal scale, as the name implies, is simply some placing of data into categories, without any order or structure. A physical example of a nominal scale is the terms we use for colours. The underlying spectrum is ordered but the names are nominal. In research activities a YES/NO scale is nominal. It has no order and there is no distance between YES and NO.

Example of a Nominal Scale

Sex	1. Male	2. Female
Area	1. Rural	2. Urban

Statistically any arithmetic operations performed on nominally scaled data can only be carried out on the count in each category. Numbers assigned to represent the categories cannot meaningfully be added, subtracted, or divided. A mean or a median cannot be calculated for nominal data. A mode can be used, however. The percentages of items falling within each category also can be determined. A chi-square statistical test can be conducted to; determine if differences between the numbers falling in the various categories is likely to be the result of chance or randomness. There are also highly sophisticated modeling techniques available for nominal data.

Nominal Scale Features

1. The numeric values are merely the names of categories.
2. The numbers are used only to make categories distinct.
3. The values don't indicate any magnitudes.
4. The values don't indicate any relationships.
5. No arithmetic operations can be used on the numbers.
6. Statistical manipulation is extremely limited.

Ordinal Scale

An ordinal scale is next up the list in terms of power of measurement. The simplest ordinal scale is a ranking. This scale represents numbers, letters, or other symbols used to rank items. Items can be classified not only as to whether they share some characteristic with another item but also whether they have more or less of this characteristic than some other object. This scale does not provide information on how much more or less of the characteristic various items possess. When a market researcher asks you to rank 5 types of beer from most flavourful to least flavourful, he/she is asking you to create an ordinal scale of preference. There is no objective distance between any two points on your subjective scale. For you the top beer may be far superior to the second preferred beer but, to another respondent with the same top and second beer, the distance may be subjectively small. An ordinal scale only lets you interpret gross order and not the relative positional distances.

An example of an ordinal scale used to determine consumer's preferences among 5 brands of Televisions

Videocon ____________________

Onida ______________________

Aviva ____________________

Sony ____________________

Sharpe ____________________

Statistically Ordinal data would use non-parametric statistics. These would include: median and mode, rank order correlation. Non-parametric analysis of variance modeling techniques can also be used with ordinal data. For example, if we want to measure an individual attitude towards particular colour television by requesting him or her to answer the following questions. After answering, the researcher assigns numbers to reflect the relative rating of each of the statements that will be used to interpret relative differences. The ordinal data indicates the relative position of two or more items but not the magnitude of the differences between the numbers. A mode or a median may be used but not a mean. The percentages may be calculated and are meaningful. The branch of statistics that deals with ordinal measurements is non-parametric statistics.

Ordinal Scale Features

1. The numeric values show the order or sequence.
2. The values are not a measure of magnitude.
3. The interval between values doesn't indicate magnitude.
4. The values do show relationships by order or sequence.
5. The values can't be used in mathematical equations.
6. Statistical manipulation is somewhat limited.

Interval Scale

The standard survey rating scale is an interval scale. This scale represents numbers used to rank items such that numerically equal distances on the scale represent equal distances in the property being measured. In this scale the location of zero point is not fixed. Both the zero point and the unit of measurement are arbitrary. It is an interval scale because it is assumed to have equidistant points between each of the scale elements. This means that we can interpret differences in the distance along the scale. We contrast this to an ordinal scale where we can only talk about differences in order, not differences in the degree of order. Interval scales are also scales which are defined by metrics such as logarithms. In these cases, the distances are noted equal but they are strictly definable based on the metric used.

Statistically interval scale data would use parametric statistical techniques: mean and standard deviation, correlation-regression, analysis of variance, factor analysis plus a whole range of advanced multivariate and modeling techniques. It can use non-parametric techniques with interval and ratio data. But non-paramteric techniques are less powerful than the parametric ones. The most frequent form of interval measurement in marketing is index numbers, another common type of marketing research data generally treated as interval scale data is attitude measures. Some descriptive measures as the mean, median, mode, range, and standard deviation are applicable. Bivariate correlation analyses, t-tests, analysis of variance tests applied for purpose of drawing inferences can be used on internally scaled data.

Interval Scale Features

1. The numeric values show both order and magnitude.
2. The interval between integer values is equal.
3. A zero value doesn't indicate absolute zero.
4. The values show relationships by order and magnitude.
5. The values can't be used to form ratios.
6. Statistical manipulation isn't very limited.

Ratio Scale

A ratio scale is the top level of measurement and is not often available in social research. The factor which clearly defines a ratio scale is that it has a true zero point. This scale consists of numbers that rank items such that numerically equal distances on the scale represent equal distances in the property being measured and have a meaningful zero. This scale is typically used in calculating sales, units produced, number of customers, to know the costs, etc. The simplest example of a ratio scale is the measurement of length. The best way to contrast interval and ratio scales is to look at temperature. The Centigrade scale has a zero point but it is an arbitrary one. The Farenheit scale has its equivalent point at 32°. (Physicists would probably argue that Absolute Zero is the zero point for temperature but this is a theoretical concept.) So, even though temperature looks as if it would be a ratio scale it is an interval scale. Interval scales may be either numeric or semantic.

Statistically the same as for interval data, a common feature of marketing research is the attempt to have respondents communicate their feelings, attitudes, opinions, and evaluations in some measurable form. To this end, marketing researchers have developed a range of scales. Each of these has unique properties. What is important for the marketing analyst to realise is that they have widely differing measurement properties. Some scales are at very best, limited in their mathematical properties to the extent that they can only establish an association between variables. Other scales have more extensive mathematical properties and some, holdout the possibility of establishing cause and effect relationships between variables.

Features of Ratio Scale

1. The numeric values show both order and magnitude.
2. The interval between integer values is equal.
3. A zero value does indicate absence of the thing measured.
4. The values show relationships by order and magnitude.
5. The values can be used to form ratios.
6. Statistical manipulation isn't limited.

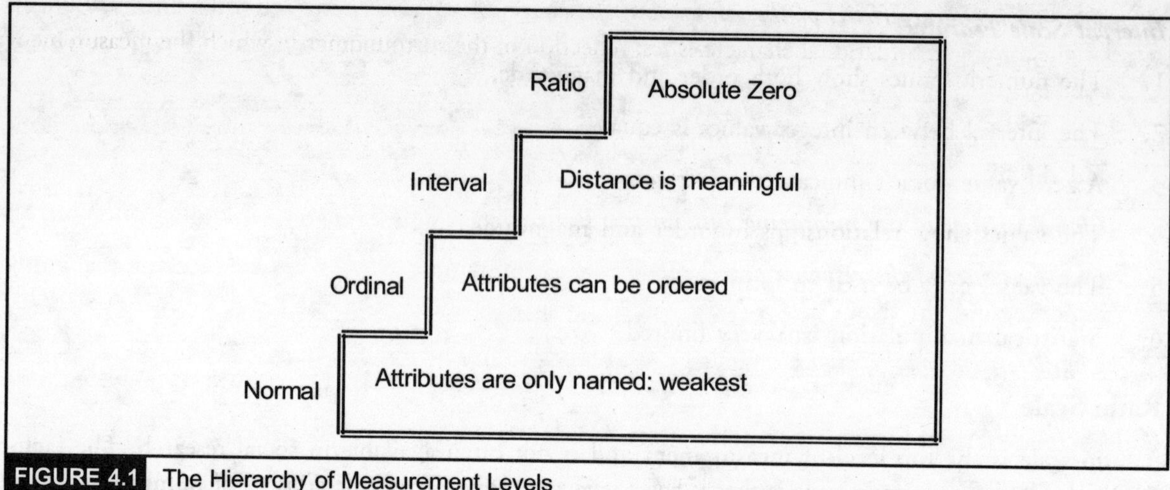

FIGURE 4.1 The Hierarchy of Measurement Levels

To Identify the Scale Data Type

1. Are the values only names to designate independent categories? If so, and the categories don't represent some order of magnitude, the scale data are nominal.
2. Do the values indicate only sequence or order of magnitude? If so, and they don't indicate the actual magnitude or interval between values, the scale data are ordinal.
3. Do the values indicate actual magnitudes with equal intervals between the scale points? If so, and zero doesn't represent absolute zero or complete absence of the thing measured, the scale is interval.
4. Do the values indicate actual magnitudes with equal intervals between the scale points? If so and a value of zero does represent absolute zero or complete absence of the thing measured, the scale is ratio.

All descriptive measures and inferential techniques are applicable to ratio scaled data.

❖ Criteria for Good Measurement

Reliability is the property of producing consistent results when certain research methods are repeated. If the same techniques are applied on similar population it doesn't yield the same measurements as the first data gathering. Reliability is very desirable. Validity is more extensive objective than reliability. Hughes defined "Validity" as, "An instrument is valid when it measures what it is supposed to measure, but since attitudes are elusive, attitude scales Validation is difficult". Sensitivity is the ability of a measurement to indicate changes or differences between the methods applied. Relevance to the decision is to be made or problem to be solved in practical consideration.

❖ Components of Measurement

The researcher must be concerned about the extent to which any single measurement reflects the characteristic under consideration versus other characteristics. The components are as follows:

1. ***True characteristic:*** Direct reflection of the characteristic of interest.
2. ***Additional stable characteristics of the respondent:*** Reflection of other permanent characteristics, such as social class to intelligence.

3. *Short-term characteristics of the respondent:* Reflection of temporary characteristics such as hunger, fatigue, or anger. Situational characteristics: reflection of the surroundings in which the measurement is taken.
4. *Characteristics of the measurement process:* Reflection of the interviewer, interviewing method, and the like.
5. *Characteristics of the measuring instrument:* Reflection of ambiguous or misleading questions.
6. *Characteristics of the response process:* Reflection of mistaken replies caused by checking the wrong response, and the like.
7. *Characteristics of the analysis:* Reflection of mistakes in coding, tabulating, and the like.

❖ Measurement Development

To develop a measurement for a particular concept such as brand image, customer satisfaction, or opinion leadership. In this section we present a sound general method for developing such a measurement. The proposed measurement development methodology is discussed in the following.

Step 1

Specify domain of concept: It involves providing a conceptual answer to the question "Exactly what do we mean by brand image, customer satisfaction and so on".

Step 2

Generate sample of items: This step involves generating a list of specific items like questions, phrases, statements for each dimension of the concept as specified in the step 1.

Step 3

Collect data for measure purifying: The edited items should be placed in an appropriate format and data collected from members of the target market of interest.

Step 4

Purify the measure: This basically involves eliminating those items that do not correlate highly with the total score for the overall measure or the specific dimensions with which they are associated.

Step 5

Collect data for reliability and validity assessment: Once the measure has been satisfactorily purified by clearing the unrelated items removed with several items remaining for each dimension of the concept, a new data set should be collected with the revised instrument.

Step 6

Assess reliability: The new data set should be analyzed to test for reliability. To the extent several different reliability assessments should be used. Unreliable items should be eliminated from the overall measurement instrument.

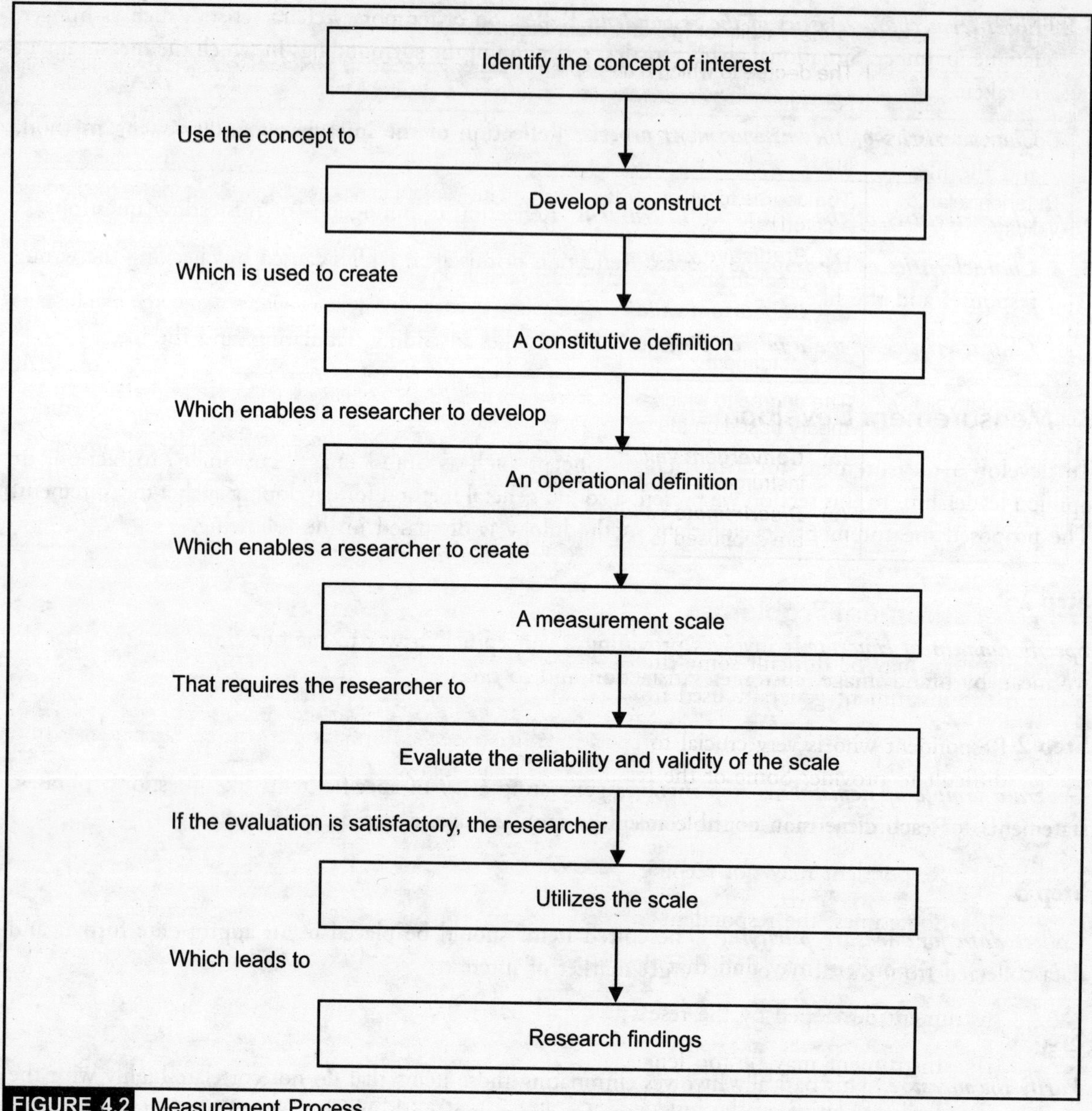

FIGURE 4.2 Measurement Process

Step 7

Assess validity: Once the reliability of the measurement has been established, its validity needs to be determined. Although any method of validation can be used, construct validation is preferred.

Step 8

Develop norms: Once a satisfactory measurement has been developed, it should be administered to various groups of people and averages and variances determined. This will allow one to interpret better the meaning of a score obtained by an individual or group in a subsequent application of the instrument.

TABLE 4.3 Assessing the Validity of Measurement Instrument

Face validity	The degree to which a measurement instrument seems to measure what it is supposed to, as judged by researchers.
Content validity	The degree to which measurement items represent the universe of the concept under study.
Criterion related validity	The degree to which a measurement instrument can predict a variable that is designated a criterion. (a) ***Predictive validity:*** The extent to which a future level of a criterion variable can be predicted by a current measurement on a scale. (b) ***Concurrent validity:*** The extent to which a criterion variable measured at the same point in time as the variable of interest can be predicted by the measurement instrument.
Construct validity	The degree to which a measurement instrument confirms a hypothesis created from a theory based on the concepts under study. (a) ***Convergent validity:*** The degree of association among different measurement instruments that purport to measure the same concept. (b) ***Discriminate validity:*** A measure of the lack of association among constructs that are supposed to be different.

❖ Measurement Problems

Measurement may be difficult some times due to two important factors. One is respondent and other one is the instrument generally used in gathering data.

1. Respondent who is very crucial to provide the necessary information to the researcher may find it difficult to provide? Some of the reasons may be as follows:
   (i) Respondent may not able to understand the intention of the investigator.
   (ii) Respondent may not recollect the required information.
   (iii) Sometimes, the respondent may not like to share the information with the investigator.
   (iv) Respondent may find that the environment is not congenial to share the information.
2. Instrument developed by the researcher may have some problems. Some of them are:
   (i) Instrument may be too lengthy
   (ii) Lack of clarity on the instructions
   (iii) Lack of sequence in the instrument
   (iv) Clarity about the purpose of the research
   (v) Poor language.

❖ Attitude Scales

Attitude scales are those that measure an individual's predisposition toward any person, object or other phenomenon. These scales are different from rating scales, where they are generally more complex, multi-item scales. Attitudes are widely believed to be a key determinant of behaviour, although the behaviour can also lead to changed attitudes. Attitudes can only be inferred and cannot be directly ascertained.

Several measurable responses can offer clues about people's attitudes.

1. Measures in which inferences are drawn from self-report of beliefs, feelings, behaviour, and so forth toward an object or class of objects.
2. Measures in which inferences are drawn from observed overt behaviour towards the object.
3. Measures, in which inferences are drawn from the individual's reaction to, or interpretations of, partially structured material relevant to the subject.
4. Measures in which inferences are drawn from performance on objective tasks where functioning may be influenced by disposition towards the object.
5. Measures in which inferences are drawn from physiological reactions to the object.

SCALING

Scaling is the term commonly used to refer to the process of measuring attitudes. Scales are devised for measuring variables. Scaling refers to the procedure by which numbers or scores are assigned to the various degrees of opinion, attitude and other concepts. When scales are used, reports describe the distribution of respondents along the scale or in the categories. The positions of various individuals or groups can then be compared with one another. Scales can be coded with numbers. The numeric codes that represent answers to questions are more easily manipulated than words. The use of numeric database saves time and money and helps to ensure accuracy, reliability and validity. Scales can be arranged so they capture answers to many questions quickly and in very little space. They are both efficient and practical.

❖ Measurement Scales

The measurement scales, commonly used in marketing research, can be divided into two groups: comparative and non-comparative scales. In comparative scaling, the respondent is asked to compare one brand or product against another. Examples of such scales include; paired comparison, dollar metric, unity-sum-gain and line marking scales. While in non-comparative scaling, respondents need only evaluate a single product or brand. Their evaluation is independent of the other product and/or brands which the marketing researcher is studying. Non-comparative scaling is frequently referred to as monadic scaling and this is the more widely used type of scale in commercial marketing research studies.

❖ Specificity of Scales

Scales are used to obtain data that will be comparable to one another. All data should be expressed in the same terms. Sometimes, the scale will be obvious to the respondent, and sometimes it will be necessary only to name the scale. There are also times when the scales will have to be clearly portrayed.

1. *Implicit scale dimensions:* In some cases, scale is already present in the minds of the respondents. For example, age of the respondent. In this case, there is a common understanding between the investigator and the respondent about the scale to be used.
2. *Explicit scale dimensions:* In some cases, there is no common understanding between the investigator and the respondent. For example, how many days have it been since you visited this place.
3. *Depicted scale dimensions:* When scales can't be specified within the question, they must be depicted as response options, verbally, numerically, or graphically. For example, where are you going from here? Respondent may be going home, friend's home, etc.

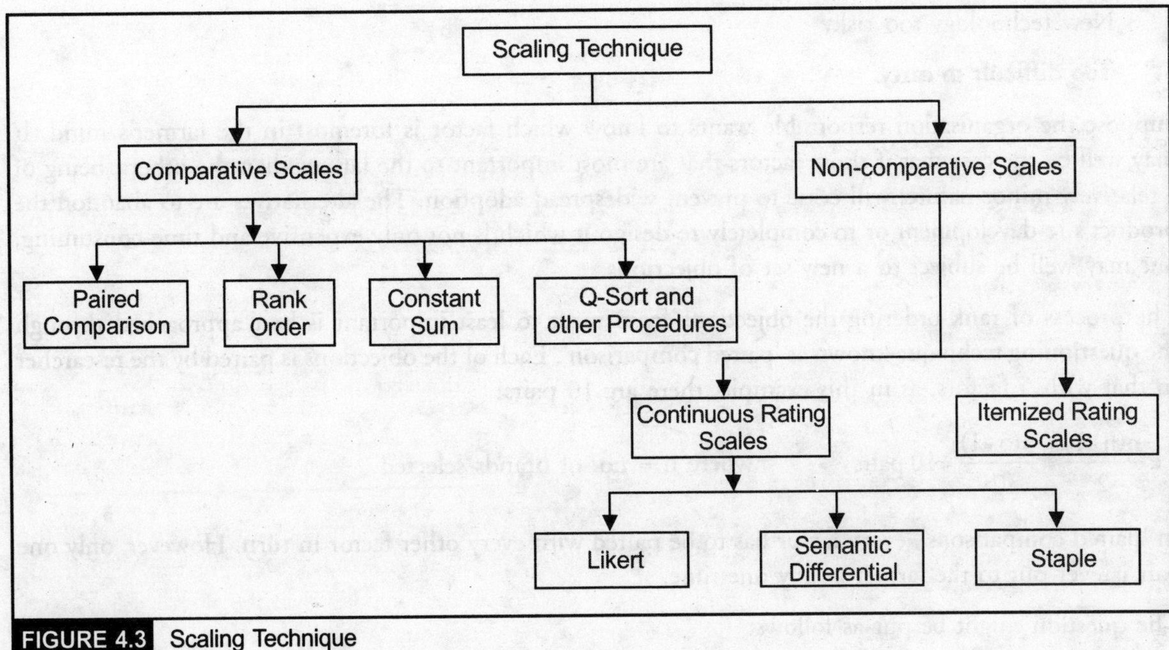

FIGURE 4.3 Scaling Technique

CLASSIFICATION OF SCALING TECHNIQUES

Figure 4.3 gives the different types of scales which are to be selected based on the type of data the researcher is intending.

❖ Comparative Scales

A comparative rating scale provides all respondents with a common frame of references. A comparative rating scale, by virtue of its common frame of references, allows the researcher to be confident that all respondents are answering the same question. However, in the context of measuring attitudes, a standard frame of references imposed by the researcher may not necessarily be meaningful to all respondents. Under such circumstances, the validity of the comparative ratings may be questionable. Under comparative rating scales, there are four types, these are Paired comparison, Rank order, Constant sum, and Q sort procedure.

Paired Comparison

It is sometimes the case that marketing researchers wish to find out which are the most important factors in determining the demand for a product. Conversely they may wish to know which of the most important factors are acting to prevent the widespread adoption of a product. Take, for example, the very poor farmer response to the first design of an animal-drawn mould board plough. A combination of exploratory research and shrewd observation suggested that the following factors played a role in the shaping of the attitudes of those farmers who feel negatively towards the design:

1. Does not ridge
2. Does not work for inter-cropping
3. Far too expensive

4. New technology too risky
5. Too difficult to carry.

Suppose the organisation responsible wants to know which factor is foremost in the farmer's mind. It may well be the case that if those factors that are most important to the farmer than the others, being of a relatively minor nature, will cease to prevent widespread adoption. The alternatives are to abandon the product's re-developmènt or to completely re-design it which is not only expensive and time-consuming, but may well be subject to a new set of objections.

The process of rank ordering the objections from most to least important is best approached through the questioning technique known as 'paired comparison'. Each of the objections is paired by the researcher so that with 5 factors, as in this example, there are 10 pairs:

i.e $\frac{n(n-1)}{2} = \frac{5(5-1)}{2} = 10$ pairs where n = no. of brands selected

In 'paired comparisons', every factor has to be paired with every other factor in turn. However, only one pair is ever put to the farmer at any one time.

The question might be put as follows:

Which of the following was the more important in making you decide not to buy the plough?

1. The plough was too expensive
2. It proved too difficult to transport

In most cases the question, and the alternatives, would be put to the farmer verbally. He/she then indicates which of the two was the more important and the researcher ticks the box on his questionnaire. The question is repeated with a second set of factors and the appropriate box ticked again. This process continues until all possible combinations are exhausted, in this case 10 pairs. It is good practice to mix the pairs of factors so that there is no systematic bias. The researcher should try to ensure that any particular factor is sometimes the first of the pair to be mentioned and sometimes the second. The researcher would never, for example, take the first factor (on this occasion 'Does not ridge') and systematically compare it to each of the others in succession. That is likely to cause systematic bias.

Below labels have been given to the factors so that the worked example will be easier to understand. The letters A – E have been allocated as follows:

A = Does not ridge

B = Far too expensive

C = New technology too risky

D = Does not work for inter-cropping

E = Too difficult to carry.

The data is then arranged into a matrix. Assume that 200 farmers have been interviewed and their responses are arranged in the grid below. Further assume that the matrix is so arranged that we read from top to side. This means, for example, that 164 out of 200 farmers said the fact that the plough was too expensive was a greater deterrent than the fact that it was not capable of ridging. Similarly, 174 farmers said that the plough's inability to inter-crop was more important than the inability to ridge when deciding not to buy the plough.

A Preference Matrix

	A	B	C	D	E
A	100	164	120	174	180
B	36	100	160	176	166
C	80	40	100	168	124
D	26	24	32	100	102
E	20	34	76	98	100

If the grid is carefully read, it can be seen that the rank order of the factors is:

Most important	E	Too difficult to carry
	D	Does not inter-crop
	C	New technology/high risk
	B	Too expensive
Least important	A	Does not ridge.

It can be seen that it is more important for designers to concentrate on improving transportability and, if possible, to give it an inter-cropping capability rather than focusing on its ridging capabilities (remember that the example is entirely hypothetical).

One major advantage to this type of questioning is that whilst it is possible to obtain a measure of the order of importance of five or more factors from the respondent, he is never asked to think about more than two factors at any one time. This is especially useful when dealing with illiterate farmers. Having said that, the researcher has to be careful not to present too many pairs of factors to the farmer during the interview. If he does, he will find that the farmer will quickly get tired and/or bored. It is as well to remember the formula of $n(n - 1)/2$. For ten factors, brands or product attributes this would give 45 pairs. Clearly, the farmer should not be asked to subject himself to having the same question put to him 45 times. For practical purposes, six factors is possibly the limit, giving 15 pairs.

It should be clear from the procedures described in these notes that the paired comparison scale gives ordinal data.

Dollar Metric Comparison

This type of scale is an extension of the paired comparison method in that it requires respondents to indicate both their preference and how much they are willing to pay for their preference. This scaling technique gives the marketing researcher an interval - scaled measurement. An example is given in figure.

An example of a dollar metric scale

Which of the following types of fish do you prefer?		How much more, in cents, would you be prepared to pay for your preferred fish?		
Fresh		Fresh (gutted)		$0.70
Fresh (gutted)		Smoked		0.50
Frozen		Smoked		0.60
Frozen		Fresh		0.70
Smoked		Fresh		0.20
Frozen(gutted)		Frozen		
From the data above the preferences shown below can be computed as follows:				
Fresh fish	0.70	+ 0.70	+ 0.20	=1.60
Smoked fish	0.60	+ (-0.20)	+ (-0.50)	=(-1.10)
Fresh fish(gutted)	(-0.70)	+ 0.30	+ 0.50	=0.10
Frozen fish	(-0.60)	+ (-0.70)	+ (-0.30)	=(-1.60)

Rank Order Scale

A comparative scaling method in which respondents are presented with several objects simultaneously and asked to order or rank them according to some criterion. In this scale, the respondent is supposed to rank the object with respect to some designated property of interest. Rank order scaling is commonly used to measure preferences for brands as well as attributes of the brands. Rank order data are frequently obtained from respondents in conjoint analysis because rank order scaling forces the respondent to discriminate among the stimulus objects. This type of scaling process more closely resembles the shopping environment. For example, the investigator is interested in knowing the consumers' preference about the detergent and its various properties, the respondent is asked to rank the detergent soaps with respect to that property or attributes.

Preference for detergent brands using rank order scaling.

Brand	**Rank Order**
Nirma Super	________
Wheel	________
Arial	________
Surf Excel	________
Rin	________
Tide	________

Instructions: Rank the various brands of detergents in order of preference. Start by picking out the one brand that you like most and assign it a number 1. Then find the second most preferred brand and assign it a number 2. Continue this procedure until you have ranked all the brands of detergents in order of preference. Least preferred one should be assigned a rank of 6.

Constant Sum Scales

Measurement scales that ask the respondent to divide a given number of points, typically 100, among two or more attributes, based on their importance to him or her. A common problem with launching new products is one of reaching a decision as to what options, and how many options one offer. Whilst a company may be anxious to meet the needs of as many market segments as possible, it has to ensure that the segment is large enough to enable him to make a profit. It is always easier to add products to the product line but much more difficult to decide which models should be deleted. One technique for evaluating the options which are likely to prove successful is the unity-sum-gain approach.

The procedure is to begin with a list of features which might possibly be offered as 'options' on the product, and alongside each you list its retail cost. A third column is constructed and this forms an index of the relative prices of each of the items. The table below will help clarify the procedure. For the purposes of this example, the basic reaper is priced at ₹ 20,000 and some possible 'extras' are listed along with their prices.

The total value of these hypothetical 'extras' is ₹ 7,460 but the researcher tells the farmer, he has an equally hypothetical ₹ 3,950 or similar sum. The important thing is that he should have considerably less hypothetical money to spend, than the total value of the alternative product features. In this way, the farmer is encouraged to reveal his preferences by allowing researchers to observe how he trades one additional benefit off against another. For example, would he prefer a side rake attachment on a 3 meter head rather than have a transporter trolley on either a standard or 2.5m wide head? The farmer has to be told that any unspent money cannot be retained by him so he should seek the best value-for-money he can get.

In cases where the researcher believes that mentioning specific prices might introduce some form of bias into the results, then the index can be used instead. This is constructed by taking the price of each item over the total of ₹ 7,460 and multiplying by 100. Survey respondents might then be given a maximum of 60 points and then, as before, are asked how they would spend these 60 points. In this crude example, the index numbers are not too easy to work with for most respondents, so one would round them as has been done in the adjusted column. It is the relative and not the absolute value of the items which is important so the precision of the rounding need not overly concern us.

The Unity-sum-gain Technique

Item	Additional Cost (₹)	Index	Adjusted Index
2.5 wide rather than standard 2m	2,000	27	30
Self-lubricating chain rather than belt	200	47	50
Side rake attachment	350	5	10
Polymer heads rather than steel	250	3	5
Double rather than single-edged cutters	210	2.5	5
Transporter trolley for reaper attachment	650	9	10
Automatic leveling of table	300	4	5

The unity-sum-gain technique is useful for determining which product features are more important to farmers. The design of the final market version of the product can then reflect the farmers' needs and preferences. Practitioners treat data gathered by this method as ordinal.

Q-Sorting Scales

The Q-sorting scale is generally used to compare individuals. Q-sorting scaling was developed to discriminate among a relatively large number of objects quickly. This scaling uses a rank order procedure in which objects are sorted into scale based on similarity with respect to the attitude being measured.

This method is parallel to the judgment of Thrustone's equal appearing interval except that the subjects respond to each stimulus in terms of their attitudes towards it and not in terms of its degree of favorableness and the subjects are instructed to place a specific number of statements in each category. The respondents are given a large number of items and are asked to place them in eleven scales from most favourable to least favourable. The Q-sort scale requires the respondent to express his degree of agreement or disagreement with the item. If the respondent agrees most favorably the item is placed in one extreme. The respondent should place a preassigned number in each scale usually preset so as to result in an approximately normal distribution over the whole range. Each scale is given a score value. Interest centres not on total subject scores but the degree of similarity among various subjects. The similarity may be determined by correlation analysis. The Q-sort procedure is used to classify subjects in terms of similarity with regard to the attitude being measured.

❖ Non-comparative Scales

A non-comparative scale implicitly permits respondents to use any frame of reference or even none at all. Non-comparative scales are broadly classified into continuous rating scales and itemized rating scales. Itemized rating scales are further classified into three. These are Likert scale, Semantic Differential scale and Stapel scale.

Continuous Rating Scales

The respondents are asked to give a rating by placing a mark at the appropriate position on a continuous line that runs from one extreme of the criterion variable to the other. The scale can be written on a card and shown to the respondent during the interview. Two versions of a continuous rating scale are depicted in figure.

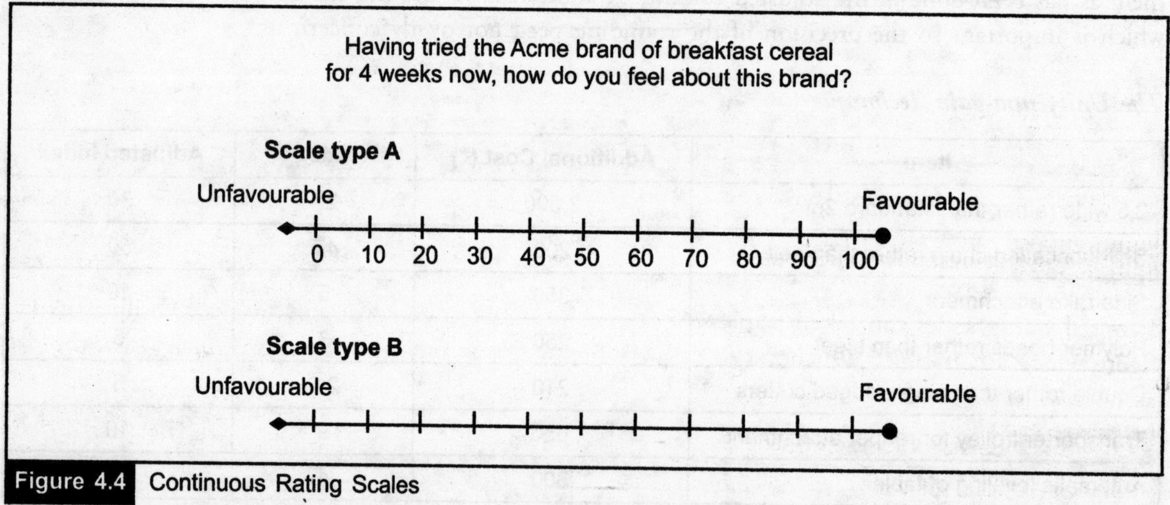

Figure 4.4 Continuous Rating Scales

When version B is used, the respondent's score is determined either by dividing the line into as many categories as desired and assigning the respondent a score based on the category into which his/her mark falls, or by measuring the distance, in millimeters or inches, from either end of the scale. Whichever of these forms of the continuous scale is used, the results are normally analysed as interval scaled.

Line marking scale

The line marked scale is typically used to measure perceived similarity differences between products, brands or other objects. Technically, such a scale is a form of what is termed a semantic differential scale since each end of the scale is labeled with a word/phrase (or semantic) that is opposite in meaning to the other. For some types of respondent, the line scale is an easier format because they do not find discrete numbers (e.g. 5, 4, 3, 2, 1) best reflect their attitudes/feelings. The line marking scale is a continuous scale. Consider the products which can be used when frying food. In the case of each pair, indicate how similar or different they are in the flavour which they impart to the food.

Itemised Rating Scales

With an itemised scale, respondents are provided with a scale having numbers and/or brief descriptions associated with each category and are asked to select one of the limited numbers of categories, ordered in terms of scale position that best describes the product, brand, company or product attribute being studied. Examples of the itemised rating scale are illustrated in the following Figure 4.5.

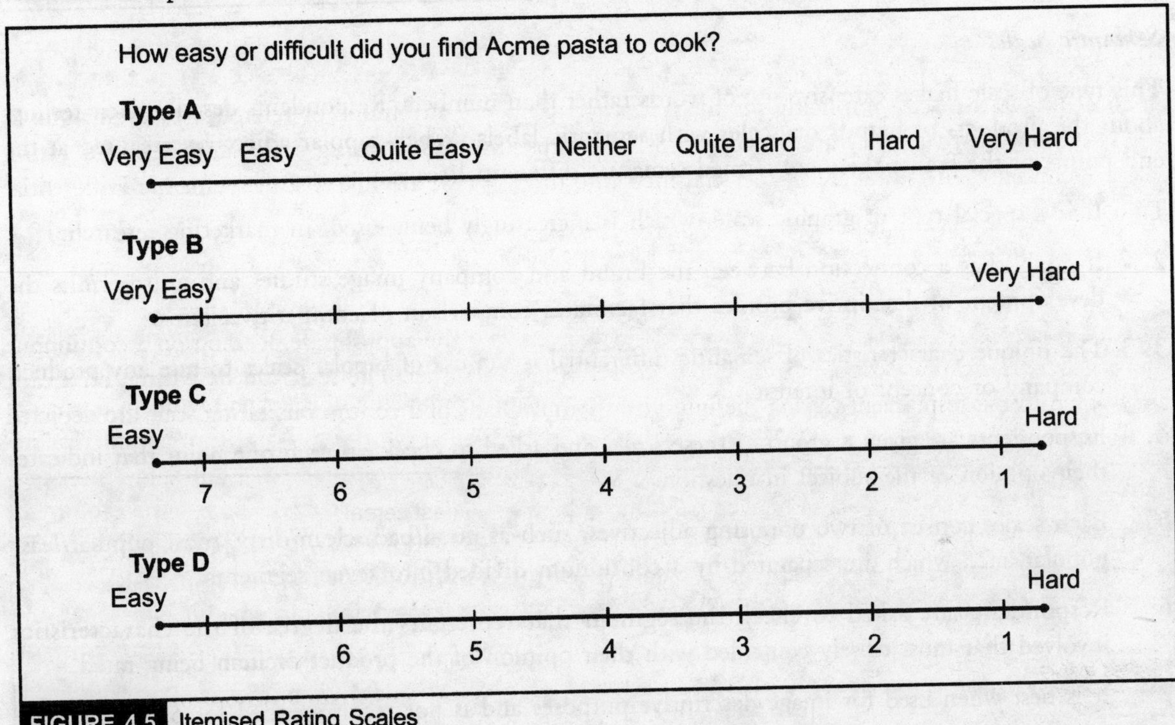

FIGURE 4.5 Itemised Rating Scales

Itemised rating scales can take a variety of innovative forms as demonstrated by the two illustrated in figure which are graphic. Whichever form of itemised scale is applied, researchers usually treat the data as interval level.

TABLE 4.4 Selected Itemized Rating Scales

Purchase Intent	Definitely will buy	Probably will buy	Probably will not buy	Definitely will not buy	
Level of Agreement	Strongly agree	Somewhat agree	Neither agree nor disagree	Somewhat disagree	Strongly disagree
Quality	Very good	Good	Neither good nor bad	Fair	Poor
Dependability	Completely dependable	Somewhat dependable	Not very dependable	Not dependable at all	

Contd...

Style	Very stylish	Somewhat stylish	Not very stylish	Completely unstylish	
Satisfactions	Completely satisfied	Somewhat satisfied	Neither satisfied nor dissatisfied	Somewhat dissatisfied	Completely dissatisfied
Cost	Extremely expensive	Expensive	Neither expensive nor inexpensive	Slightly inexpensive	Very High
Ease of use	Very easy to use	Somewhat easy to use	Not very easy	Difficulty to use	Inexpensive
Color Brightness	Extremely bright	Very bright	Somewhat bright	Slightly bright	Not bright at all
Modernity	Very modern	Somewhat modern	Neither modern nor old-fashioned	Somewhat old fashioned	Very old fashioned

Semantic Scales

This type of scale makes extensive use of words rather than numbers. Respondents describe their feelings about the products or brands on scales with semantic labels. When bipolar adjectives are used at the end points of the scales, these are termed semantic differential scales.

1. It is a special type of graphic scale, which is increasingly being used, in marketing research.
2. It establishes a connection between the brand and company image studies and also permits the development of descriptive profiles that facilitates comparison of competitive items.
3. The unique characteristics of semantic differential is the use of bipolar scales to rate any product, company or concept of interest.
4. Respondents are given a group of these scales and asked to check on each one point that indicates their opinion of the subject in question.
5. Each scales consist of two opposing adjectives, such as good/bad, clean/dirty, most popular/least popular, etc., which are separated by a continuum divided into seven segments.
6. Respondents are asked to check the segment that represents the degree of the characteristics involved that most closely coincided with their opinion of the product or item being rated.
7. It is best when used for image descriptive purposes and is not recommended for overall attitude measurement.
8. The advantage of using semantic differential is its simplicity, while producing results comparable with those of the more complex scaling methods.
9. The method is easy and fast to administer, but it is also sensitive to small differences in attitude, highly versatile, reliable and generally valid.

The semantic scale and the semantic differential scale are illustrated in the following Figure 4.6.

Perception of national brands and private brands:

High quality	3	2	1	0	1	2	3	Low quality
Lower price	3	2	1	0	1	2	3	High price
Higher value	3	2	1	0	1	2	3	Low value
Attractive	3	2	1	0	1	2	3	Unattractive
Packaging								No Packaging

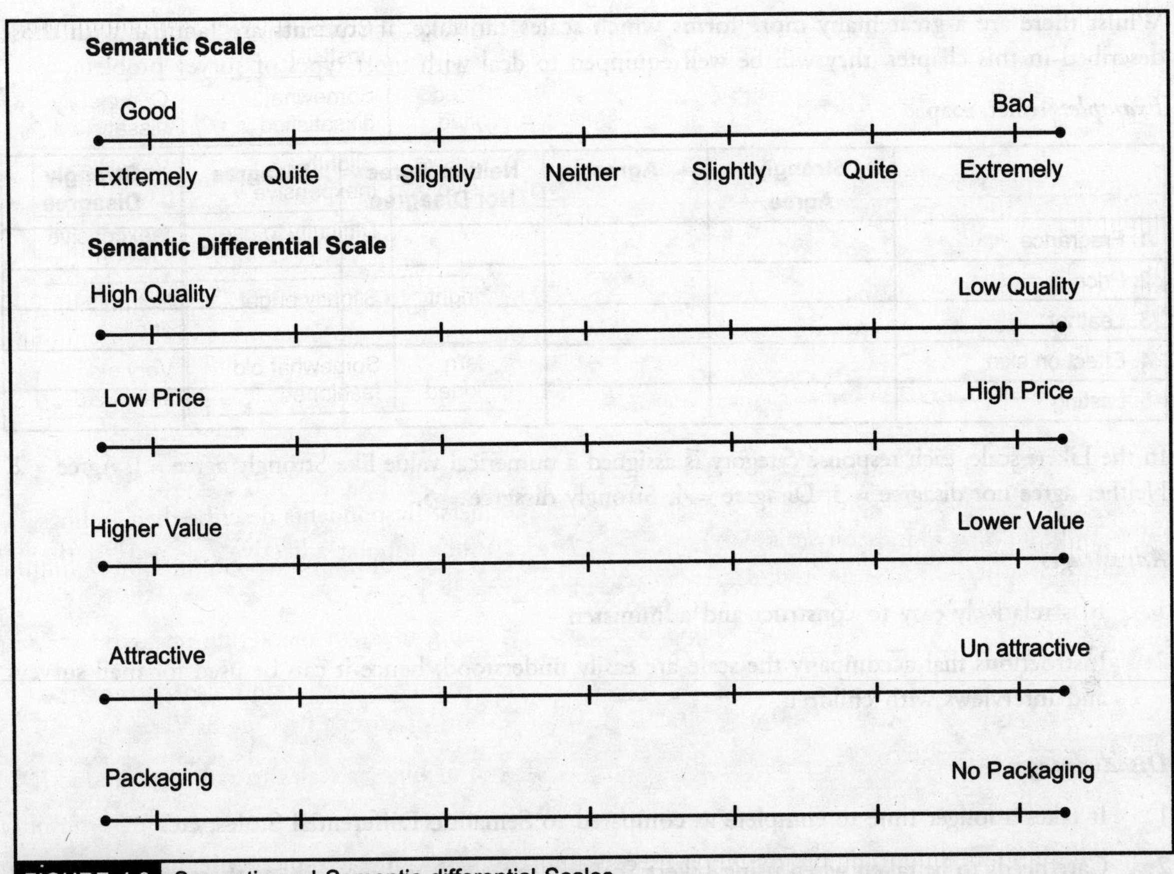

FIGURE 4.6 Semantic and Semantic differential Scales

Likert Scales

A Likert scale is what is termed a summated instrument scale. This means that the items making up a Likert scale are summed to produce a total score. In fact, a Likert scale is a composite of itemised scales. Typically, each scale item will have 5 categories, with scale values ranging from –2 to +2 with 0 as neutral response. This explanation may be clearer from the example.

Example: The Likert Scale

	Strongly Agree	Agree	Neither	Disagree	Strongly Disagree
If the price of raw materials fell, firms would reduce the price of their food products.	1	2	3	4	5
Without government regulation the firms would exploit the consumer.	1	2	3	4	5
Most food companies are so concerned about making profits they do not care about quality.	1	2	3	4	5
The food industry spends a great deal of money making sure that its manufacturing is hygienic.	1	2	3	4	5
Food companies should charge the same price for their products throughout the country.	1	2	3	4	5

Likert scales are treated as yielding Interval data by the majority of marketing researchers. The scales which have been described in this chapter are among the most commonly used in marketing research.

Whilst there are a great many more forms which scales can take, if students are familiar with those described in this chapter, they will be well equipped to deal with most types of survey problem.

Example: Toilet Soap

	Strongly Agree	Agree	Neither Agree Nor Disagree	Disagree	Strongly Disagree
1. Fragrance					
2. Price					
3. Leather					
4. Effect on skin					
5. Lasting					

In the Likert scale, each response category is assigned a numerical value like Strongly agree = l, Agree = 2, Neither agree nor disagree = 3, Disagree = 4, Strongly disagree = 5.

Advantages

1. It is relatively easy to construct and administer.
2. Instructions that accompany the scale are easily understood; hence it can be used for mail surveys and interviews with children.

Disadvantages

1. It takes a longer time to complete as compared to Semantic Differential Scales, etc.
2. Care needs to be taken when using Likert Scales in cross-cultural research, as there may be cultural variations in willingness to express disagreement.

Stapel Scale

Modified and simplified version of differential scale. Stapel scale is unipolar, interval rating scale with values ranging from +5 to -5 the respondent is asked to select a numerical category, which best describes his attitudes. Unlike the semantic differential, the scale values are used to indicate how accurately one adjective describes the concept in question. The respondent is instructed to indicate how accurately each term describes the concept by selecting a numerical response category. The higher the numerical response category, the more the term describes the concept.

The stapel scale produces results similar to the semantic differential and the results can be analyzed in the same ways. The advantages of this technique lie in the ease of administration and the absence of any need to protest the adjectives or phrases to ensure true bipolarity. In addition, the stapel scale can be administered over the telephone.

Example:

Stapel Scale Abundance of Exhibits	Complex User Registration	Low Commission	Good Response to Complaints	Poor Protection of Personal Information	Confusing Support System
+5	+5	+5	+5	+5	+5
+4	+4	+4	+4	+4	+4
+3	+3	+3	+3	+3	+3

Contd...

+2	+2	+2	+2	+2	+2
+1	+1	+1	+1	+1	+1
-1	-1	-1	-1	-1	-1
-2	-2	-2	-2	-2	-2
-3	-3	-3	-3	-3	-3
-4	-4	-4	-4	-4	-4
-5	-5	-5	-5	-5	-5

SCALES COMBINATIONS

The multiple Rating list: The multiple rating list is a commonly used variation of the linear, numeric scale but there is an important distinction. With the linear, numeric scale, the respondent has to pick a number from the scale and then write the number beside the item. The multiple rating list has the labels of the scale extremes at the top. The scale itself is listed beside each item. This has two advantages (1) All the respondent has to do is circle a number, and that's easier than writing it; and (2) The responses form a visual pattern, so the juxtaposition of the responses on a horizontal spectrum is a closer mapping to the way people actually think about the evaluations they are making.

Several savings or investment vehicles are listed below. Please indicate how safe or risky you feel each one is by circling a number beside. If you feel it is very safe, circle a number towards the left. If you feel it's very risky, circle one towards the right, and if you think it's someplace in between, circle a number from the middle range that indicates your opinion.

	Extremely Safe				Extremely Risky		
	1	2	3	4	5	6.	7
Savings account	1	2	3	4	5	6	7
Loan saving account	1	2	3	4	5	6	7
Certificates of deposit	1	2	3	4	5	6	7
Corporate common stocks	1	2	3	4	5	6	7
Precious metals	1	2	3	4	5	6	7

The Diagram Scale: Some times, a diagram scale may be useful in getting right responses from the respondents. Respondents' preference in identifying locations, preferring road lanes, buildings, etc.

Non-verbal Scales: It may be difficult to collect the preferences most of the time. In such cases, non-verbal patterns need different scales. In such situations, non-verbal scales may be useful. Under non-verbal scales, there are mainly two types of scales are used. These are picture scales and graphic scales.

CONSIDERATIONS IN SELECTING A SCALE

While selecting a scale the following have to be considered:

1. ***The nature of the construct being measured:*** What is that we are measuring is most important while selecting the scale. This is purely based on the scope of research that the researcher is initiating.

2. ***Type of scale:*** Type of scale selection is purely based on decision-maker of the research. Most of the time, researchers prefer to opt for the easy one and most economical one. This doesn't mean to

compromise the out come of the study. Depending upon the nature of the study, researcher may prefer rank-order one which can be completed quickly or he may prefer semantic differential scale which require large amount of time and effort.

3. ***Balanced versus non-balanced scale:*** Measurement scales that have the same number of positive and negative categories is balanced scale. Whereas non-balanced scales are weighted toward one end or the other of the scale. Again this is depending upon researcher expecting wide range of opinions or limited range of opinions. If it is related to wide range of opinions then the researcher has to opt for balanced scale other wise non-balanced scale may be preferred.
4. ***Number of scale categories:*** The marketing researcher has to decide how many number of categories has to be included in a scale. If more number of categories is to be considered then the scale will have richness. Otherwise, if little number of categories is to be considered then it naturally lacks that richness. It is always better to have more number of categories to generate data about the intensity of the respondent.
5. ***Forced versus non-forced choice:*** Similarly, it is always better to decide even number or odd number. In the case of even number, there is no scope for neutral point. If there is neutral point, the respondent is forced to indicate the respondent opinion some degree of positive or negative feelings on the subject. A scale without a neutral point or don't know option forces even those persons with no information about an object to state an opinion. The argument for forced choice is that the respondent has to concentrate his or her feelings. The arguments against forced choice are that inaccurate data are recorded and that some respondents' may refuse to answer the question.

CRITERIA FOR A GOOD TEST RELIABILITY

In research, the term reliability means repeatability and consistency. A measure is considered reliable if it would give you the same result over and over again under constant conditions. This can be undertaken by using the same scale or test on the same set of respondents, using the same methods. However, in practice, this becomes difficult especially as the same set of respondents may not be inclined to answer the same questions again. Another point to note is that same respondents may remember their previous answers to the question and give the same answers. Another factor that might distort the criterion of reliability is that the respondents may become extremely cautious and careful the second time, may avoid giving accurate answers or their attitude might have changed during the intervening period. Thus, one has to choose the timing of the retest in such a way so as to strike a balance between the memory effect and the effect of changes in views.

❖ Validity

Validity means the success of the scale in measuring what it sets out to measure, so that differences between individuals' scores can be taken as representing true differences in the characteristic under study.

According to Moser and Kalton, there are four approaches that can be commonly distinguished. They are:

Content Validity

In content validity, one has to check the operationalisation against the relevant content domain for the construct. This approach assumes that one has to have a good detailed description of the content that includes definition of the problem, items to be measured, suitable scale to measurement. Despite all this care, he may be criticized on the ground that the scale developed by him lacks validity. This happens because, whether or not a given scale contains the content validity will depend on the judgment of the researcher and, this is likely to vary from individual to individual. To avoid this, it may be preferable to approach a group of knowledgeable persons, rather than leaving it to one person alone.

Construct Validity

Construct validity refers to the degree to which inferences can legitimately be made from the operationalisations in a study to the theoretical constructs on which those operationalisations were based. The concept of construct validity is more complex than that of content validity. In order to apply construct validity, the researcher postulates the nature and extent of association between the attitude and other specified variables. He then examines whether these relationships exist. If not, there could be two possible explanations. First, his scale might be invalid as it does not satisfactorily measure what it sets out to measure. Second, his theory might be deficient in some way and it may be difficult for him to identify it. The point to emphasize is that the construct validity is based on theoretical considerations.

Predictive Validity

In predictive validity, researcher assesses the operationalisation's ability to predict something it should theoretically be able to predict. Predictive validity signifies how best the researcher can guess the future performance, from his knowledge of the attitude score. The procedure for predictive validity first measures the attitude and then predicts the future behavior on the basis of this measurement. This is followed by the measurement of the future behavior at an appropriate time. Finally, the obtained scores are compared with the earlier predicted scores. If the two series of scores are closely associated, the scale is said to have predictive validity.

Concurrent Validity

In concurrent validity, researcher assesses the operationalisation's ability to distinguish between groups that it should theoretically be able to distinguish between. It may be noted that a high degree of concurrent validity may sometimes be spurious as the collection of one set of data may influence the collection of another set. As in any discriminating test, the results are more powerful if you are able to show that the researcher can discriminate between two similar groups.

S. No.	Approach	Description
1.	Content validation	Involves assessing the representativeness or the sampling adequacy of the items contained in the measuring instrument.
2.	Criterion-related validation	Involves inferring an individual's score or standing on some measurement, called a criterion, from the measurement at hand.
3.	Concurrent validation	Involves assessing the extent to which the obtained score may be used to estimate an individual's present standing with respect to some other variable.
4.	Predictive validation	Involves assessing the extent to which the obtained score may be used to estimate an individual's future standing with respect to the criterion variable.
5.	Construct validation	Involves understanding the meaning of the obtained measurements.

REVIEW QUESTIONS

1. What is measurement and scaling? Explain the difference with examples.
2. What are the scaling techniques that are generally available for the marketing researchers?
3. What is the importance of attitude scales in marketing research? Explain various types of attitude scales.
4. What are the various characteristics of a good scale?
5. What is attitude scale? Discuss Likert scaling technique.
6. Explain the reliability and validity of a scale.

Case Study

Ice cream giant of India Anand want to set up various soft cones vending machines at various shopping malls and other shopping places. The USP of the ice cream is that it is less sweet, low calories and yet very thick and creamy. They have 5 flavours i.e. Vanilla, dark cocoa, coffee, butterscotch and strawberry. They also have unique real fruit flavours in orange, kiwi, black current and mixed fruit.

Before they launch the ice cream they need to know the taste preferences, buyers' behaviour towards their spending power and frequency of eating ice cream. The ice cream is targeted to health conscious consumers.

Questions

1. What is research process? Explain the research process for the above case.
2. As a researcher which research design would you use? Justify your choice.
3. Which scaling technique you would recommend for the measurement of the data collected?
4. Which technique you would use to test the "value for money" satisfaction?

CHAPTER FIVE

DECISION-MAKING TOOLS

INTRODUCTION

Decision-making means selection of one course of action from among various alternative courses of action, one of which is judged to be the best under given circumstances according to the decision-maker. Decision-maker may be an individual or group or a company, etc. There are several statistical techniques which help us in the process of decision-making, some of which were discussed earlier. For example, the inferential statistics helps in acceptance or rejection of a hypothesis at certain level of significance. The techniques of correlation and regression help in establishing suitable functional relationship between variables, forecasting helps in scientific prediction. But decision-making in the present context refers to an optimal choice under conditions of uncertainty. In this regard the probability theory has to play a vital role. In the present chapter, probability theory will be used more meaningfully in the process of decision-making under state of uncertainty and risk.

Statistical decision theory consists of a large number of quantitative techniques which help in analyzing a decision situation and enable us to arrive at a strategy which is the best under given circumstances of the case.

Decision analysis refers to logical and quantitative analysis of all factors that influence a decision. The theory tries to uncover the logical structure of the problem through proper analysis and classification of a decision problem into the alternative courses of action.

❖ Linear Programming and Decision Theory

Almost all are done under linear programming too. But, decision theory is different in one important respect i.e., whereas in linear programming, the constraints of the choice are known and given, in decision theory, the probabilities of occurrence of events on which outcomes of each action depend are not precisely known. The probability theory, therefore, has to play an important role especially, the Beyesian rule of revising prior probability with more information being made available in that regard. Therefore, the peculiarity of statistical decision theory is the process of decision-making under the state of uncertainty and risk. Also, in linear programming, and other statistical methods discussed earlier the pay-off of a decision in terms of money value or the time and cost of saving, was not taken into account.

TYPES OF DECISION-MAKING ENVIRONMENT

Decision are made based upon the information available about the occurrence of events as well as the decision situation (or environment).

The types of decision-making environment are:

1. ***Decision-making under certainty:*** In this type the decision-maker has the complete knowledge (perfect information) of consequence of every decision choice (course of action) with certainty. Hence, the decision-maker will choose an action that yields the largest return (pay-off) for the known future (state of nature). For example, the decision to purchase either (a) NSC (National Saving Certificate); (b) Indira Vikas Patra; (c) deposit in NSS (National Saving Scheme). Deposit in a public sector bank is one in which it is reasonable to assume complete information about the future because there is no doubt that the Indian Government will pay the interest as it falls due and the principal at maturity. In this decision model assumed certainty means that only one possible state of nature (future) exists.
2. ***Decision-making under risk:*** In decision-making under risk, the decision-maker has less than the knowledge under certainty about the consequences of every decision choice (course of action). In other words, there is more than one state of nature (future). It is assumed that the decision-maker has the knowledge about the probability with which each state of nature will occur. For example, the probability of getting digits 1, 2, 3, 4, 5 or 6 when a dice is thrown is 1/6 and the probability of getting head or tail in the toss of a coin is ½, and the probability of the birth of a female or male child is 50% each.
3. ***Decision-making under uncertainty:*** In this case the decision-maker is unable to specify the probabilities with which the various states of nature will occur. Thus, decisions under uncertainty are taken with even less information than decision under risk. For example, the probability that Mr. A will become the Prime Minister of the country, 15 years from now is not known. Launching of a new product in the market, drilling a rig for the exploration of oil, etc. fall under this category.

❖ Decision-making under Condition of Uncertainty

Here only pay-offs are known and nothing is known about the likelihood of each state of nature – situation like launching a new product in the market, drilling a rig for the exploration of oil and purchase of shares of companies (fluctuating in nature), etc. fall under this category. Under decisions of uncertainty, a few decision criteria are available which could help the decision-maker immensely. These are the following:

Maximin Criterion (Pessimistic Approach)

Here the decision-maker adopts a pessimistic attitude and plays safe. The decision-maker should always be pessimistic or conservative, resulting in a maximin criterion. The strategy of the decision-maker would be the one which results in the best of worst outcomes. We shall discuss the various decision criteria with the help of one example.

Example 1

The research department of a consumer products division has recommended to the marketing department to launch a soap with three different perfumes. The marketing manager has to decide the type of perfume to be launched under the following estimated payoffs for the various levels of sales called states of nature.

TABLE 5.1

Type of Perfume	Estimated Level of Sales (units)		
	S_1 = 20,000	S_2 = 10,000 (pay offs)	S_3 = 2,000
A	25	15	10
B	40	20	5
C	60	25	3

In the above example, the worst outcomes in terms of payoffs for each type of perfume A, B and C is when the sales are the lowest, i.e., 10, 5 and 3 for S_3 = sales of 2000 units. With the lowest possible sales, the best payoff is obtained with perfume of type A. Thus, the manager can maximise the minimum payoff by launching the soap with perfume of type A.

Minimax Criterion (Optimistic Approach)

The attitude of the decision-maker is somewhat optimistic and choice of the strategy is exactly opposite to that of maximum criterion. For different types of perfumes under the condition of largest sales, the payoffs are 25, 40 and 60. The minimum payoff under the conditions of maximum sales is again obtained with type A perfume. The decision-maker is content with a payoff of 25 although he expects maximum sales and chooses type A perfume.

Maximax Criterion

The decision-maker becomes completely optimistic and chooses a strategy that is expected to give the best of the payoffs. So for the sales at maximum level, to obtain the maximum payoff the choice would be type C perfume, which gives payoff of 60.

Laplace Criterion (Criterion of Rationality of Jacob Bernoulli Method)

As the decision-maker has no information about the probability of occurrence of various events he makes a simple assumption that each is equally likely. Using the Laplace Criterion, expected values are worked out in Table 5.2.

TABLE 5.2

Type	Probability	Expected Pay-off
A	1/3	1/3 × 25 + 1/3 × 15 + 1/3 × 10 = 50/3
B	1/3	1/3 × 40 + 1/3 × 20 + 1/3 × 5 = 65/3
C	1/3	1/3 × 60 + 1/3 × 25 + 1/3 × 3 = 88/3

The strategy would be to launch the product with type C perfume which gives the maximum expected pay off of 88/3.

Hurwicz Criterion (Criterion of Realism)

The decision-maker would be pragmatic to take an attitude falling somewhere in between the two extremes of maximin criterion and the maximax criterion. Leonid Hurwicz, therefore, propounds a combination of the two criteria. In this, the decision-maker's degree of optimism is represented by α, the coefficient of optimism. The value varies between 0 and 1. α = 0 corresponds to the maximin criterion (total pessimism) and α = 1 to the maximax criterion (total optimism).

Decision index $D_i = \alpha M_1 + (1 - \alpha)m_1$ where

M_1 = maximum payoff from any of the outcome resulting from the ith strategy.

m_1 = minimum payoff from any of the outcomes resulting from the ith strategy.

For each strategy, the value of the decision index is found and the strategy with the highest D_i is chosen. The decision-maker will specify the value of a depending upon his level of optimism. This will be a matter of judgement.

For the example of 1 on launching a soap, let us assume that α = 0.6

$\therefore \quad D_1 = 0.6 \times 25 + (1 - 0.6) \times 10 = 19.0$

$D_2 = 0.6 \times 40 + (1 - 0.6) \times 5 = 26.0$

$D_3 = 0.6 \times 60 + (1 - 0.6) \times 3 = 37.2$ (maximum)

The decision will be to launch a product with type C perfume.

Minimax Regret Criterion (Savage Criterion)

Developed by L.J. Savage the criterion is based on the concept of regret (or opportunity loss) and calls for selecting the course of action that minimises the maximum regret. While the other decision rules do not take into account the cost of opportunity lost by making the wrong decision, the minimax regret criterion does so. The following example will illustrate the criterion.

If the payoffs represent profit, then i^{th} regret = max payoff = i^{th} pay off for the jth event,

Choose the minimum of the maximum regret.

If the payoffs represent costs, then i^{th} regret = i^{th} pay off – Maximum pay off (i.e., minimum cost) for the jth event.

Choose the minimum of the maximum regret.

The following examples will illustrate the application.

Example 2

A businessman has 3 alternatives open to him each of which can be followed by any of the four possible events. The conditional payoffs (in ₹) for each action event combinations are given below:

Alternatives	Payoffs conditional on events			
	a	b	c	d
A	7	0	-10	5
B	-4	11	18	-2
C	13	5	0	7

Find out which alternative should be adopted. If the businessman adopts the minimax regret criterion.

Solution:

Alternatives	Regret payoff amount				Maximum Regret
	a	b	c	d	
A	13 – 7 = 16	11 – 0 = 11	18 – (– 10) = 28	7 – 5 = 2	28
B	13 – (– 4) = 17	11 – 11 = 0	18 – 18 = 0	7(– 2) = 9	17
C	13 – 13 = 0	11 – 5 = 6	18 – 0 =18	7 – 7 = 0	18

Since alternative B corresponds to minimum of the maximum possible regrets, the businessman (the decision-maker) would choose this alternative.

Example 3

Given the following pay-off function for each act a_1 and a_2

$Qa_1 = -30 + 50x$

$Qa_2 = -90 + 20x$

1. What is the break-even value of x?
2. If $x = 10$, which is the better act?
3. If $x = 10$, what is the regret of the poor strategy?
4. If $x = -5$, which is the better act?
5. If $x = -5$, what is the regret of the poorer strategy?

Solution:

1. Equation Qa_1 and Qa_2

   $-30 + 50x = -90 + 20x$

   or $\quad x = -2$

   $\therefore \quad -2$ is the break even point
2. Substitution x = 10 in Qa_1 and Qa_2

   $Qa_1 = 470 \qquad Qa_2 = 110$

   Hence a_1 is a better strategy
3. Regret with $x = 10$ is equal to $470 - 110 = 360$

   This happens when strategy a_2 is adopted
4. For $x = -5$ $Qa_1 = -280$

   $Qa_1 = -190$

   a_2 is a better strategy
5. Regret in (iv) = 90 = (+ 280 – 190)

Example 4

M/s Reddy & Company has three alternative courses of action open, each of which can be followed by any of the four possible events. The conditional payoffs (in ₹) for each action and event combination are given below:

Conditional Payoffs on Events

Alternatives ↓	E_1	E_2	E_3	E_4 → Events
A_1	8	0	–10	6
A_2	-4	12	18	-2
A_3	14	6	0	8

Determine which alternative should the company choose, if they adopt the:

1. Maximin criterion (Pessimistic)
2. Maximax criterion (Optimistic)
3. Hurwicz criterion (The degree of optimism being 0.70)
4. Laplace criterion (Equally likely)
5. Minimax regret criterion (Regret)

Solution:

Alternative	Maximum payoff	Minimum payoff	H = a × maximum + (1–α) minimum for α = 0.70
A_1	8	–10	2.6
A_2	18	–4	11.4
A_3	14	0	9.8

1. The maximum of the minimum payoffs (–10, –4, 0) = 0; which is for alternative A_3, hence A_3 would be chosen.
2. For maximax criterion A_2 will be chosen (maximum of the maximum payoffs) of (8, 18, 14)
3. Under Hurwicz criterion A_2 will be chosen (maximum of 2.6, 11.4 and 9.8)
4. Under Laplace Criterion, assigning equal probabilities to the payoffs of each strategy results in the following expected payoffs.

Alternative	Payoffs				Expected Payoff Value
	E_1	E_2	E_3	E_4	(¼)A + (¼)B + (¼)C + (¼) D
A_1	8	0	–0	6	1
A_2	–4	12	18	–2	6
A_3	14	6	0	8	7

Since expected value Z is the highest, the decision-maker will choose A_3.

5. Minimax Regret Criterion.

Alternative	Regret –		Payoffs Amount		Maximum Regret
	E_1	E_2	E_3	E_4	
A_1	14 – 8 = 6	12-0=12	18-(-10)=28	8-6=2	28
A_2	14–(–4)=18	12-12=0	18-18=0	8-(-2)=10	18
A_3	14 – 14 =0	12-6=0	18-0=18	8-8=0	18

Since alternatives A_2 and A_3 both correspond to the minimum of the maximum possible regrets, the decision-maker would choose either of these two.

Example 5

The following matrix gives payoff of different strategic alternatives A_1, A_2, A_3 against conditions (events) N_1, N_2, N_3 and N_4. Indicate the decision under the following approach.

1. Pessimistic
2. Optimistic
3. Regret and
4. Hurwicz criterion, the degree of optimism being 0.7

$$\begin{array}{c} \\ A_1 \\ A_2 \\ A_2 \end{array}\begin{array}{cccc} N_1 & N_2 & N_3 & N_4 \\ \left[\begin{array}{cccc} ₹\,4{,}000 & -100 & 6{,}000 & 18{,}000 \\ 20{,}000 & 5{,}000 & 400 & 0 \\ 20{,}000 & 15{,}000 & -2{,}000 & 1{,}000 \end{array}\right] \end{array}$$

Solution:

$$\begin{array}{c} \\ A_1 \\ A_2 \\ A_2 \end{array}\begin{array}{cccc} N_1 & N_2 & N_3 & N_4 \\ \left[\begin{array}{cccc} ₹\,4{,}000 & -100 & 6{,}000 & 18{,}000 \\ 20{,}000 & 5{,}000 & 400 & 0 \\ 20{,}000 & 15{,}000 & -2{,}000 & 1{,}000 \end{array}\right] \end{array}\begin{array}{cc} \text{Min Value} & \text{Max.Value} \\ -100 & 18000 \\ 0 & 20000 \\ -2000 & 20000 \end{array}$$

1. Pessimistic is Maximin criterion

   Maximin = Max (-100, 0, -2000) = 0 – alternative A_2 will be chosen

   The decision-maker will adopt A_2 strategy under pessimistic criteria

2. Optimistic is Maximax criterion

   Maximax = Max (18000, 20000, 20000) = 20,000 – alternatives either A_2 or A_3 will be chosen

   The decision-maker will adopt either A_2 or A_3 strategy under pessimistic criteria

3. Regret criterion is Minimax regret criterion

   The above pay-off table need to be converted into regret table

Regret payoff = (Maximum payoff from each condition coloumn – payoff)

Regret Table

Strategy	Condition			
	N_1	N_2	N_3	N_4
A_1	20000-4000	15000-(-100)	6000-6000	18000-18000
A_2	20000-20000	15000-5000	6000-400	18000-0
A_3	20000-20000	15000-15000	6000-(-2000)	18000-1000

Regret Table

Strategy	Condition			
	N_1	N_2	N_3	N_4
A_1	16000	15100	0	0
A_2	0	0	5600	18000
A_3	0	0	8000	17000

Strategy	Maximum Value (Rupees)
A_1	16000
A_2	18000
A_3	17000

Minimax = Min (16000, 18000, 17000) = 16000

The decision-maker will select A_1 strategy under Minimax regret criteria.

6. Hurwitcz criteria (H value): given $\alpha = 0.7$

H = α (Maximum payoff in strategy + (1– α) (Minimum payoff in strategy)

Strategy	Hurwitcz H value (Rupees)
A_1	HA = (16000x0.7) + (1-0.7)x100 = **11170**
A_2	HB = (20000x0.7) + (1-0.7)x0 = **14000**
A_3	HC = (20000x0.7) + (1-0.7)x(-2000) = **13400**

Hence, the decision-maker will select A_2 strategy as the highest value of H for A_2 startegy is ₹ 14,000 as compared to other strategies.

❖ Decision-making under Conditions of Risk

When the decision-maker has to select from among several possible options whose probabilities of occurrence are known, he is said to take decision under risk. The probabilities of various outcomes may be determined objectively from the past data or from the experience and judgement of the decision-maker. Under conditions of risk, the most popular decision criterion for finalising the alternatives is the expected monetary value/expected opportunity loss of the expected payoff.

Expected Monetary Value (EMV) Criterion

The Expected Monetary Value (EMV) is the expected value of the conditional payoff for a given course of action. It is obtained for each action by considering various act-event combinations. The following steps would explain the EMV criterion.

1. Conditional profit for each act-event combination is to be listed first along with the corresponding probabilities.
2. The expected conditional profits for each act are to be determined secondly.
3. Thirdly EMV for each act is to be determined.
4. Finally choose the act which corresponds to the optimal EMV.

Example 6

XYZ company is trying to decide about the size of the plant to be built in Hyderabad. Three alternatives of annual capacity, viz. (i) 10,000 units (ii) 20,000 units (iii) 30,000 units are under consideration. Demand for the product is not known with certainty but the management has estimated the probabilities for 5 different levels of demand. The profit for each size of the plant at different levels of demand is as follows:

Level of Demand	Probability	Profit (₹ in Lakhs) for different actions (Built plant with capacity of)		
		10,000	20,000	30,000
Very high	0.15	–4	–6	–8
High	0.30	1	0	–2
Moderate	0.25	1	7	5
Low	0.20	1	7	11
Very Low	0.10	1	7	11

What plant capacity would you suggest to the management?

Solution:

Level of Demand	Probability	Profit (₹ in Lakhs) for different actions (Built plant with capacity of)		
		10,000	20,000	30,000
Very high	0.15	–4×0.15 = –0.60	–6×0.15 = –0.9	–8×0.15 = –1.20
High	0.30	1×0.30 = 0.30	0×0.3 = 0.0	–2×0.30 = –0.60
Moderate	0.25	1×0.25 = 0.25	7×0.25 = 1.75	5×0.25 = 1.25
Low	0.20	1×0.20 = 0.20	7×0.20 = 1.40	11×0.20 = 2.20
Very Low	0.10	1×0.10 = 0.10	7×0.10 = 0.70	11×0.10 = 1.10
		EMV = 0.25	2.95 (max)	2.75

Since plant with capacity of 20,000 units is likely to yield highest EMV of ₹ 2.95 lakhs, the company should decide to build a plant of this capacity.

Expected Opportunity Loss (EOL) Criterion

An alternative approach to expected Monetary Value (EMV) is to minimize Expected Opportunity Loss (EOL). The expected opportunity loss or expected value of regrets represents the amount by which maximum possible profit will be reduced under various possible stock actions. The steps to calculate EOL are as follows:

1. The conditional profit table for each act-event combination with the corresponding event probabilities are listed.
2. For each event, find out the Conditional Opportunity Loss (COL) by subtracting the pay off from the maximum payoff for that event.
3. For each act, determine the expected COL values and sum these values to get the EOL for that act.
4. Lastly choose the act which corresponds to the minimum COL value.

Example 7

A small industry finds from the past data that the cost of making an item is ₹ 25, the selling price of the item is ₹ 30 if it is sold within a week, and it could be disposed off at ₹ 20 per item at the end of the week if unsold. Frequency of weekly sales is given below:

Weekly sales:	<3	4	5	6	7	>8
No. of weeks:	0	10	20	40	30	0

Find the optimum number of items per week the industry should make.

Solution:

Cost of producing an item = ₹ 25

Selling price = ₹ 30

Profit if it is sold = 30 – 25 = ₹ 5

If unsold, disposal price = ₹ 20

Loss if an item is unsold = 25 – 20 = 5

Sales	Probability	Production			
		4	5	6	7
4	0.10	₹ 20	20–5 =15	20–2×5 =10	20–3×5=5
5	0.20	20	25	25–5=20	25–2×5=15
6	0.40	20	25	30	30–5=25
7	0.30	20	25	30	35

Explanation of above computation: Figures under production 4 are all ₹ 20, i.e., if 4 are manufactured and sale is of 4, then profit is ₹ 20, we cannot sell more than 4 in this case even if chances of sales are 5, 6, or 7 and so conditional profit is the same ₹ 20 under this column.

Figures under production 5. If we make 5 but sale is of 4 only then profit = 20 – 1× 5=15. If 5 are sold, then profit = 25, we cannot sell more than 5 since production is of 5 only and so other figures are all 25. (conditional profit is 25).

Likewise figures under production 6 and production 7.

Expected profit Table (figures brought forward from previous table)

Possible demand	Probability	Expected profit from making (₹)			
		4	5	6	7
4	0.10	20×0.1=2.0	15×0.1=1.5	1.0	0.5
5	0.20	20×0.2=4.0	25×0.2=5.0	4.0	3.0
6	0.40	20×0.4=8.0	25×0.4=10.0	12.0	10.0
7	0.30	20×0.3=6.0	25×0.3=7.5	9.0	10.5
Total expected profit		20.0	24.0	26.0(max)	24.0

Hence optimum number of items to be produced = 6 Ans.

Conditional Profit Table

Sale	Probability	Possible Production action (alternative)			
		4	5	6	7
4	0.10	₹ 20	15	10	5
5	0.20	20	25	20	15
6	0.40	20	25	30	25
7	0.30	20	25	30	35

Conditional Loss Table

Sale	Probability	Possible Production action (alternative)			
		4	5	6	7
4	0.10	20-20=0	20-15=5	20-10=10	20-5=15
5	0.20	25-20=5	25-25=0	25-20=5	25-15=0
6	0.40	30-20=10	30-25=5	30-30=0	30-25=5
7	0.30	35-20=15	35-25=10	35-30=5	35-35=0

Expected Opportunity Loss (EOL) can now be calculated by multiplying the probabilities of each of state of nature with the appropriate loss value and adding the resulting products.

Expected Loss Table

Sale	Probability	Possible Production action (alternative)			
		4	5	6	7
4	0.10	0×0.10=0.0	5×0.10=0.50	10×0.10=1.00	15×0.10=1.50
5	0.20	5×0.20=1.00	0×0.20=0.0	5×0.2=1.00	10×0.20=2.00
6	0.40	10×0.40=4.00	5×0.40=2.00	0×0.4=0	5×0.4=2.00
7	0.30	15×0.3=4.50	10×0.3=3.00	5×0.3=1.50	0×0.3=0

The optimum stock position is one which will minimize the expected opportunity losses. Thus, the optimum number of items to be produced = 6 Ans.

Note: Both EMV and EOL criteria produce the same optimal decision alternatives. But EOL is based on finding the minimum EOL value under EOL criterion irrespective of whether the problem is of maximizing expected profit or minimizing expected loss whereas EMV criterion is based on either largest EMV or smallest EMV depending on the problem of maximization or minimization.

Expected Value of Perfect Information (EVPI)

After making prior analysis the decision-maker must decide either to collect additional information regarding the states of nature or to take the action as suggested by the prior analysis. Prior distribution is not always a perfect predictor regarding the states of nature. This is more so in business decision problems. However, if somehow, the decision-maker finds a perfect predictor, he would prefer action based on perfect predictor for it would enable him to maximise his profits or minimise his losses. The highest expected profits resulting in the presence of perfect predictor is called the Expected Payoffs of Perfect Information (EPPI). EPPI is often called the expected value of payoff under certainty. The perfect prediction reduces the opportunity losses due to uncertainty to zero. The highest payoff in the absence of perfect predictor is EMV of the optimal action.

The difference between EPPI and EMV is called the Expected Value of Perfect Information (EVPI). EVPI represents the maximum amount of money which a decision-maker could spend to obtain additional information regarding the states of nature. It may be noted that EVPI is always equal to the EOL of selecting the optimum action under uncertainty. The identity EMV + EOL = EPPI follows from the result EVPI = EOL and EVPI = EPPI – EMV.

This will be explained with the help of following examples.

Example 8

In the previous problem of production in the industry, the occurrence of the states of nature was known with the probability. If we know accurately the information about the future demand referred to as perfect information, the problem will be solved. In the event of accurately knowing the demand, the industry would stock exactly the same number and realise a known profit. If the industry stocks 4 items and all are sold, it will realise a profit of ₹ 20, if 5 items then ₹ 25 and so on. We will make two tables one for conditional profit under certainty and expected profit with perfect information.

Conditional Profit Table under Uncertainty (₹)

Possible Demand	Possible Stock Action (alternative)			
	4	5	6	7
4	20	–	–	–
5	–	25	–	–
6	–	–	30	–
7	–	–	–	35

The Expected Profit under Perfect Information (EPPI) can now be calculated.

Expected Profit table with perfect information(₹)

Market Size (no. of items)	Conditional Profit under Certainty	Probability of Market Size	Expected profit with perfect information
4	20	0.1	20 × 0.1=2.0
5	25	0.2	25 × 0.2=5.0
6	30	0.4	30 × 0.4=12.0
7	35	0.3	35 × 0.3=10.5
			EPPI = 29.5

The best expected profit without information was calculated out to be ₹ 26 [see example (6)] and here it is ₹ 29.50. The difference of ₹ 3.50 is the maximum amount, the industry will be willing to pay in the week for a perfect predictor because this is the maximum amount by which the industry can increase its expected weekly profit. The difference (₹3.50) is the expected value of perfect information and is known as EVPI. If the industry pays more than ₹ 3.50 to the predictor, it will lower the expected weekly profit. It may be noted that in example (8), ₹3.50 was the minimum expected loss (EOL). It may be concluded that EVPI = Minimum EOL = EPPI –Max. EMV.

DECISION TREE ANALYSIS

Decision means selection of one course of action from several courses of action available to the decision-maker in solving a problem keeping in mind the objectives of the problem environment. Decision-making as a process is an amalgam of both rational and psychological factors. The analysis does not make the decision-makers' role superfluous. The decision-maker, having analyzed the decision problem normatively via decision theory analysis, must introspectively apply the blend of rational and psychological factors ignored to come to a decision about the problem under consideration.

Decision analysis makes the decision-maker aware of the elements in the decision problem and various possible strategies that he must consider. It provides a framework for the logical analysis of any business decision situation. Most business decisions are made in an uncertain environment. Some examples of business problems needing decision analysis are:

1. Plant Modernisation decision
2. Installation of new manufacturing plant
3. Installation of new products
4. Alternative possible distribution channel

All the above situations can be regarded as investment decision problems because in each of these, the firm has to make some expenditure which should provide a financial return over some future time horizon, the exact length of which is generally unknown. Uncertainty about the future creates most of the difficulty.

In addition, often managers need to make decisions in a sequence, i.e., one after the other. Decision tree analysis provides a structure, which a decision-maker can use to integrate the contribution from the various functional areas to the analysis of the decision problem. It helps in obtaining an analytical method for determining the best strategy to adopt in given decision problem.

❖ Decision Tree Concept

A decision tree is a graphic representation of the decision process indicating the decision alternatives, states of nature along with probabilities attached to these states of nature and conditional benefits or losses. It consists of a network of nodes and branches. Two types of nodes are used, one, a decision node represented by a square □ and a chance (or state of nature or event) node represented by a circle ○. Alternative courses of action (strategies) originate from the decision node as main branches (decision branches). At the end of each decision branch, there is a state of nature node from which emanates chance events in the form of sub-branches (chance branches). The respective payoffs and the probabilities associated with the alternative courses and the chance events are shown alongside these branches. At the terminal of the chance branches are shown the expected values of the outcome.

A decision tree contains:

1. Decision Nodes,
2. Chance or Event nodes,
3. Payoff,
4. Logic of roll back (move back /folding back).

The general approach used in decision tree analysis is to work backward through the tree from right to left, computing the expected value of each chance node. We then choose the particular branch leaving a decision node, which leads to the chance node with the highest expected value. This is known as roll-back or fold back process.

❖ Steps in Decision Tree Analysis

1. Identify the decision points and the alternative courses of action at each decision point systematically.
2. If we are analysing a chance node, we calculate the expected value at that node by multiplying the probability on each branch emanating from that node by the payoff at the end of that branch and then summing the products for all of the branches emanating from the node.
3. If we are analyzing a decision node, we get the expected values of all the alternative strategies at that node and choose the strategy having the maximum of the expected values for all of the branches emanating from the node. In this way we choose the action with the largest expected value and we discard the branches corresponding to the less profitable actions. We mark those branches with a double slash (//) to indicate that they have been not considered.
4. Proceed backwards to the next stage of decision point.
5. Repeat above steps till the first decision point is reached.
6. Finally, identify the course of action to be adapted from the beginning to the end under different possible outcomes for the situation as a whole.
7. Decision problem can be single stage decision or sequential multi stage logic of a problem environment.

Advantages

1. It structures the decision process and helps decision-making in an orderly, systematic and sequential manner.
2. It requires the decision-maker to examine all possible outcomes, whether desirable or undesirable.
3. It communicates the decision-making process to others in an easy and clear manner.
4. It displays the logical relationship between the parts of a complex decision and identifies the time sequence in which various actions and subsequent events occur.
5. It is especially useful in situations where the initial decision and its outcome effects the subsequent decision.

Disadvantages

1. Decision tree becomes more complicated as the number of decision alternatives increase and more variables are introduced.
2. It becomes highly complicated when interdependent alternatives and dependent variables are present in the problem.
3. It assumes that utility of money is linear and increase or decrease with money value.
4. It analyses the problem in terms of expected values and thus yields an 'average' valued solution.
5. There is often inconsistency in assigning probabilities for different events.

Decision trees are useful for representing the interrelated, sequential and multidimensional aspects of a decision-making problem. By drawing decision tree, one is in a position to visualize the entire complexity of the decision problem in all its dimensions as also the actual process and stages for arriving at the final decision. Hence this is called sequential or multistage decision analysis.

❖ Decision Situations

Decision Situations can be:

1. Single stage decision
2. Sequential and a multistage problem.

Probability tree is constructed to arrive at single stage decision and the probabilities of the events can be shown explicitly with the help of this probability tree.

Example: Tossing of a fair coin.

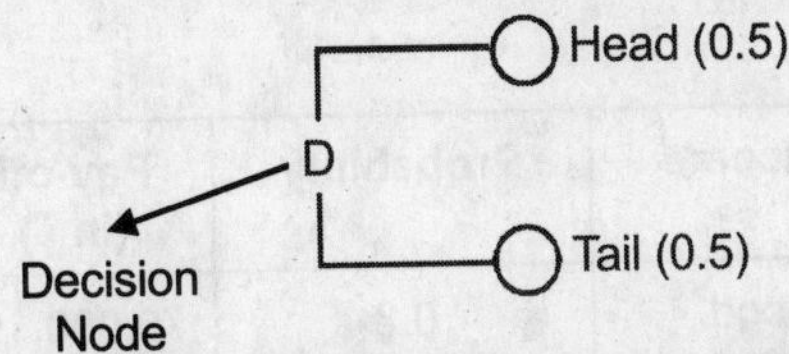

The following examples will explain the construction decision tree and the evaluation process to come out with best possible alternative.

Example 9

A manufacturer of a toy is interested to launch a deluxe or popular model of a toy. If a deluxe model is launched, the probabilities are 0.3, 0.4 and 0.3 that the market will be good, fair and poor respectively, giving rise to the pay-offs ₹ 70,000, ₹ 35,000 and ₹ (–5,000). If the popular model is introduced, the corresponding probabilities are given by 0.4, 0.3 and 0.3 with respective pay-offs ₹ 75,000, ₹ 40,000 and ₹ (–7,500). Use decision tree analysis and decide which model the manufacture should launch?

Solution:

The Decision Tree for the given problem is drawn below which is a Single stage Decision Problem.

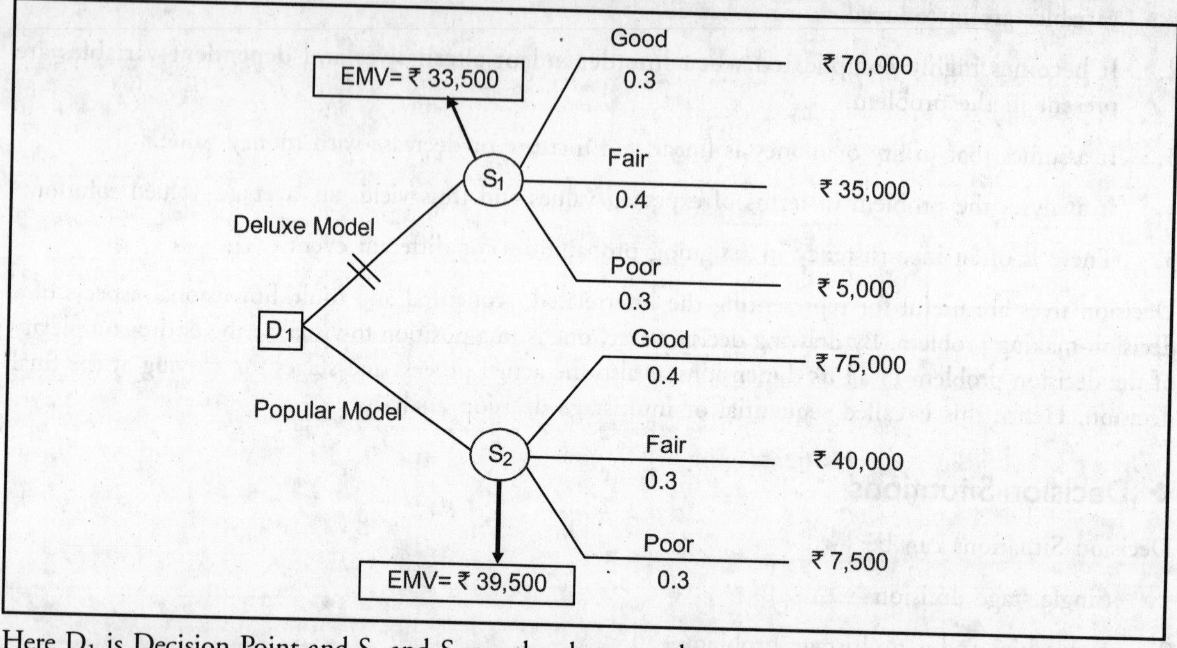

Here D_1 is Decision Point and S_1 and S_2 are the chance nodes.

To analyse the decision tree we begin at the end of the tree and work backwards. For each set of event branches, EMV is calculated and for each set of decision branches, the one with the highest EMV is selected. Following the same procedure we move back on the decision tree to the next decision point. This technique of analysing tree is called the Roll-back technique. The required calculations are shown in the following table.

Decision Point	Strategy	Outcome	Probability	Pay-off (in ₹)	Expected Payoff
D_1	Deluxe Model	Good	0.3	70,000	0.3x70,000 = 21,000
		Fair	0.4	35,000	0.4x35,000 = 14,000
		Poor	0.3	- 5,000	0.3x(-5,000) = –1,500
	Total				**₹ 33,500**
	Popular Model	Good	0.4	75,000	0.4x75,000 = 30,000
		Fair	0.3	40,000	0.3x40,000 = 12,000
		Poor	0.3	- 7,500	0.3x(-7,500) = – 2,250
	Total				**₹ 39,750**

The results are presented on the Decision Tree also.

Interpretation

With Deluxe Model, EMV is ₹ 33,500 and Popular Model EMV is ₹ 39,750. So the best strategy is Popular Model which gives highest EMV. The branch corresponding to Deluxe Model is shown with

'\\' as it is having smaller EMV compared to Popular Model and hence discarded. The table in which the calculations are shown is optional. The calculations can be performed on the decision tree directly.

Example 10

An Executive has four alternatives D_1, D_2, D_3 and D_4. Each of the alternatives may result in the events R_1, R_2, R_3 and R_4. Probabilities of occurrence of these results are R_1 = 0.5, R_2 = 0.2, R_3 = 0.2 and R_4 = 0.1. The pay-off matrix between decision and result is indicated below:

	R_1	R_2	R_3	R_4
D_1	14	9	10	5
D_2	11	10	8	7
D_3	9	10	10	11
D_4	8	10	11	13

Show the decision situation in the form of a decision tree and indicate the most preferred decision to be taken by the executive and corresponding expected value?

Solution:

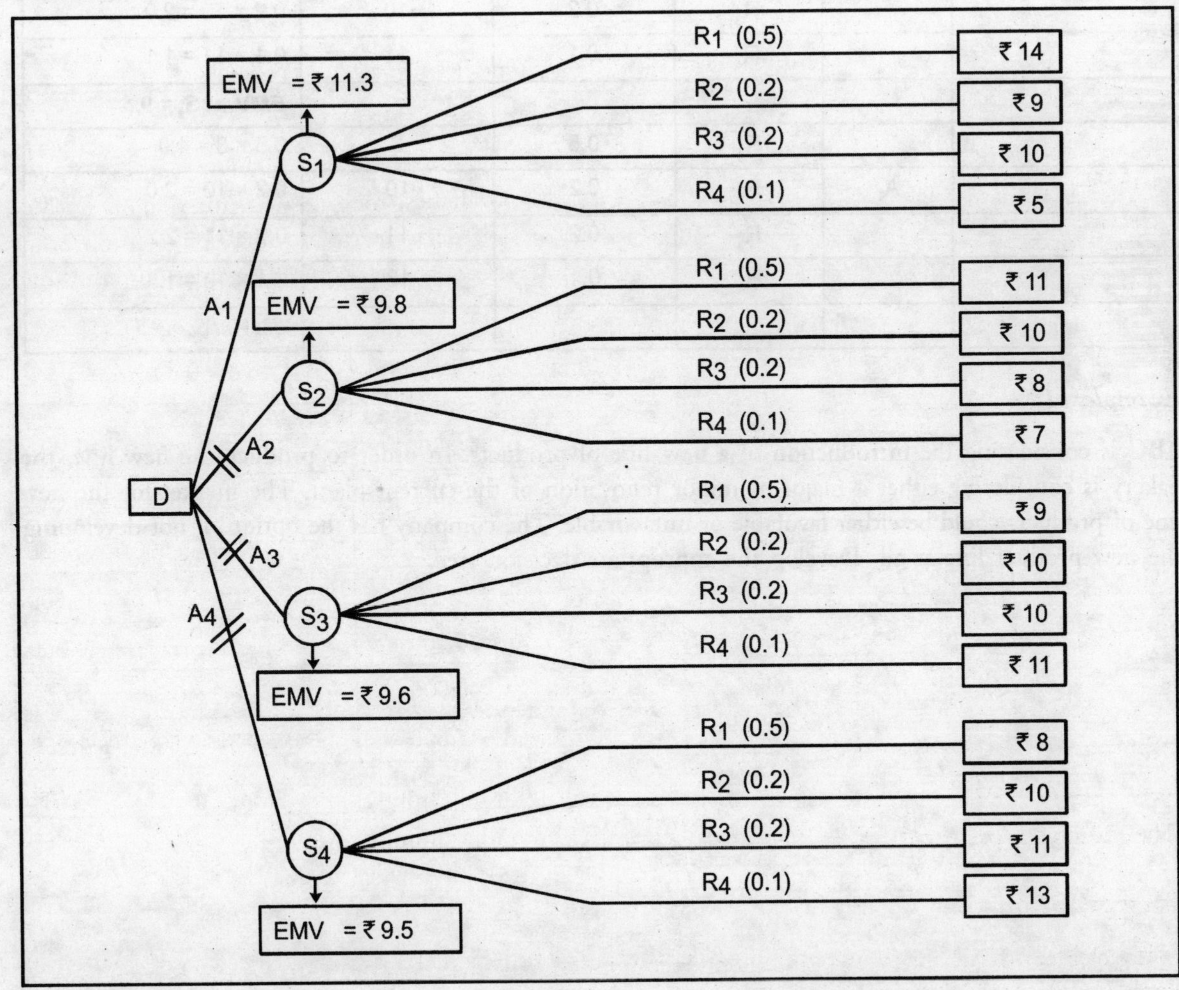

Marketing Research

Decision Point	Strategy	Outcome	Probability	Pay off	Expected Pay off
		R_1	0.5	140	0.5 × 14 = 7.0
	A_1	R_2	0.2	9	0.2 × 9 = 1.8
		R_3	0.2	10	0.2 × 10 = 2.0
		R_4	0.1	5	0.1 × 5 = 0.5
					EMV at S_1 = 11.3
		R_1	0.5	11	0.5 × 11 = 5.5
	A_2	R_2	0.2	10	0.2 × 10 = 2.0
		R_3	0.2	8	0.2 × 8 = 1.6
		R_4	0.1	7	0.1 × 7 = 0.7
					EMV at S_2 = 9.8
D		R_1	0.5	9	0.5 × 9 = 4.5
	A_3	R_2	0.2	10	0.2 × 10 = 2.0
		R_3	0.2	10	0.2 × 10 = 2.0
		R_4	0.1	11	0.1 × 11 = 1.1
					EMV at S_3 = 9.6
		R_1	0.5	8	0.5 × 8 = 4.0
	A_4	R_2	0.2	10	0.2 × 10 = 2.0
		R_3	0.2	11	0.2 × 11 = 2.2
		R_4	0.1	13	0.1 × 13 = 1.3
					EMV at S_4 = 9.5

Example 11

ABC is considering the introduction of a new line of products. In order to produce the new line, the bakery is considering either a major or minor renovation of the current plant. The market for the new line of products could be either favorable or unfavorable. The company has the option of not developing the new product line at all. Develop the appropriate decision tree.

Solution:

The following is the decision tree based on the information given in the above problem

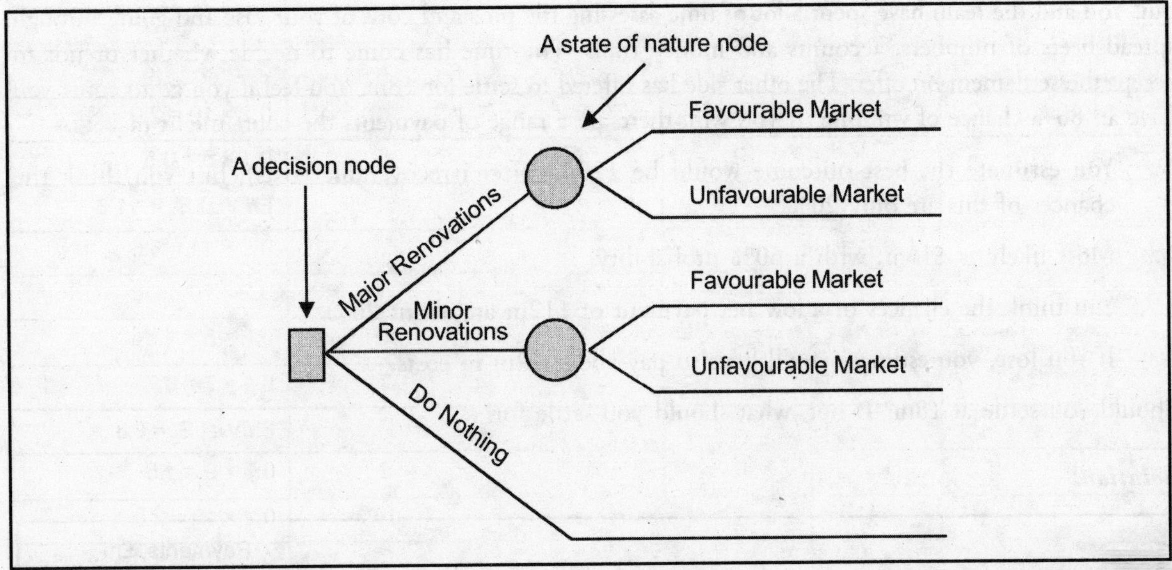

With major renovation, at ABC company the payoff from a favorable market is ₹ 100,000, from an unfavorable market ₹ 90,000. Minor renovations and favorable market has a payoff of ₹ 40,000 and an unfavorable market ₹ –20,000. Assuming that a favorable market and an unfavorable market are equally likely, solve the decision tree.

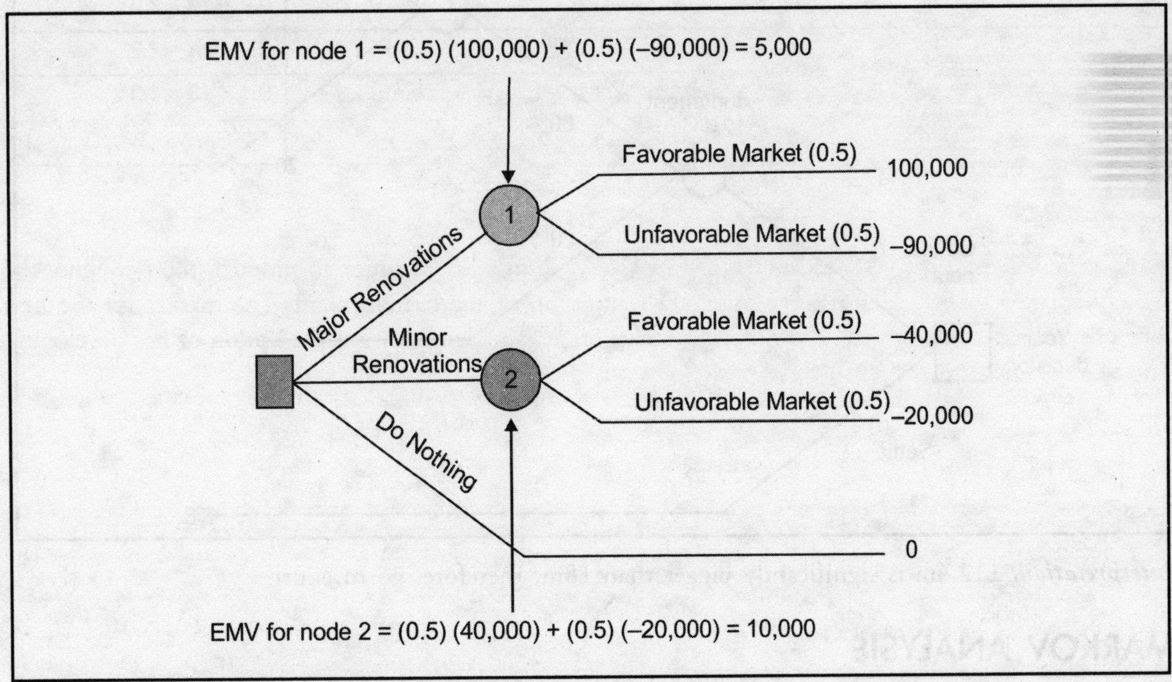

Therefore, the appropriate choice under equally likely market conditions is to make the minor modifications EMV = ₹ 10,000.

Example 12

Your client has been defrauded of a large sum of money. You are pursuing the bank which paid the money out. You and the team have spent a lot of time assessing the pros and cons of your case and going through spreadsheets of numbers, accounts and money trails. The time has come to decide whether or not to accept the settlement on offer. The other side has offered to settle for £8m. You feel if you go to court you have an 80% chance of winning. If you win, there are a range of payments the court might make:

1. You estimate the best outcome would be £20m (after irrecoverable costs), but you think the chances of this are only 20%.
2. Most likely is £16m, with a 60% probability.
3. You think the chances of a low net payment of £12m are about 20%.
4. If you lose, you estimate you'll have to pay about £2m in costs.

Should you settle at £8m? If not, what should you settle for?

Solution:

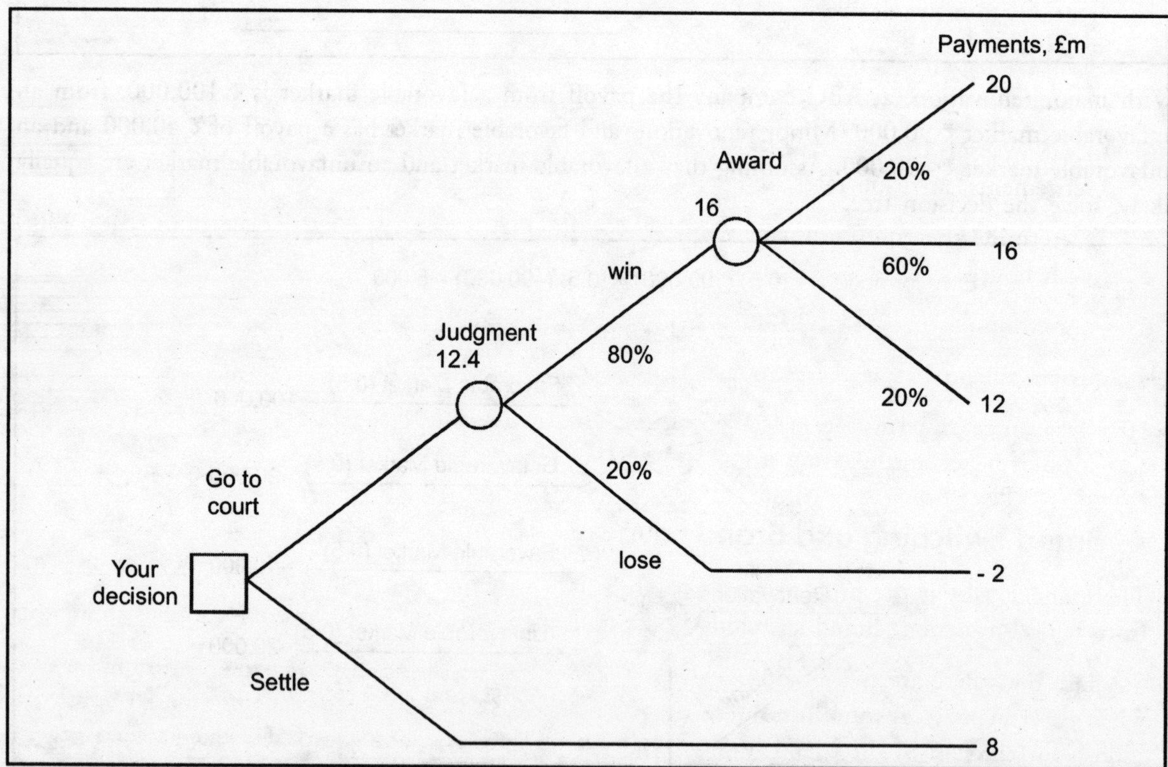

Interpretation: £12.4m is significantly bigger than £8m, therefore, go to court.

MARKOV ANALYSIS

Markov analysis is a technique that deals with the probabilities of future occurrences by analyzing presently known probabilities. The technique has numerous applications in business, including market share analysis, bad debt prediction, university enrollment predictions, and determining whether a machine will break down in the future.

Markov analysis makes the assumption that the system starts in an initial state or condition. For example, two competing manufacturers might have 40% and 60% of the market sales, respectively, as initial states. Perhaps in two months the market shares for the two companies will change to 45% and 55% of the market, respectively. Predicting these future states involves knowing the system's likelihood or probability of changing from one state to another. For a particular problem, these probabilities can be collected and placed in a matrix or table. This matrix of transition probabilities shows the likelihood that the system will change from one time period to the next. This is the Markov process, and it enables us to predict future states or conditions.

❖ Applications of Markov Analysis

1. Analyzing consumer buying patterns by examining and predicting the behaviour of consumers in terms of their brand loyalty and switching patterns to other brands.
2. Determine the market share of the company versus its competitors over a period of time.
3. Studying stock market price movements from period-to-period.
4. Analyzing behaviour of accounts receivables to know the receiving patterns and non-receiving patterns to arrive at allowance for doubtful accounts.
5. Evaluating alternative maintenance policies, queuing systems and work assignments in manufacturing industries.
6. Determining future manpower requirements of an organization taking into consideration retirements, attrition rates, resignations, etc.
7. Determine the equilibrium or stable, traffic flow conditions at a particular traffic point during rush hours.
8. Determining the probability that a machine will properly function next week.
9. Useful in predicting the electorate behaviour in elections.
10. Determine on term faction (stable) of trucks at each location and the mean number of trips a truck would make, starting from a location before returning to that location.

❖ Brand Switching and Brand Loyalty

The brand loyalty is the propensity of a consumer to continue to purchase the same brand of product from period-to-period. Brand switching is the movement of customers form one supplier to another.

Suppose that there are two brands of soaps X and Y selling in the market in the beginning of a year when third brand Z is introduced into market. The market is then observed continuously month-after-month for changes in the brand loyalty – that is, whether and how customers change their brand of soap over time. The steady state probabilities can be determined for each of the brand after a long time assuming that the conditions of the market are same.

❖ Transition Probability

Transition probability is the conditional probability that will be in future state given a current or existing state. A matrix shows probabilities of staying in the same state (retention probabilities), moving to another state (loss probability), and arriving from another state (gain probabilities) from one period to the next is called transition matrix.

Markov processes follow the four assumptions:

1. There are a limited or finite number of possible states.
2. The probability of changing states remains the same over time.
3. We can predict any future state from the previous state and the matrix of transition probabilities.
4. The size and makeup of the system (e.g., the total number of manufacturers and customers) do not change during the analysis.

❖ States and State Probabilities

States are used to identify all possible conditions of a process or a system. For example, a machine can be in one of two states at any point in time. It can be either functioning correctly or not functioning correctly. We can call the proper operation of the machine the first state, and we can call the incorrect functioning the second state. Indeed, it is possible to identify specific states for many processes or systems. If there are only three grocery stores in a small town, a resident can be a customer of any one of the three at any point in time. Therefore, there are three states corresponding to the three grocery stores. If students can take one of three specialties in the management area (let's say management science, management information systems, or general management), each of these areas can be considered a state.

In Markov analysis we also assume that the states are both collectively exhaustive and mutually exclusive. Collectively exhaustive means that we can list all of the possible states of a system or process. Our discussion of Markov analysis assumes that there is a finite number of states for any system. Mutually exclusive means that a system can be in only one state at any point in time. A student can be in only one of the three management specialty areas and not in two or more areas at the same time. It also means that a person can only be a customer of one of the three grocery stores at any point in time. After the states have been identified, the next step is to determine the probability that the system is in this state. Such information is then placed into a vector of state probabilities.

P (i) = vector of state probabilities for period *i*

$$= (P_1, P_2, P_3, \ldots\ldots, P_n)$$

where

n = number of states

$P_1, P_2, \ldots, P_n$ = probability of being in state 1, state 2,...., state n

In some cases, in which we are only dealing with one item, such as one machine, it is possible to know with complete certainty what state this item is in. For example, if we are investigating only one machine, we may know that at this point in time the machine is functioning correctly. Then the vector of states can be represented as follows:

P (1) = (1,0)

where

P (1) = vector of states for the machine in period 1

$P_1 = 1$ = probability of being in the first state

$P_2 = 0$ = probability of being in the second state

This shows that the probability the machine is functioning correctly, state 1, is 1, and the probability that the machine is functioning incorrectly, state 2, is 0 for the first period. In most cases, however, we are dealing with more than one item.

The Vector of State Probabilities for Three Grocery Store Example

Let's look at the vector of states for people in the small town with the three grocery stores. There could be a total of 1,00,000 people who are shopping at three grocery stores during any given month. Forty thousand people may be shopping at Food Mart A, and 30,000 people each may be shopping at Food Mart B and Food Mart C. The probability that a person will be shopping at one of these three grocery stores is as follows:

State 1 – Food Mart A: 40,000/100,000 = 0.40 = 40%

State 2 – Food Mart B: 30,000/100,000 = 0.30 = 30%

State 3 – Food Mart C: 30,000/100,000 = 0.30 = 30%

These probabilities can be placed in the vector of state probabilities shown as follows:

P(1) = (0.4, 0.3, 0.3)

Where

P(1) = vector of state probabilities for the three grocery stores for period 1

P_1 = 0.4 = probability that a person will shop at Food Mart A, state 1

P_2 = 0.3 = probability that a person will shop at Food Mart B, state 2

P_3 = 0.3 = probability that a person will shop at Food Mart C, state 3

You should also notice that the probabilities in the vector of states for the three grocery stores represent the market shares for these three stores for the first period. Thus, Food Mart A has 40% of the market, Food Mart B has 30%, and Food Mart C has 30% of the market in period 1. When we are dealing with market shares, the market shares can be used in place of probability values.

Management of these three groceries should be interested in how their market shares change over time. Customers do not always remain with one store, but they may go to a different store for their next purchase. In this example, a study has been performed to determine how loyal the customers have been. It is determined that 80% of the customers who shop at Food Mart A Store one month will return to that store next month. However, of the other 20% of American's customers, 10% will switch to Food Mart B and the other 10% will switch to Food Mart C for their next purchase. For customers who shop this month at Food Mart B, 70% will return, 10% will switch to Food Mart A Store, and 20% will switch to Food Mart C. Of the customers who shop this month at Food Mart C, 60% will return, but 20% will go to Food Mart A Store and 20% will go to Food Mart A Store and 20% will switch to Food Mart B.

The below figure provides a tree diagram to illustrate this situation. Notice that of the 40% market share for Food Mart A Store this month, 32% (0.40 x 0.80 = 0.32) will return, 4% will shop at Food Mart B, and 4% will shop at Food Mart C. To find the market share for American next month, we can add this 32% of returning customers to the 3% that leave Food Mart B to come to American and the 6% that leave Food Mart C to come to American. Thus, Food Mart A Store will have a 41% market share next month.

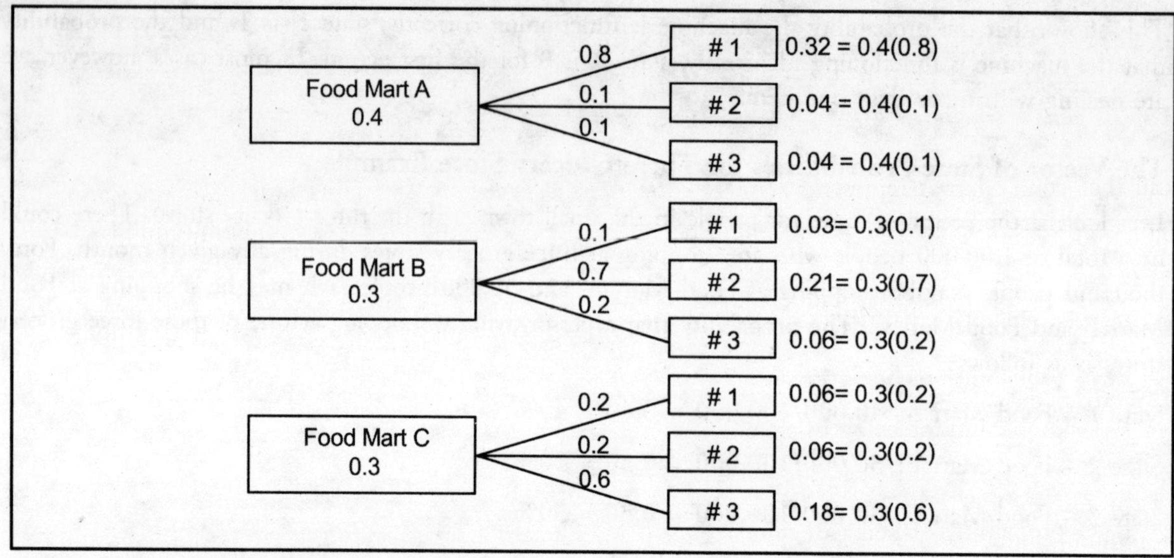

Although a tree diagram and the calculations just illustrated could be used to find the state probabilities for the next month and the month after that, the tree would soon get very large. Rather than using a tree diagram, it is easier to use a matrix of transition probabilities. This matrix is used along with the current state probabilities to predict the future conditions.

❖ Matrix of Transition Probabilities

The concept that allows us to get from a current state, such as market shares, to a future state is the matrix of transition probabilities. This is a matrix of conditional probabilities of being in a future state given a current state. The following definition is helpful:

Let P_{ij} = conditional probability of being in state j in the future given the current state of i.

For example, P_{12} is the probability of being in state 2 in the future given the current state 1 in the period before.

Let P = matrix of transition probabilities

$$P = \begin{bmatrix} P_{11} & P_{12} & P_{13} & \text{L} & P_{1n} \\ P_{21} & P_{22} & P_{23} & \text{L} & P_{2n} \\ \text{M} & & & & \text{M} \\ P_{m1} & P_{m2} & P_{m3} & & P_{mn} \end{bmatrix}$$

Individual P_{ij} values are usually determined empirically. For example, if we have observed over time that 10% of the people currently shopping at store 1 (or state 1) will be shopping at store 2 (state 2) next period, then we know that P_{12} = 0.1 or 10%.

Transition Probabilities for the Three Grocery Stores

We used historical data with the three grocery stores to determine what percentage of the customers would switch each month. We put these transitional probabilities into the following matrix:

$$P = \begin{bmatrix} 0.8 & 0.1 & 0.1 \\ 0.1 & 0.7 & 0.2 \\ 0.2 & 0.2 & 0.6 \end{bmatrix}$$

Recall that Food Mart A represents state 1, Food Mart B is state 2, and Food Mart C is state 3. The meaning of these probabilities can be expressed in terms of the various states, as follows:

Row 1

$0.8 = P_{11}$ = probability of being in state 1 after being in state 1 the preceding period

$0.1 = P_{12}$ = probability of being in state 2 after being in state 1 the preceding period

$0.1 = P_{13}$ = probability of being in state 3 after being in state 1 the preceding period

Row 2

$0.1 = P_{21}$ = probability of being in state 1 after being in state 2 the preceding period

$0.7 = P_{22}$ = probability of being in state 2 after being in state 2 the preceding period

$0.2 = P_{23}$ = probability of being in state 3 after being in state 2 the preceding period

Row 3

$0.2 = P_{31}$ = probability of being in state 1 after being in state 3 the preceding period

$0.2 = P_{32}$ = probability of being in state 2 after being in state 3 the preceding period

$0.6 = P_{33}$ = probability of being in state 3 after being in state 3 the preceding period

Note that the three probabilities in the top row sum to 1. The probabilities for any row in a matrix of transition probabilities will also sum to 1. After the state probabilities have been determined along with the matrix of transition probabilities, it is possible to predict future state probabilities.

❖ Predicting Future Market Shares

One of the purposes of Markov analysis is to predict the future. Given the vector of state probabilities and the matrix of transition probabilities, it is not very difficult to determine the state probabilities at a future date. With this type of analysis, we are able to compute the probability that a person will be shopping at one of the grocery stores in the future. Because this probability is equivalent to market share, it is possible to determine future market shares for Food Mart A, Food Mart B, and Food Mart C. When the current period is 0, calculating the state probabilities for the next period (period 1) can be accomplished as follows:

$$P(1) = P(0)P \tag{1}$$

Furthermore, if we are in any period n, we can compute the state probabilities for period n + 1 as follows:

$$P(n + 1) = P(n)P \tag{2}$$

Equation 1 can be used to answer the question of next period's market shares for the grocery stores. The computations are:

$$P(1) = P\ (0)\ P$$

$$= (0.4, 0.3, 0.3)\begin{bmatrix} 0.8 & 0.1 & 0.1 \\ 0.1 & 0.7 & 0.2 \\ 0.2 & 0.2 & 0.6 \end{bmatrix}$$

$$= [(0.4)(0.8) + (0.3)(0.1) + (0.3)(0.2),$$

$$(0.4)(0.1) + (0.3)(0.7) + (0.3)(0.2),$$

$$(0.4)(0.1) + (0.3)(0.2) + (0.3)(0.6)]$$

$$= (0.4, 0.31, 0.28)$$

As you can see, the market share for Food Mart A and Food Mart B has increased while the market share for Food Mart C has decreased. Will this trend continue in the next period and the one after that? From Equation 2, we can derive a model that will tell us what the state probabilities will be in any time period in the future. Consider two time periods from now:

$$P(2) = P\ (1)\ P$$

Since we know that

$$P(1) = P\ (0)\ P$$

we have

$$P(2) = [P\ (1)\ P] = [P\ (0)\ P]\ P = P\ (0)\ PP = P\ (0)\ P^2$$

In general,

$$P(n) = P\ (0)\ P^n \tag{3}$$

Thus, the state probabilities n periods in the future can be obtained from the current state probabilities and the matrix of transition probabilities.

In the three grocery store examples, we saw that Food Mart A and Food Mart B had increased market shares in the next period, while Atlas Food lost market share. Will Atlas eventually lose its entire market share? Or will a stable condition be reached by all three groceries? Although Equation 3 provides some help in determining this, it is better to discuss this in terms of equilibrium or steady state conditions. To help introduce the concept of equilibrium, we present a second application of Markov analysis: machine breakdowns.

❖ Equilibrium or Steady State Market Shares

The market shares that each product would capture after some period of time has passed and that would not change, assuming the transition probability matrix remain unchanged.

Equilibrium Conditions

Looking at the earlier example, it is easy to think that eventually all market shares or state probabilities will be either 0 or 1. This is usually not the case. Equilibrium share of the market values or probabilities are normally encountered. One way to compute the equilibrium share of the market, or equilibrium state probabilities, is to use Markov analysis for a large number of periods. It is possible to see if the future values are approaching a stable value.

Table State(s) Probabilities

Period	State 1	State 2
1	1.0	0.0
2	0.80	0.2
3	0.66	0.34
4	0.562	0.438
5	0.4934	0.5066
6	0.44538	0.55462
7	0.411766	0.588234
8	0.388236	0.611763
9	0.371765	0.628234
10	0.360235	0.639754
11	0.352165	0.647834
12	0.346515	0.653484
13	0.342560	0.657439
14	0.339792	0.660207
15	0.337854	0.662145

The machine starts off functioning correctly (in state 1) in the first period. In period 5, there is only a 0.4934 probability that the machine is still functioning correctly, and by the period 10, this probability is only 0.360235. In period 15, the probability that the machine is still functioning correctly is about 0.34. The probability that the machine will be functioning correctly at a future period is decreasing but it is decreasing at a decreasing rate. What would you expect in the long run? If we made these calculations for 100 periods, what would happen? Would there be equilibrium in this case? If the answer is yes, what would it be? Looking at the below table, it appears that there will be an equilibrium at 0.333333 or 1/3. But how can we be sure?

By definition, an equilibrium condition exists if the state probabilities or market shares do not change after a large number of periods. Thus, at equilibrium, the state probabilities for a future period must be the same as the state probabilities for the current period. This fact is the key to solving for the equilibrium state probabilities. This relationship can be expressed as follows:

From Equation 2 it is always true that

P(next period) = P(this period) P

or

$$P(n + 1) = P(n)\,P$$

At equilibrium, we know that

$$P(n + 1) = P(n)$$

Therefore, at equilibrium

$$P(n + 1) = P(n)\,P = P(n)$$

So

$$P(n) = P(n)\,P$$

or, dropping the n term,

$$P(n) = PP$$

At equilibrium, the state probabilities for the next period are the same as the state probabilities for the current period. For Tolsky's machine, this can be expressed as follows:

$$P = P\,P$$

$$(P_1 + P_2) = (P_1 + P_2)\begin{bmatrix} 0.8 & 0.2 \\ 0.1 & 0.9 \end{bmatrix}$$

Using matrix multiplication, we get

$$(P_1 + P_2) = [(P_1)(0.8) + (P_2)(0.1), (P_1)(0.2) + (P_2)(0.9)]$$

The first term on the left-hand side, P_1, is equal to the first term on the right-hand side $(P_1)(0.8) + (P_2)(0.1)$. In addition, the second term on the left-hand side, P_2, is equal to the second term on the right-hand side $(P_1)(0.2) + (P_2)(0.9)$. This gives us the following:

$$P_1 = 0.8\,P_1 + 0.1P_2$$

$$P_2 = 0.2\,P_1 + 0.9P_2$$

We also know that the state probabilities, P_1 and P_2 in this case, must sum to 1. (Looking at the above table, you note that P_1 and P_2 sum to 1 for all 15 periods.) We can express this property as follows:

$$P_1 + P_2 + \ldots + P_n = 1$$

$$P_1 + P_2 = 1$$

Thus, we will be solving the following two equations:

$$P_2 = 0.2\,P_1 + 0.9P_2$$

$$P_1 + P_2 = 1$$

Rearranging the first equation, we get

$$0.1\,P_2 = 0.2\,P_1$$

or

$$P_2 = 2P_1$$

Substituting this into the following equation, we have

$$P_1 + P_2 = 1$$

or

$$P_1 + 2P_1 = 1$$

or

$$3P_1 = 1$$

$$P_1 = 1/3 = 0.33333333$$

thus

$$P_2 = 2/3 = 0.66666667$$

It the results are compared with the table ,the equilibrium state probability for state 1 is 0.33333333, and the equilibrium state probability for state 2 is 0.66666667. These values are what you would expect by looking at the tabled results. This analysis indicates that it is only necessary to know the matrix of transition in determining the equilibrium market shares. The initial values for the state probabilities or the market shares do not influence the equilibrium state probabilities. The analysis for determining equilibrium state probabilities or market shares is the same when there are more states. If there are three states (as in the grocery store example), we have to solve three equations for the three equilibrium states; if there are four states, we have solve four simultaneous equations for the four unknown equilibrium values, and so on.

You may wish to prove to yourself that the equilibrium states we have just computed are, in fact, equilibrium states. This can be done by multiplying the equilibrium states times the original matrix of transition. The results will be the same equilibrium states. Performing this analysis is also an excellent way to check your answers to end-of-chapter problems or examination questions.

Example 13

The 'School of International Studies for Population' found out by its survey that the mobility of the population of a state to a village, town and city is in the following percentages:

		To		
		Village	Town	City
From	Village	50%	30%	20%
	Town	10%	70%	20%
	City	10%	40%	50%

What will be the proportion of population in village, town and city after two years, given that the present populations has proportions of 0.7, 0.2 and 0.1 in the village, town and city respectively?

Solution:

The problem can be solved with a first order Markov chain.

Calculation for First Year

The expected proportion of population in a village, town and city after the first year is obtained by multiplying the matrix of transition probabilities by the matrix of the present population proportion of the village, town and city:

$$\underset{\text{Present Proportion}}{\begin{bmatrix} 0.70 & 0.20 & 0.10 \end{bmatrix}} \underset{\text{Transition Matrix}}{\overset{\text{Village Town City}}{\begin{bmatrix} 0.50 & 0.30 & 0.20 \\ 0.10 & 0.70 & 0.20 \\ 0.10 & 0.40 & 0.50 \end{bmatrix}}} = \underset{\text{Proportion after one year}}{\overset{\text{Village Town City}}{\begin{bmatrix} 0.38 & 0.39 & 0.23 \end{bmatrix}}}$$

The proportion of population after one year is obtained by multiplying the present population row by each column in the transition matrix.

Calculation for Second Year

The expected proportion of population for the second year can be determined in the same manner. The transition matrix is multiplied by the population proportion after the first year.

$$\begin{bmatrix} 0.38 & 0.39 & 0.23 \end{bmatrix} \begin{bmatrix} 0.50 & 0.30 & 0.20 \\ 0.10 & 0.70 & 0.20 \\ 0.10 & 0.40 & 0.50 \end{bmatrix} = \begin{bmatrix} 0.252 & 0.479 & 0.269 \end{bmatrix}$$

Present Proportion First Year — Transition Matrix — Proportion after one year / Second Year

Remark: Alternative method of calculation for period n.

The determination of population proportion for any period n could also have been made by raising the transition matrix to the power n – 1 and multiplying by the initial share of population:

$$\begin{bmatrix} 0.70 & 0.20 & 0.10 \end{bmatrix} \begin{bmatrix} 0.50 & 0.30 & 0.20 \\ 0.10 & 0.70 & 0.20 \\ 0.10 & 0.40 & 0.50 \end{bmatrix}^{n-1} = \text{[Proportion after n years]}$$

Initial Proportion — Transition matrix

Example 14

For the following transition probability matrix, determine the steady state probabilities and comment.

$$\begin{pmatrix} 0.6 & 0.3 & 0.1 \\ 0.4 & 0.5 & 0.1 \\ 0.2 & 0.1 & 0.7 \end{pmatrix}$$

Solution:

Let P = Transition probability matrix

S = Steady sate probability matrix

$$\text{Therefore, } P = \begin{pmatrix} 0.6 & 0.3 & 0.1 \\ 0.4 & 0.5 & 0.1 \\ 0.2 & 0.1 & 0.7 \end{pmatrix}$$

$S = (p_1, p_2, p_3)$ where p_1, p_2, p_3 are steady state probabilities

Steady state condition: SP = S

$$(p_1, p_2, p_3) = (p_1, p_2, p_3) \begin{pmatrix} 0.6 & 0.3 & 0.1 \\ 0.4 & 0.5 & 0.1 \\ 0.2 & 0.1 & 0.7 \end{pmatrix}$$

$(p_1, p_2, p_3) = [(0.6p_1 + 0.42p_2 + 0.2p_3), (0.3p_1 + 0.5p_2 + 0.1p_3), (0.1p_1 + 0.1p_2 + 0.7p_3)]$

Then by equating left hand side and right hand side terms, we get the following three equations:

$p_1 = 0.6p_1 + 0.42p_2 + 0.2p_3 \Rightarrow 0.4p_1 - 0.4p_2 - 0.2p_3 = 0$ (1)

$p_2 = 0.3p_1 + 0.5p_2 + 0.1p_3 \Rightarrow -0.3p_1 + 0.5p_2 - 0.1p_3 = 0$ (2)

$p_3 = 0.1p_1 + 0.1p_2 + 0.7p_3 \Rightarrow -0.1p_1 - 0.1p_2 + 0.3p_3 = 0$ (3)

Since the total probabilities of steady state equal to one, the following equation will represent this property

$p_1 + p_2 + p_3 = 1.0$ (4)

Taking into account of first (1), (2) and (4) equations for simplification

$0.4p_1 - 0.4p_2 - 0.2p_3 = 0$ (1)

$-0.3p_1 + 0.5p_2 - 0.1p_3 = 0$ (2)

$p_1 + p_2 + p_3 = 1.0$ (4)

Rearrange equation (4) as : $p_1 = (1 - p_2 - p_3)$

Substituting p_1 value in equation (1) to eliminate p_1

$0.4(1 - p_2 - p_3) - 0.4p_2 - 0.2p_3 = 0$ (1)

Simplifying the above equation, we get

$0.8p_2 + 0.6p_3 = 0.4$ (5)

Substituting p_1 value in equation (2) to eliminate p_1

$-0.3(1 - p_2 - p_3) + 0.5p_2 - 0.1\,p_3 = 0$ (2)

Simplifying the above equation, we get

$0.8p_2 + 0.2p_3 = 0.3$ (6)

By solving (5) and (6) equations consisting of p_2, p_3 variables

Subtracting (6) from (5)

$0.8p_2 + 0.6p_3 = 0.4$ (5)

(–) $0.8p_2 + 0.2p_3 = 0.3$ (6)

$0.4p_3 = 0.1$

Hence $p_3 = 0.25$

Substituting p_3 value in equation (5) to get p_2 value

$0.8p_2 + 0.6(0.25) = 0.4$ (5)

Hence $p_2 = 0.3125$

Substituting p_2, p_3 values in equation (4) to get p_1 value

$p_1 + 0.3125 + 0.25 = 1.0$

Hence $p_1 = 0.4375$

Computed steady state probabilities for this problem are summarized as follows:

State 1 : $p_1 = 0.4375$

State 2 : $p_2 = 0.3125$

State 3 : $p_3 = 0.25$

SUMMARY

With the assumptions discussed in this chapter, it is possible to use Markov analysis to predict future states and to determine equilibrium conditions. We also explore a special case of Markov analysis in which there is one or more absorbing states. This involves using the fundamental matrix to determine equilibrium conditions.

In this chapter, only three applications of Markov analysis are explored. We examined machine, the market shares for three grocery stores, and an accounts receivable system. The applications of the method are far reaching, and any dynamic system that meets the model's assumptions can be analyzed by the Markov approach.

REVIEW QUESTIONS

1. What is Decision Theory? Discuss the importance of Decision Theory.
2. Explain the types of decision-making environments with examples.
3. Explain the criteria of different decision-making environments.
4. What is equilibrium market share? Explain the applications of Markov model in marketing research.
5. What is Decision Tree? How decision tree analysis will help the decision-makers to take right decisions?
6. A marketer buys a lot of fruits for ₹ 3000 each and sells for ₹ 8000. Construct the pay off table for the marketer assuming a range of variation of 17 – 20 lots. If the frequency of sale of lots for 17–20 are 25, 40, 20 and 15 weeks. Using decision tree analysis, find out the optimum stock the marketer must have?
7. A management is faced with the problem of choosing one of three products for manufacturing. The potential demand for each product may turn out to be Good, Moderate or Poor. The Probability for each of the states of nature were estimated as follows:

Product	Nature of Demand		
	Good	Moderate	Poor
X	0.60	0.25	0.15
Y	0.55	0.30	0.15
Z	0.40	0.50	0.10

The estimated profit or loss in rupees under three states may be taken as:

Product	Good	Moderate	Poor
X	30,000	20,000	10,000
Y	60,000	30,000	20,000
Z	40,000	10,000	–15,000

Advise the management by using decision tree analysis.

8. A person has two independent investments – A and B available to him, but he can undertake only one at a time, due to certain constraints. He can choose A first and then stop, or if A is successful then take B or vice-versa. The probability of success of A is 0.6, while for B it is 0.4. Both the investments require a initial capital outlay of ₹ 10,000 and both return nothing if the venture is unsuccessful. Successful completion of A will return ₹ 20,000 (over cost) and successful completion of B will return ₹ 24,000 (over cost). Draw decision tree and determine the best strategy.

9. A client asks an estate agent to sell three properties A, B and C for him and agrees to pay him a 5% commission on each scale. He specifies certain conditions. The estate agent must sell property A first, and this he must do within 60 days. If as and when A is sold, the agent receives his 5% commission on that sale. He can then either back out at this stage or nominate and try to sell either of the two remaining properties within 60 days. If he doesn't succeed in selling the nominated property in that period, he is not given the opportunity to sell the other. If he does sell in that period, he is given the opportunity to sell the third property on the same conditions. The following table summaries the price, selling costs (incurred whenever a sale is attempted in ₹) and the estate agents estimated probability of making a sale. Find the optimal strategy using decision tree approach for the estate agent?

Property	A	B	C
Price of Property	12,000	25,000	50,000
Selling Cost	400	225	450
Probability of Sale	0.7	0.6	0.5

10. Bimetal Company is considering manufacture of a new product. If manufacturing is started without research, there is a 65% chance of good sales giving a net profit of ₹ 3,00,000 and 35% chance of poor sales leading to a loss of 3,00,000. If research is undertaken at a cost of ₹ 60,000 it is estimated that there is 90% chance of its indicating high sales and 10% chance of indicating low sales. Experience shows that when research indicated high sales, 70% of the times sales may be really good giving a profit of ₹ 4,00,000 and 30% of the times sales may be really bad leading to a loss of ₹ 50,000. On the other hand, if the research indicates low sales, 80% of the times sales may be bad leading to a loss of ₹ 1,00,000 and 20% of the times sales may be good leading to profit of ₹ 80,000. Prepare a decision tree and indicate the optimal strategies of Bimetal Company.

11. A company has two options to either invest in a large plant (investment ₹ 50 lakhs) or a small plant (outlay ₹ 25 lakhs). In the latter option, after one year, depending on market response it can expand by Investing ₹ 30 lakhs further. Market survey puts the market response into two categories, good and bad. The chances of good response initially is 0.6 and bad response is 0.4. However, if the initial response is good, subsequent response will be good with probability 0.9. Similarly, if initial response is bad, subsequent response is likely to be bad with probability 0.9. The estimated pay-offs are:

	Small Plant		Large Plant	
	Good	Bad	Good	Bad
Initial Year	15	5	20	5
Subsequent years (Cumulative)	60	20	80	20

What option the company should adopt?

12. The number of units of an item that are withdrawn from inventory on a day-to-day basis is a Markov chain process in which requirements for tomorrow depend on today's requirements. A one-day transition matrix is given below:

Number of units withdrawn from inventory

$$\text{Today}\quad \begin{array}{c} 5 \\ 10 \\ 12 \end{array} \overset{\text{Tomorrow}}{\overset{\begin{array}{ccc} 5 & 10 & 12 \end{array}}{\begin{bmatrix} 0.6 & 0.4 & 0.0 \\ 0.3 & 0.3 & 0.4 \\ 0.1 & 0.3 & 0.6 \end{bmatrix}}}$$

(a) Construct a tree diagram showing inventory requirements on two consecutive days.

(b) Develop a two-day transition matrix.

(c) Comment on how a two-day transition matrix might be helpful to a manager who is responsible for inventory management.

Case Study

ABC Electronics Ltd. was a company incorporated in 1983 by Mr. Viswam and over the years had emerged as one of the forerunners in the growing segment of the electronics and home appliances market in India. Presently it has a market share of 30 per cent of the home appliances market. The company's product strategy has been to offer a wide product range right from mono stereo, two-in-ones, sophisticated music system, televisions, refrigerators, washing machines, and microwave ovens. ABC Electronics marketing strategy also included offering the above products so as to match the needs and budget of the middle class and upper strata of the society.

In 1991 Raghu, son of Mr. Viswam took over as the Managing Director of the company. Seeing the intense competition in the market in the post liberalization scenario, Raghu was keen to go by the principle that once you have targeted your customer , you follow him/her relentlessly with attractive offerings. In 1994 he started with a well focused promotion and distribution strategies. The promotion included spending ₹ 10 crores in advertising through holding exhibitions, organizing special training programmes for their sales force, using mass media appeal, offering freebies and various other sales promotion techniques. For distribution, Raghu went about the task of selecting exclusive showrooms and franchisees to display their wide range of products. The location for the exclusive retail outlets was also selected so as to match the perception of the consumers as an "exclusive showroom" for them.

Even after two years of the operating the new promotion and distribution strategy, the sales of ABC Electronics, was not picking up to the extent the company had thought it would. Raghu directed the marketing manager to do a study of the other retail outlets to know the trend. The results indicated that there was a change in the consumers' perception about purchasing consumer durables. There was seen a preference for purchasing goods from retail outlets having more than one brand.

Questions

1. Where do you think Raghu went wrong in his analysis of consumer behaviour?
2. Discuss the change in the role of consumers today as compared to the consumers five years ago.

CHAPTER SIX

DESIGN OF QUESTIONNAIRE

INTRODUCTION

Surveys of any kind are expensive and time-consuming to conduct, it is important that the data analysis is as extensive and well-prepared for as possible. The strength of the analysis depends on good quality data that in turn stems from good design of the data collection instrument, i.e. the questionnaire, and of the collection procedures.

This section provides a compilation of do's and don'ts for good questionnaire design that will, if followed, make data analysis easier and faster than otherwise. The survey process is outlined to place questionnaire design in context. Also covered in this document are a number of ways in which the computer fits into various elements of the overall survey process.

A crucial part of good research is concerned with making sure that the questionnaire design addresses the needs of the research. To move from the research aims to deciding what are the right questions to put on a questionnaire is a key aspect that needs to be addressed by the researcher. This document makes some comments about this important area but does mainly concentrate on the mechanics of designing the questionnaire.

Unfortunately, too many researchers complete the data collection before they have given sufficient thought to the data analysis. This can lead to inadequate data and inadequate inferences from the data, and can disappoint and frustrate the researcher. Ideally, the method of analysis should be known, and it should inform the preceding stages of the research.

This is the information age. More information has been published in the last decade than in all previous history. Everyone uses information to make decisions about the future. If our information is accurate, we have a high probability of making a good decision. If our information is inaccurate, our ability to make a correct decision is diminished. Better information usually leads to better decisions.

QUESTIONNAIRE DESIGN

Questionnaire research design proceeds in an orderly and specific manner. Each item in the flow chart depends upon the successful completion of all the previous items. Therefore, it is important not to skip a single step. Notice that there are two feedback loops in the flow chart to allow revisions to the methodology and instruments.

No survey can achieve success without a well-designed questionnaire. Unfortunately, questionnaire design has no theoretical base to guide the marketing researcher in developing a flawless questionnaire. All the researcher has to guide him/her is a lengthy list of do's and don'ts born out of the experience of other researchers past and present. Hence, questionnaire design is more of an art than a science.

❖ Steps in the Development of a Questionnaire

1. *Decide the information required:* It should be noted that one does not start by writing questions. The first step is to decide 'what are the things one needs to know from the respondent in order to meet the survey's objectives?' These, as has been indicated in the opening chapter of this textbook, should appear in the research brief and the research proposal. One may already have an idea about the kind of information to be collected, but additional help can be obtained from secondary data, previous rapid rural appraisals and exploratory research. In respect of secondary data, the researcher should be aware of what work has been done on the same or similar problems in the past, what factors have not yet been examined, and how the present survey questionnaire can build on what has already been discovered. Further, a small number of preliminary informal interviews with target respondents will give a glimpse of reality that may help clarify ideas about what information is required. Start your survey by setting down the aims for the survey. To define the aims for academic, as opposed to market, research you will need to review the relevant literature and you may need to do some preliminary research amongst your target subjects. Fulfilling these aims should then drive the design of your questionnaire and help select questions that are relevant, concise and efficient.

2. *Define the target respondents:* At the outset, the researcher must define the population about which he/she wishes to generalise from the sample data to be collected. For example, in marketing research, researchers often have to decide whether they should cover only existing users of the generic product type or whether to also include non-users. Secondly, researchers have to draw up a sampling frame. Thirdly, in designing the questionnaire we must take into account factors such as the age, education, etc. of the target respondents. A key issue in choosing the sample relates to whether the members you have chosen are representative of the population. Often the sample is chosen randomly from a list that contains all the members of the population; such a list is called a sampling frame. Some methods of selecting samples, e.g. quota sampling, do not require a sampling frame. To determine the sample size it is usual to work back from how many responses (completed questionnaires) are required for the analysis. One rough and ready rule is to look for about 20-30 responses in each of the major sub-categories of the sample.

3. *Choose the method(s) of reaching target respondents:* It may seem strange to be suggesting that the method of reaching the intended respondents should constitute part of the questionnaire design process. However, a moment's reflection is sufficient to conclude that the method of contact will influence not only the questions the researcher is able to ask but the phrasing of those questions. The main methods available in survey research are:

   (i) Personal interviews

   (ii) Group or focus interviews

   (iii) Mailed questionnaires

   (iv) Telephone interviews.

   Within this region the first two mentioned are used much more extensively than the second pair. However, each has its advantages and disadvantages. A general rule is that the more sensitive or personal the information, the more personal the form of data collection should be.

   Where the questionnaire is administered by post, or e-mail or some other indirect means, it is usual practice to provide a letter that explains what the questionnaire is about and why its completion is of value.

4. ***Decide on question content:*** Researchers must always be prepared to ask, "Is this question really needed?" The temptation to include questions without critically evaluating their contribution towards the achievement of the research objectives, as they are specified in the research proposal, is surprisingly strong. No question should be included unless the data it gives rise to is directly of use in testing one or more of the hypotheses established during the research design.

   There are only two occasions when seemingly "redundant" questions might be included:

   (i) Opening questions that are easy to answer and which are not perceived as being "threatening", and/or are perceived as being interesting, can greatly assist in gaining the respondent's involvement in the survey and help to establish a rapport.

   (ii) This, however, should not be an approach that should be overly used. It is almost always the case that questions which are of use in testing hypotheses can also serve the same functions.

   (iii) "Dummy" questions can disguise the purpose of the survey and/or the sponsorship of a study. For example, if a manufacturer wanted to find out whether its distributors were giving the consumers or end-users of its products a reasonable level of service, the researcher would want to disguise the fact that the distributors' service level was being investigated. If he/she did not, then rumors would abound that there was something wrong with the distributor.

5. ***Develop the question wording***

   (i) Survey questions can be classified into three forms, i.e. closed, open-ended and open response-option questions. So far only the first of these, i.e. closed questions has been discussed. This type of questioning has a number of important advantages.

   (ii) It provides the respondent with an easy method of indicating his answer – he does not have to think about how to articulate his answer.

   (iii) It 'prompts' the respondent so that the respondent has to rely less on memory in answering a question.

   (iv) Responses can be easily classified, making analysis very straightforward.

   (v) It permits the respondent to specify the answer categories most suitable for their purposes.

6. ***Putting questions into a meaningful order and format***

   (i) *Opening questions:* Opening questions should be easy to answer and not in any way threatening to the respondents. The first question is crucial because it is the respondent's first exposure to the interview and sets the tone for the nature of the task to be performed. If they find the first question difficult to understand, or beyond their knowledge and experience, or embarrassing in some way, they are likely to break off immediately. If, on the other hand, they find the opening question easy and pleasant to answer, they are encouraged to continue.

   (ii) *Question flow:* Questions should flow in some kind of psychological order, so that one leads easily and naturally to the next. Questions on one subject, or one particular aspect of a subject, should be grouped together. Respondents may feel it disconcerting to keep shifting from one topic to another, or to be asked to return to some subject they thought they gave their opinions about earlier.

   (iii) *Question variety:* Respondents become bored quickly and restless when asked similar questions for half an hour or so. It usually improves response, therefore, to vary the respondent's task from time-to-time. An open-ended question here and there (even if it is not analysed) may provide much-needed relief from a long series of questions in which respondents have been forced to limit their replies to pre-coded categories. Questions involving showing cards/ pictures to respondents can help vary the pace and increase interest.

(iv) *Closing questions:* It is natural for a respondent to become increasingly indifferent to the questionnaire as it nears the end. Because of impatience or fatigue, he may give careless answers to the later questions. Those questions, therefore, that are of special importance should, if possible, be included in the earlier part of the questionnaire. Potentially sensitive questions should be left to the end, to avoid respondents cutting off the interview before important information is collected.

In developing the questionnaire, the researcher should pay particular attention to the presentation and layout of the interview form itself. The interviewer's task needs to be made as straightforward as possible.

(a) Questions should be clearly worded and response options clearly identified.

(b) Prescribed definitions and explanations should be provided. This ensures that the questions are handled consistently by all interviewers and that during the interview process, the interviewer can answer/clarify respondents' queries.

Ample writing space should be allowed to record open-ended answers, and to cater for differences in handwriting between interviewers.

7. ***Check the length of the questionnaire:*** In general it is best for a questionnaire to be as short as possible. A long questionnaire leads to a long interview and this is open to the dangers of boredom on the part of the respondent (and poorly considered, hurried answers), interruptions by third parties and greater costs in terms of interviewing time and resources. In a rural situation an interview should not last longer then 30-45 minutes.

8. ***Run a pilot survey:*** Test the questionnaire on a small sample of your subjects first. If this is not possible, at least test it on some colleagues or friends. The aim here is to detect any flaws in your questioning and correct these prior to the main survey. The piloting may enable you to convert an open-ended question into a closed question by determining the range of possible answers. You may also be able to perform a trial analysis on your pilot sample and hence test out all your analysis procedures. Having done your pilot survey, you can make amendments that will help to maximize your response rate and minimize your error rate on answers.

9. ***Develop the final form:*** If the questionnaire has been subjected to a thorough pilot test, the final form of the questions and questionnaire will have evolved into its final form. All that remains to be done is the mechanical process of laying out and setting up the questionnaire in its final form. This will involve grouping and sequencing questions into an appropriate order, numbering questions, and inserting interviewer instructions.

10. ***Carry out the main survey:*** It means designed questionnaire will be administered among the selected sample respondents to the study.

11. ***Analyze the data:*** A precursor to analysis is the coding, entry and checking of data. Some comments were made earlier about the statistical analysis packages that are available. In all instances, data can either be entered direct or imported from other packages such as Excel, provided the instructions for the receiving package are adhered to. In all cases, a similar approach is used for coding and formatting data.

❖ Types of Questionnaries

Structured Interview Schedules

This document mainly gives advice on the construction of questionnaires for direct reply; the structured interview questionnaire can be dealt with in a similar but slightly different way. For example, questions asked orally are usually phrased differently from those written down and it is important to include detailed conversational text when an interview is conducted face to face or by telephone.

Self-administered Questionnaire

There are several ways to minimize position bias in a self-administered survey. One good way is to print several versions of the questionnaire, each with a different ordering of the items on the list. This is however often impractical because of the high cost involved in printing several different versions of your questionnaire.

1. One can also randomly or alphabetically order list items and indicate in the instructions how they are ordered. This reduces the likelihood that respondents will see the first items as most important. For interviewer-administered surveys, interviewers modify the order in which the attributes are presented to the respondent.
2. Put demographic questions at the end of the questionnaire, if possible. There are at least two reasons for this. First, some demographic questions such as age and income can be sensitive and should be placed at the end, as discussed in guideline number. Second, it is better to keep respondents' minds on the purpose of the survey at the beginning, while you have their attention. Demographic questions rarely require much thought, so wait until the end when respondents might be tired.
3. Try to minimize the number of times the respondent or the interviewer has to follow a skip rule. For example, "If the answer to question 3 is 'None of the Above,' skip to question 6." When there are too many skips or when skips become too complicated, researchers run the risk of introducing error and confusion.

❖ Physical Appearance of the Questionnaire

The physical appearance of a questionnaire can have a significant effect upon both the quantity and quality of marketing data obtained. The quantity of data is a function of the response rate. Ill-designed questionnaires can give an impression of complexity, medium and too big a time commitment. Data quality can also be affected by the physical appearance of the questionnaire with unnecessarily confusing layouts making it more difficult for interviewers, or respondents in the case of self-completion questionnaires, to complete this task accurately. Attention to just a few basic details can have a disproportionately advantageous impact on the data obtained through a questionnaire.

❖ Decision on Sequence in Questionnaire

1. Do not clutter the form up with unnecessary headings, and numbers. However, it is good practice to ensure that the questionnaire has a title and that the revision or date of the version is printed on the questionnaire.
2. A brief introductory statement is useful, especially if the introductory letter could go adrift. Contact and return information should be included on the questionnaire, irrespective of whether addressed

return envelopes are provided; these can easily become separated. Similarly it is good practice to number or otherwise identify individual questions for reference purposes; this is particularly helpful to deal with queries during the data entry and analysis stage.

3. Lay out the questions and answer choices attractively and neatly. Try to be consistent in aspects such as wording and try to standardize by using as few question types as possible.
4. Avoid switching between landscape and portrait for the text layout.
5. Avoid overfilling the page, with lots of lines, borders and boxes since these can make the page look too 'dense'.
6. A key factor that affects the response rate is the length of the questionnaire; questionnaires perceived as long will deter respondents. Using a small font may cut down the number of pages and hence make the questionnaire look shorter; but remember that small fonts can put people off – particularly those with less than perfect eyesight.
7. Symbol fonts can be useful for characters such as "o"? If you are relying on the respondent to complete the questionnaire, begin with questions that will raise interest. Maintain logical sequence, e.g. group together all questions that relate to similar areas. You should try to keep the flow through a questionnaire logical and very simple, i.e. avoid complex branching.

❖ General Guidelines for Questionnaire Layout

1. ***Create professional, attractive and uncluttered questionnaires:*** Fonts should be large enough to avoid eye strain; instructions for completing the survey should be easy to understand. If your survey has multiple pages, it should be bound in a booklet so that pages cannot get mixed up. And, if respondents are to see the survey, it should have an attractive cover.
2. ***Make the survey easy to complete:*** The check boxes or lines easy to see; and the numbers to be circled far enough apart so the respondent or interviewer will not inadvertently circle two numbers. If you are using scanable forms, where bubbles need to be filled in completely and with a specific writing utensil such as a number 2 pencil, make sure the instructions are clear and easy to find.
3. ***Number your questions clearly:*** This will lessen the chance, particularly in longer surveys, of respondents or interviewers getting lost.
4. ***Start with a brief introduction:*** Describe the survey's purpose, the topics being covered and how the results will be used. Also, mention any incentive for completing the survey, such as a drawing entry, the opportunity to have a copy of the results and so on.
5. ***No direct approach:*** If you are conducting a telephone survey, do not have the interviewer say "How are you?" in the introduction. This will irritate respondents who, at such an early stage in the interview, have been given no reason to want to talk to the interviewer, much less tell them how they are. Keep the introduction short, polite and to the point. Normally, the only question that should be asked in the introduction is if respondents are willing to participate.
6. ***Interviewer instruction:*** For interviewer-administered surveys, make any interviewer instructions (that is, anything that is not supposed to be read to the respondent), easy to distinguish. Put interviewer instructions in upper case, color or italics.
7. ***Leave plenty of room:*** Respondents must get opportunity to write answers to open-ended questions. Do not supply lines because this could constrain any comments.

❖ Advantages of Written Questionnaires

1. Questionnaires are very cost effective when compared to face-to-face interviews. This is especially true for studies involving large sample sizes and large geographic areas. Written questionnaires become even more cost effective as the number of research questions increases.

2. Questionnaires are easy to analyze. Data entry and tabulation for nearly all surveys can be easily done with many computer software packages.

3. Questionnaires are familiar to most people. Nearly everyone has had some experience completing questionnaires and they generally do not make people apprehensive.

4. Questionnaires reduce bias. There is uniform question presentation and no middle-man bias. The researcher's own opinions will not influence the respondent to answer questions in a certain manner. There are no verbal or visual clues to influence the respondent.

5. Questionnaires are less intrusive than telephone or face-to-face surveys. When a respondent receives a questionnaire in the mail, he is free to complete the questionnaire on his own time-table. Unlike other research methods, the respondent is not interrupted by the research instrument.

❖ Disadvantages of Written Questionnaires

1. One major disadvantage of written questionnaires is the possibility of low response rates. Low response is the curse of statistical analysis. It can dramatically lower our confidence in the results. Response rates vary widely from one questionnaire to another (10% - 90%), however, well-designed studies consistently produce high response rates.

2. Another disadvantage of questionnaires is the inability to probe responses. Questionnaires are structured instruments. They allow little flexibility to the respondent with respect to response format. In essence, they often lose the "flavor of the response" (i.e., respondents often want to qualify their answers). By allowing frequent space for comments, the researcher can partially overcome this disadvantage. Comments are among the most helpful of all the information on the questionnaire, and they usually provide insightful information that would have otherwise been lost.

3. Nearly ninety per cent of all communication is visual. Gestures and other visual cues are not available with written questionnaires. The lack of personal contact will have different effects depending on the type of information being requested. A questionnaire requesting factual information will probably not be affected by the lack of personal contact. A questionnaire probing sensitive issues or attitudes may be severely affected.

4. When returned questionnaires arrive in the mail, it's natural to assume that the respondent is the same person you sent the questionnaire to. This may not actually be the case. Many times business questionnaires get handed to other employees for completion. Housewives sometimes respond for their husbands. Kids respond as a prank. For a variety of reasons, the respondent may not be who you think it is. It is a confounding error inherent in questionnaires.

5. Finally, questionnaires are simply not suited for some people. For example, a written survey to a group of poorly educated people might not work because of reading skill problems. More frequently, people are turned off by written questionnaires because of misuse.

❖ Questionnaire Design: General Considerations

1. Most problems with questionnaire analysis can be traced back to the design phase of the project. Well-defined goals are the best way to assure a good questionnaire design. When the goals of a study can be expressed in a few clear and concise sentences, the design of the questionnaire becomes considerably easier. The questionnaire is developed to directly address the goals of the study.
2. One of the best ways to clarify your study goals is to decide how you intend to use the information. Do this before you begin designing the study. This sounds obvious, but many researchers neglect this task. Why do research if the results will not be used?
3. Be sure to commit the study goals to writing. Whenever you are unsure of a question, refer to the study goals and a solution will become clear. Ask only questions that directly address the study goals. Avoid the temptation to ask questions because it would be "interesting to know".
4. As a general rule, with only a few exceptions, long questionnaires get less response than short questionnaires. Keep your questionnaire short. In fact, the shorter the better. Response rate is the single most important indicator of how much confidence you can place in the results. A low response rate can be devastating to a study. Therefore, you must do everything possible to maximize the response rate. One of the most effective methods of maximizing response is to shorten the questionnaire.
5. If your survey is over a few pages, try to eliminate questions. Many people have difficulty knowing which questions could be eliminated. For the elimination round, read each question and ask, "How am I going to use this information?" If the information will be used in a decision-making process, then keep the question... it's important. If not, throw it out.
6. One important way to assure a successful survey is to include other experts and relevant decision-makers in the questionnaire design process. Their suggestions will improve the questionnaire and they will subsequently have more confidence in the results.
7. Formulate a plan for doing the statistical analysis during the design stage of the project. Know how every question will be analyzed and be prepared to handle missing data. If you cannot specify how you intend to analyze a question or use the information, do not use it in the survey.
8. Make the envelope unique. We all know how important first impressions are. The same holds true for questionnaires. The respondent's first impression of the study usually comes from the envelope containing the survey. The best envelopes (i.e., the ones that make you want to see what's inside) are colored, hand-addressed and use a commemorative postage stamp. Envelopes with bulk mail permits or gummed labels are perceived as unimportant. This will generally be reflected in a lower response rate.
9. Provide a well-written cover letter. The respondent's next impression comes from the cover letter. The importance of the cover letter should not be underestimated. It provides your best chance to persuade the respondent to complete the survey.
10. Give your questionnaire a title that is short and meaningful to the respondent. A questionnaire with a title is generally perceived to be more credible than one without.
11. Include clear and concise instructions on how to complete the questionnaire. These must be very easy to understand, so use short sentences and basic vocabulary. Be sure to print the return address on the questionnaire itself (since questionnaires often get separated from the reply envelopes).

12. Begin with a few non-threatening and interesting items. If the first items are too threatening or "boring", there is little chance that the person will complete the questionnaire. People generally look at the first few questions before deciding whether or not to complete the questionnaire. Make them want to continue by putting interesting questions first.

13. Use simple and direct language. The questions must be clearly understood by the respondent. The wording of a question should be simple and to the point. Do not use uncommon words or long sentences. Make items as brief as possible. This will reduce misunderstandings and make the questionnaire appear easier to complete. One way to eliminate misunderstandings is to emphasize crucial words in each item by using bold, italics or underlining.

14. Leave adequate space for respondents to make comments. One criticism of questionnaires is their inability to retain the "flavor" of a response. Leaving space for comments will provide valuable information not captured by the response categories. Leaving white space also makes the questionnaire look easier and this increases response.

15. Place the most important items in the first half of the questionnaire. Respondents often send back partially completed questionnaires. By putting the most important items near the beginning, the partially completed questionnaires will still contain important information.

16. Hold the respondent's interest. We want the respondent to complete our questionnaire. One way to keep a questionnaire interesting is to provide variety in the type of items used. Varying the questioning format will also prevent respondents from falling into "response sets". At the same time, it is important to group items into coherent categories. All items should flow smoothly from one to the next.

17. If a questionnaire is more than a few pages and is held together by a staple, include some identifying data on each page (such as a respondent ID number). Pages often accidentally separate.

18. Provide incentives as a motivation for a properly completed questionnaire. What does the respondent get for completing your questionnaire? Altruism is rarely an effective motivator. Attaching a dollar bill to the questionnaire works well. If the information you are collecting is of interest to the respondent, offering a free summary report is also an excellent motivator. Whatever you choose, it must make the respondent want to complete the questionnaire.

19. Use professional production methods for the questionnaire—either desktop publishing or typesetting and key lining. Be creative. Try different colored inks and paper. The object is to make your questionnaire stand out from all the others the respondent receives.

20. Make it convenient. The easier it is for the respondent to complete the questionnaire the better. Always include a self-addressed postage-paid envelope. Envelopes with postage stamps get better response than business reply envelopes (although they are more expensive since you also pay for the non-respondents).

21. The final test of a questionnaire is to try it on representatives of the target audience. If there are problems with the questionnaire, they almost always show up here. If possible, be present while a respondent is completing the questionnaire and tell her that it is okay to ask you for clarification of any item. The questions she asks are indicative of problems in the questionnaire (i.e., the questions on the questionnaire must be without any ambiguity because there will be no chance to clarify a question when the survey is mailed).

QUESTION TYPES

Different types of questions can be used, e.g. open vs. closed, single vs. multiple responses, ranking, and rating.

Open vs. Closed Questions

Many advise against using open-ended questions and advocate using closed questions. However, open questions can be useful. For example, the open question:

What do you think are the reasons for football hooliganism?

Would elicit a whole range of replies of varying length and articulation. If you are interested in making very precise judgments of each individual respondent this may well be useful. If, however, you are concerned, as most surveys are, in summarizing replies to produce a picture of your population, a better approach may be …

Do you think football hooliganism is caused by: (tick if appropriate)

Lack of discipline at home ☐

Players' behaviour on pitch ☐

Family breakdown ☐

Youth unemployment ☐

Poor schooling ☐

Violence on T.V. ☐

Other (please specify) ☐

Plan to make your categories exhaustive, i.e. covering all possibilities, by making fairly broad suggestions that will still satisfy your objectives. However, you could include the catch-all type option (other) as above.

If you still feel that your questions cannot be categorized until all the replies are returned then ensure that sufficient space is included for the question and leave a space in the margin to code a numeric response.

e.g. What was the main problem you encountered with your wheelchair?

Single vs. Multiple Response

When designing questions make sure you have thought through whether you want the respondent to give a single or a multiple response. For example, if you ask the question:

Which of the following means do you use to travel to college?

Bus ☐

Car ☐

Bike ☐

You might get someone who thinks that only one box should be ticked while another respondent might believe they are at liberty to tick as many boxes as they like. If you intend that the respondent treat these as a series of independent dichotomous yes/no questions then the question could be clarified by inserting the text "tick all boxes that apply". Note that treating the question in this way would require three separate variables to be set up on the computer and for each variable coding might be 0 for no and 1 for yes. Consider the following question:

What is your most usual means of traveling to college?

(Tick one box only)

Bus ☐

Car ☐

Bike ☐

The above should elicit one response, i.e. the answers form mutually exclusive categories. For the computer the above would be coded as one variable with Bus represented by 1, Car by 2 and Bike by 3. If the respondent omitted to answer then this could be coded as 0 or some other missing value. However, note the problem with both the above questions if someone travels by train or just walks. Either all the possibilities have to be anticipated in advance or an additional box has to be offered for the respondent to tick and specify the mode of transport.

Never be tempted to use the following structure:

Select up to three of the options below and enter in the boxes opposite

Option A	Option B	Option C	
Option D	Option E	Option F	☐☐☐

Whilst this may be logically sound you will have problems when summarizing these results. A very tedious and finally unsatisfactory search is required to determine how any given option performs.

Ranked Responses

Sometimes it is useful for the respondent to rank a set of options by numbering them in order from 1 to the maximum number you are interested in. For example, to a question like:

Place in order of importance to you the following features of a camping holiday:

(Indicate by numbering from 1-4 in order where 1 is the most important)

Open air ☐

Mobility ☐

Cost ☐

People ☐

Atmosphere ☐

Note that each option will need to be coded as a separate variable and in the above case five variables are required (even though only four ranks are to be identified). This approach can generate a lot of data and so the number of options used should not be excessive. Apart from this respondents find it difficult to discriminate meaningfully between lots of options.

Rated Responses

A popular approach in the social sciences is to use Likert scales such as the example below: (Circle the number under the initials that applies. VI=Very Important; I=Important; N=Neutral; U=Unimportant; VU=Very Unimportant).

Indicate your view of the following aspects of a camping holiday

	VI	I	N	U	VU
Community Life	1	1	2	4	5
Low cost	1	2	3	4	5
Outdoor Life	1	2	3	4	5
Ability to move around	1	2	3	4	5

Note that each of the four rows will form a separate variable that contains the appropriate numeric code from 1 to 5.

CHOOSING A RESPONSE FORMAT

When you have devised your questions, the next step is to choose the most appropriate response format. The most common formats used are open and closed questions. Open ended questions have no predetermined response schedule, meaning more detailed responses are elicited. However, they are less structured, responses are difficult to encode and they are more difficult and take longer to complete.

Closed questions provide respondents with a list of response options. The responses are tightly structured and easily encoded and analysed. Less time is needed to complete them. The disadvantages are that answers have less depth and responders may be frustrated if their desired response does not fit the options available.

Alternatively, you could choose a response scale, such as Likert or forced choice scale. A Likert Scale has five or seven points and the respondent chooses just one, e.g. 1 = strongly agree, 2= agree, 3 = undecided, 4 = disagree, 5 = strongly disagree. Therefore, it allows a middle or undecided response, however, acquiescent responses are also allowed. A forced choice scale has four points, e.g. 1= strongly agree, 2= agree, 3= disagree, 4 = strongly disagree. Therefore, respondents are forced to give either a positive or negative response and an undecided response is not allowed. Other response formats are available, such as ranked responses, visual analogue scales and Guttman Scale.

❖ Response Rate and Following up on Non-respondents

Response rate is the single most important indicator of how much confidence can be placed in the results of a survey. A low response rate can be devastating to the reliability of a study.

One of the most powerful tools for increasing response is to use follow-ups or reminders. Traditionally, between 10 and 60 per cent of those sent questionnaires respond without follow-up reminders. These rates are too low to yield confident results, so the need to follow up on non-respondents is clear.

Researchers can increase the response from follow-up attempts by including another copy of the questionnaire. When designing the follow-up procedure, it is important for the researcher to keep in mind the unique characteristics of the people in the sample. The most successful follow-ups have been achieved by phone calls.

Many researchers have examined whether postcard follow-ups are effective in increasing response. The vast majority of these studies show that a follow-up postcard slightly increases response rate, and a meta-analysis revealed an aggregate gain of 3.5 per cent. The postcard serves as a reminder for subjects who have forgotten to complete the survey.

Non-response Bias

Many studies have attempted to determine if there is a difference between respondents and non-respondents. Some researchers have reported that people who respond to surveys answer questions differently than those who do not. Others have found that late responders answer differently than early responders, and that the differences may be due to the different levels of interest in the subject matter. One researcher, who examined a volunteer organization, reported that those more actively involved in the organization were more likely to respond.

Demographic characteristics of non-respondents have been investigated by many researchers. Most studies have found that non-response is associated with low education. However, one researcher reported that demographic characteristics such as age, education, and employment status were the same for respondents and non-respondents. Another study found that non-respondents were more often single males.

Most researchers view non-response bias as a continuum, ranging from fast responders to slow responders (with non-responders defining the end of the continuum). In fact, one study used extrapolation to estimate the magnitude of bias created by non-response. Another group of researchers argue that non-response should not be viewed as a continuum, and that late respondents do not provide a suitable basis for estimating the characteristics of non-respondents.

❖ General Guidelines for Question Ordering

1. The first few questions should be easy for respondents to understand, be important to the study's purpose, engage the attention and interest of your respondent. Do not begin with an open-ended question or one which respondents might feel has a "right" answer.
2. It is important to get your respondent interested in the survey at the very beginning. In cases where the topic is already of interest or importance to the respondent, start with general questions, then funnel to more specific ones. If the topic is of low importance to respondents, start with specific questions. This gives respondents a frame of reference; then ask broader, more general questions.
3. Group questions in sections, and position sections or questions in a logical order.
4. Introduce new sections with a sentence or phrase so that participants have a chance to switch mental gears.
5. Place questions about sensitive issues such as income, sexual habits or drug abuse toward the end of the document, or section. This helps avoid alienating, taxing or in other ways worrying participants.
6. Consider lists of similar items carefully. For example, you might ask about product satisfaction using 10 different attributes (price, availability, delivery, color, fit and so on). The first items on a list such as this usually get treated differently by respondents than the last items do. This is called position bias.

REVIEW QUESTIONS

1. Summarise the qualities of a good questionnaire.
2. Where should interviewer instructions pertaining to responses to a particular question be placed on the questionnaire?
3. The textbook says that one does not start by writing questions. How should the researcher begin?
4. What are the two occasions when apparently "redundant" questions should be found in a questionnaire?
5. Name the three advantages of open-ended questions.
6. What could be the three reasons why a respondent is unable to answer a question?
7. What is the recommended duration of interviews carried out in rural situations?
8. What are the key characteristics of opening questions in a questionnaire?
9. Explain the purpose of a questionnaire as a measurement instrument.
10. Describe the process of designing a questionnaire, the steps involved, and guidelines which must be followed at each step.
11. Identify the major design differences between phone, mail, and personal interview questionnaires.
12. Discuss the appropriateness of the various data collection methods for addressing different populations and different measurement tasks.
13. Describe the design and proper use of computerized data collection instruments and distinguish between Computer Assisted Telephone Interviews (CATI) and computer-assisted personal interviews.

MODEL QUESTIONNAIRE 1

Questionnaire for the study of buying behaviour of motorbike:

Name :

Age :

Place :

Occupation : Business Service

1. Do you own a bike

   Yes No

2. Which bike do you have or you are intending to buy?
3. According to your perception which is the best among these bikes?

   (i) Hero Honda (ii) Rajdoot (iii) Yamaha (iv) Suzuki

4. Please rank these bikes according to your choice from (i) to (vi). ((i) for best & (vi) for least preferable)

   (i) Hero Honda Splender (ii) Suzuki Samurai
   (iii) Hero Honda CBZ (iv) Yamaha Rx-135
   (v) Rajdoot (vi) Bajaj Kawasaki

5. Are you aware of the various models of Hero Honda motorcycles?

   (i) Splender (ii) CD 100
   (iii) CD 100 SS (iv) CBZ
   (v) Street (vi) Sleek

6. What normally encourages you the most when you make a purchase decision?

   (i) Advertisements (ii) Recommendations
   (iii) Past experience (iv) Any Other (Please Specify)

7. To what extent advertisements normally affect your purchase decision?

   (i) Absolutely (ii) Many a times
   (iii) Sometimes

8. What are the factors which influence your buying decision?
9. Which bike would you prefer among these pairs? (Select one from each pair)

   (i) Splender vs. Yamaha Rx-13
   vs. Suzuki Samurai
   vs. Rajdoot

   (ii) CBZ vs. Yamaha Rx-13
   vs. Suzuki Samurai

vs. Rajdoot

vs. Bajaj Kawasaki

(iii) Sleek vs. Yamaha Rx-13

vs. Suzuki Samurai

vs. Rajdoot

vs. Bajaj Kawasaki

(iv) CD vs. Yamaha Rx-13

vs. Suzuki Samurai

vs. Rajdoot

vs. Bajaj Kawasaki

(v) CD 100 SS vs. Yamaha Rx-13

vs. Suzuki Samurai

vs. Rajdoot

vs. Bajaj Kawasaki

10. Why do you prefer a bike instead of a scooter?

 (i) Comfort (ii) Style (iii) More economical

Questions

1. Was the research design appropriate for obtaining information to determine if an opportunity existed?
2. Were the right question being asked to gather the needed information?
3. Were the questions properly worded?

MODEL QUESTIONNAIRE 2

Questionnaire Construction to Study Advertising Effectiveness:

Dear Respondent,

Any information provided by you will be strictly used for academic purposes only. Your cooperation in this regard will be highly appreciated.

Thank you,

1. Are you aware of advertising effectiveness?

   Yes No

2. What is the type of effect of advertisement on you?

   (i) Positive effect (ii) Negative effect

   (iii) Not much effect (iv) Great effect

3. What is the effect of advertisement on the purchase of consumer goods.

   (i) High (ii) Moderate

   (iii) Low

4. Manner of advertisement which have an effect on purchase?

   (i) Seeing an advertisement on T.V. (ii) A person coming at your door

   (iii) Sales with discounts, free gifts, etc. (iv) Friends and relatives

5. Type of advertisement preferred for consumer goods

   (i) Print media (ii) Vision media

   (iii) Mural/outdoor advertisement (iv) Publicity

6. What is your purchase pattern for consumer goods which are introduced in the market.

   (i) Purchase immediately (ii) Purchase after survey

   (iii) Wait for results (iv) Any other, (place specify)

7. What is the most attractive feature in an advertisement? Rank in order of your preference. (1 being the best)

   (i) Product information (ii) Celebrities

   (iii) Music (iv) Slogans

   (v) Overall presentation

8. Why advertisements are sometimes harmful?

   (i) Increase price of the product (ii) Waste resources

   (iii) Motivate youngsters to consume harmful things to health

9. Have you ever been deceived by an advertisement?
   (i) Have been deceived
   (ii) Have not been deceived
   (iii) If option is (i) then go to 16 else go to 17
10. What was the reason for deception
   (i) Product feature wrongly stated
   (ii) Price was under stated
   (iii) Product was hyped
11. What is the effect of an advertisement on price?
   (i) Increase in price (ii) Decrease in price
   (iii) No effect
12. What is the effect of celebrities on advertisement?
   (i) Increase in price (ii) Emotional encashment
   (iii) Promote things harmful to health
13. Did advertisements effect your consumption?
   (i) Increased consumption considerably (ii) Increased consumption marginally
   (iii) No effect on consumption (iv) Decreased consumption marginally
   (v) Decreased consumption considerably
14. Effectiveness of advertisement with regards to following parameters:

Cost

Low	1	2	3	4	5	High

Message content

Bad	1	2	3	4	5	Good

Celebrities endorsement

Negative	1	2	3	4	5	Positive

Media vehicle

Low	1	2	3	4	5	High

Recall value

Poor	1	2	3	4	5	High

15. Make paired comparison from the following

	T.V.	Radio	Print	Mural/Outdoor advertisement
T.V.				

Radio

Print

Mural/Outdoor advertisement

Consumer profile

Name:

Age:

(i) Below 25 (ii) 25-35 (iii) 35-50 (iv) 50 & above

Sex:

Occupation

Business

Profession

Service

If any other please specify ——————————

Income group —————— yearly

(i) 100,000 – 150,000 (ii) 150,000 – 300,000 (iii) 300,000 & above

Questions

1. Was the research design appropriate for obtaining information to determine if any opportunity existed?
2. Were the right questions being asked to gather the needed information?
3. Were the questions properly worded?

MODEL QUESTIONNAIRE 3

Patient satisfaction survey for the inpatient service of multispeciality hospital:

Name: Age:

Sex: Address:

Monthly Income:

Date of Admission: Room Number:

Expected Length of stay According to Doctor:

Nature of Illness PR cause of Admission

(i) Medical (ii) Surgical (iii) Obstetric/Gynaec

(iv) Pediatric (v) Dental/Eye/ENT (vi) Investigations

(vii) Emergency (viii) Accident (a) Domestic, (b) Road (ix) Others (Please specify)

1. How do you become aware of the multi specialty hospital?

   Through

   (i) Advertisement (ii) Friends and relatives

   (iii) Family Doctor (iv) Others, specify

2. Do you visit hospital every time you or your family members need medical attention?

   (i) Always (ii) Sometimes (iii) Emergency conditions only

3. Is this the first time you or any of your family members is admitted into hospital?

   Yes No

   If no, how many times earlier you or any of your family members were admitted into OPD of Hospital?

   Yourself:

   Your family members:

   (i) When were you/your family members admitted into the hospital?

   (ii) What was the ailment?

   (iii) Was the treatment?

   (a) Effective (b) Partially effective (c) Ineffective? (Specify reasons)

4. How were you admitted this time? Please tick appropriate choice:

   (i) Referred by OPD (ii) Referred by EMD From other hospital

   (iii) Corporate tie up with any hospital (iv) Friends or family physician recommended for the same.

5. Were you admitted into any other hospital for any kind of aliment in past 7 years? If yes, where and when? For what kind of illness?

   Was the treatment effective? Yes No

   If no, any special cause?

   If the patient is admitted for the first time and none of his family members was admitted here before, please follow the following questions.

6. Did you get your choice of room? Yes No

   If yes, did you get the room instantaneously? Yes No

7. Were you informed about the nature of treatment given by doctors or nurse?

   Yes No

8. Were you informed about the expected length of stay in the hospital?

   Yes No

9. How do you rank your satisfaction level w.r.t. the following services:

   5. Highly satisfied 4. Satisfied 3. Average 2. Unsatisfied 1. Highly unsatisfied

Service/staff	1	2	3	4	5	Remarks
Ease of admission						
Treatment received						
Nursing						
Housekeeping						
F & B						
Patient care						
Transportation						
Staff courtesy a) Admn. Counter b) Billing c) Patient care d) Others						
Doctors						
Cleanliness & hygiene						

10. Was there any incidence that happened so as to cause harm to the patient during his/her stay in the hospital? (Like – patient fall, administering wrong medicine, not giving specific medicine of required precautions not being taken care of).

    If yes, please specify:

11. Do you think at any point of time, you are charged more than your expectations?

    (i) Some points (ii) Everywhere (iii) No idea (Please specify)

12. How do you perceive the quality of treatment-received w.r.t. cost of treatment?

    (i) Highly expensive (ii) Expensive (iii) Average/value for services received

13. How do you rank the Cost vs quality of treatment w.r.t. other similar hospitals where you or your family have received treatment before?

    (i) Above (ii) At par (iii) Below

14. Suggestions for improvement/areas that caused most dissatisfaction to you:

15. If the patient or his/her family members were admitted into the hospital for any kind of treatment before?

    Please indicate your satisfaction level at the time of discharge w.r.t. following aspects:

	Highly Satisfied	Satisfied	Average	Unsatisfied	Highly Unsatisfied
Time taken	1	2	3	4	5
Diet counseling	1	2	3	4	5
Billing process	1	2	3	4	5
Dr. Consultation	1	2	3	4	5
Handover of discharge	1	2	3	4	5

16. How do you consider the quality of treatment received this time as compared to previous time?

    (i) Better (ii) Same (iii) Worse

17. Have you recommended any hospital to your friends or relatives earlier?

    Yes No

18. Would you still recommend any multispeciality hospital to other people?

    I will Strongly recommend

    Hestitantly recommend

    Not recommend

    Recommendations/Comments:

MODEL QUESTIONNAIRE 4

Changes in women's dress preference: An in-depth study based on lifestyle and age.

Friends, This questionnarie is to conduct a survey on lifestyle, age and dress preference of Indian women. Please spend a few minutes to answer the following questions. I assure you that your answers will be kept completely confidential.

1. Your name:
   (i) Mrs. (ii) Miss
2. City/Town where you have been residing for the last three years:
3. You are best described as a
   (i) Student (ii) Working professional
   (iii) Housewife (iv) Others (pl. specify)
4. Education
   (i) Doing high School (ii) Doing Graduation
   (iii) Doing Postgraduation (iv) Did Graduation
   (v) Did Postgraduation
5. Do you like to dress
   (i) According to other people's choice
   (ii) Sometimes according to your choice, sometime according to other's choice
   (iii) According to your choice only
6. Do you like to spend sometime on hairstyle?
   (i) Yes (ii) No
   If Yes, how much do you spend?
7. Do you prefer to color your hair?
   (i) Yes (ii) No
   If yes, which color do you like?
8. Which statement do you agree the most?
   (i) I believe in maintaining a simple life.
   (ii) I don't care for others negative comments.
   (iii) I want to remain busy with my work and assignments.
   (iv) I believe men and women may use same dress, have same hairstyle and do same jobs.
   (v) I believe that different roles need to be played on different occasions.

9. If you are working in an organization, which type of dress do you prefer?
   (i) Always sari (ii) Always salwar kurta
   (iii) Always trouser and blazer (iv) Varies from time to time
10. Reason for choosing this dress.
   (i) I prefer Indian traditional values.
   (ii) I like dresses, which are comfortable and can be maintained in journey.
   (iii) I prefer dresses, which help to build professional, look.
   (iv) I prefer economy pricing.
   (v) Others (please mention it).
11. What is your preferred casual dress?
   (i) Salwar kurta (ii) Jeans and T-shirt
12. Which type of magazines do you go through?
   (i) Vanita (ii) Saras Salil
   (iii) Femina/Cosmopolitan (iv) Others (please mention the name)
13. Which type of TV programs do you prefer?
   (i) Family shows (ii) News channels in Hindi
   (iii) English news channels (iv) General entertainment
14. Do you feel that marriage is essential for a woman's life?
   (i) Always yes (ii) Sometimes it is necessary
   (iii) Never needed (iv) Part of the culture
15. How do you comment on living together?
   (i) It's very bad (ii) Sometimes it is necessary
   (iii) It is modern day's demand (iv) Against to the culture
16. How do you want to greet your guest?
   (i) By preparing home made food (ii) By purchasing fast food from outside
   (iii) Some times purchase food (iv) Sometimes prepare it at home
17. Suppose one of your friends or a relative takes liquor regularly, in you opinion he is
   (i) Doing a crime (ii) Doing unhealthy social activity
   (iii) Maintaining high status (iv) Spoilling his health
18. If you don't offer prayer/puja, do you feel guilty?
   (i) Always (ii) Sometime
   (iii) Often sometimes (iv) Never

19. In which age group do you belong

(i) Below 19	(ii) 20-24	(iii) 25-29
(iv) 30-34	(v) 35-39	(vi) Above 40

20. Which group best identifies your family's monthly income?

(i) Less than ₹ 10,000	(ii) 10,000-15,000	(iii) 15,000-20,000
(iv) 20,000-25,000	(v) Above ₹ 25,000	

Exercises

1. A company wishes to launch a new toothpaste which can effectively prevent cavities and tooth decay as well make teeth whiter. But the toothpaste markets are highly crowed with multiple brands. Design a questionnaire to identify product attributes important to consumers and consumer purchase behaviour. Also decide target group on whom the questionnaire can be executed.

2. You have been asked to develop a survey questionnaire to determine consumers' attitudes toward the health care provided by the public hospitals in your capital city. What type of questions (i.e., disguised/non-disguised/combination; open-ended/closed ended, etc.) would be preferable in this situation? How many questions should you ask? Explain your answer.

Case Study India Telephones

Bharathi is management trainee with India Telephones. She was looking at the questionnaire she had formulated for the value added services which were to be provided by India Telephones. The questionnaire is as follows:

1. How many long distance calls do you make per week?

   0-3, 3-5, 5-10, more than 10.

2. What is your income?

   10000-15000, 15000-20000, 20000-30000.

3. How much money do you spend on your telephone bill?

   Less than 800, 1000-1500,1500-2000, above 2000.

4. Have you shopped in a telephone store?

   Yes/No

5. Do you own your telephone?

   Yes/No

6. Are you aware of special discount rates for long distance calls?

   Yes/No

7. Do they influence when you make long distance call?

   Yes/No

8. If your telephone rates increased, would you cut back on telephones purchased or usage?

   Yes/No

9. Do you plan to install more lines in future?

   Yes/No

10. Do you have any sp. phones like car phones, call waiting, phone for deaf, picture phone, wireless phone, push button?

Questions

1. She was wondering how would the respondents react to the mail questionnaire.
2. Examine the subjects that are brought up in the questionnaire and their sequence. How would you alter it to make it more result oriented?
3. When this questionnaire comes back, what problems do you foresee to understand the responses and tabulate them?
4. Which other methods of the questionnaire do you suggest? Justify your answer.

CHAPTER SEVEN

SAMPLING

INTRODUCTION

Sample planning and sampling methodology are key skills of the marketing research. Once the researcher has clearly specified the problem and developed an appropriate research design and data collection instruments, the next step in the research process is to select those elements from which the information will be collected. It is in this context that an understanding of those elements from which information is collected and procedure to be followed in identifying those elements becomes important. The basic question that the researcher naturally faces is whether the data should be collected from the total elements or a set of total elements. In other words, total elements are called population and set of elements are called sample. Data collection from all elements of the population is called census method. A census is an investigation of all individual elements making up the population, i.e., it involves a total enumeration. Data collection from a sub set of the population is called sampling. A population or universe is a complete group of people, sales territories, stores, etc. Sharing some common set of characteristics. When a distinction is made between population and universe, it is made on the basis of whether the group is finite (population) or infinite (universe). The population is defined in keeping with the objectives of the study. Some times, the entire population will be sufficiently small, and the researcher can include the entire population in the study. This type of research is called a census study because data is gathered on every member of the population. Usually, the population is too large for the researcher to attempt to survey all of its members. Therefore, researcher prefers to select a portion of the population, it is called sample.

SAMPLING

A sample is a subset or some part of the larger population. The purpose of sampling is to estimate some characteristics of the population. A small, but carefully chosen sample can be used to represent the population. The sample reflects the characteristics of the population from which it is drawn. In research parlance characteristics of a population are termed parameters whereas the sample estimates of the population parameters are termed statistics.

The relationships among population parameter, sample, and statistics can be illustrated by means of a schematic diagram as shown in Figure 7.1.

❖ Importance of Sampling

1. Sampling reduces the time and cost of research studies. Because of sampling, it has become possible to undertake a national or global studies at a reasonable cost and time. Such economy in time and cost improves the viability of several field studies.

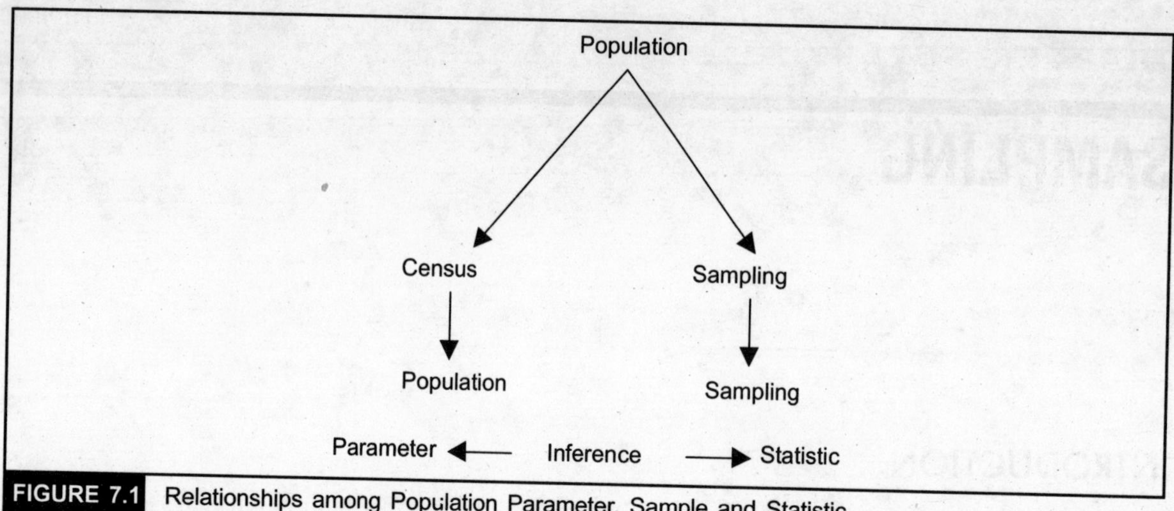

FIGURE 7.1 Relationships among Population Parameter, Sample and Statistic

2. Sampling requires smaller staff both for field work and for processing and analyzing the data.
3. The quality of a study is often better with sampling to a complete coverage. The possibility of better interviewing, more thorough investigation of missing, wrong or suspicious information, better supervision, and better processing is greater in sampling than in complete coverage.
4. Sampling provides much quicker results than does a census. The speed of execution minimizes the time between the recognition of a need for information and the availability of that information. The speed of execution is vital in feasibility studies, evaluation studies, and business research. Timely execution of a study is essential for making use of its findings.
5. Sampling is the only procedure possible, if the population is infinite, e.g., throws of dice, consumer behaviour surveys, etc.
6. Statistical sampling yields a crucial advantage over any other way of choosing a part of the population for a study. That is, when the estimates of the population characteristics are made from the sample results, the precision of these estimates can also be gauged from the sample results themselves.

DEVELOPING A SAMPLING PLAN

The process of developing an operational sampling plan can be summarized in seven steps. These steps are as follows.

Step 1: Define the Population

The basic issue in developing a sampling plan is to specify the characteristics of those individuals or things (for example, customers, companies, stores) from whom or about whom information is needed to meet the research objectives. A properly designated population must be defined in terms of elements, sampling units, extent and time. For example, a survey of consumers might specify the population as:

Element:	Men and women
Sampling Units:	Households
Extent:	New Delhi
Time:	April-July 2010.

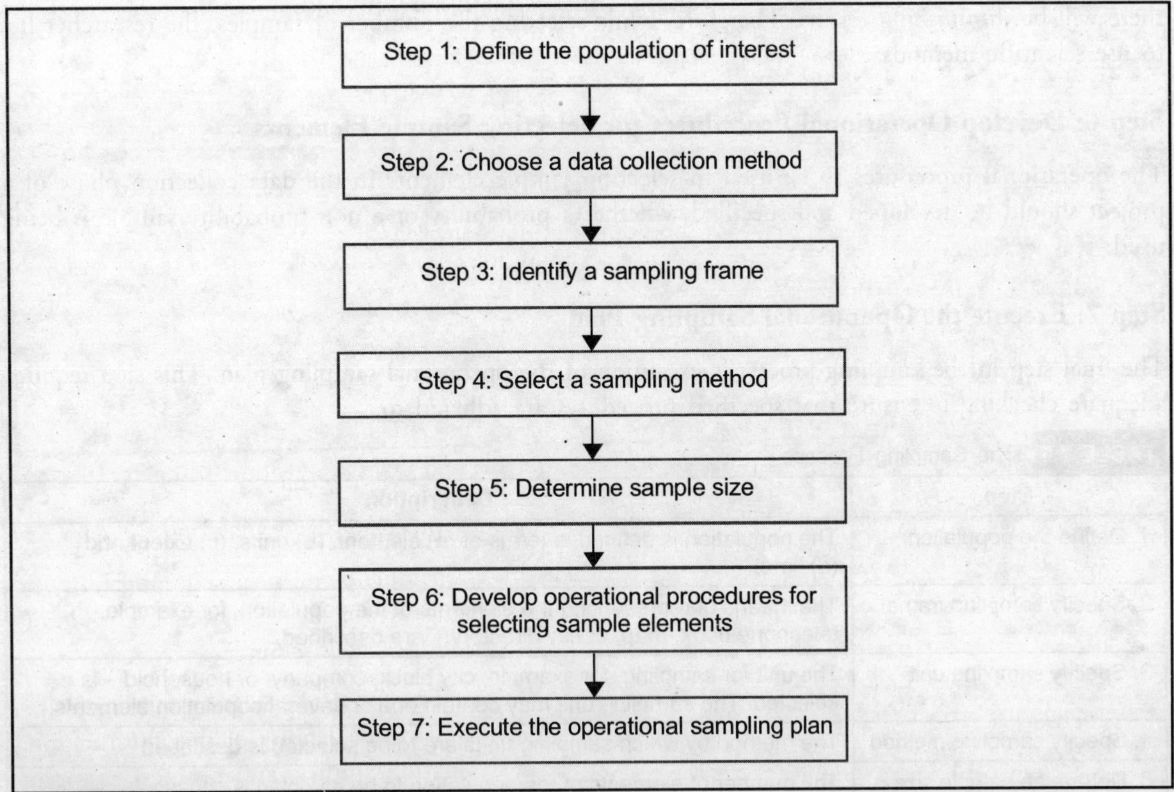

FIGURE 7.2 Developing a Sampling Plan

Step 2: Choose a Data Collection Method

The selection of a data collection method has implications for the sampling process. For example, both telephone interviews and mall-intercept surveys have certain inherent disadvantages in regard to sampling.

Step 3: Identify a Sampling Frame

The third step in the process is to identify the sampling frame, which is a list of the members or elements of the population from which units to be sampled are to be selected. A sampling frame is a means, representing the elements of the population. Identifying the sampling frame may simply mean specifying a procedure for generating such a list. The list may be telephone directory, list of registered voters, city directories, city maps, etc. In the ideal situation, the list of population members complete and accurate. Unfortunately, there usually is no such list.

Step 4: Select a Sampling Method

The fourth step in developing a sampling plan is selection of a sampling method, which will depend on the objectives of the study, the financial resources available, time limitations, and the nature of the problem under investigation. The major alternative sampling methods can be grouped under two headings – probability sampling methods and non-probability sampling methods.

Step 5: Determine Sample Size

Once a sampling method has been chosen, the next step is to determine the appropriate sample size. Generally, the larger the sample, the more accurate the research results. However, beyond certain number, there will be diminishing results. Therefore, while selecting the number of samples, the researcher has to use scientific methods.

Step 6: Develop Operational Procedures for Selecting Sample Elements

The operational procedures to be used in selecting sample elements in the data collection phase of a project should be developed and specified, whether a probability or a non-probability sample is being used.

Step 7: Execute the Operational Sampling Plan

The final step in the sampling process is execution of the operational sampling plan. This step requires adequate checking to ensure that specified procedures are adhered to.

TABLE 7.1 The Sampling Process

Step	Description
1. Define the population	The population is defined in terms of (a) element, (b) units, (c) extent and (d) time.
2. Specify sampling frame	The means of representing the elements of the population, for example, telephone book, map, or city directory – are described.
3. Specify sampling unit	The unit for sampling, for example, city block, company, or household – is selected. The sampling unit may contain one or several population elements.
4. Specify sampling method	The method by which sampling units are to be selected is described.
5. Determine sample size	The number of elements of the population to be sampled is chosen.
6. Specify sampling plan	The operational procedures for selection of the sampling units are selected.
7. Select the sample	The office and fieldwork necessary for the selection of the sample are carried out.

CHARACTERISTICS OF A GOOD SAMPLE DESIGN

A good sample design requires the judicious balancing of four broad criteria – goal orientation, measurability, practicality and economy.

1. *Goal orientation:* This suggests that a sample design "should be oriented to the research objectives, tailored to the survey design, and fitted to the survey conditions". If this is done, it should influence the choice of the population, the measurement as also the procedure of choosing a sample.

2. *Measurability:* A sample design should enable the computation of valid estimates of its sampling variability. Normally, this variability is expressed in the form of standard errors in surveys. However, this is possible only in the case of probability sampling. In non-probability samples, such as quota sample, it is not possible to know the degree of precision of the survey results.

3. *Practicality:* This implies that the sample design can be followed properly in the survey, as envisaged earlier. It is necessary that complete, correct, practical, and clear instructions should be given to the interviewer so that no mistakes are made in the selection of sampling units and the final selection in the field is not different from the original sample design. Practicality also refers to simplicity of the design, i.e. it should be capable of being understood and followed in actual operation of the field work.

4. *Economy:* Finally, economy implies that the objectives of the survey should be achieved with minimum cost and effort. Survey objectives are generally spelt out in terms of precision, i.e. the

inverse of the variance of survey estimates. For a given degree of precision, the sample design should give the minimum cost. Alternatively, for a given per unit cost, the sample design should achieve maximum precision (minimum variance).

It may be pointed out that these four criteria come into conflict with each other in most of the cases, and the researcher should carefully balance the conflicting criteria so that he is able to select a really good sample design.

SAMPLING METHODS OR TECHNIQUES

Sampling methods are classified as either probability or non-probability. Probability sampling method is one where samples in which every element of the population have a known, non-zero likelihood of selection. In other words, the sample is selected in such a way that each unit within the population or universe has a known chance of being selected. It is this concept of "known chance" that allows for the statistical projection of characteristics based on the sample to the population. Whereas non-probability sampling method is one where the samples in which specific elements from the population have been selected in a non-random manner. In probability samples, each member of the population has a known non-zero probability of being selected.

Probability methods include random sampling, systematic sampling, and stratified sampling. In non-probability sampling, members are selected from the population in some non-random manner. These include convenience sampling, judgment sampling, quota sampling, and snowball sampling. The advantage of probability sampling is that sampling error can be calculated. Sampling error is the degree to which a sample might differ from the population. When inferring to the population, results are reported plus or minus the sampling error. In non-probability sampling, the degree to which the sample differs from the population remains unknown.

TABLE 7.2 Non-probability versus Probability Sampling

Factors	Conditions favoring the use of	
	Non-probability Sampling	**Probability Sampling**
Nature of research	Exploratory	Conclusive
Relative magnitude of sampling	Non sampling errors are larger	Sampling errors are larger
Variability in the population	Homogeneous (low)	Heterogeneous (high)
Statistical considerations	Unfavorable	Favorable
Operational considerations	Favorable	Unfavorable

❖ Probability Sampling

Random Sampling

Random sampling is the purest form of probability sampling. Each member of the population has an equal and known chance of being selected. When there are very large populations, it is often difficult or impossible to identify every member of the population, so the pool of available subjects become biased. A sampling procedure that assures that each element in the population has an equal chance of being selected is referred to as simple random sampling.

Let us assume you had a school with a 1000 students, divided equally into boys and girls, and you wanted to select 100 of them for further study. You might put all their names in a drum and then pull

100 names out. Not only does each person have an equal chance of being selected, we can also easily calculate the probability of a given person being chosen, since we know the sample size (n) and the population (N) and it becomes a simple matter of division:

$$n/N \times 100 \text{ or } 100/1000 \times 100 = 10\%$$

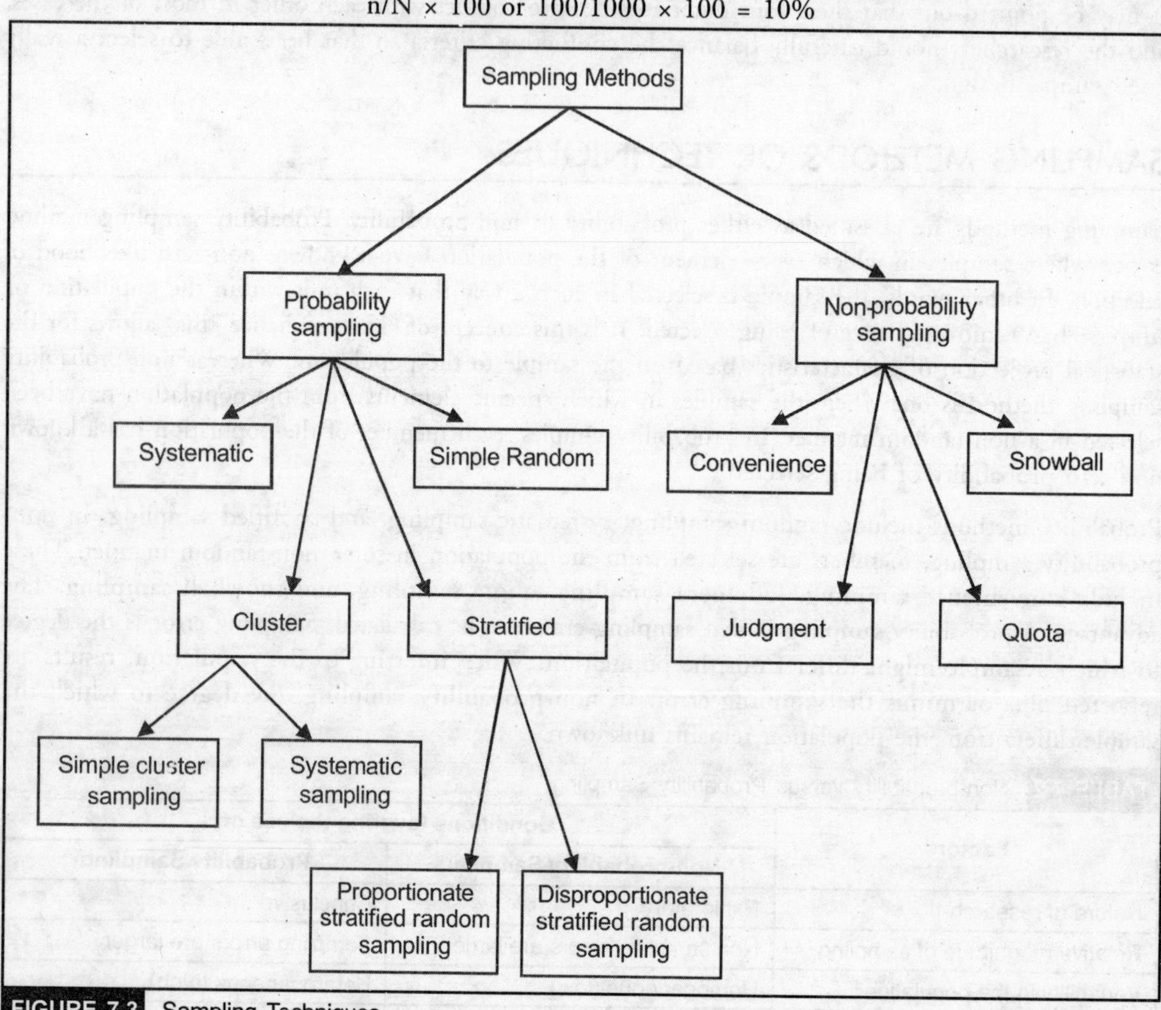

FIGURE 7.3 Sampling Techniques

This means that every student in the school has a 10% or 1 in 10 chance of being selected using this method. There are a number of potential problems with simple and systematic random sampling. If the population is widely dispersed, it may be extremely costly to reach them. On the other hand, a current list of the whole population we are interested in (sampling frame) may not be readily available. Or perhaps, the population itself is not homogeneous and the sub-groups are very different in size. In such a case, precision can be increased through stratified sampling. Some problems that arise from random sampling can be overcome by weighting the sample to reflect the population or universe. For instance, if in our sample of 100 students we ended up with 60% boys and 40% girls, we could decrease the importance of the characteristics for boys and increase those of the girls to reflect our universe, which is 50/50.

Systematic Sampling

Systematic sampling is often used instead of random sampling. It is also called an Nth name selection technique. After the required sample size has been calculated, every Nth record is selected from a list of population members. As long as the list does not contain any hidden order, this sampling method is as good as the random sampling method. Its only advantage over the random sampling technique is simplicity. Systematic sampling is frequently used to select a specified number of records from a computer file.

Stratified Sampling

Stratified sampling is commonly used probability method that is superior to random sampling because it reduces sampling error. A stratum is a subset of the population that shares at least one common characteristic. Examples of stratums might be males and females, or managers and non-managers. The researcher first identifies the relevant stratums and their actual representation in the population. Random sampling is then used to select a sufficient number of subjects from each stratum. "Sufficient" refers to a sample size large enough for us to be reasonably confident that the stratum represents the population. Stratified sampling is often used when one or more of the stratums in the population have a low incidence relative to the other stratums. Let us assume that Mr. X wanted to determine the spending patterns of a hotel's guests. Knowing that the business clientele behaves quite differently from the leisure guests, Mr. X might want to separate them into different groups or strata. He is, however, dealing with a downtown property where 80% of the clientele stays in fact on business, with only 20% of the guests there for leisure purposes.

In simple random sampling, there is no assurance that a sufficient number of leisure travellers would actually be included in the sample. Using the rule of thumb about sample size determination, we need at least 100 respondents for our leisure segment. This means that we would need four times as many business travellers, since they represent four times as many guests at the hotel, for a total of 500 respondents. This is referred to as "proportionate stratified sampling". Disproportionate sampling is only undertaken if a particular strata is very important to the research project but occurs in too small a percentage to allow for meaningful analysis unless its representation is artificially boosted. In this technique you over sample and then weight your data to re-establish the proportions. Let us assume you only have enough budgets to survey 300 guests, but you still want at least 100 leisure travelers to have a sufficient number for further analysis. This means that you over sample for leisure travelers at a ratio of 2:1. Therefore, you would need to weight each of your business travelers by 2 (i.e. 2 × 2 = 4) to end up with the proper proportions.

1. ***Proportionate stratified random sampling:*** In this type of sampling procedure the number of objects or sampling units chosen from each group is proportional to the number in the population. Proportional stratified sampling can further be classified as directly proportional and inversely proportional stratified sampling. Examples of both types of proportional stratified sampling are provided here.
2. ***Disproportionate stratified random sampling:*** In stratified sampling, when the sample size in each group is not proportional to the respective group sizes, it is known as disproportional stratified sampling. When multiple groups are compared and their respective group sizes are small, a proportional stratified sampling will not yield a sample size large enough for meaningful comparisons, and disproportional stratified sampling is used.

Cluster Sampling

This method refers to selection of clusters or groups instead of individual units. Contrary to simple random sampling and stratified sampling, where single subjects are selected from the population, in cluster sampling the subjects are selected in groups or clusters. This approach allows overcoming the constraints of costs and time associated with a very dispersed population. It involves two stages (a) cluster elements are so formed as to include in a single cluster, and (b) a given number of clusters are shown randomly to form the sample. Clusters may and may not be equal in size. Clusters of equal size are generally the result of the planned conditions chosen by the sampler. Smaller the size of the cluster, the greater will be the precision of estimate for a given size of the sample.

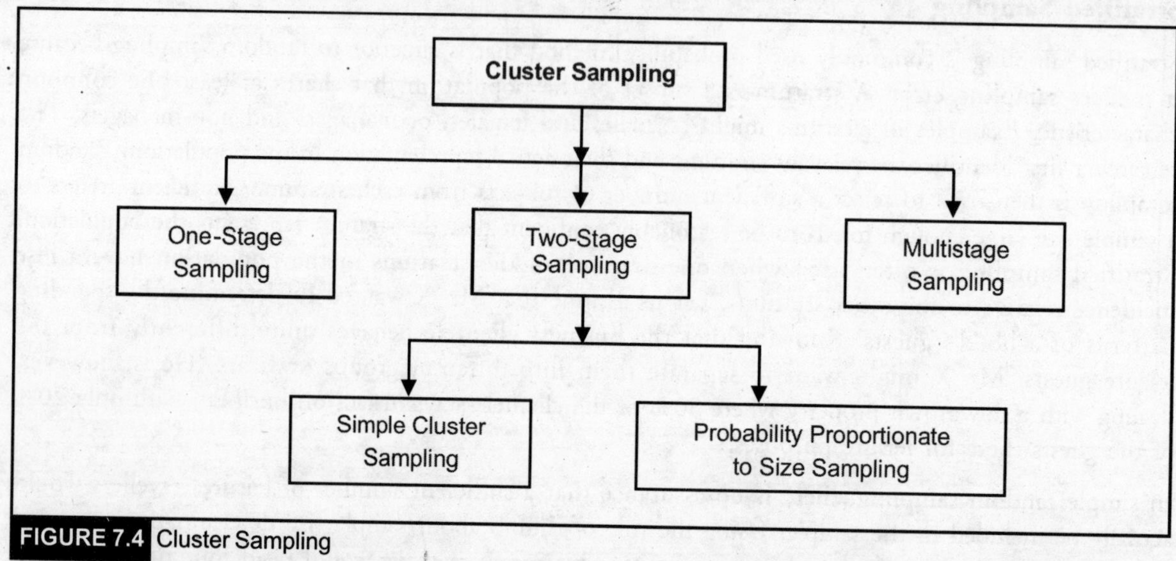

FIGURE 7.4 Cluster Sampling

Assume that researcher wanted to conduct interviews with hotel managers in a major city about their training needs. You could decide that each hotel in the city represents one cluster, and then randomly select a small number, e.g. 10. You would then contact the managers in these 10 properties for interviews. When all units of the selected cluster are interviewed, this is referred to as "one-stage cluster sampling". If the subjects to be interviewed are selected randomly within the selected clusters, it is call "two-stage cluster sampling". This technique might be more appropriate if the number of subjects within a unit is very large (e.g., instead of interviewing managers, you want to interview employees). You could also combine cluster sampling with stratified sampling. For instance, in the above example of wanting to interview employees in randomly selected clusters, you might want to stratify the employees based on some characteristic deemed most relevant to your study (e.g., seniority, job function, etc.) and then randomly select employees from each of these strata. This type of sampling is referred to as "multistage sampling".

Classification of one and two stage sampling: If all the elements in each selected cluster are included in the sample, the procedure is called one stage cluster sampling. If the sample of element is drawn probabilistically from each selected cluster the procedure is two stage cluster sampling. Two stage cluster sampling can be either simple cluster sampling involving SRS (Simple Random Sampling) or Probability Proportionate to Size (PPS) sampling. Furthermore, a cluster sample can have multiple (more than two) stages, as in multistage cluster sampling.

A common form of cluster sampling in area sampling: In this sampling the clusters, consist of geographic areas, such as countries, housing tracts, or blocks. If only one level of sampling takes place in selecting the basic elements (for example, the researcher samples blocks and then all the households within the selected blocks are included in the sample), the design is called single-stage area sampling. If two (or more) levels of sampling take place before the basic elements are selected (the researcher samples blocks, and then samples households within selected blocks), the design is called two (multi) – stage area sampling. The distinguishing feature of the one-stage area sample is that all of the households in the selected blocks (or geographic areas) are included in the sample. Cluster sampling economy is shown in Figure 7.5 and 7.6.

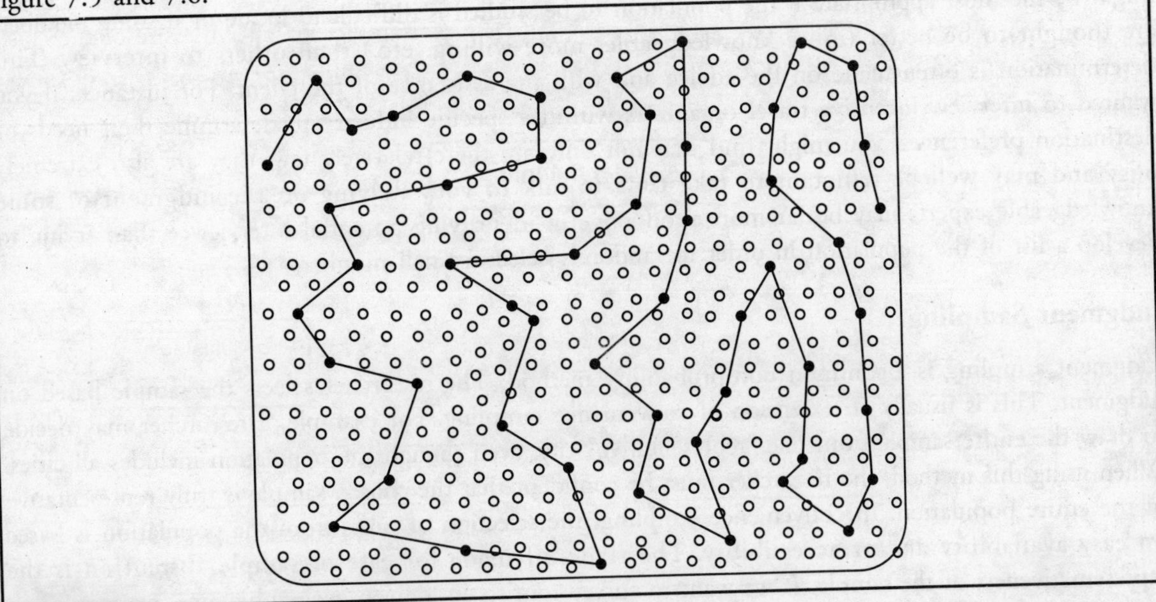

FIGURE 7.5 Unclustered Random Sample

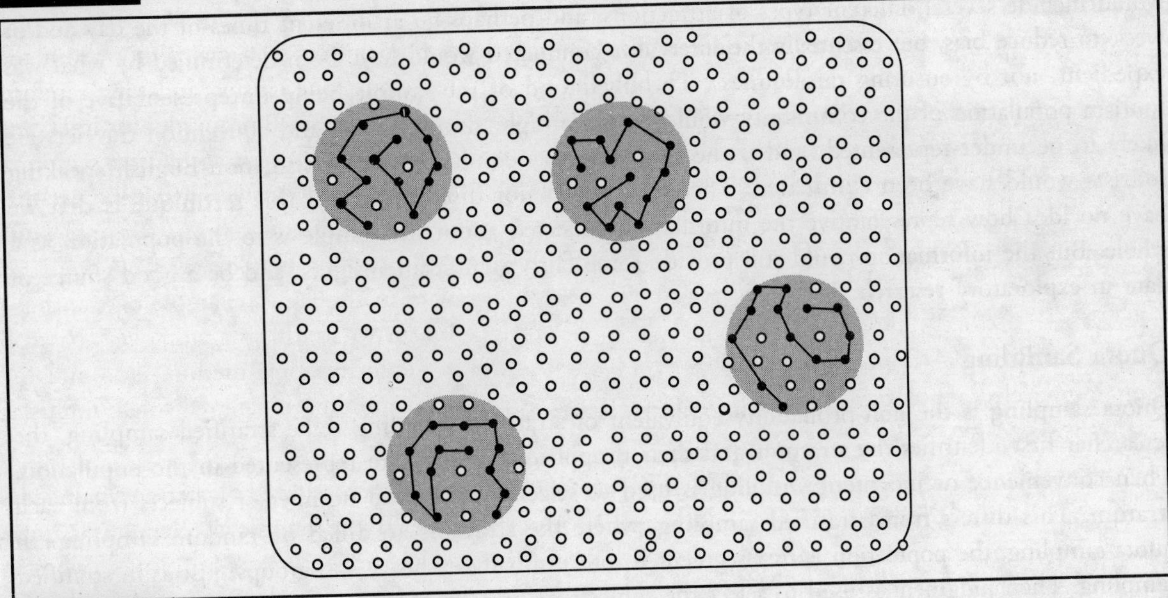

FIGURE 7.6 Clustered Random Sample

❖ Non-Probability Sampling

Convenience Sampling

Convenience sampling is used in exploratory research where the researcher is interested in getting an inexpensive approximation of the truth. As the name implies, the sample is selected because they are convenient. This non-probability method is often used during preliminary research efforts to get a gross estimate of the results, without incurring the cost or time required to select a random sample. In judgment sampling, the researcher or some other "expert" uses his/her judgment in selecting the units from the population for study based on the population's parameters. This type of sampling technique might be the most appropriate if the population to be studied is difficult to locate or if some members are thought to be better (more knowledgeable, more willing, etc.) than others to interview. This determination is often made on the advice and with the assistance of the client. For instance, if you wanted to interview incentive travel organizers within a specific industry to determine their needs or destination preferences, you might find that not only are there relatively few, they are also extremely busy and may well be reluctant to take time to talk to you. Relying on the judgment of some knowledgeable experts may be far more productive in identifying potential interviewee than trying to develop a list of the population in order to randomly select a small number.

Judgment Sampling

Judgment sampling is a common non-probability method. The researcher selects the sample based on judgment. This is usually an extension of convenience sampling. For example, a researcher may decide to draw the entire sample from one "representative" city, even though the population includes all cities. When using this method, the researcher must be confident that the chosen sample is truly representative of the entire population. In convenience sampling, the selection of units from the population is based on easy availability and/or accessibility. The trade-off made for ease of sample abstention is the representativeness of the sample. If we want to survey tourists in a given geographic area, we may go to several of the major attractions since tourists are more likely to be found in these places. Obviously, we would include several different types of attractions, and perhaps go at different times of the day and/or week to reduce bias, but essentially the interviews conducted would have been determined by what was expedient, not by ensuring randomness. The likelihood of the sample being unrepresentative of the tourism population of the community would be quite high, since business and convention travelers are likely to be under-represented, and if the interview was conducted in English, non-English speaking tourists would have been eliminated. Therefore, the major disadvantage of this technique is that we have no idea how representative the information collected about the sample is to the population as a whole. But the information could still provide some fairly significant insights, and be a good source of data in exploratory research.

Quota Sampling

Quota sampling is the non-probability equivalent of stratified sampling. Like stratified sampling, the researcher first identifies the stratums and their proportions as they are represented in the population. Then convenience or judgment sampling is used to select the required number of subjects from each stratum. This differs from stratified sampling, where the stratums are filled by random sampling. In quota sampling, the population is first segmented into mutually exclusive sub-groups, just as in stratified sampling. Then judgment is used to select the subjects or units from each segment based on a specified proportion. It is the second step which makes the technique one of non-probability sampling. Let us assume you wanted to interview tourists coming to a community and to study their activities and spending. Based on national research you know that 60% come for vacation/pleasure, 20% are VFR (Visiting Friends and Relatives), 15% come for business and 5% for conventions and meetings. You also know that 80% come from within the province, 10% from other parts of Canada, and 10% are international. A total of 500 tourists are to be intercepted at major tourist spots (attractions, events, hotels, convention centre, etc.), as you would in a convenience sample. The number of interviews could, therefore, be determined based on the proportion a given characteristic represents in the population.

For instance, once 300 pleasure travelers have been interviewed, this category would no longer be pursued, and only those who state that one of the other purposes was their reason for coming would be interviewed until these quotas were filled. Obvious advantages of quota sampling are the speed with which information can be collected, the lower cost of doing so and the convenience it represents.

Snowball Sampling

Snowball sampling is a special non-probability method used when the desired sample characteristic is rare. It may be extremely difficult or cost prohibitive to locate respondents in these situations. Snowball sampling relies on referrals from initial subjects to generate additional subjects. While this technique can dramatically lower search costs, it comes at the expense of introducing bias because the technique itself reduces the likelihood that the sample will represent a good cross section from the population.

Snowball sampling (also called network, chain referral, or reputational sampling) is a method for identifying and sampling (or selecting) cases in the network. It is based on an analogy to a snowball, which begins small but becomes larger as it is rolled on wet snow and picks up additional snow. It begins with one or a few people or cases and spreads out on the basis of links to the initial cases.

This design has been found quite useful where respondents are difficult to identify and are best located through referral networks. In the initial stage of snowball sampling, individuals are discovered and may or may not be selected through probability methods. This group is then used to locate others who possess similar characteristics and who, in turn, identify others. The "snowball" gathers subjects as it rolls along.

For example, a researcher examines friendship networks among teenagers in a community. He or she begins with three teenagers who do not know each other. The researcher approaches each teenager and asks names of four close friends. The researcher then goes to the four friends and asks each to name four close friends, then goes to those four and does the same thing again, and so forth. A large number of people are involved in the process. Each person in the sample is directly or indirectly tied to the original teenagers, and several people may have named the same person. The researcher eventually stops, in selecting the sample.

Panel sampling: In this method of sampling, same units or elements are measured on subsequent occasions. In some type of research studies, there may be a necessity to contact the same unit or element after some time to have a comparison between two timings. In such cases, this type of sampling places an important role to generate the data on a continuous basis.

Multi-phase sampling or double sampling: Under this method, information will be gathered generally from the selected units and then depending upon the nature of data collected, a more intensive study can be done by gathering the data from the same units but not from all.

RANDOM-DIGIT DIALING (RDD)

If truly accurate or representative, current sampling frames are not available, a researcher would have to employ an alternate method such as random-digit dialing, if conducting telephone interviews. The only solution to the problem of unlisted telephone numbers is to generate phone numbers by some random process. This practice, referred to as Random-Digit Dialing involves generation of random numbers at random. But practical considerations complicate the problem greatly. The foremost is the relatively small proportion of the working numbers among all possible 10-digit telephone numbers. Only about 1 in 170 of all possible telephone numbers is actually in use. The proportion of the working residential numbers in RDD samples can be increased dramatically by selecting from only the 103 working area codes (first three digits). The approach yields approximately 1 working residential number for every 17 randomly generated. From a cost stand point, this rate is still low, entailing too many unproductive dialings while including a proportionate number of unlisted phone homes in the sample. There are three alternative approaches built around the use of a telephone book.

❖ Four-Digit Approach

Taking the four-digit approach, the researcher must, in addition to restricting the sample to the 103 working area codes, select numbers only from working central offices or exchanges. The last four digits of the number are generated via some process that approaches randomness. Problem with this approach is that all exchanges have an equal probability of being selected, while some have a high proportion of all possible numbers in service and others have only a small proportion in service.

❖ Three-Digit Approach

The next logical progression in RDD is the three-digit dialing approach. This method increases the proportion of working numbers to better than one in three. Consulting the section of a criss-cross directory where phone numbers are listed numerically will show that within a particular exchange, certain sequences of 1000 numbers are totally unused while other groups of 1000 are in use. Generate the last three digits of each exchange by means of some random process. This method is more efficient in eliminating non-working numbers, but increases bias due to missing new exchanges that have been activated.

The four digit method is safer from the standpoint of avoiding bias, but more expensive due to the greater number of calls that must be made. It is suggested that three-digit method is most appropriate when the directories for the area of interest are relatively current or when there has been little growth in the area since the publication of the recent directory. In other cases, the four digit method should be used.

❖ Using Telephone Books

RDD samples can also be generated from the telephone book. This is accomplished by selecting numbers at random from the book and adding a random number as the sixth or seventh digit. Somewhere between one in two and one in three of the numbers generated will be working residential numbers. This is a viable approach because; all exchanges are proportionately represented in the book. The phone book is recommended as an RDD sample source only in those cases where the appropriate computer hardware and software are not available. There are two major reasons for making this recommendation. First, the construction of sample by this approach is time-consuming and expensive. Second, if the interviewers are given directions and left to generate numbers themselves, the researcher loses all control over the validity of the sample. Computer programmes can incorporate three-or four-digit approaches and generate RDD samples at a very low cost. The print-out can be set up to capture additional data and to help the researcher control field costs and proper execution of the sampling plan.

RELIABILITY AND VALIDITY

The extent to which results are consistent over time and an accurate representation of the total population under study is referred to as reliability. In other words, if the results of a study can be reproduced under a similar methodology, then the research instrument is considered to be reliable. The consistency with which questionnaire items are answered can be determined through the test-retest method, whereby a respondent would be asked to answer the same question(s) at two different times. This attribute of the instrument is actually referred to as stability. If we are dealing with a stable measure, then the results should be similar. A high degree of stability indicates a high degree of reliability, since the results are repeatable. The problem with the test-retest method is that, it may not only sensitize the respondent to the subject matter and hence influence the responses given, but also one cannot be sure that there were no changes in extraneous influences such as an attitude change that has occurred that could lead to a difference in the responses provided. Probing for attitudes usually requires a series of questions that are similar, but not the same. This battery of questions should be answered consistently by the respondent. This can be tested using the split-half method, whereby the researcher takes the results obtained from one-half of the scale items and checks them against the results of the other half. Although the researcher may be able to prove the research instrument's repeatability and internal consistency, and therefore, reliability, the instrument itself may not be valid. In other words, it may consistently provide similar results, but it does not measure what the research proposed to determine.

Validity determines whether the research truly measures that which it was intended to measure or how truthful the research results are. In other words, does the research instrument allow you to hit "the bull's eye" of your research object? Researchers generally determine validity by asking a series of questions, and will often look for the answers in the research of others. Starting with the research question itself, you need to ask yourself whether you can actually answer the question you have posed with the research instrument selected. For instance, if you want to determine the profile of Goan eco-tourists, but the database that you are using only asked questions about certain activities, you may have a problem with the face or content validity of the database for your purpose. Similarly, if you have developed a questionnaire, it is a good idea to pre-test your instrument. You might first ask a number of people who know little about the subject matter whether the questions are clearly worded and easily understood (whether they know the answers or not). You may also look to other research and determine what it has found with respect to question wording or which elements need to be included in order to provide an answer to the specific aspect of your research. This is particularly important when measuring more subjective concepts such as attitudes and motivations. Sometimes, you may want to ask the same question in different ways or repeat it at a later stage in the questionnaire to test for consistency in the response. This is done to confirm criterion validity. All of these approaches will increase the validity of research instrument. Probing for attitudes usually requires a series of questions that are similar, but not the same. This battery of questions should be answered consistently by the respondent. If it is, the scale items are said to have high internal validity. What about the sample itself? Is it truly representative of the population chosen? If a certain type of respondents was not captured, even though they may have been contacted, then your research instrument does not have the necessary validity. In a door-to-door interview, for instance, perhaps the working population is severely under-represented due to the times during which people were contacted. Or perhaps those in upper income categories, more likely to live in condominiums with security could not be reached. This may lead to poor external validity since the study results are likely to be biased and not applicable in a wider sense. Most field research has relatively poor external validity since the researcher can rarely be sure that there were no extraneous factors at play that influenced the study's outcomes. Only in experimental settings can variables be isolated sufficiently to test their impact on a single dependent variable. Although an instrument's validity presupposes that its reliability, the reverse is not always true. Indeed, you can have a research instrument that is extremely consistent in the answers it provides, but the answers are wrong for the objective the study sets out to attain.

DETERMINATION OF SAMPLE SIZE

In sampling the real challenge before the researcher is to decide the size of the sample. The sample size depends on the budget and degree of confidence required. The researcher can buy higher reliability, lower sampling error, and greater confidence for additional time, money, and effort. Ordinarily, though there is some minimum sample size, below which the data are worthless. Similarly, there is point of diminishing returns, above which additional confidence is negligible. The objective of sample size determination is to find the optimum point between those two extremes for the survey project at hand. The decision to decide the sample size must be scientifically made and should not be done arbitrarily because of the risks involved. Size of the sample should be determined by a researcher keeping in view the following points.

1. *Nature of universe:* Universe may be either homogenous or heterogeneous in nature. If the items of the universe are homogenous, a small sample can serve the purpose. But if the items are heterogeneous, a large sample would be required. Technically, this can be termed as the dispersion factor.
2. *Number of classes proposed:* If many class-groups are to be formed, a large sample would be required because a small sample might not be able to give a reasonable number of items in each class-group.
3. *Nature of study:* If items are to be intensively and continuously studied, the sample should be small. For a general survey, the size of the sample should be large, but a small sample is considered appropriate in technical surveys.
4. *Type of sampling:* Sampling technique plays an important part in determining the size of the sample. A small random sample is apt to be much superior to a larger but badly selected sample.
5. *Standard of accuracy and acceptable confidence level:* If the standard of accuracy or the level of precision is to be kept high, we shall require relatively large sample. For doubling the accuracy for a fixed significance level, the sample size has to be increased fourfold.
6. *Availability of finance:* In practice, size of the sample depends upon the amount of money available for the study purposes. This factor should be kept in view while determining the size of sample for large samples result in increasing the cost of sampling estimates.
7. *Other considerations:* Nature of units, size of the population, size of questionnaire, availability of trained investigators, the conditions under which the sample is being conducted, the time available for completion of the study are a few other considerations to which a researcher must pay attention while selecting the size of the sample.

The statistical determination of sample size requires knowledge of (a) variance of the population, (b) the magnitude of acceptable error and (c) the confidence level. Several computational formulas are available for determining sample size; the following are some of the formulas.

❖ Determining Sample Size for Estimating Means

1. *Sample size when estimating a mean:* The confidence interval for the universe mean, μ, is given by

$$\overline{X} \pm z \frac{\sigma_p}{\sqrt{n}}$$

where

$\overline{X}$ = sample mean;

z = the value of the standard variate at a given confidence level (to be read from the table giving the areas under normal curve) as shown in appendix and it is 1.96 for a 95% confidence level;

n – size of the sample;

σ_p = standard deviation of the population (to be estimated from past experience or on the basis of a trial sample). Suppose, we have $\sigma_p = 4.8$ for our purpose.

If the difference between μ and $\overline{X}$ or the acceptable error is to be kept within ±3 of the sample mean with 95% confidence, then we can express the acceptable error, 'e' as equal to

$$e = z \cdot \frac{\sigma_p}{\sqrt{n}}$$

or

$$3 = 1.96 \frac{4.8}{\sqrt{n}}$$

Hence,

$$n = \frac{(1.96)^2 (4.8)^2}{(3)^2} = 9.834 \cong 10.$$

2. ***Sample size when estimating a percentage or proportion:*** If we are to find the sample size for estimating a proportion, our reasoning remains similar to what we have said in the context of estimating the mean. First of all, we shall have to specify the precision and the confidence level and then we will work out the sample size as under:

Since the confidence interval for universe proportion, $\hat{p}$ is given by

$$p \pm z \cdot \sqrt{\frac{p \cdot q}{n}}$$

where

p = sample proportion, q = 1-p;

z = the value of the standard variate at a given confidence level and to be work out from the table showing area under Normal Curve; (See appendices)

n = size of sample;

Since $\hat{p}$ is actually what we are trying to estimate, then what value we should assign to it? One method may be to take the value of p = 0.5 in which case 'n' will be the maximum and the sample will yield at least the desired precision. This will be the most conservative sample size. The other method may be to take an initial estimate of p which may either be based on personal judgment or may be the result of a pilot study. In this context, it has been suggested that a pilot study of something like 225 or more items may result in a reasonable approximation of p value.

Then with the given precision rate, the acceptable error, 'e' can be expressed as under:

$$e = z \cdot \sqrt{\frac{pq}{n}}$$

or

$$e^2 = z^2 \frac{pq}{n}$$

or $$n = \frac{z^2 \cdot p \cdot q}{e^2}$$

The formula gives the size of the sample in case of infinite population when we are to estimate the proportion in the universe. But in case of finite population the above stated formula will be changed as under:

$$n = \frac{z^2 \cdot p \cdot q \cdot N}{e^2 (N-1) + z^2 \cdot p \cdot q}$$

Illustration

What would be the size of the sample if a simple random sample from a population of 4000 items is to be drawn to estimate the per cent defective within 2 per cent of the true value with 95.5 per cent probability? What would be the size of the sample if the population is assumed to be infinite in the given case?

Solution:

In the given question we have the following:

N = 4000

e = .02 (since the estimate should be within 2% of true value);

z = 2.005 (as per table of area under normal curve for the given confidence level of 95.5%).

As we have not been given the p value being the proportion of defectives in the universe, let us assume it to be p = .02 (This may be on the basis of our experience or on the basis of past data or may be the result of a pilot study).

Now we can determine the size of the sample using all this information for the given question as follows:

$$n = \frac{z^2 \cdot p \cdot q \cdot N}{e^2 (N-1) + z^2 \cdot p \cdot q}$$

$$\frac{(2.005)^2 (.02)(1-.02)(4000)}{(.02)^2 (4000-1) + (2.005)^2 (.02)(1-.02)}$$

$$= \frac{315.1699}{1.5996 + .0788} = \frac{315.1699}{1.6784} = 187.78 \simeq 188$$

But if the population happens to be infinite, then our sample size will be as under:

$$n = \frac{z^2 \cdot p \cdot q}{e^2}$$

$$= \frac{(2.005)^2 \cdot (.02)\,(1-.02)}{(.02)^2}$$

$$= \frac{.0788}{.0004} = 196.98 \simeq 197$$

❖ Stratified Sample Size

The sampling study has depended much on the stratified sample to reduce the sampling error. Sample size may have a number of strata or clusters. The researcher will have to deal within strata variability, and within and between cluster variability in calculating the sample size. Since allocation of the population members into strata confines each sub sample's variance within the range of values in each stratum, the sampling error is reduced to a very nominal level. The standard error has a determining affect on the sample size. The stratified sample size may be proportional or disproportional. While one stratum may contain 0.05% of the population size, the other may contain 0.08%, 0.10% and so on. The percentage may vary as per requirements and situations. In case of stratified sampling, only the size of the stratum is used as a guide for allocating the total sample. The size of stratified sampling may be calculated as below:

$$n_1 = \frac{N_i}{N} - n$$

where

n_i = Number of sample units from Stratum i

N_i = Total number of units in the stratum i

N = Total number of units in the Population

n = Sample size desired

The advantage of proportional allocation is that it leads to an estimate which is computationally simple. For calculating the weighted estimates, the weighted calculation of each stratum is totaled. Thus, standard deviation of all the stratum is given by

$$\sigma\overline{x}st = \sqrt{\sum_{i=1}^{k} W_i^2 \frac{\sigma i^2}{ni}}$$

Where

Wi = Weight of Stratum i = $\frac{Ni}{N}$

σi = standard Deviation of the I stratum

k = Total number of strata

The disproportional stratified sample may be a more desirable method if the standard deviation of the observation in each stratum is known. Thus, the standard deviation of the mean of a disproportionate stratified sample is

$$\sigma = \sigma\sqrt{\frac{(W\sigma)^2}{n}}$$

The cost per observation did not enter into the formula for calculating the sample size although cost exerts a direct impact. If the cost per observation or variability is not the same for each stratum, there is need of determining sample size by considering the precision. Cost per observation by subgroup is considered for calculation of sample size.

❖ Sample Size in Non-Probability

Besides the probability selection, non-probability selection is also taken into account. The probability selection does not apply to purposive selection. The size of the non-probability sample is selected in a subjective manner. The researcher selects a size because he feels that the size will be appropriate and the response pattern will be formed. In many studies, the financial factor is the single factor to decide the sample size based on non-probability judgment. In the quota sample, some criteria are taken into account for deciding the sample size. In many theories of non-probability sampling, the researcher considers the statistical significance, sampling error, method of sample selection, representation of sampling and other factors. The researchers should base their sampling size in relation to the statistical significance of the findings.

Other Determinants of Sample Size

The probability and non-probability sample size may be decided by some other method. The variability of elements within the population has become a very important factor to decide the sample size. The more variable the strata or cluster, the larger the sample taken from the population. The research budget and cost per unit of researcher are very important factors in all sorts of probability and non-probability samples to decide the sample size. Cost exerts a direct impact on the stratified or cluster samples. Unequal costs per observation by strata or by cluster are also taken into consideration for deciding the sample size.

ERROR

A survey aims at estimating or inferring selected population characteristics or parameters by studying either the entire population or a sample of the population. The research results may differ from the true values of the parameters under study. Such differences are known as errors and biases. There are broadly two types of errors in connection with the sampling errors. One is random error and the second one is systematic error, sometimes called bias. Error that results from chance variation is called random error or random sampling error. The chance variation is the difference between the sample value and the true value of the population mean. Systematic error or bias is the result of mistakes or problems in the research design or flaws in the execution of the sample design. Systematic error exists in the results of a sample if those results show a consistent tendency to vary in one direction from the true value of the population parameter. These errors are also called non-sampling errors. The non-sampling errors can be categorized as sample design error and measurement error.

❖ Sampling and Non-Sampling Errors

Marketing research studies are based on samples of people or products or stores. The results emerging from such studies are then generalized, i.e., applied to the entire population. For example, if a study is done amongst Tata Nano car owners in a city to know their average monthly expenditure on the maintenance of their car, it can be done either by covering all Tata Nano car owners residing in that city or by choosing a sample, say 10%, of the total Tata Nano car owners. In the latter case, the study may give a different average than the actual average if the entire population is covered. The difference between the sample value and the corresponding population value is known as the sampling error. In other words, the errors which arise because of studying a part of the total population are called sampling errors.

Non-sampling errors, as the name implies, are all those errors which occur in different stages of research. It can also occur in any of the subsequent stages such as in designing a questionnaire, non-response of the questionnaire, in the analysis and interpretation of data, etc. It is not easy to measure a non-sampling error. The chances of non-sampling errors are several during the course of a study, the marketing researcher has to be very careful to ensure an effective control over them.

❖ Types of Sampling Design Errors

Sample design error is a systematic error that results from a problem in the sample design or sampling procedures:

1. ***Selection error:*** Selection error occurs when sampling procedures are incomplete or improper or when appropriate selection procedures are not properly followed. For example, door to door interviewers might decide to avoid houses that do not look neat and tidy because they think the inhabitants will not be agreeable to doing a survey. If people who live in messy houses are systematically different from those who live in tidy houses, then selection error occur in the results of the survey.

2. ***Defective population definition:*** If the population is not well-defined and does not fit to the objects of research study, then an error occurs. In other words, selection of an inappropriate population causes this error. Suppose a study is undertaken to know the views of industrial workers on incentives offered by a company. The study defines its population as male employees and interviews are held amongst them. The exclusion of female employees would be a source of error.

3. ***Frame error:*** The sampling frame is the list of all units comprising the population from which a sample is to be drawn. If the sampling frame is incomplete or inaccurate, its use will give rise to this type of error. A common source of frame error in marketing research is the use of a published telephone directory as a sampling frame for a telephone survey. Many households are not listed in a current telephone directory.

❖ Types of Measurement Errors

Error that results from incorrectly defining the population or universe from which a sample is chosen. Measurement error is caused when the information gathered is different from the information sought. For example, respondents are asked to indicate whether they own a colour television set. Some of them may respond in the affirmative just to boost their image before an interviewer, even though they may not own a colour television set. Such responses will result in measurement error. This type of error occurs frequently in research studies. Moreover, it is difficult to control it as it can arise from several sources. Various types of measurement errors are as follows:

1. ***Surrogate information error:*** This type of error occurs when the information sought by the researcher is different for the information needed to solve the problem. A simple example of this error is when price of a brand is taken to represent its quality. In such a case, it is presumed that higher the price of the product, the better is its quality. This may or may not be true.

2. ***Non-response error:*** It is almost impossible to obtain data from each and every respondent covered in the sample. There are always some respondents who refuse to give any information. Thus, non-response error occurs when respondents refuse to cooperate with the interviewer by not answering his questions. This error also occurs when respondents are away from home when the interviewer calls on them. In case of mail survey particularly, the extent of non-response is usually high.

3. ***Measurement instrument (questionnaire) error:*** A questionnaire is an instrument to collect data from respondents in a survey. If the questionnaire is defective, the data collected on that basis will be misleading. For example, if one or more questions are wrongly worded conveying a different

meaning than what was sought to be conveyed, wrong data will be collected through responses to such questions

4. *Interviewer bias:* This error occurs on account of interviewer's influence in conducting an interview or wrong recording by him. By putting emphasis on a certain word or phrase in a questionnaire, interviewers can influence respondents to answer in a particular way. Interviewers sometimes even resort to filling up questionnaire without contacting the respondents.

5. *Data processing error:* After the data have been collected, they are to be processed. This involves coding the responses, recording the codes, etc., so that data collection can be transformed into suitable tables. Mistakes can occur during the processing stage of data. As in the case of data processing, errors can occur on account of wrong analysis of data. Apart from simple mistakes in summation, division, etc., more complex errors can occur. For example, the application of a wrong statistical technique can cause such errors.

6. *Interpretation errors:* Sometimes wrong interpretation of data can cause this type of error. In order to support a particular line of action, the researcher may deliberately mis-interpret data. Wrong interpretation of data may occur at times without one being aware of it.

7. *Response error:* If there is a tendency for people to answer a particular question in a certain way, then there is a response bias. Response bias can result from deliberate falsification or unconscious misrepresentation.

8. *Experimental error:* An experiment aims at measuring the impact of one or more independent variables on a dependent variable. For example, take the case of the impact of training on the performance of salesmen. During the period when the training is given, there may be a decline in competition and as a result sales performance may improve. The results of such an experimental study will be misleading.

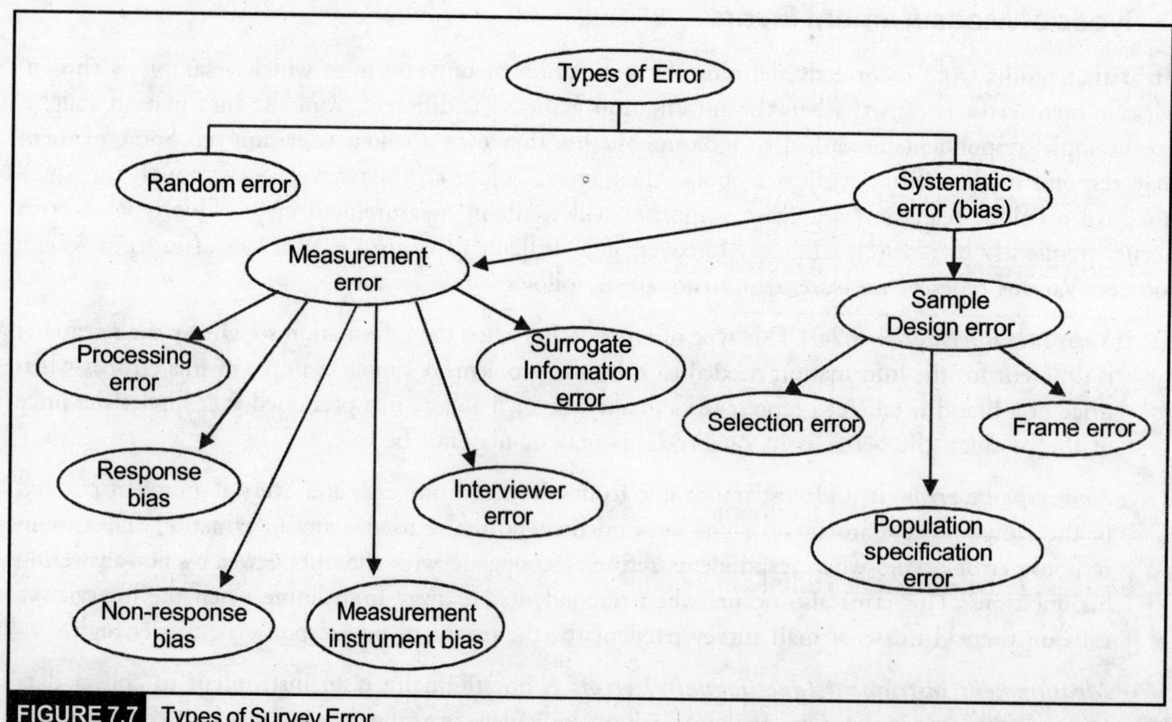

FIGURE 7.7 Types of Survey Error

❖ Strategies for Handling Research Errors

The purpose of research design is to maximize the accuracy of the information that can be obtained for a given expense. Maximizing the accuracy of information requires minimizing errors in the information. There are three basic strategies for dealing with potential errors:

1. Minimize individual error through effective research design,
2. Minimize total error through error trade-offs, and
3. Measure or estimate residual error.

I. Random error	This error can be reduced by increasing sample size.
II. Systematic error	This error can be reduced by minimizing sample design and measurement errors.
A. Sample design error	
Frame error	This error can be minimized by getting the best sampling frame possible and doing preliminary quality control checks to evaluate the accuracy and completeness of the frame.
Population specification error	It can be reduced or minimized only by more careful consideration and definition of the population of interest.
Selection error	It is minimized by developing selection procedures that will ensure randomness and by developing quality control checks to make sure that these procedures are followed in the field.
B. Measurement error	
Surrogate information error	This error results from seeking and basing decisions on the wrong information. It results from poor design and can be minimized only by paying more careful attention to specification of the types of information required to fulfill the objectives of the research.
Interviewer error	This error occurs because of interactions between the interviewer and the respondent that affect the responses given. It is minimized by careful interviewer selection and training. In addition, quality control checks should involve unobtrusive monitoring of interviewers to ascertain whether they are following prescribed guidelines.
Measurement instrument error	Also referred to as questionnaire bias, this error is minimized only by careful questionnaire design and pretesting.
Processing error	It is minimized by developing and following rigid quality control procedures for transferring data and supporting quality control checks.
Non-response error	It is minimized by doing everything possible (e.g., shortening the questionnaire, making the questionnaire more respondent friendly, doing callbacks, providing incentives, contacting people when they are most likely to be at home) to encourage those chosen for the sample to respond.
Response bias	It can be minimized by paying special attention to questionnaire design. In particular, questions those are hard to answer, might make the respondent look uninformed, or questions dealing with sensitive issues should be modified.

Strategy 1: Minimizing Individual Error

Increasing sample size can reduce the probability and magnitude of sampling error; but increasing sample size also increases costs. However, it may be possible to reduce sampling error by moving from a simple random sample to a stratified sample.

Strategy 2: Trade-off Individual Errors to reduce Total Error

Assume that a researcher has initially selected a large sample for a mail survey. The sample is large enough to provide a low level of sampling error, but it has taken such a large proportion of the research budget that there are sufficient funds remaining for only one follow-up mailing. Past experience with surveys of this type indicates that, with one follow-up mailing, the total response rate will reach 40%, with four follow-ups; it will climb to 55%. Given the nature of the survey, the researcher thinks that the non-respondents may differ significantly from the respondents. One solution would be to ask for an increase in the budget. However, such funds may not be available or the resultant data may not justify additional expenditures. A second solution is to "trade off" sampling error for non-response error. Sample size could be reduced, which would increase the probable amount of sampling error. However, the funds thus freed could provide additional mailed follow-up questionnaires and telephone calls to the final group of non-respondents. These errors may reduce non-response error more than enough to offset the increase in sampling error. Thus, the result is a reduction in total error and an increase in total accuracy.

Strategy 3: Measure or Estimate Residual Error

Statisticians and others have recognized this with respect to sampling error. Virtually all studies dealing with random samples report confidence intervals and confidence levels. Unfortunately, many researchers have tended to ignore the presence of other types of errors. Potential errors should never be completely ignored. At a minimum, the researcher should explicitly, if not subjectively, estimate the extent of each type of potential error. If individual errors or the combined effects of the errors are large, they should be reduced by means of the research design or their effects taken into account in the analysis of the data.

❖ Sources of Sampling Bias

1. *Accessibility bias:* Some respondents are more readily selected or included in the sample so they're over selected.
2. *Affinity bias:* Respondents who are most attractive to the interviewer are more often selected, so they're overrepresented.
3. *Cluster bias:* The respondents selected are too closely clustered, so they're more similar to one another than to the population as a whole.
4. *Non-response bias:* Respondents of a certain type more often refuse to participate, so they're underrepresented.
5. *Order bias:* The order of respondent selection over selects or under selects those of a certain type because they're in a certain place.
6. *Self-selection bias:* Respondents are allowed to volunteer and those of a certain type more often do so, so they're overrepresented.
7. *Termination bias:* Respondents of a certain type more often prematurely withdraw their participation in a continuing task, so they're underrepresented.
8. *Visibility bias:* Some types of respondents are more easily identified or recognized than others, so they're more often selected.

REVIEW QUESTIONS

1. What is sampling? Why is sampling important in marketing research?
2. Explain the Sampling Techniques.
3. What is Sampling Design? What are the steps involved in Sampling Design?
4. What is Sampling Error? Explain in detail various sampling errors.
5. What is Sampling Bias? What are the sources of Sampling Bias?
6. Explain the differences between probability and non-probability sampling techniques.
7. What is sampling size? Why sample size is important in research?
8. What factors influence in deciding sampling size?

Case Study 1

The Rayalaseema Ruchulu is a chain of five entertainment restaurants located in four major cities in the South India. The original one was opened in 1985 in Hyderabad by Nivvi. The restaurant offers "a taste of Traditional Royalaseema" in the form of a six-course Drama fest and "ASTAPADULU" entertainment from epic's plays. All is provided by serving wenches bearing pots of pullets and puddings and tapsters wielding mighty spigots.

The unique aspect of this restaurant is that the audience becomes involved in the show that is conducted throughout the meal, with members at each table being appointed Keeper of the food and Keeper of the Traditional Drink. Adding to the authenticity of the atmosphere, Nivvi has hired entertainers from England.

Ms. Nivvi feels that "the key to the continued success of this type of operation is the maintenance of a friendly, lively ambience with a royal feast fit for kings and queens". In the past she has always been personally involved in the operations of each tavern, but that has become impossible since the chain has grown. As a result, Ms. Nivvi has had to pay a premium to hire top-quality tavern managers who have come from England. Despite the care Ms. Nivvi has taken to ensure the quality of the operation,s he still feels that she needs some mechanism that would permit the patrons of the tavern to express their feelings as to the quality of the food and entertainment. Ms. Nivvi is considering three alternative forms of marketing research:

Option 1: A short questionnaire will be placed on each table. The customers who wish to criticize, praise, or offer suggestions would be asked to complete the form and give it to their waiter or waitress.

Option 2: A trained interviewer will visit each tavern in each city on an unannounced basis where he or she will select customers to be interviewed as they are leaving the Restaurant.

Option 3: A marketing research firm will be hired to conduct a telephone interview of a random sample of adults in each of the four cities.

Questions

1. Discuss the types of non-sampling errors, if any, that would likely be present in each of the sampling options that might distort the results.
2. Which option, if any, would you recommend to Ms. Nivvi?

Case Study 2

A business firm, engaged in the manufacture of sports goods, is interested to know the changing patterns of family expenditures for recreation in a metropolitan city. The firm finds it difficult to use simple random sampling, as suitable lists of families are not available apart from excessive cost of contacting families spread over a wide area. Faced with this situation, they approached you for a suitable sampling method. Which method you suggest and why?

Case Study 3

Shyamala who is considering starting her own online grocery service. Two weeks ago, she ran a focus group consisting of 12 of her known friends, some of whom use an online grocer, and some of whom do not. She kept the moderator questions broad, just trying to get a sense of what e-visitors are looking for in their online grocery trips. Some of the verbata statements from the focus group is given at the end of this case.

Those data indicate variance on satisfaction with the current system, and even for loyal users, different levels of satisfaction with different features of the system. Though people seem generally happy, there is clearly room for improvement in elements of online grocery shopping.

In addition, Shyamala is trying to think long-term, knowing that she wants one arm of her business to focus on grocery delivery, and one arm of her business to grow into a profitable consumer research business, offering in-depth insight into the consumer-decision processes for grocery shopping and online shopping more generally. Shyamala figures additional research will be required to understand how to set priorities in potentially improving the software, and the broader questions of how to understand the consumer's behavior and infer the thought processes underlying their behavior.

Shyamala had studied Marketing Research and so she knows that there are many research methodologies to choose from. She is fresh off of her experience running the focus group that yielded the information given below. Although it was fun and she thinks she learned a lot, she doubts that she could run another focus group that could be shaped to address these fairly specific concerns. She's thought about doing a survey-just asking people, "Do you care about brands?" or "Are you price sensitive" and so on. However, she doubts that people would admit to being overly influenced by brand or price, even though their purchases may indicate that they are. She's also rejected an observational technique-a friend had suggested that she sit down next to a person who is about to do an online grocery run and just watch what they do and take notes. She's afraid that her presence would be off-putting and the person doing the grocery shopping might behave differently from how they normally would.

A computer-geeky friend tells her that every mouse click gets stored into a user file and that she should look at what people actually do rather than what they say. She is intrigued by this but understandably is having difficulty in obtaining such data from current online grocery providers. She decides to invest in having a programmer create a smaller-scale simulation of an online grocer. She will ask participants to pretend they are grocery shopping online. She'll strip off each user file and analyze the click stream data. She might run a survey, too, but with the click streams, she'll know just what people did, not just what they say they would do.

Verbatim accounts from Focus group on Online grocery trips.

1. It's great I don't need a car (Current User)
2. It's difficult to just browse, like if I'm not sure what I'm in the mood for (had tried online shopping but is no longer a user)
3. I cant' touch the fruits. I can't read the side of the box of cereals (current user)
4. They chose my vegetables better than I would have (current user)
5. I wish they could pick up my dry cleaning too (not a user but intends to begin)
6. It's kind of expensive. There's a big annual fee, a delivery charge each time and you know you've got to tip the delivery guy. (Current user)
7. This is terrific-I don't like to shop for food even if I had the time, which I certainly do not (Current User)
8. I guess it's Okay . Thing is, there's a <name of grocery> on my way home from work, so that's just convenient for me (Non-user, does not intend to begin)
9. Don't I get any , you know, frequent flyer points things? (Non-user getting used to the concept)

Contd...

Questions

1. Shyamala has considered a number of marketing research approaches. List out the various approaches that she has considered. Do you agree with her assessment or do you feel she was hasty in dismissing any of the techniques? Which method would you recommend?
2. What did you learn from the focus groups verbatim accounts? Was the sample suitable? When would it be important to run two different focus groups, one for users and one for non-users?

Case Study 4

A Company is marketing a new teeth cleaning kit to the dentists in a large metropolitan area. The kit is designed for dentists to use on their patients when they come into the clinic for check-up. The new kit is being advertised heavily in the professional journals read by dentists. The Company's management would like to keep advertising expenditures at a high level until approximately 70% of the dentists in the area are aware of the new kit. They would like you to undertake a telephone survey to determine the level of awareness of the new kit among dentists. They would like to be 95.4% confident that the survey findings are within 6 per cent of the true awareness level among dentists. (Assume that the Dental Council in the area has a list of doctors registered in the area and is known to be 5400 dentists. Assume also that at any time approximately 10% of the area's dentists are not available due to vacation, illness and so on and that all contacted dentists will cooperate to your telephonic query. What sample size you would choose for this study. (Z value for this can be taken as 2).

CHAPTER EIGHT

DATA PROCESSING

INTRODUCTION

Once the data have been collected, the researcher has to process, analyze and interpret the same. All this effort however will be in vain if the collected data are not properly processed and analyzed. Data Processing is a series of steps involved in refining the raw data into a meaningful form for further analysis. If sufficient attention is often not given to these aspects, quality of the result suffers. It is desirable to have a well thought out framework for the processing and analysis of data prior to their collection. Dummy tables should be prepared in order to illustrate the nature and extent of tabulation as also the comparisons of data that will be undertaken. At the same time, it may be noted that certain changes in such a framework may become necessary at a later stage. The researcher should not hesitate to introduce such changes as may be necessary to improve the quality of tabulation and analysis of data.

STEPS IN DATA PROCESSING

The steps involved in data processing are as follows:

❖ Validation

Validation means the process of ascertaining that interviews actually were conducted as specified. In other words, validation process is to ensure that interviews were administered properly and completely. The researcher must determine, to the extent possible, that each of the questionnaires to be processed represents a valid interview. The goal of validation is solely to detect interviewer fraud or failure to follow key instructions. Certain types of interviewing offers no opportunity to observe or monitor the interviewing process while it is taking place. One may have noticed various questionnaires presented throughout the text almost always have a place to record the respondent's name, address, and telephone number. This information is seldom used in any way in the analysis of the data; it is collected only to provide a basis for validation. Interviewer cheating may not be uncommon. For this reason, validation is an integral and necessary step in the data processing stage of a marketing research project. In other words, before undertaking the coding, tabulating and analysis of responses contained in questionnaires, they should be checked for completeness, accuracy and uniformity, which are important. This validation helps the researcher to know:

1. Whether the questionnaires are complete and do not have any omissions or partial responses,
2. Whether the interviewers have interpreted questions and instructions uniformly,
3. Whethter Interviewer was courteous,

4. About the client and purpose of the survey,
5. About the investigator from the respondent side.

❖ Editing

Editing is the process by which data are prepared for subsequent coding. As it is a very subjective process, it is necessary that persons, who are well qualified and trained in the job of editing, should alone be entrusted with this responsibility. Editing is the process of examining errors and omissions in the collected data and making necessary corrections in the same. This is desirable when there is some inconsistency in the response or responses as entered in the questionnaire or when it contains only a partial or a vague answer. We have to very carefully edit the data in order to avoid errors. We have to identify the omissions, ambiguities and errors in the responses. It should be done before data is analysed and many times in the field itself.

Some of the examples of editing are as follows:

1. The respondent has given answers which are inconsistent with each other. In such a case, the editor has to change one of the answers so as to make it consistent with others. He has to use his judgment to decide which answer is correct so that the other one can be suitably changed.
2. The respondent has marked two answers instead of one for a particular question. In such a case, the editor has to carefully examine which of the two answers would be more accurate. Sometimes, when a decision cannot be made categorically, he may prefer to code 'no information' for that question. Editing is of two types. These are:
   (i) *Field editing:* Editing can be undertaken both at the time when the field survey is in progress and when it has been completed. In the former case, it is known as field editing.
   (ii) *Central editing:* Another type of editing is central editing, which is undertaken after the questionnaires have been received at the headquarters. As far as possible, a single editor should carry out this task so that consistency in editing can be ensured. However, in the case of large studies, this may not be physically possible. An alternative way would be to split the entire task into two or more parts so that each part of the work can be looked after by one single editor. In such a case, chances of inconsistencies pertaining to the responses of a particular part can be almost fully avoided.

   Editing demands vigilance and patience; obvious inaccuracies, some of which may be facetious or extremely doubtful, should be rejected. Surveys often include 'check' questions to test the validity of other responses. The consistency and accuracy of the responses over the entire questionnaire are checked during this important phase of the research process.

❖ Coding

After editing, the next task is the coding of answers for analytical purposes. Questionnaires are usually printed with coding so that interviewers can complete these during interviews. Coding is the procedure of classifying the answers to a question into meaningful categories. The symbols used to indicate these categories are called codes. Coding is necessary to carry out the subsequent operations of tabulating and analyzing data. If coding is not done, it will not be possible to reduce a large number of heterogeneous responses into meaningful categories with the result that the analysis of data would be weak and ineffective, and without proper focus. Coding involves two steps. The first step is to specify the different categories or classes into which the responses are to be classified. The second step is to allocate individual answers to different categories. It is desirable to follow some guidelines to ensure the utility and rationality of the code. One of the most important points in this is that the categories must be all inclusive and exclusive. The 'all- inclusive' concept can be taken care of by adding one or more such categories as 'other', 'no information' and 'none'. The other aspect is that categories must be 'mutually exclusive', i.e., they must not be overlapping and ambiguous. It should be possible to classify each response in one and only one category. However, this requirement is often violated when more than one dimension is embodied in a single case.

To give an example, a person may, by occupation, be an industrial worker as well as unemployed. Here two concepts of dimensions have been used. The first is the occupational category and the second is the current employment mutually, exclusive. It would, therefore, be advisable to use two category-sets, one for the occupation and the other for the current employment status.

There is no definite rule for number of categories or classes that can be used. This will be depending on the research problem as also the extent of analysis the researcher proposes to carry out. In large surveys, where mostly structured questionnaires are used, the response categories are predetermined and are contained in the questionnaires themselves. The categories are in the form of multiple-choice answers to the questions.

For Example

The respondent may be asked: To which age group do you belong? 15-30 years, 45-60 years, 60+ years. Here, four distinct categories are indicated and the respondent is supposed to indicate by checking the category in which his age falls. It is obvious that in such a case, the respondent himself chooses the category which is applicable to him.

At times the questionnaires are wholly or partially pre-coded. These questionnaires contain a numeric code for each of the response categories.

Some examples of pre-coded questions are given below:

Questions	Answers	Codes
1. How often these days do you go to your relatives?	More than once a week	I
	Once a week	2
	Once a month	3
2. House?	Three or four times a year	1
	Less often	2
	Never	3
3. Which type of wrist watch do you own?	Hand wound	1
	Automatic	2
	Electronic	3

Sometimes data are transferred from the questionnaire to a coding sheet and then punched into cards. A practice which is frequently followed is to edit and code the data simultaneously. These two operations are regarded as one operation which is looked after by one person.

The respondent has given answers which are inconsistent with each other. In such a case, the editor has to change one of the answers so as to make it consistent with others. He has to use his judgment to decide which answer is correct so that the other one can be suitably changed.

❖ Data Entry

It is the process of converting data from the questionnaires to a form that can be read by the researcher. This process requires a data entry device, such as a computer, and a storage medium. The validated, edited, and coded questionnaires have to be given to data entry operator. The data are entered directly from the questionnaires, because experience has shown that large number of errors are introduced when questionnaire data are transposed manually to coding sheets. Going directly from the questionnaire to the data entry device and associated storage medium is much more accurate and efficient.

❖ Cleaning of Data

Once the data from all questionnaires have been entered and stored in the device then that will be used to process them. It is time to do final error checking before proceeding to the tabulation and statistical analysis of the survey results. Irrespective of the package used to enter the data, it is important to do a final error check of the data or what is sometimes, referred to as machine cleaning of data. This may be done through error checking routines and/or marginal reports. Computer programs that accept instructions from the user to check for logical errors in the data are called error checking routines. Marginal report is a computer generated table of the frequencies of the responses to each question, used to monitor entry of valid codes and correct use of skip patterns.

❖ Classification

Most research studies result in a large volume of raw data which must be reduced into homogeneous groups to get meaningful relationships. This fact necessitates classification of data which happens to be the process of arranging data in groups or classes on the basis of common characteristics. Data having a common characteristic are placed in one class and in this way, the entire data gets divided into a number of groups or classes. Classification can be one of the following two types depending upon the nature of the phenomenon involved.

Classification according to Attributes

Data are classified on the basis of common characteristics which can either be descriptive (such as literacy, sex, honesty, etc.) or numerical (such as weight, height, income, etc.). Descriptive characteristics refer to qualitative phenomenon which cannot be measured quantitatively; only their presence or absence in an individual item can be noticed. Data obtained this way on the basis of certain attributes are known as statistics of attributes and their classification is said to be classification according to attributes.

Classification according to Class-intervals

Unlike descriptive characteristics, the numerical characteristics refer to quantitative phenomenon which can be measured through some statistical units. Data relating to income, production, age, weight, etc. come under this category. Such data are known as statistics of variables and are classified on the basis of class intervals. For instance, persons whose incomes, say, are within ₹ 201 to ₹ 400 can form one group; those whose incomes are within ₹ 401 to ₹ 600 can form another group and so on. In this way, the entire data may be divided into a number of groups or classes or what are usually called "class intervals." Each group or class-interval has an upper limit as well as a lower limit which are known as class limits. The difference between the two class limits is known as class magnitude. The number of items which fall in a given class is known as the frequency of the given class. All the classes or groups, with their respective frequencies taken together and put in the form of a table, are described as group frequency distribution or simply frequency distribution.

❖ Tabulation

Tabulation comprises sorting of the data into different categories and counting the number of cases that belong to each category. Counting the number of responses to one common question is called as univariate tabulation. Tabulation of responses to two questions simultaneously is known as bivariate tabulation and more than two is called multivariate tabulation.

The main objective is to organise the information and prepare the summary that highlights the salient features. While tabulating mainly the responses of open ended questions, special care must be taken in formation of distinct categories.

1. Categories should be mutually exclusive, that is, there should not be any overlap or ambiguity in description of any two categories.
2. Grouping of similar responses. If a set of responses are found to convey similar information, they should be grouped together.
3. Exhaustive responses, it is desirable to construct an exhaustive set of responses for any issue.

The simplest way to tabulate is to count the number of responses to one question. This is also called uni-variate tabulation. The analysis based on just one variable is obviously meager. Where two or more variables are involved in tabulation, it is called bi-variate or multivariate tabulation. In marketing research projects, generally both types of tabulation are used. The tabulation may be done by hand or by machine or some part by hand and the other by machine. The number of tabulations will depend on the number of variables, while the number of responses to a question will depend on the sample size. If the number of variables in a survey is not large and the sample size is small, then tabulation by hand is preferable. On the other hand, when the number of variables involved is large as a result of which there may be several relationships and if the sample size is large, it will be more appropriate to opt for machine tabulation. In marketing research projects, generally both type of tabulations are used.

The various types of tabulation methods are as follows:

Hand Tabulation

If the number samples in a survey is not large and the sample size is small, then tabulation by hand is preferable. Normally, hand tabulation is carried out with the help of a tally sheet.

Example:

	No. of Books Read	**Frequency**
0	~~IIII~~ IIII	9
1	~~IIII~~ ~~IIII~~ ~~IIII~~	15
2	~~IIII~~ ~~IIII~~ III	13
3	~~IIII~~ ~~IIII~~	10
4	~~IIII~~ III	8
5	~~IIII~~	5
		60

Machine Tabulation

On the other hand, when the number of variables involved is large as a result of which there may be several relationships and the sample size is large, it will be more appropriate to opt for machine tabulation. For this purpose, mechanical sorting and tabulating equipments available with such concerns as the Hindustan Computers Ltd and Remington Rand are used. These equipments include key punches, sorting machines and tabulating machines.

For example, the relationship between the economic status and the no. of movies seen:

No. of Movies seen	Rich	Middle	Poor	Total
0	-	~~IIII~~	IIII	9
1	-	~~IIII~~ II	~~IIII~~ III	15
2	II	IIII	~~IIII~~ II	13
3	III	III	IIII	10
4	I	I	~~IIII~~ I	8
5	IIII	I	-	5

The main advantages of mechanical tabulation are:

1. Extensive and large scale survey can be handled conveniently.
2. It takes much less time than hand tabulation.
3. Greater accuracy in the sorting and counting is achieved with the help of machine tabulation.
4. In the case of large scale tabulation, mechanical tabulation eventually turns out to be cheaper than hand tabulation.
5. The inter-relationship between two or more variables can be undertaken easily.

One-way Tabulation

A one way tabulation shows both the absolute frequencies and the percentages of responses. Although it may not be responsible to give percentages, it is good practice to include them, as they facilitate comparisons. The researcher ensures that the percentage figures add up to 100. He has also decide up to what decimal point percentage should be given. Generally, figures may be given in one decimal place. Rarely, if ever, do they need to be given to two decimal places. While such figure would be more accurate, they would be more confusing to the reader. The guiding principle in reporting percentages is that unless decimals serve a useful purpose, they should be avoided. Sometimes only percentages are shown in the table and corresponding frequencies are omitted. In such cases, it is necessary to indicate the total number of cases on which the percentages are based.

It can be explained with the help of the following example:

No. of Movies seen per week	Number of Respondents	Percentage of Respondents (%)
0	9	15
1	15	25
2	13	27
3	10	17
4	8	13
5	5	18

In this example both frequencies and percentages are used so that information can be more clearly understood.

In constructing cross classification tables, one has to first determine which data has to be given primary emphasis and which data has to be given secondary emphasis. Data with primary emphasis are normally given in columns while those with secondary emphasis are shown in rows. This order is repeated for higher order tables, i.e., those having three or more dimensions. This convention is almost invariably followed because it is easier to see data when figures follow one another in a column rather than in a row. It can be explained with the following example:

Income Level	Shopping Center		Total no. of Households
	A	B	
Up to ₹ 1000	100	200	300
₹ 1000 +	120	80	200
Total	220	280	500

The above example gives the break-up of respondent households, both by income level and by their preference for shopping center. A table of this type is also known as a contingency table. This is the simplest contingency table with two rows and two columns.

Cross-tabulation or Two-way Tabulation

Cross-tabulation or two-way tabulation or bivariate or multivariate tabulation is that form of presentation of data which includes two or more variables. The multiresponse questions are properly treated. Cross-tabulation consists of multiple variables and are used for summary analysis of all factors. The cross-tabulation is used to indicate data in which both the dependent variable and the independent variables are categorical. When you want to know how respondents answered on two or more questions at the same time, you will need to run a cross-tabulation. In order to do so, you must first determine which is your independent variable, and which is your dependent variable, since the first is traditionally used as column headings and the latter are found in the row. Independent variables explain or predict a response or an outcome, which is the dependent variable under study. As a basic rule, demographic information is usually considered independent, since characteristics such as gender, age, education, etc., will normally determine the responses we make. If the variables being studied are not demographic, then the independent variable is determined by the study's objectives. For example if the study's objective is to determine whether the level of satisfaction with the past holiday at a destination influences the likelihood of return, then level of satisfaction is our independent variable and the likelihood to return the dependent one.

Identification of Factors to be Cross-tabulated

The cross-tabulation can be successful only if the researcher is able to identify those factors crucial to relationships and then workout the cross-tabulation along those lines. The type and nature of factors used will vary according to the nature of the study, such as:

1. In a simple fact gathering research, the factors to be considered are usually spelled out and the researcher has to merely put the data in the desired form.

2. In the case of applied research, the researcher will select the factors. For instance, the HRM department interested in identifying those key factors resulting in variation in the performance appraisal of its first level executives. The company suggests factors to consider like age, experience

and the package of in-house aptitude tests. The intuitive probing also makes the researcher include certain other factors such as – institute of graduation, curriculum exposed to in the college, nature of summer training/project undertaken by the executive while in college.

3. In a basic research, the researcher will select all the factors to be cross-tabulated. For instance, in a customer purchase behaviour analysis, the researcher may select certain factors such as age, sex, family life cycle, net income, education, occupation, benefit-usage, etc., as those possibly influence the purchase habits of customers.

Limitations of Cross-tabulation

There are two major limitations associated with cross-tabulations:

1. The sample must be large enough to enable simultaneous analysis. This means that sufficient units have to be considered so as to give a proper representation to each cell in the data matrix.
2. In spite of preliminary investigations and familiarity with the situation (to facilitate intuitive feeling of the key factors), it is difficult to be sure whether all the pertinent tabulations have been considered.

Higher Order Tabulation

Higher order tabulation generally incorporates several kinds of information whether related or unrelated. It is a composite tabulation ready for other operation tabulation. This type of tabulation may provide unlimited information. It serves several purposes. This covers comprehensive subject matters and data of all sorts of information of a subject.

REVIEW QUESTIONS

1. What is data processing? Explain briefly the steps involved in data processing.
2. What is cross tabulation? Explain the importance of cross tabulation with suitable examples.
3. What is Editing and Coding? Explain the importance of Editing and Coding in data processing.
4. What is higher order table? Why higher order tables are essential?
5. Describe the main elements of a data analysis plan.
6. Describe the procedure for selecting a data analysis strategy and the factors influencing the process.
7. Explain the data preparation process and the methods used to prepare raw data for analysis.
8. Explain and discuss the frequencies procedure and the use of cross tabulations.

CHAPTER NINE

CENTRAL TENDENCY AND DISPERSION: ANALYSIS OF DATA (UNIVARIATE ANALYSIS)

INTRODUCTION

Statistical test is a formal technique, based on some probability distribution, for arriving at a decision about the reasonableness of an assertion or hypothesis. The test technique makes use of one or more values obtained from sample data to arrive at a probability statement about the hypothesis. But such a test technique also makes use of some more assertions about the population from which the sample is drawn.

Statistical procedures generally require metric scales and non-metric scales. It is understood that there are four measuring scales generally used to present the data. Nominal and ordinal scales are sometimes referred to as non-metric scales. Whereas interval and rating scales are referred to as metric scales.

In performing basic data analysis, the research analyst is faced with the decision of whether to use measures of central tendency or percentages (one way frequency tables, cross tabulation). Responses to questions either are categorical or take the form of continuous variables. Categorical variables, such as occupation (coded 1 for professional/managerial, 1 for clerical, etc.) limit the analyst to reporting the frequency and relative percentage with which each category was encountered. Variables such as age can be continuous or categorical, depending on how the information was obtained. Statistical tests are available that can indicate whether two means – for example, average expenditures by men and average expenditures by women at fast food restaurants – or two percentages differ to a greater extent than would be expected by chance (sampling error) or whether there is a significant relationship between two variables in a cross tabulation table.

AN OVERVIEW OF STATISTICAL TECHNIQUES

The entire gamut of statistical techniques can be broadly classified as univariate and multivariate techniques, based on the nature of the problem. Univariate techniques are appropriate when there is a single measurement of each of the sample objects, or when there are several measurements of each of the observations but each variable is analysed in isolation. On the other hand, Multivariate techniques are appropriate for analyzing data when there are two or more measurements of each observation and the variables are to be analysed simultaneously. Univariate techniques can be further classified based on the type of data – whether they are non-metric or metric. Non-metric data are measured on a nominal or ordinal scale, whereas metric data are measured on an interval or ratio scale. Non-parametric statistical tests can be used to analyse non-metric data. Non-parametric data do not require any assumptions regarding the distribution of data. For both non-metric and metric data, the next level of classification involves determining whether a single sample or multiple samples are involved. Further, in the case of multiple samples, the appropriate statistical test depends on whether the samples are independent or dependent.

❖ Statistical Significance

The basic motive for making statistical inferences is to generalize from sample results to population characteristics. A fundamental tenet of statistical inference is that it is possible for numbers to be different in a mathematical sense but not significantly different in a statistical sense. For example, suppose cola drinkers are asked to try two cola drinks in a blind taste test and indicate which they prefer; the results show that 51 per cent prefer one test product and 49 per cent prefer the other. There is a mathematical difference in the results, but the difference would appear to be minor and unimportant. The difference probably is well within the range of accuracy of researchers' ability to measure taste preference and thus, probably is not significant in a statistical sense. Three different concepts can be applied to the notion of difference.

1. ***Mathematical differences:*** By definition, if numbers are not exactly the same, they are different. This does not, however, mean that the difference is either important or statistically significant.
2. ***Statistical significance:*** If a particular difference is large enough to be unlikely to have occurred because of chance or sampling error, then the difference is statistically significant.
3. ***Managerially important differences:*** One can argue a difference is important from a managerial perspective only if results or numbers are sufficiently different. For example, the difference in consumer responses to two different packages in a test market might be statistically significant but yet so small as to have little practical or managerial significance.

TABLE 9.1 Qualitative versus Quantitative Research

	Qualitative Research	Quantitative Research
Types of questions	Probing	Limited probing
Sample size	Small	Large
Amount of information from each respondent	Substantial	Varies
Requirements for administration	Interviewer with special skills	Interviewer with fewer special skills
Type of analysis	Subjective, interpretive	Statistical, summation
Hardware	Tape recorders, projection devices, video recorders, pictures, discussion guides	Questionnaires, computers, printouts
Degree of explicability	Low	High
Researcher training	Psychology, sociology, social psychology, consumer behaviour, marketing, marketing research	Statistics, decision models, decision marketing, marketing research
Type of research	Exploratory	Descriptive or causal

TABLE 9.2 Applications of Qualitative and Quantitative Research

Topic Area	Settings Best for Qualitative Research	Settings Best for Quantitative Research
Advertising	A company, marketer of Harpic cleaning products wants to come up with ideas for creatively communicating through a television commercial.	Two different commercials for Harpic cleaner have been developed; management wants to know which of the two will be more effective in favorably influencing target customers' preferences for harpic

Contd...

Product Planning and Promotion	The brand manager in charge of Kitchen Aid small appliances wishes to develop an understanding of how, when, where and why consumers use kitchen appliances.	The brand manager wants to conduct a large-scale segmentation study to identify heavy users of kitchen appliances.
Personal Selling	Sales of Ford Explorer have been dropping steadily; the sales manager wants to identify possible reasons for this decline.	From discussions with several dealers, the sales manager suspects that customer satisfaction with Ford Explorer is low and wants to confirm by using a customer satisfaction questionnaire.
Services Marketing	The administrators of Bhagyanagar Memorial Hospital, Hyderabad, want to develop a feel for the nature and the extent of apprehension experienced by patients when they are in the hospital.	The administrators want to ascertain patients' rating of specific attributes of such things as patient care, food service, and medical treatment.
Politics	Environmental researcher wants to understand the environmental concerns of Indian citizens before unveiling his Energy Plan to the public.	He wants to determine the support for oil exploration in the Godavari Basin, and possibly in waters off the beaches Bay of Bengal (% of Indians in favor of it).

ANALYSIS OF DATA

The data is collected, then the sampling is done, simultaneously the interviews are carried out. The collected data then goes for processing. After the data have been processed, it is necessary that these data are analysed.

At this stage, there is a need to understand what is analysis and interpretation. Analysis refers to computation of certain indices or measures along with searching for patterns of relationship that exist among the data groups. From the viewpoint of data collected from survey or experiments, analysis involves converting raw data into information which is meaningful. This usually takes the pattern of estimating the values of unknown parameters of the population and testing of hypothesis for drawing inferences. Interpretation is to convert the new information emerging from the analysis into information that is pertinent or relevant to the study. The researcher has to work out how the new information is related to one another or the existing information and draw conclusions from the gathered data. It means, interpretation gives explanation or finding out the meaning. It involves drawing conclusions from the analysis of data. In other words, interpretation means explaining the figures and facts in the context of theory on which the investigation is done. It serves two purposes. First, it gives an understanding of the general factors that seem to explain what has been observed and the second is, it provides theoretical conception which can serve as a guide for further research. Analysis and interpretation are interlinked. Often, analysis of data and interpretation of results are done simultaneously. The purpose of data analysis and interpretation is to answer a vital question: Does the findings from the data relate to the objectives and hypotheses of the study?

There are several statistical techniques available to do this, the researcher has to decide which of these will be used. The data can be analysed by using: (a) the measures of central tendency, (b) the measures of dispersion (Univariate) (one way or single variable frequency tables), (c) the bivariate analysis (studies the pattern of relationship between two variables), and (d) Multivariate analysis (studies the pattern of relationships between three or more variables at the same time for analysis).

There are two types of tests basically available for data analysis, viz., parametric and non-parametric. The parametric tests can be used if the parameters such as mean standard deviation, etc., exist and are used to develop a test. The basic assumption in such tests is that the source of data is normally distributed. Sometimes the population may not have a normal distribution. However, in research, sample is most frequently used as the sample distribution is very close to normal distribution. That is why parametric tests are used. The parametric tests that are commonly used are: (1) Z-test, (2) T-test, (3) χ^2-test and (4) F-test. Whereas in some situations like psychological research studies, the underlying assumption of parametric tests is not valid. In such cases, non-parametric tests can be used. These are also known as distribution free tests viz., Chi-square test, the McNemar test, Rank-sum test, etc.

❖ Criteria for Selecting the Appropriate Analytic Method

Since so many different analytic methods are available, the researcher may find it difficult to select one which is appropriate for his or her data. In order to help the researcher in the selection of analytic method, Suji Nair suggested the following criteria:

1. ***What is the purpose of analysis:*** If the analysis is meant for summarising the collected data, then the lower level techniques, such as, measures of central tendency or measures of dispersion are appropriate. Whereas if the analysis is to identify whether a significant difference exists between groups of data or if some type of association exists between two or more variables, then higher level methods are needed.

2. ***The type of measurement scales to be involved:*** The scale represented by the number usually determines the analytic methods that are to be used. There are metric (interval, ratio), non-metric (nominal, ordinal) data.

3. ***The number of samples to be involved:*** The study may be pertaining to using a single sample and comparison to be made among units within that sample. Or the study could involve more than one separate samples. A vital question to be answered by the researcher would be – does the analysis involve a sample and a population or two or more sample? Are the samples being studied independent or one another? If yes, the selection of the members for one sample will not limit the selection of members for the second sample. Otherwise, the sample members could be same and used twice or so as the study demands.

4. ***The number of variables to be analysed:*** This is one of the most important aspects which will help the researcher to select the appropriate statistical method. The number of variables could either involve a univariate situation, bivariate situation or a multivariate analysis. So accordingly there will be differences in the type of statistical methods involved.

UNIVARIATE ANALYSIS

Data analysis begins with univariate analysis. Univariate analysis also is the foundation for the bivariate and multivariate analysis. Univariate analysis is the assessment of the distributional properties of a variable. It serves two broad purposes: description and preparation for multivariate analysis. These functions correspond to the two primary forms of univariate analysis, the assessment of central tendency and of dispersion, or convergence and divergence. This mainly deals with the meaning of a typical value and to what extent do values differ from this typical value. Descriptive research focuses on identifying what is the most characteristic of a set of observations. Any variation from this typical value usually is the most important concern with regard to subsequent multivariate analysis. There is a possibility that many times univariate analysis itself is the research goal. For example, we might calculate the percentage of women going for work. Descriptive research emphasizes what are most typical using estimates of central tendency. When univariate analysis is preliminary to multivariate analysis, dispersion takes center stage. This analysis often uncovers at least some technical problems that need to be resolved before other forms of analysis can proceed.

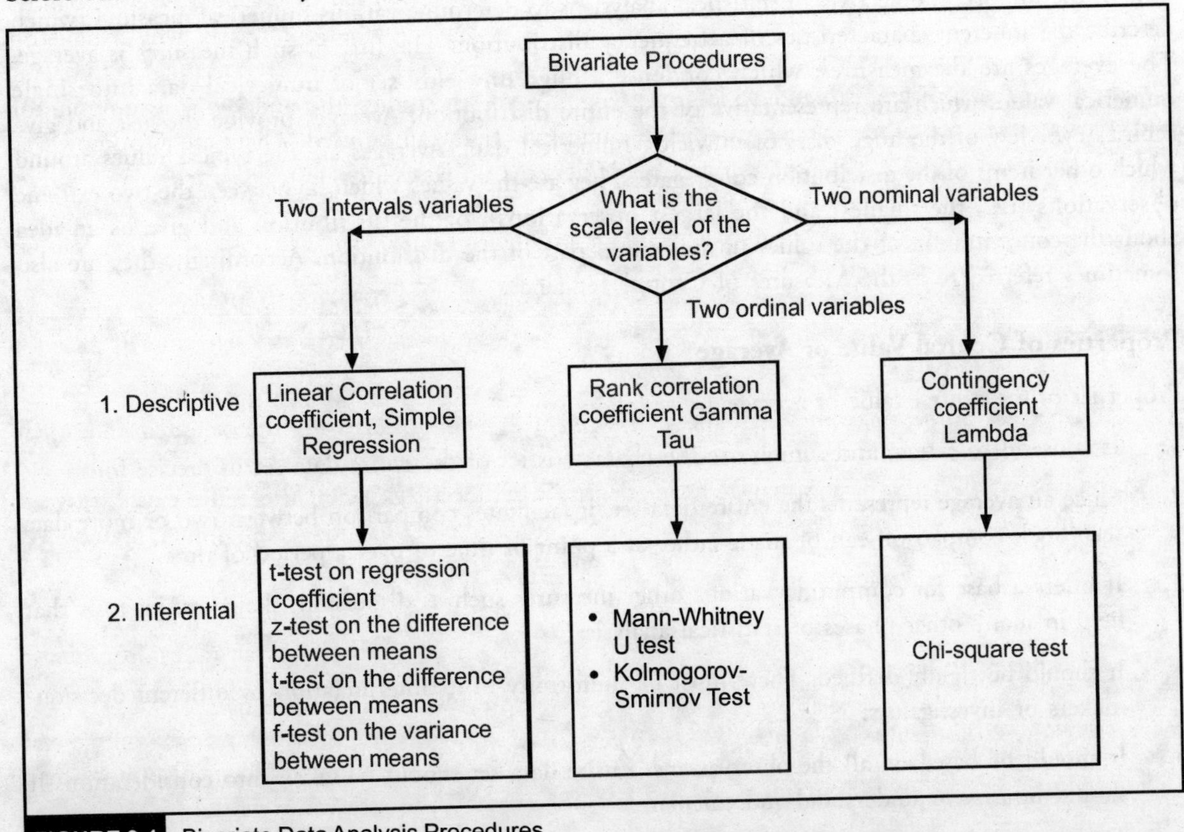

FIGURE 9.1 Bivariate Data Analysis Procedures

Univariate Procedures
What is the scale level of the variables?
Intervals
Nominal
Ordinal
1. Descriptive
a) Central Tendency
b) Dispersion
a. Mean
b. Standard Deviation
a. Median
b. Interquartile range
a. Mode
b. Relative and absolute frequencies by category
2. Inferential
z-test
t-test
Kolmogorov-Smirnov Test
Chi-square test

FIGURE 9.2 Univariate Data Analysis Procedures

❖ Measures of Central Tendency

One of the important objectives of statistical analysis is to determine various numerical measures, which describe the inherent characteristics of a frequency distribution. The first of such measures is average. The averages are the measures, which condense a huge unwieldy set of numerical data into single numerical values which are representative of the entire distribution. Averages provide the gist and give a bird's eye view of the huge mass of unwieldy numerical data. Averages are the typical values around which other items of the distribution congregate. They are the values which lie between the two extreme observations (i.e., the smallest and the largest observations), of the distribution and give us an idea about the concentration of the values in the central part of the distribution. Accordingly, they are also sometimes referred to as the Measures of Central Tendency.

Properties of Central Value or Average

Properties of the central value or average are as follows:

1. It is useful to extract and summarize the characteristics of the entire data set in precise form.
2. Since an average represents the entire data set, it facilitates comparison between two or more data sets. Such comparison can be made either at a point of time or over a period of time.
3. It offers a base for computing various other measures such as dispersion, skewness, kurtosis that help in many other phases of statistical analysis.
4. It should be rigidly defined. There must be uniformity in its interpretation by different decision-makers or investigators.
5. It should be based on all the observations. Entire data set should be taken into consideration. It should be easy to understand and calculate.
6. It should have sampling stability.
7. It should be capable of further algebraic treatment.
8. It should not be unduly affected by extreme values.

The following are the various measures of central tendency or measures of location, which are commonly used in practice.

Mathematical Averages

The measures computed for a sample are called statistics. These are denoted by lower case letters.

E.g: 'n' → no. of observations, $\overline{X}$ → Mean

Measures computed for the entire population are called parameters, and denoted by Greek letters.

E.g: N → Size of the population, μ → population mean.

Arithmetic Mean (AM)

Arithmetic Mean is the first average and is most widely used in statistics. There are two methods to calculate Arithmetic Mean.

1. Direct method
2. Indirect or short-cut method

Above two methods can be applied on three different data series.

They are:

1. Ungrouped Data
2. Grouped – Discrete series
3. Grouped – Continuous series

Direct Method: Ungrouped Data

Arithmetic mean:

$$\overline{X} = \frac{\Sigma X}{n}$$

$\Sigma X \longrightarrow$ Sum of values of all observations

$n \longrightarrow$ No. of elements in the population

In this method, A.M. is calculated by adding the values of all observations and dividing the total by the no. of observations.

$$\overline{X} = \frac{X_1 + X_2 + X_3 + ...X_n}{n} = \frac{\Sigma X}{n}$$

Example 1

Calculate the arithmetic Mean of the numbers 30, 41, 47, 54, 23, 34, 37, 51, 53, 47

$$\overline{X} = \frac{30+41+47+54+23+34+37+51+53+47}{10} = \frac{417}{10} = 41.7$$

Direct Method: Grouped Data – Discrete Series

If data are grouped as frequency distribution, then mean

$$\overline{X} = \frac{\Sigma fx}{\Sigma f}$$

Where,

f = frequency

X = Variable

Σf = Sum of the frequency = N

Example 2

Calculate the mean for the following data.

Marks obtained (X)	4	8	12	16	20
No. of students (f)	6	12	18	15	9

$$\overline{X} = \frac{\Sigma fn}{\Sigma f}$$

Σf = 6+12+18+15+9 = 60

$$\overline{X} = \frac{(6)(4)+(12)(8)+(18)(12)+(15)(16)+(9)(20)}{6+12+18+15+9} = \frac{24+96+216+240+180}{60}$$

$$= \frac{758}{60} = 12.6$$

Direct Method: Grouped Data-Continuous Series

The following assumptions are made to calculate Arithmetic Mean from grouped data.

1. The class intervals must be closed.
2. The width of each class interval should be equal.
3. The values of the observation in each class interval must be uniformly distributed between its lower and upper limits.
4. The mid-value of each class interval must represent the average of all values in that class interval.

$$\overline{X} = \frac{\Sigma fm}{\Sigma f}$$

where,

f = frequency of the class

Σm = mid-value of the class or X

Σf = Sum of the frequency

Example 3

Calculate A.M. for the following data

Income (₹)	10-20	20-30	30-40	40-50	50-60	60-70
No. of persons	4	7	16	20	15	8

Income (₹)	No. of Persons (f)	Mid value (m)	fm
10-20	4	15	60
20-30	7	25	175
30-40	16	35	560
40-50	20	45	900
50-60	15	55	825
60-70	8	65	520
	Σ f = 70		**Σ f m=3040**

$$\overline{X} = \frac{\Sigma fm}{\Sigma f}$$

$$\overline{X} = \frac{3040}{70} = 43.43$$

Hence, the income of men is ₹ 43.43 per person

Short-cut Method: Ungrouped Data

In this method, an arbitrary assumed mean is used as a basis for calculating deviations from individual values in the data set.

Let "A" be the assumed Mean and let

$$d = X - A$$

or

$$X = A + d$$

$$\therefore \overline{X} = \frac{\Sigma X}{n} = \frac{\Sigma(A+B)}{n} = A + \frac{\Sigma d}{n}$$

$$\therefore \overline{X} = A + \frac{\Sigma d}{n}$$

Example 4

Calculate the Arithmetic Mean of the numbers 8, 3, 5, 12, 10

Let assumed mean A = 8

X	d = X – A
8	0
3	– 5
5	– 3
12	4
10	2
Total	**Σ d = – 2**

$$n = 5$$

$$\therefore \overline{X} = A + \frac{\Sigma d}{n}$$

$$\therefore \overline{X} = 8 + \frac{(-2)}{5}$$

$$= 7.6$$

Short-cut Method: Grouped Data-discrete Series

In this case also, arbitrary mean A to be assumed.

$$\overline{X} = A + \frac{\Sigma fd}{\Sigma f}$$

Example 5

Calculate A.M. for the following data

Income (₹)	10-20	20-30	30-40	40-50	50-60	60-70
No. of persons	4	7	16	20	15	8

Take assumed Mean 'A' = 45

$$\overline{X} = A + \frac{\Sigma fd}{\Sigma f}$$

$$\overline{X} = 45 + \frac{-110}{60} = ₹\ 43.43$$

Income (₹)	No. of Persons (f)	Mid value (m)	d=x-a	fd
10-20	4	15	–30	–120
20-30	7	25	–20	–140
30-40	16	35	–10	–160
40-50	20	45	0	0
50-60	15	55	10	150
60-70	8	65	20	160
	Σ f =70			**Σ f m = –110**

Average income = ₹ 43.43 per person

Short-cut Method: Grouped Data – Continuous Series

The difference between earlier and this problem is Class width.

$$\overline{x} = A + \frac{\Sigma fd}{\Sigma f} * i$$

where,

A = Assumed value for the A.M

i = width of the class

d = $\frac{m - A}{i}$, deviations from assumed mean.

m = mid value of the class

Example 6

Calculate A.M. for the following data

Income (₹)	10-20	20-30	30-40	40-50	50-60	60-70
No. of persons	4	7	16	20	15	8

Let assumed mean (A) be 45 and divisible common factor(i) be 10

Income (₹)	No. of persons(f)	Mid value (m)	d=(x–a)/i =(x–45)/10	fd
10-20	4	15	–3	–12
20-30	7	25	–2	–14
30-40	16	35	–1	–16
40-50	20	45	0	0
50-60	15	55	1	15
60-70	8	65	2	16
	Σ f =70			Σ f m =–11

$$\overline{x} = A + \frac{\Sigma f d}{\Sigma f} * i$$

$$= 45 + \left(\frac{-11}{70}\right) * 10 = 43.43 \text{ (Same as earlier)}$$

Weighted Arithmetic Mean

One of the limitations of AM discussed above is that it gives equal importance to all the items. But there are cases where relative importance of the different items is not same. When this is so, Weighted AM is calculated. The weighted means enables us to calculate an average that takes into account the importance of each value to the overall total.

$$\overline{X}_w = \frac{\Sigma(w \times X)}{\Sigma w}$$

where,

$\Sigma(w \times X)$ → Sum of the weight of each element times that element

Σw → Sum of all the weights

$\overline{X}_w$ → Weighted mean

w → Weight assigned to each observation

Example 7

A contractor employs three types of workers, male, female and children. To a male worker, he pays ₹ 100 per day, to female worker ₹ 75 and to a child worker ₹ 35 per day. What is the average wage per day, if there are 20 male, 15 female and 5 children.

Wage per day (₹) X	No. of Workers W	WX
100	20	2000
75	15	1125
35	5	175
	Σw = 40	ΣwX = 3300

$$\overline{X}_w = \frac{\Sigma(w \times X)}{\Sigma w}$$

Weighted AM = 3300/40 = ₹ 82.50

Advantages of Arithmetic Mean

1. The concept is familiar to most people and intuitively clear.
2. Mean is useful for performing statistical procedures such as comparing the means.
3. It is rigidly defined by algebraic formula.
4. It is capable for further algebraic treatment.

Disadvantages of Arithmetic Mean

1. Arithmetic Mean may be affected by extreme values that are not representative of the rest of the data.
2. Unable to compute mean for a data set that has open ended classes at either the high or low end of the scale.

The Geometric Mean

The geometric Mean 'G' of a set of 'n' numbers x_1, x_2, x_3 ... x_n is the Nth root of the products of the numbers.

$$\text{G.M} = \sqrt[n]{(x_1 x_2 x_3 \ldots\ldots\ldots)}$$

The geometric Mean of the numbers 2, 4, 8 is $= \sqrt[3]{(2*4*8)} = 4$

Calculation of Geometric mean – Discrete series

$$\text{GM} = \text{Anti log}\left\{\frac{\Sigma f \log x}{\Sigma f}\right\}$$

Calculation of Geometric mean – continuous series

$$\text{GM} = \left\{\frac{\Sigma f \log x}{\Sigma f}\right\}\text{Anti log}$$

where,

f = Frequency

x = Variable

m = Mid value of the class

Σf = Sum of the frequency.

Merits

1. It is rigidly defined.
2. It is useful in average ratios and percentages and in determining rates of increase or decrease.
3. It is capable of algebraic manipulation.
4. It gives less weight to large items and more to small ones than does the arithmetic average.

Demerits

1. It is difficult to understand.
2. It is difficult to compute and interpret.
3. It cannot be computed when there are negative values in a series or one or more of the values are zero.

The Harmonic Mean

The harmonic mean is based on the reciprocals of the numbers averaged. It is defined as the reciprocal of the arithmetic mean or the reciprocal of the individual observations for a set of 'n' positive values x_1, x_2 ... x_n. The harmonic mean is equal to

$$\text{HM} = \frac{N}{\Sigma \frac{1}{X}}$$

Example 8

The harmonic mean of the numbers 2, 4, 8 is

$$\text{HM} = \frac{3}{\frac{1}{4}+\frac{1}{5}+\frac{1}{6}} = \frac{3}{\frac{37}{60}} = \frac{3 \times 60}{37} = 4.87$$

Calculation of harmonic mean – Discrete series

$$\text{HM} = \frac{\Sigma f}{\Sigma \left(\frac{f}{x}\right)}$$

Calculation of harmonic mean – Continuous series

$$\text{HM} = \frac{\Sigma f}{\Sigma \left(\frac{f}{m}\right)}$$

where

Σf = Total frequency

f = Individual frequencies

m = Mid point of class

Merits

1. Its value is based on every item of the series.
2. It leads itself to algebraic manipulation.
3. In problems relating to time and rates, it gives betters results than other averages.

Demerits

1. It is difficult to understand and compute.
2. Its value cannot be computed when there are both positive and negative items in a series.
3. It gives largest weight to smallest items. This is generally not a desirable feature and as such, this average is not very useful for the analysis of economic data.

Relation between Arithmetic, Geometric and Harmonic Mean

The Geometric mean of a set of positive numbers x_1, x_2,... x_n is less than or equal to their Arithmetic mean but is greater than or equal to their Harmonic Mean.

In Symbols

$$HM \leq GM \leq AM$$

They all will be equal, only if all the values x_1, x_2, x_3 ... x_n are identical

Averages of Position

1. Median
2. Mode
3. Quartiles
4. Deciles
5. Percentiles

The Median

The median is a single value that measures the central item in the data. This single item is the middle most or most central item in the set of numbers. Half of the items lie above this point, and the other half lie below it.

Calculating the Median from Ungrouped Data

To find the median of a data set, first array the data in ascending or descending order. If the data set contains an odd number of items, the middle item of the array is the median. If there is an even number of items, the median is the average of the two middle items.

$$\text{Median} = \frac{n+1}{2} th \text{ item in a data array.}$$

Example 9

Calculate Median for the following data

Data items are to be arranged either ascending order or descending order.

Item	1	2	3	4	5	6	7
Time in minutes	4.2	4.3	4.7	4.8	5.0	5.1	9.0

$$\text{Median} = \frac{n+1}{2}th \text{ item} = \frac{7+1}{2}th \text{ item} = \text{4th item} = 4.8 \text{ (data items are even)}$$

Example 10

Data items are to be arranged either ascending order or descending order

Item	1	2	3	4	5	6	7	8
Time in minutes	86	52	49	43	35	31	30	11

$$\text{Median} = \frac{n+1}{2}th \text{ item} = \text{item} = \frac{8+1}{2}th \text{ 4.5th item} = \text{Average of 4th and 5th items.}$$

$$= \frac{43+35}{2} = 39 \text{ (data items are even)}$$

Calculating the Median from Grouped Data

To find the median value, first identify the class interval which contains the median value or the observation of the data set. To identify such class interval, find the cumulative frequency of each class until the class for which the cumulative frequency is equal to or greater than the value of the observation. The value of the median within that class is found by using interpolation.

$$\text{Median} = 1 + \frac{(n/2 - cf)}{f} \times i$$

where,

$l \rightarrow$ Lower class limit (or boundary) of the median class interval

$cf \rightarrow$ Cumulative frequency of the class prior to the median class interval

$f \rightarrow$ Frequency of the median class

$i \rightarrow$ Width of the median class

$n \rightarrow$ Total no. of observations in the distribution

Example 11

Calculate the median for the following data

Earnings (₹)	0-10	10-20	20-30	30-40	40-50	50-60	60-70
No of persons	7	18	34	50	35	20	6

Earnings	No. of Persons	Cumulative Frequency
0 - 10	7	7
10 - 20	18	25
20 - 30	34	59
30 - 40	**50**	**109 (Median class)**
40 - 50	35	144
50 - 60	20	164
60 - 70	6	170
	N = 170	

Median observation = $(N/2)th = 170/2 = 85th$

This observation lies in the class 30 – 40

$$\text{Median} = 1 + \frac{(n/2) - cf}{f} * i$$

$$= 30 + \frac{109 - 85}{170} \times 10$$

$$= 30 + 1.41 = ₹\ 31.4$$

The Median earnings is ₹ 31.4 per day.

Advantages of Median

1. Extreme values do not affect the median as strongly as they do the mean.
2. The median is easy to understand and can be calculated from any kind of data even for grouped data with open-ended classes, unless the median falls in the open-ended class.
3. The median can be found even for data of qualitative descriptions such as colour or sharpness, rather than numbers. Suppose there are fine runs of printing press, the results from which must be rated according to sharpness of image. They can array the results from best to worst.

Disadvantages of Median

1. Statistical procedures are more complex for finding mean.
2. The data should be arranged before calculating median. If the data is large, time is consumed for arranging data.

Applications of Median

The median is helpful in understanding the characteristics of data when:

1. Observations are qualitative in nature,
2. Extreme values are present in the data set,
3. A quick estimate of average is desired.

Mode

The mode of a set of numbers is that value which occurs with the greatest frequency. It is the most common value. In some contexts, the mode may not exist, and even if it does exist, it may not be unique.

For example:

The set 2, 2, 5, 7, 9, 9, 10, 10, 10, 11, 12, 18 has mode 10.

For example:

The set 3, 5, 8, 10, 12, 15, 16 has no mode.

For example:

The set 2, 3, 4, 5, 5, 7, 7, 7, 9 has two modes 5 and 7 and is called "bimodal", since it has two modes.

A distribution having only one mode is called unimodal distribution.

Mode for Grouped Data

In the case of grouped data when a frequency curve has been constructed to fit in data, the mode will be the value (or values) of x corresponding to the maximum point (or points) on the curve. From a frequency distribution (or) histogram, the mode can be obtained from the following formula:

$$\text{Mode} = L_1 + \frac{(\Delta_1)}{(\Delta_1)+(\Delta_2)} \times i$$

Where, L_1 = Lower boundary class of modal class (i.e. class containing the mode)

Δ_1 = Excess of modal frequency over frequency of preceding class.

Δ_2 = Excess of modal frequency over frequency of succeeding class.

i = Size of modal class

$$\text{Mode} = 1 + \frac{f_1 - f_0}{2f_1 - f_o - f_2} \times i$$

Where,

l = Lower limit of the modal class

f_1 = Frequency of the modal class

f_0 = frequency of the class preceding the modal class

f_2 = frequency of the class succeeding the modal class

i = class interval

Example 12

Earnings (₹)	0-10	10-20	20-30	30-40	40-50	50-60	60-70
No of persons	7	18	34	50	35	20	6

Earnings	No. of Persons
0-10	7
10-20	18
20-30	34(f_0)
30-40(modal class)	**50 (f_1)**
40-50	35(f_2)
50-60	20
60-70	6
	N = 170

Since the highest frequency is in 201-250 class, it is called as modal class.

$$l = 30$$

$$f_1 = 50$$

$$f_0 = 34$$

$$f_2 = 35$$

$$i = 10$$

$$\text{Mode} = 1 + \frac{f_1 - f_0}{2f_1 - f_o - f_2} \times i$$

$$\text{Mode} = 30 + \frac{50 - 34}{2 * 50 - 34 - 35} \times 10$$

$$\text{Mode} = 30 + 5.16 = 35.16$$

Merits of Mode

1. By definition, mode is the most typical value or representative value of a distribution.
2. It is not unduly affected by extreme values.
3. Its value can be determined in open-ended distributions without ascertaining the class-limits.
4. It can be used to describe qualitative phenomenon. For example, if we want to compare the consumer preferences for different types of products, we should take into account the modal preferences expressed by different groups of people.

Demerits of Mode

1. The value of the mode cannot always be determined sometimes there may be a bi-modal series.
2. It is not capable of algebraic manipulations.
3. It is not based on each and every item of the series.
4. It is not a rigidly defined measure. There are several formulas for calculating the mode, usually all of which give somewhat different answers.

Relation between Mean, Median and Mode

For Unimodal frequency curves which are moderately skewed (asymmetrical) the empirical relation is

Mean-Mode = 3(Mean-Median) or

Mode = 3 Median- 2 Mean

❖ Measures of Dispersion

The various measures of central tendency like Mean, Median and Mode give us one single figure that represents the entire data. But the average alone cannot adequately describe a set of observations unless all the observations are the same. It is hence necessary to describe the variability or dispersion of the observations. In two or more distributions the central value may be the same but still there can be wide disparities in the formation of distribution.

Definitions of Dispersion

1. Dispersion is the measure of the variation of the items. **—A.L. Bowley**
2. The degree to which numerical data tend to spread about an average value is called the variation or dispersion of the data. **—Spiegel**
3. Dispersion is the degree of the scatter or variation of the variable about a central value. **—Brooks & Dick**
4. The measurement of the scatteredness of the mass of figures in a series about an average is called measure of variation or dispersion. **—Simpson & Kafka**

Significance of Measuring Dispersion

Measures of dispersion are needed for four basic purposes:

1. To determine the reliability of an average.
2. To serve as a basis for the control of the variability.
3. To compare two or more series with regard to their variability.
4. To facilitate the use of other statistical measures.

Properties of a good Measure of Dispersion

A good measure of dispersion should possess as far as possible the following properties:

1. It should be simple to understand.
2. It should be easy to compute.
3. It should be rigidly defined.
4. It should be based on each and every item of the distribution.
5. It should be amenable to further algebraic treatment.
6. It should have sampling stability.
7. It should not be unduly affected by extreme items.

❖ Methods of Studying Dispersion

The following are the important methods of studying variation:

Of these the first two, namely the range and quartile deviations are positional measures because they depend on the values at a particular position in the distribution. The other two, the average deviation and the standard deviation are called calculation measures of deviation because all the values are employed in their calculation and the last one is a graphic method.

Range

It is the simplest method of studying dispersion. It is defined as the difference between the value of the smallest item and the value of the largest item included in the distribution.

$$\text{Range} = L - S$$

Where,

L = Largest item

S = Smallest item

$$\text{Coefficient of Range} = \frac{L-S}{L+S}$$

Uses of Range in Business

1. ***Quality control:*** The object of quality control is to keep a check on the quality of the product without 100% inspection. The idea basically is that if the range, i.e. the difference between the largest and smallest mass produced items, increases beyond a certain point, the production machinery should be examined to find out why the items produced have not followed their usual consistent pattern.
2. ***Fluctuations in the share prices:*** Range is useful in studying the variations in the prices of stocks and shares and other commodities that are sensitive to price changes from one period to another.
3. ***Weather forecasts:*** The meteorological department does make use of the range in determining say the difference between the minimum temperature and the maximum, temperature. This information is of great concern to the general public.

Quartile Deviation (QD) or Interquartile Range

Quartile Deviation represents the difference between the third quartile and the first quartile.

$$\text{Inter Quartile range} = Q_3 - Q_1$$

$$\text{Quartile Deviation} = \frac{Q_3 - Q_1}{2}$$

Quartile Deviation is an absolute measure of dispersion. The relative measure corresponding to this measure, called the coefficient of quartile deviation.

$$\text{Coefficient of Quartile deviation} = \frac{Q_3 - Q_1}{Q_3 + Q_1}$$

Quartiles divide a series in four equal parts. For any series, there are three quartiles.

First quartile (Q_1) divides the distribution in such a way that one-fourth (25%) of the total terms lie below it, and three-fourth lie above it.

$$Q_2 = \text{Median} = 1 + \frac{(n/2 - cf)}{f} \times i$$

for discrete series Q_1 = (N+1)/4th item

$$\text{for grouped data } Q_1 = 1 + \frac{(n/4 - cf)}{f} \times i$$

$l \rightarrow$ Lower class limit (or boundary) of the median class interval (N/4)th item

$cf \rightarrow$ Cumulative frequency of the class prior to the median class interval

$f \rightarrow$ Frequency of the median class

$i \rightarrow$ Width of the median class

$n \rightarrow$ Total no. of observations in the distribution

Second quartile (Q_2) divides entire distribution in such a way that fifty per cent of the terms below it and remaining fifty above it. This is equivalent to Median.

For discrete series Q_2 = (N+1)/2th item

$$Q_2 = \text{Median} = 1 + \frac{(n/2 - cf)}{f} \times i$$

where,

$l \rightarrow$ Lower class limit (or boundary) of the median class interval (N/2th item)

$cf \rightarrow$ Cumulative frequency of the class prior to the median class interval

$f \rightarrow$ Frequency of the median class

$i \rightarrow$ Width of the median class

$n \rightarrow$ Total no. of observations in the distribution

Third quartile (Q_3) divides the distribution in such a way that 3/4th (75%) of total items fall below it and 1/4th (25%) of total items above it.

For discrete series Q_1 = 3(N+1)/4th item

$$\text{For grouped data } Q_1 = 1 + \frac{(3n/4 - cf)}{f} \times i$$

where,

$l \rightarrow$ Lower class limit (or boundary) of the median class interval (3N/4)th item

$cf \rightarrow$ Cumulative frequency of the class prior to the median class interval

$f \rightarrow$ Frequency of the median class

$i \rightarrow$ Width of the median class

$n \rightarrow$ Total no. of observations in the distribution

Uses of Quartile Deviation

1. As compared to range, it is considered a superior measure of dispersion.
2. In case of open-ended distribution, it is quite suitable.
3. Sine it not influenced by the extreme values in a distribution, it is particularly suitable to highly skewed or erratic distributions.

❖ Mean Deviation (MD)

The Mean Deviation is also known as the average deviation. It is the average difference between the items in a distribution and the Median or Mean of that series.

For Individual observations,

$$\text{M.D.} = \frac{1}{N}\Sigma|X - A|$$

$$= \frac{\Sigma|D|}{N} \text{ where } |D| = |X - A|$$

Where, A = Any Average

D = Deviation from average

For discrete series,

$$\text{M.D.} = \frac{\Sigma f|D|}{N}$$

$|D|$ Denotes deviation from average ignoring signs.

For continuous series,

$$\text{M.D.} = \frac{\Sigma f|D|}{N}$$

$|D|$ denotes deviation of mid values from average ignoring signs.

Uses of MD in Business

It is especially effective in reports presented to the general public or to groups not familiar with statistical methods. This measure is useful for small sample with no elaborate analysis required. Incidentally, it may be mentioned that the National Bureau of Economic Research has found, in its work on forecasting business cycle, that the average deviation is the most practical measure of dispersion to use for this purpose.

❖ Standard Deviation (SD)

Standard Deviation was introduced by Karl Pearson in 1823. It is by far the most important and widely used measure of studying dispersion. It is the square root of the mean of the squared deviation from the arithmetic mean.

Calculation of Standard Deviation

Individual Series

$$\sigma = \sqrt{\frac{\Sigma x^2}{N}}$$

Where, $x = (X - \overline{X})$

X = individual observation

$\overline{X}$ = Mean

from Assumed Mean, $\sigma = \sqrt{\left(\frac{\Sigma d^2}{n} - \left(\frac{\Sigma d}{n}\right)^2\right)}$

d = deviations of the items from an assumed mean

Discrete Series

$$\sigma = \sqrt{\frac{\Sigma fx^2}{\Sigma f}} \text{ where } x = (X - \overline{X})$$

From Assumed Mean, $\sigma = \sqrt{\left(\frac{\Sigma fd^2}{\Sigma f} - \left(\frac{\Sigma fd}{\Sigma f}\right)^2\right)}$

Where d = (x – A)

A = assumed Mean

Continuous Series

Direct Method

$$x = \sqrt{\frac{\Sigma fx^2}{\Sigma f}}, \text{ where } x = (m - \overline{x})$$

from Assumed Mean

$$\sigma = \sqrt{\left(\frac{\Sigma fd^2}{\Sigma f} - \left(\frac{\Sigma fd}{\Sigma f}\right)^2\right)} * 1$$

$$d = \frac{(m - A)}{i}$$

i = class interval

Example 13

Find out the Standard Deviation for the following data of sales per day. 25, 27, 31, 32, 35

Direct Method

$$\text{Mean} = (25 + 27 + 31 + 32 + 35)/5 = 150/5 = 30 = \overline{X}$$

$$\Sigma(X - \overline{X})^2 = (25\text{-}30)^2 + (27\text{-}30)^2 + (31\text{-}30)^2 + (32\text{-}30)^2 + (35\text{-}30)^2$$

$$= 25 + 9 + 1 + 4 + 25 = 64$$

$$\sigma = \sqrt{\frac{64}{5}} = 3.578$$

Assumed Mean Method

Let Assumed Mean = 31

$$\sigma = \sqrt{\left(\frac{\Sigma d^2}{n} - \left(\frac{\Sigma d}{n}\right)^2\right)}$$

$$\Sigma d = (25\text{-}31) + (27\text{-}31) + (31\text{-}31) + (32\text{-}31) + (35\text{-}31)$$

$$= -6 + (-4) + 0 + 1 + 4 = -5$$

$$\Sigma d^2 = (25 - 31)^2 + (27 - 31)^2 + (31 - 31)^2 + (32 - 31)^2 + (35 - 31)^2$$

$$= 36+16+0+1+16 = 69$$

$$\sigma = \sqrt{\left(\frac{69}{5} - \left(\frac{-5}{5}\right)^2\right)}$$

$$SD = \sigma = \sqrt{12.8} = 3.578 \text{ (same as earlier)}$$

Example 14

Suppose that a prospective buyer tests the bursting pressure of samples of rubber tubes received from the manufacturer. Find out the standard deviation of the bursting pressure of the tubes.

Bursting Pressure in lbs	5-10	10-15	15-20	20-25	25-30
Number of tubes	2	9	29	54	6

Direct Method

Bursting Pressure	Number of Tubes (f)	m	fm	m- $\bar{x}$	$(m-\bar{x})^2$	$f(m-\bar{x})^2$
5-10	2	7.5	15	-12.65	160	320
10-15	9	12.5	112.5	-7.65	58.5	527
15-20	29	17.5	507.5	-2.65	7	204
20-25	54	22.5	1215	2.35	5.5	298
25-30	6	27.5	165	7.35	54	324
Total	**100**		**2015**			**1673**

$$\sigma = \sqrt{\frac{\Sigma f(m-\bar{x})^2}{\Sigma f}}$$

$$= \frac{\Sigma fm}{\Sigma f} = \frac{2015}{100} = 20.15$$

$$\sigma = \sqrt{\frac{1673}{100}} = 4.09$$

Assumed Mean Method:

Let assumed mean = 22.5

Bursting Pressure	Number of Tubes (f)	m	d = (m–22.5)/5	fd	fd^2
5-10	2	7.5	-3	-6	18
10-15	9	12.5	-2	-18	36
15-20	29	17.5	-1	-29	29
20-25	54	22.5	0	0	0
25-30	6	27.5	1	6	6
Total	**100**			**Σ fd = – 47**	**$\Sigma fd^2 = 89$**

$$\sigma = \sqrt{\left(\frac{\Sigma fd^2}{\Sigma f} - \left(\frac{\Sigma fd}{\Sigma f}\right)^2\right)}$$

$$d = \frac{(m-A)}{i}$$

i = class interval

$$\sigma = \sqrt{\left(\frac{89}{100} - \left(\frac{-47}{100}\right)^2\right)} * 5$$

σ = 4.09 (same as earlier)

Mathematical Properties of SD

1. *Combined SD:*

$$\sigma_{12} = \sqrt{\frac{n_1\sigma_1^2 + n_2\sigma_2^2 + n_1\sigma_1^2 + n_2\sigma_2^2}{n_1 + n_2}}$$

σ_{12} = combined SD

σ_1 = SD of 1st group

σ_2 = of 2nd group

$\sigma_1 = |\bar{x}_1 - \bar{x}_{12}|$

$\sigma_2 = |\bar{x}_2 - \bar{x}_{12}|$

2. *Standard Deviation of 'n' natural numbers:*

$$\sigma = \sqrt{\frac{(N^2 - 1)}{12}}$$

Variance: The standard deviation is an absolute measure of dispersion. The corresponding relative measure is known as the coefficient of variation. It is used in such problems where we want to compare the variability of two or more than two series. That series for which, the coefficient of variation is greater is said to be more variable or conversely less consistent, less uniform, less stable or less homogeneous.

$$\text{Variance} = \sigma^2$$

$$\text{Coefficient of variance} = \frac{\sigma}{\bar{x}} \times 100$$

❖ Skewness

Measures of variation describe the dispersion of individual values in data around central value. Such descriptive analysis of a frequency distribution remains incomplete until we measure the degree to which these individual values in the data set deviate from symmetry on both sides of the central value and the direction in which these are distributed. This analysis is important due to the fact that data sets may have the same mean and standard deviation but the frequency curves differ in their shape.

A frequency distribution of the set of values that is not 'symmetrical (normal)' is called asymmetrical or skewed. In a skewed distribution, extreme values in a data set move towards one side or tail of a distribution, thereby lengthening that tail. When extreme values move towards the upper or right tail, the distribution is positively skewed. When such values move towards the lower or left tail, the distribution is negatively skewed. For symmetrical distribution mean = median = mode.

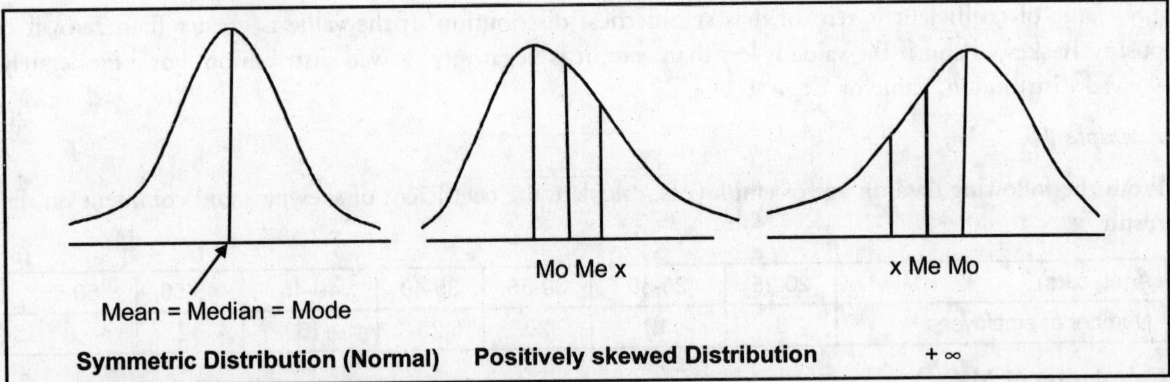

For a positively skewed distribution, AM > Median > Mode, and for a negatively skewed distribution, AM < Median < Mode. The relationship between these measures of central tendency is used to develop a measure of skewness called the coefficient of skewness to understand the degree to which these measures differ.

Measures of Skewness

Measures of skewness can be both absolute as well as relative. As mean, median and mode are identical in a symmetric distribution, the more the mean moves away from the mode, the larger the asymmetry or skewness. Karl Pearson made distance between the mean and the mode as basis for measuring skewness. A measure of absolute skewness cannot be used for the purpose of comparison because the same amount of skewness has different meanings in distribution with small variation and in distribution with large variation. In order to make valid comparison between the skewness in two or more distributions, it is to eliminate the distributing influence of variation. This can be accomplished by dividing the absolute skewness by standard deviation. The following are two important methods of measuring relative skewness:

1. *Karl Pearson's Coefficient of Skewness:* The method is most widely used for measuring skewness. This can be calculated using the formula:

   $$Sk_P = \frac{Mean - Mode}{\sigma}$$

   Sk_P = Karl Pearson's coefficient of skewness

   If mode is ill-defined, the modified formula can be using the relationship:

   Mode = 3 Median – 2 Mean.

   $$Sk_P = \frac{3(Mean - Median)}{\sigma}$$

   Theoretically, the value of Sk_P varies between ± 3. But for moderately skewed distribution, value of Sk_P = ± 1

2. *Bowley's Coefficient of Skewness:* This method is based on quartiles. The formula for calculating coefficient of skewness is:

   $$Sk_B = \frac{(Q_3 + Q_1 - 2Med)}{Q_3 - Q_1}$$

The value of coefficient is zero of it is symmetrical distribution. If the value is greater than zero, it is positively skewed and if the value is less than zero, it is negatively skewed distribution. For a moderately skewed distribution, value of $Sk_B = \pm 1$

Example 15

From the following data on age of employees, calculate the coefficient of skewness and comment on the result.

Age(years)	20-25	25-30	30-35	35-40	40-45	45-50	50-55
Number of employees	8	12	20	25	15	12	8

Calculation of Mean

Let assumed mean (A) be 37.5 and divisible common factor(i) be 5

Age (years)	No. of Persons (f)	Mid Value (m)	d = (x-A)/i = (x-37.5)/5	fd	fd^2
20-25	8	22.5	-3	-24	72
25-30	12	27.5	-2	-24	48
30-35	20(f_0)	32.5	-1	-20	20
35-40 (modal class)	25(f_1)	37.5	0	0	0
40-45	15(f_2)	42.5	1	15	15
45-50	12	47.5	2	24	48
50-55	8	52.5	3	24	72
	$\Sigma f = 100$			$\Sigma fd = -5$	$\Sigma fd^2 = 275$

$$\bar{x} = A + \frac{\Sigma fd}{\Sigma f} * i$$

$$= 37.5 + \left(\frac{-5}{100}\right) * 5 = 37.25$$

Calculation of Mode

$$\text{Mode} = 1 + \frac{f_1 - f_0}{2f_1 - f_o - f_2} \times i$$

Mode lies in the class interval 35 – 40

$$\text{Mode} = 35 + \frac{25 - 20}{2 \times 25_1 - 20 - 15} \times 5$$

$$= 36.67$$

Calculation of Standard deviation:

$$\sigma = \sqrt{\left(\frac{\Sigma fd^2}{\Sigma f} - \left(\frac{\Sigma fd}{\Sigma f}\right)^2\right)}$$

$$\sigma = \sqrt{\left(\frac{275}{100} - \left(\frac{-5}{100}\right)^2\right)} * 5$$

$= 8.29$

$$\text{Karl Person's coefficient of skewness } (Sk_p) = \frac{3(Mean - Median)}{\sigma}$$

$$= \frac{3(37.5 - 36.67)}{8.29} = +0.07$$

The value of coefficient is positive and indicates that the distribution is slightly positively skewed.

❖ Normal Distribution

The Normal Distribution was discovered by De Moivre as the limiting case of Binomial model in 1733. It was also known to Laplace no later than 1774, but through a historical error, it has been credited to Gauss who first made reference to it in 1809. Throughout the 18th and 19th centuries, various efforts were made to establish the Normal model as the underlying law ruling all continuous random variables—thus the name Normal. The Normal model has, nevertheless, become the most important probability model in statistical analysis.

Normal distribution in which the random variable can take on any value within a given range. This is the normal distribution, which is an important continuous probability distribution. This distribution is also known as the Gaussian distribution after the name of the eighteenth century mathematician-astronomer Karl Gauss, whose contribution in the development of the normal distribution was very considerable. As a vast number of phenomena have approximately normal distribution, it has to make inferences by drawing samples. The normal distribution has certain characteristics, which make it applicable to such situations.

Normal Probability Distribution Function

A random variable X is said to have a Normal Distribution with parameters μ (mean) and σ^2 (Variance), if the density function is given by:

$$y = f(x) = \frac{1}{\sigma\sqrt{2\pi}} e^{-\frac{1}{2}\left(\frac{x-\mu}{\sigma}\right)^2}; \quad -\infty < x < \infty$$

where y is the computed height of an ordinate at a distance of x units from the mean μ.

$\pi = \frac{22}{7} = 3.1416$ (is a constant)

e = 2.7 183 (the base of the system of natural logarithms and is a constant).

μ = Mean and

σ^2 = Variance of the given random variable X.

In symbols, it can be expressed as: $X \sim N(\mu, \sigma^2)$

This is read as: The Random Variable X follows a Normal Distribution with mean m and Variance σ^2.

Characteristics of Normal Probability Distribution

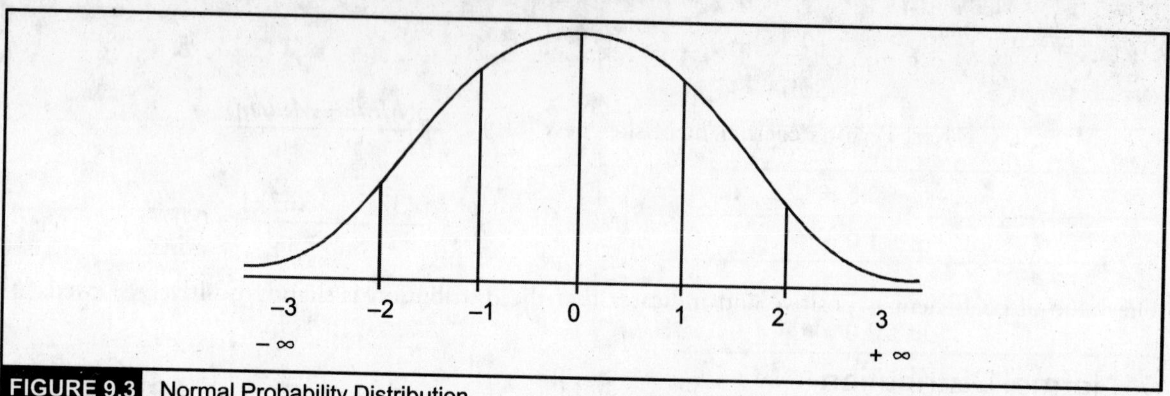

FIGURE 9.3 Normal Probability Distribution

Let us see what this figure indicates in terms of characteristics of the normal distribution. It indicates the following characteristics.

1. The curve is bell-shaped, that is, it has the same shape on either side of the vertical line from mean.
2. It has a single peak. As such it is unimodal.

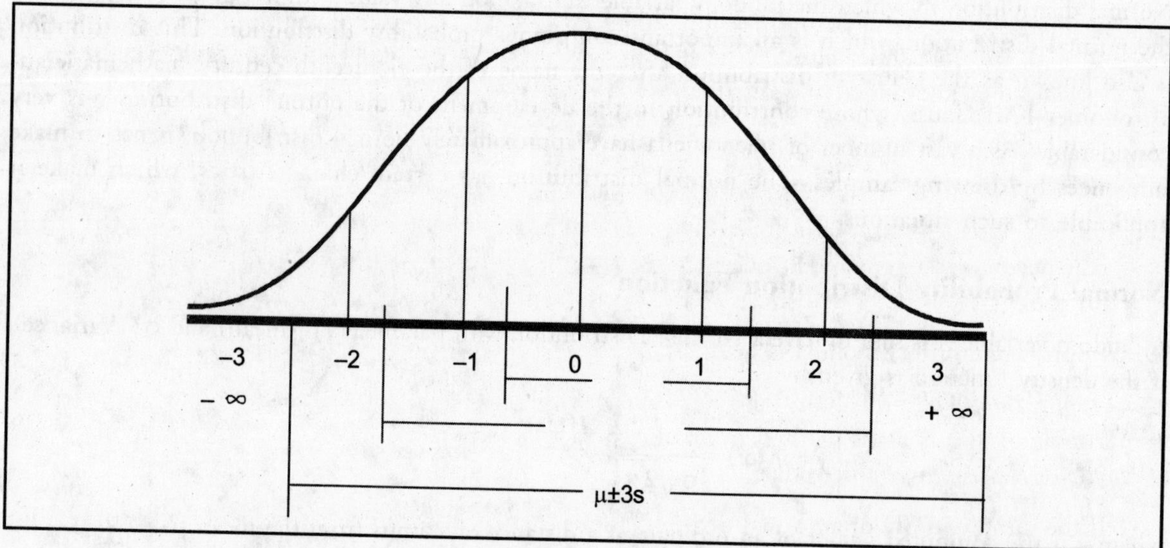

3. The mean is located at the centre of the distribution.
4. The distribution is symmetrical.
5. The two tails of the distribution extend indefinitely but never touch the horizontal axis.
6. Since the normal curve is symmetrical, the lower and upper quartiles are equidistant from the median, that is, Q_3 – Median=Median – Q_1.
7. The mean, median, and mode have the same value, that is, mean = median – mode

Area under the normal curve:

Area between $\mu + 1\sigma$ to $\mu - 1\sigma$ is 68.27%

Area between $\mu + 2\sigma$ to $\mu - 2\sigma$ is 95.45%

Area between $\mu + 3\sigma$ to $\mu - 3\sigma$ is 99.73%

Limits	Area in %
$\mu \pm 0.5\ \sigma$	38.30
$\mu \pm 1.0\ \sigma$	68.27
$\mu \pm 1.5\ \sigma$	86.64
$\mu \pm 2.0\ \sigma$	95.45
$\mu \pm 2.5\ \sigma$	98.76
$\mu \pm 3.0\ \sigma$	99.73
$\mu \pm 3.5\ \sigma$	99.96

The most Important Reasons for its Applicability

1. Normal distribution is important because, a wide variety of naturally occurring random variables such as heights and weights of all creatures are distributed evenly around a central value, average, or norm (hence the name normal distribution). Although the distributions are only approximately normal, they are quiet close. Whenever too many factors influence the outcome of a random variable then the underlying distribution is normal.

   Ex.: Height of a tree is determined by the "sum" of such factors as rain, soil quality, sunshine, disease, etc.,

2. All the statistical tables are limited by size of their parameters (mostly). However, when these parameters are large enough, one may use normal distribution for calculating the critical values-for these tables. Ex.: F-statistic is related to standard normal Z-statistic as follows: $F=Z^2$;

3. Approximation to Binomial is made by taking $\mu = np$; $\sigma^2 = npq$

   Application: The probability of a defective item coming off a certain assembly line is p=0.25. A sample of 400 items is selected from a large lot of these items. What is the probability of getting 90 (or) less items are defective.

4. If the mean and SD of a normal distribution are known. It is easy to convert back and forth from raw scores to percentiles.

5. It has been proven that the underlying distribution is normal if and only if the sample mean is independent of sample variance, this characterizes the normal distribution. Therefore, many effective transformations can be applied to convert almost any shaped distribution into a normal one.

6. The most important reason for popularity of normal distribution is the Central Limit Theorem (CLT). The distribution of the sample averages of a large number of independent variables (random) will be approximately normal regardless of the distributions of the individual random variables. The CLT is useful especially when you are dealing with a population with an unknown distribution.

7. The normality condition is required by almost all kinds of parametric statistical tests. Using most statistical tables, such as T-table, and F-table all require the normality condition of the population.

8. This condition should be tested before using the tables, otherwise the conclusion will be wrong. A normal curve with mean and standard deviation σ can be converted into a standard normal distribution by performing the change of the scale and origin. The original $\overline{X}$ and σ will be converted to o and 1 respectively. The units for the standard normal distribution curve are denoted by Z and are called the Z values or Z scores. They are also called standard units or standard scores. The Z score is known as a 'standardized' variable because it has a zero mean and a standard deviation of one.

$$z = \frac{X - \overline{X}}{\sigma}$$

This transformation will be used widely in Z test in hypothesis testing.

Example 16

The Rural Bank is reviewing its service charges and interest paying policies on cheque accounts. The bank has found that the average daily balance on personal cheque accounts is ₹ 550.00, with a standard deviation of ₹ 150.00. In addition, the average daily balances have been found to be normally distributed.

1. What percentage of personal cheque account customers carry average daily balances in excess of ₹ 800.00
2. What percentage of these customers carry a balance of ₹ 600.00 or lower.
3. The bank is considering paying interest to customers carrying average daily balances in excess of a certain amount. If the bank does not want to pay interest to more than 5% of its customers, what is the minimum daily balance it should pay interest on?

Identifying the Problem

Our random variable represents the daily balance on cheque accounts held with the bank. We know the balances are normally distributed with a mean of ₹ 550 and standard deviation of ₹ 185.

The mean has been calculated on all balances so is the population mean μ = 550.

The standard deviation has been calculated on all balances so is a population standard deviation σ = 185.

1. What percentage of personal cheque account customers carry average daily balances in excess of ₹ 800.00.

First, convert ₹ 800 to a z score by the formula $z = \dfrac{x-\mu}{\sigma} = \dfrac{800-550}{150} = 1.67$

Second, look up table to find the area between the centre and the z score 1.67

= 0.4525

Third, find $P(x > 800) = P(z > 1.67)$ by subtracting 0.4525 from 0.5

$$P(x > 800) = P(z > 1.67) = 0.5 - 0.4525 = 0.0475$$

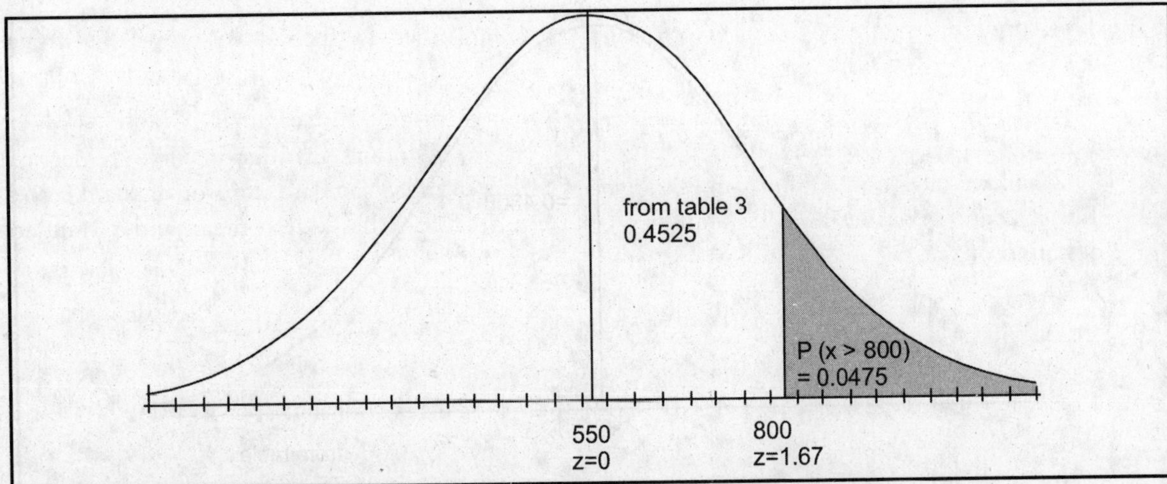

2. What percentage of these customers carry a balance of ₹ 600.00 or lower.

$$z = \frac{x-\mu}{\sigma} = \frac{600-550}{150} = 0.33$$

So $P(x < 600) = P(z < 0.33) = 0.5 + 0.1293 = 0.6293$

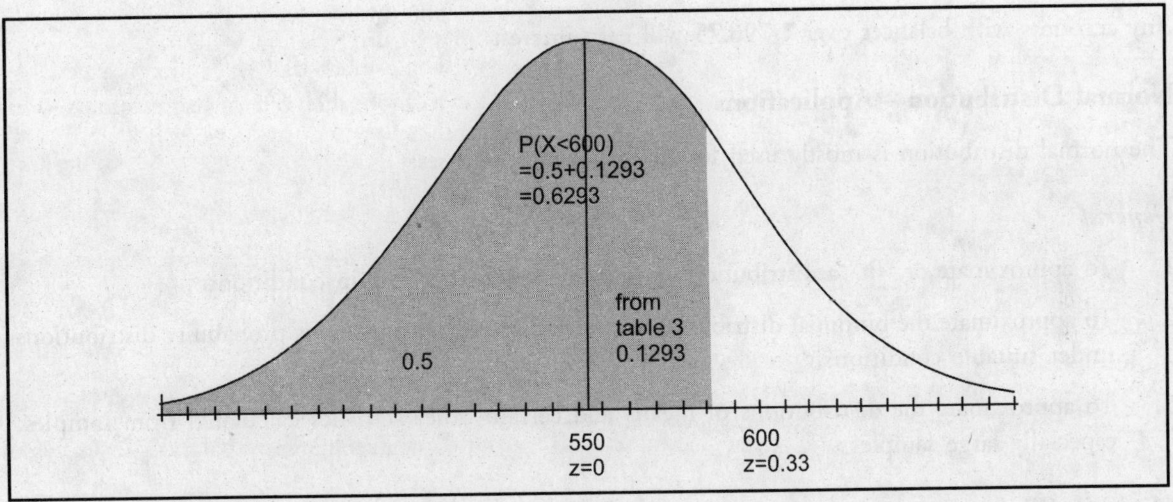

3. The bank is considering paying interest to customers carrying average daily balances in excess of a certain amount. If the bank does not want to pay interest to more than 5% of its customers, what is the minimum daily balance it should pay interest on?

   The bank will only want to pay interest to a few customers so the daily balance limit will be in the top end of the balances. 5% represents an area under the bell curve – in this case the area in the right hand tail.

   First, find the rest of the area on the right hand side of the bell: 50% – 5% = 45% = 0.4500

   Second, look up the area 0.4500 (or nearest area to it) in table 3 to find the z score that corresponds with this area: z = 1.645

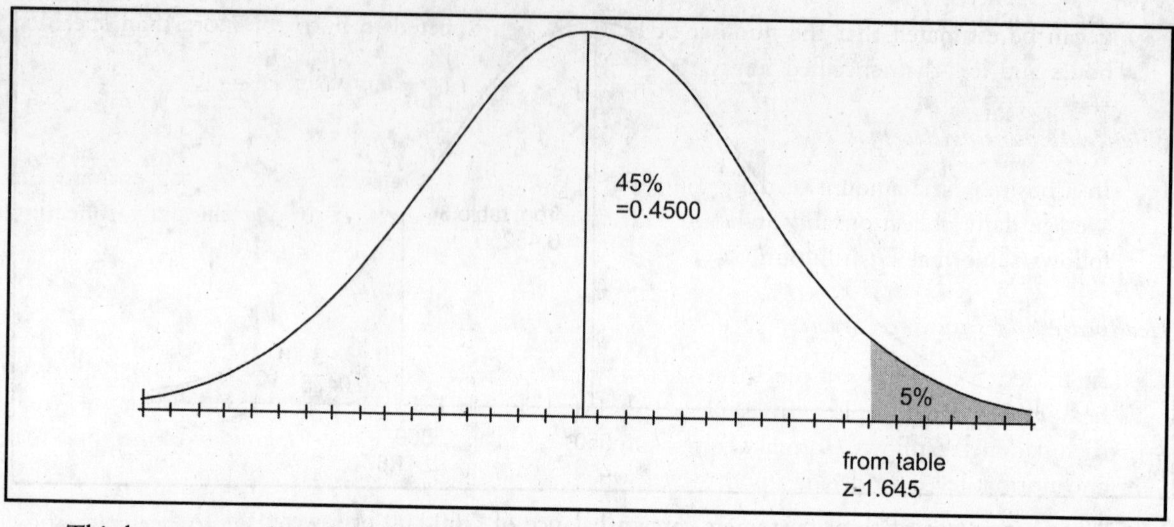

Third, rearrange the z formula to find the value of x

$$\text{rearrange } z = \frac{x-\mu}{\sigma} \text{ to find } x: \; x = z\sigma + \mu$$

$$x = 1.645 \times 150 + 550 = 796.75$$

Any accounts with balances over ₹ 796.75 will earn interest.

Normal Distribution – Applications

The normal distribution is mostly used for the following purposes:

General

1. To approximate or "fit" a distribution of measurement under certain conditions.
2. To approximate the binomial distribution to other discrete or continuous probability distributions under suitable conditions.
3. To approximate the distributions of means and certain other statistics calculated from samples, especially large samples.

Marketing/Economics

1. Estimation of sales in different ranges given the average daily sales along with Variance of sales for 50 branches of a particular company, the Normal Distribution can be applied.
2. For estimation of income levels of group of persons and no. of persons drawing at different range of income, the income distribution can be approximated to normal distribution.

Production/Operations

1. A workshop produces a known quantity of units per day. The average weight of unit and standard deviation are given. Assuming normal distribution, we can find how many units are expected to weigh less than greater than some given weight.
2. A company manufactures Electric bulbs and find that lifetime of the bulbs is normally distributed with some average life in hours and standard deviation in hours. On the basis of the information,

it can be estimated that the number of bulbs that is expected to burn for more than specified hours and less than specified hours.

Finance/Accounting/Receivables

1. In a business, the amount of daily collection is given for a particular period, we can estimate the average daily collection and Standard Deviation of this business. Assuming the daily collection follows a Normal Distribution.

Healthcare and Insurance Services

1. In patient's medical sample information, many parameters like cholesterol, urea in blood, hemoglobin, sugar, lipid profile, blood pressure, etc., are used for diagnostic testing purpose. If each parameter follows Normal Distribution, we can calculate number of patients having abnormal and normal levels to decide upon the treatment to be followed.
2. In insurance industry, if insurance premium follows normal distribution, we can calculate how many persons fall above or below a certain insured amount to plan marketing strategies by the management.

Personnel

1. Given with average and variance of a wage distribution of a group of workers, one can estimate the number of workers in different wage ranges.
2. Given a distribution of training hours of a category of employees, it can be planned for the number of hours required for training an employee to suit a particular work requirement.

REVIEW QUESTIONS

1. "Every average has its own peculiar characteristics, it is difficult to say which average is the best." Explain with examples.
2. What do you mean by Dispersion? What are the different measures of dispersion?
3. Bennett Distribution Company, a subsidiary of a major appliance manufacturer, is forecasting regional sales for next year. The Atlantic branch, with current yearly sales of ₹ 193.8 million, is expected to achieve a sales growth of 7.25 per cent; the Midwest branch, with current sales of ₹ 79.3 million is expected to grow by 8.20 per cent; and the Pacific branch, with sales of ₹ 57.5 million, is expected to increase sales by 7.15 per cent. What is the average rate of sales growth forecasted for next year?
4. Six hundred candidates appeared for an entrance test for admission to a management course. The marks obtained by the candidates were found to be normally distributed with a mean of 152 marks and a standard deviation of 18 marks.

   If the top 60 performers were given confirmed admission, what are the minimum marks (to the nearest integer) above which a candidate would be sure of being admitted?

   Further, those obtaining at least 170 marks, but not qualified for confirmed admission were included in a provisional list. How many candidates were included in this list? (Answer to the nearest integer.)

5. The customer accounts at a certain departmental store have an average balance of ₹ 480 and a standard deviation of ₹ 160. Assuming that the account balances are normally distributed

   (i) What proportion of the accounts is over ₹ 600?

   (ii) What proportion of the accounts is between ₹ 400 and ₹ 600?

   (iii) What proportion of the accounts is between ₹ 240 and ₹ 360?

6. As a result of testing 20,000 Electric Bulbs manufactured by a company, it was found that the lifetime of the bulbs was normally distributed with a mean life of 2040 hours with a Standard Deviation of 60 hours. On the basis of the information, estimate the number of bulbs expected to burn for (i) More than 2150 hours, (ii) More than 2000 hours, (iii) Less than 1960 hours, (iv) Less than 2175 hours, and (v) Between 1950 and 2200 hours.

7. The daily wages of 1,000 workmen are Normally distributed with a mean of ₹ 70 and with a Standard Deviation of ₹ 5. Estimate the number of workers whose daily wages will be (i) More than ₹ 80, (ii) More than ₹ 65, (iii) Less than ₹ 73, (iv) Less than ₹ 55, (v) Between ₹ 54 and ₹ 84, and (vi) Between ₹ 68 and ₹ 82.

8. In a certain business, the value of daily sales follow a normal distribution with a mean of ₹ 20,000 and a Standard Deviation of ₹ 500. Find the percentage of days on which the daily sales will be (i) Below ₹ 16,500, (ii) Beyond ₹ 24,500, (iii) Between ₹ 17,000 and ₹ 23,000.

   The income of a group of 10,000 persons was found to be normally distributed with mean ₹ 1750 p.m. and standard deviation ₹ 50. Show that this group 95% had income exceeding ₹ 1668 and only 5% had income exceeding ₹ 1832. What was the lowest income among the richest 100.

9. The number of solar heating systems available to the public is quite large, and their heat-storage capacities are quite varied. Here is a distribution of heat-storage capacity (in days) of 28 systems that were tested recently by University Laboratories, Inc.

Days	Frequency
0 – 0.99	2
1 – 1.99	4
2 – 2.99	6
3 – 3.99	7
4 – 4.99	5
5 – 5.99	3
6 – 6.99	1

   University Laboratories, Inc. knows that its report on the tests will be widely circulated and used as the basis for tax legislation on solar-heat allowances. It therefore, wants the measures it uses to be as a reflective of the data as possible.

   (i) Compute the mean for these data

   (ii) Compute the mode for these data

   (iii) Compute the median for these data

   (iv) Select the answer among parts (a) (b), and (c) that best reflects the central tendency of the test data and justify your choice.

10. In a small company, two typists are employed. Typist A types one page in ten minutes while typist B takes twenty minutes for the same.

(i) Both are asked to type 10 pages. What is the average time taken for typing one page?

(ii) Both are asked to type for one hour. What is the average time taken by them for typing one page?

11. The following data gives the saving bank accounts balances of nine sample households selected in a survey. The figures are in rupees.

745; 2,000; 1,500; 68,000; 461; 549; 3,750; 1,800; 4,795;

Find the mean and the median for these data.

12. The prices of a Tea Company shares in Mumbai and Kolkata markets during the last ten months are recorded below:

Month (2000)	Mumbai	Kolkata
January	105	108
February	120	117
March	115	120
April	118	130
May	130	100
June	127	125
July	109	125
August	110	120
September	104	110
October	112	135

Determine the Arithmetic Mean and Standard Deviation of the price of shares. In which market are the share prices more stable?

13. Southeastern Stereos, a wholesaler, was contemplating becoming the supplier to three retailers, but inventory shortages have forced Southeastern to select only one. Southeastern credit manager is evaluating the credit record of these three retailers. Over the past 5 years, these retailers, accounts receivable have been outstanding for the following average number of days. The credit manager feels that consistency, in addition to lowest average, is important. Based on relative dispersion, which retailer would make the best customer?

Lee	62.2	61.8	63.4	63.0	61.7
Forrest	62.5	61.9	62.8	63.0	60.7
Davis	62.0	61.9	63.0	63.9	61.5

14. Realistic Stereo shops marks up its merchandise 35 per cent above the cost of its latest additions to stock. Until 4 months ago, the Dynamic 400-S VHS recorder had been ₹ 300. During the last 4 months, Realistic has received 4 monthly shipments of this recorder at these unit costs: ₹ 275, ₹ 250, ₹ 240 and ₹ 225. At what average rate per month has Realistic's retail price for this unit been decreasing during these 4 months?

15. From the following data on the profits (in thousands) of 1000 companies, calculate the coefficient of skewness and comment on the result.

Profit	100-120	120-140	140-160	160-180	180-200	200-220	220-240
Number of companies	17	53	199	194	327	208	2

16. What is analysis of data? Why analysis of data is important in marketing research?

17. Compare and contrast Univariate and Bivariate analysis techniques in marketing research.

18. What is the difference between parametric and non-parametric test.

19. What are the non-parametric tests? Explain the importance of non-parametric tests in marketing research.

20. The following are the responses obtained from 100 individuals about the usage of a brand of a Company X against Competitors before and after a promotion campaign and data is cross-tabulated as below.

Before the Promotion, Brand Used	**After Promotion, Brand Used**	
	Company X	**Competitors**
Company X	15	5
Competitors	16	64

Test at 5% Level of Significance whether there is any significant change in the purchase pattern before and after the conducting of promotion campaign?

21. Two dentists gave the following ratings on a rating scale of 1 to 7 for 12 patients with respect to the degree of cavity on teeth.

Patient	1	2	3	4	5	6	7	8	9	10	11	12
Dentist A	4	5	7	6	3	1	6	4	3	3	5	1
Dentist B	3	6	7	6	7	4	6	7	3	5	5	6

Test for the significant difference in the ratings by two Dentists at 5% LOS. Use Wilcoxon Matched Pairs Test.

22. Instructors A and B both teach a first course in chemistry at a particular university. On a common final examination, their students received the grades as shown below. Test at the 0.05 significance level the hypothesis that there is no difference between the two instructors' grades. Apply The Mann – Whitney U test.

A	88	75	92	71	63	84	55	64	82	96				
B	72	65	84	53	76	80	51	60	57	85	94	87	73	61

23. In sample of 120 persons in a village, 76 persons were administered a new drug for preventing influenza out of whom, 24 persons were attacked by influenza. Amongst those not administered the new drug, 12 persons were not affected by influenza. Prepare:

(i) 2 × 2 tables showing the actual and expected frequencies.

(ii) Use chi-square test for finding out whether the new drug is effective at 5% level of Significance. [Ans: Chi-Square Value=18.968]

24. A certain drug was administered to 456 males out of a total 720 in a certain locality to test its efficacy against typhoid. The incidence of typhoid is shown below. Find out the effectiveness of the drug against the disease. (The table value of χ^2 for 1 d.f. at 5% level of significance is-3.84).

	Infection	**No Infection**
Administering the drug	144	312
Without administering	192	12

25. A salesman of a firm manufacturing a type of cosmetics hypothesized that a type of cosmetic was favored more by boys than by girls. Accordingly, a sample study was made and the result was tabulated below. Apply the Chi-square test and find out whether the hypothesis is justified by the sample study.

	Most liked	**Liked**	**Not liked**
Boys	120	250	100
Girls	110	190	90
Total	320	70	110

26. The number of automobile accidents per week in a certain community were as follows: 12, 8, 20, 2, 14, 10, 15, 6, 9, 4. Are these frequencies in agreement with the belief that accident conditions were the same during the 10 weeks period?

27. A personnel manager is interested in trying to determine whether absenteeism is greater on one day of the week than on another. His records for the past year yield this sample distribution.

Day of Week	**Number of Absentees**
Monday	66
Tuesday	57
Wednesday	48
Thursday	54
Friday	75

28. A sample of 400 managers is found to have a mean height of 171.38 cms can it be reasonably regarded as a sample from a large population of mean height 171.17 cms and standard deviation of 3.3 cms?

29. I.Q. test on two groups of boys and girls gave the following results: Mean of Girls=78, S.D.=10, n=30; Mean of Boys=75, S.D.=13, n=70. Is there any significance in the mean scores of girls and boys at 5% level of significance?

30. A sales clerk in the departmental store claims that 65% of the shoppers entering the shop leave without making a purchase. A random sample of 50 shoppers showed that 35 of them left without buying anything. Are these sample results consistent with the claim of the sales clerk? Use a level of significance of 0.05.

31. A soap manufacturer wanted to know what percentage of the citizens of Mumbai use his soap. He conducted a survey and found that out of 500 persons selected at random for the purpose, only 10% use his soap. He spent ₹ 5 lakh on an advertisement campaign to attract more customers. In order to know the results of his campaign conducted another survey and found that out of 600 persons, 15% are using his soap. Do you think that the expenditure has really increased the percentage of citizens of Mumbai using his soap?

32. You are given the following data about the life of two brands of bulbs:

	Sample size	Mean life (in hours)	Standard deviation (in hours)
Brand A	12	2,000	250
Brand B	15	2,230	300

Do you think that there is a significant difference in the quality of the two brands of bulbs?

33. Twelve persons are appointed in clerical position in an office. Their performance is noted by giving a test and the marks recorded out of 10. They are given 3 month's training and again they are given a test and marks recorded out of 12 are as given below.

Employee	A	B	C	D	E	F	G	H	I	J	K	L
Before	4	5	3	7	8	6	5	9	10	6	4	3
After	5	4	6	8	7	5	9	9	10	6	5	4

Can we conclude that the training has improved the performance of the employees?

Case Study

Consider the following data obtained from a survey conducted by an Internal Tourism restaurant in India.

Respondent	Sex	Age	Race	Preferences for lunch time meal		Average Consumption per week of preferred	
				Food	Drink	Food	Drink
1	M	24	Malaysian	Malaysian	Cola	3	6
2	M	32	Indian	Indian	Cola	2	4
3	M	20	Chinese	Indian	Non-cola	6	5
4	F	22	Indian	Chinese	Cola	1	3
5	M	19	Chinese	Indian	Cola	3	2
6	F	25	Chinese	Indian	Non-cola	4	7
7	M	36	Indian	Chinese	Non-cola	8	6
8	M	18	Chinese	Chinese	Cola	3	9
9	F	35	Chinese	Chinese	Cola	3	2
10	M	23	Malaysian	Malaysian	Non-cola	4	7
11	F	18	Indian	Malaysian	Cola	3	4
12	F	19	Chinese	Malaysian	Cola	4	8
13	F	27	Malaysian	Indian	Non-cola	4	2
14	M	30	Malaysian	Indian	Cola	5	4
15	M	32	Indian	Indian	Cola	6	6
16	M	26	Malaysian	Chinese	Non-cola	5	1
17	F	25	Malaysian	Chinese	Cola	8	2
18	M	27	Indian	Chinese	Cola	9	6
19	F	28	Indian	Indian	Cola	5	5
20	M	33	Indian	Chinese	Non-cola	3	6

Analyze the data and write a short report. Your report must contain.

1. A frequency distribution of respondents' age, gender and race.
2. Total consumption of three types of foods and two types of drinks.
3. Cross-tabulation of the respondent's: Age and sex with drink preference, and race and sex with food and drink preference.
4. Other observations about the data.

CHAPTER TEN

HYPOTHESIS TESTING

INTRODUCTION

Hypothesis may be defined as a proposition or a set of propositions, set forth as an explanation for the occurrence of some specified group of phenomenon either asserted merely as a provisional conjecture to guide some investigation or accepted as highly probable in the light of established facts. A research hypothesis is quite often a predictive statement, which is capable of being tested using scientific methods that involve an independent and some dependent variables. Hypothesis is a proposition temporarily accepted as true in the light of what is, at the time, known about a phenomenon. It is adopted as a tool for action in the search for truth.

Lundberg defines hypothesis as a "*tentative generalisaton, the validity of which remains to be tested. In its most elementary stages, the hypothesis may be any hunch, guess, imaginative idea which becomes a basis for action or investigation*".

Johson described hypothesis as "*Islands in the uncharted seas of thought to be used as bases for consolidation and recuperation as we advance into the unknown*".

In other words, hypothesis gives the researcher a basis for the meaning. For instance, the following statements may be considered:

1. Students who take tuitions perform better than the others who not receive tuitions.
2. The female students perform as well as the male students.
3. Officers in my organization have higher than average level of commitment (variable).
4. Level of job commitment of the officers is associated with their level of efficiency.
5. Level of job commitment of the officers is positively associated with their level of efficiency.
6. The higher the level of job commitment of the officers, the lower their level of absenteeism.

These statements are hypotheses that can be objectively verified and tested. Thus, they indicate that a hypothesis states what one is looking for. Besides, it is a proposition that can be put to test in order to examine its validity.

CONCEPT OF HYPOTHESIS

In order to make decisions, it is necessary to make certain assumptions about the population parameters. These assumptions are referred to as "Hypothesis". Then a sample or samples are taken to estimate the values of these population parameters. If these estimates coincide with our assumptions, then we accept the "Hypothesis" as being correct. If the value of the sample statistic, thus, calculated is different from the assumption about the population parameter, then a decision must be made whether this difference was purely a matter of chance with which it happens in nature or whether this difference is significant so that it is the real difference and our assumptions about the population parameter are wrong. Since we are testing for our assumptions on "Hypothesis" being correct or not, this field of decision-making is known as "Hypothesis testing".

❖ Characteristics of Hypothesis

A hypothesis should have the following characteristic features:

1. A hypothesis must be precise and clear. If it is not precise and clear, then the inferences drawn on its basis would not be reliable.
2. A hypothesis must be capable of being put to test. Quite often, the research programmes fail owing to its incapability of being subject to testing for validity. Therefore, some prior study may be conducted by the researcher in order to make a hypothesis testable. A hypothesis "is tested if other deductions can be made from it, which in turn can be confirmed or disproved by observation".
3. A hypothesis must state relationship between two variables, in the case of relational hypotheses.
4. A hypothesis must be specific and limited in scope. This is because a simpler hypothesis generally would be easier to test for the research. And therefore, he/she must formulate such hypotheses.
5. As far as possible, a hypothesis must be stated in the most simple language, so as to make it understood by all concerned, however, it should be noted that simplicity of a hypothesis is not related to its significance.
6. A hypothesis must be consistent and derived from the most known facts. In other words, it should be consistent with a substantial body of established facts. That is, it must be in the form of a statement which judges accept as being the most likely to occur.
7. A hypothesis must be amenable to testing within a stipulated or reasonable period of time. No matter how excellent a hypothesis, a researcher should not use it if it cannot be tested within a given period of time, as none can afford to spend a life-time on collecting data to test it.
8. A hypothesis should state the facts that gave rise to the necessity of looking for an explanation. This is to say that by using the hypothesis, and other known and accepted generalizations, a researcher must be able to derive the original problem condition. Therefore, a hypothesis should explain what it actually wants to explain, and for this, it should also have an empirical reference.
   (i) *Clarity:* The hypothesis must be conceptually clear. The concepts embodied in the hypothesis be defined in a way commonly communicable and acceptable.
   (ii) *Testable:* Hypothesis should be empirically testable. Hypothesis must be framed to draw logical inferences which can be tested with the help of available techniques.
   (iii) *Precise:* The hypothesis should be precise and specific. The hypothesis should be narrow in its scope and precise in its expression.
   (iv) *Related to existing theory:* The hypothesis should be related to the existing knowledge and framed based on the present situation.
   (v) *Known facts:* The hypothesis should be consistent with known facts.

❖ Importance of Hypothesis

Hypothesis plays an important role in the research field. The research problem that is to be investigated must be based on the hypothesis. In other words, there may not be any systematic research without hypothesis. The hypothesis will act as a guide to the researcher. Hypothesis clears fog and clarifies certain doubts. The hypothesis gives confidence to the researcher to go ahead into the unknown environment. The hypothesis tries to establish rapport from past to the future and finally hypothesis gives aimful and gainful search for the researcher.

❖ Role of Hypothesis in Research

In research, a hypothesis serves several important functions:

1. ***It guides the direction of the study:*** Quite frequently, one comes across a situation when the researcher tries to collect all possible information on which he could lay his hands on. Later on, he may find that only part of it he could utilize. Hence, there was an unnecessary use of resources on trivial concerns. In such a situation, hypothesis limits what shall be studied and what shall not be.
2. ***It identifies facts that are relevant and those that are not:*** Who shall be studied (married couples), in what context, they shall be studied (their consumer decision-making), and what shall be studied (their individual perceptions of their roles).
3. ***It suggests which form of research design is likely to be the most appropriate:*** Depending upon the type of hypothesis, a decision is made about the relative appropriateness of different research designs for the study under consideration. The design could be a survey design, experimental design, content analysis, case study, participation observation study, and/or Focus Group Discussions.
4. It provides a framework for organizing the conclusions of the findings.

❖ Formulations of Hypothesis

The formulation of hypothesis foı the purpose of the study will be from any one of the following sources:

1. Existing knowledge about the field of the study.
2. The findings of the previous research studies.
3. The existing environment and culture.
4. Pre-study findings or Pilot study findings.
5. Experiences of the researchers in the relevant field of study.

These are testable propositions. First hypothesis contains only one variable. The second one has two variables, which have been shown to be associated with each other but the nature of association has not been specified (non-directional relationship). In the third hypothesis, we have gone a step further where in addition to the relationship between the two variables, the direction of relationship (positive) has also been given. In the fourth hypothesis, level of efficiency has been replaced with level of absenteeism, the direction of relationship between the two variables has been specified (which is negative). In the following discussion, you will find these hypotheses being quoted as part of the examples.

❖ Types of Hypothesis

Hypothesis is classified into the following categories:

1. ***Descriptive Hypothesis:*** Descriptive hypothesis contains only one variable and thereby it is also called as univariate hypothesis. Descriptive hypothesis typically state the existence, size, form, or distribution of some variable.

   The first hypothesis contains only one variable. It only shows the distribution of the level of commitment among the officers of the organization which is higher than average. Such a hypothesis is an example of a Descriptive Hypothesis.

   Researchers usually use research questions rather than descriptive hypothesis. For example, a question can be: What is the level of commitment of the officers in your organization?

2. ***Relational Hypothesis:*** These are the propositions that describe a relationship between two variables. The relationship could be non-directional or directional, positive or negative, causal or simply correlational. While stating the relationship between the two variables, if the terms of positive, negative, more than, or less than are used then such hypotheses are directional because the direction of the relationship between the variables (positive/negative) has been indicated. These hypotheses are relational as well as directional. The directional hypothesis is the one in which the direction of the relationship has been specified. Non-directional hypothesis is one in which the direction of the association has not been specified. The relationship may be very strong but whether it is positive or negative has not been postulated.

   (i) *Correlational Hypotheses:* State merely that the variables occur together in some specified manner without implying that one causes the other. Such weak claims are often made when we believe that there are more basic causal forces that affect both variables. For example: Level of job commitment of the officers is positively associated with their level of efficiency.

   Here we do not make any claim that one variable causes the other to change. That will be possible only if we have control on all other factors that could influence our dependent variable.

   (ii) *Explanatory (causal) Hypotheses:* Imply the existence of, or a change in, one variable causes or leads to a change in the other variable. This brings in the notions of independent and the dependent variables. Cause means to "help make happen." So the independent variable may not be the sole reason for the existence of, or change in the dependent variable. The researcher may have to identify the other possible causes, and control their effect in case the causal effect of independent variable has to be determined on the dependent variable. This may be possible in an experimental design of research.

   Different ways to state Hypotheses:

   (a) Hi motivation causes hi efficiency.

   (b) Hi motivation leads to hi efficiency.

   (c) Hi motivation is related to hi efficiency.

   (d) Hi motivation influences hi efficiency.

   (e) Hi motivation is associated with hi efficiency.

   (f) Hi motivation produces hi efficiency.

   (g) Hi motivation results in hi efficiency.

(h) If hi motivation then hi efficiency.

(i) The higher the motivation, the higher the efficiency

3. ***Null Hypothesis:*** If a hypothesis asserts that there is no difference between sample statistic and parameter then it is called "Null Hypothesis" or a claim or Hypothesis about the values of population parameters is known as "Null Hypothesis" and is usually denoted by H_o.

4. ***Alternative Hypothesis:*** Any hypothesis which is complementary to the null hypothesis is called an "Alternative hypothesis" and is usually denoted by H_1. The alternative hypothesis is the hypothesis that sample observations are influenced by some non-random cause. For example, suppose we wanted to determine whether a coin was fair and balanced. A null hypothesis might be that half the flips would result in Heads and half, in Tails. The alternative hypothesis might be that the number of Heads and Tails would be very different. Suppose we flipped the coin 50 times, resulting in 40 Heads and 10 Tails. Given this result, we would be inclined to reject the null hypothesis and accept the alternative hypothesis. The term "null" means nothing or invalid. It may be written as: H_0: $\mu = \mu_0$, where, H_0 is the null hypothesis and μ_0 is the mean of the population. The alternative hypothesis is H_A: $\mu = \mu_0$. The rejection of the null hypothesis will show that the mean of the population is not µ0. If this happens, then it implies that the alternative hypothesis is accepted. There can be more than two or more alternative hypothesis though only one can be tested at a time against the null hypothesis.

Null Hypothesis:

(i) There is no difference between the mean height of men and women.

(ii) There is no relationship between highest education level achieved and yearly salary.

Alternative Hypothesis:

(i) Men are taller than women.

(i) Increasing the education level achieved increases one's yearly salary.

5. ***Simple Hypothesis:*** If the hypothesis completely specifies the population or its parameters, then it is known as simple hypothesis.

6. ***Composite Hypothesis:*** Any hypothesis, which is complementary to the simple hypothesis, is known as Composite Hypothesis. In sampling from a normal population $N(\mu, \sigma^2)$, the hypothesis

H_0: $\mu = \mu_0$ and $\sigma^2 = \sigma_0^2$

is a simple hypothesis since it completely specifies the distribution. On the other hand, each of the following hypothesis is a composite hypothesis.

(i) H_0: $\mu = \mu_0$ (Nothing is known about σ^2)

(ii) H_0: $\mu < \mu_0$ (Given $\sigma^2 = \sigma_0^2$)

(iii) H_0: $\mu > \mu_0$, (Given $\sigma^2 = \sigma_0^2$) and so on.

❖ Process of Hypothesis Testing

The general procedure followed in testing hypothesis comprises of the following six steps.

1. ***Setup a hypothesis:*** The first step in hypothesis testing is to establish the hypothesis to be tested. Since statistical hypothesis are usually assumptions about the value of some unknown parameter,

the hypothesis specifies a numerical value or range of values for the parameter. The conventional approach to hypothesis testing is not to construct single hypothesis about the population parameter, but rather to set up two different hypothesis. These hypotheses are normally referred to as (i) null hypothesis denoted by H_0 and (ii) alternative hypothesis denoted by H_1.

If the sample information leads us to reject H_0, then we will accept the alternative hypothesis H_1. Thus, the two hypotheses are constructed so that if one is true, the other is false and vice-versa.

The rejection of the null hypothesis indicates that the difference has statistical significance and the acceptance of the null hypothesis indicates that the difference is due to chance. As against the null hypothesis, the alternative hypothesis specifies those values that the researcher believes to hold true. The alternative hypothesis my embrace the whole range of values rather than single point.

2. ***Setup a suitable significance level:*** Having set up a hypothesis, the next step is to select a suitable level of significance. The confidence with which an experimenter rejects or retains null hypothesis depends on the significance level adopted. The level of significance usually denoted by "a" is generally specified before any samples are drawn, so that results obtained will not influence our choice. Though any level of significance can be adopted, in practice we either take 5 per cent or 1 per cent level of significance. When we take 5 per cent level of significance, then there are about 5 chances out of 100 that we would reject the null hypothesis when it should be accepted, i.e., we are about 95 per cent confident that we have made the right decision. When we test a hypothesis at a 1 per cent level of significance, there is only one chance out of 100 that we would reject the null hypothesis. When it should be accepted, i.e., we are about 99 per cent confident that we have made the right decision. When the null hypothesis is rejected at $\alpha = 0.05$, the test result is said to be "significant". When the null hypothesis is rejected at $\alpha = 0.01$, the test result is said to be "highly significant".

3. ***Determination of a suitable test statistic:*** The third step is to determine a suitable test statistic and its distribution. Many of the test statistics that we shall encounter will be of the following form:

$$\text{Test Statistic} = \left[\frac{\text{(Sample Statistic)} - \text{(Hypothesized Population Parameter)}}{\text{Standard Error of the Sample Statistic}}\right]$$

State the test statistic (Z, t, χ^2, F, etc.) that will be used to conduct the hypothesis test (the appropriate test statistics for the different kinds of hypothesis tests are given in the tables of the reference page, "Statistical Inference for Values of Population Parameters").

Calculate the value of the test statistic, using the sample data. (If you are using Excel or SAS, or some similar computer package, you will calculate the value of the test statistic, along with a p-value.)

"p" value

A p-value (or probability value) is the probability of getting a value of the sample test statistics that is at least as extreme as the one found from the sample data, assuming the null hypothesis is true. Traditionally, statisticians used "alpha" values that set up a dichotomy: reject/fail to reject conclusion. P-values measure how confident we are in rejecting a null hypothesis. If a p-value is less than 0.01, we say this is "highly statistically significant" and there is very strong evidence against the null hypothesis. P-values between 0.01 and 0.05, indicate that it is statistically significant and adequate evidence against the null hypothesis. For p-values greater than 0.05, there is, generally, insufficient evidence against the null hypothesis.

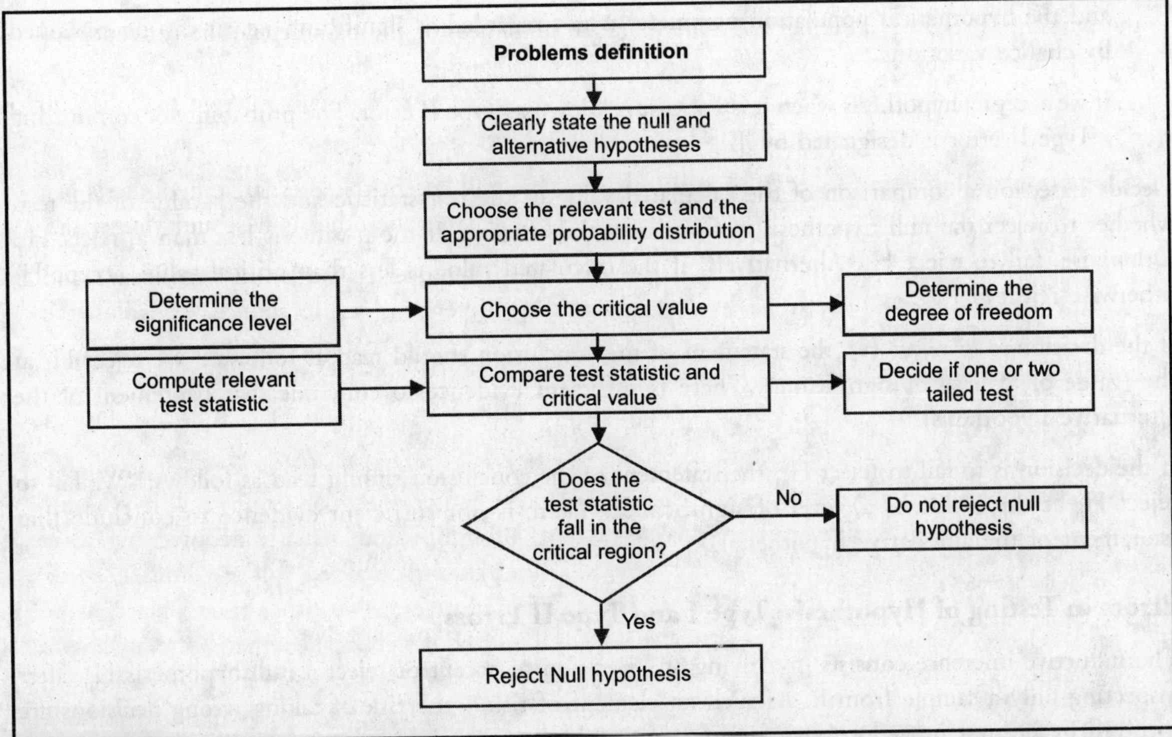

FIGURE 10.1 Steps of Hypothesis Testing

4. *Determination of Critical Region:* It is important to specify, before the sample is taken, which values of the test statistic will lead to rejection of H_0 and which values of the test statistic will lead to the acceptance of H_0. The former is called the critical region. The value of α, the level of significance indicate the importance that one attaches to the consequences associated with incorrectly rejecting H_0. It can be shown that when the level of significance is a, the optimal critical region for a two-sided test consists of that $\frac{\alpha}{2}$ per cent of the area in the right-hand side of the distribution plus that $\frac{\alpha}{2}$ per cent in the left hand side. Thus, establishing a critical region is similar to determining a 100(1-α)% confidence interval. In general, one uses a level of significance of $\alpha = 0.05$ indicating that one is willing to accept a 5 per cent chance of being wrong to reject H_0.
5. *Performing computations:* The fifth step in testing hypothesis is the performance of various computations from a random sample of size n; necessary for the test statistic obtained in Step (3). Then we need to see whether sample result falls in the critical region or in the acceptance regions.
6. *Making decisions:* Finally, in the Sixth Step, we may draw statistical conclusions and the management may take decisions. A statistical decision or conclusion comprises either accepting the null hypothesis or rejecting it. The decision will depend on whether the computed value of the test criterion falls in the region of rejection or the region of acceptance. If the hypothesis is being tested at 5 per cent level of significance and the observed set of results have a probability less than 5 per cent, we reject the null hypothesis and the differences between the sample statistic and the hypothetical population parameter is considered to be significant. On the other hand, if the test statistic falls in the region of non-rejection, the null hypothesis is accepted and the difference between the sample statistic

and the hypothetical population parameter is not regarded as significant, i.e., it can be explained by chance variations.

If we accept a hypothesis when it is False, it is known as Type II error. The probability of committing a Type II error is designated by 'β'.

Decide based on a comparison of the calculated value of the test statistic and the p-value of the test, whether to reject the null hypothesis in favor of the alternative. If the p-value is less than a, reject H_0. Otherwise, fail to reject H_0. Alternatively, if the calculated value is less than critical value, accept H_0 otherwise reject H_0.

If the decision is to reject H_0, the statement of the conclusion should read as follows: "We reject H_0 at the (value of a) level of significance. There is sufficient evidence to conclude that (statement of the alternative hypothesis)."

If the decision is to fail to reject H_0, the statement of the conclusion should read as follows: "We fail to reject H_0 at the (value of a) level of significance. There is not sufficient evidence to conclude that (statement of the alternative hypothesis)."

Errors in Testing of Hypothesis: Type I and Type II Errors

The inductive inference consists in arriving at a decision to accept or reject a null hypothesis H_0, after inspecting only a sample from it. As such an element of risk – the risk of taking wrong decisions are involved in any test procedure; there are four possible mutually disjoint and exhaustive results:

1. The hypothesis is **true** and our test **accepts** it i.e., accept H_0 when it is true.
2. The hypothesis is **true** but our test **rejects** it i.e., reject H_0 when it is true.
3. The hypothesis is **false** but our test **accepts** it i.e., accept H_0 when it is false.
4. The hypothesis is **false** and our test **rejects** it i.e., reject H_0 when it is false

The decisions in (i) and (iv) are correct decisions while the decisions (ii) and (iii) are wrong decisions. These decisions may be expressed in the following table.

	Decisions from the sample is	
	Reject H_0	**Accept H_0**
H_0 True	Wrong Decision (**Type I error**) **α**	Correct Decision (confidence level) 1-α
H_0 False	Correct Decision (Power of the test) 1- β	Wrong Decision (**Type II error**) **β**

Type I error: If we Reject a hypothesis when it is True it is known as Type I error. The probability of committing a type I error is designated as 'α' and is called level of significance i.e., Pr [Reject H_0 when it is true] = Pr [Type I error] = α.

Type II error: If we Accept a hypothesis when it is False, it is known as Type II error. The probability of committing a Type II error is designated by 'β'.

i.e., Pr[Accept H_0 when it is false] = Pr [Type II error] = β

Type I error: wrong rejection of H_0 (H_0 is true but is rejected).

Type II error: wrong rejection of H_a (H_a is true but is rejected).

⇒ A sensible statistical procedure should result in small chance of making both type I and type II errors.

However, it is impossible to have as small chance of making both types of errors simultaneously. The larger the chance of making a Type I error is, the smaller is the chance of making a Type II error.

Let

α = the probability of making a Type I error.

β = the probability of making a Type II error.

$\Rightarrow$The larger α is, the smaller β is.

Usually, we control α to some predetermined numerical value, called the level of significance. Then, a sensible or good statistical procedure should result in as small value of β as possible with a controlled to the predetermined level of significance. Some commonly used level of significance include 0.1, 0.05, 0.01.

Since most applications of hypothesis testing control the probability of making a Type I error, the probability of making a Type II error would not be controlled. Since the probability of making a Type II error can not be controlled, "not reject H_0" can still have high probability of making a Type II error. Therefore, we do not "accept H_0" since the probability of making an error is still high. We do "not reject H_0" so far because we can not find enough evidence to "reject H_0".

Power of the Test: If we reject a hypothesis when it is false, the decision is correct. Then it is known as the **power** of the test. The probability of not committing Type II error is designated by $(1 - \beta)$

i.e., $$Pr\text{ (Reject } H_0 \text{ when it is false)} = (1 - \beta)$$

Critical Region: A region (corresponding to a statistic) in the sample space which amounts to rejection of H_0 is termed as critical region or region of rejection. It will be established on the basis of the choice of the value of the level of significance.

Critical Value: The value of test statistic, which separates the critical (or rejection) region and acceptance region is called the critical value or significant value. It depends upon:

1. The level of significance used, and
2. The alternative hypothesis, whether it is two-tailed or single-tailed.

It is important to specify which value of the test statistic will reject the null hypothesis and which will accept it. When computed test statistic falls in the region of acceptance. We accept the null hypothesis at a per cent level of significance. When the value falls in the region of rejection, we reject H_0. So we determine the region of acceptance and rejection. The values which lead to rejection of H_0 are called critical values and the region is called critical region. The various critical regions for two-tailed and one (single) tailed are shown in the following figures.

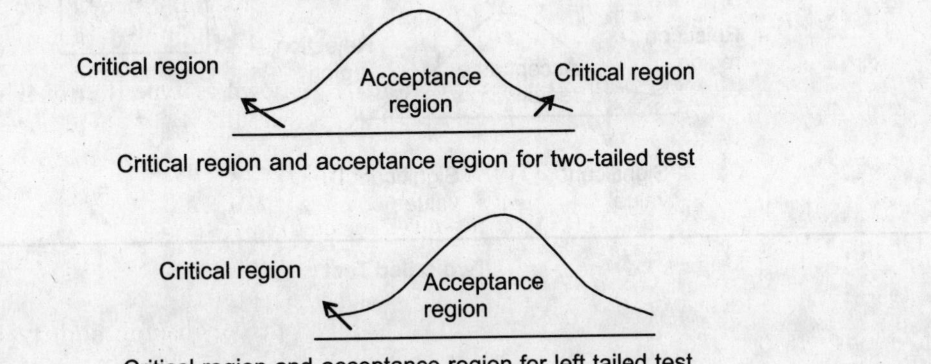

Critical region and acceptance region for two-tailed test

Critical region and acceptance region for left tailed test

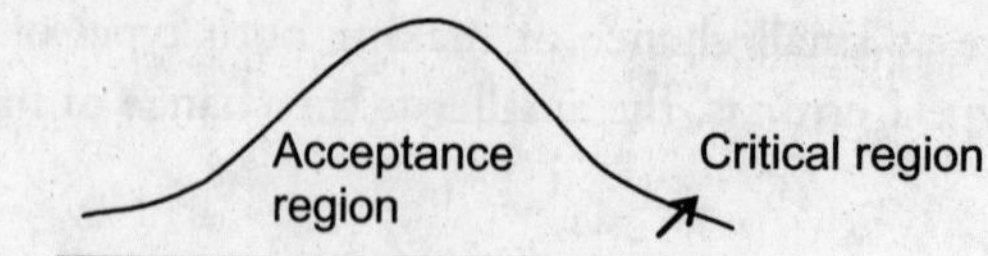

Critical region and acceptance region for right tailed test

Level of Significance: The maximum size of the Type I error which we are prepared to risk is known as the level of significance. Therefore,

$$Pr[\text{Type I error}] = \alpha$$

$$Pr[\text{Reject } H_0 \text{ when } H_0 \text{ is true}] = \alpha$$

One-tailed and Two-tailed Tests

In any test, the critical region is represented by a portion of the area under the probability curve of the sampling distribution of the test statistic. Basically, there are three kinds of problems associated in testing of hypothesis. They are:

1. *Two-tailed test* is a test where the alternative hypothesis leads to have the critical region in two-tails of the distribution:

   $$H_0: \mu_1 = \mu_2 \text{ (or } \mu = \mu_0\text{)}$$

   against $$H_1: \mu_1 \neq \mu_2 \text{ (or } \mu \neq \mu_0\text{)}$$

   is known as two-tailed test. The diagram presents the critical region into two tails.

2. **One tailed test** is a test where the alternative hypothesis leads to have the critical region in right side or left side of the distribution. This is also usually called as one (single) tailed test.

   (i) *Right-tailed test:*

   $$H_0: \mu_1 = \mu_2 \text{ (or } \mu = \mu_0\text{)}$$

   against $$H_1: \mu_1 > \mu_2 \text{ (or } \mu > \mu_0\text{) Right-tailed test}$$

   (ii) *Left-tailed test:*

   $$H_0: \mu_1 = \mu_2 \text{ (or } \mu = \mu_0\text{)}$$

   against $$H_1: \mu_1 < \mu_2 \text{ (or } \mu < \mu_0\text{) Left-tailed test.}$$

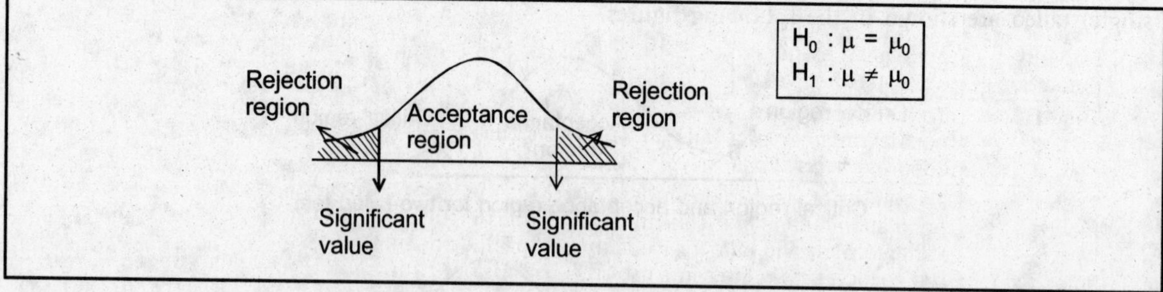

Two-tailed Test

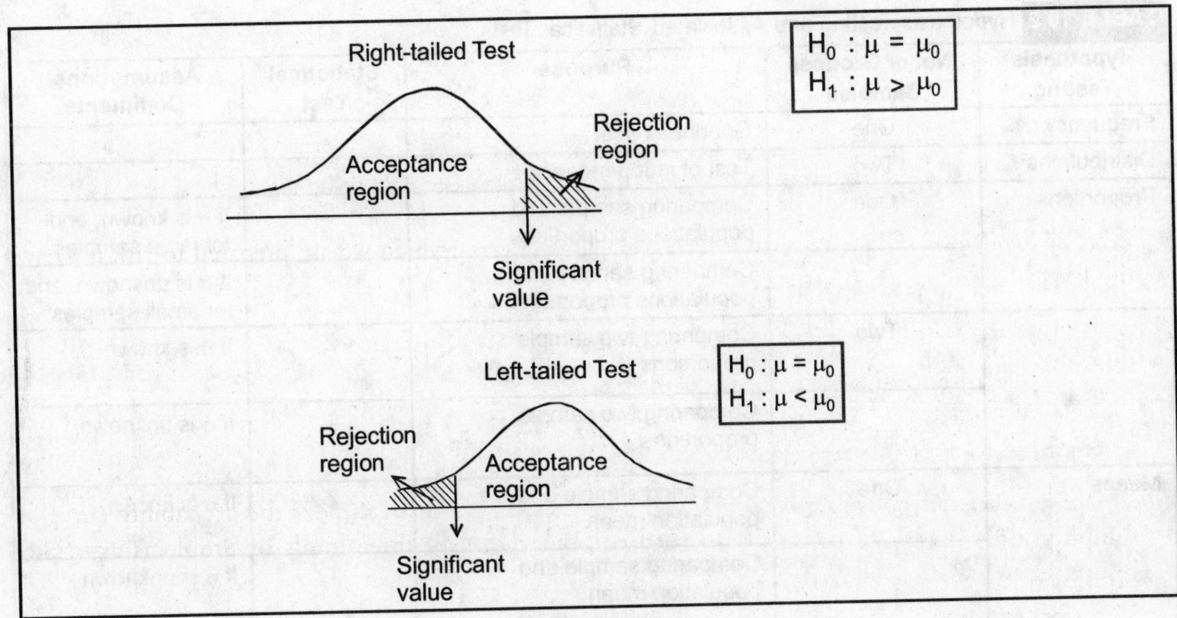

One-tailed Test

❖ Statistical Hypothesis

A statistical hypothesis is an assumption about a population parameter. This assumption may or may not be true. The best way to determine whether a statistical hypothesis is true is to examine the entire population. Since this is often impractical, researchers typically examine a random sample from the population. If the sample data are consistent with the statistical hypothesis, the hypothesis is accepted; if not, the hypothesis is rejected. There are two types of statistical hypothesis.

TABLE 10.1 Univariate Hypothesis Tests

Type of Test	Primary Purpose of Test	Illustrative Research Question Test is Designed to Answer
Chi-square contingency test	When then association between two categorical (nominal or ordinal) variables is to be examined	Is there a significant relationship between customers' highest level of schooling (education) (measured, say, as a four-category ordinal variable) and whether or not they recommend National Insurance Company to a friend? (measured as an ordinal variable)
Test for a single mean	To test hypotheses that compare the population mean of a variable to a prespecified value	Is the average waiting time for Ace Super market's customers at the store's checkouts significantly greater than 10 minutes?
Test for a single proportion	To test hypotheses that compare the population proportion of a variable to a prespecified value	Is the proportion of households owning DVDs in Dallas significantly less than .3?
Test of two means	To test hypotheses that compare the population mean of a variable for two separate populations	Is the average expenditure per household on eating out significantly higher in Detroit than in Des Moines?
Test of two means when samples are dependent	To test hypotheses that compare two population means of the same variable when the data for the test are collected from the same set of sample units	On the basis of data collected from a panel of households before and after the special ad campaign for Suds detergent, is the mean purchase volume of Suds per household significantly higher after the campaign than before?
Test of two proportions	To test hypotheses that compare the population proportion of a variable for two separate populations	Is the proportion of two-income households significantly lower in the Midwest states than in the northeast states?

TABLE 10.2 Hypothesis Testing and Associated Statistical Tests

Hypothesis Testing	No. of Groups/ Samples	Purpose	Statistical Test	Assumptions/ Comments
Frequency	One	Goodness of fit	χ^2	
Distributions	Two	Test of independence	χ^2	
Proportions	One	Comparing sample and populations proportions	Z	If σ is known, and for large samples
		Comparing sample and populations proportions	t	If σ is unknown, and for small samples
	Two	Comparing two sample proportions	Z	If σ is known
		Comparing two sample proportions	t	If σ is unknown
Means	One	Comparing sample and population mean	Z	If σ is known
		Comparing sample and population mean	t	If σ is unknown
	Two	Comparing two sample means	Z	If σ is known
		Comparing two sample means (from independent samples)	t	If σ is unknown
		Comparing two sample means (from related samples)	t	If σ is unknown
	Two or more	Comparing multiple sample means	F	Using analysis of variance framework (discussed in next chapter)
Variance	One	Comparing sample and population variances	χ^2	
	Two	Comparing sample variances	F	

Legend: σ = population standard deviation

Statistical Hypothesis Testing

Any hypothesis can be subjected to test with known statistical method. The rest is core otherwise the research study will be incomplete. Thus, testing of hypothesis is an essential part of the research study for the reasons that the study of statistical inference enables researcher to so much confidently examine the accuracy of the study results. Data with experimental nature require to undergo a comparison of two or more relating to statistics. An evaluation of the difference between two statistics, say mean is desired. Both means are subject to error. The difference between the two means may be ascribed to sampling error or may be due to different structures. A decision in this regard is required between these alternatives. Statistical procedure which leads to decision of this kind is called Test of significance. It may be applied to the difference between statistics of independent samples or between statistics obtained under different conditions for the sample. Sometimes it is applied to test the difference between a single sample statistic and fixed value. There are two important means of testing hypothesis 1. The study of hypothesis for logical consistency and 2. The study of hypothesis for agreement with fact.

Statistical Hypothesis Testing, or Tests of Significance, is used to determine if the differences between two or more descriptive statistics (such as a mean, per cent, proportion, standard deviation, etc.) are statistically significant or more likely due to chance variations. It is a method of testing claims made about populations by using a sample (subset) from that population.

In hypothesis testing, descriptive numbers are standardized so that they can be compared to fixed values, which are found in tables and in computer programs, which indicate how "unusual" it is to obtain the data collected. A statistical hypothesis to be tested is always written as a null hypothesis (no change). Generally, the null hypothesis will contain the symbol "=" to indicate the status quo, or no change. An appropriate test will tell us to either reject the null hypothesis or fail to reject (accept) the null hypothesis.

Confidence Limits – Population Proportion

If we consider a large sample of size n from an infinite population with a population proportion P and the sample proportion is p, then the Standard normal variate will be

$$Z = \frac{P - E(P)}{S.E.(P)} = \frac{p - P}{\sqrt{\frac{PQ}{n}}} \sim N(0,1)$$

But, in general population proportion will be unknown. So, the population proportion will be estimated on the basis of sample proportion. Then the standard error will be $\sqrt{\frac{pq}{n}}$. Then the confidence limits for the population proportion (P) are given by

$$\text{p} \pm Z_\alpha\, S.E.(p) \Rightarrow p \pm Z_\alpha \sqrt{\frac{pq}{n}}$$

i.e.,

$$P_r\left[p - Z_\alpha\sqrt{\frac{pq}{n}} < P < p + Z_\alpha\sqrt{\frac{pq}{n}}\right] = (1-\alpha)$$

If $\alpha = 0.01$, then the confidence limits for population proportion are

$$P_r\left[p - 2.58\sqrt{\frac{pq}{n}} < P < p + 2.58\sqrt{\frac{pq}{n}}\right] = 0.99$$

Example 1

The Director, Human Resources of a large organisation wanted to know what proportion of all persons who had ever been interviewed for a job in his organisation had been hired? He was willing to settle for 95 per cent confidence interval. A random sample of 500 interview records revealed that 76 of them had been hired.

Solution:

The 95 per cent confidence interval for the population proportion is given by

$$p \pm 1.96\sqrt{\frac{pq}{n}}$$

Since the sample proportion = p = (76/500) = 0.152

Then, the confidence interval will be

$$0.152 \pm 1.96\sqrt{\frac{0.152 \times 0.848}{500}}$$

$$\Rightarrow \quad 0.152 + 1.96(0.016)$$

$$\Rightarrow \quad 0.152 + 0.031 = (0.121,\ 0.183)$$

Hence, the required proportion varies between 0.121 and 0.183

Confidence Limits – Difference of Two Population Proportions

If p_1 and p_2 are sample proportions in large and independent random samples of sizes n_1 and n_2 respectively from two infinite population with population proportions P_1 and P_2 respectively, then the Standard normal variate will be

$$Z = \frac{(p_1 - p_2) - E(p_1 - p_2)}{S.E.(p_1 - p_2)}$$

where $$E(p_1 - p_2) = E(p_1) - E(p_2) = P_1 - P_2$$

and $$S.E.(p_1 - p_2) = \sqrt{\text{Var}(p_1 - p_2)}$$

$$= \sqrt{\text{Var}(p_1) + \text{Var}(p_2)} = \sqrt{\frac{P_1Q_1}{n_1} + \frac{P_2Q_2}{n_2}}$$

Thus, for large samples by Central Limit Theorem

$$Z = \frac{(p_1 - p_2) - E(p_1 - p_2)}{S.E.(p_1 - p_2)} = \frac{(p_1 - p_2) - (P_1 - P_2)}{\sqrt{\frac{P_1Q_1}{n_1} + \frac{P_2Q_2}{n_2}}} \sim N(0, 1)$$

Hence, the confidence limits for the difference of population proportions at α% level of significance are given by (since P_1 and P_2 are unknown their unbiased estimates p_1 and p_2 are used instead). Thus, giving the (1 - α)% confidence limits for $(P_1 - P_2)$ as

$$(p_1 - p_2) \pm Z_\alpha S.E(p_1 - p_2)$$

i.e., $$(p_1 - p_2) \pm Z_\alpha\sqrt{\frac{P_1Q_1}{n_1} + \frac{P_2Q_2}{n_2}}$$

i.e., $$P_r\left[(p_1-p_2) - Z_\alpha\sqrt{\frac{P_1Q_1}{n_1} + \frac{P_2Q_2}{n_2}} < (P_1-P_2) < (p_1-p_2) + Z_\alpha\sqrt{\frac{P_1Q_1}{n_1} + \frac{P_2Q_2}{n_2}}\right] = 1 - \alpha$$

Example 2

A random sample of 160 people from a city A showed that 50 are smokers. Another sample of 250 people from another city B showed that 50 are smokers. At 95% confidence, what is difference of proportion of smokers? (Z_a = 1.96)

Solution:

Given that n_1 = 160 and

p_1 = Proportion of smokers in city A

= 50/160 = 0.3125 and

n_2 = 250 and

p_2 = Proportion of smokers in city B

= 50/250 = 0.20

$q_1 = 1 - p_1 = 1 - 0.3125 = 0.6875$

$q_2 = 1 - p_2 = 1 - 0.20 = 0.80$

Then, $$\text{S.E.}(p_1 - p_2) = \sqrt{\frac{p_1q_1}{n_1} + \frac{p_2q_2}{n_2}} = \sqrt{\frac{0.3125 \times 0.6875}{160} + \frac{0.2 \times 0.8}{250}} = 0.0445$$

(Since P_1, P_2 are unknown, their unbiased sample estimates p_1, p_2 are used). Therefore, 95% confidence limits are given by

$$(p_1 - p_2) \pm Z_\alpha \sqrt{\frac{p_1q_1}{n_1} + \frac{p_2q_2}{n_2}}$$

$$\Rightarrow \quad (0.3125 - 0.2) \pm 1.96 \sqrt{\frac{0.3125 \times 0.6875}{160} + \frac{0.2 \times 0.8}{250}}$$

$$\Rightarrow \quad 0.1125 \pm 1.96 \times 0.0445 = 0.1125 \pm 0.0873$$

$$\Rightarrow \quad (0.0253 \text{ to } 0.1997)$$

Hence, the difference of population proportion of smokers with 95% confidence limits are: (0.0253 to 0.1997)

Confidence Limits – Population Standard Deviation

In a random sample of size n from an infinite population with variance σ^2, the variance of the sampling distribution of standard deviation is given by Var $(s) = \frac{\sigma^2}{2n}$

Hence (1 – α)% confidence limits for the population standard deviation s is given by

$$s \pm Z_\alpha S.E.(s) = s \pm Z_\alpha \sqrt{\frac{\sigma^2}{2n}}$$

Where the values of z_α for different levels of significance are given in the tables. But, in general, the population variance is unknown. It is estimated from the corresponding sample variance. Then, the confidence limits for population standard deviation are given by

$$s \pm Z_\alpha \sqrt{\frac{s^2}{2n}}$$

i.e.,

$$P_r\left[s - Z_\alpha \sqrt{\frac{s^2}{2n}} < \sigma < s + Z_\alpha \sqrt{\frac{s^2}{2n}}\right] = (1-\alpha)$$

If α = 0.05, the confidence limits will be

$$P_r\left[s - 1.96\sqrt{\frac{s^2}{2n}} < \sigma < s + 1.96\sqrt{\frac{s^2}{2n}}\right] = 0.95$$

i.e.,

$$s \pm 1.96\sqrt{\frac{s^2}{2n}}$$

❖ Hypothesis Testing – Large Samples

Though it is difficult to draw a clear-cut line of demarcation between large and small samples, it is generally agreed that if the size of sample exceeds 30, it should be regarded as a large sample. The tests of significance used for large samples are different from the one used for small samples for the reason that the assumptions we make in case of large samples do not hold for small samples. Tests of hypothesis involving large samples are based on the following assumptions.

1. The sampling distribution of a sample statistic is approximately normal.
2. Values given by the samples are sufficiently close to the population value and can be used in its place for the standard error of the estimate.

Hypothesis Testing – Single Mean

Let $X_1, X_2 \ldots\ldots X_n$ be a random sample of size n from a population with mean m and variance σ^2. Assume that σ^2 is known and m is unknown. In developing the test of significance for a single mean we are interested, to test if the mean of the population has a specified value m_0 (say), i.e., $\mu = \mu_0$.

Example 3

The mean lifetime of a sample of 100 light tubes produced by a company is found to be 1,560 hours with a population standard deviation of 90 hours. Test the hypothesis that the mean lifetime of the tubes produced by the company is 1580 hours.

Solution:

The null hypothesis is that there is no significant difference between the sample mean and hypothetical population mean. The population mean has a specified value.

Null Hypothesis (H_0): $\mu = \mu_0$

Alternative Hypothesis(H_1): $\mu \neq \mu_0$

Let α = 0.05

Then the test statistics

$$Z = \frac{\overline{x} - \mu_0}{\sigma / \sqrt{n}} \sim N(0,1)$$

$$Z = \frac{1560 - 1580}{90 / \sqrt{100}} = \frac{20}{90/10} = \frac{20}{9} = -2.22$$

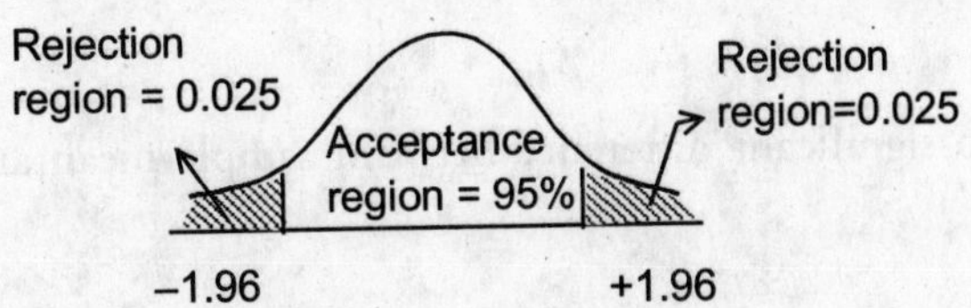

Since it is two-tailed test, the critical value of $Z_\alpha = \pm 1.96$ for a two-tailed test at a=5% level of significance.

Conclusion: Since the computed value of Z = -2.22 falls in the rejection region, we reject the null hypothesis. Hence, the mean lifetime of the tubes produced by the company may not be 1,580 hours.

Example 4

The mean weight of 200 male students in a college is 62 kgs with a standard deviation of 4 kgs. Test the hypothesis that the mean weight in the population is greater than 58 kgs. Use α = 1%.

Solution:

The null hypothesis is that the population mean has a specified value i.e.,

$H_0 : \mu = 58$ kgs $(= \mu_0)$

against $H_1 : \mu > 58$ kgs

$\alpha = 0.01$

the test statistic

$$Z = \frac{\overline{x} - \mu_0}{\sigma / \sqrt{n}} \sim N(0,1)$$

$$Z = \frac{60 - 58}{4 / \sqrt{200}} = \frac{2}{4/14.14} = \frac{28.28}{4} = 7.07$$

Rejection
region = 0.05
Acceptance
region = 95%
2.33

The critical value of $Z_\alpha = 2.33$ for a right-tailed test at 1% level of significance.

Conclusion: Since computed value of Z = 7.07 falls in the rejection region, we reject the null hypothesis. Hence, the mean weight of the students is greater than 58 kgs.

Example 5

A bakery in a city was fined ₹ 1210 for selling cakes that were underweight. The city prosecutor collected 200 cakes from the bakery, to test the average weight of the cake. It is known that the population standard deviation (weight of the cake) is 2 kgs. The sample (n = 200) they obtained has a mean weight is 23.75 kgs. Will you conclude that the bakery was selling cakes that were underweight. The bakery was expected to sell cake of weight 24 kgs.

Solution:

Null hypothesis: There is no significant difference between sample mean and hypothetical population mean (μ = 24kgs)

$H_0 : \mu = 24$ and

$H_1 : \mu < 24$ (left tailed test)

Let $\alpha = 0.01$. The test statistic

$$Z = \frac{\bar{x} - \mu_0}{\sigma / \sqrt{n}} \sim N(0,1)$$

$$= \frac{23.75 - 24}{2/\sqrt{200}} = \frac{-0.25 \times 14.14}{2} = \frac{-3.555}{2} = -1.7678$$

Rejection region =0.01

Acceptance region = 99%

-2.33

Conclusion: Since the computed value of Z = – 1.7678 falls in the acceptance region, we may accept the null hypothesis. Hence, the bakery was selling cakes of correct weight of 24 kgs, only.

Hypothesis Testing – Two Means

Two sample means are taken from two populations or same population. The hypothesis testing is the significant difference between two sample means.

Example 6

Two types of new cars produced in India are tested for petrol mileage. One sample consisting of 36 cars averaged 13 kmpl (kilometers per litre). While the other sample consisting of 72 cars averaged 11.5 kmpl, with population variances as $\sigma_1^2 = 1.5$ and $\sigma_2^2 = 2.0$ respectively. Test whether there is any significant difference in the petrol consumption of these two types of cars. Use $\alpha = 0.01$.

Solution:

We are given the following information

$n_1 = 36$ $\bar{X}_1 = 13$ $\sigma_1^2 = 1.5$

$n_2 = 72$ $\bar{X}_2 = 11.5$ $\sigma_2^2 = 2.0$

Null hypothesis: There is no significant difference in the petrol consumption of the two types of cars, i.e.,

$H_0 : \mu_1 = \mu_2;\ H_1 : \mu_1 \neq \mu_2$ and $\alpha = 0.01$ (given)

The test statistic

$$Z = \frac{\bar{X}_1 - \bar{X}_2}{\sqrt{\frac{\sigma_1^2}{n_2} + \frac{\sigma_2^2}{n_2}}} \sim N(0, 1) \text{ (under } H_0)$$

$$Z = \frac{13 - 11.5}{\sqrt{\frac{1.5}{36} + \frac{2.0}{72}}} = \frac{1.5}{0.204} = 5.68$$

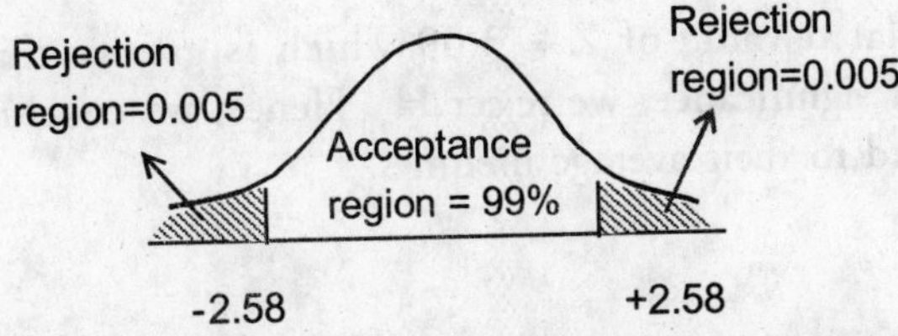

Conclusion: Since the calculated value of Z = 5.68 which is greater than the tabulated value of Z_a = 2.58 at 1% level of significance, the null hypothesis is rejected. Hence, there is a significant difference in the petrol consumption of the two types of cars.

Example 7

Two brands of bulbs are quoted at the same price. A buyer tested a random sample of 60 bulbs of Brand A which gave a mean lifetime of 86 hours with a standard deviation of 6 hours. Another sample of 5 bulbs of Brand B which gave a mean lifetime of 82 hours with a standard deviation of 9 hours. Test whether the two brands of bulbs are same with regard to their average life? Use α = 0.10

Solution:

We are given the following information

$n_1 = 60$ $\quad \bar{X}_1 = 86$ hours $\quad s_1 = 6$ hours (sample standard deviation)

$n_2 = 75$ $\quad \bar{X}_2 = 82$ hours $\quad s_2 = 9$ hours (sample standard deviation)

Null hypothesis: The two brands are similar with regard to their average lifetimes, i.e., H_0: $\mu_1 = \mu_2$ against the alternative hypothesis that the samples have come from different populations

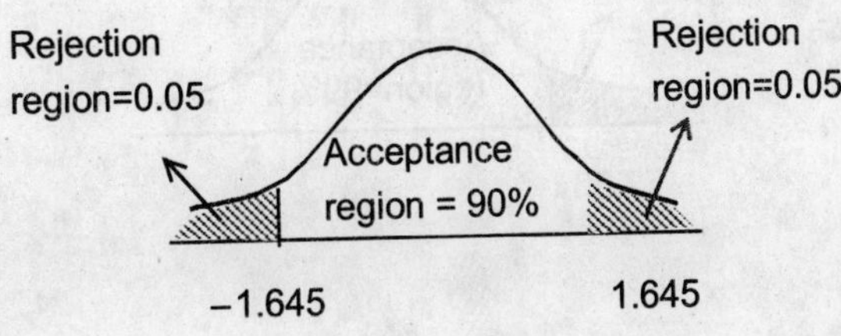

H_0: $\mu_1 = \mu_2$ H_1: $\mu_1 \neq \mu_2$ and $\alpha = 0.10$

Test statistic

$$Z = \frac{\bar{X}_1 - \bar{X}_2}{\sqrt{\frac{s_1^2}{n_1} + \frac{s_2^2}{n_2}}} \sim N(0,1)$$

by using Central Limit Theorem for large sample theory

$$Z = \frac{86 - 82}{\sqrt{\frac{36}{60} + \frac{81}{75}}} = \frac{4}{1.296} = 3.09$$

Conclusion: Since the calculated value of Z = 3.09 which is greater than the tabulated value of $Z_\alpha = \pm\ 1.645$ at 10% level of significance, we reject H_0. Hence, we conclude that the two brands of bulbs are not same with regard to their average lifetimes.

Example 8

A research investigator was interested in studying whether there is a significant difference in the salaries of MBA grades in two metropolitan cities. A random sample size 100 from Mumbai yields an average income of ₹ 20,150. Another random sample of 60 from Chennai results in an average income of ₹ 20,250. If the variances of both the populations are given as σ_1^2 = ₹ 40,000 and σ_2^2 = ₹ 32,400 respectively. Test whether the Mumbai mean salaries are less than the Chennai salaries. Use α as 0.01

Solution:

We are given that

$n_1 = 100$; $X_1 = 20{,}150$; $\sigma_1^2 = 40{,}000$

$n_2 = 60$; $X_2 = 20{,}250$; $\sigma_2^2 = 32{,}400$

The null hypothesis is that both Mumbai mean salaries and Chennai mean salaries are equal, i.e., H_0: $\mu_1 = \mu_2$

against H_1: $\mu_1 < \mu_2$

left-tailed test and $\mu = 0.01$, then the test statistic will be

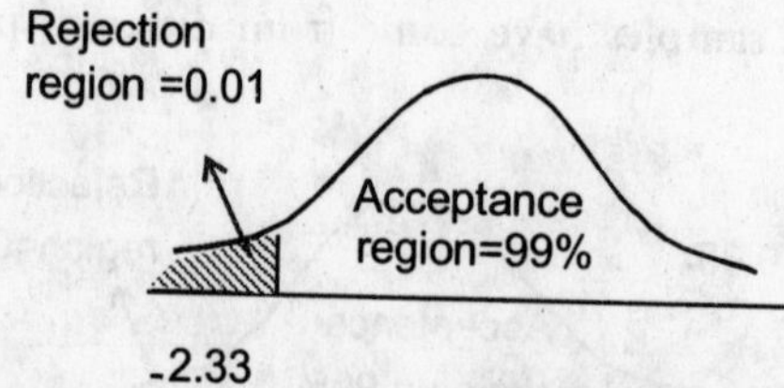

$$Z = \frac{\bar{x}_1 - \bar{x}_2}{\sqrt{\frac{\sigma_1^2}{n_1} + \frac{\sigma_2^2}{n_2}}} \sim N(0,1) \qquad \text{(Under } H_0\text{)}$$

$$= \frac{20150 - 20250}{\sqrt{\frac{40000}{100} + \frac{32400}{60}}} = -\frac{100}{30.66} = -3.26$$

Since the calculated value of Z = -3.26 which is less than

Z_α = -2.33, we reject H_0. Hence we conclude that the Mumbai mean salaries are less than Chennai mean salaries.

Example 9

A researcher wants to know the intelligence quotient of students in a school. He selected two groups of students. In the first group, there are 150 students having mean IQ of 75 with a standard deviation of 15. In the second group, there are 250 students having mean IQ of 70 with a standard deviation of 20. Test whether the groups have come from some population. Use α as 1% level of significance.

Solution:

We are given the following information:

$n_1 = 150$; $\bar{X}_1 = 75$; $s_1 = 15$

$n_2 = 250$; $\bar{X}_2 = 70$; $s_2 = 20$

The null hypothesis is that there is no significant difference in the mean scores obtained by students in both the groups.

$H_0: \mu_1 = \mu_2$

$H_1: \mu_1 \neq \mu_2$ and $\alpha = 0.01$,

Then the test statistic is

$$Z = \frac{\bar{x}_1 - \bar{x}_2}{\sqrt{\hat{\sigma}^2\left(\frac{1}{n_1} + \frac{1}{n_2}\right)}} \sim N(0,1)$$

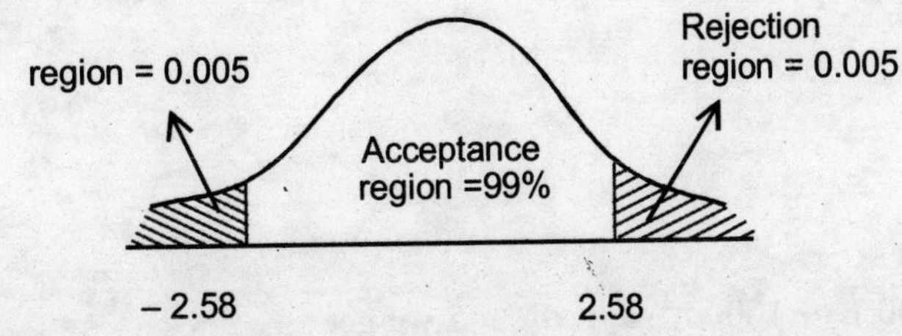

Since σ^2 is unknown, it can be estimated by the corresponding standard deviation as

$$\hat{\sigma}^2 = \frac{n_1 s_1^2 + n_2 s_2^2}{n_1 + n_2}$$

$$= \frac{150 \times (15)^2 + 250 \times (20)^2}{150 + 250}$$

$$= \frac{150 \times 225 + 250 \times 400}{400}$$

$$= \frac{133750}{400} = 334.375$$

$$Z = \frac{75 - 70}{\sqrt{334.375\left(\frac{1}{150} + \frac{1}{250}\right)}} = \frac{5}{\sqrt{3.5666}} = \frac{5}{1.8886} = 2.648$$

Conclusion: Since the calculated value of Z = 2.648 which is greater than the tabulated value of $Z_\alpha = \pm$ 2.58 at 1% level of significance, we reject H_o. Hence, we conclude that the mean score obtained by students in both the groups are different.

Example 10

The MBA department is concerned that dual degree students may be receiving lower grades than the regular MBA students. Two independent random samples have been selected. 100 observations from population 1 (dual degree students) and 100 from population 2 (MBA students). The sample means obtained are X_1 (bar)=84 and X_2 (bar)=87. It is known from previous studies that the population variances are 4.0 and 5.0 respectively. Using a level of significance of .10, is there evidence that the dual degree students are receiving lower grades? Fully explain your answer.

Solution:

To Test

Ho : $\mu_1 = \mu_2$ Vs H1 : $\mu_1 < \mu_2$ (one tailed test)

Test Statistics: As n is large >30 so we use Normal Test

$$z = \frac{\bar{x}_1 - \bar{x}_2}{\sqrt{\frac{\sigma_1^2}{n_1} + \frac{\sigma_2^2}{n_2}}}$$ follows Standard Normal distribution N(0,1)

= -10

Putting

$\bar{x}_1 = 84$ $\bar{x}_2 = 87$ $n_1 = 100$ $n_2 = 100$ $\sigma_1^2 = 4$ $\sigma_2^2 = 5$ we get

P-value = P (z < -10) = 0

Since the P-value 0 < 0.1, we reject H0. It is statistically significant.

Conclusion: At the 10% level of significance, the data provides enough evidence to reject the null hypothesis. Thus, we conclude at 0.1 level of significance that the dual degree students are receiving lower grades.

Test of Proportions

Tests of proportion are used to compare proportions or percentages against either a hypothesized value (one-sample test) or comparing two populations.

One-sample Test

Example 11

In a city A, out of 600 men, 325 men were found to be smokers. Does this information support the statement that 'Majority of men in this city are smokers'? Draw your conclusion using α = 5% and α =10% separately.

Solution:

We are given that n = 600, X = 325

Sample proportion of smokers is $p = \frac{X}{n} = \frac{325}{600} = 0.5417$

The null hypothesis is that the number of smokers and non-smokers are equal in the city so that

P_0 = Population proportion of smokers in the city $= \frac{1}{2} = 0.5$

$$\Rightarrow \qquad Q_0 = 1 - P_0 = 1 - \frac{1}{2} = 0.5$$

i.e., $\quad H_0: p = P_0 = \frac{1}{2} = 0.5$

Against the alternative hypothesis is that the majority of men in the city are smokers, i.e.,

$H_1: p > P_0\ (=0.5)$ (Right tailed) and α = 0.05 and α = 0.10 then the test statistic will be

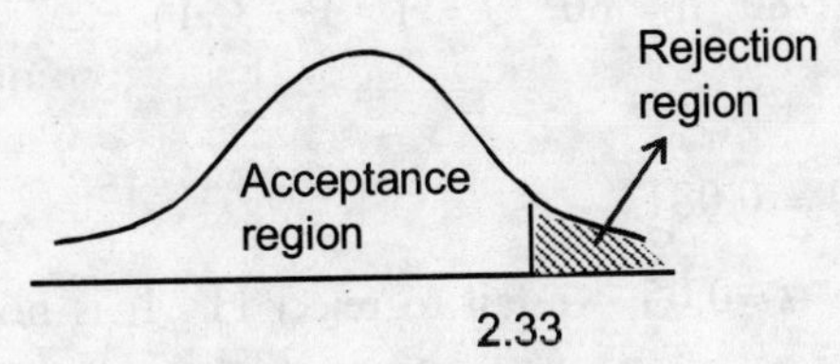

$$Z = \frac{p - P_0}{\sqrt{\frac{P_0 Q_0}{n}}} \sim N(0,1) \qquad \text{(under } H_0\text{)}$$

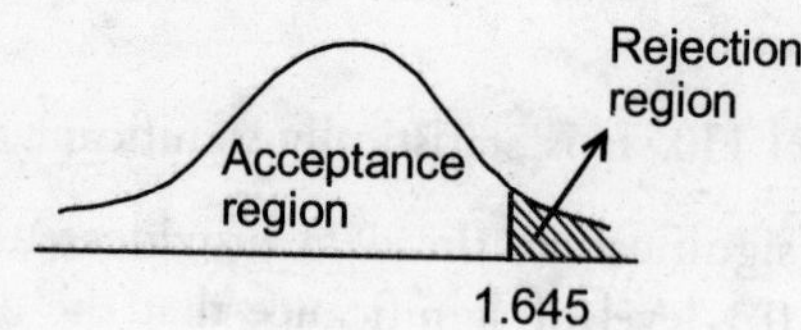

Therefore, $$Z = \frac{0.5417 - 0.5}{\sqrt{\frac{0.5 \times 0.5}{600}}}$$

$$= \frac{0.0417}{\sqrt{0.0004165}} = \frac{0.0417}{0.0204} = 2.04$$

1. Since the calculated value of Z = 2.04 is less than the tabulated value of Z_α = 2.33, we may accept H_0 at 10% level of significance. Hence, we may conclude that the number of smokers and non-smokers are equal in the city.
2. Since the calculated value of Z=2.04 is greater than the tabulated value of Z_α =1.645 at 5% level of significance, we reject H_o. Hence, we conclude that the majority of men in the city are smokers.

Example 12

The board of real estate developers claims that 56% of all voters will vote for a bond issue to construct a massive new water project. A random sample of 80 voters was taken and 51 said that they would vote for the new water project. (note: carry out the calculations for this problem to 3 dec. places). Test to see if this data indicates that more than 56% of all voters favor the project. Use a 5% significance level.

Solution:

To Test

H_o : P= 0.56 Vs H_1 : P > 0.56 (One tailed test)

Test Statistics

We use the standard normal distribution.

$$z = (p\text{-}P)/\sqrt{(PQ/n)} \text{ follows } N(0,1)$$
$$= 1.4$$

where

$$P = 0.56,\ p = 51/80\ \ n = 80\ \ Q = 1 - P = 0.44$$

P Value

$$\text{P-value} = P\ (z > 1.4\ ) = 0.0813$$

Since the P-value is greater than α =0.05, we fail to reject H_0. It is not statistically significant.

Conclusion: At the 5% level of significance, the data does not provide enough evidence to reject the null hypothesis. Thus, we conclude that data does not indicate that more than 56% of all voters favor the project.

Two sample test of Proportions

Example 13

In a simple random sample of 600 men taken from a big city, 450 are found to be the users of a product 'x'. In another simple random sample of 900 men taken from another city 450 are found to be the users of a product 'x'. Do the data indicate that there is a significant difference in the habit of usage of the product 'x' in the two cities?

Solution:

We are given that n_1 = 600; x_1 = 450; n_2 = 900 and x_2 = 450

$$p_1 = \frac{X_1}{n_1} = \frac{450}{600} = 0.75$$

$$p_2 = \frac{X_2}{n_2} = \frac{450}{900} = 0.5$$

The null hypothesis is that the proportion of users of the product x in both the cities are equal.

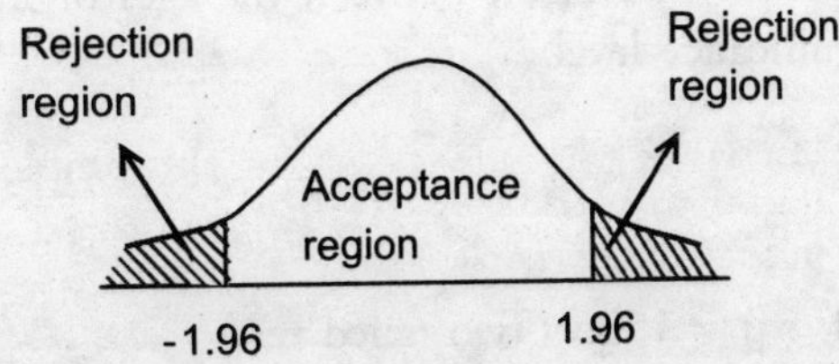

i.e., $H_o : P_1 = P_2$

against $H_1 : P_1 \neq P_2$ (two tailed test).

Let α = 0.05, then the test statistic will be

$$Z = \frac{(p_1 - p_2) - (P_1 - P_2)}{\sqrt{\frac{P_1Q_1}{n_1} + \frac{P_2Q_2}{n_2}}} \sim N(0,1)$$

$$\therefore \quad Z = \frac{(0.75 - 0.5) - (0)}{\sqrt{\frac{0.75 \times 0.25}{600} + \frac{0.5 \times 0.5}{900}}}$$

$$Z = \frac{0.25}{\sqrt{0.00059}} = \frac{0.25}{0.02429} = 10.29$$

Since the calculated value of Z = |10.29| which is much greater than the tabulated value of Z_α = 1.96, we reject H_0. Hence, we conclude that there is a significant difference between proportion of users of the product x in both the cities.

❖ Hypothesis Testing – Small Samples

If the sample size is small (say 30, or less), then the sample statistic will follow a **t-distribution.**

The Student's *t*-distribution was obtained by W.S. Gosset and was published under the pen name of 'Student' in the year 1908. It is reported that Gosset was a Statistician for a brewery and that the management did not want him to publish his scholarly theoretical work under his real name and bring shame to this employer. Consequently, he selected the pen name of **Student**.

As a matter of fact, procedures of Statistical inference for small samples are the same as those presented in preceding chapters. The study of statistical inference with the small samples is called small sampling theory or exact sampling theory.

One Sample t-test

In this, one sample mean is compared with hypothesized mean.

Example 14

Statistical abstract report that the average annual expenditure for healthcare by individuals 25 to 34 years old is \$1,596. A random sample of 34 people in Detroit between the ages of 25 and 34 had a sample mean expenditure of \$1,425 with sample standard deviation of \$425. Test to see if the mean expenditure for healthcare for people in Detroit between the ages of 25 and 34 is different from the national average. Use α 1% significance level.

Solution:

To Test

$H_o : \mu = 1596$ Vs $H_1 : \mu \neq 1596$ (Two tailed test)

Test Statistics

$$t = \frac{\bar{x} - \mu}{s / \sqrt{n}}$$ follows Student's t-distribution with d.f. = n –1 = 33.

$$= -2.35$$

Where

$\bar{x} = 425 \quad \mu = 1596 \quad s = 425 \quad n = 34$

We use t-distribution as σ is unknown.

P Value

P-value = 2*P(z <-2.35) = 0.0251

Since P-value of 0.0251 > 0.01 we do not reject H_0. It is statistically not significant.

Conclusion: At 1% level of significance, the data does not provide enough evidence to reject the null hypothesis. Thus, we conclude that the mean expenditure for healthcare for people in Detroit between the ages of 25 and 34 is not different from the national average?

Example 15

Prices of shares (in ₹) of a company on different days in a month are given as: 66, 65, 64, 63, 61, 60, 59, 71, 72, 67. Will you conclude that the mean price of the shares is less than ₹ 65 in the month?

Solution:

1. Null hypothesis H_0: m = m_0 (= 65)
2. Alternative hypothesis m_1 : m < m_0
3. Let level of significance α = 0.05.

The tabulated value of *t* for 9 degrees of freedom at 5% level of significance is -1.833.

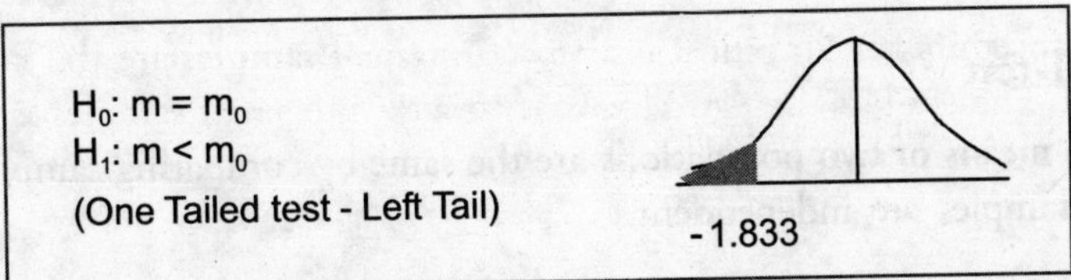

Assuming the population is Normally Distributed and the population standard deviation is unknown, then the test statistic will be

$$t = \frac{\bar{x} - \mu_0}{S/\sqrt{n}}$$

$\bar{x}$ and *S* can be computed from the sample values as shown in the following table:

x	*d* = *x*–65	d^2
66	1	1
65	0	0
64	–1	1
63	–2	4
61	–4	16
60	–5	25
59	–6	36
71	6	36
72	7	49
67	2	4
Total	**–2**	**172**

$$\bar{x} = A + \frac{\sum d}{n} = 65 + \frac{-2}{10} = 64.8$$

$$S^2 = \frac{1}{n-1}\Sigma(x_i - \bar{x})^2$$

Since we have taken deviations, we should calculate S^2 for the deviation data using the following formula.

$$S = \sqrt{\frac{\sum d_i^2}{n-1} - \frac{(\sum d_i)^2}{n(n-1)}} = 4.367$$

$$S = \sqrt{\frac{172}{9} - \frac{(-2)^2}{10 \times 9}} = \sqrt{19.11 - 0.04}$$

$$= \sqrt{19.07} = 4.367$$

$$t = \frac{\overline{x} - \mu_0}{S/\sqrt{n}} = \frac{64.8 - 65}{4.367/\sqrt{10}} = \frac{(-0.2)(3.16)}{4.367} = \frac{-0.632}{4.367} = -0.1447$$

Conclusion: Since the computed value of $t = -0.1447$ is greater than the tabulated value of $t_a = -1.833$, we may accept H_0 at 5% level of significance for 9 degrees of freedom.

Two Sample Mean T-test

This tests whether the means of two populations are the same by comparing sample means. In this case, assume that the two samples are independent.

Example 16

A random sample of 15 families in one city showed an average monthly food expenditure of ₹ 1320 with a standard deviation of ₹ 120 and a random sample of 12 families in another city showed on average monthly food expenditure of ₹ 1380 with a standard deviation of ₹ 100. Test whether the city I food expenditure is less than the city II food expenditure at a level of significance of 0.01.

Solution:

1. Setup null hypothesis as $H_0: \mu_1 = \mu_2$
2. Setup alternative hypothesis as $H_1: \mu_1 < \mu_2$
3. $\alpha = 0.01$

1. Test statistic $$t = \frac{\overline{x}_1 - \overline{x}_2}{S\sqrt{\frac{1}{n_1} + \frac{1}{n_2}}}$$

where $$S = \sqrt{\frac{n_1 s_1^2 + n_2 s_2^2}{n_1 + n_2 - 2}}$$

$$S = \sqrt{\frac{15(120)^2 + 12(100)^2}{15 + 12 - 2}} = \sqrt{\frac{15 \times 14400 + 12 \times 10000}{25}}$$

$$= \sqrt{\frac{216000 + 120000}{25}} = \sqrt{\frac{336000}{25}} = \sqrt{13440} = 115.93$$

$$t = \frac{-60}{115.93\sqrt{0.15}} = \frac{-60}{115.93 \times 0.3873} = \frac{-60}{44.8997} = -1.3363$$

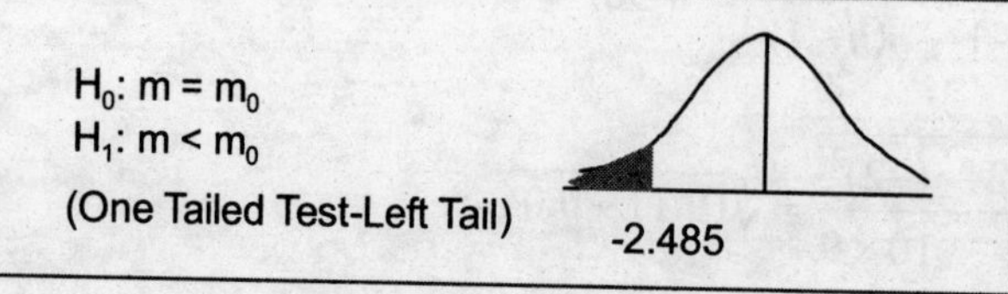

The table value of *t* for 25 D.F. at 1% LOS is -2.485.

Conclusion: Since computed value of t = –1.3363 is falling in the Acceptance Region, we may accept H_0.

Paired t-Test

This tests the equality of means of two samples from the same population by calculating the difference in the two readings. This example uses data of sales before and after an advertising campaign. Suppose a business concern is interested to find, whether a particular media of promoting sales of a product is really effective or not. Example, door to door canvassing or advertisement in papers or through Television. Suppose we want to find if advertisement is really effective in promoting sales of a particular product.

Example 17

Ten workers were given a training programme with a view to shorten their assembly time for a certain mechanism. The results of the time and motion studies before and after the training programme are given below:

X_i = Time taken for assembling before training and Y_i = Time taken for assembling after training

Workers	1	2	3	4	5	6	7	8	9	10
X_i	15	18	20	17	16	14	21	19	13	22
Y_i	14	16	21	10	15	18	19	16	14	20

On the basis of this data can it be concluded that the training programme has shortened the average assembly time.

Solution:

We setup $H_0: \bar{d} = 0$ against $H_1: \bar{d} \neq 0$,

then the test statistic will be

$$t = \frac{\bar{d}}{\frac{S}{\sqrt{n}}} \sim \text{a t-Distribution with (n-1) D.F.}$$

Calculations for $\bar{d}$ and S

Worker	**X_i**	**Y_i**	**$d_i = X_i - Y_i$**	**d_i^2**
1	15	14	1	1
2	18	16	2	4
3	20	21	–1	1
4	17	10	7	49
5	16	15	1	1
6	14	18	-4	16
7	21	19	2	4
8	19	16	3	9
9	13	14	-1	1
10	22	20	2	4
		Total	12	90

$$\bar{d} = \frac{\Sigma d_i}{n} = \frac{12}{10} = 1.2$$

$$s^2 = \frac{\Sigma d_i^2}{n} - (\bar{d})^2$$

$$= \frac{90}{10} - (1.2)^2 = 9 - 1.44 = 7.56$$

$$S^2 = \frac{n\,s^2}{n-1}$$

$$S^2 = \frac{10(7.56)}{10-1} = \frac{75.6}{9} = 8.4$$

$$S = \sqrt{8.4} = 2.898$$

$$t = \frac{\bar{d}\sqrt{n}}{S} = \frac{1.2\sqrt{10}}{2.898} = \frac{1.2 \times 3.162}{2.898} = 1.309$$

$H_0 : \bar{d} = 0$

$H_1 : \bar{d} \neq 0$

(*Two Tailed Test*)

−2.26 2.26

The table value of t for n = 9 D.F., at 5% level of significance is 2.26.

Conclusion: Since the computed value of t = 1.309 is less than the table value of t, the Null Hypothesis may be accepted. Hence, the training programme has not shortened the average assembly time.

Example 18

In an experiment related to clinical trials, 10 individuals are selected at random and the number of hours of sleep before and after the consumption of a medicine (which is meant for increasing the hours of sleep) are recorded and presented.

Individuals	1	2	3	4	5	6	7	8	9	10
Hours slept before consumption of Medicine(X_i)	7	9	6	8	10	9	11	4	7	8
Hours slept after consumption of Medicine(Y_i)	9	11	12	12	8	6	15	8	10	6

Apply t-test to determine whether reorganization had any effect on sales.

Solution:

Let us take the null hypothesis that the medicine has no effect in creating additional hours of sleep against the alternative hypothesis that the medicine increases the number of hours of sleep on the average.

In other words, $H_0: \bar{d} = 0$ against $H_1: \bar{d} \neq 0$,

then the test statistic will be

$$t = \frac{\bar{d}}{\frac{S}{\sqrt{n}}} \sim \text{a t-Distribution with (n-1) D.F.}$$

We apply *t*-test

Individual	X_i	Y_i	$d_i = (X_i - Y_i)$	d_i^2
1	7	9	–2	4
2	9	11	–2	4
3	6	12	–6	36
4	8	12	–4	16
5	10	8	+2	4
6	9	6	+3	9
7	11	15	–4	16
8	4	8	–4	16
9	7	10	–3	9
10	8	6	+2	4
			–18	118

$$\bar{d} = \frac{\Sigma d_i}{n} = \frac{-18}{10} = -1.8$$

$$s^2 = \frac{\Sigma d_i^2}{n} - (\bar{d})^2$$

$$= \frac{118}{10} - (-1.8)^2 = 11.80 - 3.24 = 8.56$$

$$S^2 = \frac{n\,s^2}{n-1}$$

$$S^2 = \frac{10(8.56)}{10-1} = \frac{85.6}{9} = 9.511$$

$$S = \sqrt{9.511} = 3.084$$

$$t = \frac{\bar{d}\sqrt{n}}{S} = \frac{(-1.8)\sqrt{10}}{3.084} = \frac{(-1.8)\times 3.162}{3.084} = -1.845$$

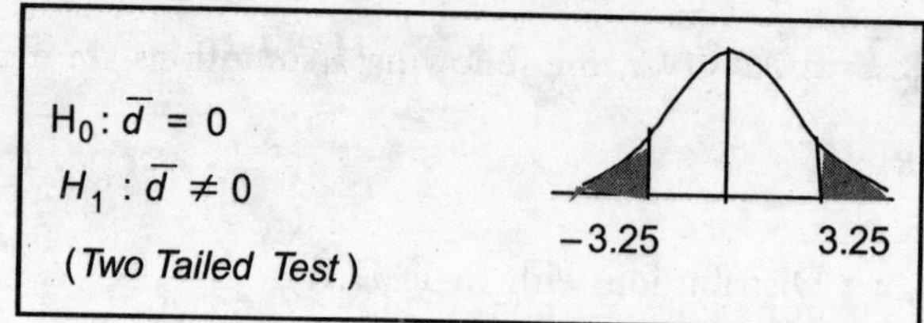

The table value of *t* for n = 9 D.F., at 1% level of significance is -3.25.

Conclusion

Since the computed value of t = -1.845 is less than the table value of t, the Null Hypothesis may be accepted. Hence, the medicine has not increased the average hours of sleep.

ANALYSIS OF VARIANCE (ANOVA)

While dealing with testing of hypothesis, we have studied the testing for two means both in large as well as small samples. In large samples, you have used 'Z' statistic and in small samples, you have used 't' statistic for testing. If we want to test more than two means simultaneously, one way is to test them by pairs, i.e., selecting two at a time and apply either a 'Z' statistic (Large sample) or a 't' statistic (small sample) depending upon their sample sizes. But there is no way in which one can say whether more than two means are equal or not simultaneously. In the present lesson, we study the testing process for testing the equality of more than two means simultaneously. This is called as Analysis of Variance, popularly known as ANOVA.

For example, four different fertilizers are applied to five plots each of rice and yield of rice in each of the plots is measured. We are interested in finding out whether the effect of these fertilizers on the yields is significantly different or not. In other words, we wish to test whether the samples have come from same Normal Population or not. The purpose of ANOVA is to test the homogeneity of several means.

The term 'Analysis of Variance' was first introduced by Prof. R. A. Fisher in 1920s while dealing with problems in the analysis of agronomical data. Variation is inevitable, unavoidable and inherent in nature. The total variation in any set of numerical data is due to a number of causes which may be classified as:

1. Assignable causes, and
2. Chance causes.

The variation due to Assignable causes can be detected and measured whereas variation due to Chance causes is beyond the control of human hand and cannot be traced separately.

Definition

Prof. R. A. Fisher defined the analysis of variance as "Separation of variance ascribable to one group of causes from the variance ascribable to other group".

ANOVA consists of the estimation of the amount of variation due to each of the independent factors (or causes) separately and then comparing these estimates due to assignable factors (or causes) with the estimate due to chance factors (or causes), the latter being known as experimental error (or error).

Assumptions:

For the validity of the 'F- Test' in ANOVA, the following assumptions are made.

1. The observations are independent.
2. The parent population from which the sample observations are taken is Normal and
3. Various treatment and environmental effects are additive in nature.

❖ ANOVA (One Way Classification)

The general format of the data presentation for analysing data to apply ANOVA is as given below. Let us suppose that N observations x_{ij}, (i = 1, 2, …, k; j =1, 2, …, n_i) of a random variable X are grouped on some basis into k classes of sizes n_1, n_2, …, n_k respectively such that, N = $\sum n_i$ for i = 1, 2, …,k is presented as below:

Class	Observations				Total
1	x_{11}	x_{12}	. . .	x_{1n1}	R_1
2	x_{21}	x_{22}	. . .	x_{2n2}	R_2
…	…	…	…	…	…
I	x_{i1}	x_{i2}	. . .	$x_{i\,n2}$	R_i
…	…	…	…	…	…
K	x_{k1}	x_{k2}	. . .	x_{knk}	R_k

Objective of ANOVA (One way)

To examine whether there is any significant difference between the class means in view of the inherent variability within the separate classes.

Null Hypothesis: We set up the null hypothesis that there is no significant difference between means of different classes. In other words, the yield of rice for four fertilizers on the average are same. Mathematically, the null and alternative hypotheses can be set as:

$$H_0: \mu_1 = \mu_2 = \mu_3 = - - - = \mu_k$$

$$H_1: \mu_1 \neq \mu_2 \neq \mu_3 \neq - - - \neq \mu_k$$

where μ_i for i =1, 2, ,.. , k classes is the mean yield of rice for i^{th} class.

Formula for Computation

1. Grand total = G = $\sum\sum x_{ij}$; for i = 1, 2,…k and j = 1, 2, .. n_i
2. Correction Factor = CF = G^2/N; where N = $\sum n_i$ for i = 1, 2, …k
3. Total Sum of Squares = TSS = $\sum\sum x^2_{ij}$ – CF;
4. Sum of Squares between Classes = SS (Between Classes)

   = $\{R^2_1/n_1 + R^2_2/n_2 + \ldots + R^2_i/n_i + \ldots + R^2_k/n_k\}$ – CF;
5. Error Sum of Squares = Residual Sum of Squares = SS(within Classes) = TSS – SS(Between Classes)

Degrees of Freedom(D.F.)

Total Degrees of Freedom = Total D.F.= N –1

Degrees of Freedom between Classes= Between D.F. =k –1

Degrees of Freedom within Classes= Within D.F.=N –k

Note:

1. Sum of Squares between Classes is also called as Sum of Squares between Treatments.
2. Error Sum of Squares or Residual Sum of Squares is also called as Sum of Squares within treatments.
3. Degrees of Freedom between Classes are also called as Degrees of Freedom between Treatments.
4. Degrees of Freedom within Classes is also called as Degrees of Freedom due to Error or Residual Degrees of Freedom.

Calculation of Mean Square:

1. Mean Square for Classes = MSC = SS (Between Classes)/ k-1
2. Mean Square for Error = MSE = SS(within Classes)/N-K

Calculation of F-Ratio:

The F- Ratio is calculated as

$$F = MSC / MSE \text{ Or } F = MSE / MSC$$

depending upon the Value of MSC and MSE. The larger of the two will be taken on the numerator for having a value of F more than '1'. The F follows an F-distribution with (K-1, N-K) D.F. Tables pertaining to F-distribution are presented in Appendix: F-tables.

ANOVA Table (One Way Classification)

Source of Variation	D.F.	Sum of Squares	Mean Square	F - Ratio
Between Classes	K–1	SS (Between Classes)	MSC = SS (Between Classes)/k-1	MSC/ MSE Or MSE/ MSC
With in Classes	N–k	SS(within Classes)	MSE = SS(within Classes)/N-k	
Total	N–1	TSS		

Example 19

Three fertilizers A, B and C are given to different number of plots of uniform area and their yields in kilograms are as given below. Test whether the average yields of three different fertilizers is same at α = 5% LOS?

Fertilizer	Yields				
A	7	11	9	-	-
B	4	6	8	5	2
C	10	8	6	8	-

Solution:

Table showing Sums of observations

Fertilizer	Yields					Total
A	7	11	9	-	-	27
B	4	6	8	5	2	25
C	10	8	6	8	-	32
Grand Total = G						84

Table showing Squares of observations

Fertilizer	Yields					Total
A	49	121	81	-	-	251
B	16	36	64	25	4	145
C	100	64	36	64	-	264
Sum of Squares						660

Formula for Computation

1. $n_1 = 3; n_2 = 5; n_3 = 4; N= n_1+ n_2 + n_3 = 3 + 5 + 4 = 12$
2. Grand total = G = $\sum\sum x_{ij} = 84$
3. Correction Factor = CF = $G^2/N = (84^2/12) = 7056/12 = 588$
4. Total Sum of Squares = TSS = $\sum\sum\sigma\ x^2_{ij} - CF = 660 - 588 = 72$
5. Sum of Squares between Classes = SS (Between Classes)

   $= \{R^2_1/n_1 + R^2_2/n_2 + \ldots + R^2_k/n_k\} - CF$

   $= \{27^2/3 + 25^2/5 + 32^2/4\} - 588$

   $= \{729/3+625/5+1024/4\} - 588$

   $= \{243+125+256\} - 588 = 36$

6. Error Sum of Square s= Residual Sum of Squares

   = SS (within Classes)

   = TSS – SS (Between Classes)

   = 72 – 36 = 36

   Degrees of Freedom (D.F.)

   Total Degrees of Freedom = Total D.F. = N – 1 = 12 – 1 = 11

   Degrees of Freedom between Classes = Between D.F. = k – 1 = 3 – 1 = 2

   Degrees of Freedom within Classes = Within D.F. = N – k = 12 – 3 = 9

   Calculation of Mean Square

7. Mean Square for Classes = MSC

   = SS (Between Classes)/k – 1

   = 36/2 =18

8. Mean Square for Error= MSE

= SS(within Classes)/N-K

= 36/9 = 4

Calculation of F-Ratio

The F-Ratio is calculated as

F = MSC/MSE = 18/4 = 4.5

~ F-distribution with (2,9) D.F. i.e., F(2,9)

ANOVA Table (One Way Classification)

Source of Variation	D.F.	Sum of Squares	Mean Square	F-Ratio
Between Classes	3 – 1 =2	36	MSC = 36/2 =18	18/4 = 4.5
Within Classes	12 – 3 = 9	36	MSE = 36/9 = 4	~ F(2,9)
Total	12 – 1 = 11	TSS		

Table Value of F-Ratio

Since the calculated value of F = 4.5 is more than the table value of F= 4.26 at α=5% LOS, the H_0: $\mu_1 = \mu_2 = \mu_3$ may not be accepted. Hence, the average yields of three fertilizers are different.

Note:

The table value of F is obtained from the corresponding F table by fixing the α at 5% LOS (It is given in the question). In general, the value of can be chosen at the convenience of the decision-maker. Usual values of α are 5% or 1%. But it can be chosen differently as well. In the present problem, Table value of F for (2,9) D.F. at α = 5% is 4.26.

Conclusion:

1. It may be noted that the data can be shifted to a different origin.
2. It may be noted that the observations in each class/treatment can be equal.

❖ Analysis of Variance – Two Way Classification

We have seen how to analyse the data for one single factor (class, Salesmen, Treatments, Operator, Machine, etc.) using analysis of variance. In this section, we study how to analyse the data using two factors simultaneously. For example, we have two factors as variety or rice and soil composition and the yields for each combination are given in the table below.

Variety of rice	Soil Composition						Total
	1	2	...	j	...	n	
1	x_{11}	x_{12}	...	x_{1j}	...	x_{1n}	R_1
2	x_{21}	x_{22}	...	x_{2j}	...	x_{2n}	R_2
...	...	...	...	...	...	...	...
i	x_{i1}	x_{j2}	...	x_{ij}	...	x_{in}	R_i
...	...	...	...	...	...	...	...
m	x_{m1}	x_{m2}	...	x_{mj}	...	x_{mn}	R_m
Total	C_1	C_2	...	C_j	...	C_n	

The objective of ANOVA (Two way) is to examine whether there is any significant difference between the means yields of rice varieties(or the appropriate cause of variation), to examine whether there is any significant difference between the means yields for different Soil Composition (or the appropriate cause of variation).

Null and Alternative Hypotheses

We set up two different null hypotheses one each for the individual causes of variation.

1. There is no significant difference between means yields of rice varieties. Mathematically, the null and alternative hypotheses can be set as:

   $H_0: \mu_1 = \mu_2 = \mu_3 = - - - = \mu_m$

   $H_1: \mu_1 \neq \mu_2 \neq \mu_3 \neq - - - \neq \mu_m$

   where $\mu_{i,}$ for i = 1, 2, ,.. , m varieties is the mean yield of rice for i^{th} variety.

2. There is no significant difference between means yields for different soil compositions. Mathematically, the null and alternative hypotheses can be set as:

   $H_0: \mu_1 = \mu_2 = \mu_3 = - - - - = \mu_n$

   $H_1: \mu_1 \neq \mu_2 \neq \mu_3 \neq - - - \neq \mu_n$

   where $\mu_{j,}$ for j = 1, 2, ,... , n is the mean yield for j^{th} soil composition.

Formula for Computation

1. Grand total = G = $\sum\sum x_{ij}$; for i = 1, 2, … m and j = 1, 2, ... n
2. Correction Factor = CF = G^2/N; where N = mn
3. Total Sum of Squares = TSS = $\sum\sum x^2_{ij}$ - CF;
4. Sum of Squares between soil composition = SS (Between Columns) = $C_1^2/m + C_2^2/m + \ldots + C_i^2/m + \ldots + C_k^2/m\} - CF$;
5. Sum of Squares between rice varieties = SS (between rows) =

   $\{R_1^2/n + R_2^2/n + \ldots + R_i^2/n + \ldots + R_k^2/n\} - CF$
6. Error Sum of Squares= Residual Sum of Squares = SS(Error)

   = TSS – {SS(Between Columns) + SS(Between Rows)

Degrees of Freedom (D.F.)

Total Degrees of Freedom= Total D.F.= (mxn-1)

Degrees of Freedom between Columns= n-1

Degrees of Freedom between Rows = m-1

Degrees of Freedom due to Error (Residual)= (n-1)(m-1)

Calculation of Mean Square

1. Mean Square for Rows = MSR = SS (Between Rows)/ m-1
2. Mean Square for Columns = MSC = SS(Between Columns)/n-1
3. Mean Square due to Error = MSE = SS(Error)/(n-1)(m-1)

Calculation of F-Ratio

There will be two F-ratios, one is between MSR and MSE and the other is between MSC and MSE. In the first case, F- Ratio is calculated as F=MSR/MSE or F=MSE/MSR depending upon the value of MSR and MSE. The larger of the two will be taken on the numerator for having a value of F more than '1'. The F follows an F-distribution with (Numerator D.F., Denominator D.F.). In the second case, F-Ratio is calculated as F=MSC/MSE Or F=MSE/MSC depending upon the Value of MSC and MSE. The larger of the two will be taken on the numerator for having a value of F more than '1'. The F follows an F-distribution with (Numerator D.F., Denominator D.F.). Tables pertaining to F-distribution are presented in Appendix: F-tables.

Note:

There are three possibilities.

1. In both the cases, the H_0 may be rejected,
2. In both the cases, the H_0 may not be rejected,
3. One May be rejected and the other may not be rejected.

The details of calculations explained above can be summarized and put into a table called ANOVA Table (Two Way Classification) which is presented below.

ANOVA Table (Two Way Classification)

Source of Variation	D.F.	Sum of Squares	Mean Square	F - Ratio
Between Rows	(m-1)	SSR	MSR = SSR / m-1	MSR/ MSE or MSE/ MSR
Between Columns	(n-1)	SSC	MSC = SSC / n-1	
Error	(m-1)x(n-1)	SSE	MSE= SSE/ (m-1)(n-1)	MSC/ MSE or MSE/ MSC
Total	(mn-1)	TSS		

Example 21

Four Technicians analyzed three samples each for the moisture content in the sample. The results are given below.

Samples	Technicians			
	A	B	C	D
X	9	12	10	11
Y	12	11	15	12
Z	9	10	12	14

Analyze the data and comment.

Solution:

1. There is no significant difference in mean moisture content between the samples. Mathematically, the null and alternative hypotheses can be set as: H_0: $\mu_x = \mu_y = \mu_z$ and H_1: $\mu_x \neq \mu_y \neq \mu_z$

   where μ_i, for i = x, y and z is the mean moisture content of the ith sample.

2. There is no significant difference in mean moisture content between technicians. Mathematically, the null and alternative hypotheses can be set as: H_0: $\mu_A = \mu_B = \mu_C = \mu_D$ and H_1: $\mu_A \neq \mu_B \neq \mu_C \neq \mu_D$ where μ_j, for j = A, B, C and D is the mean moisture content for j^{th} Technician.

Table showing Sums of observations

Samples	Technicians				Total
	A	B	C	D	
X	9	12	10	11	42
Y	12	11	15	12	50
Z	9	10	12	14	45
Total	30	33	37	37	137

Table showing Squares of observations

Samples	Technicians				Total
	A	B	C	D	
X	81	144	100	121	446
Y	144	121	225	144	634
Z	81	100	144	196	521
Total	306	365	469	461	1601

Grand total = $G = \sum\sum x_{ij} = 137$

Correction Factor = $CF = (137)^2/12 = 1564.08$

Total Sum of Squares = TSS = 1601 – 1564.08 = 36.92

Sum of Squares between Columns (SSC)

$= \{30^2/3+33^2/3+37^2/3+37^2/3\} - 1564.08$

$= 1575.66 - 1564.08 = 11.58$

Sum of Squares between Rows (SSR)

$= \{42^2/4+50^2/4+45^2/4\} - 1564.08$

$= 1572.25 - 1564.08 = 8.17$

Error Sum of Squares (SSE)

$= 36.92 - (11.58 + 8.17) = 17.17$

Degrees of Freedom (D.F.):

Total Degrees of Freedom = Total D.F. = (4 x 3 – 1) = 11

Degrees of Freedom between Columns = 4 – 1=3

Degrees of Freedom between Rows = 3 – 1= 2

Degrees of Freedom due to Error = (4 – 1)(3 – 1) = 6

Source of Variation	D.F.	Sum of Squares	Mean Square	F - Ratio
Between Rows	2	8.17	MSC = 8.17/2 = 4.09	4.09/ 2.86 = **1.43**
Between Columns	3	11.58	MSR =11.58/3 = 3.86	3.86/ 2.86 = **1.35**
Error	6	17.17	MSE = 17.17/6 = 2.86	
Total	11	36.92		

Conclusion

1. *F-Ratio (Between Technicians)*

   Calculated Value of F = 1.43; Table Value of F (2,6) D.F. at 5% LOS (assumed) = 5.14

   Since Calculated Value is less than Table Value, it can be concluded that H_0 is not rejected. Hence, there is no significant difference in mean moisture content analysed by technicians.

2. *F-Ratio (Between Samples)*

   Calculated Value of F = 1.35; Table Value of F (3,6) D.F. at 5% LOS (assumed) = 4.76

   Since Calculated Value is less than Table Value, it can be concluded that H_0 is accepted. Hence, there is no significant difference in mean moisture content between the samples.

❖ How to Choose a Statistical Tool from Available Statistical Tests

To select the right test, ask yourself two questions: What kind of data have you collected? What is your goal? Then refer to the Table.

TABLE 10.3 Table for Selecting a Statistical Test

	Type of Data			
Goal	**Measurement (from Gaussian Population)**	**Rank, Score, or Measurement (from Non-Gaussian Population)**	**Binomial (Two Possible Outcomes)**	**Survival Time**
Describe one group	Mean, SD	Median, interquartile range	Proportion	Kaplan Meier survival curve
Compare one group to a hypothetical value	One-sample *t* test	Wilcoxon test	Chi-square or Binomial test	
Compare two unpaired groups	Unpaired *t* test	Mann-Whitney test	Fisher's test (chi-square for large samples)	Log-rank test or Mantel-Haenszel
Compare two paired groups	Paired *t* test	Wilcoxon test	McNemar's test	Conditional proportional hazards regression
Compare three or more unmatched groups	One-way ANOVA	Kruskal-Wallis test	Chi-square test	Cox proportional hazard regression
Compare three or more matched groups	Repeated-measures ANOVA	Friedman test	Cochrane Q	Conditional proportional hazards regression

Contd...

Quantify association between two variables	Pearson correlation	Spearman correlation	Contingency coefficients	
Predict value from another measured variable	Simple linear regression or Non-linear regression	Non-parametric regression	Simple logistic regression	Cox proportional hazard regression
Predict value from several measured or binomial variables	Multiple linear regression or Multiple non-linear regression		Multiple logistic regression	Cox proportional hazard regression

Choosing between Parametric and Non-Parametric Tests: The Easy Cases

Choosing between parametric and non-parametric tests is sometimes easy. You should definitely choose a parametric test if you are sure that your data are sampled from a population that follows a Gaussian distribution (at least approximately). You should definitely select a non-parametric test in three situations:

1. The outcome is a rank or a score and the population is clearly not Gaussian. Examples include class ranking of students, the Apgar score for the health of newborn babies (measured on a scale of 0 to 10 and where all scores are integers), the visual analogue score for pain (measured on a continuous scale where 0 is no pain and 10 is unbearable pain), and the star scale commonly used by movie and restaurant critics (* is OK, ***** is Fantastic).

2. Some values are "off the scale," that is, too high or too low to measure. Even if the population is Gaussian, it is impossible to analyze such data with a parametric test since you don't know all of the values. Using a non-parametric test with these data is simple. Assign values too low to measure an arbitrary very low value and assign values too high to measure an arbitrary very high value. Then perform a non-parametric test. Since the non-parametric test only knows about the relative ranks of the values, it won't matter that you didn't know all the values exactly.

3. The data are measurements, and you are sure that the population is not distributed in a Gaussian manner. If the data are not sampled from a Gaussian distribution, consider whether you can transform the values to make the distribution become Gaussian. For example, you might take the logarithm or reciprocal of all values. There are often biological or chemical reasons (as well as statistical ones) for performing a particular transform.

Choosing between Parametric and Non-parametric Tests: The Hard Cases

It is not always easy to decide whether a sample comes from a Gaussian population. Consider these points:

1. If you collect many data points (over a hundred or so), you can look at the distribution of data and it will be fairly obvious whether the distribution is approximately bell-shaped. A formal statistical test (Kolmogorov-Smirnov test, not explained in this book) can be used to test whether the distribution of the data differs significantly from a Gaussian distribution. With few data points, it is difficult to tell whether the data are Gaussian by inspection, and the formal test has little power to discriminate between Gaussian and non-Gaussian distributions.

2. You should look at previous data as well. Remember, what matters is the distribution of the overall population, not the distribution of your sample. In deciding whether a population is Gaussian, look at all available data, not just data in the current experiment.

3. Consider the source of scatter. When the scatter comes from the sum of numerous sources (with no one source contributing most of the scatter), you expect to find a roughly Gaussian distribution.

When in doubt, some people choose a parametric test (because they aren't sure the Gaussian assumption is violated), and others choose a non-parametric test (because they aren't sure the Gaussian assumption is met).

Choosing between Parametric and Non-parametric Tests: Does it Matter?

Does it matter whether you choose a parametric or non-parametric test? The answer depends on sample size. There are four cases to think about:

1. Large sample. What happens when you use a parametric test with data from a non-gaussian population? The central limit theorem ensures that parametric tests work well with large samples even if the population is non-Gaussian. In other words, parametric tests are robust to deviations from Gaussian distributions, so long as the samples are large. The snag is that it is impossible to say how large is large enough, as it depends on the nature of the particular non-Gaussian distribution. Unless the population distribution is really weird, you are probably safe choosing a parametric test when there are at least two dozen data points in each group.
2. Large sample. What happens when you use a non-parametric test with data from a Gaussian population? Non-parametric tests work well with large samples from Gaussian populations. The P values tend to be a bit too large, but the discrepancy is small. In other words, non-parametric tests are only slightly less powerful than parametric tests with large samples.
3. Small samples. What happens when you use a parametric test with data from non-Gaussian populations? You can't rely on the central limit theorem, so the P value may be inaccurate.
4. Small samples. When you use a non-parametric test with data from a Gaussian population, the P values tend to be too high. The non-parametric tests lack statistical power with small samples.

Thus, large data sets present no problems. It is usually easy to tell if the data come from a Gaussian population, but it doesn't really matter because the non-parametric tests are so powerful and the parametric tests are so robust. Small data sets present a dilemma. It is difficult to tell if the data come from a Gaussian population, but it matters a lot. The non-parametric tests are not powerful and the parametric tests are not robust.

One or Two-sided P Value?

With many tests, you must choose whether you wish to calculate a one or two-sided P value (same as one or two-tailed P value). The difference between one and two-sided P values. Let's review the difference in the context of a t-test. The P value is calculated for the null hypothesis that the two population means are equal, and any discrepancy between the two sample means is due to chance. If this null hypothesis is true, the one-sided P value is the probability that two sample means would differ as much as was observed (or further) in the direction specified by the hypothesis just by chance, even though the means of the overall populations are actually equal. The two-sided P value also includes the probability that the sample means would differ that much in the opposite direction (i.e., the other group has the larger mean). The two-sided P value is twice the one-sided P value.

A one-sided P value is appropriate when you can state with certainty (and before collecting any data) that there either will be no difference between the means or that the difference will go in a direction you can specify in advance (i.e., you have specified which group will have the larger mean). If you cannot specify the direction of any difference before collecting data, then a two-sided P value is more appropriate. If in doubt, select a two-sided P value.

If you select a one-sided test, you should do so before collecting any data and you need to state the direction of your experimental hypothesis. If the data go the other way, you must be willing to attribute that difference (or association or correlation) to chance, no matter how striking the data. If you would be intrigued, even a little, by data that goes in the "wrong" direction, then you should use a two-sided P value. It recommends that you always calculate a two-sided P value.

Paired or Unpaired Test

When comparing two groups, you need to decide whether to use a paired test. When comparing three or more groups, the term paired is not apt and the term repeated measures is used instead.

Use an unpaired test to compare groups when the individual values are not paired or matched with one another. Select a paired or repeated-measures test when values represent repeated measurements on one subject (before and after an intervention) or measurements on matched subjects. The paired or repeated-measures tests are also appropriate for repeated laboratory experiments run at different times, each with its own control.

You should select a paired test when values in one group are more closely correlated with a specific value in the other group than with random values in the other group. It is only appropriate to select a paired test when the subjects were matched or paired before the data were collected. You cannot base the pairing on the data you are analyzing.

REVIEW QUESTIONS

1. When do you use large sample tests? What are the advantages of using large sample tests?
2. What is the difference between single mean test and difference of means test?
3. What do you understand by estimation? In what sense do we consider estimation as a procedure of decision-making?
4. What do mean by 'Statistical Estimation'? Briefly explain the methodology used for estimating the mean of the population from the mean of the sample.
5. What is the difference between 'Statistic' and 'Parameter'? Explain with examples.
6. Explain clearly the desirable properties of point estimate.
7. What is meant by confidence interval of a population parameter?
8. Explain clearly the procedure involved in interval estimation.
9. What is testing of hypothesis? Discuss various tests of hypothesis for the cases when the size of sample is large.
10. Explain the procedure generally followed in testing of hypothesis.
11. Describe the various steps involved in testing of hypothesis. What is the role standard error in testing of hypothesis?
12. What is meant by level of significance? What is one tailed and two tailed tests?
13. When do you use large sample tests? What are the advantages of using large sample tests?

14. What is the difference between single mean test and two means test?
15. What do you understand by estimation? In what sense do we consider estimation as a procedure of decision-making?
16. What do mean by 'Statistical Estimation'? Briefly explain the methodology used for estimating the mean of the population from the mean of the sample.
17. What is the difference between 'Statistic' and 'Parameter'? Explain with examples.
18. Explain clearly the desirable properties of point estimate.
19. What is meant by confidence interval of a population parameter?
20. Explain clearly the procedure involved in interval estimation.
21. What is testing of hypothesis? Discuss various tests of hypothesis for the cases when the size of sample is large.
22. What is the difference between parametric and non-parametric tests? Explain the importance of non-parametric test in marketing research.
23. A sample of 400 managers is found to have a mean height of 171.38 cms. Can it be reasonably regarded as a sample from a large population of mean height 171.17 cms and standard deviation of 3.3 cms?
24. In a random sample of 500 children from town A, the mean consumption of chocolate is 30 per month. In town B, a random sample of 400 children mean consumption of chocolate is 25 per month. Is there any significance between in the mean consumption of chocolates of two town children?
25. A sales clerk in the departmental store claims that 65% of the shoppers entering the shop leave without making a purchase. A random sample of 50 shoppers showed that 35 of them left without buying anything. Are these sample results consistent with the claim of the sales clerk? Use a level of significance of 0.05.
26. Past records show that 75% of a town consumes rice. A researcher has conducted a survey and found 60 out of 100 people will consume rice. Test the past records claim at a significance level of (i) 0.01, (ii) 0.05, and (iii) 0.10.
27. A soap manufacturer wanted to know what percentage of the citizens of Mumbai uses his soap. He conducted a survey and found that out of 500 persons selected at random for the purpose; only 10% use his soap. He spent ₹ 5 lakh on an advertisement campaign to attract more customers. In order to know the results of his campaign conducted another survey and found that out of 600 persons, 15% are using his soap. Do you think that the expenditure has really increased the percentage of citizens of Mumbai using his soap?
28. A new drug has been developed for the treatment of a certain disease. A group of 400 patients suffering from the disease were treated with an alternative drug. At the end of two weeks, 320 of the patients receiving the new drug recovered, while 240 of those taking the alternative drug recovered. Construct the 95 per cent confidence interval for the difference in the true proportion of patients who might be expected to the two drugs.
29. The foreman of a mining company has estimated the average quantity of one extracted per shift to be 34.6 tons and the sample standard deviation to be 2.8 tons per shift based upon a random sample of six shifts. Construct 95% and 90% confidence around sample average estimate.

30. A drug manufacturer has installed a machine which fills automatically 5grms of drug in each phial. A random sample of phials was taken and it is found to contain 5.02 grms on an average in a phial with a S.D. of 0.002 grms. Test at 5% level of significance whether the adjustment in the machine is in order?

31. You are given the following data about the life of two brands of bulbs:

	Sample size	Mean life (in hours)	Standard deviation (in hours)
Brand A	12	2,000	250
Brand B	15	2,230	300

Do you think that there is a significant difference in the quality of the two brands of bulbs?

32. Twelve persons are appointed in clerical position in an office. Their performance is noted by giving a test and the marks recorded out of 10. They are given 3 month's training and again they are given a test and marks recorded out of 12 are as given below.

Employee	A	B	C	D	E	F	G	H	I	J	K	L
Before	4	5	3	7	8	6	5	9	10	6	4	3
After	5	4	6	8	7	5	9	9	10	6	5	4

Can we conclude that the training has improved the performance of the employees?

33. A psychologist has prepared an 'Optimism Test" that is administered yearly to graduating students. The test measures how each graduating class feels about its future - the higher the score, the more optimistic the class. Last year's class had a mean score of $\mu = 15$. The scores are known to be normally distributed.

A sample of 9 seniors from this year's class was selected and tested. The scores for these seniors are as follows:

7 12 11 15 7 8 15 9 6

On the basis of this sample, can the psychologist conclude that this year's class has a different level of optimism to last year's class?

34. A statistician hires a company to input survey data into a computer. The company claims that the error rate is less than 0.1%. To test the claim, the statistician examines 10 000 numbers and discovers that three are incorrect. Do these results support the company claim? Test with α = 0.01.

35. A manufacturer sells its product by weight and states on the packaging that the weight is 375 grams with a standard deviation of 14.2 grams. The quality control inspector suspects that the average weight of the packets is, in fact, higher than this and institutes a survey to check these suspicions. In a random sample of 100 packets, the average weight is found to be 379 grams. Test at the 5% level of significance whether this result confirms the suspicions of the quality controller.

36. The number of units of a product sold in three different retail outlets are given below. Test whether the average number of units sold differ significantly across retail outlets? Use = 5% LOS.

Retail outlets	Number of units sold					
A	25	24	30	26	-	-
B	28	36	23	39	18	14
C	31	28	25	32	40	-

37. The following grades are obtained by students of a management programme in "Statistics" paper when taught in the A = Moring class and B= Afternoon class by the same professor. Can you conclude that morning class performed worse than the afternoon class by applying Mann-Whitney U test?

A	77	87	67	89	96	83	75	69	77	51	45
B	45	78	92	88	76	79	67	50	94	55	67

38. The following data relate to the costs of building comparable lots in the two resorts A and B (in cores of rupees)

Resort A	29	42	66	55	66	55
Resort B	35	57	51	51	60	60

The company owning the resort area A claimed that the median price of building lots was less in area A as compared to resort area B. You are asked to test this claim, using a non-parametric test with a 1 per cent level of significance.

39. On 15 different days Mr, X had to wait for the city bus to reach his college shown as: 15,25,12,10,23,13,15,10,13,14,16,9,15,14 and 18 minutes. Use the sign test at 5 per cent level of significance to test the bus company's claim that on an average, Mr. X should not have to wait for more than 16 minutes.

40. An experiment is conducted to judge the effect of brand name on quality perception, fifteen subjects are recruited for the purpose and are asked to taste and compare two samples of product (A and B) on a set of scale items judged to be ordinal. The following data are obtained:

pair	1	2	3	4	5	6	7	8	9	10	11	12	13	14	15
A	77	33	66	67	45	77	34	26	43	37	65	23	55	56	67
B	55	56	76	45	51	75	76	45	55	44	75	62	49	57	68

Test the hypothesis, using Wilcoxon matched – pairs test that there is no difference between perceived quality of the two samples. Use 5 per cent level of significance.

41. A company used three different methods of advertising its product in three cities. It later found increased sales (in thousand rupees) in identical retail outlets in the three cities as follows:

City A	45	66	69	59	69	55
City B	32	55	66	46	58	
City C	34	66	77	44	35	56

Use Kruskal-Wallis test to test the hypothesis that the mean increase in sales on account of three different methods of advertising was the same in the retail outlets in A,B and C cities. Use 5 per cent level of significance.

42. The outputs turned out by four operators in week are as given below. Test for the significant difference between the operators with regard to their average outputs. Use α = 5% LOS.

Operators	Outputs					
A	12	14	10	16	16	12
B	8	16	13	19	14	17
C	15	18	15	12	12	15
D	14	14	16	10	16	10

43. The number of hours of lost production for five machines in a factory for a period of six months is as given below. Test for the significant difference between the machines with regard to their average hours of lost production. Use α = 10% LOS.

Machines	**Hours of lost production**					
A	22	14	10	16	11	18
B	28	36	23	19	10	14
C	35	18	25	10	32	25
D	34	24	26	10	11	16
E	20	15	35	22	32	25

44. The Percentage of items 'out of stock' in three locations in Hyderabad operated by a Super Market are recorded and presented in the following table. Test whether the mean Percentage of items which are out of stock differ significantly? Use α = 1% LOS.

Location	**Items Out of Stock (in %)**				
Abids	2.2	3.4	10.0	6.1	11.2
Kukatpally	6.2	1.4	22.2	5.8	10.1
Begumpet	8.2	7.9	9.2	8.1	4.9

45. The following gives the monthly revenues (in ₹ lakhs) of a corporate hospital in three locations in Hyderabad.

	Month			
Location	**March**	**February**	**January**	**December**
Ameerpet	2.1	2.7	3.5	5.3
L.B. Nagar	3.4	1.8	2.9	2.6
Mehdipatnam	2.8	1.7	2.7	4.0

46. Test for the significance of interaction in the case of following information pertaining to mileage based on different brands of gasoline and cars? (Use α = 0.05)

	Brands of Gasoline			
Cars	**A**	**B**	**C**	**D**
Indica	13	14	13	12
	11	13	10	11
	11	10	10	12
Honda	14	13	12	11
	11	12	8	10
Mercedez	10	9	13	11

47. The following table gives the data on the performance of three different detergents at three different water temperatures. The performance was obtained on the 'whiteness' readings based on specially designed equipment for nine loads of washing:

	Dete detergent A	**Detedetergent B**	**Detedetergent C**
Cold water	45	43	55
Warm Water	37	40	56
Hot water	42	44	46

Perform a two-way analysis of variance, using the level of significance α =0.05

CHAPTER ELEVEN

NONPARAMETRIC OR DISTRIBUTION-FREE TESTS

INTRODUCTION

Nonparametric tests are also called *distribution-free* tests because the assumptions underlying their use are fewer and weaker than those associated with parametric tests. To put it another way, nonparametric tests require few if any assumptions about the shapes of the underlying population distributions. For this reason, they are often used in place of parametric tests if/when one feels that the assumptions of the parametric test have been too grossly violated (e.g., if the distributions are too severely skewed).

Many statistical methods apply solely to populations having a specified distribution of values, such as the normal distribution. Naturally, this assumption is not always reasonable in practical applications. The need for techniques that may be applied over a wide range of distributions of the parent population has led to the development of distribution-free or nonparametric statistical methods. In place of parameters such as means and variances and their estimators, these methods use ranks and other measures of relative magnitude hence the term "nonparametric." Distribution-free statistical procedures do not require the normality of underlying populations or that such populations have any particular mathematical form. Although they do require certain assumptions, nonparametric tests are generally valid whatever the population distribution.

Nonparametric counterparts to standard statistical testing procedures are typically used either when an assumption violation that invalidates the standard test is suspected, or in situations where the response variable of interest is not susceptible to numerical measurement, but can be ranked. A common example of this second setting is provided by studies of preference in marketing. For instance, in a taste test, a consumer may be asked to rank a new product in order of preference among several current brands. While the consumer probably has a preference for each product, the strength of that preference is difficult to measure. The best solution may be to have the consumer rank the various products (1 = best, 2 = second best, and so forth). The resulting set of ranks cannot be appropriately tested using standard procedures. Thus, nonparametric methods are often employed when measurements are available only on a nominal (categorical) or ordinal (rank) scale.

NONPARAMETRIC TESTS

Nonparametric tests, on the other hand, are the tests which do not depend upon the particular form of the basic frequency function from which the samples are drawn. Nonparametric test does not make any assumption regarding the form of the population. However, there are certain assumptions associated with Nonparametric tests are:

1. Sample observations are independent,

2. Variable(s) under study is (are) continuous,
3. Probability distribution function is continuous,
4. Lower order moments exist (mean, variance),
5. Measurement of the variable is Non-numerical (Ex.: Consumers rank a product in order of preference)
6. At the most it is ordinal (ranks).

❖ Advantages of Nonparametric Tests

The following advantages of nonparametric tests:

1. If the sample size is very small, there may be no alternative to using a nonparametric statistical test unless the nature of the population distribution is known exactly.
2. Nonparametric tests typically make fewer assumptions about the data and may be more relevant to a particular situation. In addition, the hypothesis tested by the nonparametric test may be more appropriate for the research investigation.
3. Nonparametric tests are available to analyze data which are inherently in ranks as well as data whose seemingly numerical scores have the strength of ranks. That is, the researcher may only be able to say of his or her subjects that one has more or less of the characteristic than another, without being able to say how much more or less. For example, in studying such a variable as anxiety, we may be able to state that subject A is more anxious than subject B without knowing at all exactly how much more anxious A is. If data are inherently in ranks, or even if they can be categorized only as plus or minus (more or less, better or worse), they can be treated by nonparametric methods, whereas they cannot be treated by parametric methods unless precarious and, perhaps, unrealistic assumptions are made about the underlying distributions.
4. Nonparametric methods are available to treat data which are simply classificatory or categorical, i.e., are measured in a nominal scale. No parametric technique applies to such data.
5. Nonparametric statistical tests are typically much easier to learn and to apply than are parametric tests. In addition, their interpretation often is more direct than the interpretation of parametric tests.
6. Nonparametric methods are readily comprehensible, very simple and easy to apply and do not require complicated sample theory.
7. No assumption is made about the form of the frequency function of the parent population from which sample is drawn.
8. Most of the Socio-Economic data are non-normal, in general, Nonparametric tests have found applications in Psychometrics, sociology and educational statistics.
9. Nonparametric tests are available to deal with the data which are given in ranks or whose seemingly numerical scores have the strength of ranks. For instance, no parametric test can be applied if the scores are given in grades such as A^+, A, A^-, B^+, B.

❖ Disadvantages of Nonparametric Tests

1. Nonparametric tests are less powerful. Because parametric tests use more of the information available in a set of numbers. Parametric tests make use of information consistent with interval scale measurement, whereas nonparametric tests typically make use of ordinal information only.

2. Nonparametric tests can be used only if the measurements are nominal or ordinal. Even in that case, if a parametric test exists, it is more powerful than the nonparametric test. In other words, if all the assumptions of a statistical model are satisfied by the data and if the measurements are of required strength, then the nonparametric tests are wasteful of time and data.
3. No Nonparametric tests exist for testing interactions in "Analysis of variance", so far, unless special assumptions about the additivity of the model are made.
4. Nonparametric tests are designed to test statistical hypothesis only and not for estimating the parameters.

❖ Why use Nonparametric Tests?

There are two main reasons to use nonparametric tests:

1. They apply to more kinds of data than the t-tests. Suppose the observations can be ordered, but that differences between the observations do not have a consistent meaning. For example, anxiety is sometimes measured with sets of yes-no questions and the score is the number of yes answers. A set of 36 questions gives a scale 0-36, but the difference between scores of 1 and 2 is not the same as the difference between scores of 31 and 32.
2. Even when t-testing is possible, the data may be so obviously non-normal (say, bimodal) as to rule it out.

❖ Limitations of Nonparametric Tests

In light of the preceding slide one might wonder, why not use nonparametric tests all the time?

1. Nonparametric tests cannot give significant results for very small samples as all the possible rank-sums are fairly likely.
2. They may require the use of fiddly tables and are not built into Excel (though they are available in R).
3. They do not, without the addition of extra assumptions, give confidence intervals for the means or medians of the underlying distributions.

PARAMETRIC "P" VS. NONPARAMETRIC "NP" TESTS

1. "P" tests use interval or ratio scale data while "NP" tests allow the hypothesis testing when data is nominal/ordinal – and also with numerical data.
2. "NP" tests need no assumption on population probability distributions.
3. "NP" tests are computationally less complicated in small samples than "P" tests.
4. Probability statements obtained from most "NP" tests are exact probability statements.
5. "P" tests make more efficient use of the information. If they can be carried out, they are preferable.
6. "NP" tests can be more tedious to be calculated when using large samples (however, we don't calculate any of these by hand, do we?).

❖ Nonparametric Tests and Procedures

Sums of ranks are the primary tools of nonparametric statistics. When comparing samples, the statistician ranks the observations in order, and then considers statistics based on those ranks, rather than on the 'raw data'. Most statistical computer packages will calculate a wide array of nonparametric statistical procedures. The most common rank-based tests are the Wilcoxon rank sum and Wilcoxon signed-rank statistics, used for comparing two populations independent sampling experiments and paired-difference experiments.

For independent samples, another nonparametric analog to the two-sample t-test is the Mann-Whitney test, which may be extended, in the case of more than two samples, to the Kruskal-Wallis test. The Kruskal-Wallis test (which tests location) and Friedman two-way ANOVA (which compares variation) are often used as alternatives to the analysis of variance for comparing several populations in a completely randomized experimental design. The Kolmogorov-Smirnov two-sample test is also used for testing differences between sample cumulative distribution functions. For one-sample tests, a Kolmogorov-Smirnov procedure has been developed to compare the shape and location of a sample distribution to a reference distribution, such as a normal or uniform.

List of most widely-used nonparametric tests in the business environment are:

1. Median Test
2. Run Test
3. McNemer Test
4. Sign Test for Paired Data
5. Wilcoxon Signed Rank (Matched Pairs) Test
6. Rank Sum Test (Mann-Whitney U-Test)
7. Kolmogrov-Smirnov Test
8. Kruskal-Wallis Test
9. Rank Correlation
10. Chi-square Test

These tests do not require the assumption that the population is normally distributed.

Chi-Square Test (χ^2)

1. The chi-square test is an important nonparametric known as a distribution-free test. No rigid assumptions are necessary in regard to the type of population distribution as is necessary for Normal Distribution except those stated above in regard to the nature of sample observations and the nature of events to which these observations are related.
2. It is not necessary to have the values of the parameters like the μ or s of a population distribution because it is based on the degree of freedom only.
3. This is simpler to understand as less Mathematical details are involved.
4. This can be used in simple ranking of values and, therefore, useful where data is not exactly measured.

This can be used with very small samples and is therefore useful in medical and social science research.

Applications of χ^2 Distribution

Chi-Square Distribution is used in the following situations:

1. To test if the population has a specified value of the variance σ^2.
2. Chi-Square test of goodness of fit.
3. χ^2-test for independence of attributes.

(i) *χ^2 test for Specified Population Variance*

We want to test if the given Normal Population has specified variance $\sigma^2 = \sigma_0^2$ (say).

We set up:

(a) Null Hypothesis (H_O): $\sigma^2 = \sigma_0^2$.

(b) Alternative Hypothesis (H_1): $\sigma^2 \neq \sigma_0^2$.

Test Statistic: $\chi^2 = \dfrac{\sum_{i=1}^{n}(x_i - \bar{x})^2}{\sigma_0^2} = \dfrac{ns^2}{\sigma_0^2}$ ~ a Chi Square Distribution with (n-1)df sample variance $\sigma^2 = \dfrac{1}{n}\sum_{i=1}^{n}(x_i - \bar{x})^2$ is the sample Variance.

Conclusion: By comparing the calculated value of Chi-Square with the tabulated value of Chi-Square for (n-1) df (degrees of freedom) at the selected level of Significance, we may accept or reject the $H_{0.}$

Example 1

Auto manufacturer representative claims that his company has perfected an adjustment to a machine that will reduce the variability in the diameter of the screws produced by the machine. The original variance was 0.010 inches. To determine whether or not his claim is reasonable, a random sample of 20 screws is selected from those produced after the adjustment had been made. The sample variance is 0.009. Does this evidence support the representative's claim?

Solution:

(a) Null Hypothesis (H_0): $\sigma^2 = 0.010$.

(b) Alternative Hypothesis (H_1): $\sigma^2 \neq 0.010$.

The data given is: n=20, $\sigma^2 = 0.009, \sigma_0^2 = 0.010$

Test Statistic:

$$\chi^2 = \frac{n\sigma^2}{\sigma_0^2} = \frac{20 \times 0.009}{0.010} = 18$$

Degrees of freedom = (n – 1) = (20 – 1) = 19

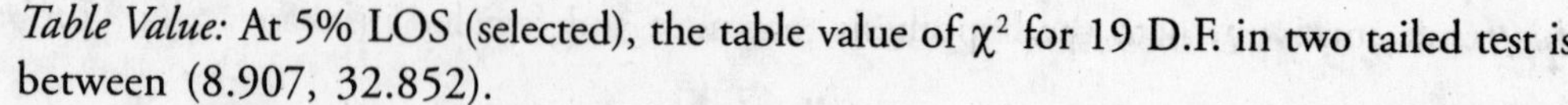

Table Value: At 5% LOS (selected), the table value of χ^2 for 19 D.F. in two tailed test is between (8.907, 32.852).

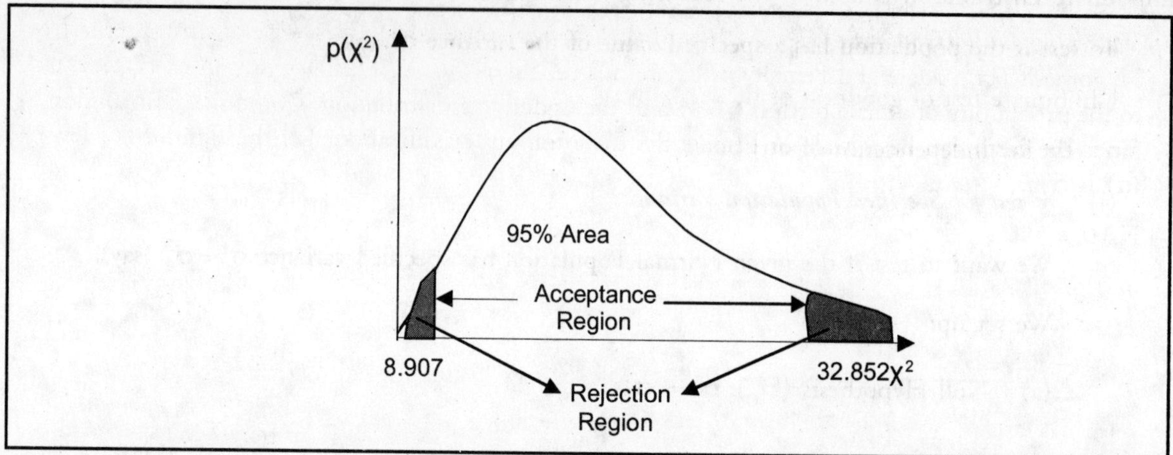

Conclusion: Since the computed value of c^2=18 is falling within the acceptance Region (limits obtained from the tables) for 19 D.F. at 5% LOS, we may accept H_0, and conclude that the sample evidence presents no reason to doubt the representative's claim.

(ii) ***χ^2 Test as a Test for Goodness of Fit***

One of the very popular applications of χ^2 test is test of goodness of fit. It enables us to ascertain how the theoretical distributions such as Binomial, Poisson, Normal etc., can fit into empirical distributions obtained from sample data. When an ideal frequency curve whether normal or some other type is fitted to the data, we are interested in finding out how well this curve fits with the observed facts. A test of the concordance (goodness of fit) of the two can be made just by inspection, but such a test is obviously inadequate.

Degrees of Freedom for Goodness of Fit

In order to determine the degrees of freedom for goodness of fit using Chi-Square test, we should first count the number of classes (symbolized by k) for which comparison between observed and expected frequencies is going to be made. As a general rule the degrees of freedom would be (k–1). However, if in addition to the total, we have to impose further restrictions, the degrees of freedom will be reduced by the number of restrictions imposed. For example, for normal distribution, if we have seven classes of observed frequencies k=7, and n =7–1=6. If we have to use the sample mean as an estimate of the population mean, we will have to subtract an additional degree of freedom which leaves us with only 5 (i.e., 6-1) D.F. In addition, if we have to use the sample standard deviation to estimate the population standard deviation, we will have to subtract one more degree of freedom leaving us with 4 (i.e., 5–1) D.F. Hence, as a general rule we should first employ the (k–1) rule and then subtract an additional degree of freedom for each population parameter that has to be estimated from the sample data.

Example 2

A market survey of 320 families with 5 children each revealed the following distribution:

Number of Boys	5	4	3	2	1	0
Number of Girls	0	1	2	3	4	5
Number of Families	14	56	110	88	40	12

Is this result consistent with the hypothesis that male and female births are equally probable?

Solution:

1. ***We set up Null Hypothesis (H_0):*** Male and Female births are equally probable against alternative Hypothesis (H_1): Male and Female births are not equally probable. This assumption of H_0 takes us to the probability of a male birth is p = ½ and the underlying distribution is Binomial distribution. Since the birth can be a Male or Female the dichotomous classification. Let the significance level (α) is 5%.

   Fix α = 5%

2. ***Test Statistic:***

$$\chi^2 = \sum_{i=1}^{k} \frac{(O_i - E_i)^2}{E_i}$$ ~ a Chi Square Distribution with (k-1) D.F., where O_i refers to

the observed frequencies and E_i refers to the expected frequencies. The probability of x male births in a family of 5 is given by

$P(x) = {}^5C_x P^x q^{5-x}$; for x = 0,1,2,3,4,5

$= {}^5C_x (½)^5$ [since p = q = ½]

To get the expected frequencies, multiply P(x) by the total number N = 320.

X	P(x)	Expected Frequency = N × P(x)
0	${}^5C_0 (½)^5 = 1/32$	320 × 1/32 = 10
1	${}^5C_1 (½)^5 = 5/32$	320 × 5/32 = 50
2	${}^5C_2 (½)^5 = 10/32$	320 × 10/32 =100
3	${}^5C_3 (½)^5 = 10/32$	320 × 10/32 =100
4	${}^5C_4 (½)^5 = 5/32$	320 × 5/32 = 50
5	${}^5C_5 (½)^5 = 1/32$	320 × 1/32 = 10

Arranging the observed and expected frequencies in the following table and calculating χ^2.

O_i	E_i	$(O_i - E_i)^2$	$(O_i - E_i)^2/E_i$
14	10	16	1.60
56	50	16	0.72
110	100	100	1.00
88	100	144	1.44
40	50	100	2.00
12	10	4	0.40
			$\chi^2 = 7.16$

Table Value (or) Critical Value from X^2 = distribution at 5% significance level, the table value of χ^2 for v = 6 – 1 = 5 is 11.070.

Conclusion: Since the computed value of χ^2=7.16 is falling within the acceptance Region for 5 df at 5% level of significance, we may accept H_0, and conclude that the Male and Female births are equally probable.

Example 3

The number of automobile accidents per week in a certain community are as follows: 12, 8, 20, 2, 14, 10, 15, 6, 9, 4. Are these frequencies in agreement with the belief that accident conditions are the same during the 10 week period?

Solution:

Null Hypothesis (H_0): The accident conditions are the same during the 10 week period against alternative.

Hypothesis (H_1): The accident conditions are not same during the 10 week period.

For α = 5%

Total Number of accidents:

$$T=12+ 8 +20+ 2+ 14+ 10+ 15+ 6+ 9+ 4 = 100$$

If the accident conditions are same, then on an average (100/10)=10 accidents per week are expected.

Test Statistic: $\chi^2 \sum_{i=1}^{k} \frac{(O_i - E_i)^2}{E_i}$ ~ a Chi-square Distribution with (k-1) D.F., where O_i refers to the observed frequencies and E_i refers to the expected frequencies.

Week	O_i	E_i	$O_i - E_i$	$(O_i - E_i)^2$	$(O_i - E_i)^2/E_i$
1	12	10	2	4	4/10
2	8	10	– 2	4	4/10
3	20	10	10	100	100/10
4	2	10	– 8	64	64/10
5	14	10	4	16	16/10
6	10	10	0	0	0/10
7	15	10	5	25	25/10
8	6	10	– 4	16	16/10
9	9	10	– 1	1	1/10
10	4	10	– 6	36	36/10
					266/10 = 26.6

χ^2_{cal} = 26.6

Table Value: At 5% significance level the table value of χ^2 for ν = 10 – 1 = 9 at 5% LOS in two tailed test is between (2.700, 19.023) (found from the tables in Appendix).

Conclusion: Since the computed value of χ^2 = 26.6 is falling in the Rejection Region (limits obtained from the tables) for 9 D.F. At 5% LOS, we may reject H_0, and conclude that the accident conditions are not same during the 10 week period.

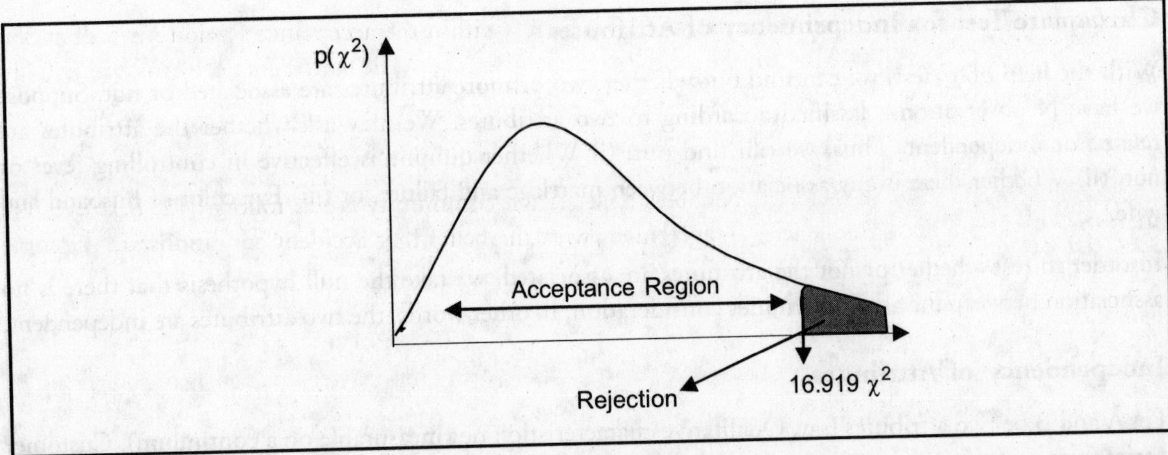

Example 4

In a particular market, there are three commercial television stations, each with its own evening news program from 6:00 to 6:30 P.M. According to a report in this morning's local newspaper, a random sample of 150 viewers last night revealed 53 watched the news on WNAE (channel 5), 64 watched on WRRN (channel 11), and 33 on WSPD (channel 13). At 5 per cent significance level, is there a difference in the proportion of viewers watching the three channels?

Solution:

We use Chi-Square goodness of fit test to test that there is a difference in the proportion of viewers watching the three channels.

Null Hypothesis: There is no difference in the proportion of viewers watching the three channels

	Observed	Expected	(O-E)^2	(O-E)^2/E
Channel 5	53	50	9	0.18
Channel 11	64	50	196	3.92
Channel 13	33	50	289	5.78
			Chi-Square	9.88
			p-value	0.007155

Test Statistics: $\chi^2 = \Sigma \frac{(O_i - E_i)^2}{E_i}$ follows Chi-Square with n-1=2 d.f

$= 9.88$

P-value: $P(\chi^2 > 9.88) = 0.007155$

Which is significant at 0.05 level of significance.

Conclusion: We reject the Null Hypothesis at 0.05 level of significance as 0.007155 <0.05. Thus, there is a difference in the proportion of viewers watching the three channels.

Chi-Square Test for Independency of Attributes

With the help of χ^2 test, we can find out whether two or more attributes are associated or not. Suppose we have N observations classified according to two attributes. We may ask whether the attributes are related or independent. Thus, we can find out: (i) Whether quinine is effective in controlling fever or not, (ii) Whether there is any association between marriage and failure, or (iii) Eye color of husband and wife.

In order to test whether or not the attributes are associated, we take the null hypothesis that there is no association between the attributes under consideration, in other words, the two attributes are independent.

Independency of Attributes

Let A and B be two attributes (say, Qualitative characteristics, not measurable on a continuum). Customer satisfaction, region, cleanliness, consumption behaviour, sex, preference, belief etc., are few non-measurable characteristics. These attributes are further sub-divided into different mutually exclusive and exhaustive categories called classes.

Example 5

A Cigarette manufacturing company interested in the effect of Sex on the type of cigarettes smoked and has collected the following data from a random sample of 150 persons.

Cigarette Size	Number of People Smoked among		Total
	Male	Female	
Small	25	30	55(A_1)
Medium	40	15	55 (A_2)
King size	30	10	40(A_3)
Total	95(B_1)	55(B_2)	150 (N)

Test whether the type of cigarette smoked and sex are independent at 2% LOS.

Solution:

1. ***Null Hypothesis:*** There is no association between the size of the cigarette smoked and Sex.

   Alternative Hypothesis: There is association between the size of the cigarette smoked and Sex.

   Degrees of Freedom: The df (degree of freedom) for the problem is {(3-1)(2-1)}= {2x1}=2. Hence, we need to calculate two expected frequencies independently as shown below.

2. Calculation of independent expected cell frequencies:

   $(A_1B_1)_e = (A_1)(B_1)/N = 55 \times 95/150 = 34.83$

   $(A_2B_1)_e = (A_2)(B_1)/N = 55 \times 95/150 = 34.83$

   Now we fill up the blanks by finding the differences as shown in the following table.

Expected Frequency Table

Cigarette Size	Number of People Smoked among		Total
	Male	Female	
Small	34.83	20.17	55
Medium	34.83	20.17	55
King Size	25.34	14.66	40
Total	95.00	55.00	150

$(A_iB_j) = O_i$	$(A_iB_j)_e = E_j$	$(O_i - E_j)^2$	$(O_i - E_j)^2/E_j$
25	34.83	96.63	2.774
40	34.83	26.73	0.767
30	25.34	21.72	0.857
30	20.17	96.63	4.791
15	20.17	26.73	1.325
10	14.66	21.72	1.481
		$\chi^2 = \Sigma(O_i - E_j)^2/E_j$	11.995

χ^2 (calculated value) = 11.995

Degrees of freedom (ν) = (r – 1) (c – 1) = (3 – 1) (2 – 1) = 2

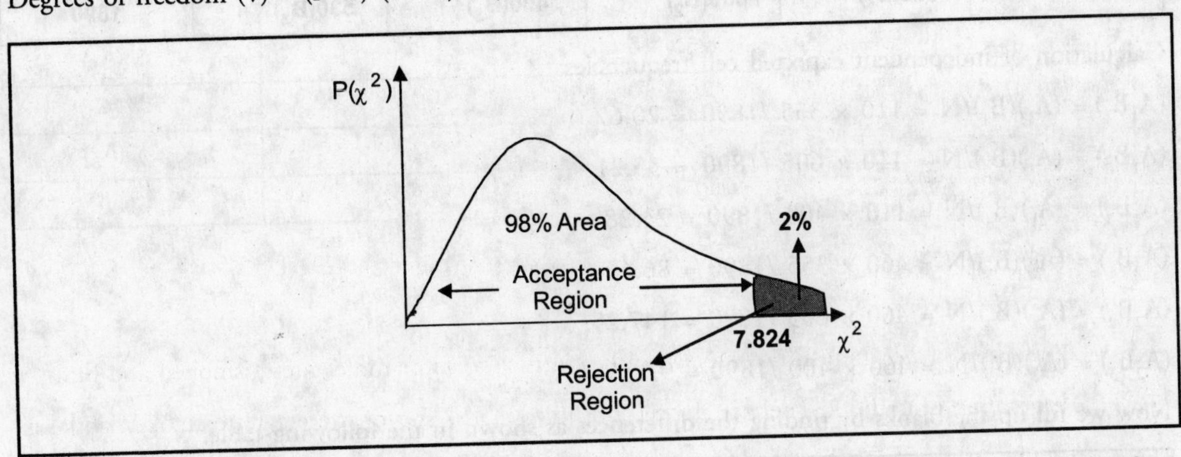

χ^2 (Critical or Table value Acceptance Range) [ν = 2 and α = 2% Level of significant = 7.824 [from chi-square distribution table]

Conclusion: As the calculated value of χ^2 = 11.995 is falling in the rejection region, i.e., the null hypothesis may be rejected. Hence, type of cigarette smoke and sex are not independent.

Example 6

The following data provide the sample information on income and the company for a cell phone connection. Apply appropriate test of significance and conclude.

Income	Company			
	BSNL	TATA	RELIANCE	AIRTEL
Low	25	35	20	30
Medium	80	120	60	200
High	250	450	320	300

Solution:

Null Hypothesis: The level of income is independent from the cell phone company for connectivity.

Alternative Hypothesis: The level of income is not independent from the cell phone company for connectivity.

Degrees of freedom: The D.F. for the problem is {(3-1) (4-1)} = {2 × 3} = 6. Hence, we need to calculate six expected frequencies independently as shown below.

Income	Company				Total
	BSNL	TATA	RELIANCE	AIRTEL	
Low	25	35	20	30	110(A_1)
Medium	80	120	60	200	460(A_2)
High	250	450	320	300	1320(A_3)
Total	**355(B_1)**	**605(B_2)**	**400(B_3)**	**530(B_4)**	**1890**

Calculation of independent expected cell frequencies:

$(A_1B_1)_e = (A_1)(B_1)/N = 110 \times 355 /1890 = 20.67$

$(A_1B_2)_e = (A_1)(B_2)/N = 110 \times 605 /1890 = 35.21$

$(A_1B_3)_e = (A_1)(B_3)/N = 110 \times 400 /1890 = 23.28$

$(A_2B_1)_e = (A_2)(B_1)/N = 460 \times 355 /1890 = 86.40$

$(A_2B_2)_e = (A_2)(B_2)/N = 460 \times 605 /1890 = 147.25$

$(A_2B_3)_e = (A_2)(B_3)/N = 460 \times 400 /1890 = 97.35$

Now we fill up the blanks by finding the differences as shown in the following table.

Income	Company				Total
	BSNL	TATA	RELIANCE	AIRTEL	
Low	20.67	35.21	23.28	30.84	110
Medium	86.40	147.25	97.35	129.00	460
High	247.93	422.54	279.37	370.16	1320
Total	**355**	**605**	**400**	**530**	**1890**

Expected Frequency Table

$(A_iB_j) = O_i$	$(A_iB_j)_e = E_j$	$(O_i - E_j)^2$	$(O_i - E_j)^2/E_j$
25	20.67	18.7489	0.9071
35	35.21	0.0441	0.0013
20	23.28	10.7584	0.4621
30	30.84	0.7056	0.0229
80	86.40	40.9600	0.4741
120	147.25	742.5625	5.0429
60	97.35	1395.0225	14.3300
200	129.00	5041.0000	39.0775
250	247.93	4.2849	0.0173
450	422.54	754.0516	1.7846
320	279.37	1650.7969	5.9090
300	370.16	4922.4256	13.2981
		$\chi^2=\Sigma(O_i-E_j)^2/E_j$	81.3269

χ^2 (calculated value) = 81.3269

Degrees of freedom (ν) = (r –1) (c – 1) = (3 –1) (4 – 1) = 2 × 3 = 6

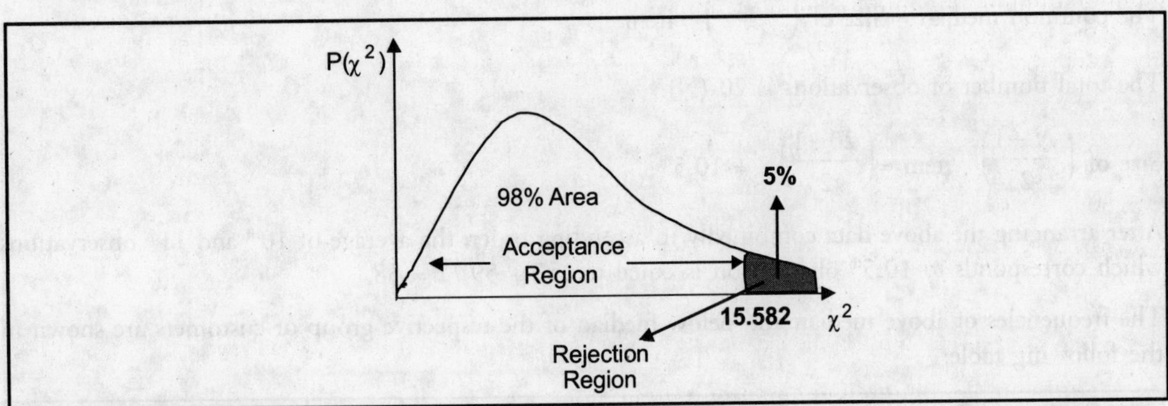

χ^2 (Critical or Table value – Acceptance Range) [ν = 6 and 5% level of significance 12.592 is from Chi-Square Distribution table].

Conclusion: As the calculated value of χ^2= 81.3269 is falling in the rejection region, the null hypothesis may be rejected. Hence, the level of income is not independent from the cell phone company for connectivity.

Median Test

One of the simplest of the order methods (ordinal data) is a procedure for testing whether two independent groups differ on the basis of deviations from the median. This test will determine if two random samples have been drawn from populations with the same median (null hypothesis).

Example 7

A Cellular Phone company wanted to determine if there is a difference in the satisfaction of services between the company's two types of customers: Individual and Corporate customers. The marketing department developed a questionnaire about its service using Liker-type statements, which are ordinarily scaled. The questionnaire was mailed to a random sample of both groups of customers. Upon returning the questionnaire to the company, the scores were recorded as shown in the following table.

Regular customers group	36	57	89	67	19	78	46	59	69	70
Corporate customers group	25	46	93	45	15	64	47	56	73	66

Using Median test, whether there is any significant difference in satisfaction of services between the two types of customers.

Solution:

Null Hypothesis: There is no significant difference in satisfaction of services between the two types of customers regular and corporate.

Alternate Hypothesis: There is significant difference in satisfaction of services between the two types of customers i.e., regular and corporate level of significance: 5 per cent (assumed).

Statistical Test: Since the data measured are ordinal and to determine whether two independent random samples are drawn from same population with same medians, Median test used.

The common median = Size of $\left(\frac{N+1}{2}\right)^{th}$ item.

The total number of observations is 20 (N).

Size of $\left(\frac{N+1}{2}\right)^{th}$ item $= \left(\frac{20+1}{2}\right)^{th} = 10.5^{th}$

After arranging the above data combinedly in ascending order, the average of 10th and 11th observations which corresponds to 10.5^{th} observation is equal to (57 + 59)/2 = 58.

The frequencies of above median and below median of the respective group of customers are shown in the following table:

Customers Group	Below Median	Above Median	Total
Individual	4 (a)	6 (b)	10 (a+b)
Corporate	6 (c)	4 (d)	10 (c+d)
Total	**10 (a+c)**	**10 (b+d)**	**20 (a+b+c+d) = n**

The calculation Chi-square (χ^2) on Median test can be done with the following formula:

$$\chi^2 = \frac{n\left(|ad - bc| - \frac{n}{2}\right)^2}{(a+b)(c+d)(a+c)(b+d)}$$

$$= \frac{20\left(|4 \times 4 - 6 \times 6c| - \frac{20}{2}\right)^2}{(10)(10)(10)(10)} = 0.2$$

χ^2 calculated = 0.2

Conclusion: Table value for 1 df at 5 per cent level of significance is 3.84. The calculated value 0.2 falls within the table value. Hence, we may accept null hypothesis. We can conclude that there is no significant difference in satisfaction of services between the two types of customers regular and corporate.

McNemer Test

McNemer test: A test applied to find the differences, if any, in before and after study environments. This test is applicable, if the data is nominal and two related samples exist. As such this test is useful for pre-test and post-test research design (Before-After environment of the same objects) when the data are measured nominally, and 2 × 2 contingency table is involved. The usual pattern of presenting the data is shown below.

Before Treatment	**After treatment**	
	Favour	**Do not Favour**
Favour	A	B
Do not favour	C	D

Test Statistic:

$$\chi^2 = \frac{\{|C - B| - 1\}^2}{(C + B)} \text{ with 1 df.}$$

Test at 5% level of significance whether the advertisement campaign was successful?

Example 8

The following are the responses obtained from 1000 families. Suppose the treatment of the advertisement is to be examined on Brand X and Brand Y (competitor's brand) of a particular product. The company has launched an advertising campaign to boost the sale of Brand X.

Before Advertisement	**After Advertisement**	
	Brand X	**Brand Y**
Brand X	200(A)	300(B)
Brand Y	400(C)	100(D)

Test at 5% Level of Significance whether the advertisement campaign was successful?

Explanation:

It should be noted that cells B and C show a change between the first and second periods. A family placed in cell B if it purchased Brand X before the advertising campaign and Brand Y after the campaign. Likewise, a family placed in cell C if it purchased Brand Y before advertising campaign but switched over to Brand X after the campaign. Cells A and D show the number of families which do not show any change in their buying behaviour, that is, these families continued to patronage the same brand X or Y during the two periods.

Solution:

Since the given data is Nominal and the data environment is before and after, we apply McNemer test.

1. ***Null and Alternate Hypothesis:***

   H_0: The advertisement campaign was not successful which would imply that the buying behavior of families did not change as a result of it. This would mean that the proportion changing from Brand Y to Brand X would be same as the proportion changing from Brand X to Brand Y.

   H_1: The advertisement campaign was successful. This would mean that the proportion changing from Brand Y to Brand X would not be same as the proportion changing from Brand X to Brand Y. The changes depicted by cells B and C.

2. ***Test Statistic:*** The McNemar test involves the calculation of Chi-square according to the following formula:

$$\chi^2 = \frac{[|400-300|-1]^2}{400+300} = \frac{99^2}{700} = 14.00 \text{ (Calculated Value)}$$

   Table value is obtained from distribution tables for 1 df at 5% level of significance as 3.84. Degrees of freedom (df) is obtained as the product of (number of Rows –1) and (number of Columns –1) = (2 – 1) × (2 – 1) = 1 × 1 = 1.

Conclusion: Since the calculated value of χ^2 =14.00 is more than the table value of χ^2 = 3.84 at 5% LOS, null hypothesis may be rejected. Hence we may conclude that advertisement campaign resulted in a positive outcome (successful) i.e., it increased the purchase rate of Brand X.

Sign Test (One Sample)

A test used to find the differences between pairs of data using + and – signs by converting the quantitative data.

This test is applicable under the following conditions:

1. The sample is drawn from a continuous symmetrical population.
2. The probability of getting a sample value less than mean is same as that of more than mean, which is equal to ½.
3. To test the Null Hypothesis, H_0: $\mu = \mu_0$ against an appropriate alternative on the basis of a random sample, we replace the values of the sample with '–' sign if μ is greater than the sample value and with '+' sign if μ is less than the sample value. If μ and sample value are equal, then we replace the observation with '0'. After changing the observed data as per the rules mentioned above, we count the following.

   Number of '+' signs = μ_1

   Number of '–' signs = μ_2

   Number of '0's = μ_3 (ignore)

   One should check that ($\mu_1 + \mu_2 + \mu_3$) = Number of sample observations.

After ignoring the signs without difference, the '+' sign and '–' sign should follow a Binomial Distribution with p (no of '+' signs) = ½ = q(no of '–' signs). For testing the significance, we calculate the theoretical value by using Binomial probabilities from,

$B(n, p, r) = P(X = r) = {}^nc_r\, p^r q^{n-r}$; r = 0, 1, 2, …., n, where

n= Sum of {'+' signs and '–' signs} and p=1/2.

The table value for testing will be the value obtained by adding Binomial Probabilities for r = 0 to μ_1. Then the table value is compared with the value of α, the LOS.

If the calculated value is less than or equal to the table value, then the H_0 may be rejected as the calculated value falls in the Critical (Rejection) region. Otherwise, the H_0 may be accepted.

Example 9

At a golf club 11 professionals scored an average ($\overline{X}$) of 280, 282, 290, 273, 283, 275, 284, 282, 279 and 281 in four rounds. Test the hypothesis that the golfers average is μ = 284 for four rounds against the alternative of average score is less than 284 at α = 5% LOS.

Solution:

Hypothesis: $H_0 : \overline{X} = \mu\ (=284) \Rightarrow p = \frac{1}{2}$

$H_1 : \overline{X} < \mu\ (=284) \Rightarrow p < \frac{1}{2}$

The difference of $\overline{X}$, μ is obtained. If the difference is less than zero put '–' sign and put '+' sign if the difference is more than zero. Put zero otherwise as shown below.

S. No.	1	2	3	4	5	6	7	8	9	10	11
$(\overline{X} = \mu)$	–	–	+	–	–	–	–	0	–	–	–

Count: Number of '+' signs = 1

Number of '–' signs = 9

Number of '0's= 1(ignore)

We observe only one '+' sign in 10 trials. Hence $\mu_1 = 1$

Probability of $(\mu_1 \le 1)$ in $B(n, p, \mu_1)$ with $n = 10$, $p = ½$ is

$$\binom{10}{0}\left(\frac{1}{2}\right)^0\left(\frac{1}{2}\right)^{10} + \binom{10}{1}\left(\frac{1}{2}\right)^1\left(\frac{1}{2}\right)^9 = 0.0010 + 0.0098$$

$$= 0.0108 \approx 0.011$$

Conclusion: Since 0.011 is less than 0.05 (the value of α, the H_0 may be rejected). In other words, it may be concluded that the golfers average score is less than 284 for four rounds.

Alternatively, we can also apply Normal approximation for the observed proportion of success based on '+' signs $= \frac{1}{10} = p$ and the observed proportion of failure based on '–' signs $= \frac{9}{10} = q$. Then the

$$\text{S.E.}\ (p) = \sqrt{\frac{pq}{n}} = \sqrt{\frac{\frac{1}{2}\times\frac{1}{2}}{10}} = 0.1581$$

For testing the $H_0 : p = \frac{1}{2}$ against $H_1 : p < \frac{1}{2}$ one tailed test must be used. The figure above presents the required information. By using the concept of confidence interval, we calculate the lower limit as

$$p - 1.645(0.1581) = \frac{1}{2} - 1.645(0.1581) = 0.2407$$

This is useful to fix the critical region as shown in the diagram.

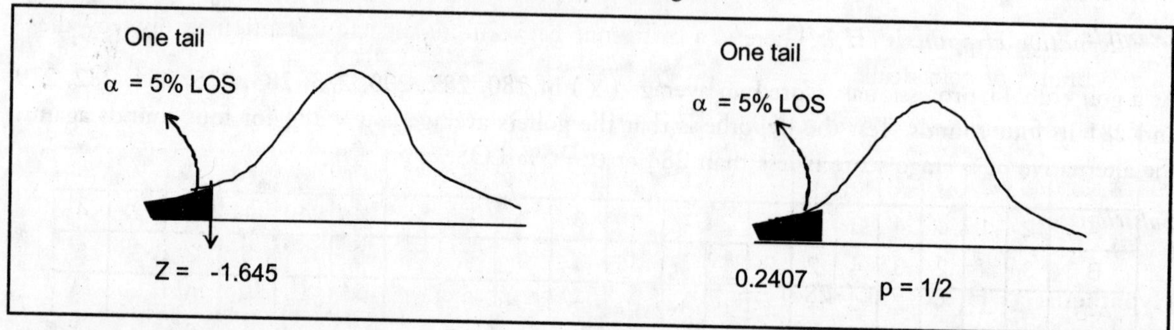

Conclusion: The observed proportion of success $p = \frac{1}{10} = 0.01$ which falls in the rejection region, we may reject H_0 at 5% LOS. In other words, it may be concluded that the golfers average score is less than 284 for four rounds.

Sign Test – Paired Data

This test is applicable under the following conditions:

1. We must have independent samples and paired-data.
2. Each pair of values can be replaced with a '+' sign if the first value of the first sample (say, X) is greater than the first value of the second sample (say, Y).
3. We take '–' sign if the first value of the first sample (say, X) is less than the first value of the second sample (say, Y).
4. In case two values are equal, the concerning pair is discarded.
5. In case, the two samples are not of equal size, then some of the values of larger sample left over after random pairing will have to be discarded.

The testing procedure remains same as in the case of one sample Sign Test. An example is presented below for illustration.

Example 10

The perceptional ratings by 40 customers to two brands of cold drink, namely, A and B are given in the following table. Each respondent was asked to taste the two brands of cold drink and then rate them. Test for the effectiveness between two types of brands A and B at α = 5% LOS. The Rating varies from 1 to 4 with a rating of 4 as excellent and rating of 1 as poor.

S.No.	1	2	3	4	5	6	7	8	9	10	11	12	13	14	15	16	17	18	19	20
A	2	1	4	4	3	3	4	2	4	1	3	3	4	4	4	1	1	2	2	4
B	3	2	2	3	4	2	2	1	3	1	2	3	4	4	3	2	3	2	3	3

S.No.	21	22	23	24	25	26	27	28	29	30	31	32	33	34	35	36	37	38	39	40
A	4	4	4	3	3	2	3	4	3	4	3	1	4	3	2	2	2	1	3	3
B	1	4	3	3	2	2	1	1	1	3	2	2	4	4	3	3	1	1	4	2

Solution:

1. ***Null Hypothesis (H_0):*** There is no difference between customers' perception about the two brands of cold drink A and B.
2. ***Alternative Hypothesis (H_1):*** There is a difference between customers' perception in taste by the two brands of cold drink.

   Level of Significance = 5%, α = 0.05

S.No.	1	2	3	4	5	6	7	8	9	10	11	12	13	14	15	16	17	18	19	20
A	2	1	4	4	3	3	4	2	4	1	3	3	4	4	4	1	1	2	2	4
B	3	2	2	3	4	2	2	1	3	1	2	3	4	4	3	2	3	2	3	3
A-B	–	–	+	+	–	+	+	+	+	0	+	0	0	0	+	–	–	0	–	+

S.No.	21	22	23	24	25	26	27	28	29	30	31	32	33	34	35	36	37	38	39	40
A	4	4	4	3	3	2	3	4	3	4	3	1	4	3	2	2	2	1	3	3
B	1	4	3	3	2	2	1	1	1	3	2	2	4	4	3	3	1	1	4	2
A-B	+	0	+	0	+	0	+	+	+	+	+	–	0	–	–	–	+	0	–	+

Number of '+' signs = 19; Number of '–' signs = 11

Number of zeros = 10

Since we are testing perceived difference, we shall exclude "Ties". Hence

n = Sum of ('+' signs and '–' signs)= 19 + 11=30

$$\bar{p} = \frac{19}{30} = 0.633; \quad \bar{q} = \frac{11}{30} = 0.367$$

S.E. of Proportions is

$$\sigma_{\bar{p}} = \sqrt{\frac{pq}{n}}$$

$$= \sqrt{\frac{(0.5)(0.5)}{30}} = \sqrt{0.00833} = 0.091.$$

Acceptance limits:

$$P_{H_0} \pm 1.96\sigma_{\bar{p}} = 0.5 \pm 1.96(0.091) = 0.5 \pm 0.178 = (0.322, 0.678)$$

The observed proportion = 0.633

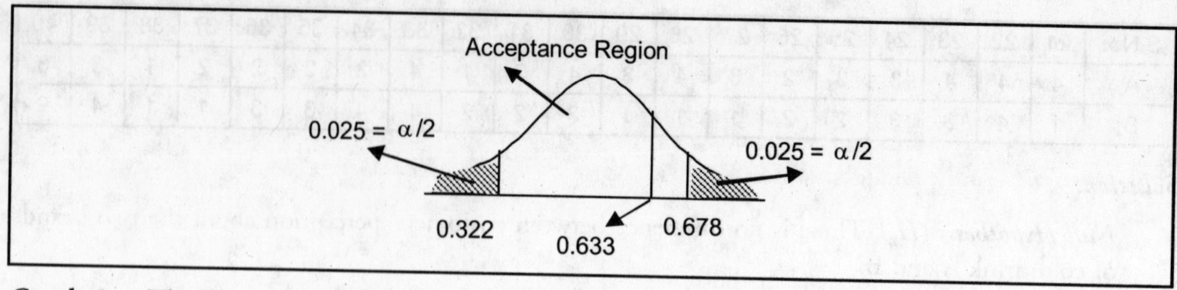

Conclusion: The H_0 may be accepted at α = 5% LOS, since the observed proportion p = 0.633, lies in between (0.322, 0.678), the acceptance limits. There is no difference between customers' perception in taste by the two types of brands of cold drink A and B.

Signed Rank Test (Wilcoxon Matched – Pairs Test)

A test applied for matched pairs by taking the differences and assigning ranks for the differences for testing the significant difference between two samples.

The following conditions to be checked before applying this test:

1. Two samples must be related and dependent so that we can have matched pairs.
2. The relationships can be wife/husband or two machines or Before/After.
3. We determine Direction and magnitude of difference between matched values.

The following are the steps involved in the process:

1. Find the difference between pairs.
2. Assign rank to the differences from smallest to the largest.
3. Without regard to sign.
4. Sum the Ranks by separating '+' and '–' differences.
5. Define T as the smaller of the two sums obtained in step-3.
6. Ignore the differences if they are 'Zero'.
7. In case of ties take "average" of those Ranks involved in tie.

If number of pairs is ≤ 25, then use table for critical values of T (critical values of T in Wilcoxon matched pairs test). If T (calculated) ≤ T(table), then Reject H_0.

Note:

If number of pairs > 25, the sampling distribution of T is taken as approximately normal (T~N) with (U_T, σ_T^2) where $U_T = \frac{n(n+1)}{4}$,

$$\sigma_T = \sqrt{\frac{n(n+1)(2n+1)}{24}}$$; n = {No. of matched pairs – No. of drop out pairs, if any}

The test Statistic is $Z = \frac{T - U_T}{\sigma_T} \sim N(0,1)$

The conclusion will be drawn based on the value of α, the selected Level of Significance.

Example 11

A retail company wants to test the effectiveness of an advertising company that is intending to enhance the awareness of the retail service features. The company administered a questionnaire before advertisement campaign, designed to measure the awareness of services offered. After the advertisement campaign, the retail company administered the same questionnaire to the same group of customers. Both before and after campaign scores are given in the following table:

Customer	1	2	3	4	5	6	7	8	9	10	11	12	13	14	15	16
Before Ad Campaign	73	43	47	53	58	47	52	58	38	61	56	56	34	55	65	75
After Ad Campaign	51	41	43	41	47	32	24	58	43	53	52	57	44	57	40	68

Test the Hypothesis that there is no significant difference in consumer awareness of retail service offered after the advertisement campaign. Use Wilcoxon matched pairs test at α = 5% LOS.

Solution:

1. ***Hypothesis (H_0):*** There is no difference in the consumer awareness of retail services after the advertisement campaign.

   Hypothesis (H_1): There is difference in the consumer awareness of retail services after the advertisement campaign.

2. Significance level (α) = 0.05

Consumer	After Ad campaign	Before Ad campaign	Difference d_i	Rank of $\|d_i\|$	Rank with + signs	Rank with – signs
1	73	51	22	13.0	13	–
2	43	41	2	2.5	2.5	–
3	47	43	4	4.5	4.5	–
4	53	41	12	11.0	11.0	–
5	58	47	11	10.0	10.0	–
6	47	32	15	12.0	12.0	–
7	52	24	28	15.0	15.0	–
8	58	58	0	No Rank	Ignore	Ignore
9	38	43	–5	6.0	–	6.0
10	61	53	8	8.0	8.0	–
11	56	52	4	4.5	4.5	–
12	56	57	–1	1.0	–	1.0
13	34	44	–10	9.0	–	9.0
14	55	57	–2	2.5		2.5
15	65	40	25	14.0	14.0	–
16	75	68	7	7.0	7.0	–
					101.5	18.5

The calculated value of T is obtained as Minimum of {Sum of Ranks with + signs, – signs}. Hence T, (Calculated) = 18.5.

For n = 15 at α = 5% (two tail) the Table value of T = 25 (obtained from Critical values of T, the Wilcoxon matched pairs test given in Appendix)

Conclusion: Since the T (calculated) = 18.5 < 25 the T (table) value, H_0 may be Rejected. Hence, we can conclude that after the advertisement campaign there is difference in the consumer awareness of retail company's services.

Mann-Whitney U-test (Rank Sum Test)

A nonparametric method used to determine whether two independent samples have been drawn from populations with the same distribution.

Mann-Whitney U-test (Rank Sum Test), which can be applied to two populations for ordinal data. The test procedure steps are given below.

Null Hypothesis: H_0: Two independent samples have been drawn from the same population {or H_0: $\mu_1 = \mu_2$ or No difference between the two populations and they have the same mean}.

Alternative Hypothesis: H_1: Two independent samples have not been drawn from the same population {H_1: $\mu_1 \neq \mu_2$ or two populations are different and their means are different}.

1. Mann-Whitney U-test uses "ranking" information rather than '+' and '–' signs. Hence, it is less wasteful of data when compared to sign test.
2. To apply Mann-Whitney U-test, we first rank the combined data after arranging the data in ascending order of magnitude.
3. The data can be arranged in descending order of magnitude also.
4. If there are ties in ranks, give each tied rank the average of the ranks they would each have had if there were no ties.

U-statistic:

$$U = n_1 n_2 + \left\{\frac{n_1(n_1+1)}{2} - R_1\right\}$$

Alternative to U-statistic:

$$U = n_1 n_2 + \left[\frac{n_2(n_2+1)}{2} - R_2\right]$$

Conclusion: For a two-tailed test, reject the equality of means, if the value of U outside the range $\{\mu_u \pm Z_{a/2\,\sigma_4}\}$ for the desired/selected LOS.

Example 12

A random sample of 15 each from two kinds of electric bulbs indicate the lifetime (in hours) is given in the following table.

Brand A	1000	1100	800	750	1300	950	1050	1250	1400	850	1150	1200	1500	600	775
Brand B	920	1120	830	1360	650	725	890	1600	900	1140	1550	550	1240	925	500

Solution:

We setup the Null and Alternative Hypothesis as follows:

H_0: $\mu_1 = \mu_2$ or No difference between the two populations and they have the same mean.

Means of ranks assigned to the values in the two groups are the same.

H_1: $\mu_1 \neq \mu_2$ or Two populations are different and their means are different.

Means of ranks assigned to the values in the two groups are not the same.

To apply Mann-Whitney U-test, we first rank the combined data after arranging the data in ascending order of magnitude.

Score	Brand	Rank	Score	Brand	Rank	Score	Brand	Rank
500	B	1	890	B	11	1150	A	21
550	B	2	900	B	12	1200	A	22
600	A	3	920	B	13	1240	B	23
650	B	4	925	B	14	1250	A	24
725	B	5	950	A	15	1300	A	25
750	A	6	1000	A	16	1360	B	26
775	A	7	1050	A	17	1400	A	27
800	A	8	1100	A	18	1500	A	28
830	B	9	1120	B	19	1550	B	29
850	A	10	1140	B	20	1600	B	30

Let R_1 = sum of the ranks in Brand 'A'

Let R_2 = sum of the ranks in Brand 'B'

$R_1 = \{3+6+7+8+10+15+16+17+18+21+22+24+25+27+28\} = 247$

$R_2 = \{1+2+4+5+9+11+12+13+14+19+20+23+26+29+30\} = 218$

n_1 = Number of items in Branch 'A' = 15

n_2 = Number of items in Branch 'B' = 15

U-statistic:

$$U = n_1 \, n_2 + \left\{\frac{n_1(n_1+1)}{2} - R_1\right\}$$

$$= 15 \times 15 + \left[\frac{15\times16}{2} - 247\right]$$

$$= 225 + [120 - 247] = 98$$

Mean of U-statistic:

$$\mu_U = \frac{n_1 n_2}{2} = \frac{15\times15}{2} = 112.5$$

S.E. of U-statistic:

$$\sigma_U = \sqrt{\frac{n_1 n_2 (n_1 + n_2 + 1)}{12}} = \sqrt{\frac{15\times15(15+15+1)}{12}} = \sqrt{581.25} = 24.11$$

Note: If n_1 and n_2 are less than or equal to 25, the tables for Mann-Whitney U Distribution can be used. If n_1 and n_2 both are larger values, then U Statistic can be approximated by Normal distribution.

LOS: Let $\alpha = 0.15$.

Acceptance limits:

$$\mu_u \pm 1.44\ \sigma_u = 112.5 \pm 1.44\ (24.11)$$

$$= (147.22,\ 77.78)$$

Conclusion: Since calculated value of U = 98 lies within the acceptance region, shown above, we conclude that there is no difference in the average lifetimes of two brands, namely, brand A and brand B.

Example 13

The following grades are obtained by students of a management programme in "MR" paper when taught in the A = Morning class and B= Afternoon class by the same professor. Can you conclude that morning class performed worse than the afternoon class by applying Mann-Whitney U test?

A	73	87	75	82	66	95	75	70	79	56	50
B	86	81	84	88	90	85	84	92	83	91	53

Solution:

We setup the Null and Alternative Hypothesis as follows:

H_0: A = B or No difference between the two populations, i.e., there is no difference between morning class (A) and afternoon class (B) as far as performance is concerned.

Means of ranks assigned to the values in the two groups are the same.

H_1: A < B or Morning class (A) is worse than Afternoon class (B) as far as performance is concerned.

To apply Mann-Whitney U-test, we first rank the combined data after arranging the data in ascending order of magnitude.

Grade	Brand	Rank	Grade	Brand	Rank
50	A	1	83	B	12
53	B	2	84	B	13.5
56	A	3	84	B	13.5
66	A	4	85	B	15
70	A	5	86	B	16
73	A	6	87	A	17
75	A	7.5	88	B	18
75	A	7.5	90	B	19
79	A	9	91	B	20
81	B	10	92	B	21
82	A	11	95	A	22

Let R_1 = sum of the ranks in Class 'A'

Let R_2 = sum of the ranks in Class 'B'

$R_1 = \{1+3+4+5+6+7.5+7.5+9+11+17+22\} = 93$

R_2 = {2+10 +12+13.5+13.5+15+16+18+19+20+21} = 160

n_1 = Number of items in Class 'A' = 11

n_2 = Number of items in Class 'B' = 11

U-statistic:

$$U = n_1 n_2 + \left\{\frac{n_1(n_1+1)}{2} - R_1\right\}$$

$$= 11 \times 11 + \left[\frac{11\times 12}{2} - 93\right]$$

$$= 121 + [66 - 93] = 94$$

Mean of U-statistic:

$$\mu_U = \frac{n_1 n_2}{2} = \frac{11\times 11}{2} = 60.5$$

S.E. of U-statistic:

$$\sigma_U = \sqrt{\frac{n_1 n_2(n_1+n_2+1)}{12}} = \sqrt{\frac{11\times 11(11+11+1)}{12}} = \sqrt{231.9166} = 15.22$$

Note: If n_1 and n_2 are less than or equal to 25, the tables for Mann-Whitney U Distribution can be used. If n_1 and n_2 both are larger values, then U Statistic can be approximated by Normal distribution.

LOS: Let α = 0.05 (Assuming)

Acceptance limits:

$\mu_u \pm Z_{crit}\ \sigma_u$ (Z_{crit} value 1.65 as 0.05 significance level from Z table)

= 60.5 ± 1 65 (15.22)

= (85.62, 35.37) → Acceptance Region

Conclusion: Since calculated value of U = 94 is not falling within the acceptance region, as shown above, we conclude that there is a difference in the class A and class B, i.e. morning class (A) is worse than afternoon class (B).

Kolmogrov-Smirnov Test

It is a test for goodness of fit similar to Chi-Square Test. It is concerned with the degree of agreement between the distribution of a set of sample values and some specified theoretical distribution. It determines whether the scores in a sample can reasonably be thought to have come from a population having theoretical distribution. It involves specifying the cumulative frequency distribution that would occur given the theoretical distribution and comparing that with the observed cumulative frequency distribution. It is used when one is interested in comparing a set of values on an ordinal scale.

The theoretical distribution represents what would be expected under H_0. The point at which the theoretical and sampling distribution are same. Kolmogrov-Smirnov(K-S) test has several advantages over χ^2 Test. It is most powerful test. It is easy to use since it does not require that data be grouped in any way.

Example 14

The following is the daily arrival distribution of cars at a automobile service station. Can we conclude that this pattern follows a Poisson distribution with μ = 3? Use 5 per cent level of significance.

Number of arrivals per day	0	1	2	3	4	5	≥ 6
Number of days	6	18	30	24	11	2	9

Solution:

For obtaining a critical value from tables, we should refer to the tables available for K-S goodness of fit. Table provides the values for D. For obtaining a critical value from tables, we should refer to the tables available for K-S goodness of fit. These tables are given in Appendix. Table provides the values for D. We want test whether the observed frequency distribution given above follows a Poisson Distribution with a specified mean value or not. For this purpose we apply Kolmogrov- Smirnov (K-S) test.

1. ***Null Hypothesis:*** H_0: The given data follows a Poisson distribution with l = 3.

   Alternative Hypothesis: H_1: The given data does not follow Poisson distribution.

Arrivals X	Observed			Probability $= \frac{e^{-m}m^x}{x!}$	Cumulative Probability (F_e)	$\|F_e - F_0\|$
	Frequency	Cumulative Frequency (CF)	Relative CF (F_0)			
0	6	6	0.06	0.050	0.050	0.010
1	18	24	0.24	0.149	0.199	0.041
2	30	54	0.54	0.224	0.423	0.117
3	24	78	0.78	0.224	0.647	**0.133**
4	11	89	0.89	0.168	0.815	0.075
5	2	91	0.91	0.101	0.916	0.006
6	9	100	1.00	0.084	1.000	0.000

Maximum value of $|F_e - F_0|$ = 0.133 (Calculated Value)

K–S statistic = D_n = Maximum $|F_e - F_0|$

= 0.133 occurring at $x = 3$

Table Value: Since, n = 100 (> 35), the critical value of D must be calculated using

$$D = \frac{1.36}{\sqrt{n}} = \frac{1.36}{10} = 0.136.$$

Conclusion: Since the calculated value of D = 0.133 is less than the table value of D = 0.136 for α = 0.05 LOS, the H_0 may be accepted. We conclude that the daily arrival distribution of cars at the automobile service centre follows a Poisson distribution with mean (m) is equal to 3.

Kruskal-Wallis Test

Mann-Whitney U-test is used to test whether two independent random samples have come from two identical populations. Kruskal-Wallis test is used to test whether r (more than two) independent random samples have come from identical populations as the null Hypothesis against the Alternative Hypothesis that r (more than two) independent random samples do not come from identical populations. Using ranked data, in this test, we test for equality of several means, which is similar to ANOVA (One Way) Classification. This test does not assume that the samples come from Normal population or the populations have the same S.D.

Method of Assigning Ranks

After pooling up of all observations, ranks are to be assigned in ascending or descending order keeping track of samples to the corresponding observations. If two or more observations got same rank, then the average rank has to be assigned to each observation.

Test Statistic:

$$H = \left\{ \frac{12}{n(n+1)} \sum_{j=1}^{r} \frac{R_j^2}{n_j} \right\} - 3(n+1)$$

R_j = Sum of the ranks in sample j; $n_j = n_1 + n_2 + n_r$

If $n_j \geq 5$ for all j = 1,2,3, then H follows a χ^2 distribution with $(r-1)$ D.F. By fixing the α at the desired level, we refer to the tables of χ^2 Distribution for obtaining the critical values for (r-1) D.F.

If any of the given samples has less than 5 items, then χ^2 distribution can not be applied and the exact test may based on table meant for it and are given in the book "Nonparametric Statistics for the Behavioral Sciences" by S. Siegel. These tables are given in Appendix.

Example 15

A company used three different methods of training to its three groups of salesmen. The method of training used was different for each group. When training was completed, the salesmen were given a test. The marks scored by them are shown below.

Training Method - A	74	88	82	93	55	70			
Training Method - B	78	80	65	57	89				
Training Method - C	68	83	50	91	84	77	94	81	92

Test at α = 5% LOS, whether the three methods of training methods yield the same result.

Solution:

1. H_o: There is no difference in the effectiveness of the three training methods.

   H_1: There is difference in the effectiveness of the three training methods.

2. Arrange the data in the ascending order of magnitude. Assign ranks for the arranged data. Keep track of the method of training.

Score	50	55	57	65	68	70	74	77	78	80
Rank	1	2	3	4	5	6	7	8	9	10
Training Method	C	A	B	B	C	A	A	C	B	B

Score	81	82	83	84	88	89	91	92	93	94
Rank	11	12	13	14	15	16	17	18	19	20
Training Method	C	A	C	C	A	B	C	C	A	C

The data and ranks are arranged by separating each training method from the above table and is tabulated as above.

Training Method A	Rank	Training Method B	Rank	Training Method C	Rank
74	7	78	9	68	5
88	15	80	10	83	13
82	12	65	4	50	1
93	19	57	3	91	17
55	2	89	16	84	14
70	6	Sum of the ranks	**42**	77	8
Sum of the ranks	**61**			94	20
				81	11
				92	18
				Sum of the ranks	**107**

$n_1 = 6;\ n_2 = 5;\ n_3 = 9;\ j = 3.$

$R_1 = 61,\ R_2 = 42,\ R_3 = 107$

$n = 6 + 5 + 9 = 20$

Test Statistic:

$$H = \left\{\frac{12}{n(n+1)}\sum_{j=1}^{3}\frac{R_j^2}{n_j}\right\} - 3(n+1)$$

R_j = Sum of the ranks in sample j; $n = n_1 + n_2 + n_3$

$$H = \left[\frac{12}{20(20+1)}\left\{\frac{(61)^2}{6} + \frac{(42)^2}{5} + \frac{(107)^2}{9}\right\}\right] - 3(20+1)$$

$$= \left[\frac{12}{20\times 21}\left\{\frac{3721}{6} + \frac{1764}{5} + \frac{11449}{9}\right\}\right] - 3(21)$$

$$= \left[(0.02857)\{620.2 + 352.8 + 1272.1\}\right] - 63 = 1.142$$

In $n_j \geq 5$ for all $j = 1, 2, 3$, then H follows a χ^2 distribution with $(r-1)$ D.F. i.e., $(r-1) = (3-1) = 2$ D.F.

If $\alpha = 0.10$, then the table value of $\chi^2(0.10) = 4.605$

Conclusion: Since the χ^2 calculated value (1.142) is less than the table value (4.605), H_0 may be accepted. Hence, there is no difference in the methods of training.

Example 16

In an experiment to determine which of three different missile systems is preferable, the propellant burning rates were determined. The data after coding is given below:

System I	24.0	16.7	22.8	19.8	18.9			
System II	23.2	19.8	18.1	17.6	20.2	17.8		
System III	18.4	19.1	17.3	17.3	19.7	18.9	18.8	19.3

Use the Kruskal-Wallis test and a significance level of = 0.05 to test the hypothesis that propellant burning rates are the same for the three missiles.

Solution:

1. H_o: There is no significant difference between three sample means (propellant burning rates) of the three different missile systems.
2. H_1: There is a significant difference between three sample means (propellant burning rates) of the three different missile systems.
3. Arrange the data in the descending or ascending order of magnitude. Assign ranks for the arranged data. Keep track of the method of training.

Burning rate	24.0	23.2	22.8	20.2	19.8	19.8	19.7	19.3	19.1	18.9	18.9	18.8
Rank	1	2	3	4	5.5	5.5	7	8	9	10.5	10.5	12
System	I	II	I	II	I	II	III	III	III	III	I	III

The data and ranks are arranged by separating each system from the above table and is tabulated as below.

System I	Rank	System II	Rank	System III	Rank
24.0	1	23.2	2	19.7	7
22.8	3	20.2	4	19.3	8
19.8	5.5	19.8	5.5	19.1	9
18.9	10.5	18.1	14	18.9	10.5
16.7	19	17.8	15	18.8	12
		17.6	16	18.4	13
Sum of the ranks (R1)	**39**	Sum of the ranks (R2)	**56.5**	17.3	17.5
				17.3	17.5
				Sum of the ranks (R3) =	**94.5**

$n_1 = 5\ n_2 = 6;\ n_3 = 8;\ j = 3.$

$R_1 = 39,\ R_2 = 56.5,\ R_3 = 94.5$

$n = 5 + 6 + 8 = 19$

Test Statistic: $H = \left\{ \dfrac{12}{n(n+1)} \sum_{j=1}^{3} \dfrac{R_j^2}{n_j} \right\} - 3(n+1)$

R_j = Sum of the ranks in sample j; $n = n_1 + n_2 + n_3$

$$H = \left[\frac{12}{19(19+1)} \left\{ \frac{(39)^2}{5} + \frac{(56.5)^2}{6} + \frac{(94.5)^2}{8} \right\} \right] - 3(19+1)$$

$$= \left[\frac{12}{19 \times 20} \{304.2 + 532.04 + 1116.28\} \right] - 60$$

$$= [(0.031578)\{1952.522\}] - 60 = 1.658$$

In $n_j \geq 5$ for all $j = 1, 2, 3$, then H follows a χ^2-distribution with $(r - 1)$ D.F. i.e., $(r - 1) = (3–1) = 2$ D.F.

If $\alpha = 0.05$, then the table value of χ^2 (0.05) = 5.991

Conclusion: Since the χ^2 calculated value (1.658) is less than the table value (5.991), H_0 may be accepted. Hence, we can conclude that there is no significant difference between three sample means (propellant burning rates) of the three different missile systems.

REVIEW QUESTIONS

1. What are the nonparametric tests? Explain the importance of nonparametric tests in marketing research.

2. The following are the responses obtained from 100 individuals about the usage of a brand of a Company X against Competitors before and after a promotion campaign and data is cross tabulated as below.

Before the promotion, brand used	**After Promotion, brand used**	
	Company X	**Competitors**
Company X	15	5
Competitors	16	64

Test at 5% Level of Significance whether there is any significant change in the purchase pattern before and after the conducting promotion campaign?

3. Two dentists gave the following ratings on a rating scale of 1 to 7 for 12 patients with respect the degree of cavity on teeth.

Patient	1	2	3	4	5	6	7	8	9	10	11	12
Dentist A	4	5	7	6	3	1	6	4	3	3	5	1
Dentist B	3	6	7	6	7	4	6	7	3	5	5	6

Test for the significant difference in the ratings by two Dentists at 5% LOS. Use Wilcoxon Matched Pairs Test.

4. Instructors A and B both teach a first course in chemistry at a particular university. On a common final examination, their students received the grades as shown. Test at the 0.05 significance level the hypothesis that there is no difference between the two instructors' grades. Apply the Mann-Whitney U-test.

A	88	75	92	71	63	84	55	64	82	96				
B	72	65	84	53	76	80	51	60	57	85	94	87	73	61

5. In sample of 120 persons in a village, 76 persons were administered a new drug for preventing Influenza out of whom, 24 persons were attacked by influenza. Amongst those not administered the new drug, 12 persons were not affected by Influenza. Prepare:

   (i) 2x2 tables showing the actual and expected frequencies.

   (ii) Use chi-square test for finding out whether the new drug is effective at 5% level of Significance.[Ans: Chi-Square Value = 18.968]

6. A certain drug was administered to 456 males out of a total 720 in a certain locality to test its efficacy against typhoid. The incidence of typhoid is shown below. Find out the effectiveness of the drug against the disease. (The table value of X^2 for 1 *d.f.* At 5% level of significance is-3.84).

	Infection	**No Infection**
Administering the drug	144	312
Without administering	192	12

7. A salesman of a firm manufacturing a type of cosmetics hypothesized that a type of cosmetic was favored more by boys than by girls. Accordingly a sample study was made and the result was tabulated below. Apply the Chi-square test and find out whether the hypothesis is justified by the sample study.

	Most liked	**Liked**	**Not liked**
Boys	120	250	100
Girls	110	190	90
Total	320	70	110

8. The number of automobile accidents per week in a certain community was as follows: 12, 8, 20, 2, 14, 10, 15, 6, 9, 4. Are these frequencies in agreement with the belief that accident conditions were the same during the 10 weeks period?

9. A personnel manager is interested in trying to determine whether absenteeism is greater on one day of the week than on another. His records for the past year yield this sample distribution.

Day of week	**Number of absentees**
Monday	66
Tuesday	57
Wednesday	48
Thursday	54
Friday	75

10. A sample of 400 managers is found to have a mean height of 171.38 cms can it be reasonably regarded as a sample from a large population of mean height 171.17 cms and standard deviation of 3.3 cms?

CHAPTER TWELVE

CORRELATION AND REGRESSION BI-VARIATE ANALYSIS

INTRODUCTION

Marketing research data analysis is a blend of statistics, psychology, information technology and art. The professional marketing researcher is not expected to have a complete understanding of all the techniques of data analysis, but is expected to manage the blending of these disciplines in order to develop and organize a complete analysis of the data that satisfies the information requirements of the project. Managers of today often need to understand and make decisions depending upon the numerical data on two or more variables simultaneously. For example,

1. Cost of production and volume of Production,
2. Expenditure on Advertising and Sales of a Product,
3. Number of Vehicles on Road and Number of Accidents,
4. Number of Colleges offering MBA Programme and number of MBA Graduates,
5. Number of Counters at an e-Seva Kendra and the waiting time of customers.
6. Number of Telephone calls and Rate per Call and so on.

In other words, one of the basic functions of a manager is to understand the relationship between these variables and make appropriate decisions keeping the future in mind known as 'Forecasting or Prediction'. The part which deals with understanding of the behaviour of variables is Correlation and the part dealing with the forecasting is Regression.

CORRELATION

Correlation is a statistical tool for studying the relationship between two or more variables and correlation analysis involves various methods and techniques used for studying and measuring the extent of relationship between the two variables. Two variables said to be correlated, if the change in one variable results in a corresponding change in the other.

Scatter Diagram: It is a diagrammatic representation of a bivariate distribution and provides a fairly and simplest way of understanding the relationship between two variables. Scatter diagram is simply the graphical presentation of pairs of observed bivariate data in the form of 'dots'. Different scatter diagrams are presented in the following discussion.

❖ Types of Correlation

Broadly speaking, there are four types of correlation, namely, (a) Positive Correlation, (b) Negative Correlation, (c) Linear Correlation and (d) Non-Linear Correlation.

Positive Correlation

If the values of two variables deviate in the same direction i.e., if increase in the values of one variable results, on an average, in a corresponding increase in the values of the other variable or if a decrease in the values of one variable results, on an average, in a corresponding decrease in the values of the other variable, the corresponding correlation is said to be positive or direct.

Examples:

1. Sales revenue of a product and expenditure on Advertising.
2. Amount of rainfall and yield of a crop (up to a point).
3. Price of a commodity and quantity of supply of a commodity.
4. Height of the Parent and the height of the Child.
5. Number of patients admitted into a Hospital and Revenue of the Hospital.
6. Number of workers and output of a factory.

Perfect Positive Correlation

If the variables X and Y are perfectly positively related to each other then, we get a graph as shown in Figure 12.1.

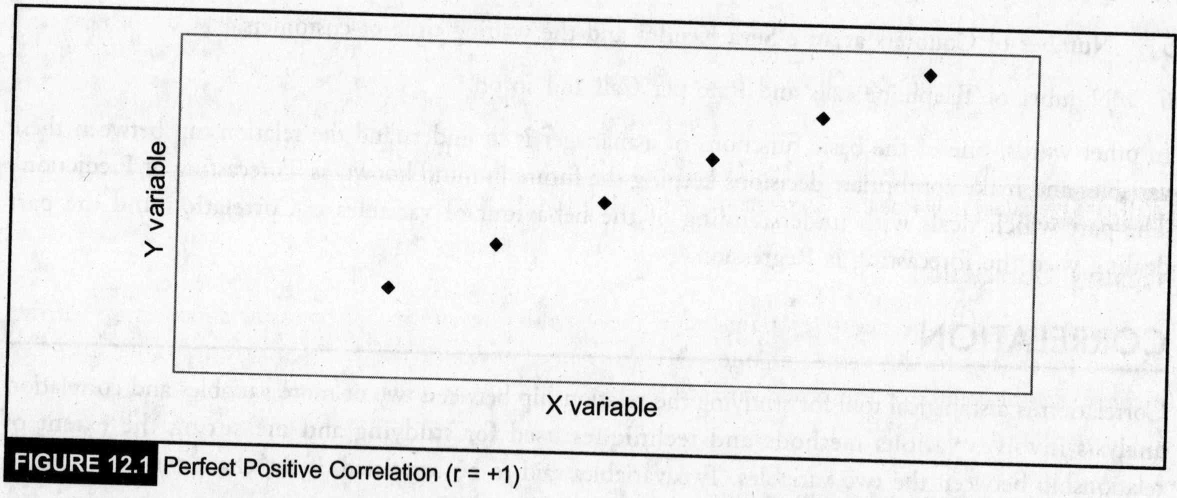

FIGURE 12.1 Perfect Positive Correlation (r = +1)

Very High Positive Correlation

If the variables X and Y are related to each other with a very high degree of positive relationship then we can notice a graph as in Figure 12.2.

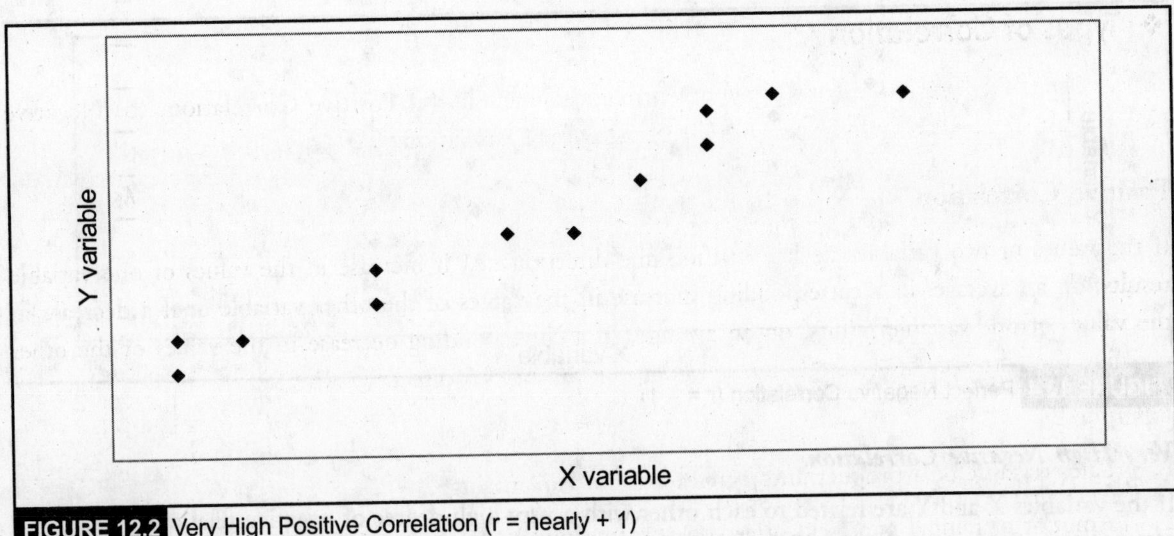

FIGURE 12.2 Very High Positive Correlation (r = nearly + 1)

Very Low Positive Correlation

If the variables X and Y are related to each other with a very low degree of positive relationship then we can notice a graph as in Figure 12.3.

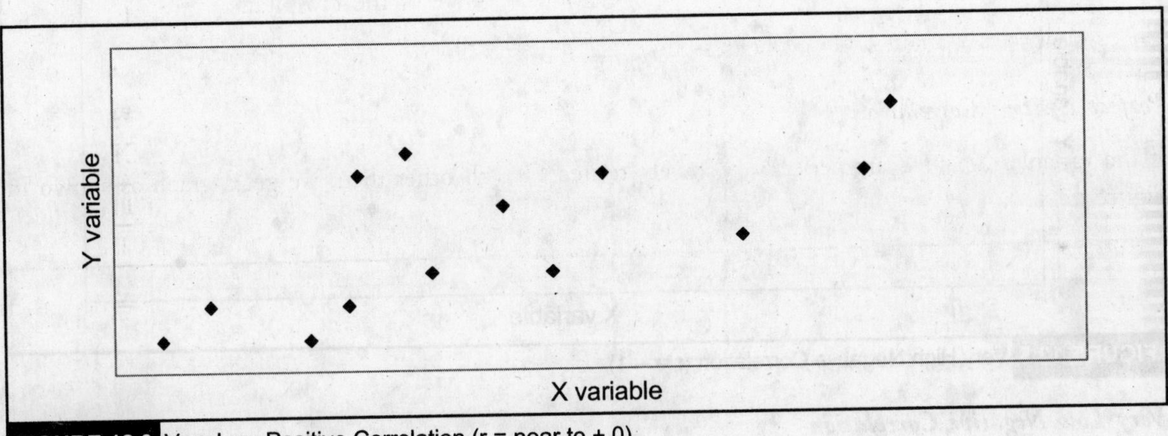

FIGURE 12.3 Very Low Positive Correlation (r = near to + 0)

Negative Correlation

Correlation is said to be negative or inverse if the variables deviate in the opposite direction i.e., if the increase (decrease) in the values of one variable results, on the average, in a corresponding decrease (increase) in the values of the other variable.

Examples:

1. Price and demand of a commodity,
2. Sale of Woolen garments and the day temperature.

Perfect Negative Correlation

If the variables X and Y are perfectly negatively related to each other then, we get a graph as shown in Figure 12.4.

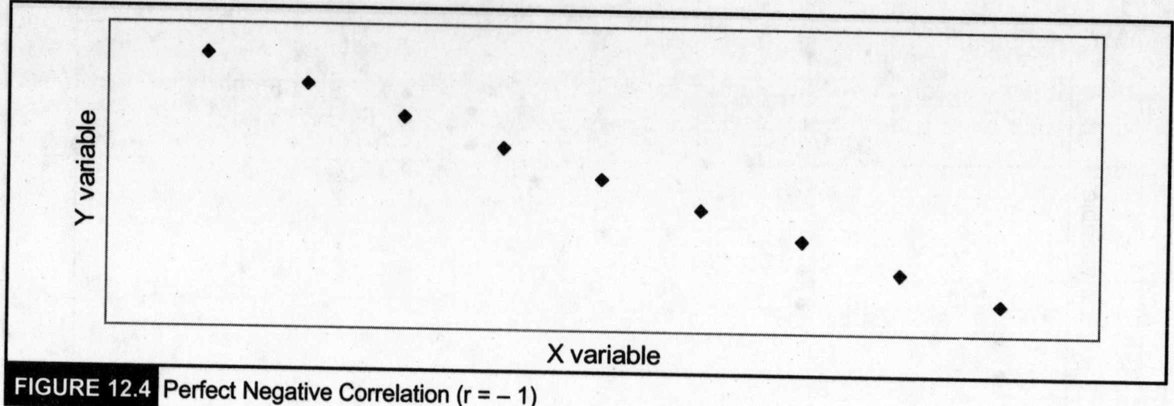

FIGURE 12.4 Perfect Negative Correlation (r = – 1)

Very High Negative Correlation

If the variables X and Y are related to each other with a very high degree of negative relationship then we can notice a graph as in Figure 12.5.

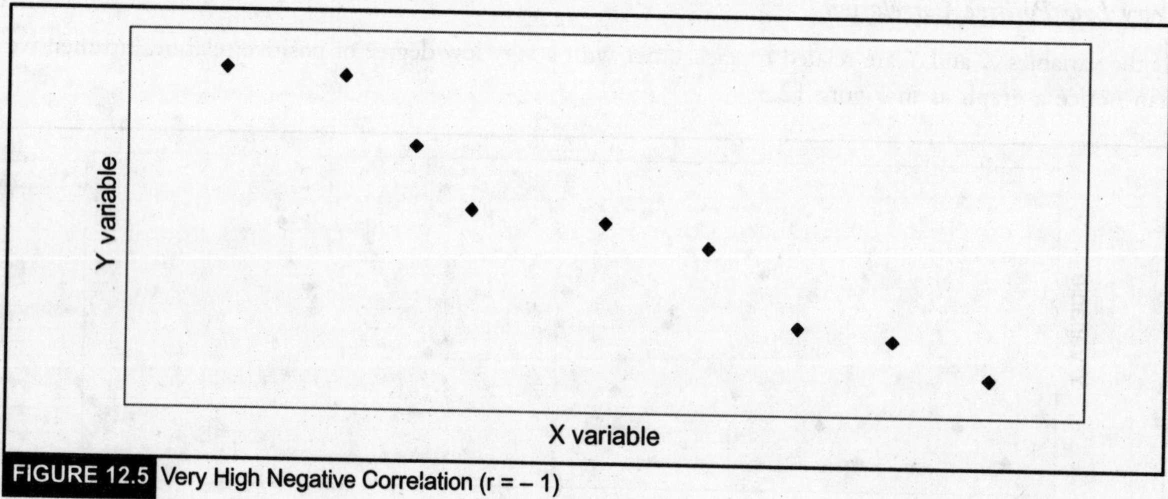

FIGURE 12.5 Very High Negative Correlation (r = – 1)

Very Low Negative Correlation

If the variables X and Y are related to each other with a very low degree of negative relationship then we can notice a graph as in Figure 12.6.

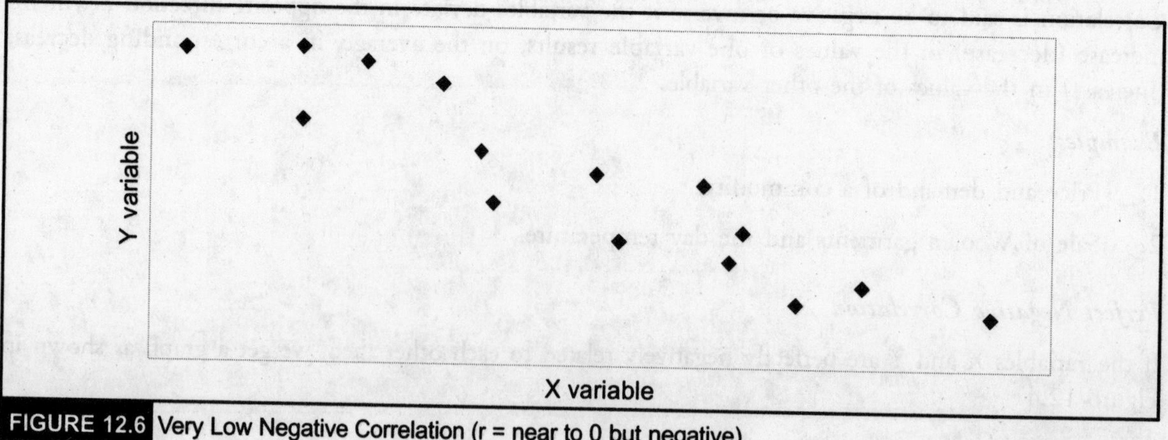

FIGURE 12.6 Very Low Negative Correlation (r = near to 0 but negative)

No Correlation

If the scatter diagram shows the points which are highly spread over and shows no trend or patterns we can say that there is no correlation between the variables. Refer to Figure 12.7.

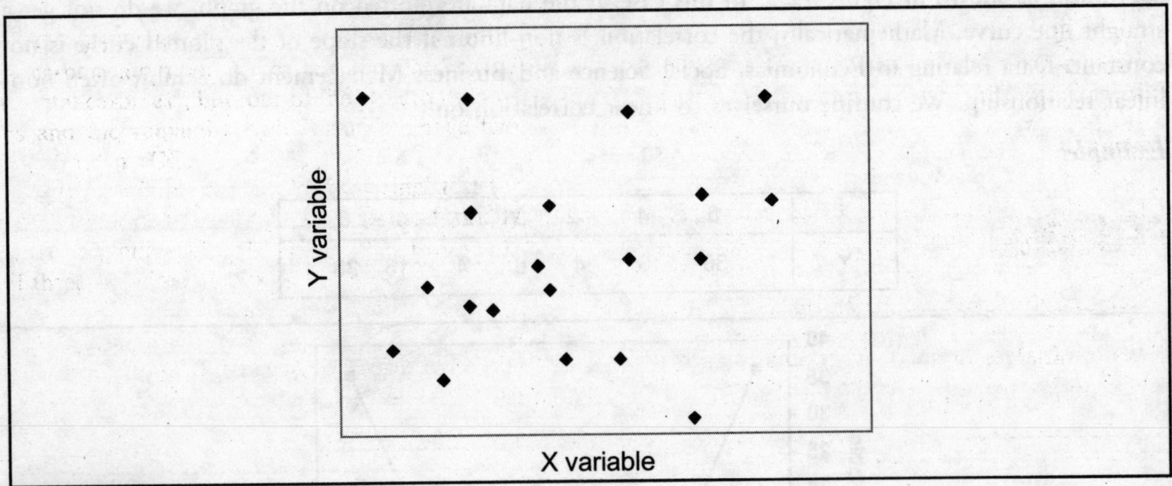

FIGURE 12.7 No Correlation (r = 0)

Linear Correlation

Two variables are said to be linearly related if corresponding to a unit change in one variable, there is a constant change in the other variable over the entire range of the values.

If two variables are related linearly, then we can express the relationship as

$$Y = a + b X$$

where 'a' is called as the "intercept" (If X= 0, then Y= a) and 'b' is called as the "rate of change" or slope.

If we plot the values of X and the corresponding values of Y on a graph, then the graph would be a straight line as shown in Figure 12.8.

Example:

X	1	2	3	4	5
Y	6	8	10	12	14

For a unit change in the value of x, a constant 2 units change in the value of y can be noticed. The above can be expressed as: $Y = 4 + 2X$

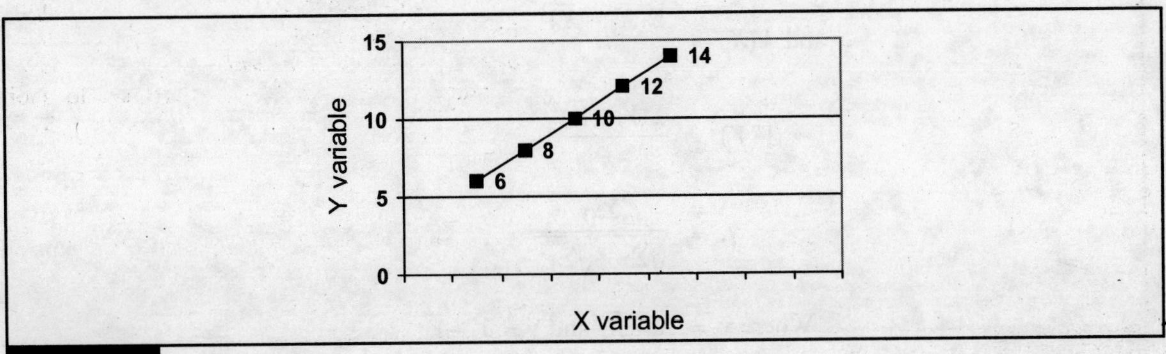

FIGURE 12.8 Linear Correlation

Non-Linear (Curvilinear) Correlation

If corresponding to a unit change in one variable, the other variable does not change in a constant rate, but change at varying rates, then the relationship between two variables is said to be non-linear or curvilinear as shown in Figure 12.9. In this case, if the data are plotted on the graph, we do not get a straight line curve. Mathematically, the correlation is non-linear if the slope of the plotted curve is not constant. Data relating to Economics, Social Science and Business Management do exhibit often non-linear relationship. We confine ourselves to linear correlation only.

Example:

X	–6	–4	–2	0	2	4	6
Y	36	16	4	0	4	16	36

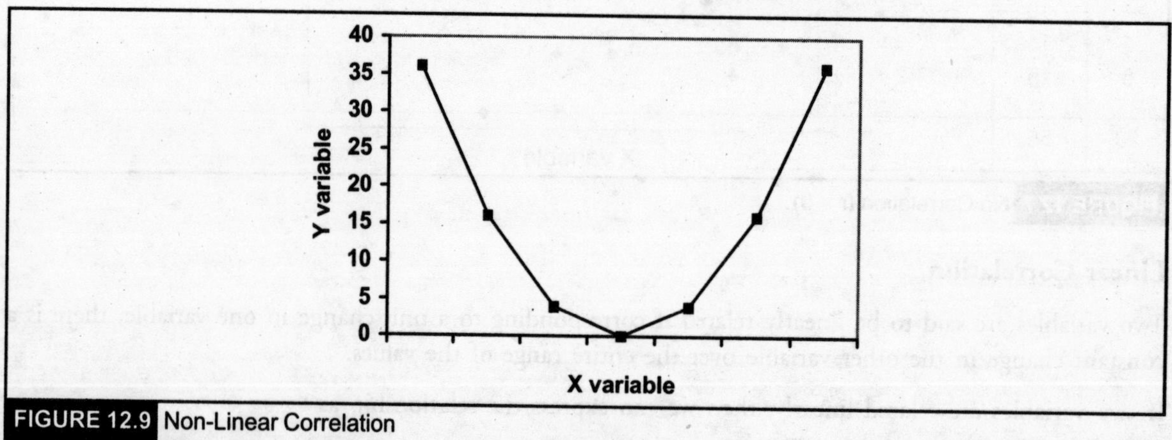

FIGURE 12.9 Non-Linear Correlation

❖ Karl Pearson's Coefficient of Correlation

To measure the degree of association between two variables X and Y, Karl Pearson defined the Coefficient of Correlation 'γ' as below. In this method, the coefficient of correlation is calculated as the ratio of the covariance of the two variables to the product of their variances.

$$\text{Correlation co-efficient } (\gamma) = \frac{Cov(X_i, Y_i)}{\sqrt{\{V(X_i)V(Y_i)\}}}$$

$$\text{where } Cov(X_i, Y_i) = \frac{\Sigma(X_i - \bar{X})(Y_i - \bar{Y})}{n}$$

$$\text{and } V(X_i) = \frac{\Sigma(X_i - \bar{X})^2}{n}$$

$$V(Y_i) = \frac{\Sigma(Y_i - \bar{Y})^2}{n}$$

$$\gamma, = \frac{\Sigma xy}{\sqrt{\Sigma x^2}\sqrt{\Sigma y^2}}$$

Where $x = X_i - \bar{X}$ and $y = Y_i - \bar{Y}$

Pearson's Method – Direct Method

We apply direct formula to find Karl Pearson's Co-efficient of correlation.

Example:

Following is the data on two variables X_i and Y_i. We find the sums and squares of products as shown in the table below.

X_i	Y_i	$(X_i-\bar{X})$ x	$(Y_i-\bar{Y})$ y	$(X_i-\bar{X})^2$ x^2	$(Y_i-\bar{Y})^2$ y^2	$(X_i-\bar{X})(Y_i-\bar{Y})$ xy
2	7	– 2	– 4	4	16	8
3	9	– 1	– 2	1	4	2
4	10	0	– 1	0	1	0
5	14	1	3	1	9	3
6	15	2	4	4	16	8
20	55			$\Sigma x^2 = 10$	$\Sigma y^2 = 46$	$\Sigma xy = 21$

$$\bar{X} = \frac{\Sigma X_i}{n} = \frac{20}{5} = 4, \qquad \bar{Y} = \frac{\Sigma Y_i}{n} = \frac{55}{5} = 11,$$

$$\gamma = \frac{\Sigma xy}{\sqrt{\Sigma x^2}\sqrt{\Sigma y^2}}$$

$$\gamma = \frac{21}{\sqrt{10}\sqrt{46}} = \frac{21}{3.16 \times 6.78} = 0.98$$

The value of γ = 0.98 shows that two series X and Y have almost perfect positive correlation.

Pearson's Method – Without Deviations (Short-cut Method)

When the arithmetic means of both sets of numerical items are not whole numbers and involve decimals, calculating the coefficient of correlation by direct method becomes tedious. To overcome this difficulty the following modified short-cut method formula is used.

$$\text{Cov(Xi,Yi)} = \frac{\Sigma X_i Y}{n} - \bar{X}\,\bar{Y}$$

$$\text{V(Xi)} = \frac{\Sigma X_i^2}{n} - \bar{X}^2; \qquad \text{V(Yi)} = \frac{\Sigma Y_i^2}{n} - \bar{Y}^2$$

$$\gamma = \frac{Cov(X_i, Y_i)}{\sqrt{\{V(X_i)V(Y_i)\}}}$$

$$\gamma = \frac{n\Sigma X_i Y_i - \Sigma X_i\,\Sigma Y_i}{\sqrt{\left[n\Sigma X_i^2 - (\Sigma X_i)^2\right]\left[n\Sigma Y_i^2 - (\Sigma Y_i)^2\right]}}$$

Example:

Calculate the Karl Pearson's coefficient of correlation for the following data between sales and advertising expenditure.

Let sales represents X_i variable and advertise expenditure represents Y_i variable to calculate the correlation coefficient using the following formula.

$$\gamma = \frac{n\Sigma X_i Y_i - \Sigma X_i \, \Sigma Y_i}{\sqrt{\left[n\Sigma X_i^2 - (\Sigma X_i)^2\right]\left[n\Sigma Y_i^2 - (\Sigma Y_i)^2\right]}}$$

X_i	Y_i	X_i^2	Y_i^2	$X_i Y_i$
1	3	1	9	3
2	15	4	225	30
3	6	9	36	18
4	20	16	400	80
5	9	25	81	45
6	25	36	625	150
$\Sigma X_i = 21$	$\Sigma Y_i = 78$	$\Sigma X_i^2 = 91$	$\Sigma Y_i^2 = 1376$	$\Sigma X_i Y_i = 326$

$$\gamma = \frac{(6 x 326) - (21 x 78)}{\sqrt{\left[(6 x 91) - (21)^2\right]\left[(6 x 1376) - (78)^2\right]}}$$

$$\gamma = \frac{318}{(10.247 x 46.605)}$$

$$\gamma = 0.667$$

This suggests that a fairly high degree of correlation between X and Y series, i.e. between sales and advertising expenditure

Pearson's Method – Shifting Origin

In case the magnitude of the data is large, using the two methods explained above will give lot of inconvenience while calculating the correlation coefficient by Karl Pearson's method. So we take deviations from some convenient numbers to reduce the magnitude of data. There will be no change in the value of correlation coefficient even if deviations are taken. We define, $u_i = X_i - A$ and $v_i = Y_i - B$, where A and B can any arbitrary and assumed values. The formulae are given below,

$$V(u_i) = \frac{\Sigma u_i^2}{n} - \bar{u}^2 \; ; \; V(vi) = \frac{\Sigma v_i^2}{n} - \bar{v}^2 \; ; \; Cov(u_i, v_i) = \frac{\Sigma u_i \, v_i}{n} - \bar{u}\,\bar{v}$$

$$\gamma = \frac{Cov(u_i, v_i)}{\sqrt{\{V(u_i)\, V(v_i)\}}}$$

$$\gamma = \frac{n\Sigma u_i v_i - \Sigma u_i \, \Sigma v_i}{\sqrt{\left[n\sum u_i^2 - \left(\sum u_i\right)^2\right]\left[n\sum v_i^2 - \left(\sum v_i\right)^2\right]}}$$

Example:

Using short cut method, we calculate 'r' for the following data of X_i = Advertising expenditure (Rupees in thousands) and Y_i = sales (Rupees in lakhs). Let us define A = 60 and B=70, two variables chosen arbitrarily. Then $u_i = X_i - 60$ and $v_i = Y_i - 70$.

X_i	Y_i	u_i	v_i	u_i^2	v_i^2	$u_i v_i$
39	47	–21	–23	441	529	+483
65	53	5	–17	25	289	– 85
62	58	2	–12	4	144	– 24
90	86	30	16	900	256	+480
82	62	22	– 8	484	64	–176
75	68	15	– 2	225	4	– 30
25	60	–35	–10	1225	100	–350
98	91	38	21	1444	441	+798
36	51	–24	–19	576	361	+456
78	84	18	14	324	196	+252
Total		$\Sigma u_i = 50$	$\Sigma v_i = -40$	$\Sigma u_i^2 = 5648$	$\Sigma v_i^2 = -2384$	$\Sigma u_i v_i = 2504$

$$\bar{u} = \frac{\Sigma u_i}{n} = \frac{50}{10} = 5\ ; \bar{v} = \frac{\Sigma v_i}{n} = \frac{-40}{10} = -4$$

$$\gamma = \frac{n\Sigma u_i v_i - \Sigma u_i\ \Sigma v_i}{\sqrt{\left[n\sum u_i^2 - \left(\sum u_i\right)^2\right]\left[n\sum v_i^2 - \left(\sum v_i\right)^2\right]}}$$

$$\gamma = \frac{(10 x 2540) - (50 x - 40)}{\sqrt{\left[(10 x 5648) - (50)^2\right]\left[(10 x 2384) - (-40)^2\right]}}$$

$$\gamma = \frac{27040}{\sqrt{(53980)(22240)}} = \frac{27040}{34647.373}$$

$$\gamma = 0.78$$

Hence, the correlation between X and Y series is fairly high as the coefficient of correlation is 0.78.

Properties of Correlation

1. The value of correlation coefficient γ varies between [–1, +1]. This indicates that the value of correction coefficient does not exceed unity.
2. Sign of γ depends on sign of the covariance.
3. If γ = –1, the variables are perfectly negatively correlated.
4. If γ = +1, the variables are perfectly positively correlated.
5. If γ = 0, the variables are not correlated in a linear fashion. There may be non-linear relationship between variables.

6. Correlation coefficient is independent of change of scale and shifting of origin. In other words, shifting the origin and change the scale do not have any effect on the value of correlation.

Let us see the following example to understand the concept, 'if $\gamma = 0$, the variables are not correlated in a linear fashion. There may be non-linear relationship between variables'.

Example:

If X_i and Y_i are given as below, we calculate the correlation coefficient.

X_i	Y_i	X_i^2	Y_i^2	X_iY_i
-3	9	9	81	–27
-2	4	4	16	–8
-1	1	1	1	–1
0	0	0	0	0
1	1	1	1	1
2	4	4	16	8
3	9	9	81	27
$\Sigma X_i = 0$	$\Sigma Y_i = 28$	$\Sigma X_i^2 = 28$	$\Sigma Y_i^2 = 196$	$\Sigma X_iY_i = 0$

$$\gamma = \frac{n\Sigma X_iY_i - \Sigma X_i \Sigma Y_i}{\sqrt{\left[n\Sigma X_i^2 - (\Sigma X_i)^2\right]\left[n\Sigma Y_i^2 - (\Sigma Y_i)^2\right]}}$$

$$\gamma = \frac{(7\times 0)-(0\times 28)}{\sqrt{\left[(7\times 28)-(0)^2\right]\left[(7\times 196)-(28)^2\right]}}$$

$$\gamma = \frac{0}{\sqrt{196\times 588}}$$

$$\gamma = \frac{0}{\sqrt{196\times 588}} = 0$$

Since $\gamma = 0$, it does not mean that the variables X_i and Y_i are uncorrelated. It can only be said that the variables are linearly uncorrelated. In fact if we closely look at the data of X_i and Y_i, it can be observed that $Y_i = X_i^2$ is the relationship existing between X_i and Y_i. This is a non-linear relationship between the variables. Karl Pearson's coefficient of correlation can not measure non-linear relationship between the variables.

❖ Rank Correlation (Spearman's Method)

It is not possible to express attributes such as character, conduct, honesty, beauty, morality, intellectual integrity, etc., in numerical terms. For example, it is easy for a class teacher to arrange the students in his class in an ascending or descending order of intelligence. This means that he can rank them according to their intelligence. Hence, in problems that involve attributes of the type mentioned above, the coefficient of correlation is entirely based on the rank differences between corresponding items.

We may have two types of numerical problems in rank correlation:

1. When actual ranks are given?
2. When ranks are not given?

Calculation of Rank Correlation

1. In the first case, when actual ranks are given, the differences of the two ranks ($R_1 - R_2$) are taken and these are denoted by 'd'.
2. The differences are squared and their total (Σd^2) obtained.
3. Then the following formula is applied to calculate the rank correlation coefficient.

$$r_s = 1 - \frac{6\Sigma d^2}{N(N^2 - 1)}$$

Where r_s denotes Spearman's Rank Correlation and N denotes number of pairs of observations.

4. In the second case, when the ranks are not given, when the actual data are given, we have to assign ranks. We may do so by taking highest value as 1 or the lowest value as 1. When the two observations are same, then the normal practice is to assign an average rank to the two observations.

When the ranks are given

Example:

The ranking of 10 students in two subjects A and B is as follows:

Student	1	2	3	4	5	6	7	8	9	10
Ranks in Subject A	4	6	1	3	9	7	10	2	8	5
Ranks in Subject B	5	8	3	1	7	6	9	2	10	4

Calculate coefficient of rank correlation and comment on the result.

Solution:

In order to calculate rank correlation, we have to calculate Σd2 and the following formula is used.

$$r_s = 1 - \frac{6\Sigma d^2}{N(N^2 - 1)}$$

The following table shows the calculations:

Student No.	Ranks in Subject A (R_1)	Ranks in Subject B (R_2)	Difference ($R_1 - R_2$) (d)	Squared Difference (d^2)
1	4	5	–1	1
2	6	8	–2	4
3	1	3	–2	4
4	3	1	2	4
5	9	7	2	4

Contd...

6	7	6	1	1
7	10	9	1	1
8	2	2	0	0
9	8	10	–2	4
10	5	4	1	1
				$\Sigma d^2 = 24$

$$r_s = 1 - \frac{6\Sigma d^2}{N(N^2-1)}$$

$$r_s = 1 - \frac{(6 \times 24)}{(10)(10^2-1)}$$

$$r_s = 1 - \frac{144}{(10)(99)} = 0.855$$

The rank correlation coefficient (0.855) shows that there is a very high degree of correlation between ranks obtained in subject A and Subject B of the ten students.

When the ranks are not given

Example:

Compute the Spearman's coefficient of correlation between marks assigned to ten students by Judges X and Y in a certain competitive test as shown below:

Student No	1	2	3	4	5	6	7	8	9	10
Marks by Judge X	43	56	29	81	96	34	73	62	48	76
Marks by Judge Y	15	26	34	86	19	29	83	67	51	58

$$r_s = 1 - \frac{6\Sigma d^2}{N(N^2-1)}$$

$$r_s = 1 - \frac{(6 \times 106)}{(10)(10^2-1)}$$

$$r_s = 1 - \frac{636}{(10)(99)} = 0.36$$

Student No.	Marks by Judge X	Ranks by Judge X (R_1)	Marks by Judge Y	Ranks by Judge Y (R_2)	Difference ($R_1 - R_2$) (d)	Squared Difference (d^2)
1	43	8	15	10	-2	4
2	56	6	26	8	-2	4
3	29	10	34	6	4	16
4	81	2	86	1	1	1
5	96	1	19	9	-8	64
6	34	9	29	7	2	4

Contd...

7	73	4	83	2	2	4
8	62	5	67	3	2	4
9	48	7	51	5	2	4
10	76	3	58	4	-1	1
						$\Sigma d^2 = 106$

The rank correlation coefficient (0.36) shows that there is a low degree of correlation between marks assigned by Judge X and Judge Y to the ten students.

Example:

Obtain the rank correlation between variables X (Price of commodity A in r_s) and Y (Price of commodity B in r_s) from the following pairs of observed values.

X	24	29	23	38	46	52	41	36	68	56
Y	110	126	145	131	163	158	131	129	154	140

X	**Ranks of X (R_1)**	**Y**	**Ranks of Y (R_2)**	**Difference ($R_1 - R_2$) (d)**	**Squared Difference (d^2)**
24	9	110	10	–1	1
29	8	126	9	–1	1
23	10	145	4	6	36
38	6	131	6.5	–0.5	0.25
46	4	163	1	3	9
52	3	158	2	1	1
41	5	131	6.5	–1.5	2.25
36	7	129	8	–1	1
68	1	154	3	–2	4
56	2	140	5	–3	9
					$\Sigma d^2 = 64.5$

In the data, there are two equal values (found in Y series), i.e., 131 which is a tie for the ranks 6 and 7 respectively. Then the average of 6 and 7 ranks (6.5) is assigned as rank for both the observations. Then the common ranks for both the observations are 6.5.

In this data, we find common ranks in the second series (Y). Therefore, the formula for the coefficient of correlation through the rank differences method has to be modified as given below:

$$r_s = 1 - \frac{6\left[\Sigma d^2 + \frac{1}{12}(m_1^3 - m_1) + \frac{1}{12}(m_2^3 - m_2) + \frac{1}{12}(m_3^3 - m_3) + \ldots\ldots\right]}{N(N^2 - 1)}$$

m_1, m_2, m_3 .... stands for number of items in the respective groups with common ranks. In this problem only one group having items two (or two common ranks in that group), hence, we can assign $m_1 = 2$)

$$r_s = 1 - \frac{6\left[\Sigma d^2 + \frac{1}{12}(m_1^3 - m_1)\right]}{N(N^2 - 1)}$$

$$r_s = 1 - \frac{6\left[64.5 + \frac{1}{12}(2^3 - 2)\right]}{10(10^2 - 1)}$$

$$r_s = 1 - \frac{6\left[64.5 + 0.5\right]}{990} = 0.61$$

The rank correlation coefficient (0.61) shows that there is a moderate correlation between X and Y.

❖ Coefficient of Determination (γ^2)

When γ = 1; or –1; or 0, the interpretation of γ does not pose any problem. When γ = 1; or –1, all the points lie on straight line in a graph showing a perfect positive or negative correlation. When the points are extremely scattered on a graph, then it becomes evident that there is almost no relationship between the two variables. However, when it comes to other values of γ, we have to be careful in its interpretation. Suppose we get a correlation of $\gamma = 0.9$, we may say that $\gamma = 0.9$ is 'twice as good' or 'twice as strong' as a correlation of $\gamma = 0.45$. It may be noted that this comparison is wrong. The strength of γ is judged by coefficient of determination, γ^2 for = 0.9, $\gamma^2 = 0.81$. We multiply it by 100, thus, getting 81 per cent. Thus, suggest that when $\gamma = 0.9$ then we can say that 81 per cent of the total variation in the Y series can be attributed to the relationship with X.

REGRESSION ANALYSIS

Literally, the word "Regression" means 'stepping back or returning to the average value'. Regression was first used by Sir Francis Galton, a British Biometrician in the 19th Century in some studies on estimating the extent to which the stature of sons of tall parents regresses back to the mean stature of the population. The interesting features of the study were:

1. Tall fathers have tall sons and short fathers have short sons.
2. The average height of the sons of a group of tall fathers is less than that of the fathers and the average height of the sons of a group of short fathers is more than that of the fathers.

In today's world, regression is used in varying fields with diversified areas of applications. It is specially used in Business Management and Economics to study the relationship between two or more economic variables that are related casually and for estimation of

1. Demand and supply curves,
2. Cost functions,
3. Production and consumption functions,
4. The effect of advertising on sales, and
5. Prediction of sales with given advertising expenditure and so on.

Prediction (estimation) is one of the major areas of interest on most of the spheres of human activity. Estimation of future production, consumption, prices, sales, income, profits, investments, demands, etc., are of paramount importance to Businessmen. Population estimation and projections are indispensable for efficient planning of an economy.

In Pharmaceutical industry, it is important and necessary to estimate the effect of a new drug on patient, its ill effects, if any, in short as well as in long run. According to M.M. Blair "Regression analysis is a mathematical measure of the average relationship between two or more variables in terms of the original units of the data".

If regression analysis is confined only to two variables then it is termed as Simple Regression.

Business examples:

1. Expenditure of a person depends on his income,
2. Yield of a crop depends on the rainfall,
3. The demand of a product depends on its price, etc.

The regression analysis for studying more than two variables at a time is known as "Multiple Regression". However, we confine ourselves to only Simple regression. In regression analysis, we come across two types of variables.

Dependent Variable: The variable whose value is influenced or is to be predicted is termed as dependent variable. Dependent variable is also known as regressed (or explained) variable.

Independent Variable: The variable which influences the dependent variable or which is used for prediction is called independent variable. Independent variable is also known as regressed (or predictor or explanatory) variable.

❖ Linear Regression

If we plot the given bivariate data on a graph paper, and obtain the scatter diagram, the points on the diagram will more or less concentrate around a curve called "curve of regression". Often, such a curve is not distinct, is quite confusing and sometimes complicated too. A graph in Figure is given below for the purpose of illustration.

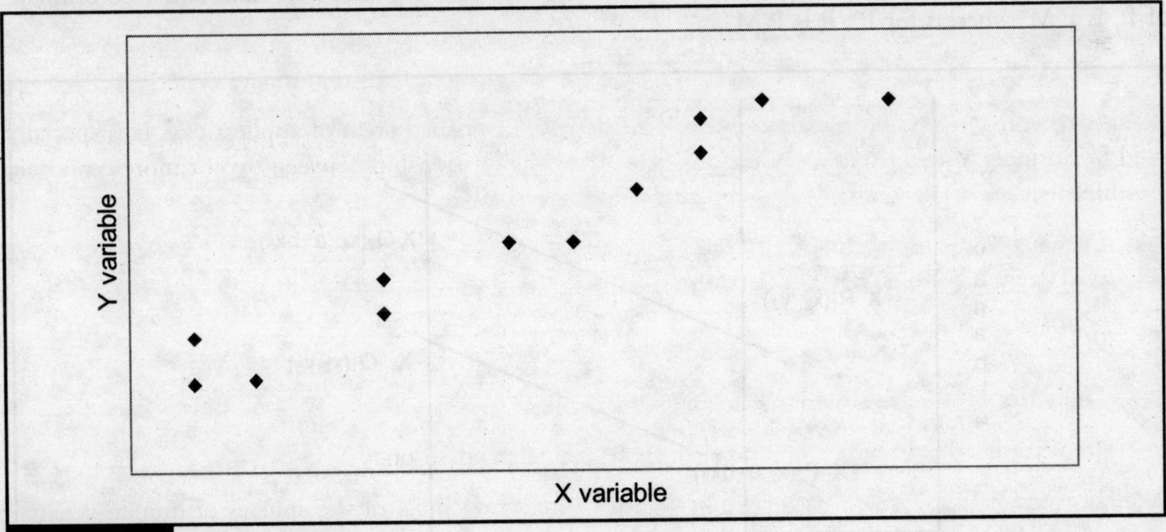

FIGURE 12.10 Regression Line

If the regression curve is a straight line, we say that the variables under study are related in linear fashion. The regression equation for such a relationship is $y_i = a + b\ x_i$, a straight line. In case of a linear regression, the values of the dependent variable increase or decrease by a constant amount for a unit change in the independent variable.

If the regression curve is not a straight line, then the regression is called as non-linear (curvy linear) regression. The regression equation will involve square terms like x^2, y^2 and/or product terms like xy, xz and so on. We confine ourselves to linear regression between two variables only.

Lines of Regression

Line of regression is the line, which gives the best estimate of one variable for any given value of the other variable. In case of two variables x and y, we shall have two lines of regression, called, (a) Regression of y on x and (b) Regression of x on y.

1. Line of regression of y on x is the line which gives the best estimate for the value of y for any specified (or given) value of x.
2. Line of regression of x on y is the line which gives the best estimate for the value of x for any specified (given) value of y.

The term best fit is interpreted in accordance with the "Principle of Least Squares" which consists of minimizing the sum of the squares of the residuals estimated. The residual is also known as error and is defined as "the deviation between the given observed value and the value of the estimate as given by the line of best fit".

Regression Equation of y on x

Let $(x_1,y_1),(x_2,y_2),...,(x_n,y_n)$ be n pairs of observations on the variables x and y under study. Let $y_i = a + bx_i$ be the line of best fit (regression) of y on x.

For the purpose of illustration, we present two points $P_2(x_2, a + bx_2)$ and $Q_2(x_5,a+bx_5)$ in the following scatter diagram. For the given point $P_1(x_2, y_2)$ in the diagram, the error is given by the line of best fit y = a + bx shown in the diagram is P_1P_2. Since the X co-ordinates for P_1 and P_2 are same and Y co-ordinate of P_1 is P_1M_1 whereas for P_2, it is P_2M_2.

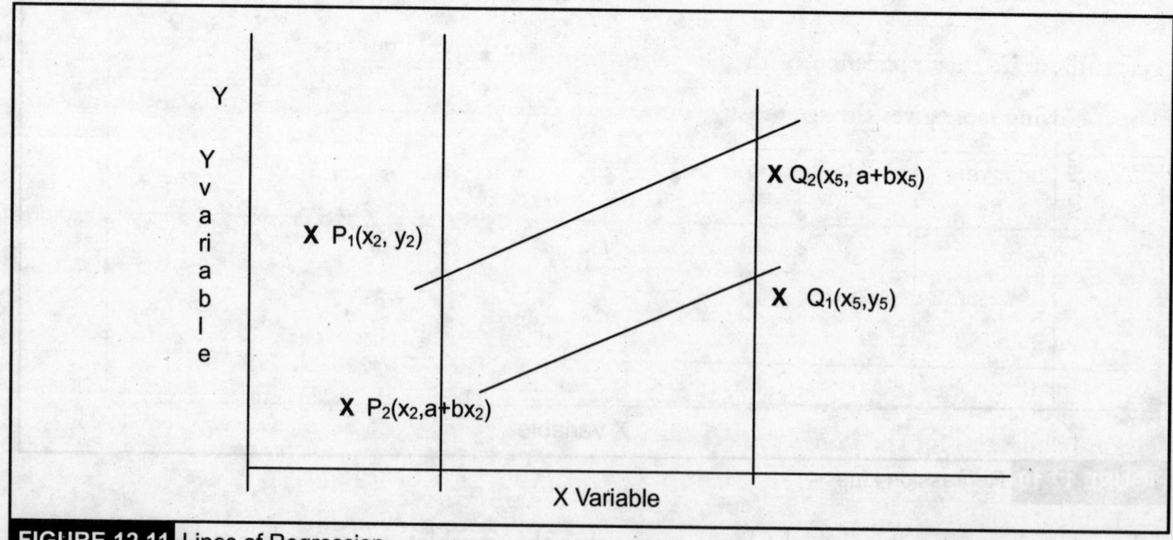

FIGURE 12.11 Lines of Regression

The difference, namely, $(P_1M_1 - P_2M_2) = P_1P_2$ which is called as error. In particular, $P_2M_2 = a + bx_2$ and $P_1M_1 = y_2$. Hence, error is: $e_2 = y_2 - (a + bx_2)$.

Similarly, for $Q_1\ (x_2, y_5)$ and $Q_2\ (x_5, a + bx_5)$, we can define the error as: $e_5 = y_5 - (a + bx_5)$.

Here, e_2 is positive and e_5 is negative. As is explained, the error can be either negative, positive or zero (if $X_2 = a + bx_2$).

Error square is defined as: $e_2^2 = (y_2 - a - b x_2)^2$

$$e_5^2 = (y_5 - a - b x_5)^2$$

Let E = sum of the squares of error for n pairs, then

$$E = \Sigma(y_i - a - bx_i)^2$$

Sometimes $\Sigma(y_i - y_e)^2$ is used to represent 'E' where y_e denotes the estimated values of y. By using maxima and minima Principles of differential calculus. We get two equations called "Normal Equations", as given below

$$\Sigma y_i = na + b\Sigma x_i$$

$$\Sigma x_i y_i = a\Sigma x_i + b\Sigma x_i^2$$

Using these two normal equations, we can solve uniquely for the value of 'a' and 'b'.

Regression equation of x on y

Similarly, the normal equations for obtaining the Regression equation of x on y is $x_i = a + by_i$ are

$$\Sigma x_i = na + b\Sigma y_i$$

$$\Sigma x_i y_i = a\Sigma y_i + b\Sigma y_i^2$$

The values of 'a' and 'b' are obtained by using the above formulae by interchanging the variables x to y and y to x.

Example:

Let us illustrate the application of the above formulae by an example:

The following table gives the age in years of cars of a certain company and its annual maintenance cost.

Age of Car in year (X_i)	Maintenance Cost (Y_i) (in ₹ '00)	$X_i Y_i$	X_i^2	Y_i^2
2	10	20	4	100
4	20	80	16	400
6	25	150	36	625
8	30	240	64	900
20	85	490	120	2025

Normal equations for the Regression equation of y on x: $y_i = a + bx_i$ are:

$$\Sigma x_i = na + b\Sigma x_i$$

$$\Sigma x_i y_i = a\Sigma x_i + b\Sigma x_i^2$$

We have $n = 4$, $\Sigma x_i = 20$, $\Sigma y_i = 85$, $\Sigma x_i y_i = 490$, $\Sigma x_i^2 = 120$

By substituting these values in the above equations, we get

$$85 = 4a + 20b \quad (1)$$

$$490 = 20a + 120b \quad (2)$$

To solve the above equations, we adopt the procedure of elimination. To eliminate 'a', we multiply the first equation by 5 to get

$$425 = 20a + 100b$$

The second equation is taken as it is. Then by subtracting the second equation from the first equation

$$\begin{array}{l} 425 = \not{20a} + 100b \\ 490 = \not{20a} + 120b \\ (-)\quad (-)\quad (-) \\ \hline -65 = 0 = -20b \\ \hline \end{array}$$

$$\Rightarrow \quad 20b = 65 \text{ or } b = \frac{65}{20} = 3.25$$

We substitute the value of $b = 3.25$ in the first equation to get

$$85 = 4a + 20\,(3.25)$$

$$\Rightarrow \quad 4a = 85 - 65.00 = 20$$

$$\Rightarrow \quad a = \frac{20}{4} = 5$$

Hence, the regression equation of y on x is

$$y_i = 5 + 3.25\,x_i$$

This equation is very useful to predict the value of y_i (maintenance cost) if we know x_i, the age (in years) of the car.

For example, we predict the annual maintenance cost for a car with 9 years age. This is obtained by substituting $x_i = 9$ in the equation $y_i = 5 + 3.25\,x_i$. Annual maintenance cost of a car with $x_i = 9$ years age is

$$y_i = 5 + 3.25 \times 9$$

$$= 5 + 29.25 = 34.25 \text{ (hundreds of ₹)}$$

Similarly, we can fit the regression equation of x on y as:

$x_i = a + b\Sigma y_i$ and the corresponding normal equations are

$$\Sigma x_i = na + b\Sigma y_i$$

$$\Sigma x_i y_i = a\Sigma y_i + b\Sigma y_i^{\ 2}$$

by substituting the sums and products obtained from the above, we have

$$20 = 4a + 85b$$

$$490 = 85a + 2025b$$

To eliminate 'a', we multiply the first equation with '85' and the second with '4'. The result is

$$1700 = 340a + 7225b$$
$$1960 = 340a + 8100b$$
$$(-) \quad (-) \quad (-)$$
$$-260 = 0 - 875b$$

$$b = \frac{260}{875} = 0.297 \approx 0.30$$

The value of 'a' can be obtained from

$$20 = 4a + 85(0.30)$$
$$4a = 20 - 25.5 = -5.5$$
$$a = \frac{-5.5}{4} = -1.375$$

The regression equation of x on y is

$$x_i = -1.375 + 0.30y_i$$

Estimation of 'a' and 'b' directly

Slope (b): It is the coefficient of the x_i term in the equation: $y_i = a + bx_i$. It shows how much the dependent variable changes for one unit change in the independent variable. When positive, it gives the increase in y_i per unit increase in x_i

y-Intercept (a): It is the value of y_i where the line $y_i = a + bx_i$ cuts Y - axis. It is the constant term in the estimation equation.

The value of 'a' (Y – intercept) and 'b' (slope) is calculated by the following formula

$$a = \frac{(\Sigma x_i^2)(\Sigma y_i) - (\Sigma x_i)(\Sigma x_i y_i)}{n\Sigma x_i^2 - (\Sigma x_i)^2} \text{ and}$$

$$b = \frac{n\Sigma x_i y_i - \Sigma x_i \Sigma y_i}{n\Sigma x_i^2 - (\Sigma x_i)^2}$$

then we substitute the values of a and b obtained above into

$y_i = a + bx_i$ which gives the Regression equation of y on x.

Example:

We have $n = 4$, $\Sigma x_i = 20$, $\Sigma y_i = 85$, $\Sigma x_i y_i = 490$, $\Sigma x_i^2 = 120$

$$a = \frac{(\Sigma x_i^2)(\Sigma y_i) - (\Sigma x_i)(\Sigma x_i y_i)}{n\Sigma x_i^2 - (\Sigma x_i)^2}$$

$$= \frac{(120)85 - 20(490)}{4(120) - (20)^2}$$

$$= \frac{(10200 - 9800)}{(480 - 400)}$$

$$= \frac{400}{80} = 5$$

$$b = \frac{n\Sigma x_i y_i - \Sigma x_i \Sigma y_i}{n\Sigma x_i^2 - (\Sigma x_i)^2}$$

$$b = \frac{(4)(490) - (20)(85)}{4(120) - (20)^2}$$

$$b = \frac{(1960 - 1700)}{(480 - 400)}$$

$$b = \frac{260}{80} = 3.25$$

The values of 'a' and 'b' obtained are same as those obtained using normal equations. Similarly, we can estimate 'a' and 'b' for the regression equation of x on y by interchanging x and y in the above formulae. Let us look at the two Regression equations obtained above.

Regression equation of y on x: $y_i = 5 + 3.25\ x_i$

Regression equation of x on y: $x_i = -\ 1.375 + 0.30\ y_i$

The regression co-efficient 3.25 is called as the regression co-efficient of y on x and is denoted by $b_{yx} = 3.25$.

Similarly, the regression co-efficient 0.30 is called as the regression co-efficient of x on y and is denoted by $b_{xy} = 0.30$.

On the basis of regression equation of Y on X, we can find out the value of Y for any value of X. Similarly, we can find out the value of X for any value of Y based on the regression equation of X on Y.

Properties of Regression Co-efficients

1. Both the regression co-efficient will take the same sign, i.e., byx and bxy will take either positive or negative sign.
2. The correlation co-efficient is the G.M. of the regression co-efficients, i.e.,

   $$\gamma = \sqrt{(b_{xy})(b_{yx})}$$

   r is positive if b_{yx} is positive and r is negative if b_{yx} is negative.
3. If one of the regression co-efficient is greater than unity (one), then the other must be less than unity.
4. The regression equations pass through their respective means.

Regression Equation using 'γ'

Sometimes we get data on x and y a below:

$\bar{x} = 15, \bar{y} = 110$, V(x) = 25, V(y) = 625 and γ (x, y) = 0.81

then we use the following procedure to get regression equations.

1. Regression equation of y on x:

$$(y_i - \bar{y}) = \gamma\sqrt{\frac{V(y)}{V(x)}}\ (x_i - \bar{x})$$

or

$$(y_i - \bar{y}) = \gamma\frac{\sigma_y}{\sigma_x}(x_i - \bar{x})$$

$$\text{Since } b_{yx} = \gamma\,\frac{\sigma_y}{\sigma_x}$$

$$(y_i - \bar{y}) = b_{yx}\,(x_i - \bar{x})$$

$$(y_i - 110) = (0.81)\sqrt{\frac{625}{25}}\ (x_i - 15)$$

$$y_i = 110 + 0.81\ \{\sqrt{25}\}(x_i - 15)$$

$$y_i = 110 + 4.05\ (x_i - 15) = 110 - 4.05\ (15) + 4.05\ x_i$$

$$y_i = 49.25 + 4.05\ x_i$$

2. Regression equation of x on y:

$$(x_i - \bar{x}) = \gamma\sqrt{\frac{V(x)}{V(y)}}\ (y_i - \bar{y})$$

$$(y_i - \bar{y}) = \gamma\,\frac{\sigma_y}{\sigma_x}\,(x_i - \bar{x})$$

$$\text{Since } b_{zy} = \gamma\,\frac{\sigma_y}{\sigma_x}$$

$$(x_i - \bar{x}) = b_{yx}\,(y_i - \bar{y})$$

$$(y_i - 15) = (0.81)\sqrt{\frac{25}{625}}\ (x_i - 100)$$

$$(x_i - 15) = (0.81)\sqrt{\frac{1}{25}}\ (\ y_i - 110)$$

$$x_i = 15 + (0.81)\ (y_i - 110)$$

$$= 15 + 0.81(0.20)\ (y_i - 110)$$

$$x_i = -2.82 + 0.162\ y_i$$

❖ Estimation – Regression Coefficients using Regression Equations

In certain situations we need to estimate the regression coefficients, means and variances of the variables directly from the given regression equations.

Example

Let the two regression equations be:

$$3X + 2Y - 26 = 0$$

$$6X + Y - 31 = 0$$

1. To find the means, we solve these two simultaneous linear equations by the process of eliminations. For this, we multiply the 2nd equation with '2' to get

   $12X + 2Y - 62 = 0$

   Subtract the 1st equation from the 2nd equation, we get

   $9X - 36 = 0$

   or $X = 36/9 = 4$.

   Substitute $X = 4$ in the 1st equation, to get

   $3(4) + 2Y - 26 = 0$

   or $2Y = 26 - 12 = 14$

   or $Y = 7$

   Since the regression equations will pass through their respective means, we can say that

   $\bar{X} = 4$ and $\bar{Y} = 7$

2. The regression equations given above are used to get 'r' the correlation coefficient.

   Let us assume $3X + 2Y - 26 = 0$ to be the regression equation of Y on X.

   Hence, $2Y = 26 - 3X$

   or $Y = 13 - \frac{3}{2} X$

   Then $b_{yx} = -\frac{3}{2} = -1.5$

   The 2nd equation $6X + Y - 31 = 0$ will be the regression equation of X on Y.

   Hence, $6X = 31 - Y$

   or $X = \frac{31}{6} - \frac{1}{6} Y$

Then $b_{xy} = -\frac{1.}{6}$

The value of r is given by

$$\gamma = \pm\sqrt{byx \,.\, bxy}$$

$$\gamma = \pm\sqrt{-\frac{1}{6}\,x - \frac{3}{2}}$$

$$= \pm\frac{1}{2}$$

Since b_{yx}, b_{xy} are negative γ will be negative. So

$$\gamma = -\frac{1}{2} = -0.5$$

3. We can use the regression equations for estimating the unknown variance (standard deviation) of one of the variables given the other variance.

$$(y_i - \bar{y}) = \gamma\frac{\sigma_y}{\sigma_x}(x_i - \bar{x})$$

Since $b_{yx} = \gamma\frac{\sigma_y}{\sigma_x}$

if $\sigma_y = 5$ then σ_x can be calculated as given below

$$b_{yx} = \gamma\frac{\sigma_y}{\sigma_x}$$

$$-\frac{1}{6} = -0.5\frac{5}{\sigma_x}$$

$$\sigma_x = -6x - 0.5x\,5 = 15$$

Example:

Compute the two regression equations on the basis of the following information:

Parameters	**x**	**y**
Mean	40	45
Standard deviation	10	9

Karl Pearson's correlation coefficient = 0.5. Also calculate the value of y for x = 48, using appropriate regression equation.

Regression equation of y on x is:

$$(y_i - \bar{y}) = \gamma\frac{\sigma_y}{\sigma_x}(x_i - \bar{x})$$

Substituting the values of : $\bar{x}$, $\bar{y}$, σ_x, σ_y, γ given in the above problem in the above equation, we get:

$$(y_i - 45) = 0.5\frac{9}{10}(x_i - 40)$$

$$y_i = 45 + 0.45\,(x_i - 40)$$

$$y_i = 45 + 0.45x_i - 18$$

$$y_i = 27 + 0.45x_i$$

Regression Equation of x on y:

$$(x_i - \bar{x}) = \gamma\frac{\sigma_x}{\sigma_y}(y_i - \bar{y})$$

Substituting the values of : $\bar{x}$, $\bar{y}$, σ_x, σ_y, γ given in the above problem in the above equation, we get:

$$(x_i - 40) = 0.5\frac{10}{9}(y_i - 45)$$

$$x_i = 40 + 0.556\,(y_i - 45)$$

$$x_i = 40 + 0.556 - 25.02$$

$$x_i = 14.98 + 0.556$$

In order to estimate the value of *y* for *x* = 48, we have to use regression equation of *y* on *x*:

$$\bar{y} = 27 + 0.45\ x_i$$

$$\bar{y} = 27 + (45 \text{ x } 48)$$

$$\bar{y} = 27 + 21.6$$

$$\bar{y} = 48.6$$

Therefore, the value of y is 48.6 when the value of x = 48.

❖ Difference between Correlation and Regression

Correlation measures the degree of relationship between two variables. Regression helps in exploiting the degree of relationship existing between two variables so that they can be linked through a regression equation. Regression equation helps in predicting the future behaviour of a dependent variable given the value of independent variable. Prediction plays a key role in formulating strategic decision framework to the management.

The following are the points of difference between Correlation and Regression:

1. Whereas coefficient of correlation is a measure of degree of co-variability between X and Y, the objective of regression analysis is to study the nature of relationship between the variables so that we may be able to predict the value of one on the basis of another.

2. Correlation is merely a tool of ascertaining the degree of relationship between two variables and, therefore, we can not say one variable is the cause and other the effect. For example, a high degree of correlation between price and demand for a certain commodity or a particular point of time

may not suggest which is the cause and which is the effect. However, in regression analysis, one variable is taken as independent while the other as independent, thus, making it possible to study cause and effect relationship.

3. In correlation analysis, coefficient of correlation is a measure of direction and degree of linear relationship between two variable X and Y. It is symmetric whether the correlation between X and Y or between Y and X. It is also immaterial which of X and Y is dependent variable and which is independent variable. In regression analysis, the regression coefficients Y on X and X on Y are not symmetric. Hence it is definitely makes a difference as to which variable is dependent and which variable is independent.

4. There may be nonsense correlation between two variables which is purely due to chance and has no practical relevance such as increase in income and increase in weight of group of people. However, there is nothing like nonsense regression.

5. Correlation coefficient is independent of change of scale and origin. Regression coefficients are independent of change of origin but not of scale.

❖ Correlation and Causation

Correlation helps us in having an idea about the degree and direction of the relationship between two variables under study. It fails to reflect upon the cause and effect relationship between the variables. If the variables have the cause and effect relationship, they are bound to vary in sympathy with each other and hence there is a high degree of correlation. In other words, causation always implies correlation but the converse is not true, i.e., even a fairly high degree of correlation between two variables need not imply a cause and effect relationship between them. For example, if X = Number of patients admitted into a super specialty hospital and Y = Number of Space shuttles launched, one may get a numerical value for r, but it does not signify the relationship between these variable.

REVIEW QUESTIONS

1. Describe common univariate and bivariate statistical tests used in marketing research and explain when they are appropriate and when they are not.

2. Explain correlation and partial correlation and their relationship to causality.

3. Find the coefficient of correlation between the sales and expenses of the ten firms given below and comment.

Sales	50	50	55	60	65	65	65	60	60	50
Expenses	11	13	14	16	16	15	15	14	13	13

(Answer: γ = + 0.7866)

4. Find Product moment coefficient of correlation between X and Y from the following data.

Marks in English (X)	65	66	67	67	68	69	70	72
Marks in Mathematics (Y)	67	68	65	68	72	72	69	71

5. Find Product moment coefficient of correlation between X and Y from the following data.

Price in ₹ (X)	100	90	85	92	90	84	88	90
Sales in Units (Y)	500	610	700	630	670	800	800	750

(Answer $\gamma = -0.85$)

6. The following frequency distribution relates to the age and salary of 100 employees working in an organisation. Find the coefficient of correlation. Grouped data

Age (years)	Salary (₹)			
	1300-1400	1400-1500	1500-1600	1600-1700
20 - 30	4	6	5	2
30 - 40	2	5	8	5
40 - 50	8	12	20	2
50 - 60	0	8	12	1

(Answer $\gamma = 0.388$)

7. Two persons were asked to watch ten specified TV programmes and offer their evaluation by rating them 1 to 10. These ratings are given below.

TV Programme	A	B	C	D	E	F	G	H	I	J
Ranks given by X	4	6	3	9	1	5	2	7	10	8
Ranks given by Y	2	3	4	9	5	7	1	10	8	6

Calculate Spearman's coefficient of correlation of the two ratings.

(Answer: $r_s = 0.685$)

8. An investigation into the demand for television sets in 7 towns has resulted in the following data:

Town	A	B	C	D	E	F	G
Population (lakh) (x)	11	14	14	17	17	21	25
No. of TV sets demanded ('000)(y)	15	27	27	30	34	38	46

Fit a linear regression of y on x and estimate the demand for TV sets for a city with population of (a) 20 lakh and (b) 32 lakh

(Answer: $y = -3 + 2x$ (a) 3,997 (b) 6,397)

9. Fit a straight line to the following data:

X (Age of a Car)	1	3	5	7	9
Y (Maintenance Cost)	15	26	34	40	52

(Answer: $Y = 11.4 + 4.4X$)

10. An enquiry into 50 families to study the relationship between Expenditure on Housing (X_i) and expenditure on food (Y_i) give the following results.

$\Sigma X_i = 8500$, $\Sigma Y_i = 8500$, $\sigma x = 60$, $\sigma y = 60$, $\gamma = +0.6$

(i) Obtain the regression lines of X on Y and Y on X

(ii) When X = 200, determine the value of Y

(Answer: (i) Y_i = 158 + 0.2 X_i; X_i = –175.6 + 1.8 Y_i; (ii) ₹198)

11. Obtain two regression equations and estimate (i) the yield of crops when the rainfall is 22 cms and (ii) the rainfall when the yield is 600 kgs.

	X = Yield (in Kg)	Y = Rainfall (in cms)
Mean	508.4	26.7
S.D	36.8	4.6

γ = + 0.52

(Answers: Y_i = – 6.346 + 0.0652 X_i ; X_i = 397.328 + 4.16 Y_i;
(i) 488.85 Kgs; (ii) 32.654 cms)

12. Estimate the sales for a given number of advertisements from the following data for X = 10

X (No. of Ads)	3	7	4	2	0	4	1	2
Y (Sales)	11	18	9	4	7	6	3	8

Develop the other regression equation also.

(Answers: Y_i = 3.33 + 1.71 X_i;
X_i = –0.11 + 0.36 Y_i; γ = + 0.786)

13. When X = 3, Y = 6, n = 4, ΣX_iY_i = 78, ΣX_i^2 = 44, ΣY_i^2 = 150:

Find both the regression equations and γ.

(Answers: Y_i = 3.75 + 0.75 X_i ;
X_i = –2.998 + 0.9996Y_i; γ = + 0.866)

14. The lines of regression are 8 X – 10 Y = 0; 40 X – 18 Y = 214 and variance of X is 9.

Find (i) Means of X and Y (ii) Correlation ‘r’ (iii) σ_y

(Answer X = 13, Y = 17, γ = + 0.6, σ_y = 4).

CHAPTER THIRTEEN

ANALYSIS OF DATA (MULTIVARIATE ANALYSIS)

INTRODUCTION

In simple correlation and simple regression analysis, the discussion was confined to two variables only. But some problems normally involve several variables. For example, the demand for television sets may depend not only on their price but also in income of households, advertising expenditure incurred by television manufacturers and other similar factors. Such problems require the use of multivariate techniques. In such cases, multiple regressions will give more accurate predictions than the bivariate regression analysis. Apart from multiple regressions, there are several methods used in multivariate analysis. This chapter focuses on the major multivariate methods.

MULTIVARIATE ANALYSIS

Multivariate analysis is the analysis of the simultaneous relationships among three or more phenomena. Some experts consider any simultaneous statistical analysis of more than two variables to be multivariate analysis. Multivariate analysis is based on three judgments regarding the nature and utilization of data that are to be made by the researcher (i) Are some of the variables dependent on others? (ii) If yes, how many variables are dependent? and (iii) Are the data qualitative (Non-metric) or quantitative (metric)? The use of a particular multivariate method will depend on the answers to these three questions.

Another approach to multivariate methods is to classify them into two broad categories: Functional methods and structural methods. The functional methods, which are also called the dependence methods, provide directionality the magnitude of relationship between one or more dependent variables and two or more independent variables. With the help of such methods, the researcher can develop predictive models which can be used for forecasting. Some of the important functional multivariate methods are multiple regression analysis, discriminant analysis, multivariate analysis of variance and canonical analysis.

The structural methods, which are also called the interdependence methods, are essentially descriptive and are not useful for reductive purposes. They are helpful in reducing large and complex data into meaningful groups and in bringing out relationships which are not otherwise apparent. Some of the structural multivariate methods are factor analysis, cluster analysis, multidimensional scaling, conjoint analysis and latent structure analysis.

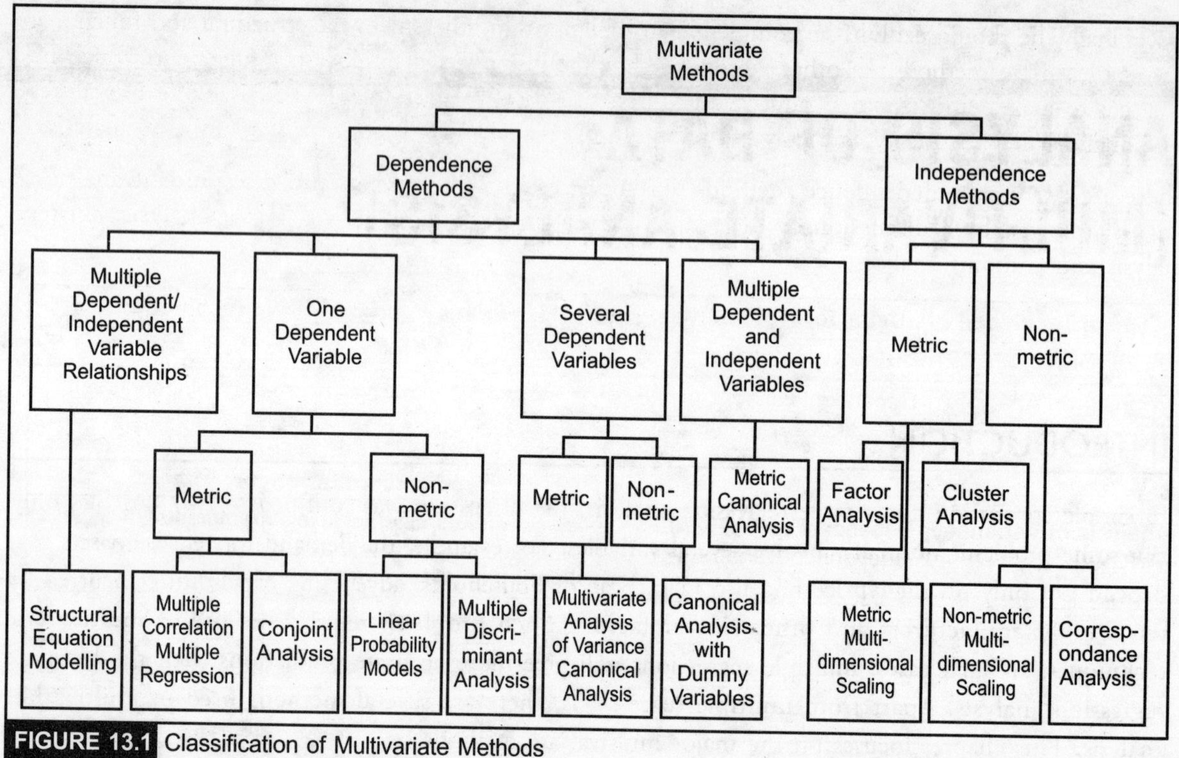

FIGURE 13.1 Classification of Multivariate Methods

❖ Guidelines for the use of Multivariate Analysis

Sheth offers a number of guidelines to the researcher who intends to use multivariate methods, to guard against their indiscriminate use. These guidelines are briefly given below:

1. The marketing researcher should not try to be technique-oriented. If he develops a fancy for one or two particular techniques and uses them indiscriminately without checking their suitability in a given case, it will harm the interests of marketing research. It may also bring about the downfall of multivariate methods.
2. He should not be carried away in building models; disregarding the fact the multivariate models are information inputs to facilitate management in the process of decision-making.
3. He should remember that multivariate methods are not substitutes for his skills and imagination in the design of research. These are necessary in conceptualization of the problem.
4. He should not overlook the need for lucid communication with management. A first rate study using sophisticated techniques may go waste if management is unable to understand it.
5. He should not make statistical inferences about the parameters of multivariate models. Such inferences are not possible on account of the sizeable existence of non-sampling or measurement errors in the data in the social sciences. Such techniques should be seen as descriptive statistical techniques for reducing large data to a summarized and meaningful form.
6. Sometimes, the researcher may be carried away by a random relationship among the variables and put substantive meanings into the data, which may not be true. This is especially true of some multivariate methods such as cluster analysis, multidimensional scaling and conjoint measurement as there is no sampling theory behind them and therefore, these are heuristics. To guard oneself against this error, it may be advisable to use at least two different techniques.

7. Finally, he should exploit the complementary relationship inherent in the structural and functional multivariate methods. In other words, he should substantiate a number of judgements which he has to make with structural multivariate analysis of data. For example, it is advisable to use cluster analysis first to specify mutually exclusive groups before using a multiple discriminant analysis.

There are two major dependence methods viz. multiple linear regression and discriminant analysis. This is followed by a discussion of the major interdependence methods viz, factor analysis, cluster analysis and conjoint analysis.

Type of Technique	Usual form of Input data	Primary purpose of the Technique
DEPENDENCY TECHNIQUES		
Regression Analysis	Dependent variable, metric Independent variable(s), metric	To ascertain the relative importance of independent variable(s) in explaining variation in the dependent variable; also to predict dependent variable values for given values of the independent variable(s)
Analysis of Variance (ANOVA)	Dependent variable, metric Independent variable(s), nonmetric	To see whether different levels (treatments) of independent variable(s) have significantly different impacts on the dependent variable
Discriminant Analysis	Dependent variable, nonmetric Independent variable(s), metric	To identify independent variables that are critical in distinguishing between sub samples defined by the dependent variable categories; also to aid in classifying new units into one of the sub sample categories
INTERDEPENDENCE TECHNIQUES		
Factor Analysis	Metric	To reduce data on a large number of variables into a relatively small set of factors; also to identify key constructs underlying the original set of measured variables
Cluster Analysis	Metric	To identify natural clusters of objects on the basis of similarities of the objects on a variety of characteristics
Multidimensional Scaling	Nonmetric (similarity ranks based on comparison of actual objects)	To identify key dimensions underlying respondent evaluations of products, brands, stores, etc.; also to determine the relative positions of the objects in multidimensional space
Conjoint Analysis	Nonmetric (preference ranks based on comparisons of hypothetical stimuli formed by systematically varying selected attribute levels)	To derive utility values that respondents implicitly assign to various levels of key attributes used in evaluating objects; the utility values themselves aid in ascertaining the relative importance of the attributes and the potential attractiveness of descriptive profiles defined by different combinations of attributes

Dependency Methods	Interdependency Methods
• Multiple Linear Regression	• Factor Analysis
• Multiple Discriminant Analysis	• Cluster Analysis
• Multivariate Analysis of Variance	• Multidimensional Scaling
• Multivariate Analysis of Covariance	• Correspondence Analysis
• Canonical Correlation	• Reliability Analysis
• Logistical Regression	
• Conjoint Analysis	

LOGISTIC REGRESSION ANALYSIS

Sometimes referred to as "choice models," this technique is a variation of multiple regression that allows for the prediction of an event. It is allowable to utilize nonmetric (typically binary) dependent variables, as the objective is to arrive at a probabilistic assessment of a binary choice. The independent variables can be either discrete or continuous. A contingency table is produced, which shows the classification of observations as to whether the observed and predicted events match. The sum of events that were predicted to occur which actually did occur and the events that were predicted not to occur which actually did not occur, divided by the total number of events, is a measure of the effectiveness of the model. This tool helps predict the choices consumers might make when presented with alternatives.

MULTIVARIATE ANALYSIS OF VARIANCE (MANOVA)

This technique examines the relationship between several categorical independent variables and two or more metric dependent variables. Whereas analysis of variance (ANOVA) assesses the differences between groups (by using T tests for 2 means and F tests between 3 or more means), MANOVA examines the dependence relationship between a set of dependent measures across a set of groups. Typically this analysis is used in experimental design, and usually a hypothesized relationship between dependent measures is used. This technique is slightly different in that the independent variables are categorical and the dependent variable is metric. Sample size is an issue, with 15-20 observations needed per cell. However, too many observations per cell (over 30) and the technique loses its practical significance. Cell sizes should be roughly equal, with the largest cell having less than 1.5 times the observations of the smallest cell. That is because, in this technique, normality of the dependent variables is important. The model fit is determined by examining mean vector equivalents across groups. If there is a significant difference in the means, the null hypothesis can be rejected and treatment differences can be determined.

MULTIPLE REGRESSION ANALYSIS

Multiple regression is the most commonly utilized multivariate technique. It examines the relationship between a single metric dependent variable and two or more metric independent variables. The technique relies upon determining the linear relationship with the lowest sum of squared variances; therefore, assumptions of normality, linearity, and equal variance are carefully observed. The beta coefficients (weights) are the marginal impacts of each variable, and the size of the weight can be interpreted directly. Multiple regression is often used as a forecasting tool.

MULTIDIMENSIONAL SCALING (MDS)

Multidimensional Scaling (MDS) is a data reduction technique, the primary purpose is to uncover the "hidden structure" of a set of data. It enables us to represent the proximities between objects spatially as in a map. The term 'proximities' means any set of numbers that express the amount of similarity or difference between pairs of objects. The term 'objects' refers to things or events. The main purpose of MDS is to map the objects in a multidimensional space such that their relative positions in the space show the degree of perceived proximity or similarity amongst them. MDS involves two aspects. First, it helps in the identification of attributes on the basis of which consumers perceive or evaluate products or brands. Second, it enables the positioning of different products of brands on the basis of these attributes. It helps generate a perceptual map, indicating the location of the brands on the basis of attributes.

❖ Approaches to Multidimensional Scaling

There are two sets of approaches that can be used for analysis of multidimensional data. One set of approaches involves the measure of attributes while the other considers proximity or preference between objects, ignoring individual attributes as factors. Regardless as to which approach is used, the results of both sets enable us to identify market clusters and their sizes. We give below an example of each of these two sets of approaches.

❖ Purpose

The use of multidimensional scale would be more appropriate than unidimensional scale. This is because consumers generally prefer a particular brand of a product not on the basis of one attribute but on a number of attributes. We briefly discuss multidimensional scaling here. The purpose of MDS is to transform consumer judgments of similarity into distances represented in multidimensional space. This is a decompositional approach that uses perceptual mapping to present the dimensions. As an exploratory technique, it is useful in examining unrecognized dimensions about products and in uncovering comparative evaluations of products when the basis for comparison is unknown. Typically, there must be at least 4 times as many objects being evaluated as dimensions. It is possible to evaluate the objects with nonmetric preference rankings or metric similarities (paired comparison) ratings. Kruskal's Stress measure is a "badness of fit" measure; a stress percentage of 0 indicates a perfect fit, and over 20% is a poor fit. The dimensions can be interpreted either subjectively by letting the respondents identify the dimensions or objectively by the researcher.

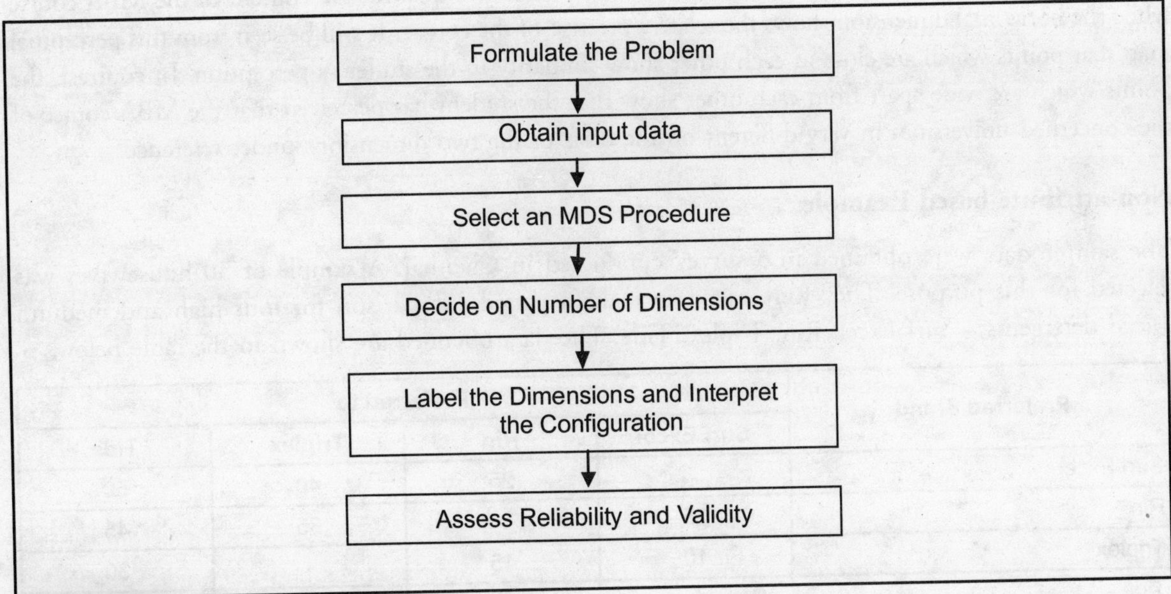

FIGURE 13.2 Conducting Multidimensional Scaling

Attribute-based Example

Let us assume that only two dimensions or attributes are involved in this example which pertains to the preferences of students of the MBA courses offered by some universities. The dimensions are: prestigious course and quantitative content. This can be shown as given above.

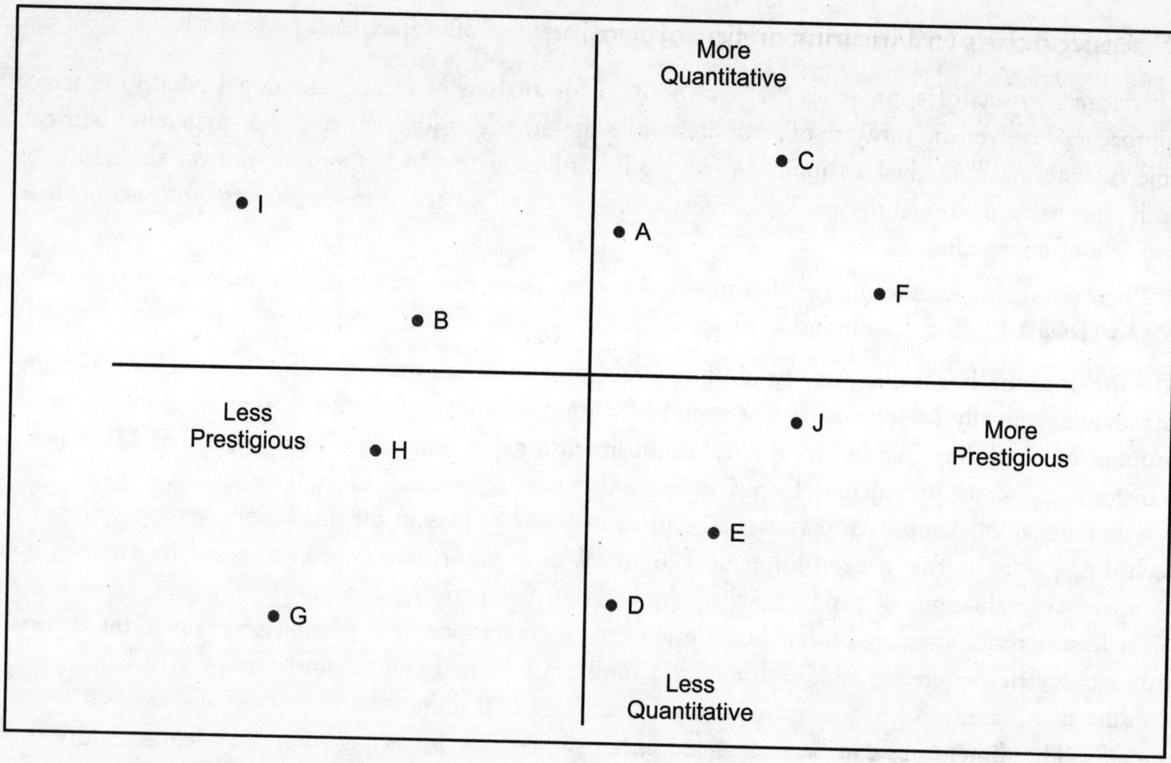

More Quantitative

• C

• I

• A

• F

• B

Less Prestigious

• J

More Prestigious

• H

• E

• D

• G

Less Quantitative

The points indicated by letters A to J show a student's comparison in the MBA programmes in ten different universities. The vertical dimension indicates the relative quantitative content of the MBA course while the horizontal dimension shows the relative prestige of the course. It will be seen from this perceptual map that points which are close to each other show similarity in the student's perception. In contrast, the points which are wide apart from each other show that the student has perceived that the MBA course of the concerned universities in very different on the basis of the two dimensions under reference.

Non-attribute based Example

The sample data were obtained in a survey conducted in Chennai. A sample of 50 housewives was selected for this purpose. They were asked to make a paired comparison for four high and medium priced detergents – Surf Excel, Rin, Triplex, Tide. The data obtained are shown in the table below.

Preferred Brand	**Preferred to**			
	Surf Excel	**Rin**	**Triplex**	**Tide**
Surf Excel	-	25	40	50
Rin	25	-	35	45
Triplex	10	15	-	30
Tide	0	5	20	-

$$D_1 = \begin{bmatrix} & \textit{Surf Excel} & \textit{Rin} & \textit{Triplex} & \textit{Tide} \\ \textit{Surf Excel} & - & 1.58 & 4.47 & 6.50 \\ \textit{Rin} & - & - & 2.92 & 4.92 \\ \textit{Triplex} & - & - & - & 2.06 \\ \textit{Tide} & - & - & - & - \end{bmatrix}$$

The table shows paired comparisons. For example, 25 out of 50 respondents preferred Rin to Surf Excel and 10 preferred Triplex to Surf Excel.

These absolute figures were then converted into a matrix of seminaries. This was done by using the following formula:

$$Sy = \frac{r_y \times r_{ji}}{N}$$

Where Sy stands for the matrix of similarity between i and j: rij stands for the number of respondents who preferred brand I to brand j: rij stands for the number of respondents who preferred brand j to brand i; and N stand for the total sample size.

The matrix of similarities was as follows:

S =

	Surf Excel	*Rin*	*Triplex*	*Tide*
Surf Excel	–	12.5	8.0	0.0
Rin	–	–	10.5	4.5
Triplex	–	–	–	12.5
Tide	–	–	–	–

As the matrix is symmetric, only the elements above the diagonal need be written.

The next step was to obtain the matrix of dissimilarities for which a simple approach of ranking was used. Thus, the metric data were converted into non-metric.

D =

	Surf Excel	*Rin*	*Triplex*	*Tide*
Surf Excel	–	1	4	6
Rin	–	–	3	5
Triplex	–	–	–	2
Tide	–	–	–	–

The above two matrices indicate that Surf Excel and Rin are closest and Surf Excel and Tide are farthest. This means that the first two brands of detergent are most similar and the other two are most dissimilar. An initial plot of the four brands in two dimensions. Using Euclidean distances, the matrix of distances became as below:

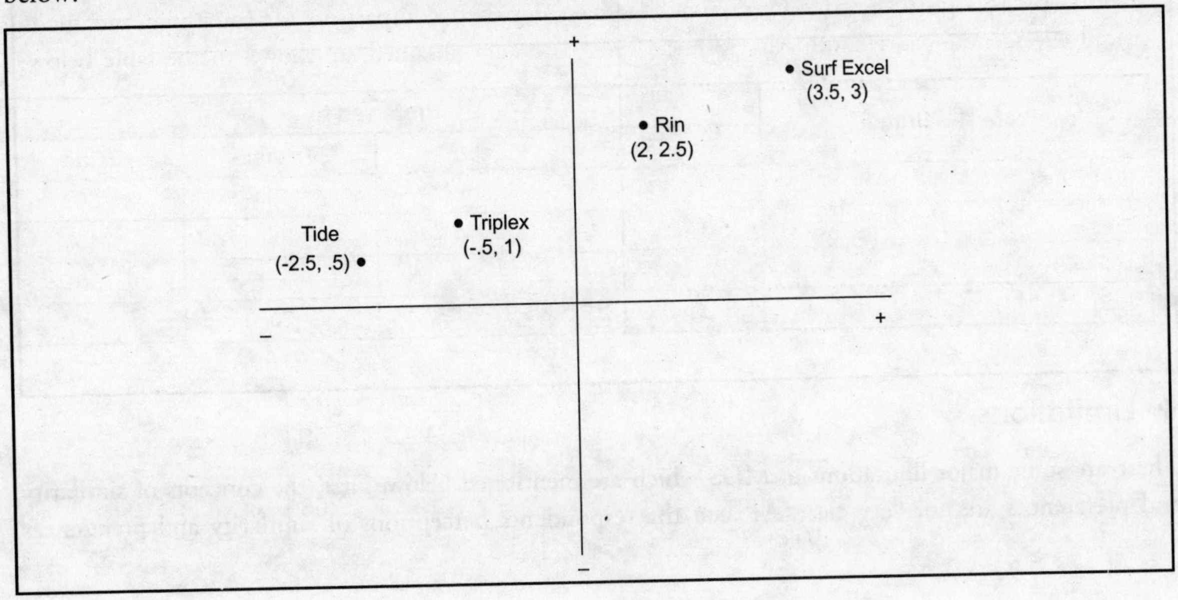

Using the formula $1 = -\frac{\Sigma \hat{d}_{ij}^2}{\Sigma \hat{d}_{ij}^2}$, the initial stress value was calculated as 0.10 or 10 per cent. It may be pointed out that this solution through satisfactory could not be regarded as ideal because the stress value was not zero. Normally, the stress value should be zero.

The process would continue until the stress value reached below the specified level. A possible solution could be arrived at by shifting the position of surf excel slightly towards the left side of the horizontal axis, as is shown in the below figure.

Using the Euclidean distances, a new matrix of distance as shown below, could be arrived at

$$S = \begin{bmatrix} & \textit{Surf Excel} & \textit{Rin} & \textit{Triplex} & \textit{Tide} \\ \textit{Surf Excel} & - & 1.12 & 4.03 & 6.04 \\ \textit{Rin} & & - & 2.92 & 4.49 \\ \textit{Triplex} & & & - & 2.06 \\ \textit{Tide} & & & & - \end{bmatrix}$$

This gave the revised stress as zero.

❖ Requirements for MDS

In order to use MDS, two requirements must be met. First, a set of numbers, called proximities, must be available. Second, a computer-based alogorithm must be available. A number of computer programmes are now available to implement an MDS analysis.

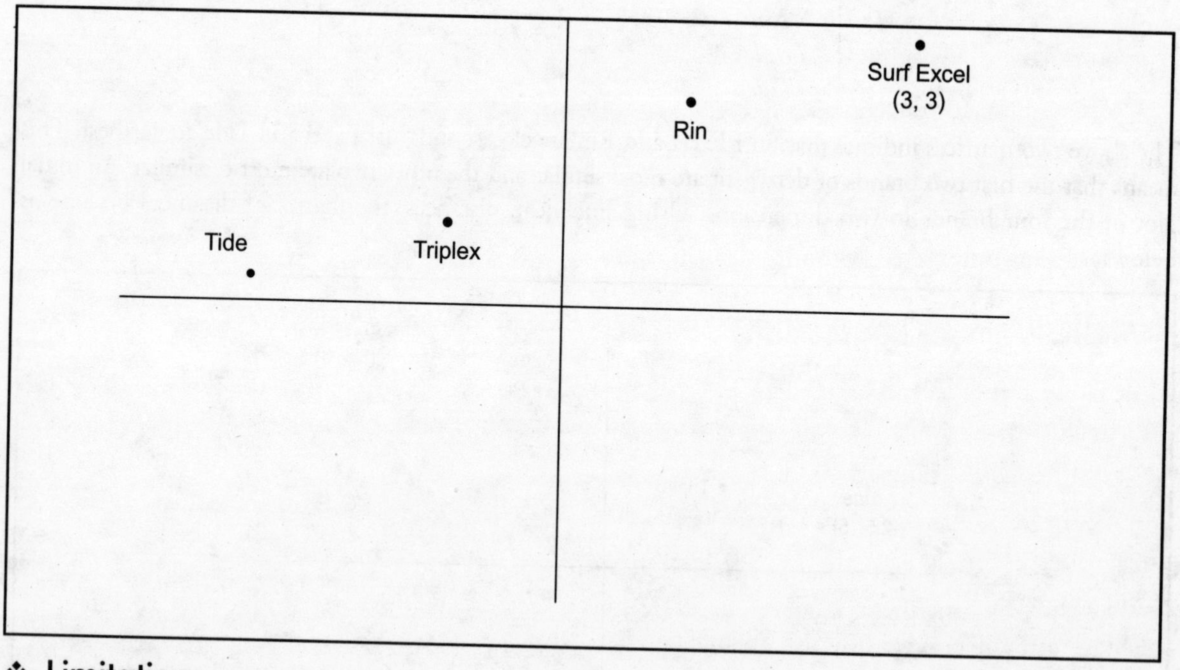

Surf Excel
(3, 3)
Rin
Tide
Triplex

❖ Limitations

There are some major limitations of MDS which are mentioned below. First, the concepts of similarity and preferences are not very clear. As such the respondents perceptions of similarity and preferences may differ. Second, there are empirical limitations. For example, the selection of various attributes or dimensions which are regarded important to respondents is subjective. One may question this selection. Third, it becomes extremely difficult to interpret the results of MDS. This is especially true when interpretation involves relating physical changes in products to psychological changes in perceptual maps. Fourth, different computer programmes often produce different results. This makes the task of interpretation of MDS results all the more difficult, apart from being confusing. At the end, it may be mentioned that MDS approach is being increasingly used by researchers. It is particularly suited for product life cycle analysis, market segmentation, vendor evaluation, measuring advertising effectiveness, test marketing, sales representative and store image research, brand-switching research and attitude scaling. The practical utility of MDS becomes most apparent when a set of data is large. In such cases MDS maps the data. It is much easier to understand the picture than the data themselves. However, the researcher must have a good understanding of MDS before he decides to use it.

CORRESPONDENCE ANALYSIS

This technique provides for dimensional reduction of object ratings on a set of attributes, resulting in a perceptual map of the ratings. However, unlike MDS, both independent variables and dependent variables are examined at the same time. This technique is more similar in nature to factor analysis. It is a compositional technique, and is useful when there are many attributes and many companies. It is most often used in assessing the effectiveness of advertising campaigns. It is also used when the attributes are too similar for factor analysis to be meaningful. The main structural approach is the development of a contingency (cross table). This means that the form of the variables should be non-metric. The model can be assessed by examining the Chi-square value for the model. Correspondence analysis is difficult to interpret, as the dimensions are a combination of independent and dependent variables.

Each of the multivariate techniques described above has a specific type of research question for which it is best suited. Each technique also has certain strengths and weaknesses that should be clearly understood by the analyst before attempting to interpret the results of the technique. Current statistical packages (SAS, SPSS, S-Plus, and others) make it increasingly easy to run a procedure, but the results can be disastrously misinterpreted without adequate care.

❖ Multiple Linear Regressions

While many formulae can be used to ascertain the relationships among more than two variables, the most frequently used method amongst social scientists is that of linear equations. The multiple linear regression takes the following form

$$Y = a + b_1X_1 + b_2X_2 + b_3X_3 + \dots b_kX_k$$

Where Y is the dependent variable which is to be predicted, X_1, X_2, X_3...and X_k are the k known variables on which predictions are to be based and a, $b_1 b_2 b_3$...and b_k are parameters, the values of which are to be determined by the methods of least squares.

An example will make the method in respect of multiple regression clear. Table gives the data on sales of a product, advertising expenditure and personal selling (number of selling agents) in respect of eight sales territories.

Sales territory	Sales (Lakh ₹)	Advertising ('000 ₹)	Personal selling (No. of selling agents)
	(Y)	(X_1)	(X_2)
1	100	40	10
2	80	30	10
3	60	20	7
4	120	50	15
5	150	60	20
6	90	40	12
7	70	20	8
8	130	60	14

The three normal equations for a linear regression are:

$\Sigma Y = na + b_1\ \Sigma X_1 + b_2 \Sigma X_2$ ...1

$\Sigma X_1 Y = a\Sigma X_1 + b_1 \Sigma X_1^2 + b_2 \Sigma X_1 X_2$ ...2

$\Sigma X_2 Y = a\Sigma X_2 + b_1 \Sigma X_1 X_2 + b_2 \Sigma X_2^2$ ...3

The totals of columns contained in table can be written with notations as follows:

$\Sigma X_1 = 320$ $\quad$ $\Sigma X_1 X_2 = 4270$

$\Sigma X_1^2 = 14600$ $\quad$ $\Sigma Y = 800$

$\Sigma X^2 = 96$ $\quad$ $\Sigma X_1 Y = 35400$

$\Sigma X_2^2 = 1278$ $\quad$ $\Sigma X_2 Y = 10480$

Substituting these values in the normal equations, given earlier:

$800 = 8a + 320b_1 + 96b_2$ (i)

Worksheet for Calculation of Multiple Regression Coefficients

X_1	X_1^2	X_2	X_2^2	X_1X_2	Y	X_1Y	X_2Y
40	1600	10	100	400	100	4000	1000
30	900	10	100	300	80	2400	800
20	400	7	49	140	60	1200	420
50	2500	15	225	750	120	6000	1800
60	3600	20	400	1200	150	9000	3000
40	1600	12	144	480	90	3600	1080
20	400	8	64	160	70	1400	560
60	3600	14	196	840	130	7800	1820
320	**14600**	**96**	**1278**	**4270**	**800**	**35400**	**10480**

$35400 = 320a + 14600b_1 + 4270b_2$ (ii)

$10480 = 96a + 4270b_1 + 1278b_2$ (iii)

Multiplying (i) by 40 and then subtracting (ii) from the resultant,

$$32000 = 320a + 12800b_1 + 3840b_2 \quad \text{(iv)}$$

$$35400 = 320a + 14600b_1 + 4270b_2 \quad \text{(ii)}$$

$$-3400 = -1800b_1 - 430b_2$$

Or $\quad 340 = 180b_1 + 43b_2 \quad$ (v)

Multiplying (i) by 12 and then subtracting (iii) from the resultant,

$$9600 = 96a + 3840b_1 + 1152b_2 \quad \text{(vi)}$$

$$10480 = 96a + 4270b_1 + 1278b_2$$

$$-880 = \quad -430b_1 - 126b_2$$

Or $\quad 440 = 215b_1 + 63b_2 \quad$ (vii)

Multiplying (v) by 43 and (vii) by 36

$$14620 = 7740b_1 + 1849\,b_2 \quad \text{(viii)}$$

$$15840 = 7740b_1 + 2268b_2 \quad \text{(ix)}$$

$$-1220 = \quad -419b_2 \quad \text{[By subtracting (ix) from (viii)]}$$

$$\therefore \quad b_2 = \frac{1220}{419} = 2.9116945$$

Substituting the value of b_2=2.9116945 in (vii) above,

$$= 440 = 215b_1 + (2.9116945 \times 3)$$

$$215b_1 = 440 - 183.43675$$

or $\quad b_1 = \dfrac{256.56325}{215}$

$$= 1.1933174$$

Substituting the value of b_1= 1.1933174 and b_2= 2.9116945 in (i) above,

$$800 = 8a + (1.1933174 \times 320) + (2.9116945 \times 96)$$

or $\quad 800 = 8a + 381.86156 + 279.52267$

or $\quad 8a = 800 - 661.38423$

or $\quad a = \dfrac{138.61577}{8}$

$$= 17.326971$$

$\therefore$ the regression equation is

$$Y = 17.327 + 1.193X_1 + 2.912X_2$$ (Rounding the values to 3 decimal places)

On the basis of this regression the likely value of sales for a given expenditure can be ascertained on advertising and a specific number of selling agents. Suppose we are interested in knowing the sales when advertising expenditure is ₹ 80,000 and when 25 selling agents are employed in a territory.

Symbolically,

$$\begin{aligned} Y &= a + b_1X_2 + b_2X_2 \\ &= 17.327 + (1.193 \times 80) + (2.912 \times 25) \\ &= 17.327 + 95.44 + 72.8 \\ &= 185.567 \end{aligned}$$

Thus, we can say that when the firm spends ₹ 80, 000 on advertising and deploys a team of 25 selling agents in a territory, it is likely to sell the product worth ₹ 185.6 lakhs in that territory.

Interpretation of the Regression Equation: The regression equation in the above example was:

$$Y_C = 17.327 + 1.193X_1 + 2.912X_2$$

The b's are called partial regression coefficients and indicate the average change in for a unit change in X, holding the other X's constant. In the above equation, for example, b_1=1.193 shows that sales increase by 1.193 units for every one thousand rupees of expenditure on advertising; b_2 = 2.912 shows that sales increase by 2.912 units for every one person employed as a selling agent. Of the two variables, personal selling is for more important than advertising for increasing sales. It may be noted that all the above calculations were carried out with absolute values. An alternative method based on deviations from the mean can be used in deriving the regression equation. The co-efficient of determination (r_2) for this multiple linear regression can be calculated by the following formula:

$$r^2 = \frac{\Sigma(Y_i - \overline{Y})^2 - \Sigma(Y_i - Y_c)^2}{(Y_i - Y)^2}$$

Where, r^2 = Co-efficient of determination

Y_i = Value of ith item in Y series

$\overline{Y}$ = Mean of the Y series

Y_c = Computed value of ith item in Y series on the basis of the regression

It has the same meaning and interpretation here as it has in the case of simple regression. The co-efficient of determination is the ratio of the explained variation to the total variation. In the above formula, the term $\Sigma(y_1 - \overline{y})^2$ shows total variation and the second term $\Sigma(y_1 - y_c)^2$ shows the explained variation. The above formula is now applied to the foregoing example.

$$\overline{Y} = \frac{800}{8} = 100$$

$$r^2 = \frac{\Sigma\left(Y_i - \overline{Y}\right)^2 - \Sigma\left(Y_i - Y_c\right)^2}{\Sigma\left(Y_i - \overline{Y}_c\right)^2}$$

$$= \frac{6800 - 190}{6800}$$

$$= 0.972 \text{ approx.}$$

X_1 ('000 ₹)	X_2 No. of selling agents	Y	Y_c	$Y - Y_c$	$(Y - Y_c)^2$	$(Y - \bar{Y})$	$(Y - \bar{Y})^2$
40	10	100	94	6	36	0	0
30	10	80	82	-2	4	-20	400
20	7	60	62	-2	4	-40	1600
50	15	120	121	-1	1	20	400
60	20	150	147	3	9	50	2500
40	12	90	100	-10	100	-10	100
20	8	70	64	6	36	-30	900
60	14	130	130	0	0	30	900
		800			**190**		**6800**

The value of r^2= 0.972 shows that 97.2 per cent of the total variation observed in the sales is explained by the regression equation. In other words, merely 2.8 per cent of the total variation in the dependent variable, Y, remains unexplained by the regression equation.

In the example of simple linear regression, only one independent variable, namely, expenditure on advertising was used as a predictor of sales. The value of r^2 calculated was 0.944. With the introduction of another independent variable, namely, personal selling (number of selling agents) the value of r^2 has increased to 0.972. This means that the introduction of another variable accounts for some improvement in explaining the variations in the dependent variable. It is because of this that the multiple linear regression is regarded as a superior analytical tool compared to the simple linear regression.

Example: Fit a multiple linear regression equation to the following data.

Family Number	Y(Annual savings in '00 of rupees)	X_1 (Annual income in '000 of rupees)	X_2 (Family size)
1	10	16	3
2	5	13	6
3	10	21	4
4	4	10	5
5	8	13	3

Solution: The multiple liner regression equation for the two independent variables X_1 and X_2 and one independent variable Y is as given below:

$$Y = a + b_1X_1 + b_2X_2$$

The three normal equations for a linear regression are:

$$\sum y = na + b_1\Sigma X_1 + b_2\Sigma X_2 \quad \text{(i)}$$

$$\Sigma X_1Y = a\Sigma X_1 + b_1\Sigma X_1^2 + b_2\Sigma X_1X_2 \quad \text{(ii)}$$

$$\Sigma X_2Y = a\Sigma X_2 + b_1\Sigma X_1X_2 + b_2\Sigma X_2^2 \quad \text{(iii)}$$

Worksheet for Calculation of Multiple Regression Coefficients

X_1	X_1^2	X_2	X_2^2	X_1X_2	Y	X_1Y	X_2Y
16	256	3	9	48	10	160	30
13	169	6	36	78	5	65	30
21	441	4	16	84	10	210	40
10	100	5	25	50	4	40	20
13	169	3	9	39	8	104	24

The totals of columns contained in table can be written with notations as follows:

n = 5

$\Sigma X_1 = 73$ $\quad \Sigma X_1X_1 = 4270$ $\quad \Sigma X_2 = 21$

$\Sigma X_1^2 = 1135$ $\quad \Sigma Y = 37$ $\quad \Sigma X_1X_2 = 299$

$\Sigma X_2^2 = 95$ $\quad \Sigma X_1Y = 579$

$\Sigma X_2^2 = 1278$ $\quad \Sigma X_2Y = 144$

Substituting these values in the normal equations, given earlier:

$37 = 5a + 73b_1 + 21b_2$ (i)

$579 = 73a + 1135b_1 + 299b_2$ (ii)

$144 = 21a + 299b_1 + 95b_2$ (iii)

Multiplying (i) by 73, (ii) by 5 and then subtracting

$2701 = 365a + 5329b_1 + 1533b_2$ (iv)

$2895 = 365a + 5675b_1 + 1495b_2$ (v)

(iv – v) $\quad -194 = -346b_1 + -38b_2$ (vi)

Multiplying (ii) by 21 (iii) by 73 and then subtracting

$12159 = 1533a + 23835b_1 + 6279b_2$ (vii)

$10512 = 1533a + 21827b_1 + 6935b_2$ (viii)

(vii) – (viii) $1647 = 2008b_1 - 656b_2$ (ix)

Solving (vi) and (ix)

$-194 = -346b_1 + -38b_2$ (vi)

$1647 = 2008b_1 - 656b_2$ (ix)

Multiplying (vi) by 656 and (ix) by 38

$-128576 = -226976b_1 + 24928b_2$ (x)

$62586 = 76304b_1 - 24928b_2$ (xi)

$-65990 = -150672b_1$ [By adding (x) from (xi)]

$$b_1 = 0.43797$$

Substituting the value of $b_1 = 0.43797$ in (vi) above,

$$-194 = -436\ (0.43797) + 38b_2$$

$$215b_2 = -42.46197$$

$$b_2 = -1.1174$$

Substituting the value of $b_1 = 0.43797$ and $b_2 = -1.1174$ in either (i) or (ii) or (iii) above,

(ii)

$$579 = 73a + 1135b_1 + 299b_2$$

$$579 = 73a + 1135(0.43797) + 299(-1.1174)$$

$$73a = 416.0113$$

$$a = 5.698$$

∴ The multiple linear regression equation is

$$Y = 5.698 + 0.43797\ X_1 - 1.1174\ X_2$$

DISCRIMINANT ANALYSIS

The purpose of discriminant analysis is to correctly classify observations or people into homogeneous groups. The independent variables must be metric and must have a high degree of normality. Discriminant analysis builds a linear discriminant function, which can then be used to classify the observations. The overall fit is assessed by looking at the degree to which the group means differ (Wilkes Lambda or D2) and how well the model classifies. To determine which variables have the most impact on the discriminant function, it is possible to look at partial F values. The higher the partial F, the more impact that variable has on the discriminant function. This tool helps categorize people, like buyers and non-buyers.

When the data are non-metric, i.e., not measurable on quantitative scales of numbers, it is not possible to determine the quantitative relationship between variables. In such cases, since correlation and regression techniques cannot be applied, the researcher has to use other techniques such as discriminant analysis.

Discriminant analysis enables the researcher to classify persons or objects into two or more categories. For example, consumers may be classified as heavy and light users. With the help of such a technique, it is possible to predict the categories or classes which are mutually exclusive in which individuals are likely to be included. In many cases the classification will be dichotomous such as users and non-users, high and low and so on.

In discriminant analysis, a scoring system is used on the basis of which an individual or object is assigned a score. This, in its turn, forms the basis for classifying an individual in the most likely class or category. Suppose an individual is 25 years of age, earns an annual income of ₹ 60,000 and has undergone formal education for a period of 17 years. Each of these three variables is given a weight, indicating its relative importance.

Symbolically,

$$Y = b_1(25) + b_2\ (60{,}00) + b_3(17)$$

Where Y is dependent variable, say, in this case, credit score or rating. A certain limit is fixed of the value of Y below which all values will be classified in Group I and all the others in Group II. The values of

b_1, b_2, and b_3 indicate their importance. The numerical value of Y can be transformed into the probability of the individual being creditworthy.

It may be noted that in the linear discriminant, the 'b' coefficients are similar to the regression coefficients. However, the main difference is that while the regression coefficients are used to predict the value of the dependent variable, the discriminant coefficients are used to classify correctly as many individuals or objects as possible.

❖ Advantages

One major advantage of linear discriminant analysis is that it enables the researcher to know, by a simple device, whether an individual is likely to belong to one of the other categories on the basis of his overall score. In this context, it is not only the values of the discriminant coefficients but also their positive or negative signs that are equally relevant. Given a certain minimum value of Z as creditworthiness, it should be clear that the higher the values of the independent variables, provided the discriminant coefficients are positive, the more chances there are for the individual to be classified under this category. The analysis on the basis of linear discriminant coefficients is simple but it becomes complex in case of a non-linear discriminant function such as $y = a + b_1X + b_2X^2$. In such a case, interpretation becomes more difficult.

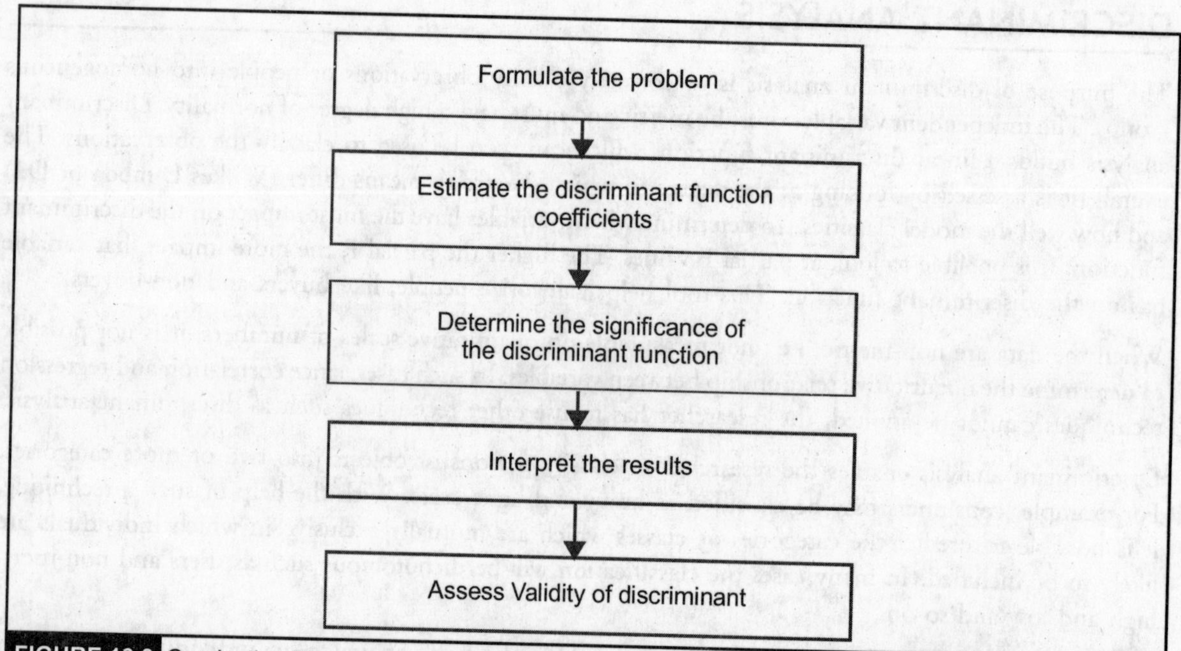

FIGURE 13.3 Conducting Discriminant Analysis

The following example gives clarity about the technique of linear discriminant analysis. Assume that a firm has developed a new industrial process which is a distinct improvement over the existing one. The firm would like to know which industrial units would be interested to buy this process. Obviously, some units which can be identified as innovators and early adopters would go in for the new process. The firm thinks that the two most important determinants for the demand for the new process would be the net profit of industrial units and their memberships of trade associations and technical societies.

Let us assume that X represents net profit (in rupees lakhs) of industrial units and Z represents the number of memberships of trade associations and technical societies held by companies. Below table shows hypothetical data on X and Z for 20 companies. Of the 20 companies for which the data are given, 12 turn out to be buyers of the new industrial process and 8 are hesitant to use the new process and they are, therefore, classified as non-buyers.

We have to determine a linear discriminant function.

$$Y_i = C_x X_i + C_z Z_i$$

and a boundary function

$$Y_c = k$$

Where,

Y_i = the discriminant value of the ith observation in the population.

C_x = a parameter specifying the relationship between Y and X

C_z = a parameter specifying the relationship between Y and Z

X_i = an explanatory variable

Z_i = an explanatory variable

Y_c = the critical value which is the boundary between the two categories.

K = a constant.

The parameter C_x is specified by the following equation:

$$C_x = \frac{S_{zz} d\bar{x} - S_{xz} d\bar{z}}{S_{zz} S_{xx} - (S_{xz})^2}$$

The parameter C_z is specified by the following equation

$$C_z = \frac{S_{xx} d\bar{z} - S_{xz} d\bar{x}}{S_{zz} S_{xx} - (S_{xz})^2}$$

In order to apply these equations, it is necessary to get the values of S_{xx},$S_{zz,}$$S_{xz}$ as also $\bar{Z}$ and $d\bar{z}$. The first three of these are sample moments which can be obtained by the following equations:

$$S_{xx} = \sum_{i=1}^{n} (X_i - \bar{X})^2$$

$$S_{zz} = \sum_{i=1}^{n} (X_i - \bar{X})^2$$

$$S_{xz} = \sum_{i=1}^{n} (X_i - \bar{X})^2 (Z_1 - \bar{Z})$$

Where,

X_i = the value of the independent variable x for observation i

$\bar{X}$ = the mean of all observations of X series

Z_i = The value of the independent variable Z for observation i

$\bar{Z}$ = the mean of all observations of Z series

The value $d\overline{x}$ of $d\overline{z}$ and can be obtained by the following equations:

$$d\overline{x} = \overline{x}^* - X^0$$

and $$d\overline{z} = \overline{z}^* - Z^0$$

Where $d\overline{x}$ = the difference between the means of X in the two categories

$d\overline{z}$ = the differences between the means of z in the two series $\overline{x}$ and $\overline{z}$ are as defined earlier * and 0 represent the two categories.

With this explanation of notations used, let us now apply the different formulas to the data given in table.

Sample Calculations for Linear Discriminant Analysis

Observations	Behaviour Buy or do not buy	Net profit (Rs.in lakhs)	Deviations of X	Square deviations of X	Membership of trade associations etc.	Deviation of Z	Square of deviations of Z	Product of X and Z deviations
(i)	(B or N)	X	$(X-\overline{X})$	$(X-\overline{X})^2$	Z	$(Z-\overline{Z})$	$(Z-\overline{Z})^2$	$(x-\overline{x})(Z-\overline{Z})$
1	N	8	-8	64	0	-3	9	24
2	N	10	-6	36	1	-2	4	12
3	N	9	-7	49	2	-1	1	7
4	B	16	0	0	4	1	1	0
5	B	15	-1	1	3	0	0	0
6	B	17	1	1	2	-1	1	-1
7	N	10	-6	36	1	-2	4	12
8	B	17	1	1	3	0	0	0
9	B	15	-1	1	4	1	1	-1
10	B	20	4	16	5	2	4	8
11	N	16	0	0	2	-1	1	0
12	B	20	4	16	4	1	1	4
13	B	19	3	9	3	0	0	0
14	N	13	-3	9	2	-1	1	3
15	N	12	-4	16	2	-1	1	4
16	B	20	4	16	6	3	9	12
17	N	18	2	4	3	0	0	0
18	B	24	8	64	6	3	9	24
19	B	22	6	36	4	1	1	6
20	B	19	3	9	3	0	0	0

$$\Sigma X = 320$$

$$\overline{X} = 16$$

$$\Sigma(X - \overline{X})^2 = 384$$

$$\Sigma Z = 60$$

$$\overline{Z} = 3$$

$$\Sigma(Z - Z) = 48$$

$$S(x - \bar{x})(Z - \overline{Z}) = 114$$

$$S_{xx} = \sum_{i=1}^{n}(X_1 - \overline{X})^2$$

$$= 384$$

$$S_{xx} = \sum_{i=1}^{n}(Z_1 - \overline{Z})^2 = 48$$

$$= 384$$

$$S_{xx} = \sum_{i=1}^{n}(X_i - \overline{X})(Z_i - \overline{Z}) = 114$$

$d\,\overline{x} = \overline{X}^* - \overline{X}^0$, where * indicates buyer companies and ^{0} non-buyer companies

$$= 18.67\text{-}12$$

$$= 6.67$$

$$d_z = \overline{Z}^* - \overline{Z}^0$$

$$= 3.92\text{-}1.62$$

$$= 2.30$$

The parameter C_x can be obtained by the following equation:

$$C_X = \frac{S_{zz}d\overline{x} - S_{xz}d\overline{z}}{S_{zz}S_{XX} - (S_{XZ})^2}$$

$$= \frac{48(6.67) - 114(2.30)}{48(384) - (114)^2}$$

$$= \frac{320.16 - 262.2}{18432 - 12996}$$

$$= \frac{57.96}{5436}$$

$$= 0.0107$$

The parameter C_z can be obtained by the following equation:

$$C_X = \frac{S_{xx}d\overline{z} - S_{xx}d\overline{x}}{S_{zz}S_{xx} - (S_{xz})^2}$$

$$= \frac{384(2.30) - 114(6.67)}{48(384) - (114)^2}$$

$$= \frac{883.2 - 760.38}{18432 - 12996}$$

$$= \frac{122.82}{5436}$$

$$= 0.0226$$

On the basis of these calculations, the linear discriminant function in this case is $Y_i = 0.0107X_i + 0.0226\ Z_i$ This discriminant function provides maximum discrimination. Since X and Z stand for net profit and the number of memberships of trade associations, etc. respectively, we find that both these variables contribute to discrimination. In order to ascertain the relative impact of the two variables in the discrimination function, the parameters C_x and C_z must be multiplied by their respective standard deviations. This is shown below:

Standard deviation of series X is $\sqrt{\frac{\Sigma(X - \bar{X})^2}{n}}$

$$= \sqrt{\frac{384}{20}} = \sqrt{19.2} = 4.38$$

Standard deviation of series Z is $\sqrt{\frac{\Sigma(Z - Z)^2}{n}}$

$$= \sqrt{\frac{48}{20}} = \sqrt{2.4} = 1.55 \text{ approx.}$$

Therefore, $\frac{\text{The discriminating effect of X}}{\text{The discriminating effect of Z}} = \frac{0.0107 \times 4.38}{0.0226 \times 1.55}$

$$\text{Relative Impact Ratio} = \frac{0.046866}{0.035030}$$

$$= 1.34 \text{ approx.}$$

It is evident from this result that the variable X indicating net profit has a greater effect on the discriminating function than the other variable Z which indicates the number of memberships of trade associating, etc.

We have now to determine the critical value of Y (i.e., Y_c) for this purpose, we have first to calculate the discriminant value for each pair of values of X and Z, the two independent variables from the discriminant function.

$$Y_i = 0.0107X_i + 0.0226Z_i$$

Table gives an array of twenty companies in descending order – the highest discriminant value shown by company No.18 which is one the top of the table and the lowest discriminant value shown by company No.1 which is at the bottom of the table. Now to determine the critical value of Y, we locate the two adjoining items where there is a change from one category to the other. We find that the first change from category B to N occurs from Company No.4 to Company No.17. Then again there is a change from category N to B, i.e. from Company No.17 to company No.9. The two adjoining items relevant for our purpose are Company No. 6 and Company No. 11. We use a judgemental approach in this regard and decide the boundary as being mid-way between the two categories. The midway between the two discriminant values. 2271 and .2164 is .22175 or .2217 approximately. This is the value of Y_c in our example.

TABLE 13.1 An Array of Twenty Companies on the Basis of a Linear Discriminant Model

Company No.(i)	Discriminant Value	Actual behaviour (buy or do not buy)	Category Predicted by Model Buyer
18	0.3924 (highest)	B	
16	0.3496	B	
10	0.3270	B	
19	0.3258	B	
12	0.3044	B	
20	0.2711	B	
13	0.2711	B	
4	0.2616	B	
17	0.2604	N (Missing Classification)	
9	0.2509	B	
8	0.2497	B	
5	0.2283	B	
6	0.2271	B	
	Boundary(y_c)		
11	0.2164	N	
14	0.1843	N	
15	0.1736	N	
3	0.1415	N	
7	0.1296	N	
2	0.1296	N	
1	0.0856 (longest)	N	Non-buyer

A confusion matrix or classification matrix is used to test the accuracy of a discriminant analysis. Such a matrix shows the actual classification along with the predicted classification arrived at on the basis of discriminant analysis. In case of our example, the confusion matrix would be as follows:

TABLE 13.2 Confusion Matrix of Actual versus Predicted Buyer/Non-buyer Categories

Actual Classification	Predicted Classification		Total
	Buyers	Non-buyers	
Buyers	12	0	12
Non-buyers	1	7	8

From the confusion matrix, it is evident that there is one mis-classification according to the discriminant model. Company No.17 which has a discriminant value of .2604 is a non-buyer of the new industrial process but gets included in the buyer category because of the high discriminant value. Thus, the discriminant model mis-classifies only one out of twenty companies. In other words, the success rate of the model is 95 per cent. In view of this, it can be very useful in distinguishing between good and bad prospects so that the company can deploy its sales force as also other resources more efficiently.

FACTOR ANALYSIS

The factor analysis was first used by Charles Spearman. Psychologists use it as a technique of indirect measurement. When they are interested to test human personality and intelligence, a set of questions and tests is developed for this purpose. They believe that a person given this set of questions and tests would respond on the basis of some structure that exists in his mind. Thus, his responses would form a certain pattern. This approach is based on the assumption that the underlying structure in answering the questions would be the same in the case of different respondents. Although it is in the filed of psychology that factor analysis has its beginning, it has since been applied to problems in different areas including marketing. Its use has become far more frequent as a result of the introduction of high-speed computers. In regression analysis, the problem is to predict the value of a dependent variable I on the basis of one or more independent variables. Unlike the regression analysis, factor analysis is not based on the usual distinction between dependent and independent variables; instead it rather considers all the variables simultaneously. There are two objects of factor analysis. First, it simplifies the data by reducing a large number of variables to a set of a small number of variables. Secondly, it analyses the interdependence of interrelationships among a total set of variables.

In marketing research, factor analysis can be useful in several ways. First, it can bring out the hidden or latent dimensions relevant in the relationships among product preferences. Sometimes, the product characteristics influencing the consumer preferences are not clear. In such cases, factor analysis can be helpful by revealing more important characteristics of the product, underlying the relationships among product preferences. Second, factor analysis can also be used to find out certain relationships among observed values which, though they exist, are obscures. Third, it is extremely useful when a large mass of data is to be simplified and condensed. Finally, it can be used in clustering of products or people.

❖ Uses of Factor Analysis

Factor analysis is a general name denoting a class of procedures primarily used for data reduction and summarization. Factor analysis is an interdependence technique in that an entire set of interdependent relationships is examined without making the distinction between dependent and independent variables.

Factor analysis is used in the following circumstances:

1. To identify underlying dimensions, or factors, that explains the correlations among a set of variables.
2. To identify a new, smaller set of uncorrelated variables to replace the original set of correlated variables in subsequent multivariate analysis (regression or discriminant analysis).
3. To identify a smaller set of salient variables from a larger set for use in subsequent multivariate analysis.

❖ Factor Analysis Model

Mathematically, each variable is expressed as a linear combination of underlying factors. The covariation among the variables is described in terms of a small number of common factors plus a unique factor for each variable. If the variables are standardized, the factor model may be represented as:

$$X_i = Ai_1F_1 + Ai_2F_2 + A_{i3}F_3 + \ldots + A_{im}F_m + V_iU_i$$

Where,

X_i = ith standardized variable

A_{ij} = standardized multiple regression coefficient of variable i on common factor j

F = common factor

V_i = standardized regression coefficient of variable i on unique factor i

U_i = the unique factor for variable i

m = number of common factors

The unique factors are uncorrelated with each other and with the common factors. The common factors themselves can be expressed as linear combinations of the observed variables.

$$\text{Fi} = W_{i1}X_1 + W_{i2}X_2 + W_{i3}X_3 + \ldots + W_{ik}X_k$$

Where,

Fi = estimate of i th factor

Wi = weight or factor score coefficient

k = number of variables

1. It is possible to select weights or factor score coefficients so that the first factor explains the largest portion of the total variance.
2. Then a second set of weights can be selected, so that the second factor accounts for most of the residual variance, subject to being uncorrelated with the first factor.
3. This same principle could be applied to selecting additional weights for the additional factors.

Statistics Associated with Factor Analysis

1. ***Bartlett's test of sphericity:*** Bartlett's test of sphericity is a test statistic used to examine the hypothesis that the variables are uncorrelated in the population. In other words, the population correlation matrix is an identity matrix; each variable correlates perfectly with itself ($r = 1$) but has no correlation with the other variables ($r = 0$).
2. ***Correlation matrix:*** A correlation matrix is a lower triangle matrix showing the simple correlations, r, between all possible pairs of variables included in the analysis. The diagonal elements, which are all 1, are usually omitted.
3. ***Communality***: Communality is the amount of variance a variable shares with all the other variables being considered. This is also the proportion of variance explained by the common factors.
4. ***Eigenvalue:*** The eigen value represents the total variance explained by each factor..
5. ***Factor loadings:*** Factor loadings are simple correlations between the variables and the factors.
6. ***Factor loading plot:*** A factor loading plot is a plot of the original variables using the factor loadings as coordinates.
7. ***Factor matrix:*** A factor matrix contains the factor loadings of all the variables on all the factors extracted.
8. ***Factor scores:*** Factor scores are composite scores estimated for each respondent on the derived factors.

9. ***Kaiser-Meyer-Olkin (KMO) measure of sampling adequacy:*** The Kaiser-Meyer-Olkin (KMO) measure of sampling adequacy is an index used to examine the appropriateness of factor analysis. High values (between 0.5 and 1.0) indicate factor analysis is appropriate. Values below 0.5 imply that factor analysis may not be appropriate.
10. ***Percentage of variance:*** The percentage of the total variance attributed to each factor.
11. **Residuals** are the differences between the observed correlations, as given in the input correlation matrix, and the reproduced correlations, as estimated from the factor matrix.
12. ***Scree plot:*** A scree plot is a plot of the Eigenvalues against the number of factors in order of extraction.

Example:

A researcher wants to determine underlying benefits customers seek from the purchase of a face cream. Thirty users of a particular brand were surveyed about their perceptions and images of a face cream they used. The respondents were asked to indicate their degree of agreement with the following statements using seven point scale (1-strongly disagree, 7-strongly agree). Conduct Factor analysis using SPSS software and analyze the data.

V_1 - I prefer to buy a face cream because it protects my skin

V_2 - I like a face cream that gives beauty to my face

V_3 - A face cream should remove pimples

V_4 - I prefer a face cream that add more complexion to my face

V_5 - Adding complexion to face is not an important benefit offered by a face cream

V_6 - Most important consideration in buying a face cream is to give glamour to face.

The obtained data is as shown below and the same is given as input to SPSS software and selecting the option as Factor Analysis.

Respondent No	V_1	V_2	V_3	V_4	V_5	V_6
1	7.00	3.00	6.00	4.00	2.00	4.00
2	1.00	3.00	2.00	4.00	5.00	4.00
3	6.00	2.00	7.00	4.00	1.00	3.00
4	4.00	5.00	4.00	6.00	2.00	5.00
5	1.00	2.00	2.00	3.00	6.00	2.00
6	6.00	3.00	6.00	4.00	2.00	4.00
7	5.00	3.00	6.00	3.00	4.00	3.00
8	6.00	4.00	7.00	4.00	1.00	4.00
9	3.00	4.00	2.00	3.00	6.00	3.00
10	2.00	6.00	2.00	6.00	7.00	6.00
11	6.00	4.00	7.00	3.00	2.00	3.00
12	2.00	3.00	1.00	4.00	5.00	4.00
13	7.00	2.00	6.00	4.00	1.00	3.00
14	4.00	6.00	4.00	5.00	3.00	6.00
15	1.00	3.00	2.00	2.00	6.00	4.00

Contd...

16	6.00	4.00	6.00	3.00	3.00	4.00
17	5.00	3.00	6.00	3.00	3.00	4.00
18	7.00	3.00	7.00	4.00	1.00	4.00
19	2.00	4.00	3.00	3.00	6.00	3.00
20	3.00	5.00	3.00	6.00	4.00	6.00
21	1.00	3.00	2.00	3.00	5.00	3.00
22	5.00	4.00	5.00	4.00	2.00	4.00
23	2.00	2.00	1.00	5.00	4.00	4.00
24	4.00	6.00	4.00	6.00	4.00	7.00
25	6.00	5.00	4.00	2.00	1.00	4.00
26	3.00	5.00	4.00	6.00	4.00	7.00
27	4.00	4.00	7.00	2.00	2.00	5.00
28	3.00	7.00	2.00	6.00	4.00	3.00
29	4.00	6.00	3.00	7.00	2.00	7.00
30	2.00	3.00	2.00	4.00	7.00	2.00

The following procedure is used to conduct Factor analysis using SPSS software options.

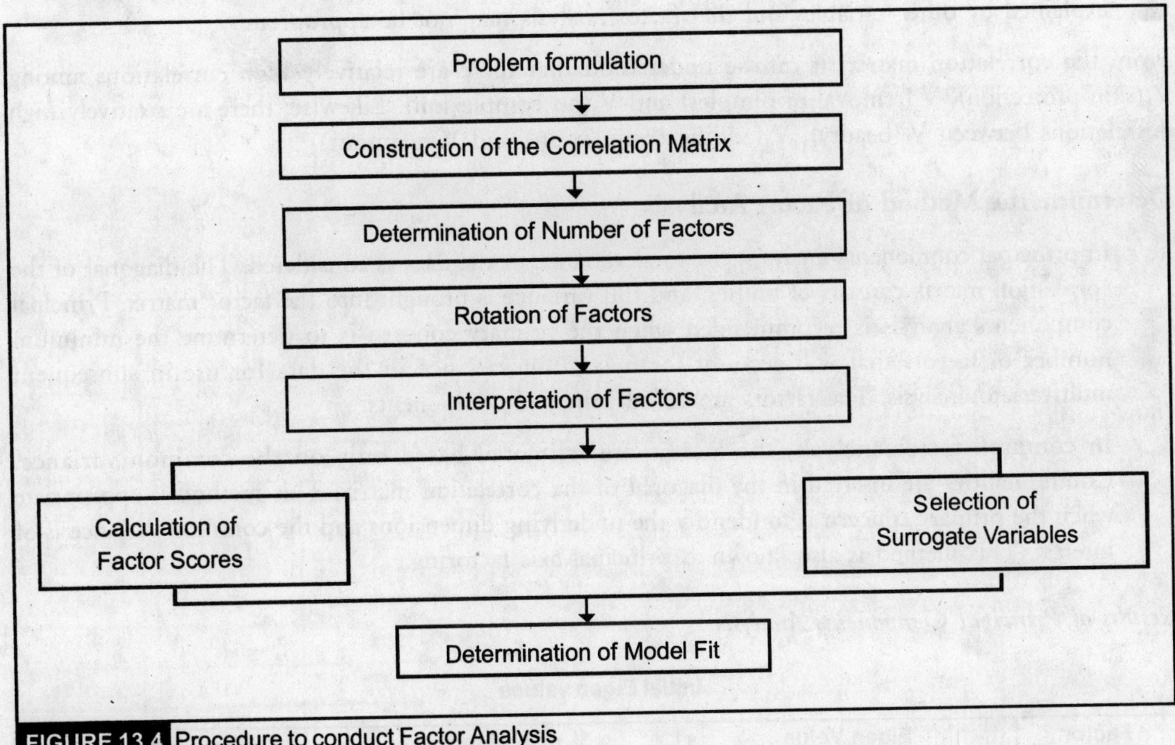

FIGURE 13.4 Procedure to conduct Factor Analysis

Formulate the Problem

1. The objectives of factor analysis should be identified.
2. The variables to be included in the factor analysis should be specified based on past research, theory, and judgment of the researcher. It is important that the variables be appropriately measured on an interval or ratio scale.

3. An appropriate sample size should be used. As a rough guideline, there should be at least four or five times as many observations (sample size) as there are variables.

Construct Correlation Matrix:

Variables	V_1	V_2	V_3	V_4	V_5	V_6
V_1	1.000					
V_2	-0.530	1.000				
V_3	0.873	-0.155	1.000			
V_4	-0.086	0.572	-0.248	1.000		
V_5	-0.858	0.020	-0.778	-0.007	1.000	
V_6	0.004	0.640	-0.018	0.640	-0.136	1.000

1. The analytical process is based on a matrix of correlations between the variables.
2. Bartlett's test of sphericity can be used to test the null hypothesis that the variables are uncorrelated in the population. In other words, the population correlation matrix is an identity matrix. If this hypothesis cannot be rejected, then the appropriateness of factor analysis should be questioned.
3. Another useful statistic is the Kaiser-Meyer-Olkin (KMO) measure of sampling adequacy. Small values of the KMO statistic indicate that the correlations between pairs of variables cannot be explained by other variables and that factor analysis may not be appropriate.

From the correlation matrix, it can be understood that there are relatively high correlations among V_1(skin protection), V_3(removal of pimples) and V_5(no complexion). Likewise, there are relatively high correlations between V_2(beauty), V_4(adding complexion) and V_6(glamour).

Determine the Method of Factor Analysis

1. In principal components analysis, the total variance in the data is considered. The diagonal of the correlation matrix consists of unities, and full variance is brought into the factor matrix. Principal components analysis is recommended when the primary concern is to determine the minimum number of factors that will account for maximum variance in the data for use in subsequent multivariate analysis. The factors are called principal components.
2. In common factor analysis, the factors are estimated based only on the common variance. Communalities are inserted in the diagonal of the correlation matrix. This method is appropriate when the primary concern is to identify the underlying dimensions and the common variance is of interest. This method is also known as principal axis factoring.

Results of Principal Components Analysis

Initial Eigen values

Factor	Eigen Value	% of Variance	Cumulative %
1	2.731	45.520	45.520
2	2.218	36.969	82.488
3	0.442	7.360	89.848
4	0.341	5.688	95.536
5	0.183	3.044	98.580
6	0.085	1.420	100.000

Communalities

Variables	Initial	Extraction
V_1	1.000	0.926
V_2	1.000	0.723
V_3	1.000	0.894
V_4	1.000	0.739
V_5	1.000	0.878
V_6	1.000	0.790

Extraction Sums of Squared Loadings

Factor	Eigen Value	% of Variance	Cumulative %
1	2.731	45.520	45.520
2	2.218	36.969	82.488

Factor Matrix

Variables	Factor 1	Factor 2
V_1	0.928	0.253
V_2	-0.301	0.795
V_3	0.936	0.131
V_4	-0.342	0.789
V_5	-0.869	-0.351
V_6	-0.177	0.871

Rotation Sums of Squared Loadings

Factor	Eigen Value	% of Variance	Cumulative %
1	2.688	44.802	44.802
2	2.261	37.687	82.488

Rotated Factor Matrix

Variables	Factor 1	Factor 2
V_1	0.962	-0.027
V_2	-0.057	0.848
V_3	0.934	-0.146
V_4	-0.098	0.845
V_5	-0.933	-0.084
V_6	0.083	0.885

Factor Score Coefficient Matrix

Variables	Factor 1	Factor 2
V_1	0.358	0.011
V_2	-0.001	0.375
V_3	0.345	-0.043
V_4	-0.017	0.377
V_5	-0.350	-0.059
V_6	0.052	0.395

Factor Score Coefficient Matrix

Variables	V_1	V_2	V_3	V_4	V_5	V_6
V_1	**0.926**	0.024	-0.029	0.031	0.038	-0.053
V_2	-0.078	**0.723**	0.022	-0.158	0.038	-0.105
V_3	0.902	-0.177	**0.894**	-0.031	0.081	0.033
V_4	-0.117	0.730	-0.217	**0.739**	-0.027	-0.107
V_5	-0.895	-0.018	-0.859	0.020	**0.878**	0.016
V_6	0.057	0.746	-0.051	0.748	-0.152	**0.790**

The lower left triangle contains the reproduced correlation matrix; the diagonal, the communalities; the upper right triangle, the residuals between the observed correlations and the reproduced correlations.

Factor loading Plot

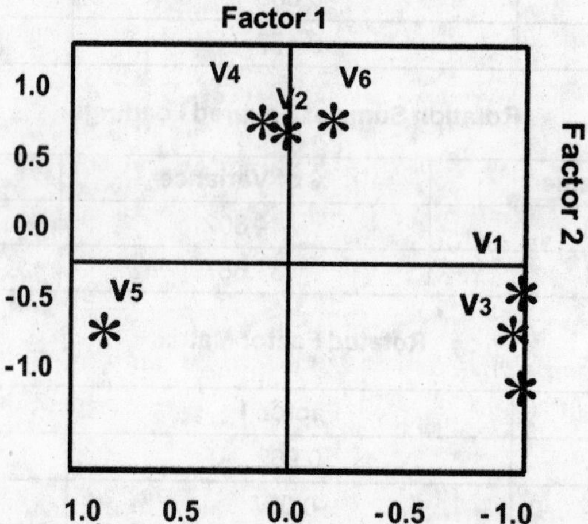

Determine the Number of Factors

1. *A Priori determination:* Sometimes, because of prior knowledge, the researcher knows how many factors to expect and thus can specify the number of factors to be extracted beforehand.

2. *Determination based on Eigenvalues:* In this approach, only factors with Eigenvalues greater than 1.0 are retained. An Eigenvalue represents the amount of variance associated with the factor. Hence, only factors with a variance greater than 1.0 are included. Factors with variance less than 1.0 are no better than a single variable, since, due to standardization, each variable has a variance of 1.0. If the number of variables is less than 20, this approach will result in a conservative number of factors.

3. ***Determination based on Scree Plot:*** A scree plot is a plot of the Eigenvalues against the number of factors in order of extraction. Experimental evidence indicates that the point at which the scree begins denotes the true number of factors. Generally, the number of factors determined by a scree plot will be one or a few more than that determined by the Eigenvalue criterion.

4. ***Determination based on Percentage of Variance:*** In this approach the number of factors extracted is determined so that the cumulative percentage of variance extracted by the factors reaches a satisfactory level. It is recommended that the factors extracted should account for at least 60% of the variance.

Scree Plot

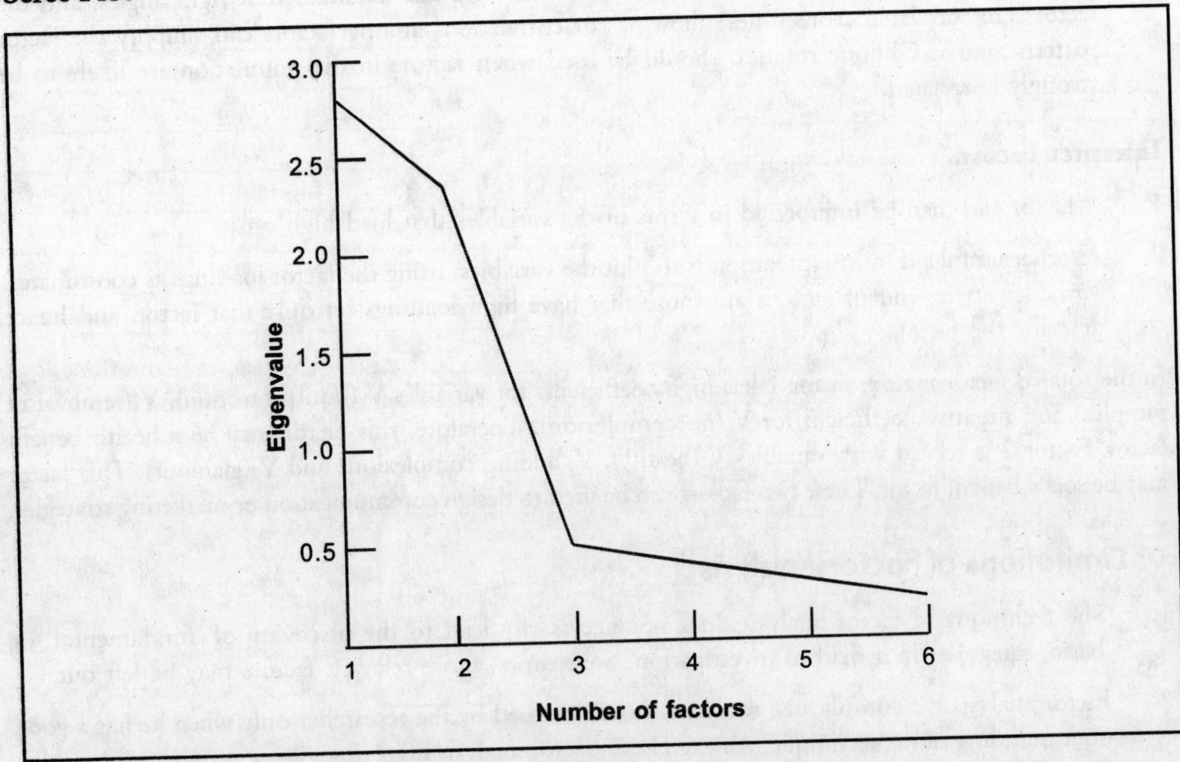

1. ***Determination based on Split-Half Reliability:*** The sample is split in half and factor analysis is performed on each half. Only factors with high correspondence of factor loadings across the two sub samples are retained.

2. ***Determination based on Significance Tests:*** It is possible to determine the statistical significance of the separate Eigenvalues and retain only those factors that are statistically significant. A drawback is that with large samples (size greater than 200), many factors are likely to be statistically significant, although from a practical viewpoint many of these account for only a small proportion of the total variance.

Rotate Factors

1. Although the initial or unrotated factor matrix indicates the relationship between the factors and individual variables, it seldom results in factors that can be interpreted, because the factors are correlated with many variables. Therefore, through rotation the factor matrix is transformed into a simpler one that is easier to interpret.

2. In rotating the factors, we would like each factor to have nonzero, or significant, loadings or coefficients for only some of the variables. Likewise, we would like each variable to have nonzero or significant loadings with only a few factors, if possible with only one.
3. The rotation is called orthogonal rotation if the axes are maintained at right angles.
4. The most commonly used method for rotation is the varimax procedure. This is an orthogonal method of rotation that minimizes the number of variables with high loadings on a factor, thereby enhancing the interpretability of the factors. Orthogonal rotation results in factors that are uncorrelated.
5. The rotation is called oblique rotation when the axes are not maintained at right angles, and the factors are correlated. Sometimes, allowing for correlations among factors can simplify the factor pattern matrix. Oblique rotation should be used when factors in the population are likely to be strongly correlated.

Interpret Factors

1. A factor can then be interpreted in terms of the variables that load high on it.
2. Another useful aid in interpretation is to plot the variables, using the factor loadings as coordinates. Variables at the end of an axis are those that have high loadings on only that factor, and hence describe the factor.

In the rotated factor matrix, factor 1 has high coefficients for variables V_1(skin protection), V_3(removal of pimples) and negative coefficient for V_5(no complexion). Therefore, this factor may be a health benefit factor. Factor 2 is related with variables V_2(beauty), V_4(adding complexion) and V_6(glamour). This factor may be social benefit factor. These two factors can be used to design communication or marketing strategies.

❖ Limitations of Factor Analysis

1. The technique of factor analysis does not necessarily lead to the discovery of 'fundamental' or 'basic' categories in a field of investigation. Sometimes, more relevant factors may be left out.
2. Factor analysis is a complicated tool and should be used by the researcher only when he has a good understanding of the technique. An exercise in factor analysis involving a large number of variables, say 50, is much bothersome and costly.
3. Another problem with factor analysis is that the reliability of results is sometimes questionable. A factor analysis carried out from one-half of the data might give quite different results from those obtained from the second-half of the data.
4. Yet another limitation of this technique is that its utility depends to a large extent on the judgement of the researcher.

In view of the foregoing limitations, the exploratory nature of factor analysis becomes clear. As Thurstone mentions the use of factor analysis should not be made where fundamental and fruitful concepts are already well-formulated and tested. It may be used especially in those domains where basic and fruitful concepts are essentially lacking and where crucial experiments have been difficult to conceive. It will thus be seen that factor analysis can be used with advantage in the case of exploratory research. Many a time factor analysis is used just because it exists, without examining its suitability.

CLUSTER ANALYSIS

The purpose of cluster analysis is to reduce a large data set to meaningful subgroups of individuals or objects. The division is accomplished on the basis of similarity of the objects across a set of specified characteristics. Outliers are a problem with this technique, often caused by too many irrelevant variables. The sample should be representative of the population, and it is desirable to have uncorrelated factors. There are three main clustering methods: hierarchical, which is a treelike process appropriate for smaller data sets; non-hierarchical, which requires specification of the number of clusters a priori, and a combination of both. There are 4 main rules for developing clusters: the clusters should be different, they should be reachable, they should be measurable, and the clusters should be profitable (big enough to matter). This is a great tool for market segmentation.

Cluster analysis is used to classify persons or objects into a small number of mutually exclusive and exhaustive groups. There should be high internal (within-cluster) homogeneity and high external (between-cluster) heterogeneity. In marketing research, cluster analysis has been increasingly used because of its utility in resolving the problem of classifying consumers, products, etc.

❖ Hypothetical Example of Cluster Analysis

Cluster analysis is illustrated by a hypothetical example of the type of vacations taken by 15 individuals-A to O. A two-dimensional perceptual map has been drawn on the basis of data relating to (i) number of vacation days, and (ii) expenditure on vacations during a given year.

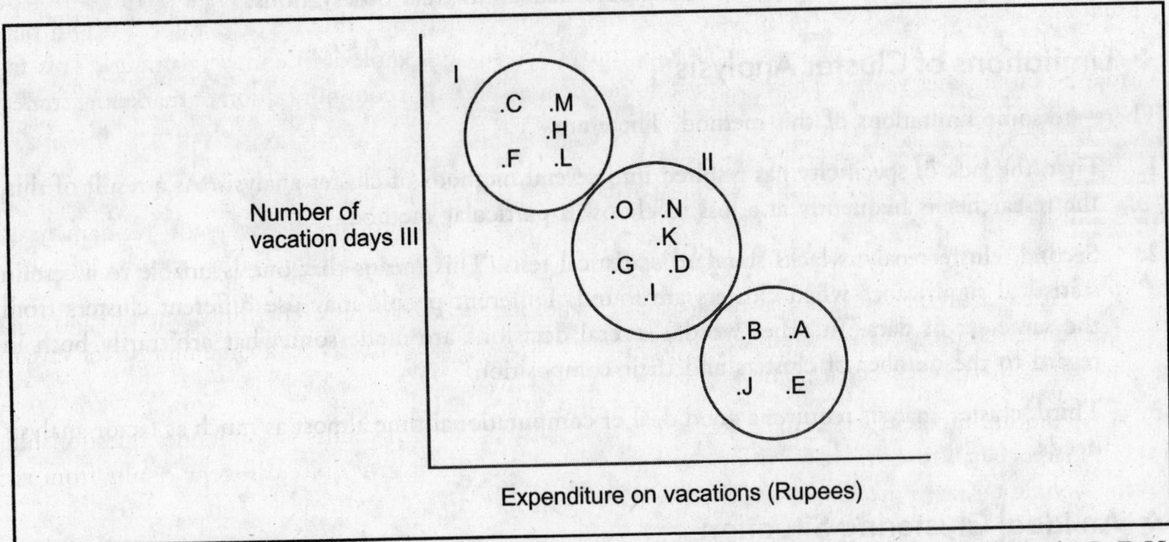

It will be seen that there are three distinct clusters. The first cluster comprising five individuals C, F, H, L and M shows that although these individuals take too many vacations, they do not spend much on their vacations. The second cluster comprising six individuals D, G, I, K, N and O shows that they take vacations moderately and also spend moderately-neither too much not too less. Finally, the third cluster comprising four individuals A, B, E and J shows that they have relatively few vacation days but spend substantially more on their vacations. On the basis of this perceptual map, the utility of classifying individuals into clusters becomes apparent. It will be seen that the points included in a cluster are close to each other and the points falling in two or more clusters are at a good distance from each other. This is the essence of cluster analysis i.e., to classify individuals or objects on the basis of their similarity or distance from each other. Distance is an inverse measure of similarity, i.e., the shorter the distance, the greater is similarity and vice-versa.

❖ Advantages of Cluster Analysis

Cluster analysis is used in marketing for different purposes:

1. ***Segmenting the market:*** Consumers may be clustered or grouped on the basis of benefits derived from the purchase of a product. Each cluster would consist of consumers who are, relatively homogeneous in terms of the benefits they seek.
2. ***Understanding the buyer behaviors:*** The main purpose of cluster analysis is to identify the homogeneous groups of buyers. From these groups, buying behaviour can be extracted to develop a suitable marketing strategy.
3. ***Identifying new product opportunities:*** In the competitive environment, clustering of brands and products would lead to identify potential new product opportunities.
4. ***Selecting test markets:*** Cities or regions can be grouped into homogeneous clusters to arrive at different marketing strategies.
5. ***Reducing Data:*** Other multivariate technique such as multiple discriminant analysis can be applied further to cluster analysis to describe differences in consumer's product usage behaviour. It enables to reduce the data that are more manageable than individual observations.

❖ Limitations of Cluster Analysis

There are some limitations of this method. These are:

1. First, the lack of specificity has resulted into several methods of cluster analysis. As a result of this, the researcher is frequently at a loss to choose a particular method.
2. Second, cluster analysis lacks standard statistical tests. This means that one is unable to ascertain statistical significance when clusters are found. Different people may use different clusters from the same set of data. In other words, several decisions are made somewhat arbitrarily both in regard to the number of clusters and their composition.
3. Third, cluster analysis requires a good deal of computational time almost as much as factor analysis needs.

❖ An Ideal Clustering Situation

Ideal clustering situation is to identify clearly the clusters which consist of homogeneous items within the cluster. There may be a difference from cluster to cluster in terms of many marketing attributes.

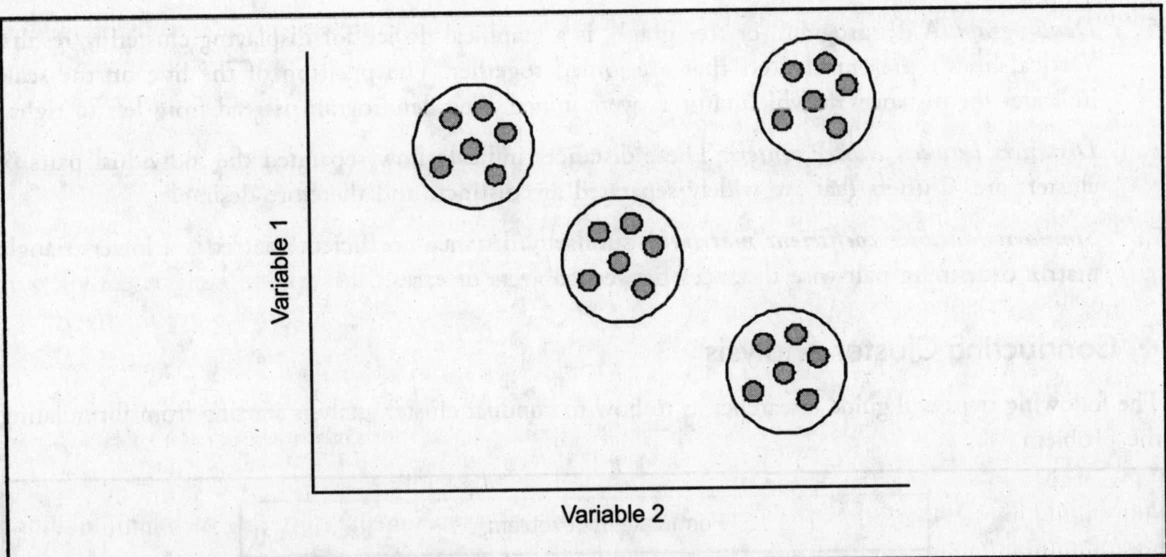

❖ A Practical Clustering Situation

In practical situation it is difficult to identify clusters where some units will be overlapping between the clusters at the interface points. Segmenting the all the units into clusters is a complex phenomena.

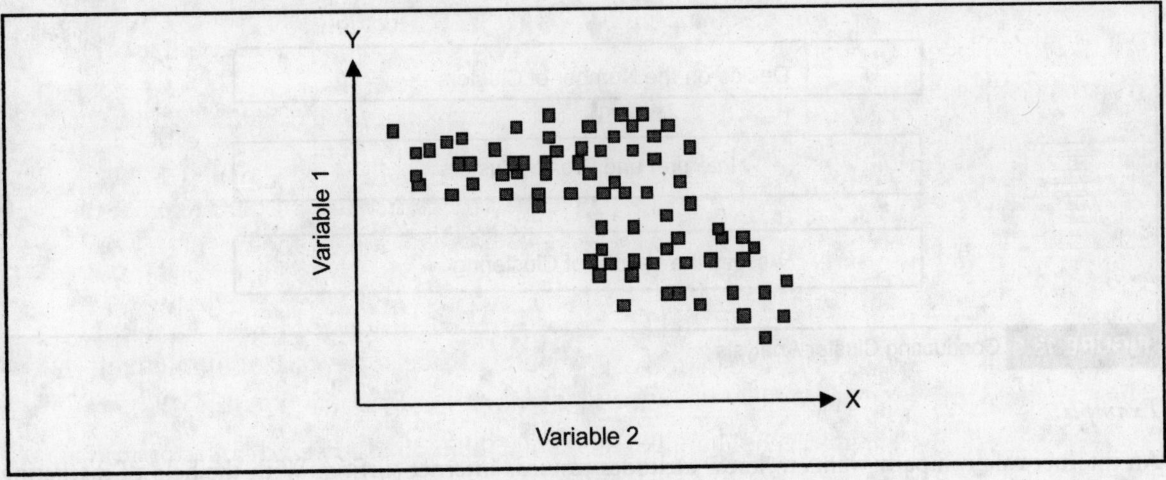

❖ Statistics Associated with Cluster Analysis

1. ***Agglomeration schedule:*** An agglomeration schedule gives information on the objects or cases being combined at each stage of a hierarchical clustering process.

2. ***Cluster centroid:*** The cluster centroid is the mean values of the variables for all the cases or objects in a particular cluster.

3. ***Cluster centers:*** The cluster centers are the initial starting points in non-hierarchical clustering. Clusters are built around these centers, or seeds.

4. ***Cluster membership:*** Cluster membership indicates the cluster to which each object or case belongs.

5. ***Dendrogram:*** A dendrogram, or tree graph, is a graphical device for displaying clustering results. Vertical lines represent clusters that are joined together. The position of the line on the scale indicates the distances at which clusters were joined. The dendrogram is read from left to right.
6. ***Distances between cluster centers:*** These distances indicate how separated the individual pairs of clusters are. Clusters that are widely separated are distinct, and therefore desirable.
7. ***Similarity/distance coefficient matrix:*** A similarity/distance coefficient matrix is a lower-triangle matrix containing pair-wise distances between objects or cases.

❖ Conducting Cluster Analysis

The following steps will guide researcher as to how to conduct cluster analysis starting from formulating the problem.

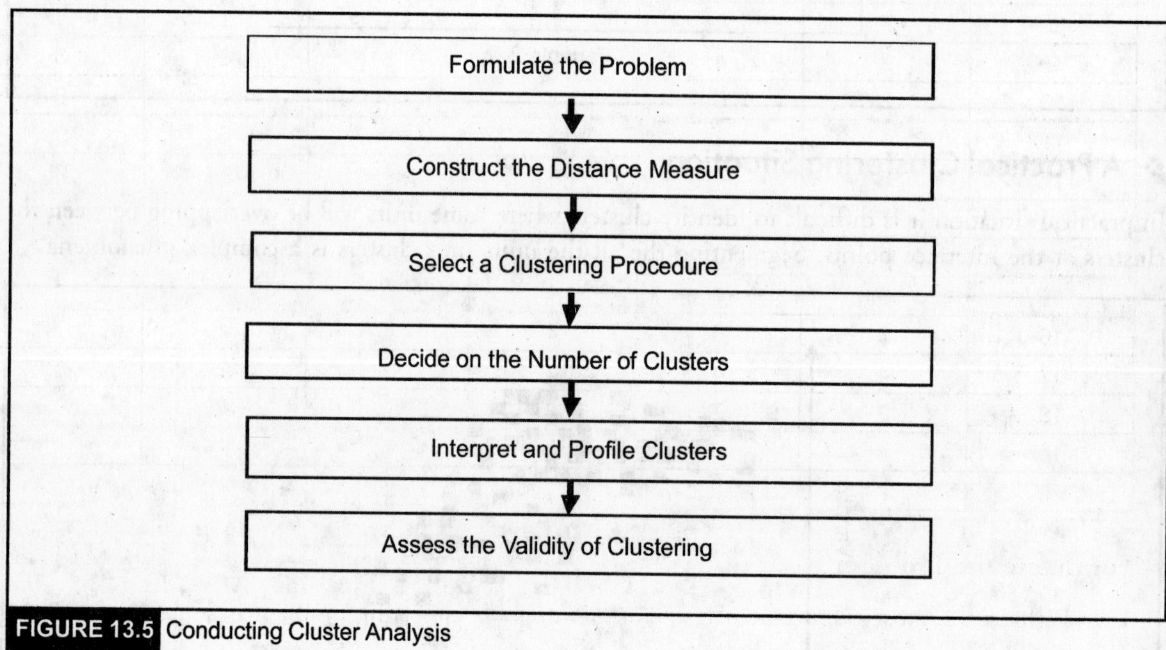

FIGURE 13.5 Conducting Cluster Analysis

Example:

An internet cafe company wants to know attitudes towards internet surfing. With the help of marketing research team, the company identified six attitude variables. Twenty respondents were asked to express their degree of agreement with the following statements on a seven point scale (1-disagree, 7-agree). Conduct cluster analysis method using SPSS to identify homogenous customer groups based on which a suitable marketing strategy can be adopted by the company.

V_1 - Internet surfing is fun.

V_2 - Surfing is bad for your budget.

V_3 - I combine surfing with music and games.

V_4 - I try to get best information I wanted while surfing.

V_5 - I don't waste time in surfing.

V_6 – I can get lot of information from various sources.

The obtained data is as shown below and the same is given as input to SPSS software and selecting the option as Cluster Analysis.

TABLE 13.3 Attitudinal Data for Clustering

Case No.	V_1	V_2	V_3	V_4	V_5	V_6
1	6	4	7	3	2	3
2	2	3	1	4	5	4
3	7	2	6	4	1	3
4	4	6	4	5	3	6
5	1	3	2	2	6	4
6	6	4	6	3	3	4
7	5	3	6	3	3	4
8	7	3	7	4	1	4
9	2	4	3	3	6	3
10	3	5	3	6	4	6
11	1	3	2	3	5	3
12	5	4	5	4	2	4
13	2	2	1	5	4	4
14	4	6	4	6	4	7
15	6	5	4	2	1	4
16	3	5	4	6	4	7
17	4	4	7	2	2	5
18	3	7	2	6	4	3
19	4	6	3	7	2	7
20	2	3	2	4	7	2

Formulate the Problem

1. Perhaps the most important part of formulating the clustering problem is selecting the variables on which the clustering is based.
2. Inclusion of even one or two irrelevant variables may distort an otherwise useful clustering solution.
3. Basically, the set of variables selected should describe the similarity between objects in terms that are relevant to the marketing research problem.
4. The variables should be selected based on past research, theory, or a consideration of the hypotheses being tested. In exploratory research, the researcher should exercise judgment and intuition.

Select a Distance or Similarity Measure

1. The most commonly used measure of similarity is the Euclidean distance or its square. The Euclidean distance is the square root of the sum of the squared differences in values for each variable. Other distance measures are also available. The city-block or Manhattan distance between two objects is the sum of the absolute differences in values for each variable. The Chebychev distance between two objects is the maximum absolute difference in values for any variable.

2. If the variables are measured in vastly different units, the clustering solution will be influenced by the units of measurement. In these cases, before clustering respondents, we must standardize the data by rescaling each variable to have a mean of zero and a standard deviation of unity. It is also desirable to eliminate outliers (cases with a typical values).

3. Use of different distance measures may lead to different clustering results. Hence, it is advisable to use different measures and compare the results.

❖ Classification of Clustering Procedures

Broadly, there are two types of clustering procedures: (1) hierarchical and (2) non-hierarchical. Both have sub-divided further. The same is presented in the following form.

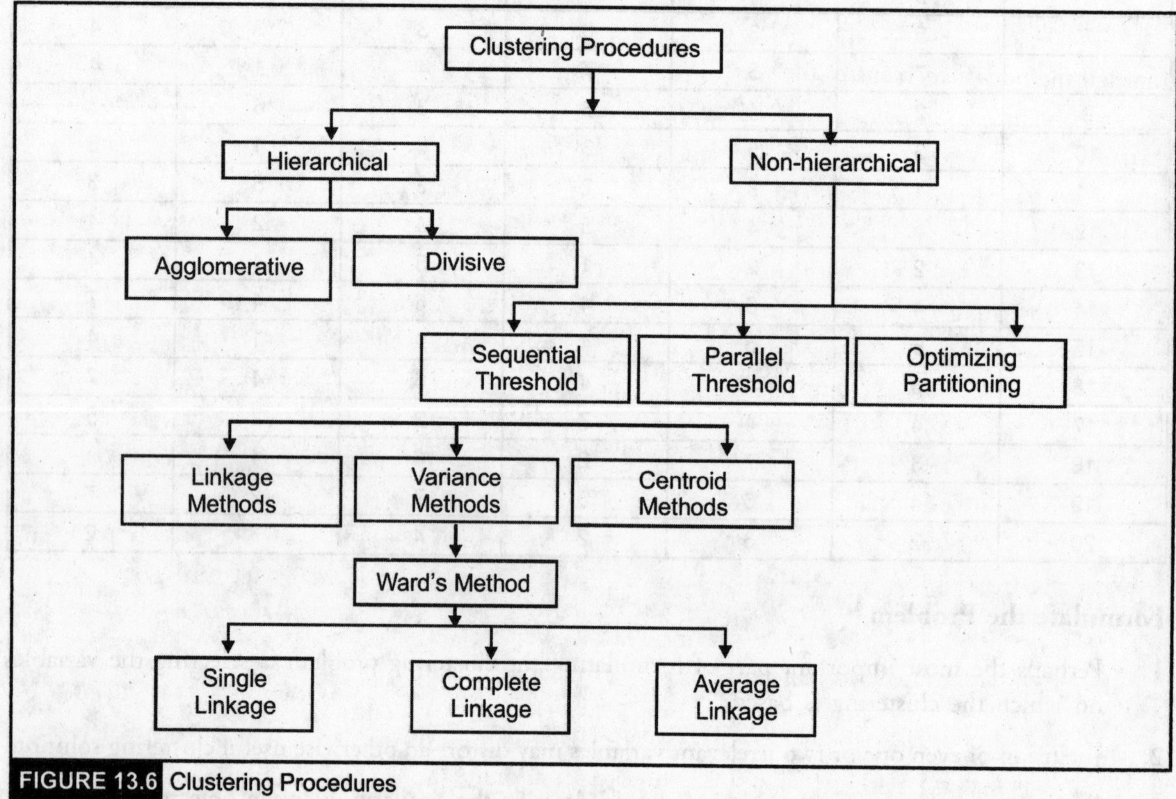

FIGURE 13.6 Clustering Procedures

Select a Clustering Procedure – Hierarchical

1. **Hierarchical clustering** is characterized by the development of a hierarchy or tree-like structure. Hierarchical methods can be agglomerative or divisive.

2. **Agglomerative clustering** starts with each object in a separate cluster. Clusters are formed by grouping objects into bigger and bigger clusters. This process is continued until all objects are members of a single cluster.

3. **Divisive clustering** starts with all the objects grouped in a single cluster. Clusters are divided or split until each object is in a separate cluster.

4. **Agglomerative methods** are commonly used in marketing research. They consist of linkage methods, error sums of squares or variance methods, and centroid methods.

Select a Clustering Procedure – Linkage Method

1. The single linkage method is based on minimum distance, or the nearest neighbor rule. At every stage, the distance between two clusters is the distance between their two closest points.
2. The complete linkage method is similar to single linkage, except that it is based on the maximum distance or the furthest neighbour approach. In complete linkage, the distance between two clusters is calculated as the distance between their two furthest points.
3. The average linkage method works similarly. However, in this method, the distance between two clusters is defined as the average of the distances between all pairs of objects, where one member of the pair is from each of the clusters.

❖ Linkage Methods of Clustering

Linkage method is to identify the units based the distance measure to identify clusters.

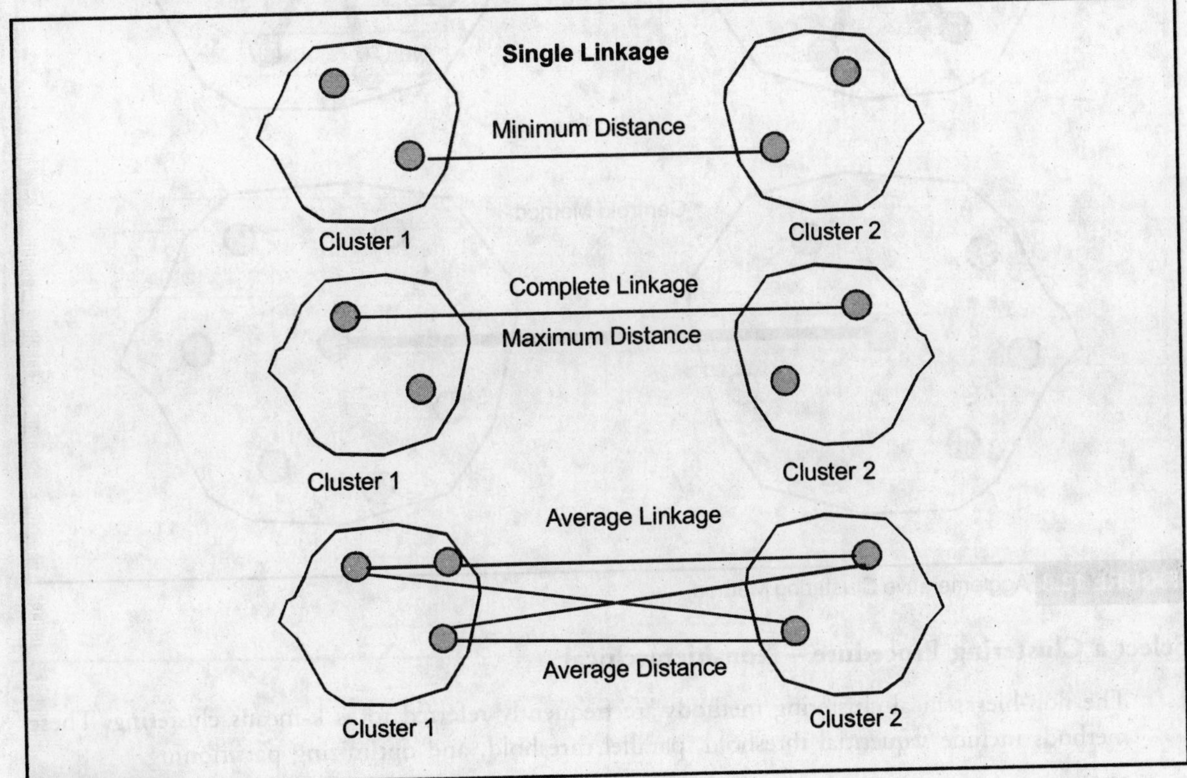

FIGURE 13.7 Linkage Method of Clustering

Select a Clustering Procedure – Variance Method

1. The variance methods attempt to generate clusters to minimize the within-cluster variance.
2. A commonly used variance method is the Ward's procedure. For each cluster, the means for all the variables are computed. Then, for each object, the squared Euclidean distance to the cluster means is calculated. These distances are summed for all the objects. At each stage, the two clusters with the smallest increase in the overall sum of squares within cluster distances are combined.

3. In the centroid methods, the distance between two clusters is the distance between their centroids (means for all the variables), Every time objects are grouped, a new centroid is computed.
4. Of the hierarchical methods, average linkage and Ward's methods have been shown to perform better than the other procedures.

❖ Other Agglomerative Clustering Methods

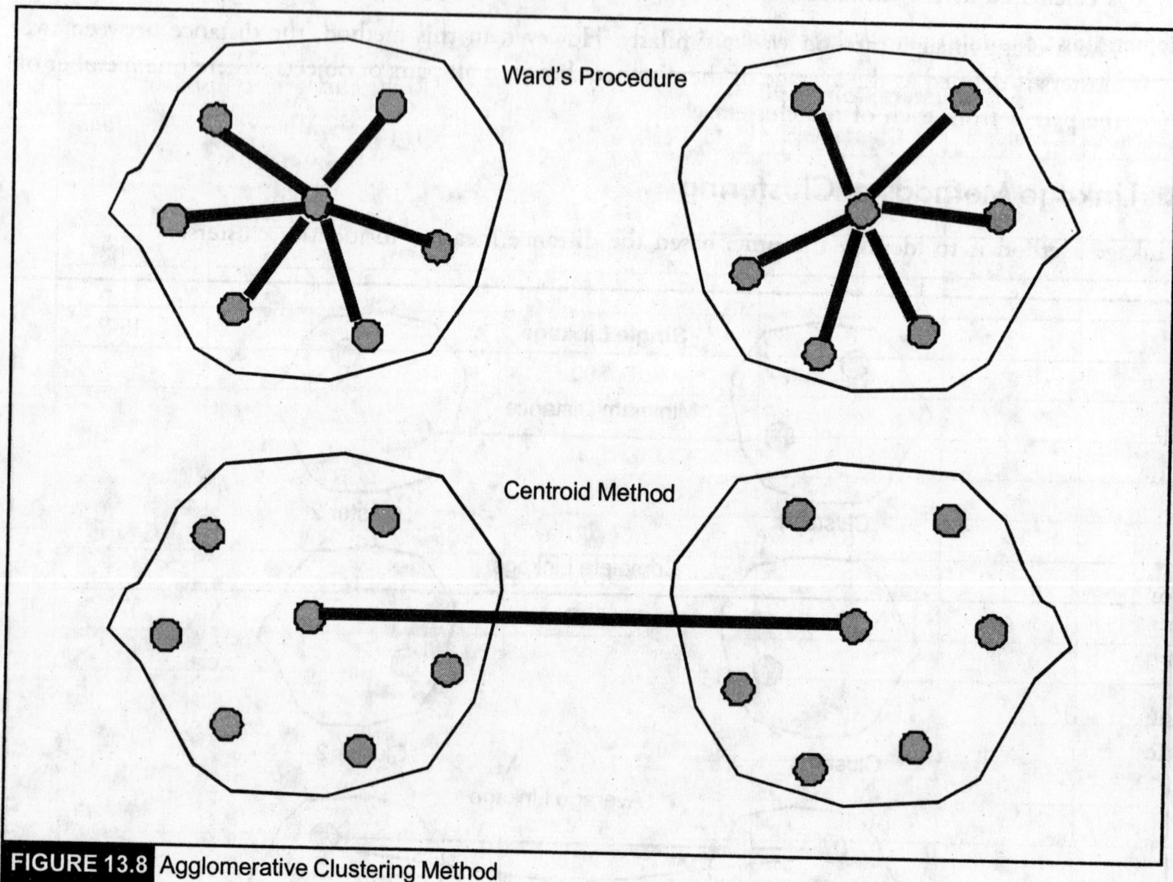

FIGURE 13.8 Agglomerative Clustering Method

Select a Clustering Procedure – Non-hierarchical

1. The non-hierarchical clustering methods are frequently referred to as k-means clustering. These methods include sequential threshold, parallel threshold, and optimizing partitioning.
2. In the sequential threshold method, a cluster center is selected and all objects within a prespecified threshold value from the center are grouped together. Then a new cluster center or seed is selected, and the process is repeated for the unclustered points. Once an object is clustered with a seed, it is no longer considered for clustering with subsequent seeds.
3. The parallel threshold method operates similarly, except that several cluster centers are selected simultaneously and objects within the threshold level are grouped with the nearest center.
4. The optimizing partitioning method differs from the two threshold procedures in that objects can later be reassigned to clusters to optimize an overall criterion, such as average within cluster distance for a given number of clusters.

It has been suggested that the hierarchical and non-hierarchical methods be used in tandem. First, an initial clustering solution is obtained using a hierarchical procedure, such as average linkage or Ward's. The number of clusters and cluster centroids so obtained are used as inputs to the optimizing partitioning method. Choice of a clustering method and choice of a distance measure are interrelated. For example, squared Euclidean distances should be used with the Ward's and centroid methods. Several non-hierarchical procedures also use squared Euclidean distances.

Results of Hierarchical Clustering

Agglomeration Schedule using Ward's Procedure

	Clusters Combined			Stage cluster first appears		
Stage	**Cluster 1**	**Cluster 2**	**Coefficient**	**Cluster 1**	**Cluster 2**	**Next stage**
1	14	16	1.000000	0	0	6
2	6	7	2.000000	0	0	7
3	2	13	3.500000	0	0	15
4	5	11	5.000000	0	0	11
5	3	8	6.500000	0	0	16
6	10	14	8.160000	0	1	9
7	6	12	10.166667	2	0	10
8	9	20	13.000000	0	0	11
9	4	10	15.583000	0	6	12
10	1	6	18.500000	6	7	13
11	5	9	23.000000	4	8	15
12	4	19	27.750000	9	0	17
13	1	17	33.100000	10	0	14
14	1	15	41.333000	13	0	16
15	2	5	51.833000	3	11	18
16	1	3	64.500000	14	5	19
17	4	18	79.667000	12	0	18
18	2	4	172.662000	15	17	19
19	1	2	328.600000	16	18	0

Cluster Membership of Cases using Ward's Procedure

	Number of Clusters		
Label case	4	3	2
1	1	1	1
2	2	2	2
3	1	1	1
4	3	3	2
5	2	2	2
6	1	1	1
7	1	1	1
8	1	1	1
9	2	2	2

Contd...

10	3	3	2
11	2	2	2
12	1	1	1
13	2	2	2
14	3	3	2
15	1	1	1
16	3	3	2
17	1	1	1
18	4	3	2
19	3	3	2
20	2	2	2

Dendrogram using Ward's Method

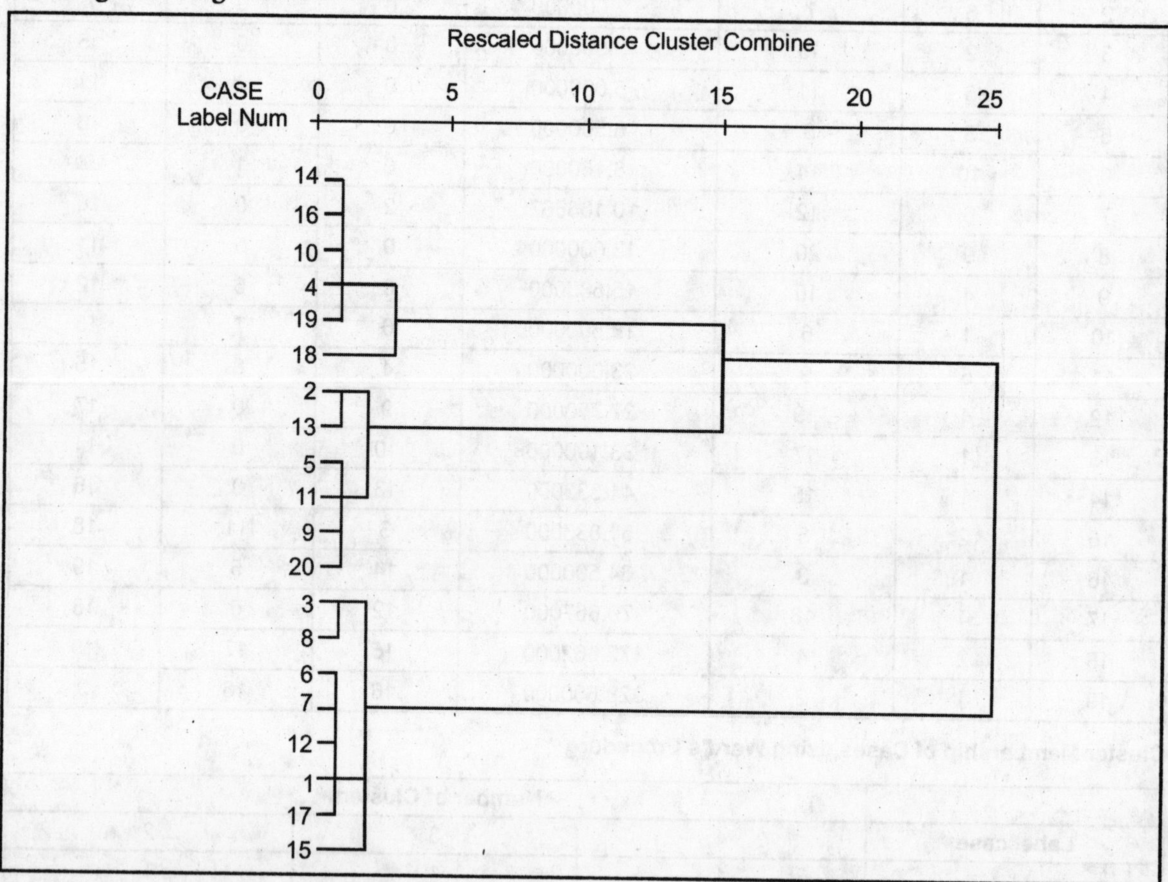

Decide on the Number of Clusters

1. Theoretical, conceptual, or practical considerations may suggest a certain number of clusters.
2. In hierarchical clustering, the distances at which clusters are combined can be used as criteria. This information can be obtained from the agglomeration schedule or from the dendrogram.
3. In non-hierarchical clustering, the ratio of total within-group variance to between-group variance can be plotted against the number of clusters. The point at which an elbow or a sharp bend occurs indicates an appropriate number of clusters.
4. The relative sizes of the clusters should be meaningful.

Interpreting and Profiling the Clusters

1. Interpreting and profiling clusters involves examining the cluster centroids. The centroids enable us to describe each cluster by assigning it a name or label.

2. It is often helpful to profile the clusters in terms of variables that were not used for clustering. These may include demographic, psychographic, product usage, media usage, or other variables.

Cluster Centroids

	Means of Variables					
Cluster No.	**V_1**	**V_2**	**V_3**	**V_4**	**V_5**	**V_6**
1	5.75.0	3.625	6.000	3.125	1.750	3.875
2	1.667	3.000	1.833	3.500	5.500	3.333
3	3.500	5.833	3.333	6.000	3.500	6.000

The above table gives the centroid or means values for each cluster. **Cluster** 1 has relatively high values on the variables V_1(Internet surfing is fun) and V_3(I combine surfing with music and games). It has low value on V_5(I don't waste time in surfing). Hence **cluster 1** can be labeled as ***"surf loving and concentrated"***. This cluster consists of cases:1,3,6,7,8,12,15,and 17. **Cluster 2** is just opposite, with low values on V_1 and V_3 and a high value on V_5 and this can be labeled as ***"apathetic surfers"***. This consists of cases 2,5,9,11,13 and 20. **Cluster 3** has high values on V_2(Surfing is bad for your budget), V_4(I try to get best information I wanted while surfing), and V_6 (You can get lot of information from various sources). Thus, this cluster can be labeled as ***"economical surfers"***. This consists of cases 4, 10,14,16,18 and 19.

❖ Assess Reliability and Validity

1. Perform cluster analysis on the same data using different distance measures. Compare the results across measures to determine the stability of the solutions.

2. Use different methods of clustering and compare the results.

3. Split the data randomly into halves. Perform clustering separately on each half. Compare cluster centroids across the two sub samples.

4. Delete variables randomly. Perform clustering based on the reduced set of variables. Compare the results with those obtained by clustering based on the entire set of variables.

5. In non-hierarchical clustering, the solution may depend on the order of cases in the data set. Make multiple runs using different order of cases until the solution stabilizes.

Results of Non-hierarchical Clustering

	Cluster		
	1	**2**	**3**
V1	1	2	7
V2	6	3	2
V3	3	2.	6
V4	7	4	4
V5	2	7	1
V6	7	2	3

Iteration	Change in Clusters		
	1	2	3
1	2.154	2.102	2.550
2	0.000	0.000	0.000

Convergence achieved due to no or small distance change. The maximum distance by which any center has changed is 0.000. The current iteration is 2. The minimum distance between initial centers is 7.746.

Cluster Membership

Case Cluster	Cluster	Distance
1	3	1.414
2	2	1.323
3	3	2.550
4	1	1.404
5	2	1.848
6	3	1.225
7	3	1.550
8	3	2.121
9	2	1.756
10	1	1.143
11	2	1.041
12	3	1.581
13	2	2.568
14	1	1.404
15	3	2.828
16	1	1.624
17	3	2.598
18	1	3.555
19	1	2.154
20	2	2.102

	Final Cluster Centers		
Cluster		2	3

Distances between Final Cluster Centers

Cluster	1	2	3
1		5.568	5.698
2	5.568		6.928
3	5.698	6.928	

It is interesting note that clusters identified from hierarchical method are same in non-hierarchical method except change in the order. The distances between the final cluster centers indicate that the pairs of clusters are well-separated.

Hierarchical clustering includes methods such as single linkage, complete linkage and average linkage. We need not to specify in advance how many clusters are to be extracted. A range of solution provided by the software from 1- cluster solution to n-cluster solution. Where as in Non-hierarchical clustering, you have to specify in advance how many clusters are required from the data. The specified number of nodes and points closest to them are used to form initial clusters and through an iterative rearrangements and the final k-clusters are determined by the package.

CONJOINT ANALYSIS

The objective of conjoint analysis is to determine what combination of a limited number of attributes is most influential on respondent choice or decision-making. A controlled set of potential products or services is shown to respondents and by analyzing how they make preferences between these products, the implicit valuation of the individual elements making up the product or service can be determined. These implicit valuations (utilities or part-worths) can be used to create market models that estimate market share, revenue and even profitability of new designs.

Marketing managers are faced with numerous difficult tasks directed at assessing future profitability, sales, and market share for new product entries or modifications of existing products or marketing strategies. These specific tasks include:

1. Predicting the profitability and/or market share for proposed new product concepts given the current offering of competitors.
2. Predicting the impact of new competitor products on profits or market share if we make no change in our competitive position.
3. Predicting customer switch rates either from our current products to new products we offer (cannibalism), or from our competitors products to our new products (draw).
4. Predicting the differential response of items 1-3 by key market segments purchasing our product.
5. Predicting competitive reaction to our strategies of introducing a new product. Specifically, should a new product be introduced, and if so, what is the optimal design configuration for this new product? Further, should pricing or other attributes of our current products be modified in response to the competition.
6. Predicting the impact of situational variables on customer preference.
7. Predicting the differential response to alternative advertising strategies and/or advertising themes.
8. Predicting the customer response to alternative pricing strategies, specific price levels, and proposed price changes.
9. Predicting competitive response to distribution strategies studying such diverse problems as determining the optimal channel of distribution, number or type of outlets, vendor selection, or sale person quotas.

Each of the identified management problems may be addressed and solved using the conjoint analysis methodology. In addition, a conjoint-based competitive strategy may be implemented by modifying the marketing mix, i.e., new product/concept identification, pricing, advertising and distribution. This competitive strategy may focus on new segments or product re-positioning. In addition to product and corporate strategy, conjoint research has been applied to family decision-making; Tourism, tax analysis; time management; direct foreign; and medicine.

Conjoint analysis is often referred to as "trade-off analysis," in that it allows for the evaluation of objects and the various levels of the attributes to be examined. It is both a compositional technique and a dependence technique, in that a level of preference for a combination of attributes and levels is developed. A part-worth, or utility, is calculated for each level of each attribute, and combinations of attributes at specific levels are summed to develop the overall preference for the attribute at each level. Models can be built which identify the ideal levels and combinations of attributes for products and services. It can be argued that conjoint analysis has become popular because it is a more powerful, more flexible, and often less expensive way to address these important issues than is the traditional concept testing approach. Conjoint Analysis is concerned with understanding how people make choices between products or services or a combination of product and service, so that businesses can design new products or services that better meet customers' underlying needs.

Although it has only been a mainstream research technique for the last 10 years or so, conjoint analysis has been found to be an extremely powerful of way of capturing what really drives customers to buy one product over another and what customers really value. A key benefit of conjoint analysis is the ability to produce dynamic market models that enable companies to test out what steps they would need to take to improve their market share, or how competitors' behaviour will affect their customers.

Conjoint analysis is concerned with the measurement of the joint effect of two or more attributes that are important from the viewpoint of the consumer. In a situation where a company would like to know the most desirable attributes or their combinations for a new product or service, the use of conjoint analysis will be most appropriate. Conjoint analysis generally used by the marketers to help determine what features a new product or service should have and how it should be priced. A typical conjoint analysis application involves a series of steps covering a variety of procedures; it is not a single procedure as is, for example, regression analysis. However, conjoint analysis is not difficult to understand.

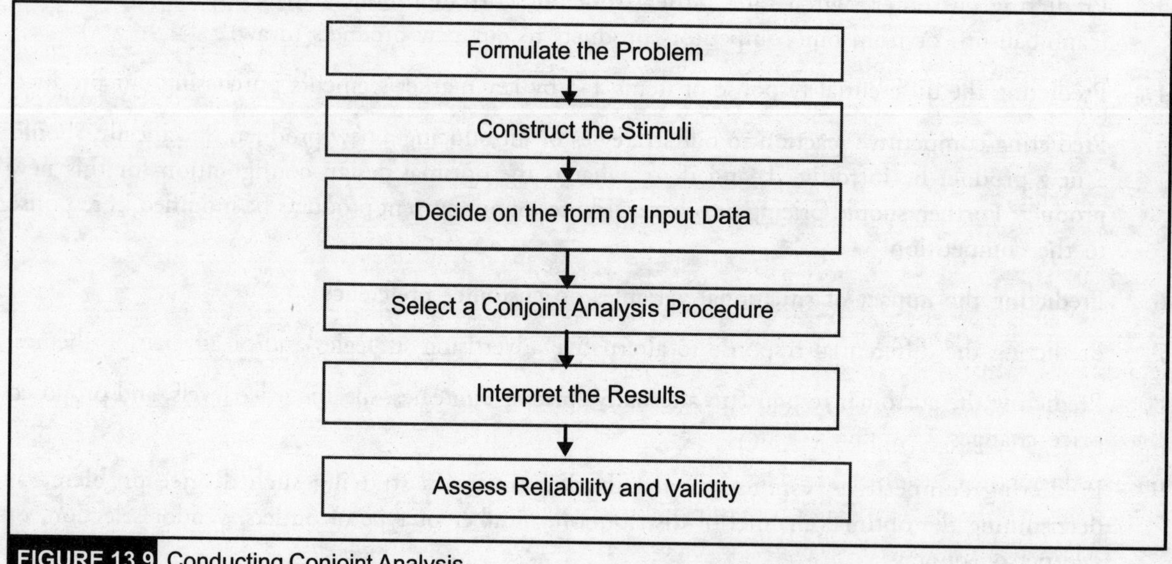

FIGURE 13.9 Conducting Conjoint Analysis

❖ Advantages

1. Estimates psychological tradeoffs that consumers make when evaluating several attributes together.
2. Measures preferences at the individual level.
3. Uncovers real or hidden drivers which may not be apparent to the respondent themselves.
4. Realistic choice or shopping task.
5. Able to use physical objects.

6. If appropriately designed, the ability to model interactions between attributes can be used to develop needs based segmentation.
7. Identification of the relevant product or service attributes.
8. Collection of data, and estimation of part-worth utility function.

Although in recent years research based on conjoint analysis has been done, it is still not used as frequently as other multivariate techniques. This is partly on account of the fact that relatively few organizations or people are fully conversant with this technique.

❖ Limitations

There are certain limitations of the conjoint analysis approach. First, it is used in predicting sales and market share. But, as its applications are not large, it is not as perfect and convincing as it should be. Second, sometimes the models of conjoint analysis fail to capture utility functions and decision rules.

1. Designing conjoint studies can be complex.
2. With too many options, respondents resort to simplification strategies.
3. Difficult to use for product positioning research because there is no procedure for converting perceptions about actual features to perceptions about a reduced set of underlying features.
4. Respondents are unable to articulate attitudes toward new categories, or may feel forced to think about issues they would otherwise not give much thought to.
5. Poorly designed studies may over-value emotional/preference variables and undervalue concrete variables.
6. Does not take into account the number items per purchase so it can give a poor reading of market share.

CANONICAL CORRELATION ANALYSIS

The most flexible of the multivariate techniques, canonical correlation simultaneously correlates several independent variables and several dependent variables. This powerful technique utilizes metric independent variables, unlike MANOVA, such as sales, satisfaction levels, and usage levels. It can also utilize non-metric categorical variables. This technique has the fewest restrictions of any of the multivariate techniques, so the results should be interpreted with caution due to the relaxed assumptions. Often, the dependent variables are related, and the independent variables are related, so finding a relationship is difficult without a technique like canonical correlation.

STRUCTURAL EQUATION MODELING (SEM)

Unlike the other multivariate techniques discussed, Structural Equation Modeling (SEM) examines multiple relationships between sets of variables simultaneously. This represents a family of techniques, including LISREL, latent variable analysis, and confirmatory factor analysis. SEM can incorporate latent variables, which either are not or cannot be measured directly into the analysis. For example, intelligence levels can only be inferred, with direct measurement of variables like test scores, level of education, grade point average, and other related measures. These tools are often used to evaluate many scaled attributes or build summated scales.

REVIEW QUESTIONS

1. What do you mean by Multivariate Techniques? Explain their significance in Marketing Research.
2. What is factor analysis? How do you conduct factor analysis? Give illustration.
3. Explain the significance of discriminate analysis. What are the steps involved in conducting discriminate analysis?
4. What is conjoint analysis? Explain its utility in marketing research with an example.
5. What is cluster analysis? Explain the steps involved in conducting cluster analysis with an example.
6. Define MDS. How do you conduct MDS?
7. In a survey on a product, data on three variables have been collected, as shown in the following table.

Respondent	Variable		
	X1	X2	X3
1	5	6	8
2	3	2	5
3	2	1	4
4	1	1	3
5	5	2	4
6	4	5	2
7	6	5	3
8	3	2	6
9	6	5	2
10	2	8	4

Perform factor analysis using controid method to identify the factors which can represent the variable of studies.

8. The performance standard of employees as a function of their age (X1) and family size (X2) is classified into 'Good' and 'Bad'. The data on 10 different employees in a company are presented in the following table.

Employee	Standards	X1 (in years)	X2 Family Size
1	Good	24	2
2	Good	12	1
3	Bad	36	2
4	Bad	24	1
5	Bad	32	3
6	Good	18	2
7	Good	45	1
8	Bad	50	3
9	Bad	35	2
10	Good	28	1

Define the discriminate function and compute discriminate ratio and identify the variable which is more important in relation to other.

9. In a marketing survey, the monthly income (in thousands of rupees) and monthly purchases of health care product (in hundreds of rupees) of respondents are summarised in the following table.

Respondent	Health Care	Months Purchase
1	12	5
2	19	4
3	13	2
4	16	8
5	18	6
6	8	3

Apply cluster analysis to the clue data and find cluster using distance measure. Draw Dendo-gram.

CHAPTER FOURTEEN

TIME SERIES

INTRODUCTION

Time series is a set of statistical observations arranged in chronological order. Time series is usually used with reference to economic data and economists are largely responsible for development of techniques of time series analysis. It can also be used for different purposes like managing production, variations of different variables, growth or decline of profits of organization, etc. Businessmen forecast future demand of sales in order to estimate proportionate production so that over stock or inadequate production can be avoided. Economists estimate future population based on time series. So that one can analyse amount of goods supply, jobs, vehicles, etc. required in future.

1. "A time series is a set of statistical observations arranged in chronological order."

   —Moris Hamburg

2. "A time series consists of statistical data which are collected, recorded or observed over successive increments."

   —Patterson

3. "A time series may be defined as a collection of magnitudes belonging to different time periods, of some variable or composite of variables, such as production of steel, per capita income, gross national product, price of tobacco, or indeed of industrial production."

   —Ya-Lun-chou

TIME SERIES ANALYSIS

There are several reasons for undertaking a time series analysis:

1. Firstly, the analysis of a time series enables us to understand the past behaviour or performance. It is possible to know how the data have changed over time and find out the probable reasons responsible for such changes. If the past performance, say of a company, has been poor, it can take corrective measures to arrest the poor performance.

2. Secondly, a time series analysis helps directly in business planning. A firm can know the long-term trend in the sale of its products. It can find out at what rate sales have been increasing over the years. This may help it in making projections of its sales for the next few years and plan the procurement of raw material, equipment and manpower accordingly.

3. Thirdly, a time series analysis enables one to study such movements as cycles that fluctuate around the trend. Knowledge of cyclical pattern in certain series of data will be helpful in making generalization in the concerned business or industry.

4. Finally, a time series analysis enables one to make meaningful comparisons in two or more series regarding the rate or type of growth. For example, growth in consumption at the national level can

be compared with that in the national income over specified period. Such comparisons are of considerable importance to business and industry.

❖ Components of a Time Series

A time series may contain one or more of the following four components:

Secular Trend (T)

We can observe steady increase or decrease in the variable over a period of time. The note of increase/ decrease can also be varying and after a period of growth or decline, reverse themselves and enter a period of decline or growth. Various types of trends can be broadly classified into:

1. Linear or straight line trend
2. Non-linear trend

Generally, the longer the period covered, the more significant the trend. When the period is short, the secular movements can not be expected to reveal themselves clearly and general drift of the series may be unduly influenced by cyclical fluctuations. This can be said by stating the minimum period to be considered in trend analysis is two to three cycles. It is not necessary that the rise or fall must continue in the same direction throughout the period. As long as we can say that the period as a whole was characterized, (excepting the year which has got different trend) we can say that a secular trend was present.

For example, an upward tendency as shown in the figure would be seen in data pertaining to population, agricultural production, money in circulation, a downward tendency will be noticed in data of births and deaths, epidemics, as a result of advancement in medical sciences, better medical facilities, literacy and higher standard of living.

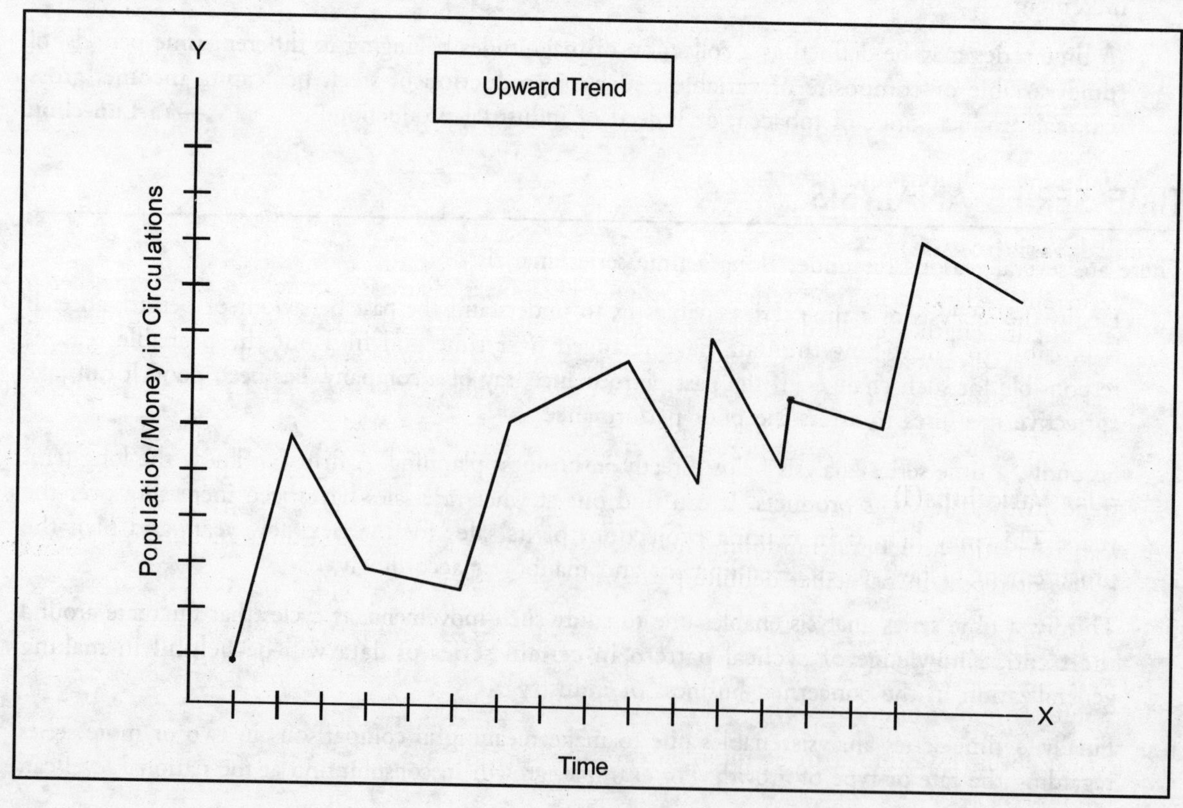

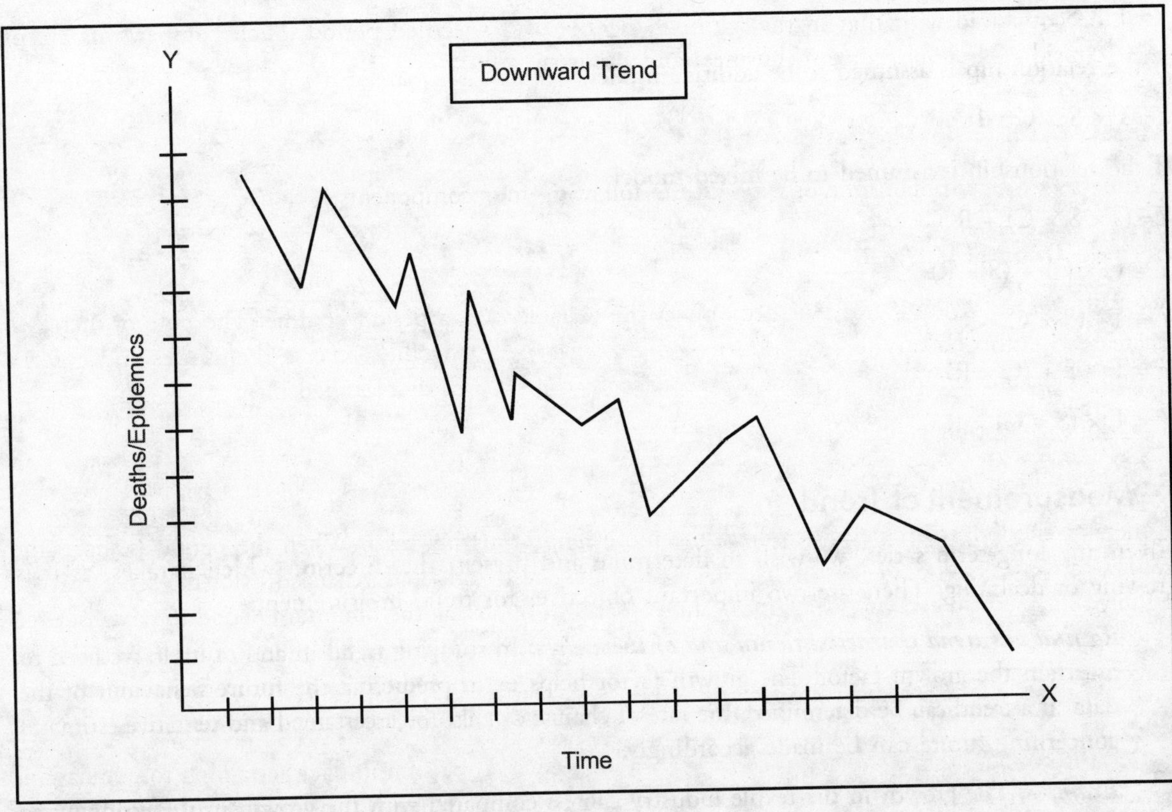

Seasonal Variations(S)

Seasonal variations are those periodic movements in business activity which occur regularly every year and have their origin in the nature of the year itself.

The factors that cause seasonal variations are:

1. Climate and weather conditions
2. Customs traditions and habits.

Cyclical Variations(C)

The recurrent variations in time series that usually last longer than a year and are regular neither in aptitude nor in length are called cyclical variations. There are four well-defined periods or phases in cycle-prosperity, decline, depression and improvement. Cyclical variations are useful in framing suitable policies for stabilizing level of business activity for avoiding booms and depressions as both are bad for an economy.

Irregular Variations(I)

Also called erratic, accidental random. These variations refer to such variations in business activity which do not repeat in particular definite pattern.

❖ Time Series Models

The result of four components (Y):

If the relationship is assumed to be multiplicative model,

$Y = T \times S \times C \times I$

If the relationship is assumed to be additive model,

$Y = T + S + C + I$

If the relationship is assumed to be mixed model,

$Y = (T \times S \times C) + R$

$Y = (T \times C) + (S \times R)$

$Y = T + (S \times C \times R)$

$Y = T + S + (C \times R)$

$Y = T \times (S + C) \times R$

❖ Measurement of Trend

Given any long-term series, we wish to determine and present the direction which it takes, as it is growing or declining? There are two important objectives for trend measurement:

1. ***To find out trend characteristics in and of themselves:*** In studying trend in and of itself, we need to ascertain the growth factor. The growth factor helps us in predicting the future behaviour of the data. If a trend can be determined, the rate of change can also be ascertained and tentative estimates concerning future can be made accordingly.

   Example: The growth in the textile industry can be compared with the growth in the economy as a whole or with the growth of other industries.

2. ***To enable us to determine trend in order to study other elements:*** The elimination of trend leaves us with seasonal, cyclical and irregular factors. These three relatively short-term elements then can be compared divorced from the long-term factor.

   Measurement of trend is in order to find out trend characteristics in and of themselves and to enable us to eliminate trend in order to study other elements. The various methods that can be used for determining trend are as follows:

   (i) Free-hand or graphical method

   (ii) Semi-averages method

   (iii) Moving average method

   (iv) Method of least squares

Free Hand or Graphical Method

This is the simplest method of studying the trend. The procedure of obtaining a straight line trend is given below:

1. Plot the time series.
2. Examine carefully the direction of hand based on the plotted information.
3. Draw a straight line which best fits the data. The line drawn should conform to following conditions:

   (i) The line should be smooth.

(ii) Some of vertical deviations from the trend of annual observation above trend line should be equal to below line.

(iii) Trend line should bisect cycles so that the area above the trend equals area below it.

(iv) The sum of squares of vertical deviations from the trend should be minimum.

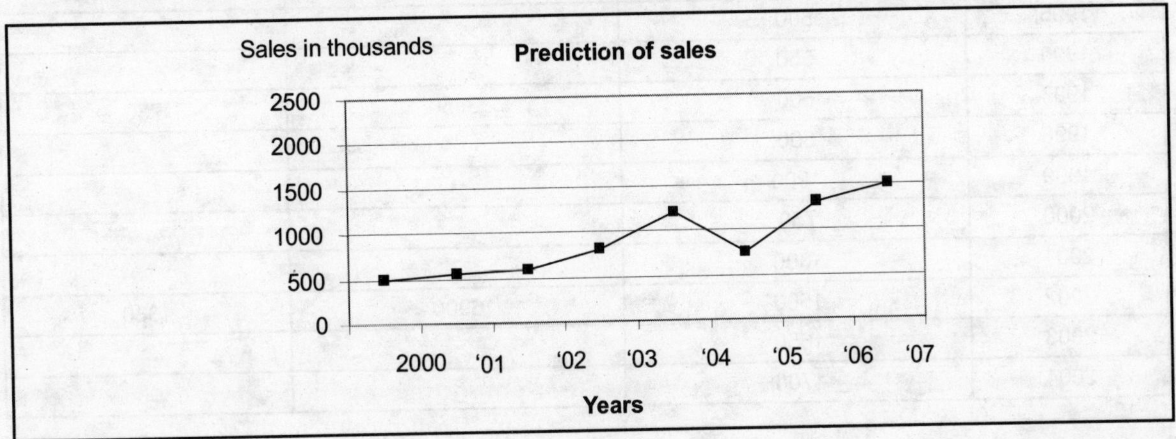

If sales in the year 2008 to be predicted, extend the graph with free hand and corresponding sales can be noted on Y axis.

Merits

1. This is the simplest method of measuring trend.
2. This method is very flexible in that it can be used regardless of whether the trend is a straight line or a curve.
3. The trend line drawn by a statistician experienced in computing the trend and having knowledge of the economic history of the concern or the industry under analysis may be a better expression of the secular movement than a trend fitted by the use of a rigid mathematical formula which while providing a good fit to the points may have no alter logical justification.

Limitations

1. This method is highly subjective because the trend line depends on the personal judgment of the investigation and therefore, different persons may draw different trend line from the same set of data.
2. Since freehand curve fitting is subjective, it cannot have much value if it is used as a basis for predictions.
3. It is very time consuming to construct a freehand trend if a careful and conscientious job is done.

Method of Semi-averages

The procedure of obtaining the trend by semi-average method is as follows:

1. The given data is divided into two parts, preferably with the same number of years. (For example, If data is given from 1995 to 2004, i.e., over a period of 10 years, the two equal parts will be each 4 years, i.e., from 1995-1999 and from 2000-2004.) In case of odd no. of years, two equal parts can be made by simply omitting the middle year.
2. After the data have been divided into two parts, (i.e., 1995-1999 and 2000-2004, an average of each part is obtained to get exactly two points).

3. Each point is then plotted at the mid point of the class interval covered by respective part and then the two points are joined by a straight line which gives us the required trend line.

Example:

Year	Sales in Thousands	Total of Four Years	Semi Averages
1995	500		
1996	550		
1997	600	3650	730
1998	800		
1999	1200		
2000	750		
2001	1300		
2002	1500	6900	1380
2003	1650		
2004	1700		

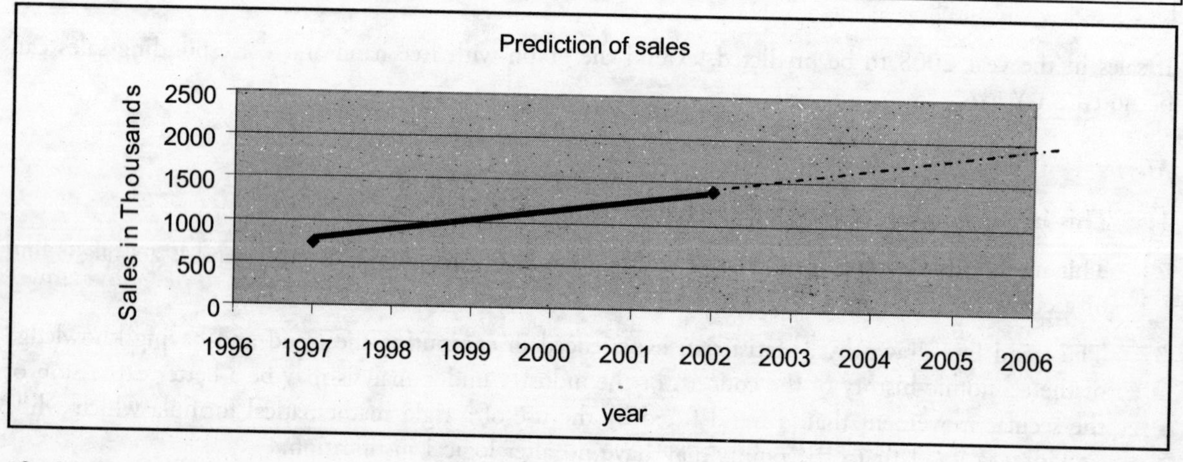

If sales in the year 2006 to be predicted, extend the graph with free hand and corresponding sales can be noted on Y axis.

Merits

1. This method is simple to understand as compared to the moving average and the method of least squares.
2. This is an objective method of measuring trend as everyone who applies the method is bound to get the same result. (having aside the arithmetic mistakes)

Limitations

1. This method assumes straight line relationship between the plotted points regardless of the fact whether that relationship exists or not.
2. The limitations of arithmetic average shall automatically apply. If there are extremes in either half or both the series. Then the trend line will not give a true picture of the growth factor.

Method of Moving-averages

When a trend is to be determined by the method of moving averages, the average value for a number of years (or months or weeks) is secured and this average is taken as the normal or trend value for the unit of time falling at the middle of the period covered in the calculation of the averages. The effect of averaging is to give a smoother curve, lessening the influence of the fluctuations that pull annual figure away from the general trend.

Note: Since the moving average method is most commonly applied to data which are characterized by cyclical movements, it is necessary to select a period for moving average which coincides with the length of the cycle. Otherwise, the cycle will not be entirely removed.

Ordinarily, the necessary period will range between three and ten years for general business series but even longer periods are required for certain types of data.

The 3 yearly moving averages shall be computed as follows:

$$\frac{a+b+c}{3}, \frac{b+c+d}{3}, \frac{c+d+e}{3}, \frac{d+e+f}{3}$$

and for 5-yearly moving average

$$\frac{a+b+c+d+e}{5}, \frac{b+c+d+e+f}{5}, \frac{c+d+e+f+g}{5} + \ldots\ldots$$

Where a,b,c,d,e,—are the data for the given period.

Example: Computation of 4-yearly moving average.

Year	Annual Sales (₹ '000)	4-yearly moving totals	4-yearly moving Average = (3)/4	2-point moving totals of column(4)	4-yearly centered moving average =(5)/2
(1)	(2)	(3)	(4)	(5)	(6)
1992	2	-			
1993	6	-			
		14	3.50		
1994	1			7.25	3.63
		15	3.75		
1995	5			7.25	3.63
		16	4.00		
1996	3			8.25	4.13
		17	4.25		
1997	7			8.75	4.38
		18	4.50		
1998	2			9.25	4.63
		19	4.75		
1999	6			9.75	4.88
		20	5.00		
2000	4			10.25	5.13
		21	5.25		
2001	8	-			
2002	3	-			

Example:

Year	Sales in Thousands	Three years moving Total	Moving Average
1995	500		
1996	550	1650	550
1997	600	1950	650
1998	800	2600	867
1999	1200	2750	917
2000	750	3250	1083
2001	1300	3550	1183
2002	1500	4450	1483
2003	1650	4850	1617
2004	1700		

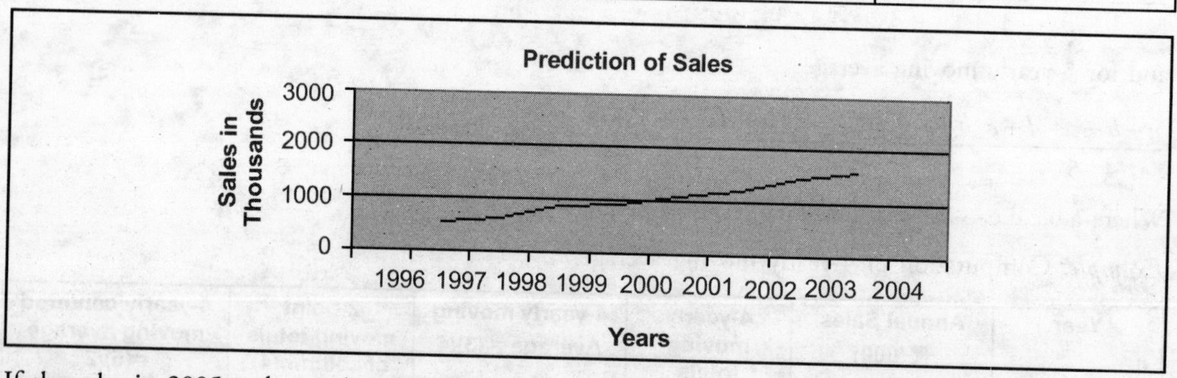

If the sales in 2005 to be predicted, the graph can be extended, and the corresponding value on Y axis is required sales value.

Merits

1. It is simple compared to method of least square.
2. It is a flexible method of measuring trend for the reason that if a few more figures are added to the data, the entire calculations are not changed-we only get some more trend values.
3. If the period of moving average happens to coincide with the period of cycle fluctuations in the data, such fluctuations are automatically eliminated.
4. It is particularly effective if the trend of a series is very irregular.

Limitations

1. Trend values can not be computed for all the years.
2. Great care has to be exercised in selecting the period of moving average.
3. The length of the various cycles in any series will usually vary considerably and therefore no moving average can completely remove the cycle.
4. The moving average is appropriate for trend computation only when:
   (i) The purpose of investigation does not call for current analysis or forecasting.

(ii) The trend is linear, and

(iii) The cyclical variations are regular both in period and amplitudes.

Unfortunately, these conditions are encountered very infrequently.

Centering

If moving average is an even period moving average, moving total are kept at centre of time span. Since the placed would not coincide with original time period, we synchronize moving averages and original data. This centering always consists of taking two period moving average of the moving averages.

Merits

1. Simple as compared to method of least squares.
2. If few more figures are added entire calculations are not changed.
3. It follows general movements of data and its shape is determined by data.
4. Effective when trend is irregular.

Demerits

1. Trend values cannot be computed for all years.
2. One has to use his own judgments for choice of period of averages.
3. Since moving average is not represented by mathematical functions, this method can't be used in forecasting.
4. Appropriate only when trend is linear, cyclical variations are regular both in period and amplitudes.

Method of Least Squares

This method is most widely used in practice. It is a mathematical method and with its help a trend line is fitted to the data in such a manner that the following two conditions are satisfied:

1. $\Sigma(y - y_c) = 0$

   It is the sum of deviations of the actual values of 'y' and the computed values of 'y' is zero.

2. $\Sigma(y - y_c)^2$ = is Least

   That is the sum of squares of the deviations of the actual and computed values is least from this line and hence the name is method of least square. The line obtained by this method is known as the line of best fit.

   The straight line is represented by the equation

   $y_c = a + bx$

   Where y_c is used to designate trend value

   x represents time

   (i) Is the computed trend figure of y variable when x = 0.

(ii) Is the slope of trend line or amount of change in 'y' variable that is associated with a change of one unit in 'x' variable.

In order to determine the values of the constants a and b, the following two normal equations are to be solved.

$$\Sigma y = Na + b\Sigma x \quad \text{(i)}$$

$$\Sigma xy = a\Sigma x + b\Sigma x^2 \quad \text{(ii)}$$

Merits

1. This is a mathematical method of measuring trend and as such there is no possibility of subjectiveness.
2. It is the line from where the sum of positive and negative deviations is zero and the sum of squares of the deviations lead.

   i.e. $\Sigma(y - y_c) = 0$

   i.e. $\Sigma(y - y_c)^2$ least
3. Trend values can be obtained for all the given time periods in the series.

Limitations

1. Great care has to be taken in selecting the type of trend curve to be fitted, i.e., linear, parabolic or some other type.
2. It is more tedious and time consuming than other methods.
3. Predictions are based only on long-term variation, i.e., trend and the impact of cyclical, seasonal and irregular variations is ignored.
4. Being a mathematical method, it is not flexible-the addition of even one more observation makes it necessary to do all the computations again.

Applications

1. Used in different situations like production, sales, exports, imports, etc., by businessmen.
2. Economists use it for forecasting population trends.
3. Avoidance of unfavorable situations based on time series can be done as we can predict (at least to some extent) based on trend so that uncertainty is reduced.
4. Certain seasonal trends help in proportionate production based on trend.
5. Sudden changes in demand, rapid technological progress cannot be known but prediction to certain extent makes it possible for the firm to cope up to the incompetency.

Example:

Year	Production Y	X	XY	X^2	Trend values Y_c
1995	20	–4	–80	16	20.98
1996	22	–3	–66	9	21.54

Contd...

1997	24	–2	–48	4	22.1
1998	21	–1	–21	1	22.66
1999	23	0	0	0	0
2000	25	1	25	1	23.75
2001	23	2	46	4	24.34
2002	26	3	78	9	24.9
2003	25	4	100	16	25.46
N = 9	$\Sigma y = 209$	$\Sigma x = 0$	$\Sigma xy = 34$	$\Sigma x^2 = 60$	$\Sigma y_c = 185.73$

$y_c = a + bX$

$$a = \frac{\Sigma Y}{N} = \frac{209}{9} = 23.22$$

$$b = \frac{\Sigma XY}{\Sigma x^2} = \frac{34}{60} = 0.56$$

$Yc = 23.22 + 0.56X$

Example:

Fit a straight line trend by the method of least squares to the following data. Assuming the same rate of change continues what would be the predicted sales for the year 2009?

Year	2000	2001	2002	2003	2004	2005	2006	2007
Sales (₹ Lakh)	76	80	130	144	138	120	174	190

Calculate trend values from 2000 to 2007 and predict the sales for 2009.

Solution: Fitting straight line trend by the method of least squares.

Year	Sales Y	Deviations from 2003.5 X	XY	X^2	$Y_{c(trend)}$
2000	76	–3.5	–266	12.25	80.16
2001	80	–2.5	–200	6.25	94.83
2002	130	–1.5	–195	2.25	109.5
2003	144	–0.5	–72	0.25	124.2
2004	138	+0.5	69	0.25	138.8
2005	120	+1.5	180	2.25	153.5
2006	174	+2.5	435	6.25	168.2
2007	190	+3.5	665	12.25	182.8
N = 8	$\Sigma y = 1052$	$\Sigma X = 0$	$\Sigma XY = 616$	$\Sigma x^2 = 42$	

$y_c = a + bX$

Since $\Sigma X = 0$

$$a = \frac{\Sigma Y}{N} = \frac{1052}{8} = 131.5$$

$$b = \frac{\Sigma XY}{\Sigma X^2} = \frac{616}{42} = 14.67$$

Y = 131.5 + 14.67X

Y_{2000}=131.5 + 14.67(–3.5) = 131.5 – 51.331 = 80.16

Thus

Y_{2009} = 131.5 + 14.67 (5.5) = 212.163

Thus, the predicted sales for 2009 are ₹ 212.163 lakhs.

REVIEW QUESTIONS

1. What is a time series? Mention its important components. Explain them briefly.
2. What are the advantages of undertaking a time series analysis to a business firm?
3. Suppose we are given a time series data for 12 years–1989 to 2000, relating to sales of a certain business firm. These data are given below.

Year	Sales (Million ₹)	Year	Sales (Million ₹)
1989	10	1995	15
1990	15	1996	24
1991	20	1997	15
1992	25	1998	21
1993	15	1999	15
1994	12	2000	24

You are asked to find out the three-year moving averages, starting from 1989.

4. Find 4 yearly moving averages and comment.

Year	Income (₹)	Year	Income (₹)
1988	15,005	1995	34,790
1989	21,568	1996	56,879
1990	34,521	1997	59,900
1991	45,566	1998	67,943
1992	35,690	1999	56,821
1993	40,523	2000	65,789
1994	27,956	2001	58,932

5. Fit a straight line trend by the method of least squares for the following and draw it on the graph paper.

Year	Reserves	Year	Reserves
2000-01	612	2004-05	1001
2001-02	719	2005-06	1106
2002-03	820	2006-07	1231
2003-04	907		

6. Calculate the three-monthly moving averages from the following data:

January	February	March	April	May	June
57	65	63	72	69	78
July	Aug.	Sep.	Oct.	Nov.	Dec.
82	81	90	92	95	97

7. Given below are the figures of production (in million tonnes) of wheat:

Year	2000	2001	2002	2003	2004	2005	2006
Production	80	90	92	83	94	99	92

Fit a straight-line trend to these figures.

8. The following data refer to annual profits of a certain business.

Year	2000	2001	2002	2003	2004	2005	2006
Profits ₹ '000	60	72	75	65	80	85	95

Find the trend values using the linear trend method. Using the trend equation, estimate the profit for 2010.

9. Assuming an additive model, apply 3-year moving averages to obtain the trend-free series for years 2 to 6 from the following data.

Year	1	2	3	4	5	6	7
Exports (₹ lakh)	126	130	137	141	145	155	159

CHAPTER FIFTEEN

STATISTICAL PACKAGE FOR THE SOCIAL SCIENCES (SPSS)

"*...The opportunity for the application of this kind of technology has barely broken the surface of the places where the technology should and could be applied to increase the effectiveness of almost everything organizations do.*"

— **Jack Noonan**
Chairman, President, and CEO
SPSS Inc.

INTRODUCTION

SPSS is a computer application that provides statistical analysis of data. It allows for in-depth data access and preparation, analytical reporting, graphics and modelling.

SPSS (originally, Statistical Package for the Social Sciences) is a software program developed in the late 1960s by graduate students at Stanford University. Although initially created to manage a large survey research project of citizen participation in seven nations, the package quickly gained popularity, and was greatly enhanced over the next few years. In 1985, a microcomputer version of SPSS for IIBM-compatible personal computers was introduced, which included many of the most popular features of the mainframe version of SPSS. Today, there are more than one million users of SPSS in academic, business, government, and non-profit organizations.

SPSS

The primary use of SPSS in educational settings is for data analysis about people, their attitudes and behaviours. SPSS is mainly used by Political Science, Communication, Sociology, Social Work and Psychology departments.

SPSS is the data analysis package of choice for people wanting to analyze quantitative data. However, most researchers find dealing with quantitative data quite daunting. Although most researchers are quite comfortable with qualitative research methods and analyses, they tend to shy away from using quantitative statistics. However, the ability to perform quantitative data analysis is increasingly becoming an important skill for researchers to possess. Actually most people's fear of statistics is unfounded. The advent of computer software programmes such as SPSS that can be used to analyze data, has meant that people do not have to know or learn mathematical formulae in order to be able to perform quantitative statistical analyses. Nowadays, all one needs to know is the appropriate analyses to perform on their data and how to do it so they can obtain the information they need to know.

Knowledge of SPSS is useful because:

1. SPSS is a leader in the field of market research and social surveys.
2. It has been in the forefront of these fields for over 40 years.
3. It is a very powerful piece of software that will enable you to carry out quantitative analysis in seconds.
4. You can legitimately see it as an extension or complement to Excel.
5. It is easier to use than other packages when it comes to handling large datasets.
6. It may help you get a job in the job market.

❖ SPSS for Windows

SPSS for Windows is a comprehensive, interactive, general-purpose package for data analysis and it includes most routine statistical techniques. SPSS is a true Windows package being mouse-driven with movable, scalable windows, drop-down menus and dialog boxes. Underlying the graphical interface is a command language consistent with previous versions of the package. A very important and useful feature is the Data Editor, which can be used to enter, view or edit data. The Data Editor makes your data immediately visible so that you can see what you are dealing with. The package also has high-resolution graphics which are easily edited and an extensive help system.

SPSS for Windows is probably one of the easiest major statistics package to use. It allows even inexperienced users to run complicated statistical analyses at the click of a few buttons. When you are at the PC, you are in charge of the package and it will attempt to do whatever you ask it, whether your instructions are sensible or not. The adage of garbage in, garbage out applies. It is, therefore, essential that you get a good understanding of the commands that you need to use and what the results mean.

SPSS for Windows provides a powerful statistical analysis and data management system in a graphical environment, using descriptive menus and simple dialog boxes to do most of the tasks for you. Simply pointing and clicking the mouse can accomplish most tasks. SPSS for Windows provides three interfaces for statistical analysis. The following are the various versions of SPSS developed over a period of time.

SPSS 17.0 for Windows consists of these modules

1. Statistics Base
2. Regression
3. Advanced Statistics
4. Custom Tables
5. Complex Samples
6. Decision Trees
7. Data Preparation
8. Categories
9. Conjoint
10. Exact Tests

11. RFM (Recency, Frequency and Monitoring)
12. Forecasting
13. Missing Values
14. Adapter for
15. Predictive Enterprise Services
16. Neural Networks
17. AMOS (Analysis of Moment Structures)

Added to SPSS 16.0

1. Mac and Linux versions of SPSS
2. Several multithreaded procedures for improved performance and scalability
3. In the Data Editor: ability to customize variable view
4. In the Data Editor: spell checking for value labels and variable labels
5. In the Data Editor: ability to sort by variable name, type, format, etc.
6. Unicode support
7. Import/export Excel 2007 data
8. Syntax to change string length and basic data type of existing variables
9. Creation of value labels and missing values on strings of any length
10. Ability to set a permanent default working directory
11. SPSS Neural Networks add-on module
12. Complex Samples Cox Regression added to SPSS Complex Samples
13. Latent Class Analysis in AMOS
14. Partial Least Squares regression
15. Support for R algorithms
16. Find and Replace feature in the Output Viewer

Added to SPSS 15.0

1. SPSS Adapter for SPSS Predictive Enterprise Services
2. Updated PMML to include transformations
3. Single administration utility for SPSS Server, Clementine Server, and SPSS Predictive Enterprise Services platform
4. Stripe temporary files over multiple disks for increased performance (in SPSS Server)
5. Export to Database Wizard
6. Custom Attributes for user-defined meta data in the SPSS Data Editor

7. Export to Dimensions Data Model
8. Optimal Binning (in SPSS Data Preparation™; this add-on module was previously called SPSS Data Validation)
9. Subset variable views
10. Python® programming language included on the SPSS CD (in SPSS Programmability Extension)
11. Ability to create first-class, user-defined procedures (in SPSS Programmability Extension)
12. Syntax control of output files (in SPSS Programmability Extension)
13. Generalized linear models (in SPSS Advanced Models)
14. Generalized estimating equations (in SPSS Advanced Models)
15. Ordinal regression to model ordinal outcomes
16. Complex samples ordinal regression (in SPSS Complex Samples)
17. Estimation and imputation of ordered-categorical and censored data (in AMOS 7.0 structural equation modeling software)
18. Dual-Y axis and overlay charts
19. Enhanced process control charts
20. Export output to PDF (in SPSS Base)
21. Data-free client (in SPSS Server)

Added to SPSS 14.0

1. Data-free client (in SPSS Server)
2. User Interface (UI) for scoring (in SPSS Server)
3. Predictor selection algorithm (in SPSS Server)
4. Naïve Bayes algorithm (in SPSS Server)
5. Clone dataset command
6. Open multiple datasets within a single SPSS session
7. Long value labels (upto 120 bytes)
8. Read/write Stata® files
9. Support for Dimensions Data Model™ and traditional market research software
10. OLE DB data access
11. Control the flow of your syntax jobs using third-party programming languages (through SPSS Programmability Extension)
12. Validate Data procedure (in SPSS Data Validation™)
13. Anomaly detection for multivariate outliers (in SPSS Data Validation)
14. Enhanced SPSS Trends™ add-on module with Expert Modeler

15. Bayesian estimation-MCMC algorithm (in AMOS™ 6.0 structural equation modeling software)
16. Data imputation, including multiple imputation (in AMOS 6.0 structural equation modeling software)
17. Run significance tests on multiple response variables (in SPSS Tables™)
18. Exclude categories used in sub-total calculations from significance tests (in SPSS Tables)
19. Preference scaling (PREFSCAL) procedure; syntax only (in SPSS Categories™)
20. Chart Builder user interface for graphics
21. Support for SPSS Inc.'s Graphics Production Language (GPL)
22. 2-D line charts and charts for multiple response sets
23. Network license reservations and priority settings
24. Network commuter license # License manager redundancy

Added to SPSS 13.0

1. In-database data preparation (sort and aggregate) to improve performance (SPSS Server only)
2. Create and save PMML models for scoring data at a later time (SPSS Server only)
3. Date and Time Wizard
4. Very long text strings (upto 32,767 bytes)
5. Interactive interface for the Output Management System (OMS)
6. Complex samples General Linear Model (GLM) (in SPSS Complex Samples add-on module)
7. Complex samples logistic regression (in SPSS Complex Samples add-on module)
8. SPSS Classification Trees™ add-on module
9. Multiple correspondence analysis (in SPSS Categories™ add-on module)
10. Population pyramids (also called mirror charts or dual charts), 3-D bar charts, and dot charts (also called dot density charts)
11. Additional chart display features/options, including paneled charts and error bars on categorical charts
12. Export output to Microsoft Power Point

Added to SPSS Base 12.0

1. 64-bit version of SPSS Server (coming soon)
2. Identify Duplicate Cases tool
3. Long variable names (upto 64 bytes)
4. Multithreaded ODBC (in SPSS Server)
5. Output Management System (turn pivot table output, such as SPSS data files, XML, and HTML into data/input)

6. Presentation graphics system
7. SPSS Complex Samples add-on module
8. SPSS Manuals on CD, featuring manuals in PDF format for SPSS Base and all add-on modules
9. Step-wise Multinomial Regression (in SPSS Regression Models add-on module)
10. Support for Open SSL
11. Visual Bander to easily create bands (e.g., break income into income "bands" of 10,000)

Added to SPSS Base 11.5

1. Export data to recent versions of Excel® and SAS®
2. Enhanced SPSS Tables™ add-on module
3. Export output to Excel
4. Export output to Word
5. Switch output language
6. Data prep tools to get your data ready for analysis

Added to SPSS Base 11.0

1. Support for communication between SPSS for Windows and SPSS Server
2. Restructure Data Wizard
3. Descriptive ratio statistics
4. Improved scalability and performance of Multinomial Logistic Regression (completed in version 10.1 in SPSS Regression Models module)
5. Improved scalability and performance of Proximities and Hierarchical Cluster Analysis (completed in SPSS 10.1)
6. Linear mixed models (a.k.a. Hierarchical Linear Models; in SPSS Advanced Models™ module)
7. Per cent change in OLAP Cubes
8. Online case studies

Added to SPSS Base 10.0

1. Each module on the desktop has a related module server available (for SPSS Server)
2. Conversion-free/copy-free data access in SQL DBMS (in SPSS Server)
3. Data stays on server, which is where procedures run (in SPSS Server)
4. Download data only if you want to (in SPSS Server)
5. SPSS client can be used with all licensed SPSS Servers
6. Actively manage temp file consolidation
7. Direct Excel interface

8. Large file capability
9. New flexible Data Editor
10. Read recent SAS files
11. Ability to run multiple SPSS sessions at one time and switch sessions
12. CATPCA and PROXSCAL (in SPSS Categories™ add-on module)
13. PLUM (in SPSS Advanced Models add-on module)
14. SPSS Maps™ add-on module
15. XML file export for model deployment with SmartScore

Added to SPSS Base 9.0

1. Text Wizard
2. Multinomial logistic regression (in SPSS Regression Models add-on module)
3. Reliability and ALSCAL Multidimensional Scaling and matrix operations (in SPSS Base)
4. ROC (Receiver-Operating Characteristic) analysis
5. Customization options: secondary axis, reference lines, hiding and reordering categories, specifying min/max values from dialog box, spikes
6. IGRAPH Scripting
7. Table to graph

Added to SPSS Base 8.0

1. Long variable labels in dialogs
2. Chart Looks
3. Chart rotation and lighting controls
4. *Chart types:* ribbon, error bar on bar chart, plotted pie, true 3-D bar and true 3-D pie
5. Interactive chart types: stacked bar, area and multiple response
6. IGRAPH (Interactive graphs)
7. Draft Viewer/Text output and control
8. Layered Reports/OLAP cubes
9. Results Coach™

Added to SPSS Base 7.0

1. 256 character-length labels
2. Customizable toolbar
3. Database Wizard
4. Cluster analysis (in SPSS Base)

5. Discriminant analysis (in SPSS Base)
6. Factor analysis (in SPSS Base)
7. GLM (in SPSS Advanced Models add-on module)
8. Varcomp (in Advanced Models add-on module)
9. HTML output
10. Output Navigator/Viewer
11. Pivot tables/Report cubes
12. Output scripting programming in BASIC
13. TableLooks
14. Statistical Coach

❖ SPSS Products

SPSS is used by market researchers, health researchers, survey companies, government, education researchers, marketing organizations and others. In addition to statistical analysis, data management (case selection, file reshaping, creating derived data) and data documentation (a metadata dictionary is stored with the data) are features of the base software.

❖ SPSS Base

Data access, manipulation, analysis, and presentation of your results. It includes extensive on-line help and tutorial sessions. Base includes all the data management and graphing facilities and the following analysis procedures which include the following:

1. ***Descriptive statistics:*** Cross tabulation, Frequencies, Descriptives, Explore, Descriptive Ratio Statistics
2. ***Bivariate statistics:*** Means, t-test, ANOVA, Correlation (bivariate, partial, distances), Nonparametric tests
3. ***Prediction for numerical outcomes:*** Correlation, Linear regression
4. ***Prediction for identifying groups:*** Factor analysis, Cluster analysis (two-step, K-means, hierarchical), Discriminant

Broadly, it consists of Reports, Frequencies, Descriptives, Explore, Crosstabs, Descriptive ratio statistics, Means-tests, Oneway ANOVA, ANOVA – two way, Correlate, Distances, Linear regression, Curve estimation, Nonparametric tests, Multiple response, Factor analysis, Two-Step cluster analysis, Cluster, Quick cluster, Discriminant analysis, Multidimensional scaling.

❖ SPSS Regression Models

Predict behaviour or events when your data go beyond the assumptions of simpler regression techniques with the following analysis procedures which include the following:

Multinomial logistic regression, Binary logistic regression, On-linear regression, Weighted least squares, Two-stage least squares, Probit regression.

❖ SPSS Advanced Models

Analyzing complex relationships with high-end modeling procedures which include the following:

Generalized linear models, Generalized estimating equations, Mixed modeling, General linear models with random or mixed effects, Repeated measures ANOVA, Variance components analysis, Loglinear analysis, Hierarchical loglinear analysis, Generalized linear loglinear and logit modeling, Survival analysis, Kaplan-Meier analysis, Cox regression.

❖ SPSS Categories

It creates perceptual maps and predicts categories. Optimal scaling procedures free you from the restrictions of two-way tables, placing the relationships among your variables in a larger frame of reference. See a map of your data not just a statistical report. Includes the following analysis procedures:

1. Categorical regression, Correspondence analysis, Multiple correspondence analysis
2. Categorical principal components analysis, Non-linear canonical correlation analysis
3. Multidimensional scaling, Preference scaling, Conjoint.

Business intelligence has become order of the day. In the highly competitive environment, organizations are generating large volumes of data internally and externally which require processing and analysis for effective decision-making in business. Using SPSS software package, the following statistical tools can be applied for effective data analysis and interpretation in business and management research.

1. Descriptive Statistics (frequency distributions, Charts and Graphs, Normal curve, Cross Tabulation, Central tendency, Measures of Dispersion)
2. Questionnaire design
3. Bivariate association (correlation, regression analysis)
4. Hypothesis testing (Parametric – large sample tests, small sample tests, ANOVA and Nonparametric tests, Chi-square Tests, Sign tests, Mann-Whitney U, Wilcoxon Matched-pairs Tests, Kruskal Wallis, McNemar)
5. Multivariate Techniques (Multiple Regression, Discriminant, ANOVA, Conjoint, Factor, Cluster analysis, Multidimensional scaling)
6. Log-linear Analysis
7. Forecasting Models
8. Probability Distribution (Normal, Binomial, Poisson)
9. Multifactorial Analysis of Variance
10. Repeated-measures Analysis of Variance

List of other statistical packages:

(i) EViews – For econometric analysis

(ii) GLIM – Early package for fitting generalized linear models

(iii) JMP – General statistics package

(iv) LISREL – Statistics package used in structural equation modeling

(v) Minitab – General statistics package

(vi) RATS – Comprehensive econometric analysis package

(vii) SAS – Comprehensive statistical package

(viii) STATISTICA – Comprehensive statistics package

(ix) Systat – General statistics package.

EXAMPLES ON SPSS WINDOWS

❖ Data Types

Before data are analysed in SPSS, it is necessary to understand the type of data as this will affect the analysis used.

Categorical: Categorical data consists of values which cannot be expressed numerically but can be grouped into categories; for example, gender which can be grouped into male and female.

Quantifiable: Quantifiable data consists of values that can be expressed numerically as quantities; for example, year of birth. Quantifiable data can further be sub-divided into two groups:

Discrete, where individual items of numeric data can have one of a finite number of values within a specified range; such as spinal column point for the variable salary scale. The value can usually be counted and it changes in discrete units, in this case whole numbers. In some instances discrete data may be rank data, for example, the order a group of people finished in a race.

Continuous, where numeric data is not restricted to specific values and is usually measured on a continuous scale; such as journey to work distance (in km).

0km Journey to work distance along here 120 km

With such data, it is possible to tell the interval between the data values for different cases; for example, the interval between a journey to work of 15 miles and another of 22 miles is 7 miles.

SPSS data are usually coded numerically (e.g. 1 = male). Although it appears less meaningful to code such responses numerically, it is better from a data manipulation point of view since SPSS allows only automatic recoding on codes which are numeric.

Example 1: To load SPSS

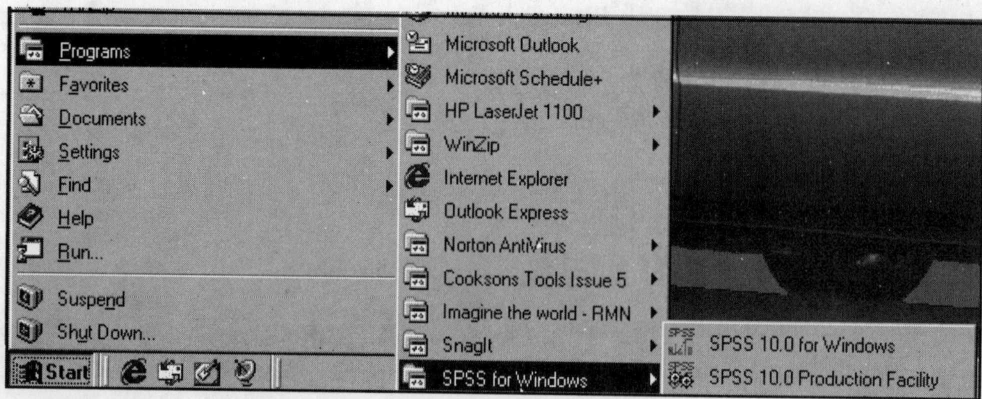

Click on the SPSS option to load and run SPSS. You may get a screen that looks like this:

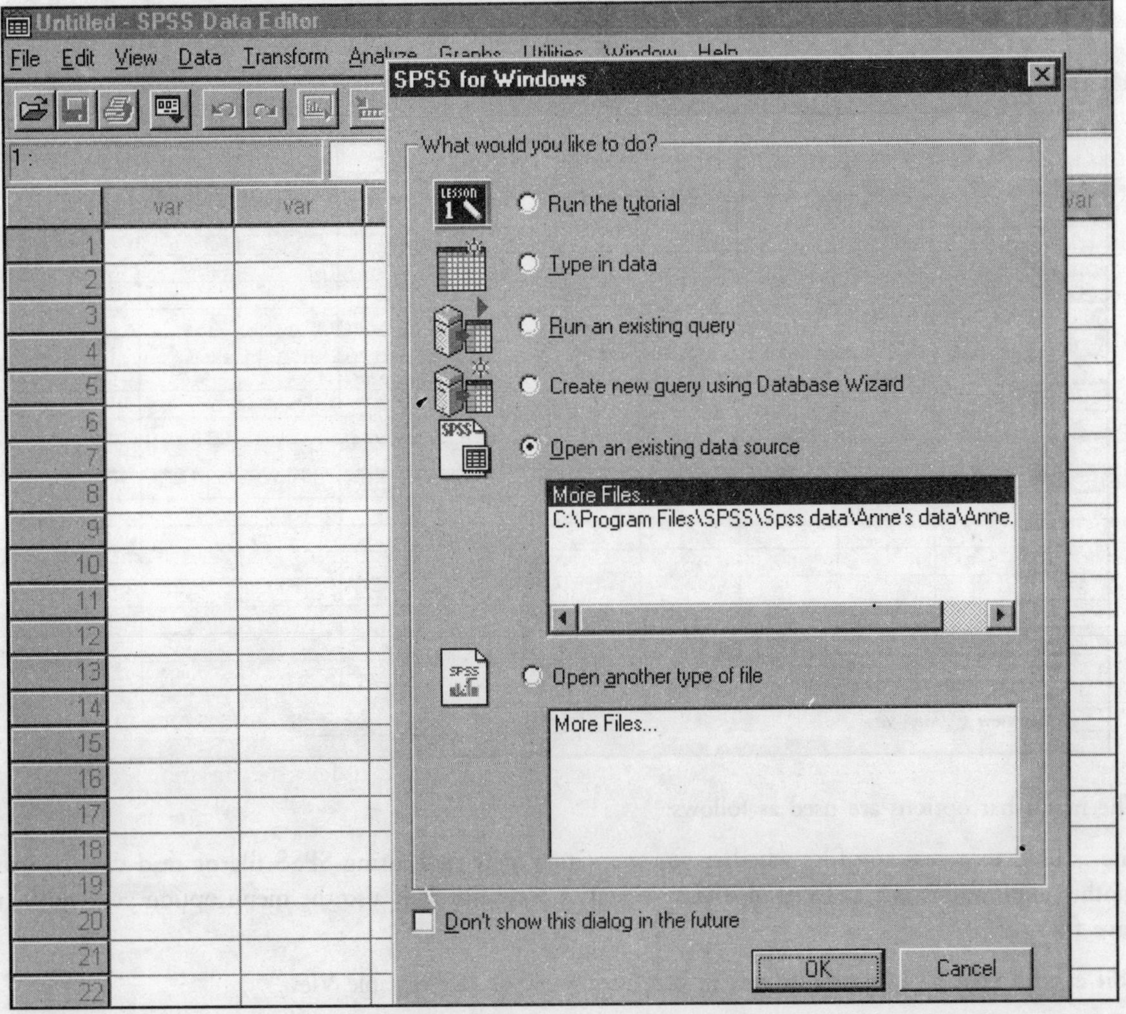

If you do, click on the cancel button at the bottom of the dialogue box to remove it. You will see Untitled SPSS Data Editor screen.

When you load and run the SPSS package it opens up a menu bar and two views. These are the Data View (currently visible) and the Variable View.

Menu Bar: This provides a selection of options (File, Edit, View, Data.....) which allow you to open files, edit data, generate graphs, create tables and perform statistical analyses. Selecting from this menu bar will, like in other windows packages, provide further pull-down menus and dialogue boxes.

Data View: This sheet contains your data (once you have entered it!), each column representing a variable for which data are available and each row representing that data for an individual or case. At present, this sheet should be blank. As this sheet is currently selected its name on the tab at the bottom is in bold.

Variable View: At present, this sheet is not visible as the variable view sheet is not active. Consequently, the name is not in bold. Don't bother to look click on the tab and look at this sheet yet, we will do that later.

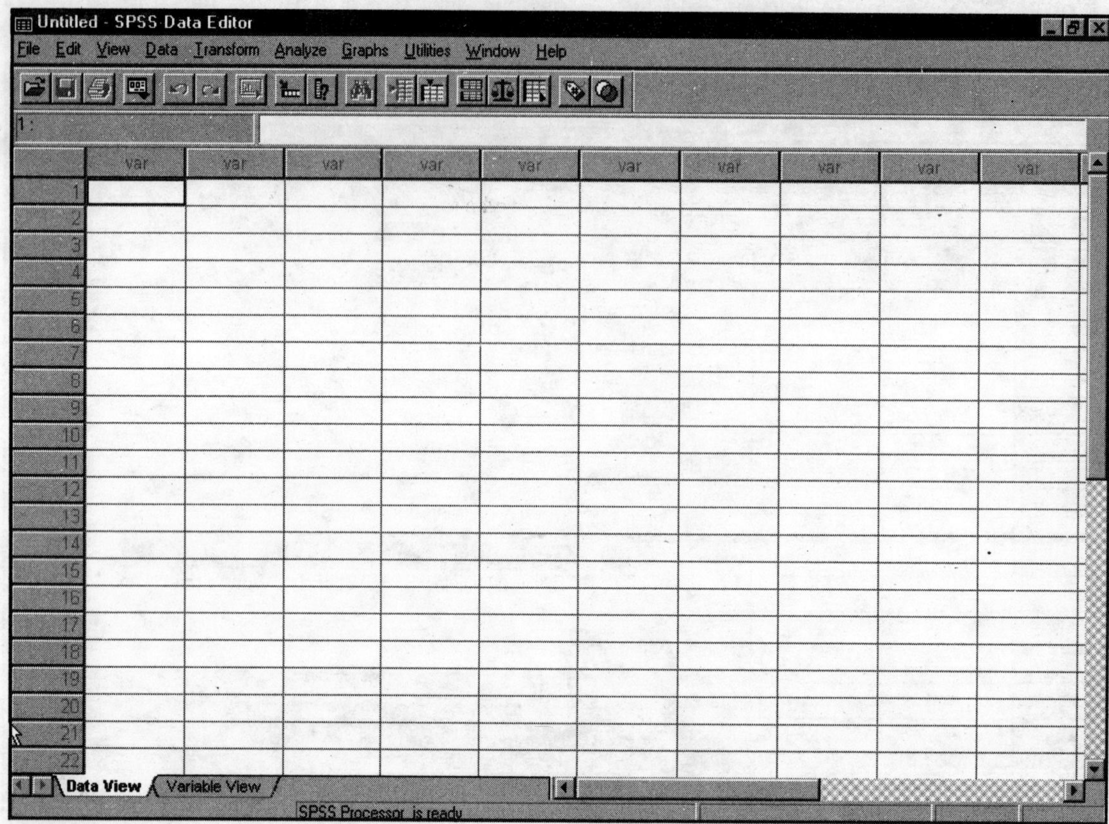

The menu bar options are used as follows:

File is used to access any files whether you want to **Open** an existing SPSS file or read data in from another application such as Excel of dBase, or start a **New** file. It is also the menu option you choose to **Save** files.

Edit can be used to alter data or text in the Data View or the Variable View.

View can be used to alter the way your screen looks. Please leave this on the default settings.

Data is used to define variables and make changes to the data file you are using.

Transform is used to make changes to selected variable(s) in the data file you are using. This can include recode(ing) existing variables and compute(ing) new variables.

Analyze is used to undertake a variety of analyses such as producing Reports, Calculating Descriptive Statistics such as Frequencies and Crosstabs (crosstabulations) and associated summary statistics, as well as various statistical procedures such as Regression and Correlation.

Graph is used to create a variety of graphs and charts such as Bar, Line and Pie charts.

Utilities are for more general housekeeping such as changing display options and fonts, displaying information on variables.

Window operates in the same way as other Windows packages.

Help is a context sensitive help feature which operates the same way as other Windows packages.

Enter the data in the SPSS data editor after creating variables. Then save the files as TEACH which will be saved as TEACH.SAV

You will now see the file appear in the Data View and the filename above the menu bar change to TEACH.SAV

TEACH.SAV - SPSS Data Editor

File Edit View Data Transform Analyze Graphs Utilities Window Help

1 : gender 2

	gender	born	marital	educate	profmemb	prevemp	preveast	prevnor	appleast	applnor
1	2	60	2	5	3	3	530	179	620	128
2	2	47	2	.	3	5	.	.	620	128
3	2	57	2	5	3	3	576	156	626	126
4	2	67	1	5	3	4	.	.	608	109
5	1	19	.	7	3	9	.	.	608	115
6	2	24	2	7	3	9	.	.	380	107
7	2	58	2	7	3	5	.	.	626	126
8	1	69	1	4	3	4	.	.	614	151
9	.	60	2	4	3	5	.	.	620	127
10	1	42	2	5	1	3	566	149	626	126
11	1	67	1	4	3	4	.	.	620	128

Example 2: To check how variables have been coded.

To check what the column heading for each variable and the codes refer to.

Click on the Variable View sheet at the bottom of the screen. You will now see:

	Name	Type	Width	Decimals	Label	Values	Missing	Columns	
1	gender	Numeric	4	0	Gender of Emp	{1, Male}...	0	8	R
2	born	Numeric	4	0	Year of Birth	None	0	8	R
3	marital	Numeric	4	0	Marital Status	{1, Single}	0	8	R

The first column contains the variable Name, in the case of the first row "gender". This is the column heading that appears in the Data View.

The second column refers to the Type of data. Although gender is categorical data, it is referred to as numeric because numeric code values have been used. The key to these code values is given in the column headed Values.

The fifth column contains the variable's Label. At present, this is partially obscured by the subsequent column. To see the full value label:

1. Move your mouse pointer in-between the Label and the Values column headings so that the ✥ appears.
2. Click and drag the column width to the right until the variable's label can be read.

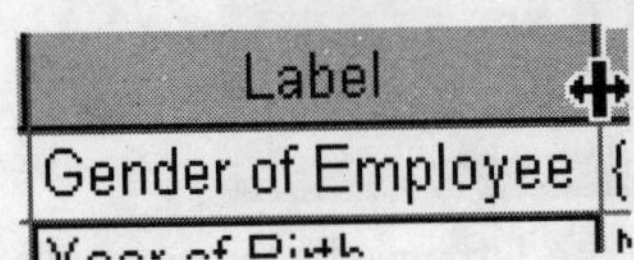

Note: If you wish to edit a variable's label just retype the label in the appropriate cell.

The sixth column contains the key to the codes used for each variable. These are known as the Values Labels.

To see the Value Labels used:

(i) Click on the cell containing the first value for the variable gender {1, Male}...

(ii) Click on the ... to the right of this cell.

The following dialogue box will be displayed:

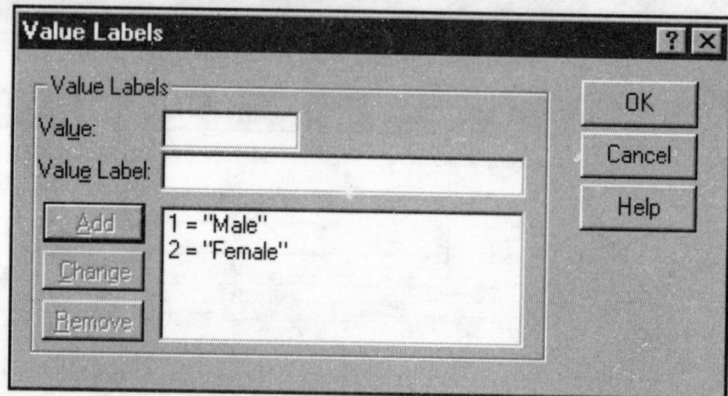

It shows the current value labels for this variable.

Note: You can also use this option to change each value label for the codes or enter new value labels.

Example 3: Frequency distribution.

Return to the Data View.

Click on Analyse then Descriptive Statistics then Frequencies.

This will usually give the Frequencies dialogue box. However, sometimes the variables in the left hand box are arranged alphabetically.

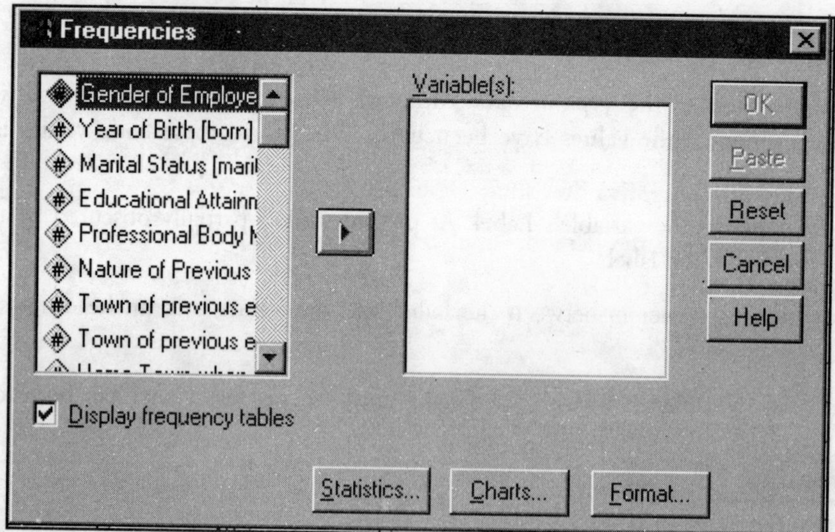

If the variables are arranged alphabetically use the downward arrow on the left hand box to scroll down until gender appears.

Highlight gender in the left hand box by clicking on it. Click on the button to move gender into the Variable(s) box and then click on OK.

You will now see a series of tables displayed in the SPSS Output Viewer. Note how SPSS first tells you if there are any missing cases. For this variable there is one missing case.

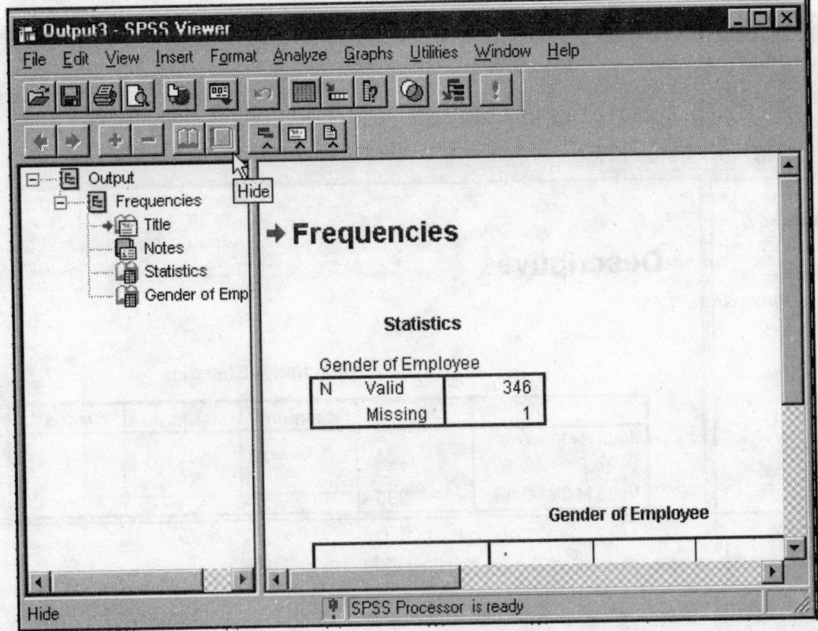

To save the contents of the SPSS Output Viewer to a file

1. Ensure that the SPSS Output Viewer window is maximised.
2. Click on File, Save as.
3. Type in the filename you wish to save it to in the File name box, making sure the file type is *.spo.
4. Ensure that the file is being saved to the correct drive and directory (N.B. please don't save output from the teach.sav file).
5. Click on the Save button.

Example 4: Calculate the arithmetic mean (average) and the standard deviation.

1. Click on Analyze, Descriptive Statistics, Descriptives
2. Scroll down to and select the jtowork variable (its at the end of the variable list), then click on the right arrow to put it in the Variable(s) box as shown below:

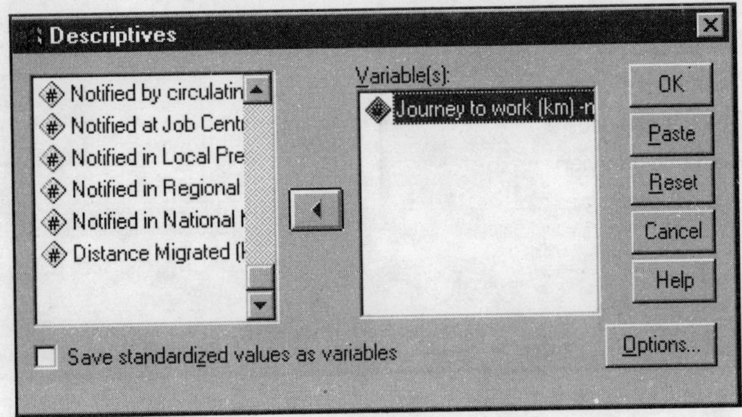

3. Click on the OK button.
4. Note how the results are added to the end of your output in the SPSS Viewer.

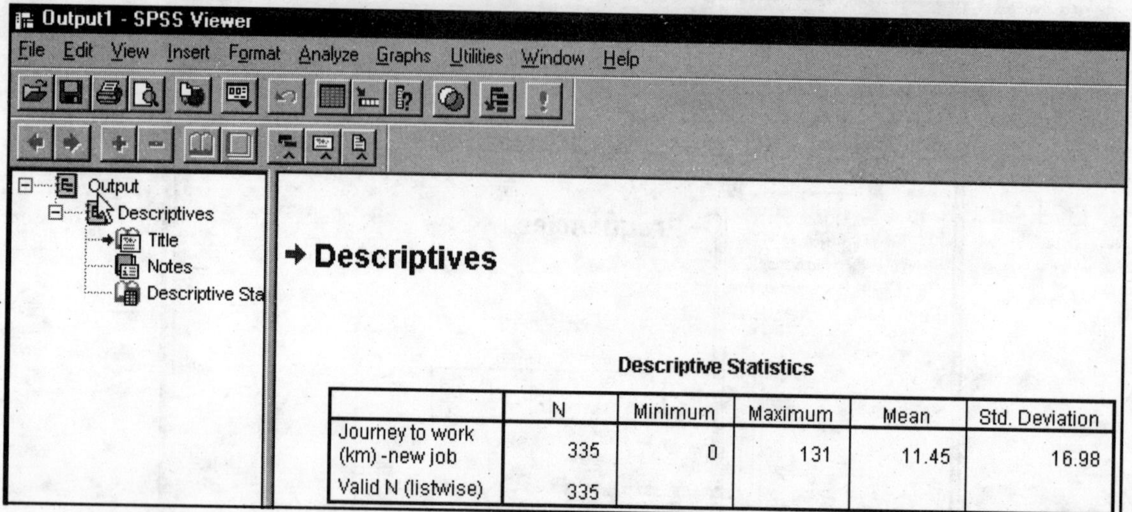

	N	Minimum	Maximum	Mean	Std. Deviation
Journey to work (km) -new job	335	0	131	11.45	16.98
Valid N (listwise)	335				

We can, therefore, see that the mean journey to work is 11.45 km.

We can also calculate the mean gender in the same way. SPSS would take the codes for male (1) and female (2), add them all up and divide by the number of observations. It is, therefore, important that you decide what statistic makes sense for the type of data.

To calculate the mode and other measures of central tendency.

To calculate the mode for the variable gender:

1. Click on Analyze, Descriptive Statistics, Frequencies.
2. Click on the reset button to empty the Variable(s) box.
3. Select gender, then click on the right arrow to put it in the Variable(s) box as shown below:

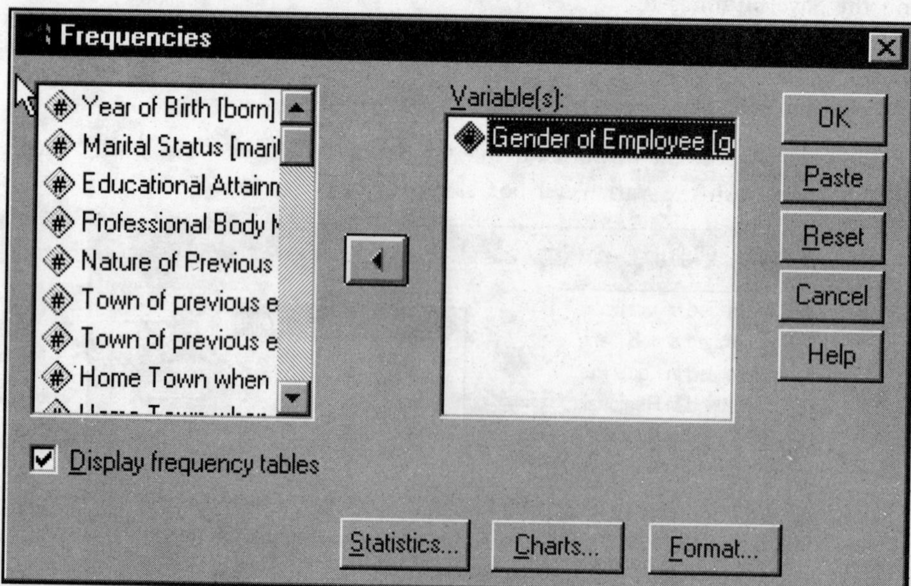

4. Click on the statistics button at the bottom and select Mode in the Central Tendency dialogue box by clicking on it.
5. Click on the continue button to return to the frequencies dialogue box.
6. This time we do not want an output table so click on the box to the left of Display frequency tables to remove the X.

7. Click on OK in the frequencies dialogue box.

   The following will be added to the SPSS Output Viewer

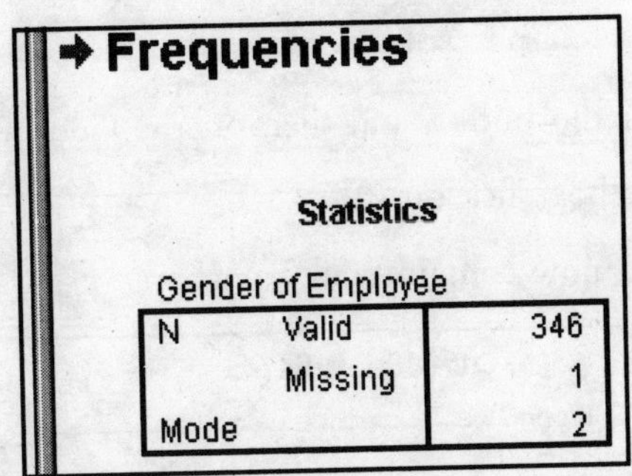

We now know that the most common gender is 2 female.

Repeat this process by calculating the most appropriate average for the following variables:

educate	Prevemp
seg	Class
Salary	three others of your choice

Choices for the most appropriate average are:

1. ***Mean:*** Normally known as the average of the data values.
2. ***Median:*** The mid point once all the data values have been ranked.
3. ***Mode:*** The data value that occurs most often.

Example 5: To produce a bar chart.

1. Click on Analyze, Descriptive Statistics, Frequencies.
2. Deselect all variables by clicking on the Reset button.
3. Scroll down and select the variable social class in the normal way.

4. Click on the charts button, you will see the following dialogue box:

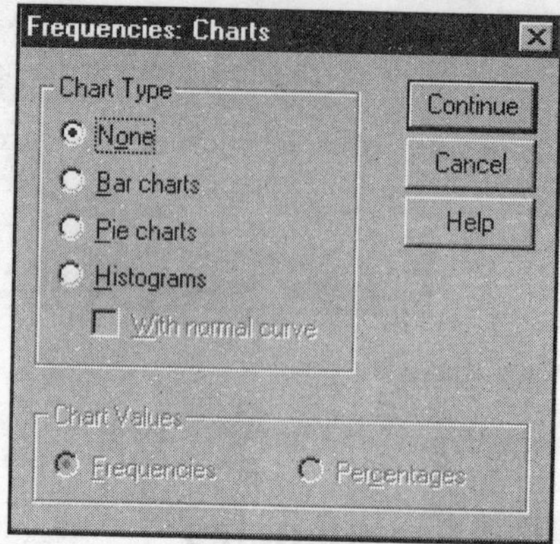

5. Click on the Bar Chart(s) radio button and then on the Continue button.
6. At the Frequencies dialogue box click on OK.

The SPSS Output Viewer should now contain your bar chart.

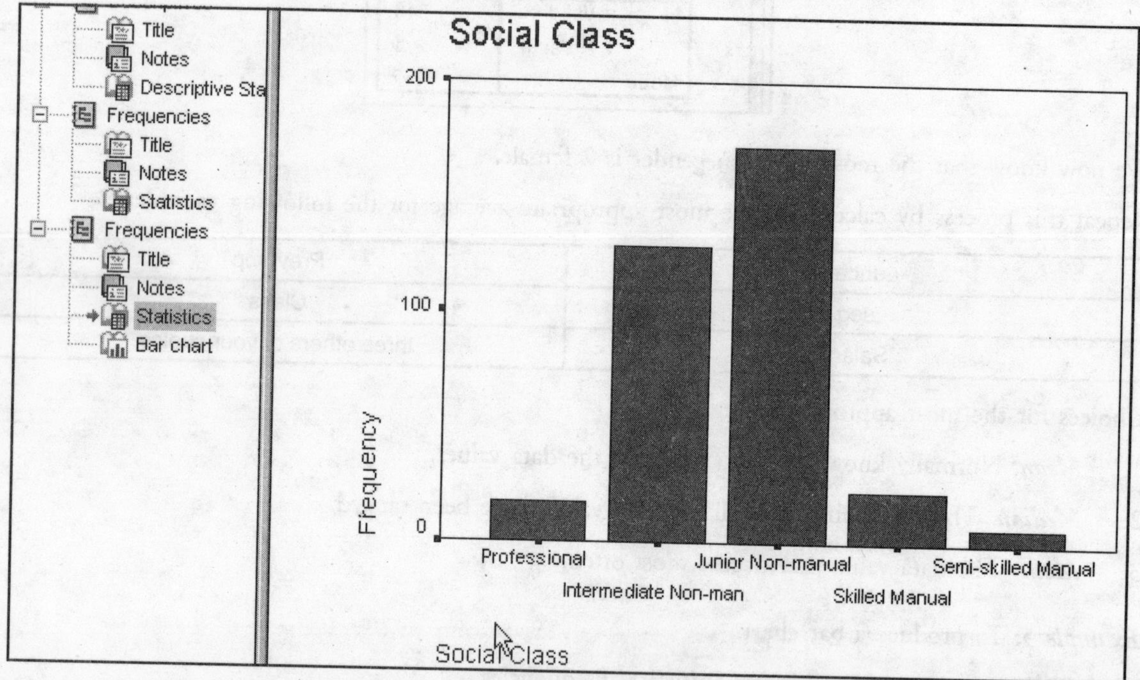

Notice that missing data are automatically excluded from the chart. Notice also that you are presented with a different menu bar which allows you to Edit the current chart and other options such as Delete.

Example 6: To create a table (crosstab) of one variable against another.

One of the most useful features of SPSS is its ability to create cross-tabulations of one variable against another.

You will now create a table of the variable educational attainment by the variable gender. You want your table to look like this:

	male	**female**
postgrad plus		
up to degree		
up to HNC/D		
up to A'level		
up to O'level (GCSE C+)		
up to CSE (GCSE D-)		
No quals.		

1. Click on Analyze, Descriptive Statistics, Crosstabs, this gives the dialogue box:

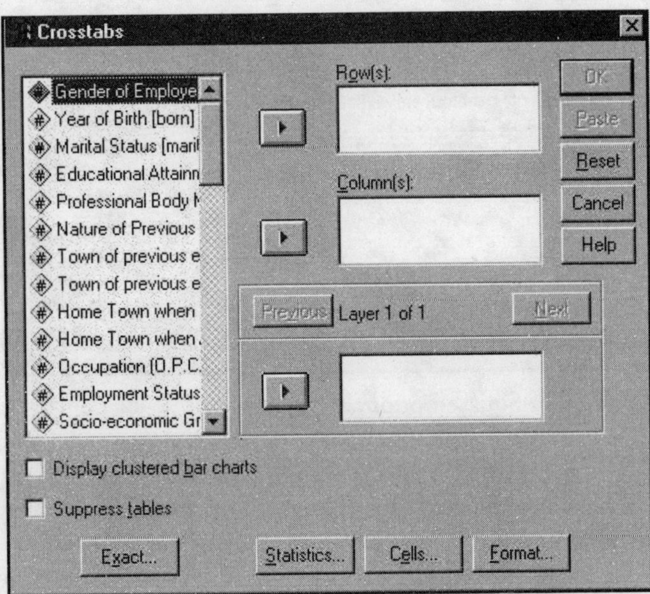

2. Select the Row(s) variable educational attainment and the Column(s) variable gender using the same principles as when selecting frequencies (hint: click on the variable and use the appropriate right arrow).
3. Once a row and a column variable have been selected you will be able to click on OK.
4. Your table will appear in the SPSS Output Viewer.

Educational Attainment * Gender of Employee Crosstabulation

Count

		Gender of Employee		
		Male	Female	Total
Educational Attainment	Postgraduate Study	11	7	18
	Up to Degree Level	17	9	26
	Up to H.N.C. / D or Diploma	27	5	32
	Up to A level	23	21	44
	Up to O level	42	57	99
	Up to C.S.E.	2	16	18
	No educational qualifications stated	23	72	95
Total		145	187	332

Example 7: Calculate a chi-square statistic for a table.

1. Click on Analyze, Descriptive Statistics, Crosstabs.
2. Select the Row(s) variable educational attainment and the Column(s) variable gender using the same principles as when selecting frequencies.
3. Click on the statistics button, a dialogue box will appear:

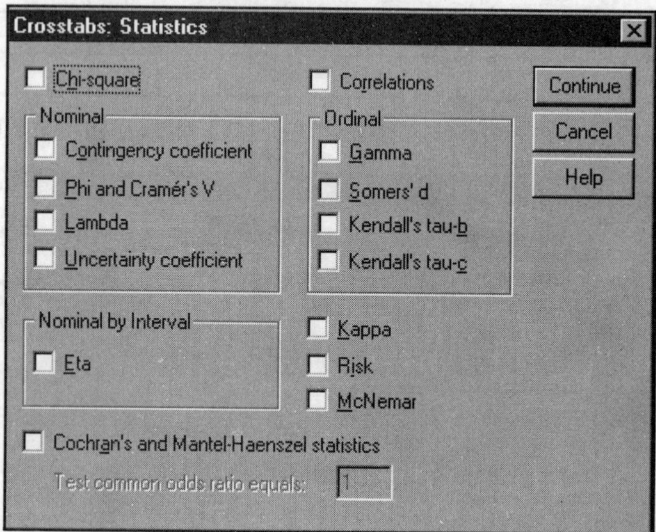

4. Click on the box to the Chi-Square option.
5. Click on Continue, OK.

SPSS will now calculate a chi-square statistic for the table you specified, placing the output at the end of the SPSS Output Viewer.

Chi-Square Tests

	Value	df	Asymp. Sig. (2-sided)
Pearson Chi-Square	52.529[a]	6	.000
Likelihood Ratio	55.996	6	.000
Linear-by-Linear Association	39.005	1	.000
N of Valid Cases	332		

a. 0 cells (.0%) have expected count less than 5. The minimum expected count is 7.86.

The key elements of your output are in the row titled Pearson Chi-Square and the associated footnote.

The chi square statistic is (the value for Pearson Chi Square), in this case, 52.529 with 6 degrees of freedom (df). This is highly significant .000. The footnote states that no cells have an expected count of less than 5 and that the minimum expected frequency for each cell in the table is 7.86. This means the assumptions of the Chi-square test are satisfied.

Example 8: Add row and column percents to a table using crosstabs.

1. Select two variables you wish to use to create a table as outlined in exercise 9.

2. Click on the cells button at the bottom of the crosstabs dialogue box.
3. Click on Row and/or Column and/or Total in the Percentages dialogue box to obtain the desired percentages.
4. Click on Continue, OK.

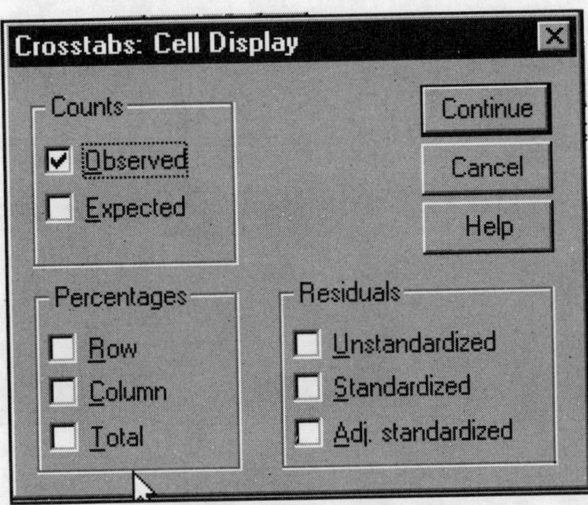

Example 9: To recode a variable's values into a new variable.

In this exercise, you are going to create a new variable educnew from the variable educational attainment by recoding the values as follows:

Postgraduate study (1)	1	Up to A level (4)	4
Up to degree level (2)	1	Up to O level or equivalent (5)	4
Up to HNC/D or diploma (3)	1	Up to CSE or equivalent (6)	4
Not stated	Missing		

This will split educational attainment into those educated upto A level (code 4) and those educated above A level (code 1).

1. Click on Transform, Recode, Into Different Variables, this gives the dialogue box:

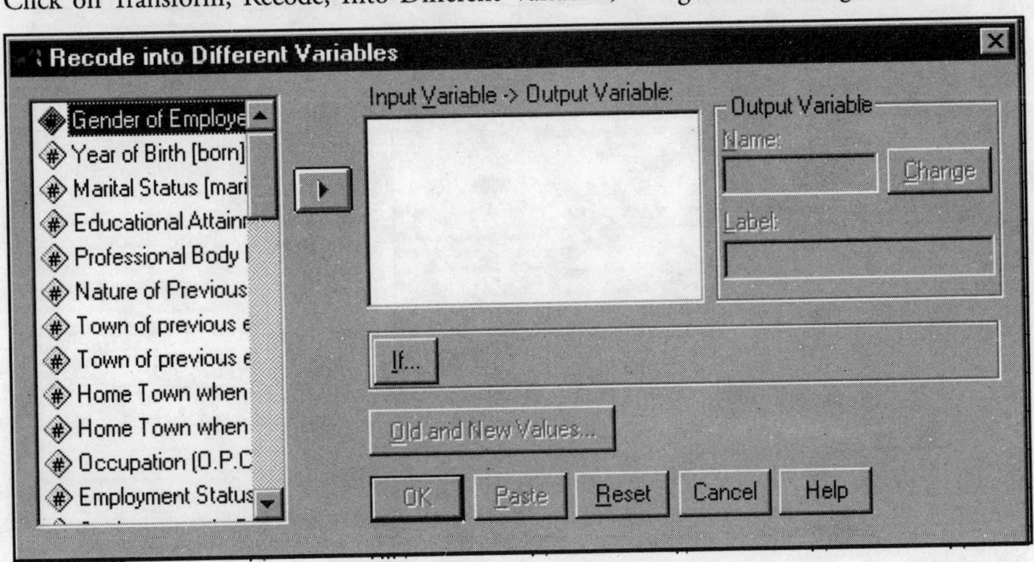

2. Click on Educational attainment in the variable list on the left hand side, it will be highlighted.
3. Click on the right arrow to transfer the variable into the Numeric Variable*Output Variable box.
4. Click on the Name box to the right of change in the Output Variable box and type in the new variable name educnew and a new variable label College Education in the Label box below.
5. Click on the change button.
6. Notice that the new variable label appears in the Numeric Variable*Output Variable box.
7. Click on the Old and New Values button and a new dialogue box opens:

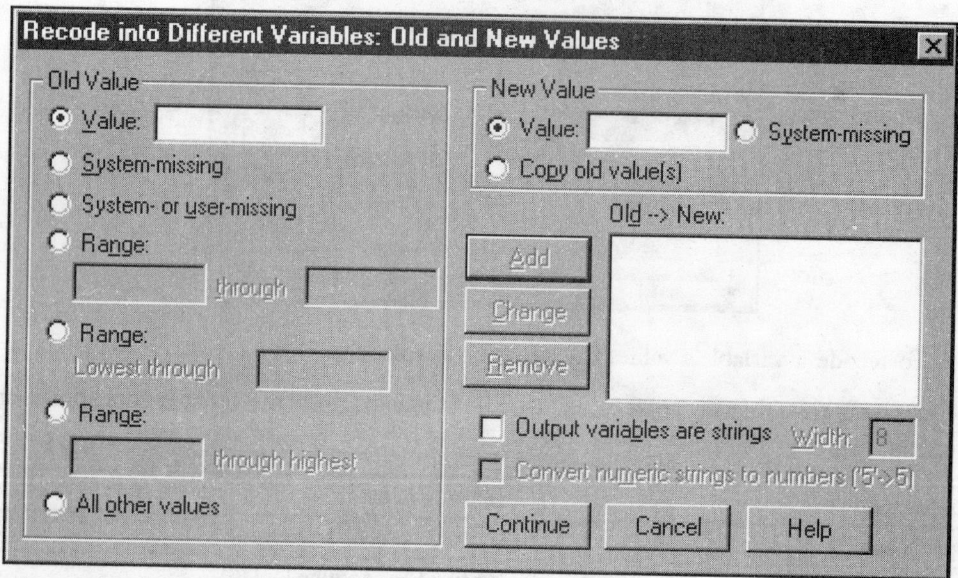

To recode the values 1, 2 and 3 into 1

1. Click on the top Range radio button in the Old Value dialogue box and type 1 in the first box and 3 in the second box.

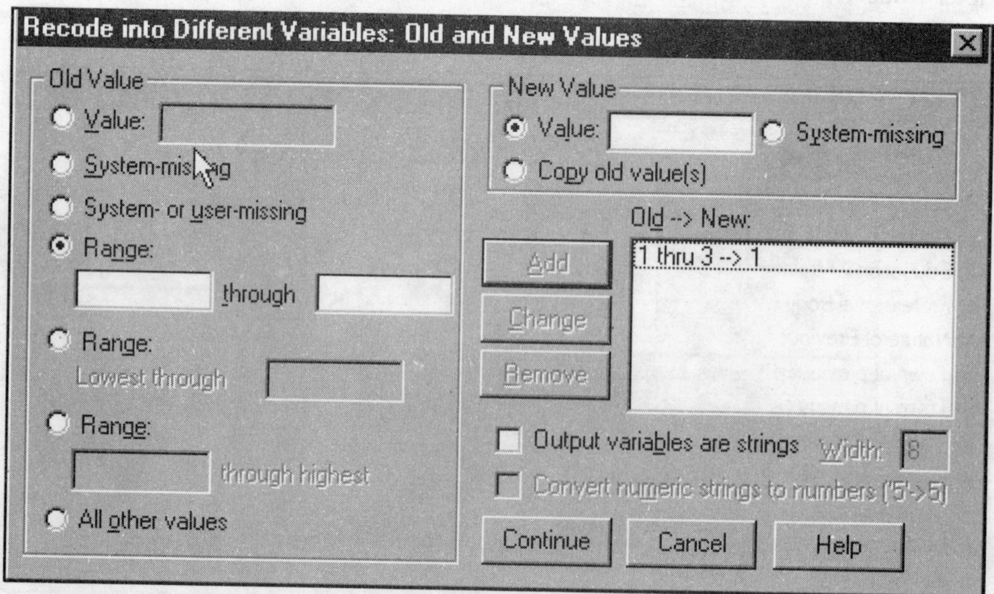

2. Click on the Value radio button in the New Value dialogue box and type 1 in the box to the right.
3. Click on Add.
4. Note that the recode has been added into the Old*New dialogue box.
5. Revise this procedure to recode the values 4, 5 and 6 to 4.
6. Revise this procedure to recode the value 7 to a missing value, using the Value and the System Missing radio buttons.
7. Check that you Old*New dialogue box looks like this:

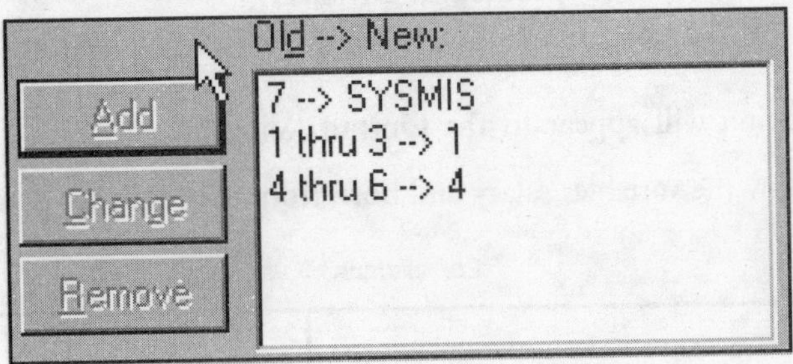

8. Click on Continue, OK.

The new variable will be created and you will be returned to the Data View.

Note: It is possible to recode a variable into the same variable, however, doing this deletes the original values for the variable. If you decide to do this make a security copy (save on to a different disc) of your data first.

Example 10: Test for a significant relationship between two variables (correlation).

Ensure that you have already opened SPSS file consisting of data on any two variables like year of birth and initial annual salary of the selected employees in an organisation.

1. Click on Analyze, Correlate, Bivariate.

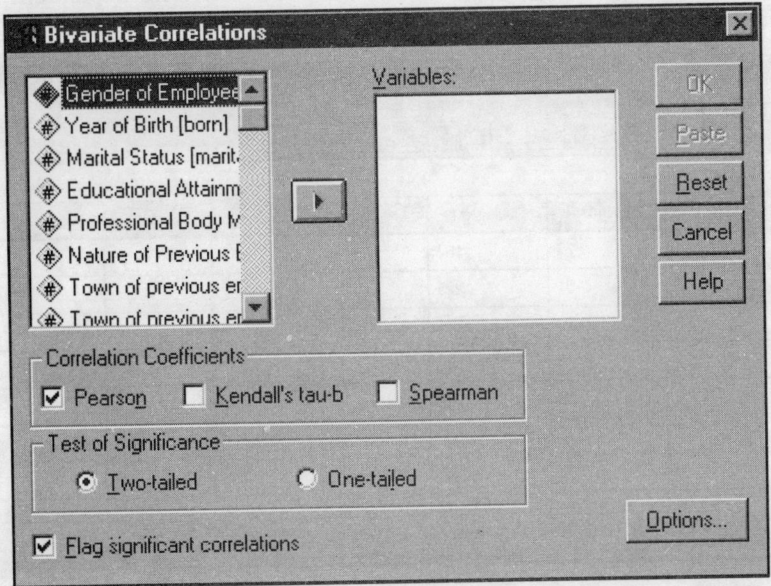

2. Point to and click on the first variable for you wish to obtain a correlation coefficient with another variable.

3. Click on to transfer the variable into the Variables box.

4. Repeat this procedure for the other variable(s) you wish to correlate with the first variable.

5. Choose the most appropriate Correlation Coefficient for your data and make sure a * is in the box.

6. Choose the most appropriate Test of Significance and click on the radio button (Use a Two-tailed test when the direction of the relationship, positive or negative, can not specified in advance. Use a One-tailed test when it can be specified in advance).

7. Click on OK.

The results of the correlation will appear in the Output Window.

In the output window below the variables salary and born from the teach.sav data set have been correlated:

Correlations

		Year of Birth	Initial Annual Salary (Spinal Column Point)
Year of Birth	Pearson Correlation	1.000	-.011
	Sig. (2-tailed)	.	.841
	N	344	333
Initial Annual Salary (Spinal Column Point)	Pearson Correlation	-.011	1.000
	Sig. (2-tailed)	.841	.
	N	333	336

SPSS has produced a correlation matrix. Obviously, there is a perfect correlation (1.0000) between the variable initial annual salary and itself. There is no correlation (-0.011) between the variable salary and the variable born and this lack of correlation is significant at the 0.841 (p=0.841) level.

Example 11: To test for a significant causal relationship between one dependent and one or more independent variables (linear regression).

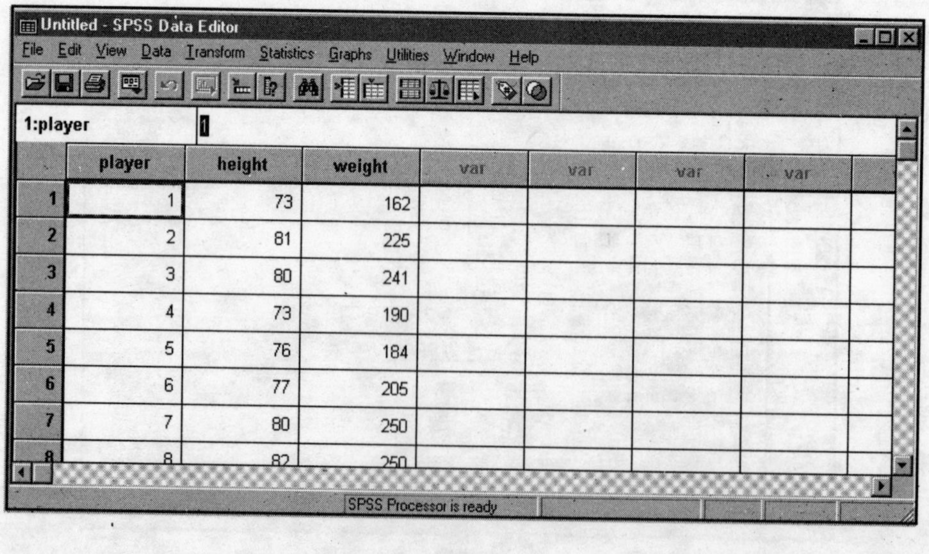

Untitled - SPSS Data Editor

File Edit View Data Transform Statistics Graphs Utilities Window Help

1:player 1

	player	height	weight	var	var	var	var
1	1	73	162				
2	2	81	225				
3	3	80	241				
4	4	73	190				
5	5	76	184				
6	6	77	205				
7	7	80	250				
8	8	82	250				

SPSS Processor is ready

Analyse the data using the following data:

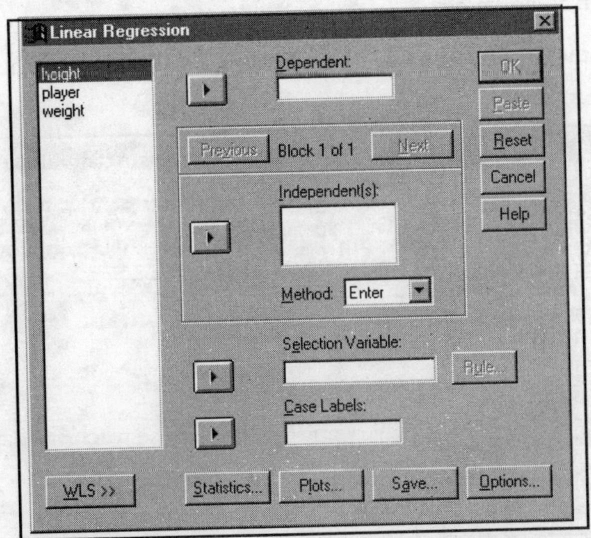

1. From the Statistics menu, select Regression. From the Regression drop down menu, select Linear. This will open the Linear Regression dialog box.
2. From the variable list, select weight. Left click on the right arrow button between the variable list and the Dependent box to move the variable, weight, to this box.
3. From the variable list, select height. Left click on the right arrow button between the variable list and the Independent(s) box to move the variable, height, to this box.
4. Select the method the independent variables are entered into the analysis. From the Method drop-down menu, there is a choice of enter, stepwise, remove, backward, and forward. In this case, we will use the enter method.
5. To limit the analysis to a subset of cases having a particular value for a variable, enter this variable into the Selection Variable box. In this case, this option is not used.
6. Determine the variable that will identify the points on plots. Select the variable and left click on the right arrow between the variable list and the Case Labels box. In this case, this option is not used.
7. To display statistics, click on the Statistics button. This will open the Linear Regression: Statistics dialog box.

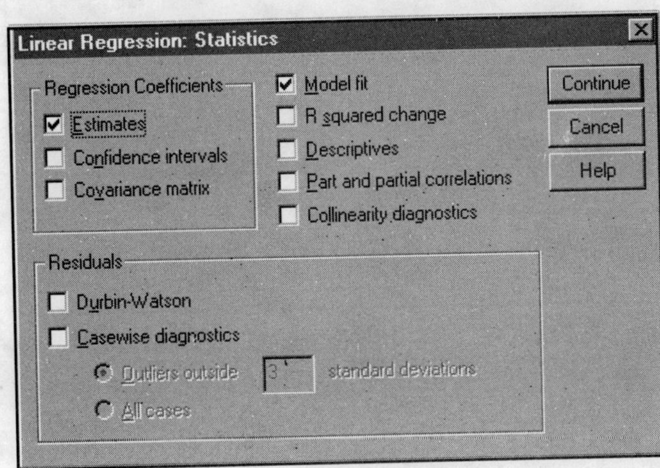

Select the appropriate statistics to be displayed and click on the Continue button when done. In this case, this option is not used.

8. To display specific plots, click on the Plots button. This will open the Linear Regression: Plots dialog box.

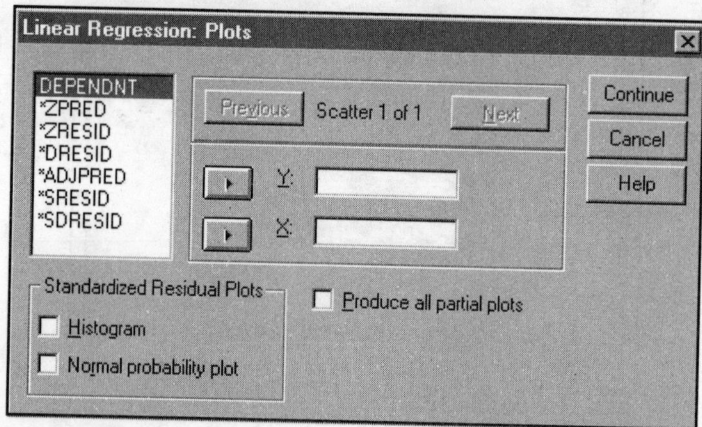

From the variable list, select the variable that will be displayed on the Y axis. Left click on the right arrow button between the variable list and the Y box. Do this also for the X axis.

When done, click on the Next button. If more plots are needed, follow the same procedure. In this case, this option is not used.

When done defining the plots, click on the Continue button.

9. To indicate which statistics should be displayed, click on the Save button. This will open the Linear Regression: Save dialog box.

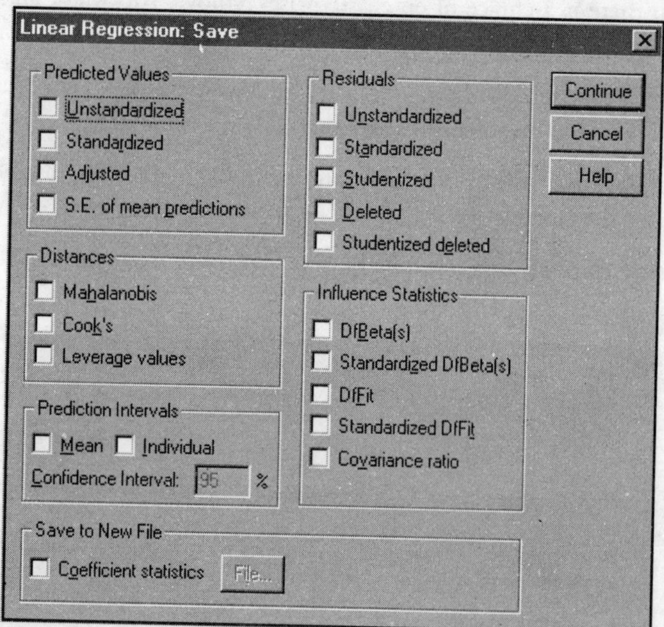

Select the appropriate statistics. To save the coefficient statistics, click on the box and indicate the file to which you want them saved. In this case, this option is not used.

10. To indicate the stepping method criteria, click the Options… button. This will open the Linear Regression: Options dialog box.

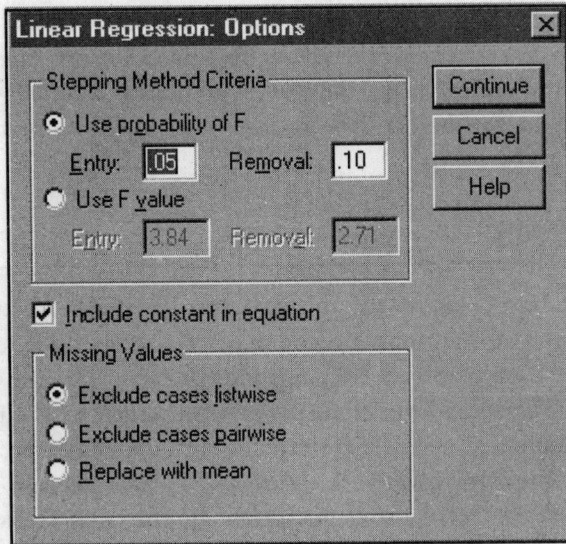

Select the method to be used. When the selection is made, click on the Continue button

11. Click OK. This will close the Linear Regression dialog box. SPSS activates the Output Navigator to display the results of the analysis.

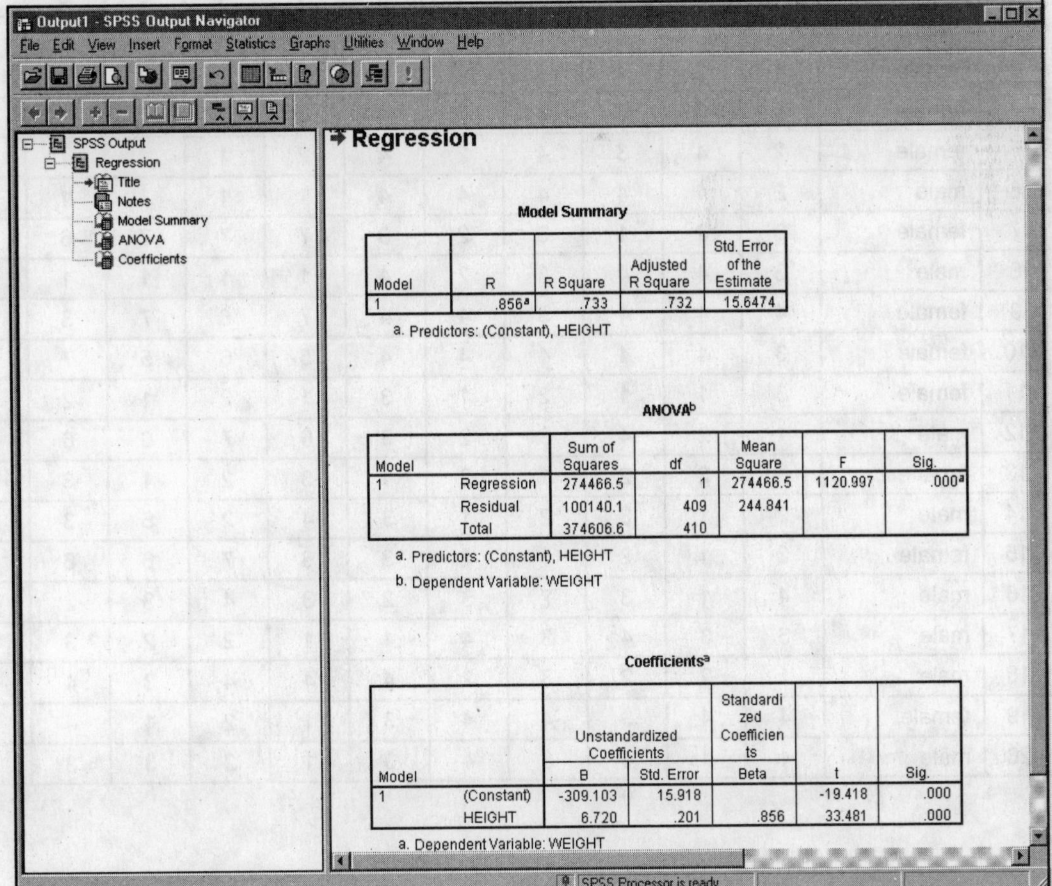

Model Summary

Model	R	R Square	Adjusted R Square	Std. Error of the Estimate
1	.856[a]	.733	.732	15.6474

a. Predictors: (Constant), HEIGHT

ANOVA[b]

Model		Sum of Squares	df	Mean Square	F	Sig.
1	Regression	274466.5	1	274466.5	1120.997	.000[a]
	Residual	100140.1	409	244.841		
	Total	374606.6	410			

a. Predictors: (Constant), HEIGHT

b. Dependent Variable: WEIGHT

Coefficients[a]

Model		Unstandardized Coefficients B	Std. Error	Standardized Coefficients Beta	t	Sig.
1	(Constant)	-309.103	15.918		-19.418	.000
	HEIGHT	6.720	.201	.856	33.481	.000

a. Dependent Variable: WEIGHT

The model is : Weight (Y) = (–309.103) + 6.720 (Height)

The standard error or standard deviation of b is estimated as 15.918, and the value of the t-statistic, t = 19.418 with n–2 = 6 degrees of freedom. From the statistical tables, the critical value of t with 6 degrees of freedom and at 5% significance level(a=0.05)1.9432 for two tailed test. Because the calculated value of t is larger than the critical value, the null hypothesis is rejected. Hence there is a significance relationship between weight and height. The positive sign of the slope coefficient indicates that this relationship is positive.

REVIEW QUESTIONS

1. *Data Description:* Listed below are the data for 20 first-year students who completed two questionnaires. The first questionnaire contained six items designed to assess attitudes toward traditional marriage. Each item had a 4-point response scale, ranging from 1 = *Very Unfavorable* to 4 = *Very Favorable*. The second questionnaire was concerned with attitudes toward abortion. This questionnaire was composed of five items tapping into different aspects of abortion, each of which used a 7-point response format, where 1 = *Extremely Unfavorable* and 7 = *Extremely Favorable*. Also given is the gender of each of the students. Below are the data. The variables casenum and gender are self-explanatory. The variables m1 through m6 are the individual item responses to the marriage questionnaire and a1 through a5 are the item responses to the abortion questionnaire.

Casenum	gender	m1	m2	m3	m4	m5	m6	a1	a2	a3	a4	a5
1	male	2	2	1	2	2	2	4	4	5	6	2
2	male	1	1	2	1	2	1	6	4	7	4	4
3	female	4	3	4	4	4	4	4	2	3	4	4
4	female	4	3	3	4	3	4	6	7	7	7	7
5	female	2	4	3	4	2	4	2	1	1	1	1
6	male	2	4	4	4	4	4	1	1	1	1	1
7	female	3	2	1	3	2	3	7	7	7	6	7
8	male	3	4	4	3	2	4	1	1	1	1	2
9	female	4	4	4	3	4	4	7	6	7	3	6
10	female	3	4	4	4	4	4	5	6	5	7	4
11	female	3	1	1	2	1	3	1	2	1	2	1
12	male	1	2	4	3	2	3	6	7	6	6	6
13	female	3	2	2	1	2	1	3	2	1	3	3
14	male	2	1	3	2	1	3	4	2	5	3	4
15	female	3	1	2	1	2	3	6	7	6	6	5
16	male	4	1	3	2	3	2	3	4	3	2	4
17	male	3	3	4	3	4	4	1	2	2	3	6
18	male	1	2	2	3	2	4	4	4	3	4	3
19	female	4	4	3	4	4	3	1	2	1	4	5
20	male	4	4	4	3	4	3	1	2	3	3	2

Activities:

(i) Create an SPSS data file for these data using the variable names given above. For the variable gender, as usual enter a1 for male and a2 for female. Save your spreadsheet. Check up the extension of the file name.

(ii) Using the COMPUTE procedure, create a new variable named marriag, which is the sum of the values for variables m1 to m6. The new computed variable will appear at the end of the data set, right after a5.

(iii) Using the same procedures, compute the new variable abortion, which is the sum of the values for variables a1 to a5. It will appear at the end of the data set, right after marriag.

(iv) You are now going to use the RECODE function described to create a new variable called m_dichot (dichotomous transformation of marriag). This variable will take the value 1 if the score for marriag is between 0 and 16, inclusive, and the value 2 if the score for marriag is greater than 16.

(v) Now, use the same procedure as in 4 to create a dichotomous variable a_dichot, which will take the value 1 for scores on abortion between 0 and 18 and 2 for scores of 19 or greater. Save your spreadsheet.

(vi) Your next task will be to use the SORT procedure described to sort your data according to the variable gender. This will cause all of the male data to be displayed in the first 10 lines of the spreadsheet and the female data to be displayed in the last 10 lines. This will facilitate comparisons between males and females.

(vii) Inspect the correlational relationship between attitudes toward marriage and attitudes toward abortion separately for the males and females. Can you draw any conclusions from your simple inspection of the data?

(viii) Prepare a cross table for the attitudes and sex. Apply chi-square test and comment on the result.

(ix) Now you are going to use the SPLIT FILE function to do separate data analyses for male and female participants. Split the file into two sub-files based on gender.

(x) Run a basic descriptive analysis of the marriag and abortion variables separately for male and female participants. Give your comment on that.

2. A psychologist was interested in self-esteem in 12 and 13-year olds. Specifically, she wanted to know if social skills training improves self-esteem.

To test her hypothesis, she gave a Self-Esteem test at the beginning of the academic year to 16 children selected at random from grade 7 at a local junior high school. The children then received two social skills lessons per week for the next ten weeks. At the end of that period, she gave the self-esteem test again.

Child	1st SE test Score	2nd SE test Score
Arthur	20	26
Jack	20	25
Nathan	21	23
Clint	21	22

Contd...

Kevin	22	21
Shaun	24	29
Sam	23	28
Jo	24	28
Gerry	26	28
Emma	29	24
Mel	26	26
Kim	27	29
Nat	23	29
Shaz	28	27
Victoria	30	34
Eliza	30	35

Using SPSS, apply appropriate test and comment.

3. 40 male and 60 female college students are queried concerning the amount of vigorous physical exercise they get each week. The students responded using the following three categories: 1 = "Little or None", 2 = "A fair amount", and 3 = "A great deal." Here are the data for the 100 students:

Males:	2	3	1	2	3	2	3	1	3	2	2
	3		2	1	2	3	2	2	1	3	3
	3	2	3		3	2	1	2	3	3	3
	3	2	3	3	3		2	1	3	2	
Females:		2	2	3	2	1	2	1	3	2	3
	1	2	1	2	2	2	3	2	2	2	1
	2	1	2	1	3	2	1	3	1	1	3
	2	3	1	2	1	2	2	3	2	3	1
	1	2	2	1	2	3	2	3	1	2	1
	1	1	2	3	1	2					

Neatly construct a frequency distribution that best summarizes these data. Include an appropriate graph for the representation of the data.

4. In a study, the researchers want to examine the relationship between different treatments and pulse. There are three groups, one control group, one group with therapy and one group with phobia training.

Control Group	**Phobia Training**	**Therapy**
72	70	61
76	64	65
68	65	63
	73	63

Perform a one-way anova. State the null hypothesis and interpret the result of your analysis.

Hints: Make two variables, treatment and pulse.

Analyze/Compare Means/One-Way anova

Dependent list: Pulse

Factor: Treatment

Options: Descriptive, Homogeneity of Variance, Means plots

Another way to do a one-way anova is to use

Analyze/General Linear Model/Univariate

Dependent variable: Pulse

Fixed factors: Treatment

Options: Descriptive statistics, Homogeneity tests

5. Explain the special significance of SPSS in the modern day research analysis.
6. What are the difficulties that are encountered by the researcher in using SPSS?

CHAPTER SIXTEEN

REPORT WRITING

INTRODUCTION

After the data have been analyzed and the conclusions reached the marketing researcher has to report his findings to the management. The reporting has to be done in a clear manner so that the chances of any misunderstandings can be minimized.

RESEARCH REPORT

A research report is a formal statement of the research process and its results. It narrates the problem studied, methods used for studying it and the findings and conclusions of the study. The reporting has to be done in a clear manner so that the chances of any misunderstanding can be minimized.

❖ Purpose of a Research Report

The Purpose of a research report is to communicate to interested persons the methodology and the results of the study in such a manner as to enable them to understand the research process and to determine the validity of the conclusions.

❖ Importance of the Report and Presentation

For the following reasons, the report and its presentation are important parts of the marketing research project:

1. They are the tangible products of the research effort. After the project is complete and management has made the decision, there is little documentary evidence of the project other than the written report. The report serves as a historical record of the project.
2. Management decisions are guided by the report and the presentation. If the first five steps in the project are carefully conducted by inadequate attention is paid to the sixth step, the value of the project to management will be greatly diminished.
3. The involvement of many marketing managers in the project is limited to the written report and oral presentation. These managers evaluate the quality of the entire project based on the quality of the report and presentation.
4. Management's decision to undertake marketing research in the future or to use the particular research supplier again will be influenced by the perceived usefulness of the report and the presentation.

❖ The Report Preparation and Presentation Process

The process begins by interpreting the results of data analysis in light of the marketing research problem, approach research design, and fieldwork. Instead of merely summarizing the statistical results, the researcher should present the findings in such a way that they can be used directly as input into decision-making.

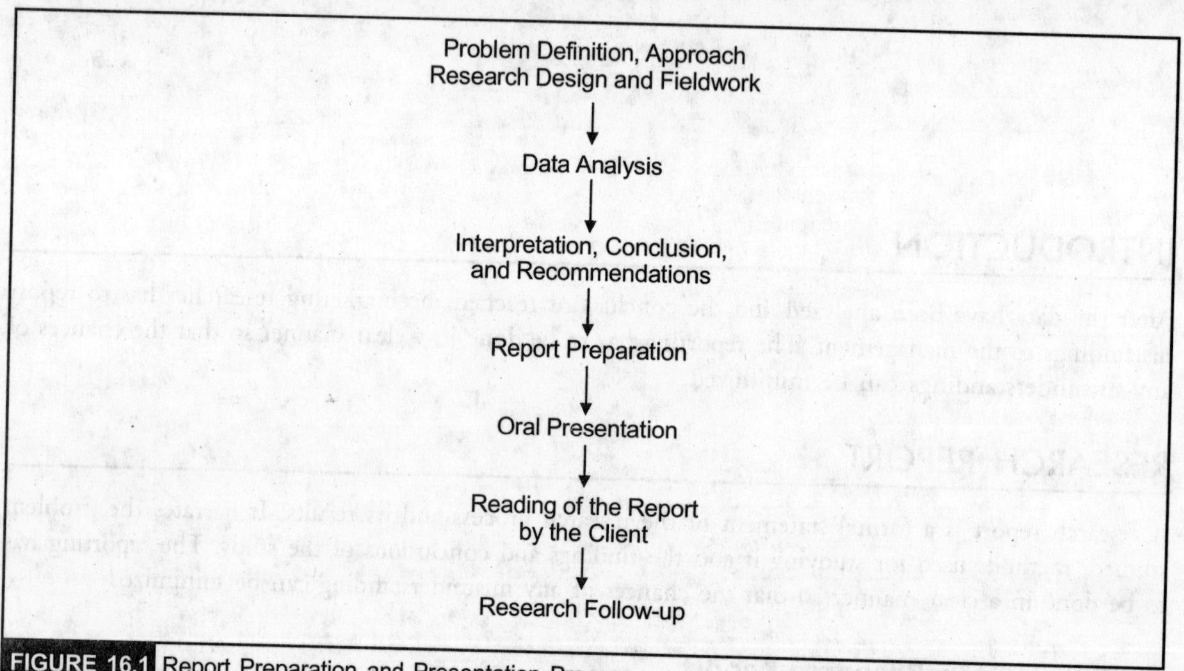

FIGURE 16.1 Report Preparation and Presentation Process

The research report should communicate the research findings effectively. All too often, the report is a complicated statement of the study's technical aspects and sophisticated research methods. If the study has been conducted for a business management, often the management is not interested in detailed reporting of the research design and statistical findings but wants only the summary of the findings. Research is only as good as the applications made of it. Nevertheless, the research report becomes a historical document, a record that may be referred to in later studies. In case of research for academic purposes, the research findings become part of the body of knowledge, and the research may produce research papers for publication in professional journals.

The report has to be presented in the format as it may have been part of the terms of reference if it is a sponsored study. In case of a dissertation, the universities have some standardized styles which have to be followed. Similarly, the research papers have to be prepared in accordance with the format specified by the professional journals.

The graphic presentation of the research process may be like Figure 16.1.

❖ Types of Research Reports

Reports can be classified by number of ways based on the function, subject matter, relationship, type of customer, nature of organization, time and formality.

Functional Classification

1. Informational,

2. Examination it is also called long-term reports.
3. Analytical (Problem-solving)

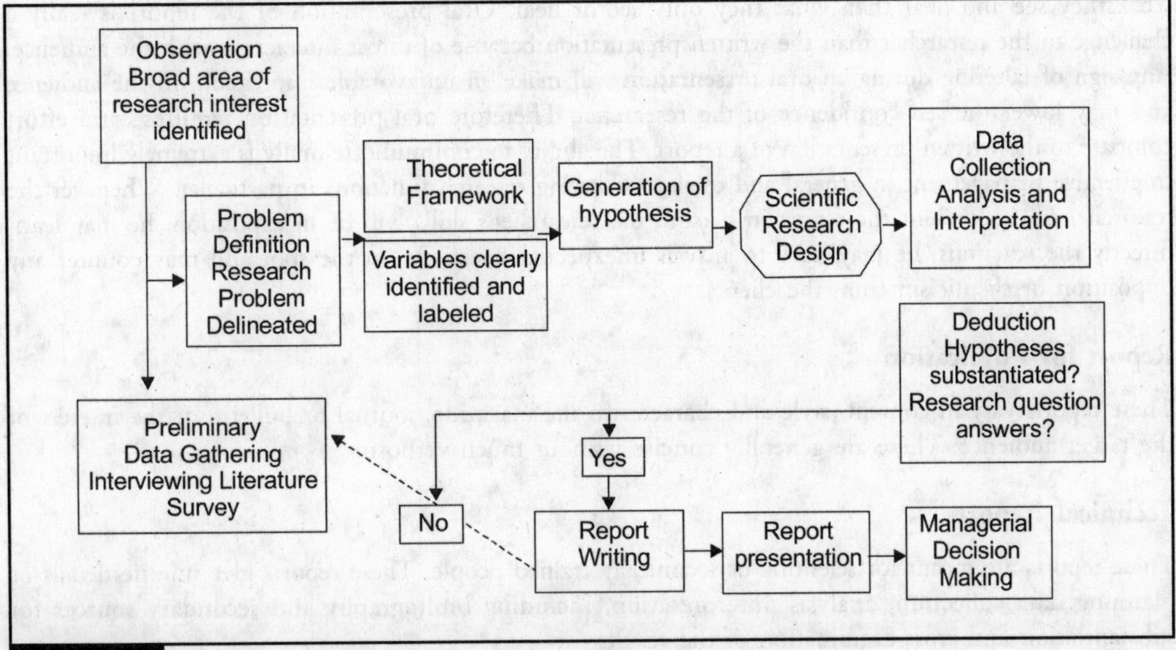

FIGURE 16.2 Graphic Presentation of the Research Process

Classification based on Subject Matter

1. Economics, commerce, etc.

Classification based on Relationship

1. Administrative report (prepared within an organization),
2. Professional report (prepared by the outsider to the organization),
3. Independent report (prepared by an independent organization for the purpose of public interest).

Classification based on Employment Status of their Authors

1. Private report prepared within the private organization,
2. Report prepared in government or public institutions are known as public reports.

Classification based on the Formality

1. Formal report
2. Informal report – (i) Short-term report and (ii) Long-term report.

Reports can be, broadly of two types: **oral and written.** An oral report is any presentation of information through the spoken word. A researcher has to consider the following when he has been asked to make an oral presentation. Consider the audience to whom the report has to be presented and prepare the same so as to incorporate the technical requirements. If the researcher has been asked to make an oral presentation of the research findings, the researcher has to prepare the report to present the same to the clients accordingly. Despite the cost, time, and effort an effective presentation requires, there are many sound reasons for doing oral and projected presentations in addition to conventional written reports. By far the most compelling and important reason is simply that people recall a vastly higher percentage of what they see and hear than what they only see or hear. Oral presentation of the report is really a challenge to the researcher than the written presentation because of direct interaction with the audience. Any sign of faltering during an oral presentation will make an unfavorable impression on the audience and may lower the self-confidence of the researcher. Therefore oral presentation requires extra effort compare to the written presentation of a report. The ability to communicate orally is extremely important to effective management in general and to the marketing research functions in particular. Whenever the researcher has to present the report in person, the researcher's skills will be in exposition, he may learn directly the reactions, he may have to answer unexpected questions on the spot and may counter any opposition or skepticism from the clients.

Report for Publication

These reports vary in content, style and character to the magazine, journal or bulletin or the interest of the target audience. These are generally concise without much verbosity.

Technical Reports

These reports are meant for scientific or technically trained people. These reports give minute details of planning data collection, analysis, interpretation, including bibliography and secondary sources for substantiation and cross-examination of the results.

Executive Reports

These reports are meant for decision-makers who are generally busy. Voluminous details are avoided in such reports or put in appendix. Key findings, assumptions, conclusions and recommendations are stated in the reports.

Advantages of Oral Presentations

1. Presentations dramatise the results of a survey, so they recalled more vividly and in greater detail than written reports.
2. They are interactive, so the presenter can listen to questions, ask for clarification, and respond immediately.
3. They provide audience feedback, so the presenter can be sure sponsors and information-seekers understand results.
4. They address a group of information-seekers simultaneously, allowing audience members to converse with one another.
5. They are compelling because the information can't be readily ignored, while written reports are often set aside.

Disadvantages of Oral Presentations

1. Report presentations are costly in terms of money, researcher time and effort, and the information-seekers' time.
2. They are perishable so they are always extra or supplementary to a written report.

3. They are demanding on the researcher's expertise, not only on technical matters, but also speaking before a group.
4. They are time and location specific, so they may require rigid scheduling and travel by the researcher or information-seekers.
5. They are complex and difficult to control, so they are many opportunities for something to go wrong or badly.

Effective Oral Presentation

1. *Research the audience:* Know who the audience are, learn about their backgrounds and information needs, and anticipate the questions they may ask.
2. *Highlight:* Choose the main points of the study to be covered during the presentation. Be careful not to select too many main points.
3. *Make good use of visual aids:* Flip charts, transparencies, slides, and so on to improve presentation clarity and maintain audience interest.
4. *Make sure the start is positive:* The start should be positive in tone, confident, and involving. Sometimes a period of silence can be used to get attention. It is useful to stimulate and involve the audience immediately, perhaps by a provocative question or statement. Absolutely never apologize at the outset, even in jest. If you tell the audience you are nervous unprepared, or unknowledgeable, even in the context of a humorous line, the audience will tend to believe you.
5. *Avoid distracting the audience:* The presenter needs to be aware that the audience is easily distracted. The following points may be kept in mind to avoid distracting: (a) Take everything out of your pockets and make sure there is nothing on the lectern other than your notes. (b) Try to avoid the extremes of either obvious pacing or hiding behind a lectern. (c) Maintain good eye contact and interact with the audience during the presentation. (d) Be concerned about the sound of your voice.
6. *Involve the audience:* An involved audience will be more interested. An effective technique is to intersperse questions throughout. If time does not permit a discussion, a pause at least gives the audience members a chance to reflect. Sometimes it is useful to ask each person to write down his or her opinion on a piece of paper a personal judgment on a key value in the data analysis. The question and answer part of the presentation is particularly important.
7. *Don't read:* The presenter should not read the presentation. The reading is usually boring for the audience. It is necessary to develop the ability to communicate orally in front of a group without a script, to prepare for those occasions when there is no time to prepare a script or when the presenter must adapt to new developments in the middle of a presentation. To heavily depending on a script will make presentation ineffective.
8. *Language:* Suitability of the language is another point worth considering while presentation. The presenter should keep the audience in mind while using the language. It is always better to use simple language, minimum phrases, no colloquial language and without many sayings and statements.
9. *It should be properly planned:* The researcher has to rehearse what he is going to say or recommend. He has to collect and organize the data in a logical manner.

Differences between Oral and Written Reports

Oral report is one which is presented to the management verbally. Written reports are documentation of the research findings.

There are three major differences between oral and written reports:

1. Oral reports are difficult to interpret as they lack visual advantage. Charts, diagrams or pictures cannot be used to stress on important points. They have to rely only on pauses and volume emphasis.

2. The pace of the presentation cannot be controlled and regulated by the audience who is being presented with the oral report. In a written report, the reader can clarify a certain point by reading it two or more times, if needed slowly and carefully.

3. A researcher will write the report very precisely and with more accuracy since he is aware that a written report is bound to receive considerable attention and scrutiny from the readers. In contrast, an oral report will not be so precise nor will the researcher give as much time in its presentation since it cannot be subjected to the same degree of scrutiny as a written report.

❖ Principles of Report Writing

A report must truly reflect the work and care that has been exercised throughout research investigation. The report writer must have a complex group of investigation and then should able to use various means of communication (words, symbols, charts, illustrations. etc.) to transmit their understandings and findings to others.

The ideas on good report writing presented in this section have been condensed from a number of authoritative sources on the subject to complete and detailed discussion can be found in several well known text devoted entirely to the subject. Though who need to develop competence in effective report writing may find the following procedural outline useful.

The fundamental medium of communication research findings is words regardless of what statistics and graphs the report may show, there should be verbal statement of every findings, as words are. It is the only precise and universal communication mode. The report writer must have a complete group of investigation and then be able to use various means of communication to bring that understanding to others. If one fails in this much of the time, effort and money spent on the research has been wasted. Good English, of course, is imperative for making good impressions but that it just the minimum requirement. As important as correctness, skillful use of language is vital in presenting ideas effectively and making their meaning clear. Such mastery is rarely possessed by University students or indeed by many in business or government it is not applied easily from reading others effective writing and practicing report preparation. Patience is needed for it may take report writing jobs to become reasonably proficient.

The following are some of the fundamental principles for writing a report:

1. ***Consider the audience:*** The nature, capacity, interest and the circumstances under which a report is likely to be read by the individuals who are likely to evaluate the report and use it, should be properly assessed, for example, that what types of information are they expecting, in what terminology and in what depth. A report written for executives should involve following consideration:

   (i) Individual preferences of executives:

      (a) Some like brief reports

(b) Some like detailed methodology

(c) Some may be interested only in statistical results rather than on conclusions and commendations.

(ii) Most of the executives are:

(a) Busy

(b) Not interested in technical and logical aspects of study

(c) Not well-versed with research technique and terminology

(d) Managers generally prefer interesting reports than dull ones

(e) Readers' interest can differ in terms of training.

Thus, it is evident from above, that the researches must make every effort to acquaint themselves with the specific references of their audience. Researchers have to be aware of such conflicts and should use their ingenuity in reconciling them.

2. ***Keep the objective of the study in mind:*** If the overall problem is understood clearly by the researcher and the information needed to achieve the objective is properly specified then the framework of the presentation has been largely determined merely to report the findings without reference to the objectives of the investigation is to present a barren piece of work. If the research is in only information gathering stage, then it will be very difficult for the Researcher' to draw conclusions and draft recommendations from the findings.

3. ***Be selective:*** If an attempt is need to include all possible details in the report, then there is always a danger that the important and significant points or results of the investigation may not be properly highlighted the assessment of important features required some degree of sense and judgment on the part of the researcher. The researcher must find a satisfactory compromise in the extent of the explanation desired for certain techniques in logic and should use his judgment that what material can be omitted. It is good to mention in the report that certain details have been omitted for the sake of brevity and that these can be supplied on request. The report should adequate enough to cover the objectives of the study.

4. ***Be objective:*** Researcher, when confident that the result of the investigation are sound and valid, should have enough courage to present and defend his findings for sound guidance to the reader, the writing should be expository. Analogies specific illustrations, comparisons drawn from experiences familiar to the research for stressing realistic of view should be used in the text by the researcher one can also use visual aids like tables, graphs, charts, etc. for this purpose.

5. ***Have a purposeful organization:*** Mere according of facts without any purpose of organization inevitably results in confusion and confusion leads to loss of interest. The purpose of report is to provide the reader, "a overall picture of the investigation" in the short possible time. Hence each paragraph in the report should be written with the thought of its position in the entire report in mind. A working outline helps the readers to comprehend the organization and also help the writer to be certain that every point is covered without duplication.

6. ***Write clearly:*** Concept of clarity has many faces and this highly subjected. The following principles with regarding to the technique of writing help in producing better reports:

(i) Use short to the point sentences

(ii) Use words the reader is likely to be familiar

(iii) Make sure that the words used are able to express the idea of the writer

(iv) Precisely

(v) Avoid mechanical flaws in presentation

(vi) Be sure that the report has uniform style and format it is wise to submit the revised draft to another researcher before the report is finalized.

❖ Precautions while Writing a Report

Research report is a channel to communicate the research findings to the readers of the report. A good research report is that which does this task efficiently and effectively the following precautions are to be taken to prepare a good research report:

1. The research report should be long enough to cover the subject and short enough to retain the readers interest.
2. A research report should not be dull and should not sustained readers interest.
3. Abstract terminology and technical Jargon should be avoided in the research report. The matter should be conveyed as simply as possible.
4. Charts, graphs and statistical tables should be used to acquire with knowledge on the content.
5. The layout of the report should be well-planned in accordance with the research problem.
6. The research report should be free from grammatical mistakes and should use techniques of composition of report writing such as quotations, foot notes, documentation, proper punctuation and use of observations.
7. The research report should present the logical analysis of the subject matter.
8. The report should show originality and should be an attempt to solve some intellectual problem.
9. The report should also indicate the policy implication relating to the problem and consideration.
10. Appendices should be enlisted in respect of all the technical data in the report.
11. Index should also be prepared and appended at the end.
12. Report must be attracted in appearance, neat and clean, whether typed or printed.
13. Bibliography of the sources of information must also be appended.
14. Confidence limits and constraints considered for the study should also be mentioned.
15. Objective of the study, nature of the problem, methods employed and analysis technique adopted must also be clearly stated in the report.

The Report Format

The following format is suggested as basic outline:

1. *Prefatory Items*

   (i) Title Page

   (ii) Researcher's declaration

   (iii) The certificate of the sponsoring authority/research supervisor

(iv) Preface and Acknowledgement

(v) Table of contents

(vi) List of Tables

(vii) List of Graphs and Charts

(viii) Abstract or Synopsis/Executive Summary

2. *Introduction*

(i) Theoretical background of the topic

(ii) Statement of the Problem

(iii) Review of Literature

(iv) Scope of the Present study

(v) The Objectives of the study

(vi) Hypotheses to be tested

(vii) Definition of concepts

3. *Research Methodology*

(i) Research design

(ii) Data collection method

(iii) Sources of Data

(iv) Sampling

(v) Field work

(vi) Data Processing and analysis plan

(vii) Chapterisation Scheme

(viii) Limitations

4. *Results Analysis and Interpretation*

5. *Summary of Conclusions and Recommendations*

6. *Bibliography, if pertinent*

7. *Appendix*

(i) Copies of forms used.

(ii) Details of sample with validation.

(iii) Tables not included in findings.

A generally useful outline of the report for executives:

1. *Letter of transmittal:* The letter of transmittal indicates to whom the report is directed, the reasons for doing the work, and the official authorization for the research.

2. *Title page:* The title page should be simple and dignified. The title page should show the subject of the report, for whom and by whom it was prepared, and the dates of completion and submittal. Ordinarily, the title page appears first.

3. *Table of contents:* If the report is lengthy, inclusion of a guide to its contents would be desirable. The table of contents is an outline of the order of appearance of the numerous divisions of the report, with page numbers.

4. *Executive synopsis:* To many executives, the synopsis is the heart of the report and cannot be underestimated. It enables an executive to grasp quickly the importance of the research. Many busy executives may read only the synopsis. It summarizes concisely all the essential parts of the report, which includes all the major facts as well as major findings and conclusions.

5. *Introduction:* The introduction serves to orient the reader to the detailed discussion of the problem at hand. Usually included in this section are the reasons for doing the work, the scope of the work, the formulation of the problem(s) to be studied, the objectives to be achieved, and the hypotheses upon which the research is based. Historical background may be included in this section.

6. *Methodology:* A description of the procedures employed to achieve the objectives follows the introductory section. The writer needs to convey to the executives some essentials of the research methodology, thus, enabling the reader to understand "why" a particular method or procedure was employed rather than another and its perceived advantages over alternative procedures.

7. *Findings:* The discussion of findings will normally be the longest section of the report. If the problem is to be solved, the data gathered must be examined as they relate to the objectives of the study. To facilitate the reader's understanding of the significance of the results, it may be quite helpful to discuss, in general terms, the method utilized in the analysis. The presentation of the findings is accomplished by a number of devices. Tables, charts, and graphs are frequently used to explain relationships of the data analyzed.

8. *Limitations:* An illustrative list of limitations might include a time constraint for completing the work, the degree the results can be generalized to a larger population, the potential effects of non-response error, or the potential effects of substituting a sampling unit in the field because of not-at-home elements. The limitations should be reported within their proper perspective, indicating the accuracy of the interpretation of the results.

9. *Conclusions and recommendations:* The conclusions are drawn by inference, either inductive or deductive, from the findings. The conclusions verify or deny the premises or hypotheses upon which the investigation has been conducted. The recommendations concerning the action to be taken follow the conclusions. Where recommendations involve policy decisions, some researchers prefer to report only conclusions and leave recommendations to those at the policy making level of management. Whether this researcher recommends action or not, it is within his or her authority to make recommendations on plans for further investigation of this or allied problems.

10. *Appendix:* The appendix provides materials supplementary to those given in the body of the report. Generally, the appendix material contains detailed and/or expanded information, such as detailed computations from which the tables in the report are generated, a copy of the questionnaire used in gathering the data, interviewer instructions, detailed statistical tables, calculations used to support the sample size chosen, and so on.

11. *Bibliography:* The bibliography is usually the final section of the report presentation. It contains detailed information on references or source materials found in various forms of communications, such as proceedings of conferences, books, pamphlets, and periodicals.

Referencing

There is a general mix up or referencing with bibliography; though the purposes are different. A bibliography is the listing of the works that are relevant to the topic of research interest arranged in alphabetical order of the last names of authors. A reference list is a subset of the bibliography, which includes details of all the citations used in literature survey and elsewhere in the report, arranged again, in the alphabetical order of the last names of authors. These citations have the goals of crediting the author and enabling the reader to find the works cited.

Giving references in the report or thesis is a must, whereas the bibliography is additional information and is certainly optional. There should be no mixing up of the meanings. There are different modes of referencing being followed by different disciplines. Find out what mode is followed in your discipline. For example, psychologists follow the publication manual of American Psychological Association (APA), and sociologists follow guidelines given in the manual of American Sociological Association. Similarly other subjects follow their professional associations. Each of these manuals specifies, with examples, how books, journals, newspapers, dissertations, and other materials are to be referenced in manuscripts. Whichever the style you pick up, follow it consistently. Since APA format is followed for referencing in many journals in management area, we shall present that here as a specimen. All the citations mentioned in the research report should find a place in the References section at the end of the report.

Specimen Format for citing different Types of References Book by a single author Leshin, C.B. (1997). Management on the World Wide Web. Englewood Cliffs, NJ: Prentice-Hall.

Start with the last name, put a comma and then initials with full stop. It is followed by the year of publication in parentheses with a full stop. Then we have the title of the publication; all in small words (unless there is some name which has to be with capital letter as it is in this title) and in italics. Give full stop at the end. It is followed by place of publication with a colon at the end. After the colon give the name of the publisher. Second line of the reference should be indented by giving five spaces.

Give two spaces for separating the references.

Book by more than one Author

Cornett, M., Wiley, B. J., & Sankar, S. (1998). The pleasures of nurturing. London: McMunster Publishing.

It is the same as the previous one except there is the use & separating the last author from its preceding one. See it is not written 'and' but being used as symbol '&.'

Edited Book

It is a book of readings or called Reader, which contains sections/articles written by a number of authors. These articles may have been published earlier in different journals/books or these may have been specially written for this book. Such a book has an editor or editors who collected these articles, edited them and published.

Pennathur, A., Leong, F. T., & Schuster, K. (Eds.) (1998). Style and substance of thinking. New York: Wilson Press.

Here after the names of the editors, the word editors is abbreviated as "Eds." And put in parentheses. Other instructions remain the same.

Chapter in an Edited Book

This is an article written by single or multiple authors and is printed in the edited book.

Riley, T., & Brecht, M. L. (1998). The success in mentoring process. In R. Williams (Ed.) Mentoring and career success. pp. 129-150. New York: Wilson Press.

We start with the name(s) of the author(s); same instructions. Then the title of the article published in this edited book. The title is in small letters except the letter of the first word. It is not to be put in italics or in bold. Give full stop at the end of the title. Then we tell about the book and its editor in which it was published. Here the editor's name does not start with the last name, but it kept straight as initials and then the last name. It is followed by the title of the book which is in italics. After the title we specify the pages of the book on which this article appeared. Rest is the same i.e. Place of publication and the publisher.

Journal Article

Jean Quart, S., & Peluchette, J. (1997). Diversity in the workforce and management models. *Journal of Social Work Studies,* 43 (3), 72-85.

The title of the article is in small letters. The name of the journal is in italics. Such professional journals are well-known in the academic community, therefore, the place of publication and the publisher is not given. Instead, its volume and number in the volume is given. All the issues published in one year are one volume. There could be number of issues in a volume. Both the volumes and issues are numbered. In this example, 43 is the volume and 3 given in the parentheses is the number in this volume. It is followed by the pages on which this article was published.

Conference Proceedings Publications

Gardezi, H. N. (2005). Population policy of India. In Z. Sathar (Ed.), Proceedings of the Third Conference on Research and Population, (pp. 100-107). New Delhi: Population Council.

Doctoral Dissertation

Chaudhary, M.A. (2004). Medical advances and quality of life. Unpublished doctoral Dissertation, Virtual University.

Paper Presented at Conference

Qureshi, Q. A. (2005, May 16). Practical tips for efficient management. Paper presented at the annual meeting Entrepreneurs, Lahore.

It is possible that the proceeding of a conference has not been published. The researcher got hold of paper that was presented at the conference and wanted to do its citation. Here along with the year of the conference, the date is also given. Title of the paper is in italics. Then give some information about owners of the conference, followed by place where the conference was held.

Unpublished Manuscript

Kashoor, M.A. (2005). Training and development in the '90s. Unpublished manuscript, Virtual University.

Newspaper Article

The GM Pact. (2005, May 16). The Dawn, p. 4.

Referencing Electronic Sources

Anand, B. (2005). Technology and immediacy of information. [On line] Available http://www.bnet.act.com

Just giving the site on the internet is not sufficient. It is necessary that the name of the author and title of the writing should be given. Internet site is actually in place of the publisher and the place of publication.

Referencing and Quotation in Literature Review

Cite all references in the body of the report using the author-year method of citation; that is, the last name of the author(s) and the year of publication are given at the appropriate places. Examples of this are as follows:

1. Ram (2005) has shown ...
2. In recent studies of dual earner families (Yadav, 2004; Pandey, 2005) it has been ....
3. In 2004, Mohantry compared dual earner and dual career families and found that ....

As can be seen from the above, if the name of the author appears as part of the narrative as in the case of (a), the year of publication alone has to be cited in parentheses. Note that in case (b), both the author and the year are cited in parentheses, separated by comma. If the year and the author are part of the textual discussion as in (c) above, the use of parentheses is not warranted.

Note also the following:

1. Within the same paragraph, you need not include the year after the first citation so long as the study cannot be confused with other studies cited in the article. An example of this is: Gutek (1985) published her findings in the book titled Sex and the Workplace. Gutek indicated ...
2. When the work is authored by two individuals, always cite both names every time the reference occurs in the text.
3. When a work has more than two authors but fewer than six authors, cite all authors the first time the reference occurs, and subsequently include only the last name of the first author followed by "*et al.*" as per example below:

   Sekaran, U., Martin, T., Trafton, N., and Osborn R. N. (1980) found ... (first citation) Sekaran *et al.* (1980) found ... (subsequent citations)
4. When a work is authored by six or more individuals cite only the last name of the first author followed by '*et al.*' and the year for the first and subsequent citations. Join the names in a multiple-author citation in running text by the word "and." In parenthetical material, in tables, and in reference list, join the names by an ampersand (&). Examples are given below:

   (i) As Tucker and Snell (1989) pointed out ...

   (ii) As has been pointed out (Tucker & Snell, 1989) ...
5. When a work has no author, cite in the text the first two or three words of the article title. Use double quotation marks around the title of the article. For example, while referring to the newspaper article, the text might be read as: While examining unions ("with GM pact," 1990).
6. When author of a work is designated as "Anonymous," cite in the text, the word Anonymous followed by a comma and the date: (Anonymous, 1979). In the reference list, an anonymous work is alphabetized by the word Anonymous.

7. When the same author has several works published in the same year, cite them in the same order as they occur in the reference list, with the in-press citations coming last. For example, Research on the mental health of dual-career family members (Sekaran, 1985a, 1985b, 1985c, 1999, in press) indicates ...

8. When more than one author has to be cited in the text, these should be in alphabetical order of the first author's last name, and the citations should be separated by semicolons as per illustration: In the job design literature (Aldag & Brief, 1976; Alderfer, 1972; Beatty, 1982; Jeanquart, 1998).

Factors that may be considered while writing the Report Introduction

1. Being with an executive summary of one or two pages.
2. Use bullets or brief paragraphs of two or three sentences each.
3. Cover only the major highlights and information needs.
4. Use headings or key phrases to identify sections.
5. The summary must stimulate interest and excite curiosity.
6. Use a response summary questionnaire, if appropriate.
7. Delete superfluous content from the response summer.
8. Type all entries and compose the summary very neatly.

Factors that may be considered while Composing Narrative Text

1. Divide the text into major sections according to the types of information needs, topics, or issues.
2. Include the tables after they have been referenced in the text, not before.
3. Avoid technical jargon used in statistics or processing in favor of the simpler, lay person's vocabulary.
4. Use short, simple, direct sentences rather than long, complex ones.
5. Use nouns repetitively to avoid any confusion about the antecedent of pronouns such as it, them, they, and so on.
6. In references to tables, figures, and other inclusions, identify them by their number or letter rather than by indefinite terms such as *"the* table."
7. Make the text interpretive rather than just descriptive of the results.
8. Introduce each major section by identifying its purpose or the reason for including it.
9. Discuss the major facts or relationships contained in each table or figure, but make the text fairly independent so it's meaningful without reference to tables.
10. Include additional ideas, conclusions, or suggestions, based on previous experience or intuition, but clearly note when they go beyond the actual results.

Factors that may be considered while composing Tables and Figures

1. Name each table and figure with a consecutive number, and preferably not with letters or Roman numerals.
2. Title each one with a brief description of exactly what's contained in the *body* of the table.

3. Label rows, columns, and sections with meaningful words, rather than codes labeled at the bottom of the table or graph.
4. Use a standard format whenever possible, so many tables are quickly recognized once the first is understood.
5. Use space and distance effectively to show relationships or provide identification.
6. Keep similar content in the same columns, rows, or sections, using space to separate distinct content.
7. Allow sufficient "white space" and don't contain too much information in one table or make it too dense.
8. Note statistical significance with an asterisk or letter superscript and note the probability level in a table footnote.
9. Use vertical rather than horizontal pages whenever possible, even if more tables or figures are needed.
10. Remember, each table or figure should virtually "stand alone," so it's meaningful without reference to text.
11. Always try to keep it clean and simple.

❖ Reading the Research Report

Advertising Research foundation developed the following guidelines for reading the report and evaluating the marketing research report.

1. ***Addresses the problem:*** The problem being addressed should be clearly identified and the relevant background information provided. The organisation sponsoring the research, as well as the one conducting the research should be clearly identified. The report should not assume that the reader has prior knowledge of the problem situation, but should give all the relevant information. A report that does not provide such information has missed the mark, as well as the readers.

2. ***Research design:*** The research design should be clearly described in non-technical terms. If the readers in the target audience of the report cannot understand the research design procedure, the fault lies with the researcher. The report should include a discussion of the information needs, data-collection methods, scaling techniques, questionnaire design and pretesting, sampling techniques, and field work. Justification should be provided for the specific methods used. Reports that do not contain, or otherwise make available, methodological details should be viewed with caution.

3. ***Execution of the research procedures:*** The reader should pay special attention to the manner in which the research procedures were executed. The people working on the project should be well-qualified and properly trained. Proper supervision and control procedures should be followed. This is particularly important with respect to data collection, data preparation, and statistical analysis.

4. ***Numbers and statistics:*** Numbers and statistics reported in tables and graphs should be examined carefully by the reader. Inappropriate numbers and statistics can be highly misleading. Consider, for example, percentages based on small samples or means reported for ordinal data. Unfortunately, the occurrence of these types of misleading statistics in reports is not uncommon.

5. *Interpretation and conclusions:* The findings should be reported in an objective and candid way. The interpretation of the basic results should be differentiated from the results *per se.* Any assumptions made in interpreting the results should be clearly identified. The limitations of the research should be discussed. Any conclusions or recommendations made without a specification of the underlying assumptions or limitations should be treated cautiously by the reader.
6. *Generalisability:* It is the responsibility of the researcher to provide evidence regarding the reliability, validity, and generalisability of the findings. The report should clearly identify the target population to which the findings apply. Factors that limit the generalisability of the findings, such as the nature and representativeness of the sample, mode and time of data collection, and various sources of error should be clearly identified. The reader should not attempt to generalize the findings of the report without explicit consideration of these factors.
7. *Disclosure:* Finally, the reader should carefully examine whether the spirit in which the report was written indicates an honest and complete disclosure of the research procedures and results. It is particularly important that procedures e.g., those used for the treatment of missing values, weighting, etc., that call for subjective judgment on the part of the researcher be made known. If any negative or unexpected findings were obtained, they should be reported. The reader should feel free to ask for any relevant information that is not contained in the report.

A careful reading of the report using these guidelines will help the client to effectively participate in research follow up.

❖ Table Presentation

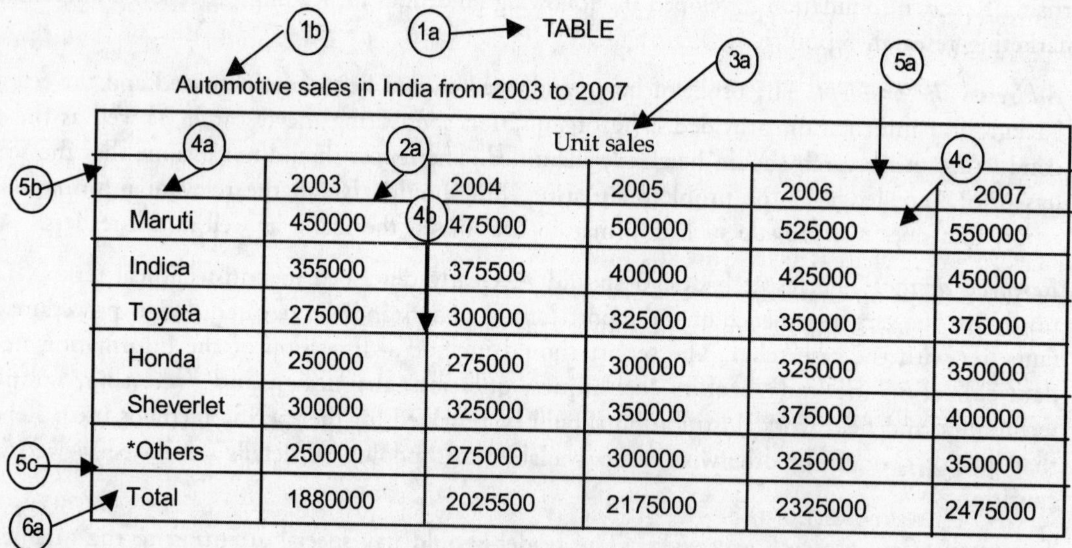

Automotive sales in India from 2003 to 2007

	Unit sales				
	2003	2004	2005	2006	2007
Maruti	450000	475000	500000	525000	550000
Indica	355000	375500	400000	425000	450000
Toyota	275000	300000	325000	350000	375000
Honda	250000	275000	300000	325000	350000
Sheverlet	300000	325000	350000	375000	400000
*Others	250000	275000	300000	325000	350000
Total	1880000	2025500	2175000	2325000	2475000

*Includes all other producers

Source: Company Websites

Guidelines for Tables

Statistical tables are a vital part of the report and deserve special attention. We illustrate the guidelines for tables using the data for US automobile sales reported in Table. The numbers in parentheses in the following section refer to the numbered sections of the table.

Title and Number: Every table should have a number (1a) and title (1b). The title should be brief yet clearly descriptive of the information provided. Arabic numbers are used to identify tables so that they can be referred to in the text.

Arrangement of Data Items: The arrangement of data items in a table should emphasize the most significant aspect of the data. Thus, when the data pertain to time, the items should be arranged by appropriate time period. When order of magnitude is most important, the data items should be arranged in that order (2a). If ease of locating items is critical, an alphabetical arrangement is not appropriate.

Basis of Measurement: The basis or unit of measurement should be clearly stated (3a).

Leaders, Rulings, and Spaces: Leaders, dots or hyphens used to lead the eye horizontally, impart uniformity, and improve readability (4a). Instead of ruling the table horizontally or vertically, white spaces (4b) are used to set off data items. Skipping lines after different sections of the data can also assist the eye. Horizontal rules (4c) are often used after the headings.

Explanations and Comments: Heading, Stubs, and Footnotes

Explanations and comments clarifying the table can be provided in the form of captions, stubs, and footnotes. Designations placed over the vertical columns are called headings (5a). Designations placed in the left-hand column are called stubs (5b). Information that cannot be incorporated in the table should be explained by footnotes (5c). Letters or symbols should be used for footnotes rather than numbers. The footnotes should come after the main table, but before the source note.

Guidelines for Graphs: As a general rule, graphic aids should be employed whenever practical. Graphical display of information can effectively complement the text and tables to enhance clarity of communication and impact. As the saying goes, a picture is worth a thousand words. The guidelines for preparing graphs are similar to those for tables. Therefore, this section focuses on the different types of graphical aids. We illustrate several of these suing the Indian automobiles sales data from table.

Line Charts: A line chart is a two-dimensional graph and is typically used to show movements on one or more items over time. The horizontal axis is customarily the time axis, and the vertical axis represents values of the items.

Pie Charts: A pie chart is a circle divided into several slices whose areas are proportionate to the quantities to be represented on the chart. The relative sizes of the slices are shown as percentages. A pie chart is excellent for showing the decomposition of a total quality into its components.

Bar Charts: A bar chart, as its name implies, consists of a series of bars (of equal thickness) whose heights (or lengths, if the bars are drawn horizontally) represent values of the items.

1. *Line Charts*
   (i) The simplest form of graphs.
2. *Pie Charts*
   (i) Appropriate for displaying marketing research results in a wide range of situations.
3. *Bar Charts*
   (i) Plain bar chart
   (ii) Clustered bar charts
   (iii) Stacked bar charts
   (iv) Multiple rows, three-dimensional bar charts.

The Simplest form of Graphs

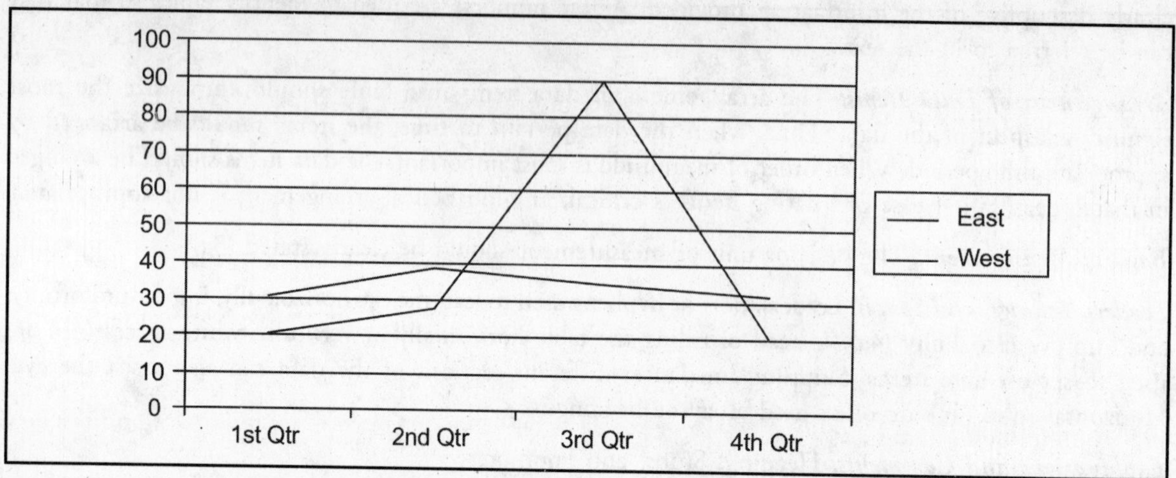

Appropriate for displaying marketing research results in a wide range of situations.

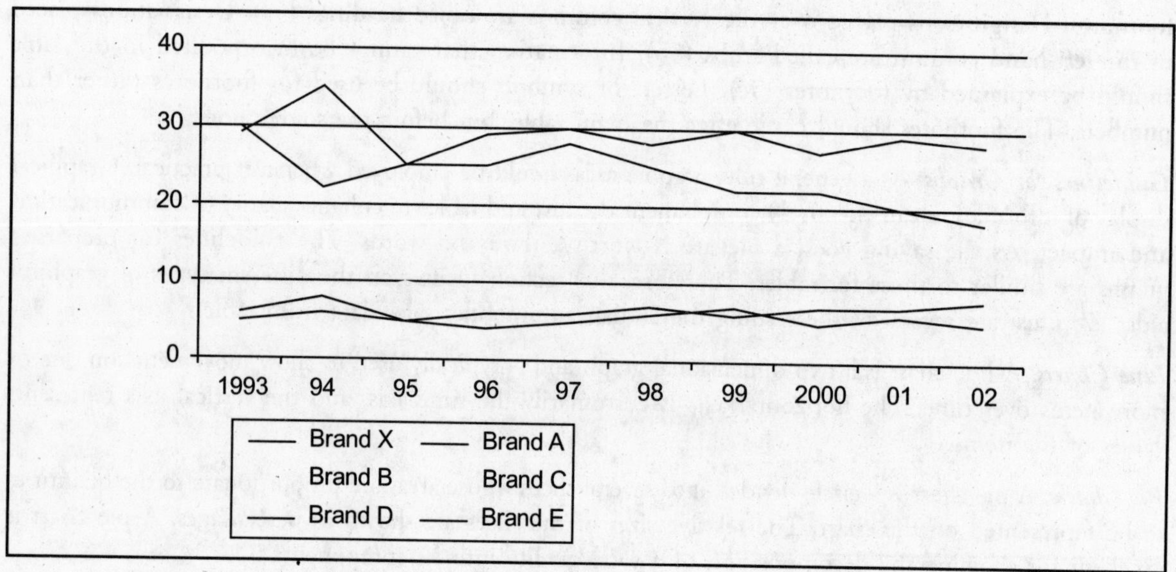

Plain Bar Chart

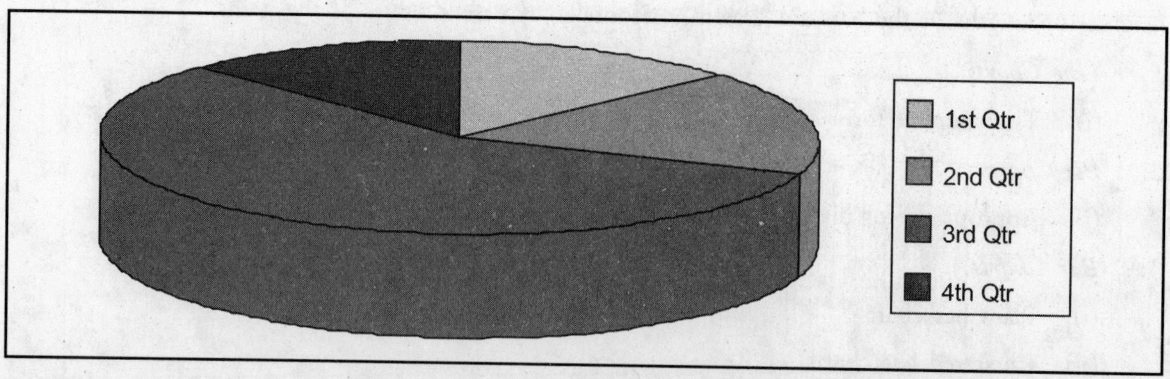

Clustered Bar Charts

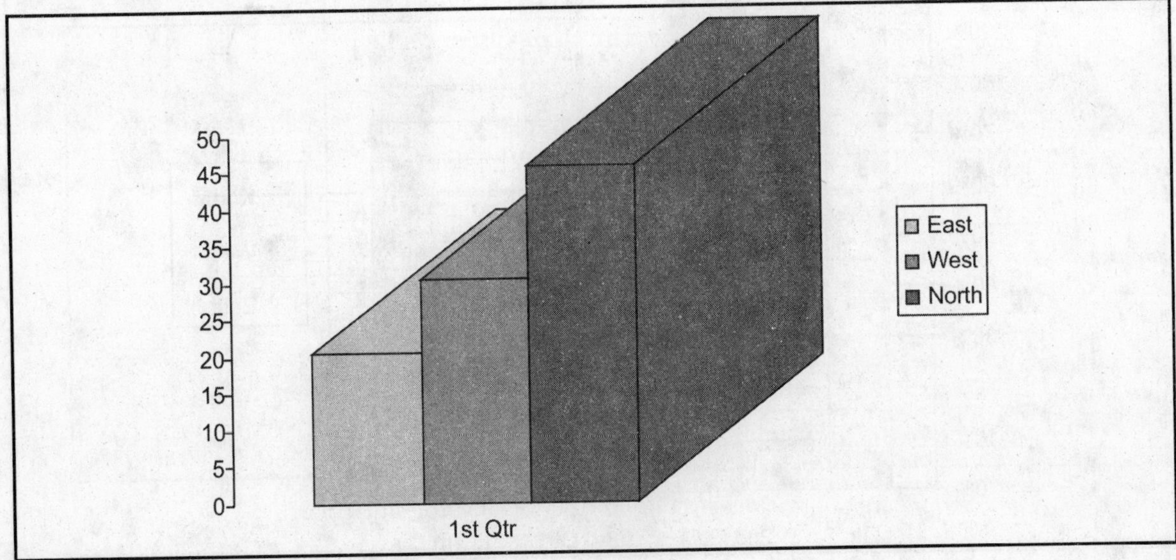

Stacked Bar Charts

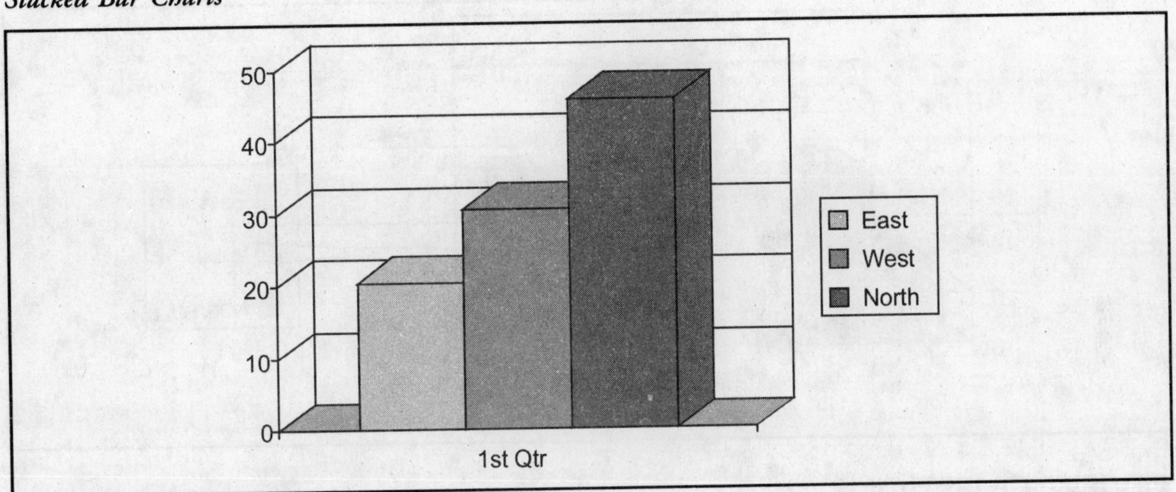

Multiple rows, three-dimensional bar charts.

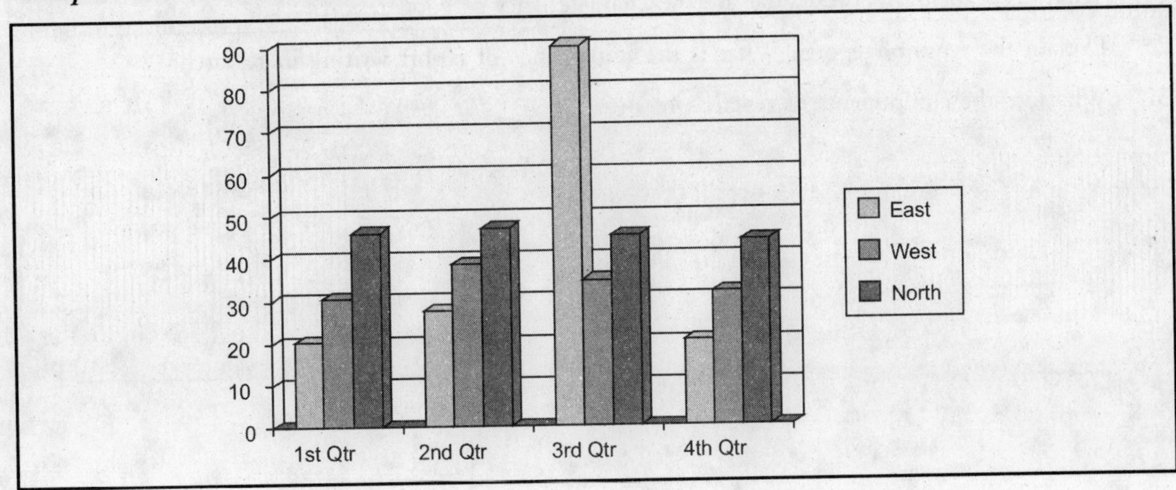

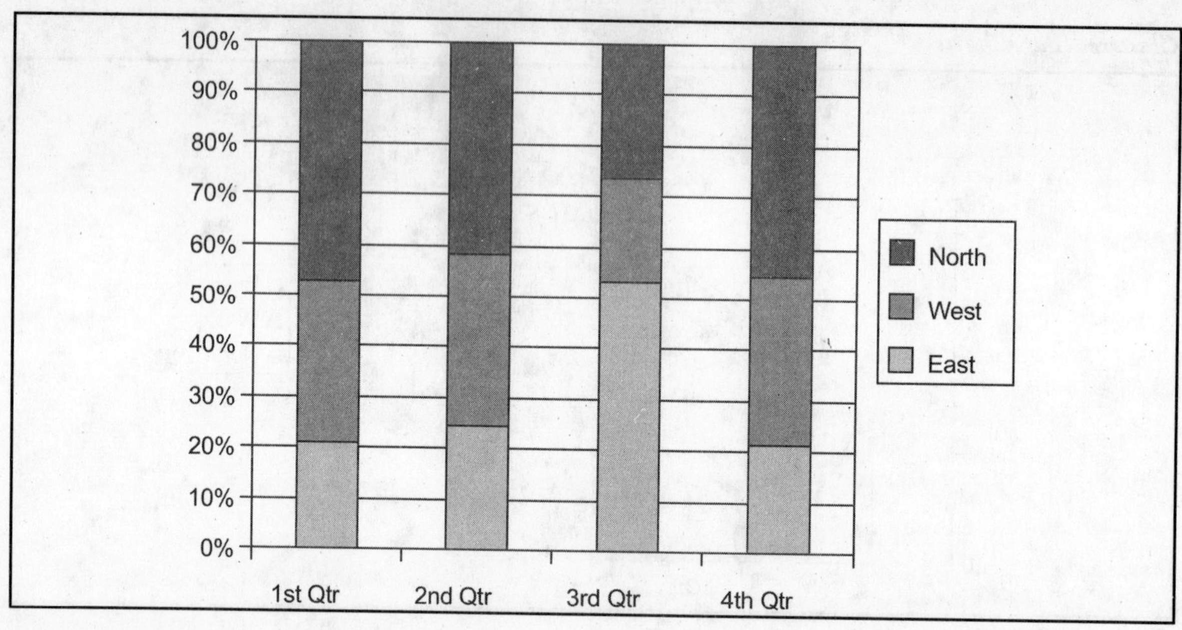

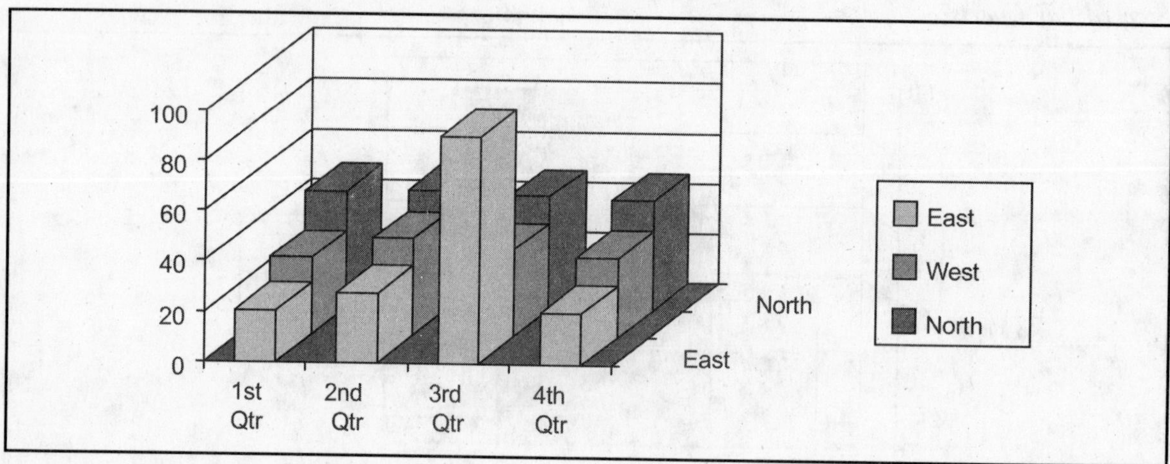

REVIEW QUESTIONS

1. What is meant by report? What are the characteristics of good report?
2. Explain the types of reports. What is the importance of report writing in research?
3. What are the components of research report?

Appendices

Appendix 1

Normal Distribution Table

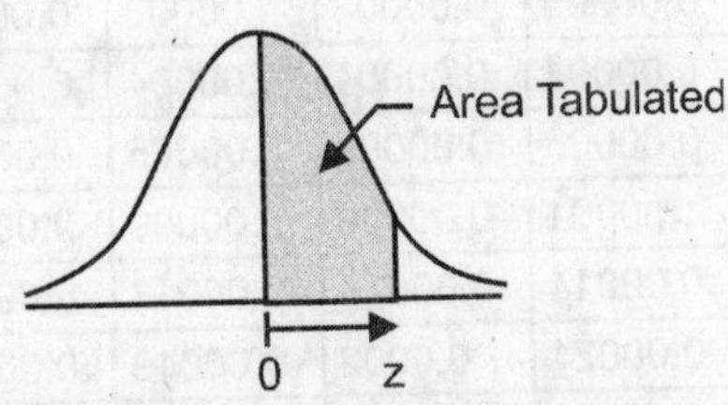

z	0.00	0.01	0.02	0.03	0.04	0.05	0.06	0.07	0.08	0.09
0.00	0.0000	0.0040	0.0080	0.0120	0.0160	0.0199	0.0239	0.0279	0.0319	0.0359
0.10	0.0398	0.0438	0.0478	0.0517	0.0557	0.0596	0.0636	0.0675	0.0714	0.0753
0.20	0.0793	0.0832	0.0871	0.0910	0.0948	0.0987	0.1026	0.1064	0.1103	0.1141
0.30	0.1179	0.1217	0.1255	0.1293	0.1331	0.1368	0.1406	0.1443	0.1480	0.1517
0.40	0.1554	0.1591	0.1628	0.1664	0.1700	0.1736	0.1772	0.1808	0.1844	0.1879
0.50	0.1915	0.1950	0.1985	0.2019	0.2054	0.2088	0.2123	0.2157	0.2190	0.2224
0.60	0.2257	0.2291	0.2324	0.2357	0.2389	0.2422	0.2454	0.2486	0.2517	0.2549
0.70	0.2580	0.2611	0.2642	0.2673	0.2704	0.2734	0.2764	0.2794	0.2823	0.2852
0.80	0.2881	0.2910	0.2939	0.2967	0.2995	0.3023	0.3051	0.3078	0.3106	0.3133
0.90	0.3159	0.3186	0.3212	0.3238	0.3264	0.3289	0.3315	0.3340	0.3365	0.3389
1.00	0.3413	0.3438	0.3461	0.3485	0.3508	0.3531	0.3554	0.3577	0.3599	0.3621
1.10	0.3643	0.3665	0.3686	0.3708	0.3729	0.3749	0.3770	0.3790	0.3810	0.3830
1.20	0.3849	0.3869	0.3888	0.3907	0.3925	0.3944	0.3962	0.3980	0.3997	0.4015
1.30	0.4032	0.4049	0.4066	0.4082	0.4099	0.4115	0.4131	0.4147	0.4162	0.4177
1.40	0.4192	0.4207	0.4222	0.4236	0.4251	0.4265	0.4279	0.4292	0.4306	0.4319
1.50	0.4332	0.4345	0.4357	0.4370	0.4382	0.4394	0.4406	0.4418	0.4429	0.4441
1.60	0.4452	0.4463	0.4474	0.4484	0.4495	0.4505	0.4515	0.4525	0.4535	0.4545
1.70	0.4554	0.4564	0.4573	0.4582	0.4591	0.4599	0.4608	0.4616	0.4625	0.4633
1.80	0.4641	0.4649	0.4656	0.4664	0.4671	0.4678	0.4686	0.4693	0.4699	0.4706
1.90	0.4713	0.4719	0.4726	0.4732	0.4738	0.4744	0.4750	0.4756	0.4761	0.4767
2.00	0.4772	0.4778	0.4783	0.4788	0.4793	0.4798	0.4803	0.4808	0.4812	0.4817
2.10	0.4821	0.4826	0.4830	0.4834	0.4838	0.4842	0.4846	0.4850	0.4854	0.4857
2.20	0.4861	0.4864	0.4868	0.4871	0.4875	0.4878	0.4881	0.4884	0.4887	0.4890
2.30	0.4893	0.4896	0.4898	0.4901	0.4904	0.4906	0.4909	0.4911	0.4913	0.4916
2.40	0.4918	0.4920	0.4922	0.4925	0.4927	0.4929	0.4931	0.4932	0.4934	0.4936
2.50	0.4938	0.4940	0.4941	0.4943	0.4945	0.4946	0.4948	0.4949	0.4951	0.4952
2.60	0.4953	0.4955	0.4956	0.4957	0.4959	0.4960	0.4961	0.4962	0.4963	0.4964
2.70	0.4965	0.4966	0.4967	0.4968	0.4969	0.4970	0.4971	0.4972	0.4973	0.4974
2.80	0.4974	0.4975	0.4976	0.4977	0.4977	0.4978	0.4979	0.4979	0.4980	0.4981
2.90	0.4981	0.4982	0.4982	0.4983	0.4984	0.4984	0.4985	0.4985	0.4986	0.4986
3.00	0.4987	0.4987	0.4987	0.4988	0.4988	0.4989	0.4989	0.4989	0.4990	0.4990

p-Values Standard Normal Probabilities (Negative)

z	0	0.01	0.02	0.03	0.04	0.05	0.06	0.07	0.08	0.09
-4	0.00003	0.00003	0.00003	0.00003	0.00003	0.00003	0.00002	0.00002	0.00002	0.00002
-3.9	0.00005	0.00005	0.00004	0.00004	0.00004	0.00004	0.00004	0.00004	0.00003	0.00003
-3.8	0.00007	0.00007	0.00007	0.00006	0.00006	0.00006	0.00006	0.00005	0.00005	0.00005
-3.7	0.00011	0.0001	0.0001	0.0001	0.00009	0.00009	0.00008	0.00008	0.00008	0.00008
-3.6	0.00016	0.00015	0.00015	0.00014	0.00014	0.00013	0.00013	0.00012	0.00012	0.00011
-3.5	0.00023	0.00022	0.00022	0.00021	0.0002	0.00019	0.00019	0.00018	0.00017	0.00017
-3.4	0.00034	0.00032	0.00031	0.0003	0.00029	0.00028	0.00027	0.00026	0.00025	0.00024
-3.3	0.00048	0.00047	0.00045	0.00043	0.00042	0.0004	0.00039	0.00038	0.00036	0.00035
-3.2	0.00069	0.00066	0.00064	0.00062	0.0006	0.00058	0.00056	0.00054	0.00052	0.0005
-3.1	0.00097	0.00094	0.0009	0.00087	0.00084	0.00082	0.00079	0.00076	0.00074	0.00071
-3	0.00135	0.00131	0.00126	0.00122	0.00118	0.00114	0.00111	0.00107	0.00103	0.001
-2.9	0.00187	0.00181	0.00175	0.00169	0.00164	0.00159	0.00154	0.00149	0.00144	0.00139
-2.8	0.00256	0.00248	0.0024	0.00233	0.00226	0.00219	0.00212	0.00205	0.00199	0.00193
-2.7	0.00347	0.00336	0.00326	0.00317	0.00307	0.00298	0.00289	0.0028	0.00272	0.00264
-2.6	0.00466	0.00453	0.0044	0.00427	0.00415	0.00402	0.00391	0.00379	0.00368	0.00357
-2.5	0.00621	0.00604	0.00587	0.0057	0.00554	0.00539	0.00523	0.00508	0.00494	0.0048
-2.4	0.0082	0.00798	0.00776	0.00755	0.00734	0.00714	0.00695	0.00676	0.00657	0.00639
-2.3	0.01072	0.01044	0.01017	0.0099	0.00964	0.00939	0.00914	0.00889	0.00866	0.00842
-2.2	0.0139	0.01355	0.01321	0.01287	0.01255	0.01222	0.01191	0.0116	0.0113	0.01101
-2.1	0.01786	0.01743	0.017	0.01659	0.01618	0.01578	0.01539	0.015	0.01463	0.01426
-2	0.02275	0.02222	0.02169	0.02118	0.02067	0.02018	0.0197	0.01923	0.01876	0.01831
-1.9	0.02872	0.02807	0.02743	0.0268	0.02619	0.02559	0.025	0.02442	0.02385	0.0233
-1.8	0.03593	0.03515	0.03438	0.03362	0.03288	0.03216	0.03144	0.03074	0.03005	0.02938
-1.7	0.04456	0.04363	0.04272	0.04181	0.04093	0.04006	0.0392	0.03836	0.03754	0.03673
-1.6	0.0548	0.0537	0.05262	0.05155	0.0505	0.04947	0.04846	0.04746	0.04648	0.04551
-1.5	0.06681	0.06552	0.06425	0.06301	0.06178	0.06057	0.05938	0.05821	0.05705	0.05592
-1.4	0.08076	0.07927	0.0778	0.07636	0.07493	0.07353	0.07214	0.07078	0.06944	0.06811
-1.3	0.0968	0.0951	0.09342	0.09176	0.09012	0.08851	0.08691	0.08534	0.08379	0.08226
-1.2	0.11507	0.11314	0.11123	0.10935	0.10749	0.10565	0.10383	0.10204	0.10027	0.09852
-1.1	0.13566	0.1335	0.13136	0.12924	0.12714	0.12507	0.12302	0.121	0.119	0.11702
-1	0.15865	0.15625	0.15386	0.1515	0.14917	0.14686	0.14457	0.14231	0.14007	0.13786
-0.9	0.18406	0.18141	0.17878	0.17618	0.17361	0.17105	0.16853	0.16602	0.16354	0.16109
-0.8	0.21185	0.20897	0.20611	0.20327	0.20045	0.19766	0.19489	0.19215	0.18943	0.18673
-0.7	0.24196	0.23885	0.23576	0.23269	0.22965	0.22663	0.22363	0.22065	0.21769	0.21476
-0.6	0.27425	0.27093	0.26763	0.26434	0.26108	0.25784	0.25462	0.25143	0.24825	0.24509
-0.5	0.30853	0.30502	0.30153	0.29805	0.2946	0.29116	0.28774	0.28434	0.28095	0.27759
-0.4	0.34457	0.3409	0.33724	0.33359	0.32997	0.32635	0.32276	0.31917	0.31561	0.31206
-0.3	0.38209	0.37828	0.37448	0.3707	0.36692	0.36317	0.35942	0.35569	0.35197	0.34826
-0.2	0.42074	0.41683	0.41293	0.40904	0.40516	0.40129	0.39743	0.39358	0.38974	0.3859
-0.1	0.46017	0.4562	0.45224	0.44828	0.44433	0.44038	0.43644	0.4325	0.42857	0.42465
0	0.5	0.49601	0.49202	0.48803	0.48404	0.48006	0.47607	0.47209	0.46811	0.46414

p-Values Standard Normal Probabilities (Positive)

z	0	0.01	0.02	0.03	0.04	0.05	0.06	0.07	0.08	0.09
0	0.5	0.50399	0.50798	0.51197	0.51596	0.51994	0.52393	0.52791	0.53189	0.53586
0.1	0.53983	0.5438	0.54776	0.55172	0.55567	0.55962	0.56356	0.5675	0.57143	0.57535
0.2	0.57926	0.58317	0.58707	0.59096	0.59484	0.59871	0.60257	0.60642	0.61026	0.6141
0.3	0.61791	0.62172	0.62552	0.6293	0.63308	0.63683	0.64058	0.64431	0.64803	0.65174
0.4	0.65543	0.6591	0.66276	0.66641	0.67003	0.67365	0.67724	0.68083	0.68439	0.68794
0.5	0.69147	0.69498	0.69847	0.70195	0.7054	0.70884	0.71226	0.71566	0.71905	0.72241
0.6	0.72575	0.72907	0.73237	0.73566	0.73892	0.74216	0.74538	0.74857	0.75175	0.75491
0.7	0.75804	0.76115	0.76424	0.76731	0.77035	0.77337	0.77637	0.77935	0.78231	0.78524
0.8	0.78815	0.79103	0.79389	0.79673	0.79955	0.80234	0.80511	0.80785	0.81057	0.81327
0.9	0.81594	0.81859	0.82122	0.82382	0.82639	0.82895	0.83147	0.83398	0.83646	0.83891
1	0.84135	0.84375	0.84614	0.8485	0.85083	0.85314	0.85543	0.85769	0.85993	0.86214
1.1	0.86434	0.8665	0.86864	0.87076	0.87286	0.87493	0.87698	0.879	0.881	0.88298
1.2	0.88493	0.88686	0.88877	0.89065	0.89251	0.89435	0.89617	0.89796	0.89973	0.90148
1.3	0.9032	0.9049	0.90658	0.90824	0.90988	0.91149	0.91309	0.91466	0.91621	0.91774
1.4	0.91924	0.92073	0.9222	0.92364	0.92507	0.92647	0.92786	0.92922	0.93056	0.93189
1.5	0.93319	0.93448	0.93575	0.93699	0.93822	0.93943	0.94062	0.94179	0.94295	0.94408
1.6	0.9452	0.9463	0.94738	0.94845	0.9495	0.95053	0.95154	0.95254	0.95352	0.95449
1.7	0.95544	0.95637	0.95728	0.95819	0.95907	0.95994	0.9608	0.96164	0.96246	0.96327
1.8	0.96407	0.96485	0.96562	0.96638	0.96712	0.96784	0.96856	0.96926	0.96995	0.97062
1.9	0.97128	0.97193	0.97257	0.9732	0.97381	0.97441	0.975	0.97558	0.97615	0.9767
2	0.97725	0.97778	0.97831	0.97882	0.97933	0.97982	0.9803	0.98077	0.98124	0.98169
2.1	0.98214	0.98257	0.983	0.98341	0.98382	0.98422	0.98461	0.985	0.98537	0.98574
2.2	0.9861	0.98645	0.98679	0.98713	0.98745	0.98778	0.98809	0.9884	0.9887	0.98899
2.3	0.98928	0.98956	0.98983	0.9901	0.99036	0.99061	0.99086	0.99111	0.99134	0.99158
2.4	0.9918	0.99202	0.99224	0.99245	0.99266	0.99286	0.99305	0.99324	0.99343	0.99361
2.5	0.99379	0.99396	0.99413	0.9943	0.99446	0.99461	0.99477	0.99492	0.99506	0.9952
2.6	0.99534	0.99547	0.9956	0.99573	0.99585	0.99598	0.99609	0.99621	0.99632	0.99643
2.7	0.99653	0.99664	0.99674	0.99683	0.99693	0.99702	0.99711	0.9972	0.99728	0.99736
2.8	0.99744	0.99752	0.9976	0.99767	0.99774	0.99781	0.99788	0.99795	0.99801	0.99807
2.9	0.99813	0.99819	0.99825	0.99831	0.99836	0.99841	0.99846	0.99851	0.99856	0.99861
3	0.99865	0.99869	0.99874	0.99878	0.99882	0.99886	0.99889	0.99893	0.99897	0.999
3.1	0.99903	0.99906	0.9991	0.99913	0.99916	0.99918	0.99921	0.99924	0.99926	0.99929
3.2	0.99931	0.99934	0.99936	0.99938	0.9994	0.99942	0.99944	0.99946	0.99948	0.9995
3.3	0.99952	0.99953	0.99955	0.99957	0.99958	0.9996	0.99961	0.99962	0.99964	0.99965
3.4	0.99966	0.99968	0.99969	0.9997	0.99971	0.99972	0.99973	0.99974	0.99975	0.99976
3.5	0.99977	0.99978	0.99978	0.99979	0.9998	0.99981	0.99981	0.99982	0.99983	0.99983
3.6	0.99984	0.99985	0.99985	0.99986	0.99986	0.99987	0.99987	0.99988	0.99988	0.99989
3.7	0.99989	0.9999	0.9999	0.9999	0.99991	0.99991	0.99992	0.99992	0.99992	0.99992
3.8	0.99993	0.99993	0.99993	0.99994	0.99994	0.99994	0.99994	0.99995	0.99995	0.99995
3.9	0.99995	0.99995	0.99996	0.99996	0.99996	0.99996	0.99996	0.99996	0.99997	0.99997
4	0.99997	0.99997	0.99997	0.99997	0.99997	0.99997	0.99998	0.99998	0.99998	0.99998

Appendix 2

t Distribution Table

Example: If you are using a two-tail test at 5% level of significance with 25 degrees of freedom, look for the *t* value under column 0.025 and 25 degrees of freedom row. The *t* value for this = 2.0595. If you are using a one tail test at 5% level of significance with 25 degrees of freedom, look for the *t* value under column 0.05 and 25 degrees of freedom row. The t value for this = 1.7081.

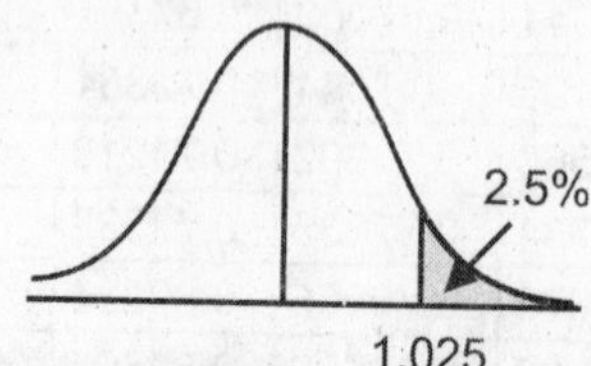

Degrees of freedom	Upper t Value									
	0.4	0.25	0.1	0.05	0.025	0.01	0.005	0.0025	0.001	0.0005
1	0.3249	1.0000	3.0777	6.3137	12.7062	31.8210	63.6559	127.3211	318.2888	636.5776
2	0.2887	0.8165	1.8856	2.9200	4.3027	6.9645	9.9250	14.0892	22.3285	31.5998
3	0.2767	0.7649	1.6377	2.3534	3.1824	4.5407	5.8408	7.4532	10.2143	12.9244
4	0.2707	0.7407	1.5332	2.1318	2.7765	3.7469	4.6041	5.5975	7.1729	8.6101
5	0.2672	0.7267	1.4759	2.0150	2.5706	3.3649	4.0321	4.7733	5.8935	6.8685
6	0.2648	0.7176	1.4398	1.9432	2.4469	3.1427	3.7074	4.3168	5.2075	5.9587
7	0.2632	0.7111	1.4149	1.8946	2.3646	2.9979	3.4995	4.0294	4.7853	5.4081
8	0.2619	0.7064	1.3968	1.8595	2.3060	2.8965	3.3554	3.8325	4.5008	5.0414
9	0.2610	0.7027	1.3830	1.8331	2.2622	2.8214	3.2498	3.6896	4.2969	4.7809
10	0.2602	0.6998	1.3722	1.8125	2.2281	2.7638	3.1693	3.5814	4.1437	4.5868
11	0.2596	0.6974	1.3634	1.7959	2.2010	2.7181	3.1058	3.4966	4.0248	4.4369
12	0.2590	0.6955	1.3562	1.7823	2.1788	2.6810	3.0545	3.4284	3.9296	4.3178
13	0.2586	0.6938	1.3502	1.7709	2.1604	2.6503	3.0123	3.3725	3.8520	4.2209
14	0.2582	0.6924	1.3450	1.7613	2.1448	2.6245	2.9768	3.3257	3.7874	4.1403
15	0.2579	0.6912	1.3406	1.7531	2.1315	2.6025	2.9467	3.2860	3.7329	4.0728
16	0.2576	0.6901	1.3368	1.7459	2.1199	2.5835	2.9208	3.2520	3.6861	4.0149
17	0.2573	0.6892	1.3334	1.7396	2.1098	2.5669	2.8982	3.2224	3.6458	3.9651
18	0.2571	0.6884	1.3304	1.7341	2.1009	2.5524	2.8784	3.1966	3.6105	3.9217
19	0.2569	0.6876	1.3277	1.7291	2.0930	2.5395	2.8609	3.1737	3.5793	3.8833
20	0.2567	0.6870	1.3253	1.7247	2.0860	2.5280	2.8453	3.1534	3.5518	3.8496
21	0.2566	0.6864	1.3232	1.7207	2.0796	2.5176	2.8314	3.1352	3.5271	3.8193
22	0.2564	0.6858	1.3212	1.7171	2.0739	2.5083	2.8188	3.1188	3.5050	3.7922
23	0.2563	0.6853	1.3195	1.7139	2.0687	2.4999	2.8073	3.1040	3.4850	3.7676
24	0.2562	0.6848	1.3178	1.7109	2.0639	2.4922	2.7970	3.0905	3.4668	3.7454
25	0.2561	0.6844	1.3163	1.7081	2.0595	2.4851	2.7874	3.0782	3.4502	3.7251
26	0.2560	0.6840	1.3150	1.7056	2.0555	2.4786	2.7787	3.0669	3.4350	3.7067
27	0.2559	0.6837	1.3137	1.7033	2.0518	2.4727	2.7707	3.0565	3.4210	3.6895
28	0.2558	0.6834	1.3125	1.7011	2.0484	2.4671	2.7633	3.0470	3.4082	3.6739
29	0.2557	0.6830	1.3114	1.6991	2.0452	2.4620	2.7564	3.0380	3.3963	3.6595
30	0.2556	0.6828	1.3104	1.6973	2.0423	2.4573	2.7500	3.0298	3.3852	3.6460
40	0.2550	0.6807	1.3031	1.6839	2.0211	2.4233	2.7045	2.9712	3.3069	3.5510
60	0.2545	0.6786	1.2958	1.6706	2.0003	2.3901	2.6603	2.9146	3.2317	3.4602
120	0.2539	0.6765	1.2886	1.6576	1.9799	2.3578	2.6174	2.8599	3.1595	3.3734
1000	0.2534	0.6747	1.2824	1.6464	1.9623	2.3301	2.5807	2.8133	3.0984	3.3002

Appendix 3

Chi-Square Distribution Table

Example: The upper x^2 value at 5% level of significance with 9 degrees of freedom is obtained at the point of intersection of 9 degrees of freedom row and 0.05 column. This x^2 value is = 16.918960.

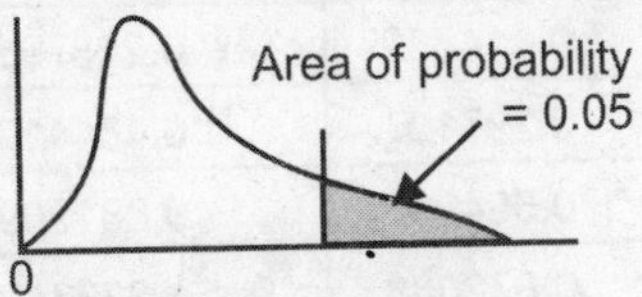

Degrees of freedom	Upper t Value 0.1	0.05	0.025	0.01	0.005
1	2.705541	3.841455	5.023903	6.634891	7.879400
2	4.605176	5.991476	7.377779	9.210351	10.596530
3	6.251394	7.814725	9.348404	11.344882	12.838073
4	7.779434	9.487728	11.143262	13.276699	14.860166
5	9.236349	11.070483	12.832492	15.086317	16.749648
6	10.644637	12.591577	14.449355	16.811872	18.547513
7	12.017031	14.067127	16.012774	18.475324	20.277738
8	13.361562	15.507312	17.534545	20.090159	21.954861
9	14.683663	16.918960	19.022778	21.666048	23.589275
10	15.987175	18.307029	20.483201	23.209287	25.188055
11	17.275007	19.675153	21.920023	24.725022	26.756864
12	18.549340	21.026055	23.336660	26.216964	28.299660
13	19.811933	22.362027	24.735581	27.688184	29.819318
14	21.064141	23.684782	26.118935	29.141163	31.319425
15	22.307121	24.995797	27.488365	30.577951	32.801491
16	23.541821	26.296221	28.845325	31.999861	34.267053
17	24.769028	27.587100	30.190983	33.408717	35.718378
18	25.989418	28.869321	31.526410	34.805237	37.156386
19	27.203565	30.143505	32.852337	36.190775	38.582122
20	28.411970	31.410420	34.169581	37.566272	39.996856
21	29.615086	32.670558	35.478856	38.932232	41.400943
22	30.813285	33.924460	36.780678	40.289448	42.795664
23	32.006890	35.172460	38.075609	41.638334	44.181385
24	33.196235	36.415026	39.364060	42.979781	45.558363
25	34.381583	37.652489	40.646498	44.314014	46.927966
26	35.563164	38.885130	41.923138	45.641636	48.289777
27	36.741228	40.113266	43.194521	46.962837	49.645035
28	37.915907	41.337152	44.460790	48.278166	50.993559
29	39.087475	42.556948	45.722279	49.587829	52.335495
30	40.256017	43.772954	46.979218	50.892181	53.671868
40	51.805044	55.758487	59.341679	63.690771	66.766047
50	63.167113	67.504805	71.420194	76.153802	79.489839
60	74.396999	79.081954	83.297706	88.379430	91.951806
70	85.527036	90.531262	95.023149	100.425051	104.214769
80	96.578196	101.879472	106.628542	112.328791	116.320928
90	107.565010	113.145234	118.135908	124.116195	128.298676
100	118.498002	124.342101	129.561252	135.806891	140.169714

Upper Chi-Square Value

Degrees of Freedom	0.995	0.99	0.975	0.95	0.9
1	0.000039	0.000157	0.000982	0.003932	0.015791
2	0.010025	0.020100	0.050636	0.102586	0.210721
3	0.071723	0.114832	0.215795	0.351846	0.584375
4	0.206984	0.297107	0.484419	0.710724	1.063624
5	0.411751	0.554297	0.831209	1.145477	1.610309
6	0.675733	0.872083	1.237342	1.635380	2.204130
7	0.989251	1.239032	1.689864	2.167349	2.833105
8	1.344403	1.646506	2.179725	2.732633	3.489537
9	1.734911	2.087889	2.700389	3.325115	4.168156
10	2.155845	2.558199	3.246963	3.940295	4.865178
11	2.603202	3.053496	3.815742	4.574809	5.577788
12	3.073785	3.570551	4.403778	5.226028	6.303796
13	3.565042	4.106900	5.008738	5.891861	7.041500
14	4.074659	4.660415	5.628724	6.570632	7.789538
15	4.600874	5.229356	6.262123	7.260935	8.546753
16	5.142164	5.812197	6.907664	7.961639	9.312235
17	5.697274	6.407742	7.564179	8.671754	10.085183
18	6.264766	7.014903	8.230737	9.390448	10.864937
19	6.843923	7.632698	8.906514	10.117006	11.650912
20	7.433811	8.260368	9.590772	10.850799	12.442601
21	8.033602	8.897172	10.282907	11.591316	13.239596
22	8.642681	9.542494	10.982330	12.338009	14.041490
23	9.260383	10.195689	11.688534	13.090505	14.847954
24	9.886199	10.856349	12.401146	13.848422	15.658679
25	10.519647	11.523951	13.119707	14.611396	16.473405
26	11.160218	12.198177	13.843881	15.379163	17.291880
27	11.807655	12.878468	14.573373	16.151395	18.113889
28	12.461281	13.564666	15.307854	16.927876	18.939235
29	13.121067	14.256406	16.047051	17.708381	19.767740
30	13.786682	14.953464	16.790756	18.492667	20.599245
40	20.706577	22.164201	24.433058	26.509296	29.050516
50	27.990825	29.706725	32.357385	34.764236	37.688637
60	35.534397	37.484796	40.481707	43.187966	46.458885
70	43.275305	45.441700	48.757536	51.739263	55.328945
80	51.171933	53.539983	57.153152	60.391459	64.277842
90	59.196327	61.754019	65.646592	69.126018	73.291079
100	67.327533	70.064995	74.221882	77.929442	82.358127

Appendix 4

F Distribution Table

Example: Upper F value at 5% level of significance with degrees of freedom (6, 8) = 3.58. Please note that n1 is the degrees of freedom for the numerator and nz is the degrees of freedom for the denominator.

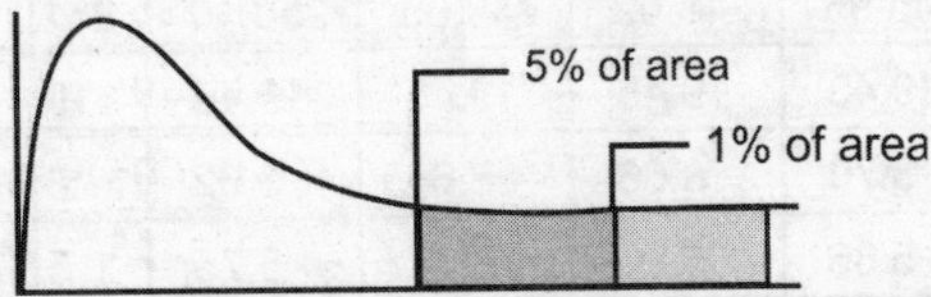

Upper F values for 5% Significance

	n									
n	**1**	**2**	**3**	**4**	**5**	**6**	**7**	**8**	**9**	**10**
1	161.45	199.50	215.71	224.58	230.16	233.99	236.77	238.88	240.54	241.88
2	18.51	19.00	19.16	19.25	19.30	19.33	19.35	19.37	19.38	19.40
3	10.13	9.55	9.28	9.12	9.01	8.94	8.89	8.85	8.81	8.79
4	7.71	6.94	6.59	6.39	6.26	6.16	6.09	6.04	6.00	5.96
5	6.61	5.79	5.41	5.19	5.05	4.95	4.88	4.82	4.77	4.74
6	5.99	5.14	4.76	4.53	4.39	4.28	4.21	4.15	4.10	4.06
7	5.59	4.74	4.35	4.12	3.97	3.87	3.79	3.73	3.68	3.64
8	5.32	4.46	4.07	3.84	3.69	3.58	3.50	3.44	3.39	3.35
9	5.12	4.26	3.86	3.63	3.48	3.37	3.29	3.23	3.18	3.14
10	4.96	4.10	3.71	3.48	3.33	3.22	3.14	3.07	3.02	2.98
11	4.84	3.98	3.59	3.36	3.20	3.09	3.01	2.95	2.90	2.85
12	4.75	3.89	3.49	3.26	3.11	3.00	2.91	2.85	2.80	2.75
13	4.67	3.81	3.41	3.18	3.03	2.92	2.83	2.77	2.71	2.67
14	4.60	3.74	3.34	3.11	2.96	2.85	2.76	2.70	2.65	2.60
15	4.54	3.68	3.29	3.06	2.90	2.79	2.71	2.64	2.59	2.54
16	4.49	3.63	3.24	3.01	2.85	2.74	2.66	2.59	2.54	2.49
17	4.45	3.59	3.20	2.96	2.81	2.70	2.61	2.55	2.49	2.45
18	4.41	3.55	3.16	2.93	2.77	2.66	2.58	2.51	2.46	2.41
19	4.38	3.52	3.13	2.90	2.74	2.63	2.54	2.48	2.42	2.38
20	4.35	3.49	3.10	2.87	2.71	2.60	2.51	2.45	2.39	2.35
21	4.32	3.47	3.07	2.84	2.68	2.57	2.49	2.42	2.37	2.32
22	4.30	3.44	3.05	2.82	2.66	2.55	2.46	2.40	2.34	2.30
23	4.28	3.42	3.03	2.80	2.64	2.53	2.44	2.37	2.32	2.27
24	4.26	3.40	3.01	2.78	2.62	2.51	2.42	2.36	2.30	2.25
25	4.24	3.39	2.99	2.76	2.60	2.49	2.40	2.34	2.28	2.24
30	4.17	3.32	2.92	2.69	2.53	2.42	2.33	2.27	2.21	2.16
40	4.08	3.23	2.84	2.61	2.45	2.34	2.25	2.18	2.12	2.08
60	4.00	3.15	2.76	2.53	2.37	2.25	2.17	2.10	2.04	1.99
120	3.92	3.07	2.68	2.45	2.29	2.18	2.09	2.02	1.96	1.91
1000	3.85	3.00	2.61	2.38	2.22	2.11	2.02	1.95	1.89	1.84

Upper F values for 5% Significance

	n									
n	10	12	15	20	24	30	40	60	120	1000
1	241.88	243.90	245.95	248.02	249.05	250.10	251.14	252.20	253.25	254.19
2	19.40	19.41	19.43	19.45	19.45	19.46	19.47	19.48	19.49	19.49
3	8.79	8.74	8.70	8.66	8.64	8.62	8.59	8.57	8.55	8.53
4	5.96	5.91	5.86	5.80	5.77	5.75	5.72	5.69	5.66	5.63
5	4.74	4.68	4.62	4.56	4.53	4.50	4.46	4.43	4.40	4.37
6	4.06	4.00	3.94	3.87	3.84	3.81	3.77	3.74	3.70	3.67
7	3.64	3.57	3.51	3.44	3.41	3.38	3.34	3.30	3.27	3.23
8	3.35	3.28	3.22	3.15	3.12	3.08	3.04	3.01	2.97	2.93
9	3.14	3.07	3.01	2.94	2.90	2.86	2.83	2.79	2.75	2.71
10	2.98	2.91	2.85	2.77	2.74	2.70	2.66	2.62	2.58	2.54
11	2.85	2.79	2.72	2.65	2.61	2.57	2.53	2.49	2.45	2.41
12	2.75	2.69	2.62	2.54	2.51	2.47	2.43	2.38	2.34	2.30
13	2.67	2.60	2.53	2.46	2.42	2.38	2.34	2.30	2.25	2.21
14	2.60	2.53	2.46	2.39	2.35	2.31	2.27	2.22	2.18	2.14
15	2.54	2.48	2.40	2.33	2.29	2.25	2.20	2.16	2.11	2.07
16	2.49	2.42	2.35	2.28	2.24	2.19	2.15	2.11	2.06	2.02
17	2.45	2.38	2.31	2.23	2.19	2.15	2.10	2.06	2.01	1.97
18	2.41	2.34	2.27	2.19	2.15	2.11	2.06	2.02	1.97	1.92
19	2.38	2.31	2.23	2.16	2.11	2.07	2.03	1.98	1.93	1.88
20	2.35	2.28	2.20	2.12	2.08	2.04	1.99	1.95	1.90	1.85
21	2.32	2.25	2.18	2.10	2.05	2.01	1.96	1.92	1.87	1.82
22	2.30	2.23	2.15	2.07	2.03	1.98	1.94	1.89	1.84	1.79
23	2.27	2.20	2.13	2.05	2.01	1.96	1.91	1.86	1.81	1.76
24	2.25	2.18	2.11	2.03	1.98	1.94	1.89	1.84	1.79	1.74
25	2.24	2.16	2.09	2.01	1.96	1.92	1.87	1.82	1.77	1.72
30	2.16	2.09	2.01	1.93	1.89	1.84	1.79	1.74	1.68	1.63
40	2.08	2.00	1.92	1.84	1.79	1.74	1.69	1.64	1.58	1.52
60	1.99	1.92	1.84	1.75	1.70	1.65	1.59	1.53	1.47	1.40
120	1.91	1.83	1.75	1.66	1.61	1.55	1.50	1.43	1.35	1.27
1000	1.84	1.76	1.68	1.58	1.53	1.47	1.41	1.33	1.24	1.11

Appendix 5

Upper F Values for 1 % Significance

Example: Upper F value at 1% level of significance with degrees of freedom (6, 8) = 6.37. Please note that n1 is the degrees of freedom for the numerator and *n2* is the degrees of freedom for the denominator.

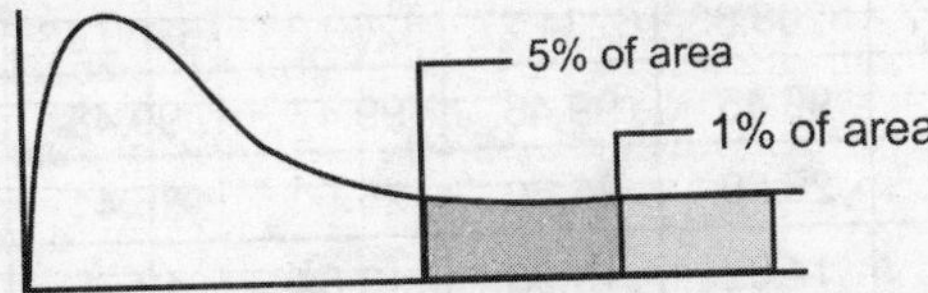

	n_1									
	1	2	3	4	5	6	7	8	9	10
n_2										
1	4052.18	4999.34	5403.53	5624.26	5763.96	5858.95	5928.33	5980.95	6022.40	6055.93
2	98.50	99.00	99.16	99.25	99.30	99.33	99.36	99.38	99.39	99.40
3	34.12	30.82	29.46	28.71	28.24	27.91	27.67	27.49	27.34	27.23
4	21.20	18.00	16.69	15.98	15.52	15.21	14.98	14.80	14.66	14.55
5	16.26	13.27	12.06	11.39	10.97	10.67	10.46	10.29	10.16	10.05
6	13.75	10.92	9.78	9.15	8.75	8.47	8.26	8.10	7.98	7.87
7	12.25	9.55	8.45	7.85	7.46	7.19	6.99	6.84	6.72	6.62
8	11.26	8.65	7.59	7.01	6.63	6.37	6.18	6.03	5.91	5.81
9	10.56	8.02	6.99	6.42	6.06	5.80	5.61	5.47	5.35	5.26
10	10.04	7.56	6.55	5.99	5.64	5.39	5.20	5.06	4.94	4.85
11	9.65	7.21	6.22	5.67	5.32	5.07	4.89	4.74	4.63	4.54
12	9.33	6.93	5.95	5.41	5.06	4.82	4.64	4.50	4.39	4.30
13	9.07	6.70	5.74	5.21	4.86	4.62	4.44	4.30	4.19	4.10
14	8.86	6.51	5.56	5.04	4.69	4.46	4.28	4.14	4.03	3.94
15	8.68	6.36	5.42	4.89	4.56	4.32	4.14	4.00	3.89	3.80
16	8.53	6.23	5.29	4.77	4.44	4.20	4.03	3.89	3.78	3.69
17	8.40	6.11	5.19	4.67	4.34	4.10	3.93	3.79	3.68	3.59
18	8.29	6.01	5.09	4.58	4.25	4.01	3.84	3.71	3.60	3.51
19	8.18	5.93	5.01	4.50	4.17	3.94	3.77	3.63	3.52	3.43
20	8.10	5.85	4.94	4.43	4.10	3.87	3.70	3.56	3.46	3.37
21	8.02	5.78	4.87	4.37	4.04	3.81	3.64	3.51	3.40	3.31
22	7.95	5.72	4.82	4.31	3.99	3.76	3.59	3.45	3.35	3.26
23	7.88	5.66	4.76	4.26	3.94	3.71	3.54	3.41	3.30	3.21
24	7.82	5.61	4.72	4.22	3.90	3.67	3.50	3.36	3.26	3.17
25	7.77	5.57	4.68	4.18	3.85	3.63	3.46	3.32	3.22	3.13
30	7.56	5.39	4.51	4.02	3.70	3.47	3.30	3.17	3.07	2.98
40	7.31	5.18	4.31	3.83	3.51	3.29	3.12	2.99	2.89	2.80
60	7.08	4.98	4.13	3.65	3.34	3.12	2.95	2.82	2.72	2.63
120	6.85	4.79	3.95	3.48	3.17	2.96	2.79	2.66	2.56	2.47
1000	6.66	4.63	3.80	3.34	3.04	2.82	2.66	2.53	2.43	2.34

Upper F Values for 1% Significance

	n_1									
n_2	10	12	15	20	24	30	40	60	120	1000
1	6055.93	6106.68	6156.97	6208.66	6234.27	6260.35	6286.43	6312.97	6339.51	6362.80
2	99.40	99.42	99.43	99.45	99.46	99.47	99.48	99.48	99.49	99.50
3	27.23	27.05	26.87	26.69	26.60	26.50	26.41	26.32	26.22	26.14
4	14.55	14.37	14.20	14.02	13.93	13.84	13.75	13.65	13.56	13.47
5	10.05	9.89	9.72	9.55	9.47	9.38	9.29	9.20	9.11	9.03
6	7.87	7.72	7.56	7.40	7.31	7.23	7.14	7.06	6.97	6.89
7	6.62	6.47	6.31	6.16	6.07	5.99	5.91	5.82	5.74	5.66
8	5.81	5.67	5.52	5.36	5.28	5.20	5.12	5.03	4.95	4.87
9	5.26	5.11	4.96	4.81	4.73	4.65	4.57	4.48	4.40	4.32
10	4.85	4.71	4.56	4.41	4.33	4.25	4.17	4.08	4.00	3.92
11	4.54	4.40	4.25	4.10	4.02	3.94	3.86	3.78	3.69	3.61
12	4.30	4.16	4.01	3.86	3.78	3.70	3.62	3.54	3.45	3.37
13	4.10	3.96	3.82	3.66	3.59	3.51	3.43	3.34	3.25	3.18
14	3.94	3.80	3.66	3.51	3.43	3.35	3.27	3.18	3.09	3.02
15	3.80	3.67	3.52	3.37	3.29	3.21	3.13	3.05	2.96	2.88
16	3.69	3.55	3.41	3.26	3.18	3.10	3.02	2.93	2.84	2.76
17	3.59	3.46	3.31	3.16	3.08	3.00	2.92	2.83	2.75	2.66
18	3.51	3.37	3.23	3.08	3.00	2.92	2.84	2.75	2.66	2.58
19	3.43	3.30	3.15	3.00	2.92	2.84	2.76	2.67	2.58	2.50
20	3.37	3.23	3.09	2.94	2.86	2.78	2.69	2.61	2.52	2.43
21	3.31	3.17	3.03	2.88	2.80	2.72	2.64	2.55	2.46	2.37
22	3.26	3.12	2.98	2.83	2.75	2.67	2.58	2.50	2.40	2.32
23	3.21	3.07	2.93	2.78	2.70	2.62	2.54	2.45	2.35	2.27
24	3.17	3.03	2.89	2.74	2.66	2.58	2.49	2.40	2.31	2.22
25	3.13	2.99	2.85	2.70	2.62	2.54	2.45	2.36	2.27	2.18
30	2.98	2.84	2.70	2.55	2.47	2.39	2.30	2.21	2.11	2.02
40	2.80	2.66	2.52	2.37	2.29	2.20	2.11	2.02	1.92	1.82
60	2.63	2.50	2.35	2.20	2.12	.2.03	1.94	1.84	1.73	1.62
120	2.47	2.34	2.19	2.03	1.95	1.86	1.76	1.66	1.53	1.40
1000	2.34	2.20	2.06	1.90	1.81	1.72	1.61	1.50	1.35	1.16

Critical Values of TIN the Wilcoxon Matched – Pairs Test

	Level of significance for one-tailed test		
	.025	.01	.005
	Level of significance for two-tailed test		
II	.05	.02	.01
6	0	-	-
7	2	0	-
8	4	2	0
9	6	3	2
10	8	5	3
11	11	‘7	5
12	14	10	7
13	17	13	10
14	21	16	13
15	25	20	16
16	30	24	20
17	35	28	23
18	40	33	28
19	46	38	32
20	52	43	38
			-
21	59	49	43
22	66	56	49
23	73	62	55
24	81	69	61
25	89	77	68

Percentage Points of D in the Two-sample Kolmogorov-Smirnov Distribution

		n_2											
nj	*a*	2	3	4	5	6	7	8	9	10	11	12	13
7	0.05	-	1.000	.857	.800	.714	.857	.714	.667	.657	.623	.631	.615
7	0.025	-	1.000	1.000	.857	.833	.857	.732	.714	.700	.675	.667	.637
7	0.01	-	-	1.000	1.000	.857	.857	.857	.778	.757	.766	.714	.714
7	0.001	-	-	-	-	-	1.000	1.000	1.000	.900	.909	.857	.857
8	0.05	1.000	.875	.875	.750	.708	.714	.750	.639	.600	.602	.625	.596
8	0.025	-	1.000	.875	.800	.750	.732	.750	.667	.675	.659	.667	.625
8	0.01	-	-	1.000	.875	.833	.857	.875	.764	.750	.727	.708	.692
8	0.001	-	-	-	-	1.000	1.000	1.000	.889	.875	.875	.833	.846
9	0.05	1.000	.889	.778	.778	.722	.667	.639	.667	.589	.596	.583	.556
9	0.025	-	1.000	.889	.800	.778	.714	.667	.778	.667	.636	.639	.615
9	0.01	-	1.000	1.000	.889	.833	.778	.764	.778	.700	.707	.694	.667
9	0.001	-	-	-	1.000	1.000	1.000	.889	.889	.889	.818	.806	.778
10	0.05	1.000	.900	.750	.800	.667	.657	.600	.589	.700	.545	.550	.538
10	0.025	-	1.000	.900	.800	.733	.700	.675	.667	.700	.618	.600	.592
10	0.01	-	1.000	.900	.900	.800	.757	.750	.700	.800	.700	.667	.646
10	0.001	-	-	-	1.000	1.000	.900	.875	.889	.900	.809	.800	.769
11	0.05	1.000	.909	.750	.709	.652	.623	.602	.596	.545	.636	.545	.524
11	0.025	-	.909	.818	.800	.727	.675	.659	.636	.618	.636	.576	.587
11	0.01	-	1.000	.909	.818	.818	.766	.727	.707	.700	.727	.652	.636
11	0.001	-	-	-	1.000	1.000	.909	.875	.818	.809	.818	.750	.755
12	0.05	1.000	.833	.750	.717	.667	.631	.625	.583	.550	.545	.583	.519
12	0.025	1.000	.917	.833	.750	.750	.667	.667	.639	.600	.576	.667	.538
12	0.01	-	1.000	.917	.833	.833	.714	.708	.694	.667	.652	.667	.609
12	0.001	-	-	-	1.000	.917	.857	.833	.806	.800	.750	.833	.750
13	0.05	1.000	.846	.750	.692	.667	.615	.596	.556	.538	.524	.519	.538
13	0.025	1.000	.923	.846	.723	.692	.637	.625	.615	.592	.587	.538	.615
13	0.01	-	1.000	.923	.800	.769	.714	.692	.667	.646	.636	.609	.692
13	0.001	-	-	1.000	1.000	.923	.857	.846	.778	.769	.755	.750	.769
14	0.05	.929	.857	.750	.657	.643	.643	.571	.556	.529	.532	.512	.489
14	0.025	1.000	.929	.786	.729	.690	.714	.625	.603	.586	.565	.560	.549
14	0.01	-	1.000	.857	.800	.762	.786	.679	.667	.643	.623	.619	.571
14	0.001	-	-	1.000	1.000	.929	.857	.804	.778	.757	.747	.714	.709
15	0.05	.933	.800	.733	.733	.633	.590	.558	.556	.533	.509	.517	.492
15	0.025	1.000	.867	.750	.733	.700	.648	.617	.600	.600	.570	.550	.533
15	0.01	-	.933	.867	.800	.767	.714	.675	.667	.667	.618	.600	.590
15	0.001	-	-	1.000	.933	.933	.857	.808	.778	.767	.727	.717	.703
16	0.05	.938	.813	.750	.675	.625	.571	.625	.542	.525	.506	.500	.486
16	CUJ25	1.000	.875	.813	.738	.667	.652	.625	.590	.563	.545	.542	.534
16	0.01	-	.938	.875	.800	.750	.688	.688	.653	.625	.602	.604	.582
16	O.cJOI	-	-	1.000	.938	.875	.857	.813	.764	.738	.722	.708	.688
17	0.05	.941	.824	.706	.647	.608	.571	.566	.536	.524	.497	.490	.475
17	0.cJ25	1.000	.882	.765	.706	.657	.647	.588	.588	.565	.545	.529	.516
17	O.C)}	-	.941	.882	.800	.716	.706	.647	.647	.624	.588	.583	.575
17	0.001	-	-	1.000	.941	.833	.824	.816	.765	.741	.706	.691	.688
18	0.05	.944	.833	.694	.667	.667	.571	.556	.556	.511	.490	.500	.470
18	0.025	1.000	.889	.750	.722	.722	.635	.597	.611	.556	.540	.556	.513
18	O.C)}		.944	.833	.778	.778	.690	.653	.667	.600	.596	.583	.560
18	0.001	-	-	1. 000	.944	.889	.802	.778	.778	.733	.707	.694	.667

Percentage Points of D in the Two-sample Kolmogorov-Smirnov Distribution

n_2													
14	**15**	**16**	**17**	**18**	**19**	**20**	**21**	**22**	**23**	**24**	**25**	***a***	**nl**
.643	.590	.571	.571	.571	.571	.564	.619	.545	.553	.548	.554	0.05	7
.714	.648	.652	.647	.635	.632	.614	.667	.623	.609	.607	.600	0.025	7
.786	.714	.688	.706	.690	.684	.664	.714	.669	.671	.667	.657	0.01	7
.857	.857	.857	.824	.802	.805	.800	.810	.812	.783	.792	.777	0.001	7
.571	.558	.625	.566	.556	.539	.550	.530	.534	.533	.542	.520	0.05	8
.625	.617	.625	.588	.597	.592	.600	.577	.580	.576	.583	.560	0.025	8
.679	.675	.688	.647	.653	.645	.650	.637	.636	.625	.667	.625	0.01	8
.804	.808	.813	.816	.778	.770	.775	.750	.750	.745	.792	.750	0.001	8
.556	.556	.542	.536	.556	.520	.517	.524	.510	.512	.514	.5071	0.05	9
.603	.600	.590	.588	.611	.573	.556	.571	.556	.556	.556	.547	0.025	9
.667	.667	.653	.647	.667	.626	.617	.619	.616	.609	.611	.600	0.01	9
.778	.778	.764	.765	.778	.737	.739	.730	.727	.734	.722	.720	0.001	9
.529	.533	.525	.524	.511	.495	.550	.500	.491	.496	.492	.500 I	0.05	10
.586	.600	.563	.565	.556	.542	.600	.552	.536	.539	.533	.540	0.025	10
.643	.667	.625	.624	.600	.595	.650	.600	.591	.596	.583	.600	0.01	10
.757	.767	.738	.741	.733	.700	.750	.710	.700	.696	.692	.700	0.001	10
.532	.509	.506	.497	.490	.488	.486	.485	.500	.470	.470	.469	0.05	11
.565	.570	.545	.545	.540	.531	.527	.532	.545	.518	.519	.509	0.025	11
.623	.618	.602	.588	.596	.584	.577	.580	.591	.561	.568	.560	0.01	11
.747	.727	.722	.706	.707	.699	.700	.680	.727	.684	.667	.669	0.001	11
.512	.517	.500	.490	.500	.474	.483	.476	.470	.453	.500	.460	0.05	12
.560	.550	.542	.529	.556	.526	.517	.512	.508	.496	.542	.500	0.025	12
.619	.600	.604	.583	.583	.570	.583	.560	.561	.540	.583	.550	0.01	12
.714	.717	.708	.691	.694	.684	.683	.667	.659	.659	.667	.640	0.001	12
.489	.492	.486	.475	.470	.462	.462	.462	.455	.452	.449	.446	0.05	13
.549	.533	.534	.516	.513	.510	.500	.502	.493	.488	.484	.486	0.025	13
.571	.590	.582	.575	.560	.559	.550	.549	.545	.538	.532	.529	0.01	13
.709	.703	.688	.688	.667	.664	.650	.656	.647	.639	.638	.615	0.001	13
.571	.467	.473	.466	.460	.455	.450	.476	.448	.441	.435	.429	0.05	14
.571	.524	.518	.513	.500	.500	.493	.500	.481	.478	.476	.474	0.025	14
.643	.586	.563	.563	.556	.556	.543	.548	.532	.528	.524	.520	0.01	14
.786	.667	.679	.668	.659	.662	.643	.643	.636	.627	.625	.626	0.001	14
.467	.533	.475	.455	.456	.446	.450	.438	.436	.432	.433	.427	0.05	15
.524	.600	.496	.506	.500	.495	.500	.486	.467	.472	.467	.467	0.025	15
.586	.600	.554	.557	.544	.533	.533	.533	.524	.519	.517	.520	0.01	15
.667	.733	.675	.647	.644	.632	.650	.629	.621	.609	.617	.613	0.001	15
.473	.475	.500	.456	.444	.438	.438	.432	.426	.427	.438	.418	0.05	16
.518	.496	.563	.500	.486	.477	.488	.467	.466	.459	.479	.453	0.025	16
.563	.554	.625	.526	.535	.526	.525	.515	.511	.508	.521	.498	0.01	16
.679	.675	.688	.640	.646	.632	.625	.619	.614	.601	.604	.595	0.001	16
.466	.455	.456	.471	.435	.437	.429	.423	.420	.417	.412	.407	0.05	17
.513	.506	.500	.529	.484	.467	.471	.465	.455	.458	.449	.447	0.025	17
.563	.557	.526	.588	.536	.514	.515	.504	.500	.501	.498	.487	0.01	17
.668	.647	.640	.706	.611	.619	.615	.608	.602	.593	.588	.586	0.001	17
.460	.456	.444	.435	.500	.415	.422	.421	.414	.411	.417	.400	0.05	18
.500	.500	.486	.484	.500	.465	.461	.460	.449	.444	.458	.436	0.025	18
.556	.544	.535	.536	.556	.515	.506	.500	.495	.493	.500	.480	0.01	18
.659	.644	.646	.611	.667	.620	.594	.595	.591	.585	.583	.571	0.001	18

Percentage Points of D in the Two-sample Kolmogorov-Smirnov Distribution

		n_s											
nl	**a**	**2**	**3**	**4**	**5**	**6**	**7**	**8**	**9**	**10**	**11**	**12**	**13**
19	0.05	.947	.789	.697	.642	.614	.571	.539	.520	.495	.488	.474	.462
19	0.025	1. 000	.895	.750	.695	.667	.632	.592	.573	.542	.531	.526	.510
19	0.01	1.000	.947	.842	.747	.728	.684	.645	.626	.595	.584	.570	.559
19	0.001	-	-	1.000	.895	.842	.805	.770	.737	.700	.699	.684	.664
20	0.05	.950	.800	.750	.650	.600	.564	.550	.517	.550	.486	.483	.462
20	0.025	1.000	.850	.800	.750	.650	.614	.600	.556	.600	.527	.517	.500
20	0.01	1.000	.950	.850	.800	.733	.664	.650	.617	.650	.577	.583	.550
20	0.001	-	-	.950	.900	.833	.800	.775	.739	.750	.700	.683	.650
21	0.05	.905	.810	.702	.657	.595	.619	.530	.524	.500	.485	.476	.462
21	0.025	.952	.857	.750	.705	.643	.667	.577	.571	.552	.532	.512	.502
21	0.01	1.000	.905	.857	.762	.714	.714	.637	.619	.600	.580	.560	.549
21	0.001	-	1.000	.952	.905	.833	.810	.750	.730	.710	.680	.667	.656
22	0.05	.909	.773	.705	.636	.591	.545	.534	.510	.491	.500	.470	.455
22	0.025	.955	.864	.750	.709	.652	.623	.580	.556	.536	.545	.508	.493
22	0.01	1.000	.909	.818	.755	.697	.669	.636	.616	.591	.591	.561	.545
22	0.001	-	1.000	.955	.909	.833	.812	.750	.727	.700	.727	.659	.647
23	0.05	.913	.783	.696	.626	.580	.553	.533	.512	.496	.470	.453	.452
23	0.025	.957	.870	.750	.696	.623	.609	.576	.556	.539	.518	.496	.488
23	0.01	1.000	.913	.826	.757	.703	.671	.625	.609	.596	.561	.540	.538
23	0.001	-	1.000	.957	.913	.826	.783	.745	.734	.696	.684	.659	.639
24	0.05	.917	.792	.708	.633	.625	.548	.542	.514	.492	.470	.500	.449
24	0.025	.958	.833	.750	.675	.667	.607	.583	.556	.533	.519	.542	.484
24	0.01	1.000	.917	.833	.750	.708	.667	.667	.611	.583	.568	.583	.532
24	0.001	-	1.000	.958	.875	.833	.792	.792	.722	.692	.667	.667	.638
25	0.05	.920	.800	.680	.640	.587	.554	.520	.507	.500	.469	.460	.446
25	0.025	.960	.840	.750	.720	.640	.600	.560	.547	.540	.509	.500	.486
25	0.01	1.000	.920	.840	.760	.713	.657	.625	.600	.600	.560	.550	.529
25	0.001	-	1.000	.960	.880	.833	.777	.750	.720	.700	.669	.640	.615
	a	I	0.05			0.025			0.01			0.001	
		I 1.36n, ± n,				nl +nz			n1 +nz			n, +n,	
	Da				1.48			1.63				1.95 -	
			n1nz			n1nz			n1nz			n1nz	

Percentage Points of D in the Two-sample Kolmogorov-Smirnov Distribution

n_2													
14	15	16	17	18	19	20	21	22	23	24	25	*a*	nl
.455	.446	.438	.437	.415	.474	.421	.409	.404	.405	.401	.394	0.05	19
.500	.495	.477	.467	.465	.526	.445	.451	.443	.435	.436	.432	0.025	19
.556	.533	.526	.514	.515	.526	.492	.499	.488	.478	.478	.472	0.01	19
.662	.632	.632	.619	.620	.632	.592	.594	.579	.579	.572	.564	0.001	19
.450	.450	.438	.429	.422	.421	.450	.412	.400	.400	.400	.400	0.05	20
.493	.500	.488	.471	.461	.445	.500	.429	.436	.433	.433	.430	0.025	20
.543	.533	.525	.515	.506	.492	.550	.474	.482	.476	.475	.470	0.01	20
.643	.650	.625	.615	.594	.592	.650	.569	.577	.570	.567	.560	0.001	20
.476	.438	.432	.423	.421	.409	.412	.429	.396	.391	.393	.385	0.05	21
.500	.486	.467	.465	.460	.451	.429	.476	.439	.427	.423	.419	0.025	21
.548	.533	.515	.504	.500	.499	.474	.524	.483	.470	.470	.465	0.01	21
.643	.629'	.619	.608	.595	.594	.569	.619	.578	.557	.560	.552	0.001	21
.448	.436	.426	.420	.414	.404	.400	.396	.409	.383	.386	.380	0.05	22
.481	.467	.466	.455	.449	.443	.436	.439	.455	.423	.420	.415	0.025	22
.532	.524	.511	.500	.495	.488	.482	.483	.500	.468	.458	.455	0.01	22
.636	.621	.614	.602	.591	.579	.577	.578	.591	.557	.553	.544	0.001	22
.441	.432	.427	.417	.411	.405	.400	.391	.383	.435	.371	.376	0.05	23
.478	.472	.459	.458	.444	.435	.433	.427	.423	.435	.409	.412	0.025	23
.528	.519	.508	.501	.493	.478	.476	.470	.468	.478	.451	.456	0.01	23
.627	.609	.601	.593	.585	.579	.570	.557	.557	.565	.536	.543	0.001	23
.435	.433	.438	.412	.417	.401	.400	.393	.386	.371	.417	.375	0.05	24
.476	.467	.479	.449	.458	.436	.433	.423	.420	.409	.458	.397	0.025	24
.524	.517	.521	.498	.500	.478	.475	.470	.458	.451	.500	.437	0.01	24
.625	.617	.604	.588	.583	.572	.567	.560	.553	.536	.583	.520	0.001	24
.429	.427	.418	.407	.400	.394	.400	.385	.380	.376	.375	.400	0.05	25
.474	.467	.453	.447	.436	.432	.430	.419	.415	.412	.397	.440	0.025	25
.520	.520	.498	.487	.480	.472	.470	.465	.455	.456	.437	.480	0.01	25
.626	.613	.595	.586	.571	.564	.560	.552	.544	.543	.520	.560	0.001	25

Lower Percentage Points of the Mann-Whitney U-Distribution

		n_2																	
n_1	a	3	4	5	6	7	8	9	10	11	12	13	14	15	16	17	18	19	20
1	0.05	-	-	-	-	-	-	-	-	-	-	-	-	-	-	-	-	0	0
1	0.025	-	-	-	-	-	-	-	-	-	-	-	-	-	-	-	-	-	-
1	0.01	-	-	-	-	-	-	-	-	-	-	-	-	-	-	-	-	-	-
1	0.001	-	-	-	-	-	-	-	-	-	-	-	-	-	-	-	-	-	-
2	0.05	-	-	0	0	0	1	1	1	1	2	2	3	3	3	3	4	4	4
2	0.025	-	-	-	-	-	0	0	0	0	1	1	1	1	1	2	2	2	2
2	0.01	-	-	-	-	-	-	-	-	-	-	0	0	0	0	0	0	1	1
2	0.001	-	-	-	-	-	-	-	-	-	-	-	-	-	-	-	-	-	-
3	0.05	0	0	1	.2	2	3	4	4	5	5	6	7	7	8	9	9	10	11
3	0.025	-	-	0	1	1	2	2	3	3	4	4	5	5	6	6	7	7	8
3	0.01	-	-	-	-	0	0	1	1	1	2	2	2	3	3	4	4	4	5
3	0.001	-	-	-	-	-	-	-	-	-	-	-	-	-	-	0	0	0	0
4	0.05	-	1	2	3	4	5	6	7	8	9	10	11	12	14	15	16	17	18
4	0.025	-	0	1	2	3	4	4	5	6	7	8	9	10	11	11	12	13	13
4	0.01	-	-	0	1	1	2	3	3	4	5	5	6	7	7	8	9	9	10
4	0.001	-	-	-	-	-	-	-	0	0	0	1	1	1	2	2	3	3	3
5	0.05	-	-	4	5	6	8	9	11	12	13	15	16	18	19	20	22	23	25
5	0.025	-	-	2	3	5	6	7	8	9	11	12	13	14	15	17	18	19	20
5	0.01	-	-	1	2	3	4	5	6	7	8	9	10	11	12	13	14	15	16
5	0.001	-	-	-	-	0	0	1	1	2	2	3	3	4	5	5	6	7	7
6	0.05	-	-	-	7	8	10	12	14	16	17	19	21	23	25	26	28	30	32
6	0.025	-	-	-	5	6	8	10	11	13	14	16	17	19	21	22	24	25	27
6	0.01	-	-	-	3	4	6	7	8	9	11	12	13	15	16	18	19	20	22
6	0.001	-	-	-	0	1	2	2	3	4	4	5	6	7	8	9	10	11	12
7	0.05	-	-	-	-	11	13	15	17	19	21	24	26	28	30	33	35	37	39
7	0.025	-	-	-	-	8	10	12	14	16	18	20	22	24	26	28	30	32	34
7	0.01	-	-	-	-	6	8	9	11	12	14	16	17	19	21	23	24	26	28
7	0.001	-	-	-	-	2	3	3	5	6	7	8	9, 10	11	13	14	15	16	
8	0.05	-	-	-	-	-	15	18	20	23	26	28	31	33	36	39	41	44	47
8	0.025	-	-	-	-	-	13	15	17	19	22	24	26	29	31	34	36	38	41
8	0.01	-	-	-	-	-	10	11	13	15	17	20	22	24	26	28	30	32	34
8	0.001	-	-	-	-	-	5	5	6	8	9	11	12	14	15	17	18	20	21
9	0.05	-	-	-	-	-	-	21	24	27	30	33	36	39	42	45	48	51	54
9	0.025	-	-	-	-	-	-	17	20	23	26	28	31	34	37	39	42	45	48
9	0.01	-	-	-	-	-	-	14	16	18	21	23	26	28	31	33	36	38	40
9	0.001	-	-	-	-	-	-	7	8	10	12	14	15	17	19	21	23	25	26

Lower Percentage Points of the Mann-Whitney U-Distribution

		n_2																	
nl	a	3	4	5	6	7	8	9	10	11	12	13	14	15	16	17	18	19	20
10	0.05	-	-	-	-	-	-	-	27	31	34	37	41	44	48	51	55	58	62
10	0.025	-	-	-	-	-	-	-	23	26	29	33	36	39	42	45	48	52	55
10	0.01	-	-	-	-	-	-	-	19	22	24	27	30	33	36	38	41	44	47
10	0.001	-	-	-	-	-	-	-	10	12	14	17	19	21	23	25	27	29	32
11	0.05	-	-	-	-	-	-	-	-	34	38	42	46	50	54	57	61	65	69
11	0.025	-	-	-	-	-	-	-	-	30	33	37	40	44	47	51	55	58	62
11	0.01	-	-	-	-	-	-	-	-	25	28	31	34	37	41	44	47	50	53
11	0.001	-	-	-	-	-	-	-	-	15	17	20	22	24	27	29	32	34	37
12	0.05	-	-	-	-	-	-	-	-	-	42	47	51	55	60	64	68	72	77
12	0.025	-	-	-	-	-	-	-	-	-	37	41	45	49	53	57	61	65	69
12	0.01	-	-	-	-	-	-	-	-	-	31	35	38	42	46	49	53	56	60
12	0.001	-	-	-	-	-	-	-	-	-	20	23	25	28	31	34	37	40	42
13	0.05	-	-	-	-	-	-	-	-	-	-	51	56	61	65	70	75	80	84
13	0.025	-	-	-	-	-	-	-	-	-	-	45	50	54	59	63	67	72	76
13	0.01	-	-	-	-	-	-	-	-	-	-	39	43	47	51	55	59	63	67
13	0.001	-	-	-	-	-	-	-	-	-	-	26	29	32	35	38	42	45	48
14	0.05	-	-	-	-	-	-	-	-	-	-	-	61	66	71	77	82	87	92
14	0.025	-	-	-	-	-	-	-	-	-	-	-	55	59	64	67	74	78	83
14	0.01	-	-	-	-	-	-	-	-	-	-	-	47	51	56	60	65	69	73
14	0.001	-	-	-	-	-	-	-	-	-	-	-	32	36	39	43	46	50	54
15	0.05	-	-	-	-	-	-	-	-	-	-	-	-	72	77	83	88	94	100
15	0.025	-	-	-	-	-	-	-	-	-	-	-	-	64	70	75	80	85	90
15	0.01	-	-	-	-	-	-	-	-	-	-	-	-	56	61	66	70	75	80
15	C). OCI1	-	-	-	-	-	-	-	-	-	-	-	-	40	43	47	51	55	59
16	0.05	-	-	-	-	-	-	-	-	-	-	-	-	-	83	89	95	101	107
16	0.025	-	-	-	-	-	-	-	-	-	-	-	-	-	75	81	86	92	98
16	0.01	-	-	-	-	-	-	-	-	-	-	-	-	-	66	71	76	82	87
16	0.001	-	-	-	-	-	-	-	-	-	-	-	-	-	48	52	56	60	65
17	0.05	-	-	-	-	-	-	-	-	-	-	-	-	-	-	96	102	109	115
17	0.025	-	-	-	-	-	-	-	-	-	-	-	-	-	-	87	93	99	105
17	0.01	-	-	-	-	-	-	-	-	-	-	-	-	-	-	77	82	88	93
17	0.001	-	-	-	-	-	-	-	-	-	-	-	-	-	-	57	61	66	70
18	0.05	-	-	-	-	-	-	-	-	-	-	-	-	-	-	-	109	116	123
18	0.025	-	-	-	-	-	-	-	-	-	-	-	-	-	-	-	99	106	112
18	0.01	-	-	-	-	-	-	-	-	-	-	-	-	-	-	-	88	94	100
18	0.001	-	-	-	-	-	-	-	-	-	-	-	-	-	-	-	66	71	76
19	0.05	-	-	-	-	-	-	-	-	-	-	-	-	-	-	-	-	123	130
19	0.025	-	-	-	-	-	-	-	-	-	-	-	-	-	-	-	-	113	119
19	0.01	-	-	-	-	-	-	-	-	-	-	-	-	-	-	-	-	101	107
19	0.001	-	-	-	-	-	-	-	-	-	-	-	-	-	-	-	-	77	82
20	0.05	-	-	-	-	-	-	-	-	-	-	-	-	-	-	-	-	-	138
20	0.025	-	-	-	-	-	-	-	-	-	-	-	-	-	-	-	-	-	127
20	0.01	-	-	-	-	-	-	-	-	-	-	-	-	-	-	-	-	-	114
20	O.OCI1	-	-	-	-	-	-	-	-	-	-	-	-	-	-	-	-	-	88

Upper Tails of the Kruskal-Wallis Distribution

Sample sizes				
nl	*n2*	*n3*	*H*	*p*
2	1	1	2.7000	.500
2	2	1	3.6000	.200
2	2	2	3.7143	.200
			4.5714	.067
3	1	1	3.2000	.300
3	2	1	3.8571	.133
			4.2857	.100
3	2	2	4.4643	.105
			4.5000	.067
			4.7143	.048
			5.3572	.029
3	3	1	4.0000	.129
			4.5714	.100
			5.1429	.043
3	3	2	4.2500	.121
			4.5556	.100
			5.1389	.061
			5.3611	.032
			6.2500	.011
3	3	3	4.6222	.100
			5.0667	.086
			5.6000	.050
			5.6889	.029
			6.4889	.011
			7.2000	.004
4	1	1	3.5714	.200
4	2	1	4.0179	.114
			4.5000	.076
			4.8214	.057
4	3	2	4.4444	.102
			4.5111	.098
			5.4000	.051
			5.4444	.046
			6.3000	.011
			6.4444	.008
4	3	3	4.7000	.101
			4.7091	.092
			5.7273	.050
			5.7909	.046
			6.7091	.013
			6.7455	.010
4	4	1	4.0667	.102
			4.1667	.082
			4.8667	.054
			4.9667	.048
			6.1667	.022
			6.6667	.010
4	4	2	4.4455	.103
			4.5545	.098
			5.2364	.052
			5.4545	.046
			6.8727	.011
			7.0364	.006
4	4	3	4.4773	.102
			4.5455	.099
			5.5758	.051
			5.5985	.049
			7.1364	.011
			7.1439	.010
4	4	4	4.5001	.104
			4.6539	.097
			5.6538	.054
			5.6923	.049
			7.5385	.011

Contd...

4	2	2	4.1667	.105				7.6538	.008
			4.4583	.100					
			5.1250	.052	5	1	1	3.8571	.143
			5.3333	.033					
			6.0000	.014	5	2	1	4.0500	.119
								4.2000	.095
4	3	1	3.8889	.129				4.4500	.071
			4.0556	.093				5.0000	.048
			5.0000	.057				5.2500	.036
			5.2083	.050					
			5.8333	.021					
5	2	2	4.2933	.122	5	4	4	4.5527	.102
			4.3733	.090				4.6187	.100
			5.0400	.056				5.6176	.050
			5.1600	.034				5.6571	.049
			6.1333	.013				7.7440	.011
			6.5333	.008				7.76.4	.009

Upper Tails of the Kruskal-Wallis Distribution - continued

Sample sizes					Sample sizes				
nl	*n2*	*n3*	*H*	*p*	*nl*	*n2*	*n3*	*H*	*v*
5	3	1	3.8400	.123	5	5	1	4.0364	.105
			4.0178	.095				4.1091	.086
			4.8711	.052				4.9091	.053
			4.9600	.048				5.1273	.046
			6.4000	.012				6.8364	.011
								7.3091	.009
5	3	2	4.4945	.101					
			4.6509	.091	5	5	2	4.5077	.100
			5.1055	.052				4.6231	.097
			5.2509	.049				5.2462	.051
			6.8218	.010				5.3385	.047
			6.9091	.009				7.2692	.010
								7.3385	.010
5	3	3	4.4121	.109					
			4.5333	.097	5	5	3	4.5363	.102
			5.5152	.051				4.5451	.100
			5.6485	.049				5.6264	.051
			6.9818	.011				5.7055	.046
			7.0788	.009				7.5429	.010
								7.5780	.010
5	4	1	3.9600	.102					
			3.9873	.098	5	5	4	4.5200	.101
			4.8600	.056				4.5229	.099
			4.9855	.044				5.6429	.050
			6.8400	.011				5.6657	.049
			6.9545	.008				7.7914	.010
								7.8229	.010
5	4	2	4.5182	.101					
			4.5409	.098	5	5	5	4.5000	.102
			5.2682	.050				4.5600	.100
			5.2727	.049				5.6600	.051
			7.1182	.010				5.7800	.049
			7.2045	.009				7.9800	.010
								8.0000	.009
5	4	3	4.5231	.103					
			4.5487	.099					
			5.6308	.050					
			5.6564	.049					
			7.3949	.011					
			7.4449	.010					

Annexure

PROJECT IN HDFC STANDARD LIFE INSURANCE COMPANY LTD.

ON

CUSTOMER-BUYING BEHAVIOUR WITH A FOCUS ON MARKET SEGMENTATION

INTRODUCTION

The liberalization of the Indian Insurance Sector has been the subject of much heated debate for some years. The policy makers where in the catch 22 situation wherein for one they wanted competition, development and growth of this insurance sector which is extremely essential for channeling the investments into the infrastructure sector. At the other end, the policy makers had the fears that the insurance premia, which are substantial, would seep out of the country; and wanted to have a cautious approach of opening for foreign participation in the sector.

As one of the rare occurrences, the entire debate was put on the back burner and the IRDA saw the day of the light thanks to the maturing polity emerging consensus among factions of different political parties. Though some changes and some restrictive clauses as regards to the foreign participation were included, the IRDA has opened the doors for the private entry into insurance.

Whether the insurer is old or new, private or public, expanding the market will present multitude of challenges and opportunities. But the key issues, possible trends, opportunities and challenges that insurance sector will have still remain under the realms of the possibilities and speculation. What is the likely impact of opening up India's insurance sector?

The large scale of operations, public sector bureaucracies and cumbersome procedures hampers nationalized insurers. Therefore, potential private entrants expect to score in the areas of customer service, speed and flexibility. They point out that their entry will mean better products and choice for the consumer. The critics counter that the benefit will be slim, because new players will concentrate on affluent, urban customers as foreign banks did until recently. This seems to be a logical strategy. Start-up costs—such as those of setting up a conventional distribution network—are large and high-end niches offer better returns. However, the middle-market segment too has great potential. Since insurance is a volumes game. Therefore, private insurers would be best served by a middle-market approach, targeting customer segments that are currently untapped.

EXECUTIVE SUMMARY

In today's corporate and competitive world, we find that insurance sector has the maximum growth and potential as compared to the other sectors. Insurance has the maximum growth rate of 70-80% while as FMCG sector has minimum 12-15% of growth rate. This growth potential attracts me to enter in this sector and 'HDFC Standard Life Insurance Company Ltd.' has given me the opportunity to work and get experience in highly competitive and enhancing sector.

- The success story of good market share of different market organizations depends upon the availability of the product and services near to the customer, which can be distributed through a distribution channel. In Insurance sector, distribution channel includes only agents or agency holders of the company. If a company like Reliance Life Insurance, Tata AIG, Max, etc. have adequate agents in the market they can capture big market as compared to the other companies.

Agents are the only way for a company of Insurance sector through which policies and benefits of the company can be explained to the customer.

RESEARCH METHODOLOGY

The study deals mainly with studying the buying pattern in the insurance industry with a special focus on HDFC Standard Life Insurance. The various segments of the markets divided in terms of Insurance needs, Age groups, Satisfaction levels, etc. will also studied.

Objectives

Objective One

1. To determine reasons behind opting for an insurance.
2. To provide the company with information of customer's Insurance policy if they have any and reasons for opting for that particular policies.
3. To know the most preferred policy.

Objective Two

1. To determine customer's perception towards private insurance companies and their expectation from private insurance companies.
2. To determine the feedback on services provided by any other insurance agent.
3. To study the types of benefits provided by insurance services.
4. To determine the use of Internet for valuable information and decision-making process.

Scope of the Study

A big boom has been witnessed in Insurance Industry in recent times. A large number of new players have entered the market and are vying to gain market share in this rapidly improving market. The study deals with HDFC Standard Life in focus and the various segments that it caters to. The study then goes on to evaluate and analyse the findings so as to present a clear picture of trends in the Insurance sector.

Significance of the Study

Significance to the Industry

This is a limited study which takes into consideration the responses of 100 people. This data can be explored to take in the trends across the industry. The significance for the industry lies in studying these trends that emerge from the study. It is a rapidly changing and evolving sector. People are only beginning to wake up to its vast possibilities. A study like this can attempt to guide the future of the industry based on current trends.

Significance for the Researcher

To facilitate and provide all the useful information of the study, the company, the insurance industry and also provide marketing ways, methods of HDFC Standard Life Insurance.

Research Design

1. Non-probability
2. Exploratory and descriptive experimental research

The research is primarily both exploratory as well as descriptive in nature. The sources of information are both primary and secondary.

A well-structured questionnaire was prepared and personal interviews were conducted to collect the customer's perception and buying behaviour, through this questionnaire.

Sampling Methodology

Sampling Technique: Initially, a rough draft was prepared keeping in mind the objective of the research. A pilot study was done in order to know the accuracy of the Questionnaire. The final Questionnaire was arrived only after certain important changes were done. Thus, our sampling came out to be judgemental and convenient.

Sampling Unit: The respondents who were asked to fill out questionnaires are the sampling units. These comprise of employees of MNCs, Govt. Employees, Self Employed, etc.

Sample Size: The sample size was restricted to only 100, which comprised of mainly people from different regions of Chennai due to time constraints.

Sampling Area: The area of the research was Chennai, Tamil Nadu, India.

Limitations of the Research

1. The research is confined to a certain parts of Chennai (Madras) and does not necessarily show a pattern applicable to all of country.
2. Some respondents were reluctant to divulge personal information which can affect the validity of all responses.
3. In a rapidly changing industry, analysis on one day or in one segment can change very quickly. The environmental changes are vital to be considered in order to assimilate the findings.

Questionnaire

1. Are you employed?

   Yes No

   If yes, only then proceed.
2. Do you have any insurance policy?

   Yes No
3. Which insurance policy do you have?

   Life Non-life Both
4. Which company's insurance policy you prefer the most? (Rank them)

   (i) LIC ☐

   (ii) ICICI Prudential ☐

   (iii) SBI Life Insurance ☐

   (iv) ING VYSYA Life ☐

   (v) Reliance Life Insurance ☐

   (vi) Tata AIG Life ☐

   (vii) Any other ________ (Specify)

5. For how many years do you have insurance policy? (Please tick)

   (i) <5yrs (ii) 5-10 yrs (iii) 10-15 yrs (iv) any other_______ (Specify)

6. What do you think are the benefits of insurance cover? (Rank them)

   (i) Cover future uncertainity ☐

   (ii) Tax deductions ☐

   (iii) Future investment ☐

   (iv) Any other __________ (Specify)

7. Which feature of your policy attracted you to buy it? (Rank them)

   (i) Low premium ☐

   (ii) Larger risk coverance ☐

   (iii) Money back guarantee ☐

   (iv) Reputation of company ☐

   (v) Easy access to agents ☐

   (vi) Any other __________ (Specify)

8. Your monthly income?

   (i) <4k (ii) 4k-8k (iii) 8k-12k (iv) 12k-16k (v) other_______(Specify)

9. Do you really think insurance policy cover in today's scenario is not essential?

   ____

10. What's your perception about insurance? (Rank them)

    (i) A saving tool ☐

    (ii) A tax saving device ☐

    (iii) A tool to protect future ☐

11. How has/would you bought/buy an insurance?

    (i) Customer approached insurance companies ☐

    (ii) Insurance companies approached customer ☐

12. Are you satisfied with the policy?

    (i) Satisfied saving tool ☐

    (ii) Not satisfied ☐

    (iii) Not responding ☐

13. Are you satisfied with the service agent?

(i) Satisfied saving tool

(ii) Not satisfied

(iii) Not responding

14. Do you pay taxes?

Yes No

15. Where have you invested for tax saving? (Rank them)

(i) LIC

(ii) NSC

(iii) Bonds

(iv) PPF

(v) PF

(vi) EPF

16. Which is the best form of investments? (Rank them)

(i) Fixed assets

(ii) Bank deposits

(iii) Jewellery

(iv) Securities, i.e., Bonds, MFS

(v) Shares

(vi) Insurance

17. What do you intent to gain from investments?

(i) Saving and returns

(ii) Security

(iii) Tax benefits

18. What's the right age to buy insurance?

(i) After 25 Yrs

(ii) After 35 Yrs

(iii) After 45 Yrs

(iv) Any time

19. How would you rate Indian Insurance companies?
    - (i) Rigid plans
    - (ii) Non-user friendly
    - (iii) Unsatisfactory services
    - (iv) Non-aggressive
    - (v) Satisfactory
    - (vi) Good
    - (vii) Very good

20. What would you look for in an insurance companies? (Rank them)
    - (i) A trusted name
    - (ii) Friendly service and responsiveness
    - (iii) Good plans
    - (iv) Accessibility

21. Are you planning for new investments?

    Planning ☐ Not planning ☐

22. Would you go for insurance if a service provider away from the city offers better service and products?
    - (i) Yes
    - (ii) No
    - (iii) Uncertain

Thank you

Name:__________

Address:__________

____

Occupation:__________

DATA ANALYSIS AND INTERPRETATION

Data gives Preference of Respondents of Insurance Companies

Company's Name	No. of Respondent	Share (%)
L.I.C.	78	78
HDFC	2	2
ICICI Prudential	10	10
SBI Life	7	7
Reliance Life Insurance	3	3
Total	**100**	**100**

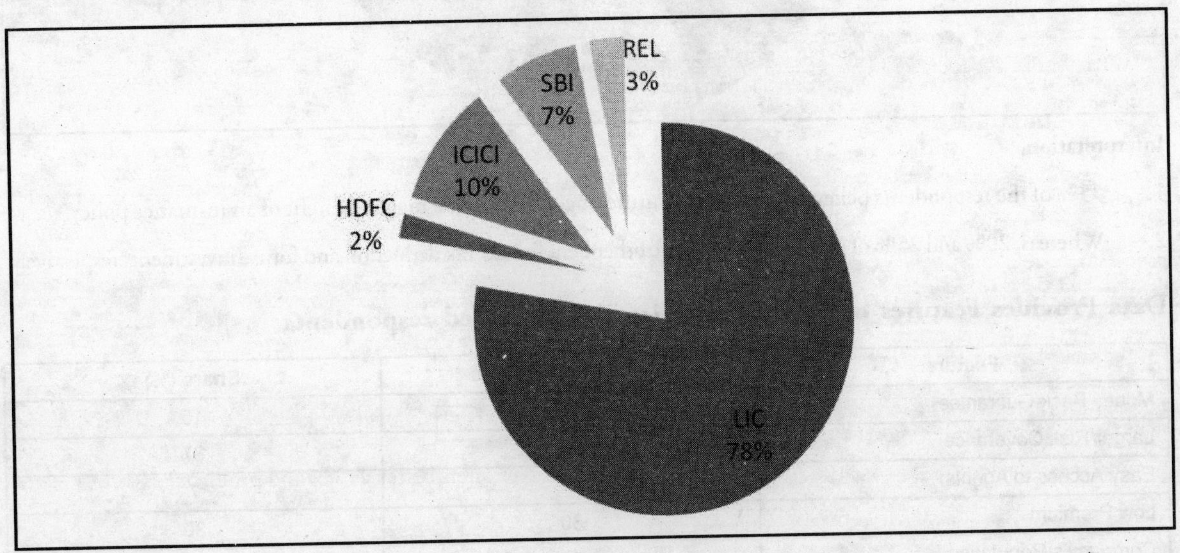

Interpretation

1. 78% of the people contacted prefer LIC policy to any other and therefore, it is ranked no.1 by that per cent of respondents.

Data gives Benefits of Insurance Perceived by Respondents

Benefits	No.of Respondents	Share (%)
Cover Future Uncertainty	55	55
Tax Deductions	20	20
Future Investment	25	25
Total	100	100

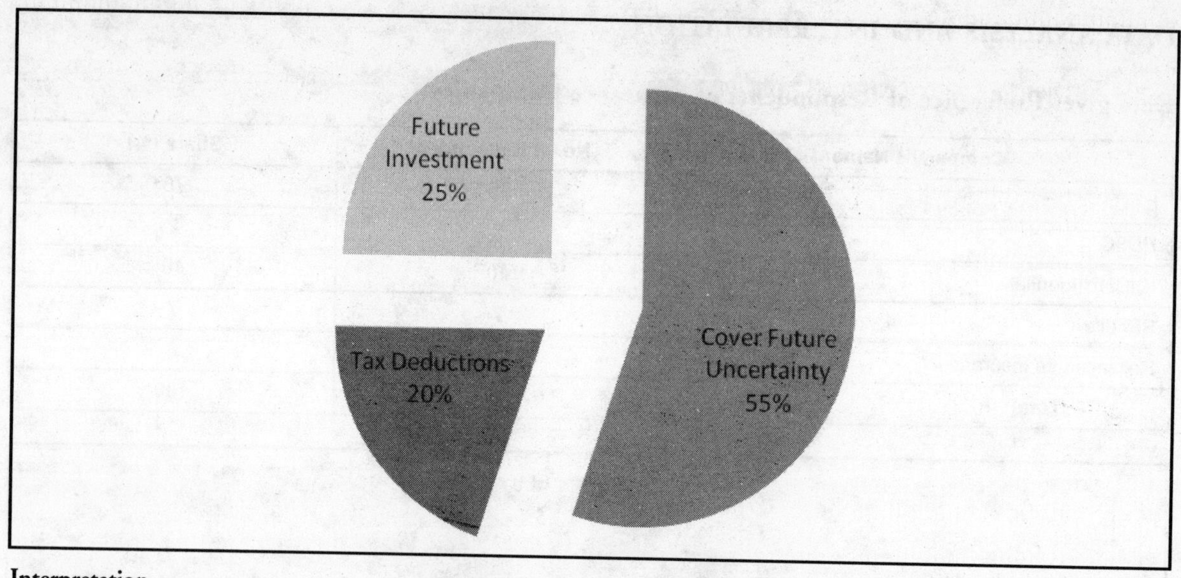

Interpretation

1. 55% of the respondents believe that covering future uncertainty is the biggest benefit of an insurance policy.
2. Whereas, 20% and 25% of them believe that the other benefits are Tax deduction and future investments respectively.

Data Provides Features of Insurance policy that attracted respondents

Feature	No. of Respondents	Share (%)
Money Back Guarantee	15	15
Larger Risk Coverance	37	37
Easy Access to Agents	7	7
Low Premium	30	30
Company's Reputation	11	11
Total	100	100

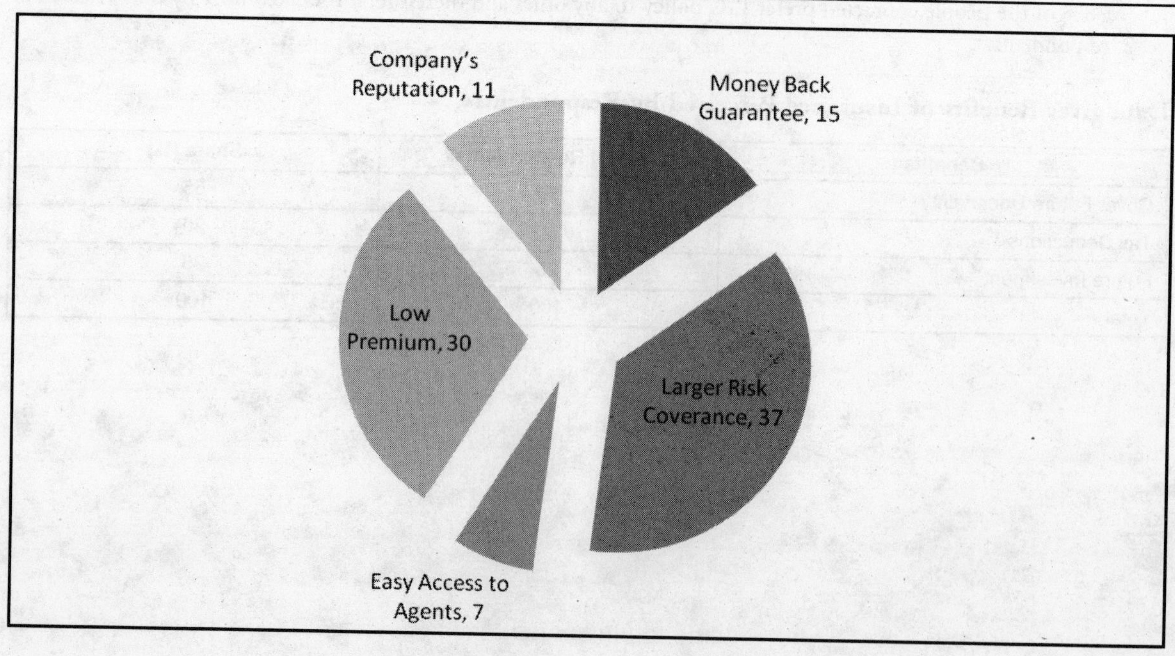

Interpretation

1. Majority of the respondents (37%) found Larger risk coverance as the most attracted feature of the all.

Data Provides Number of Insurance policy type Respondents

Policy Type	No. of Respondents	Share (%)
Life policy	52	52
Non life policy	17	17
Both	31	31

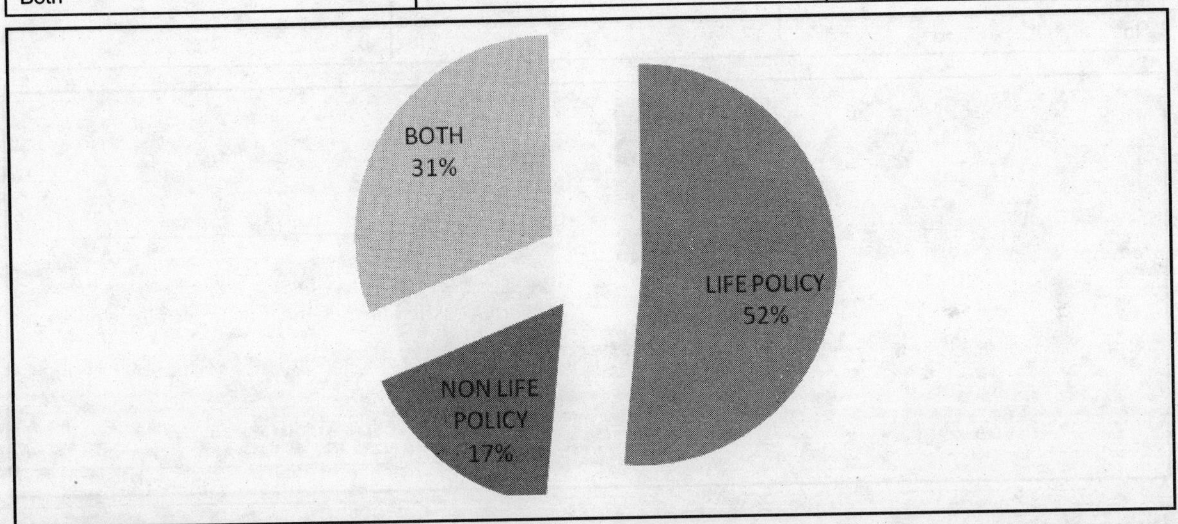

Interpretation

1. 75% of the respondents have Life Insurance Policy while 45% have both. (The % is calculated out of 280 positive response)

Data gives people perception about insurance

Response	No. of Respondents	Share (%)
A saving tool	32	32
A tax saving device	29	29
A tool to protect your family	39	39

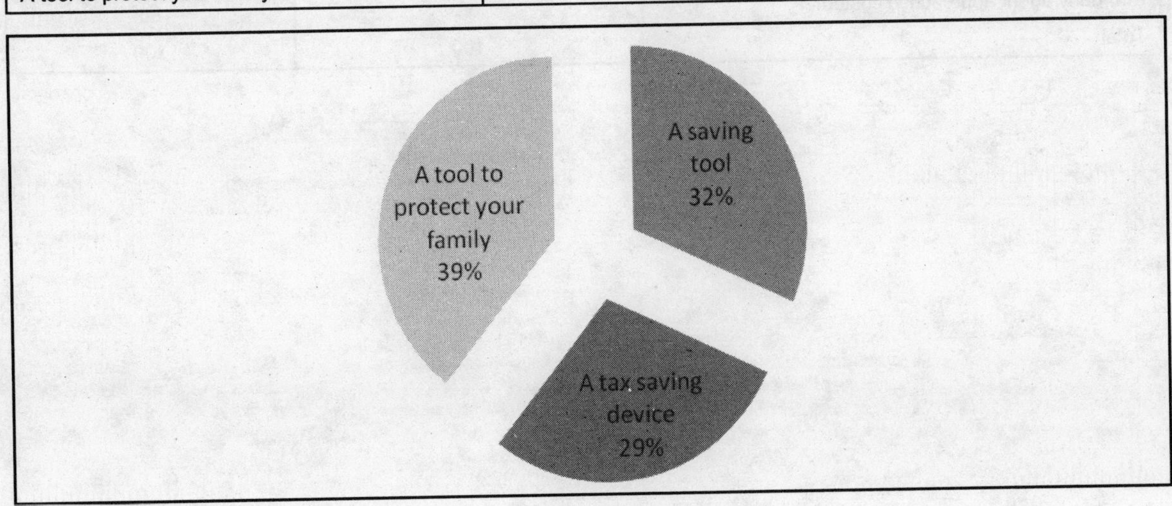

Interpretation

1. 81% of the respondents have perception of Insurance being a saving tool.
2. And 74% of the respondents have perception of Insurance being a tax saving device.
3. But 100% of the respondents are with the view that Insurance is a tool to protect your family.

Data shows people having Insurance

Response	No. of Respondents	Share (%)
Yes	70	70
No	30	30

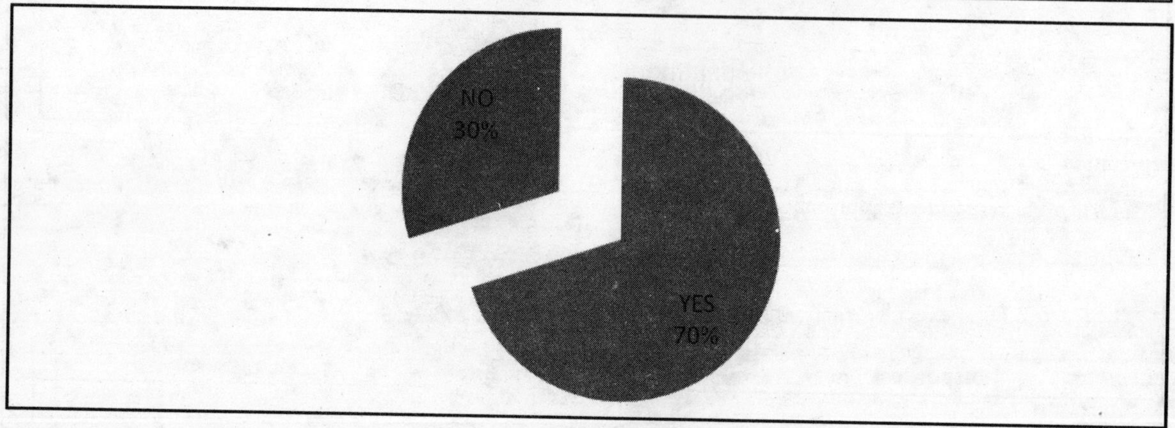

Interpretation

1. Of the sample size of 400 surveyed respondents, 70% of the respondents are having Insurance policy.
2. 30% of the respondents are either not having any Insurance policy at present or their policy is already matured.
3. And at present, 100% of the respondents are with the view that Insurance is a tool to protect your family.

Data shows buying Process of the People

Buying Process	No. of Respondents	Share (%)
Customer approached Insurance company/Agent	44	44
Company/agent approached customer	56	56
Total	100	100

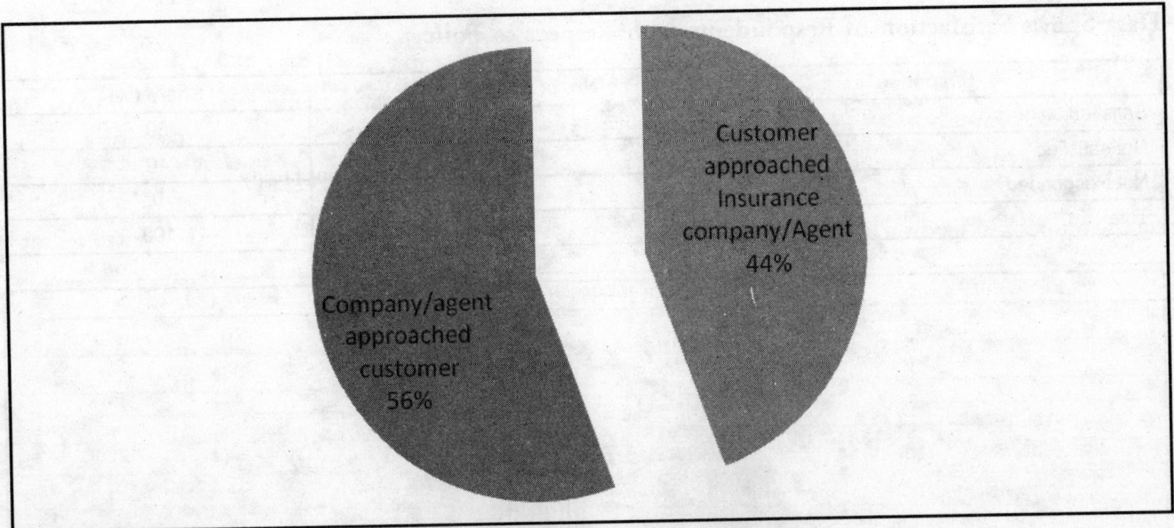

Interpretation

1. 44.5% of the respondents approached the Insurance Company/Agent.
2. Whereas, 55.5% of the respondents were approached by the Company/Agent.

Data shows Reasons behind Insurance

Response	No. of Respondents	Share (%)
Tax saving	31	31
Saving/Investment	31	31
Family protection	38	38

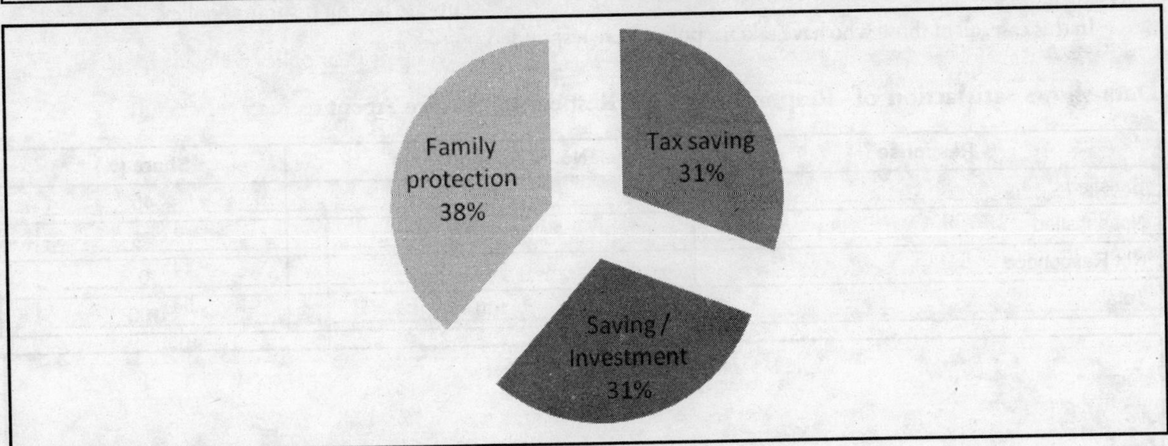

Interpretation

1. 80.71% of the Respondents opted for Insurance for tax saving benefits.
2. 80.71% of the Respondents opted for saving/Investments.
3. But all of them, i.e., 100% of the respondents have opted for insurance for their family protection.

Data Shows Satisfaction of Respondents with Respect to Policy

Response	No. of Respondents	Share (%)
Satisfied	60	60
Not satisfied	40	40
Not Responded	0	0
Total	100	100

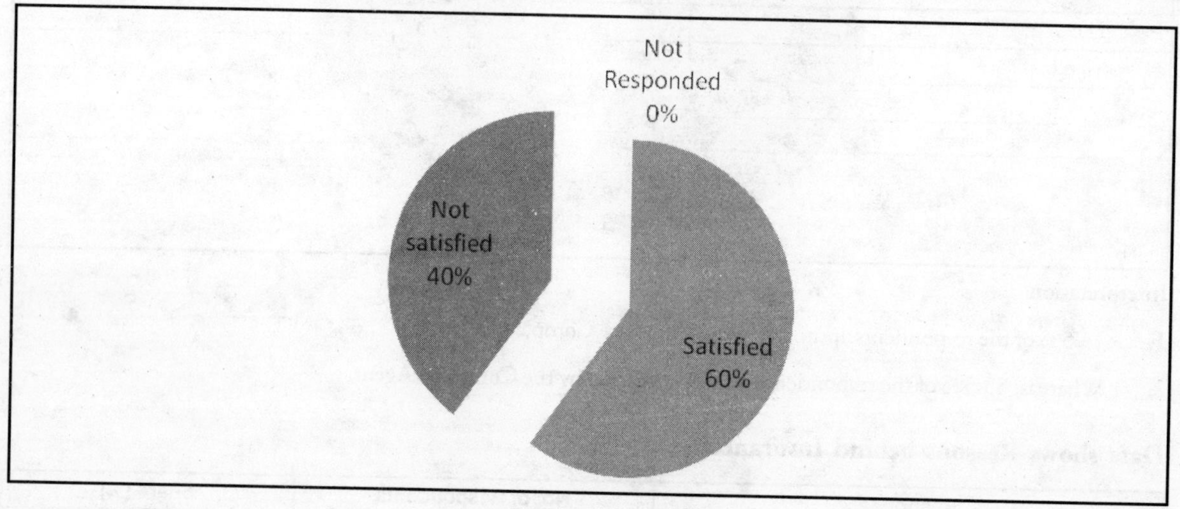

Interpretation

1. 60% of the respondents are more or less satisfied with their existing policy.
2. 40% of the respondents are not satisfied with their existing policy.
3. In this case, all of those who have taken a policy have responded.

Data shows satisfaction of Respondents with Respect to Service Agent

Response	No. of Respondents	Share (%)
Satisfied	45	45
Not satisfied	55	55
Not Responded	0	0
Total	100	100

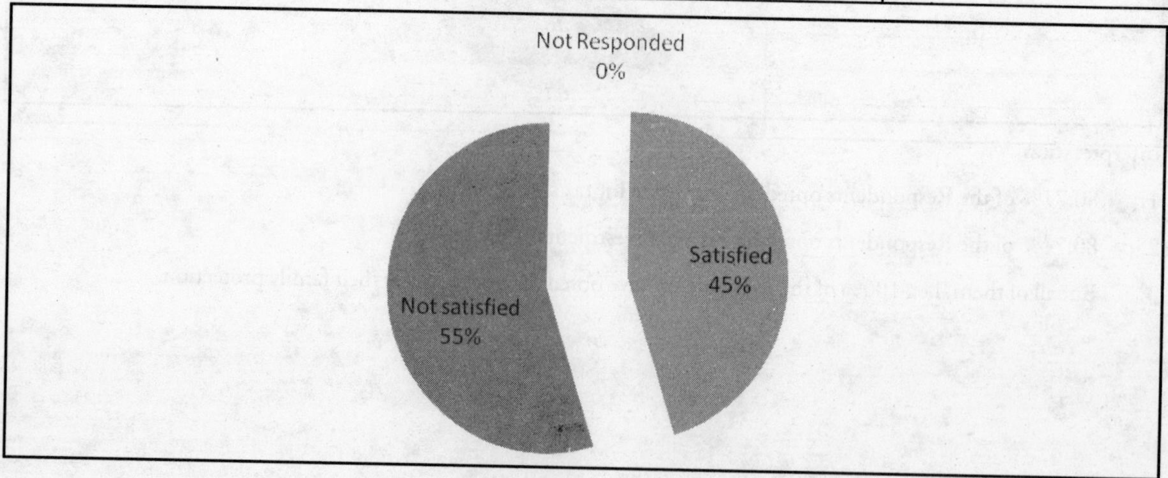

Interpretation

1. 45% of the respondents are satisfied with their existing service agent.
2. 55% of the respondents are not satisfied with their existing insurance agent.
3. All of those who have taken a policy have responded.

Data shows Number of Respondents Paying Tax

Response	No. of Respondents	Share (%)
Paying tax	100	100
Not paying tax	-	0
Total	100	100

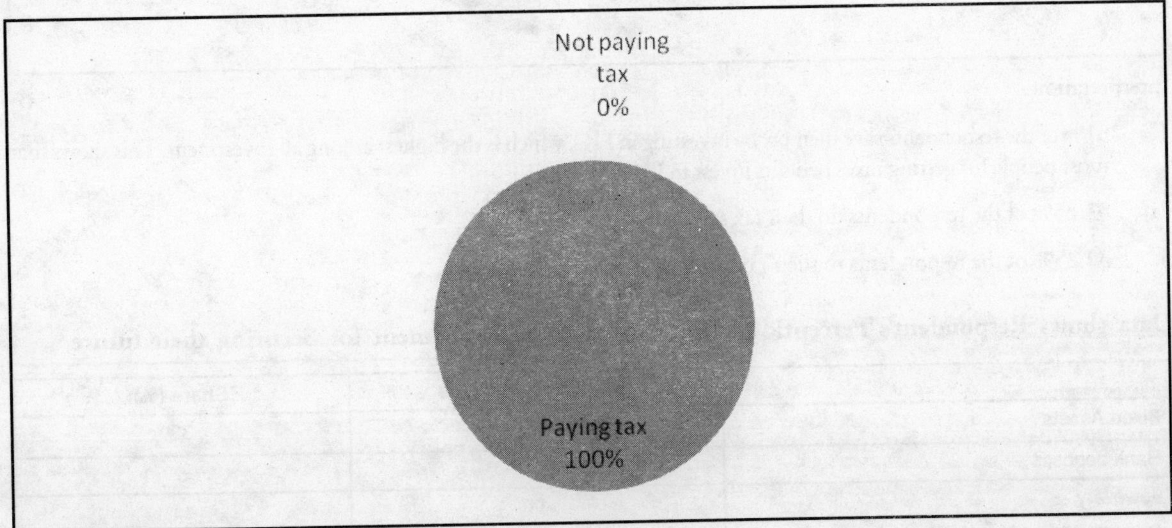

Interpretation

Of the sample size of 400 respondents, all the respondents are paying tax.

Data shows Respondent's Investments for Tax Saving

Investments	No. of Respondents	Share (%)
LIC	30	30
NSC	19	19
Bonds	19	19
PPF	14	14
PF	12	12
EPF	6	6

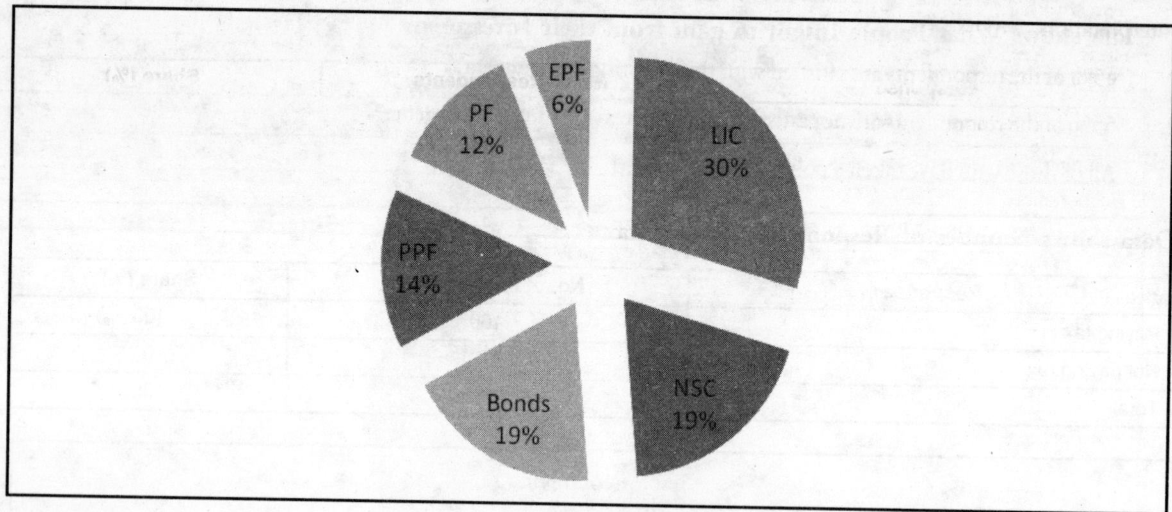

Interpretation

1. 51% of the respondents save their tax by investing in LIC, which is the highest among all Investment. This shows that most people for getting taxes benefits invest in LIC.
2. 33.25% of the respondents do their tax saving by investing in NSC.
3. 32.25% of the respondents to their tax saving by investing in bonds.

Data shows Respondent's Perception about best form of Investment for Securing their future

	No. of Respondents	Share (%)
Fixed Assets	33	33
Bank deposits	5	5
Jewellery	11	11
Securities i.e., bonds, MFs	17	17
Shares	4	4
Insurance	30	30

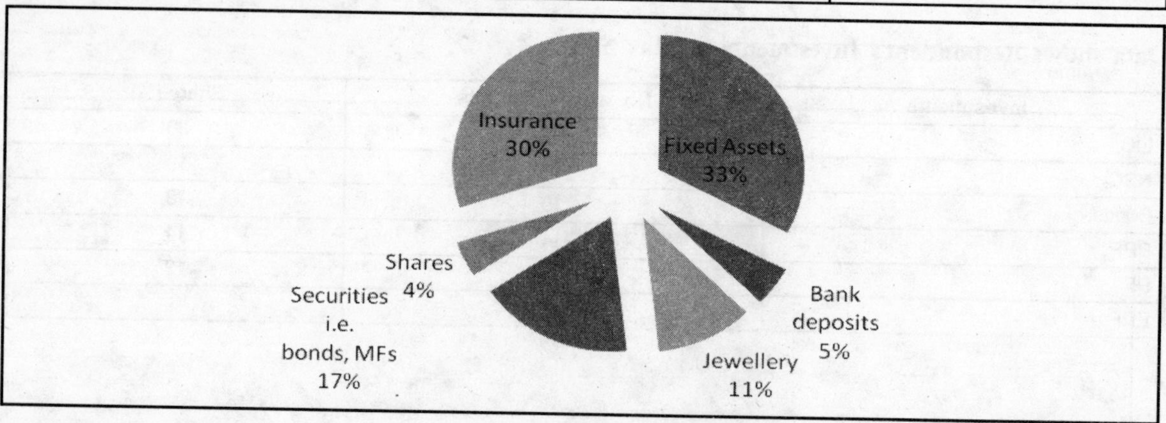

Interpretation

1. 75.25% of the respondents as with the view that Fixed Assets is the best form of investment for securing their future.
2. 70.5% of the respondents are with the perception that Insurance is the best form of investment for securing their future, which is one of the highest and this shows that insurance is an important key for securing your future.

Data shows What People Intent to gain from their Investment

Response	No. of Respondents	Share (%)
Saving and Returns	38	38
Security	35	35
Tax benefits	27	27

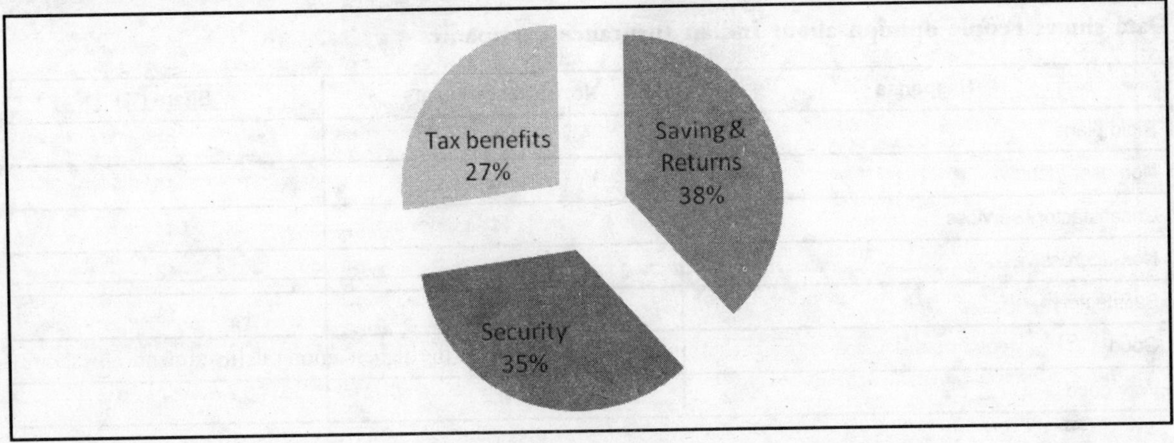

Interpretation

1. 100% of the respondents intent to gain saving and returns from their investment.
2. 90% of the respondent's intent to gain security from their investments.
3. Whereas, 71.75% of the respondent's intent to gain tax benefits from their investments.

Data gives People's Perception on Appropriate age for Buying Insurance

Response	No. of Respondents	Share (%)
After 25 years	29	29
After 35 years	10	10
After 45 years	0	0
Anytime	61	61

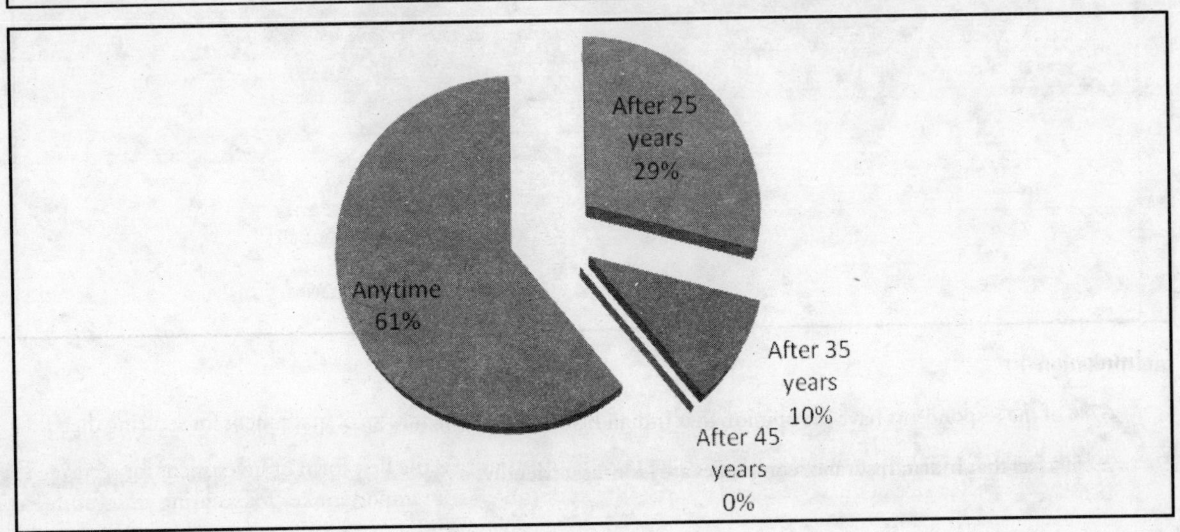

Interpretation

1. 29% of the respondents are with the view that insurance should be bought after the age of 25 years.
2. 10.5% of the respondents are with the view that insurance should be bought after the age of 35 years.
3. Whereas, 60.5% of the respondents are with the view that buying of insurance do not have anything to do with age, i.e. there is no age limitations. It can be purchased any time according to the need.

Data shows People opinion about Indian Insurance Companies

Response	No. of Respondents	Share (%)
Rigid plans	35	35
Non-user friendly	15	15
Unsatisfactory services	14	14
Non-aggressive	18	18
Satisfactory	13	13
Good	5	5
Very good	0	0

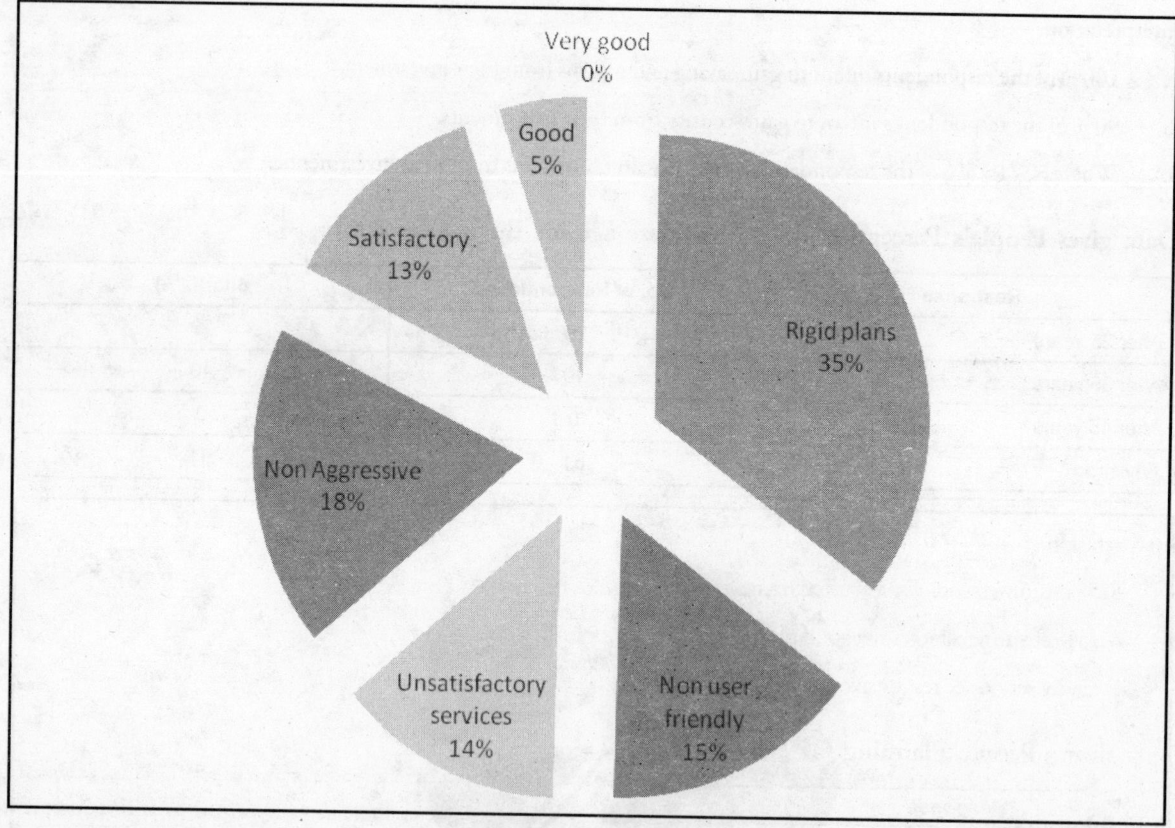

Interpretation

1. 67% of the respondents have the opinion that Indian Insurance Companies have Rigid plans.
2. 29.5% feel that Indian Insurance companies are Non-user friendly.

3. 26.5% feel that services of Indian Insurance companies are Unsatisfactory.

4. 35.75% of the respondents are with the view that Indian Insurance companies are Non-aggressive.

5. 24% of the respondents feel that products and services of Indian Insurance companies is Satisfactory.

6. Whereas only 10.25% feel that it is good enough.

7. And according to the data, no single person has felt that it is very good.

Data Shows what people would look for in an Insurance Company

Response	No. of Respondents	Share (%)
A trusted name	29	29
Friendly service and responsiveness	25	25
Good plans	29	29
Accessibility	17	17

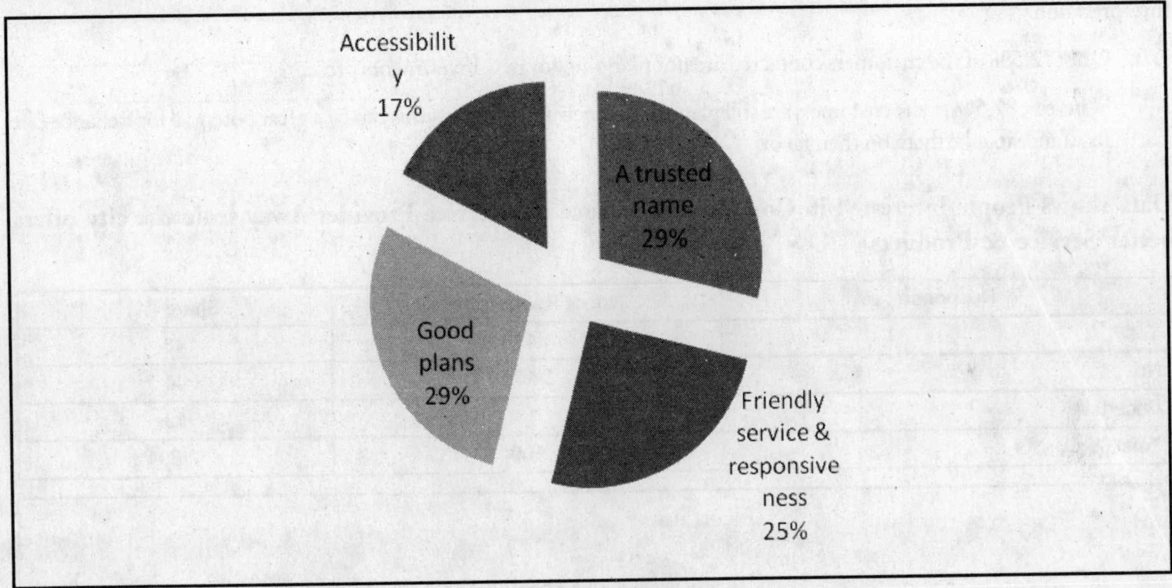

Interpretation

1. 82% customers look for a Trusted name in a company for insurance.
2. 81.5% customers look for a good plan in a company for insurance.
3. Friendly service & responsiveness and accessibility are also important factors looked by customers in a company.

Data shows People Planning for New Investments

Response	No. of Respondents	Share (%)
Planning	87	87
Not planning	13	13
Total	100	100

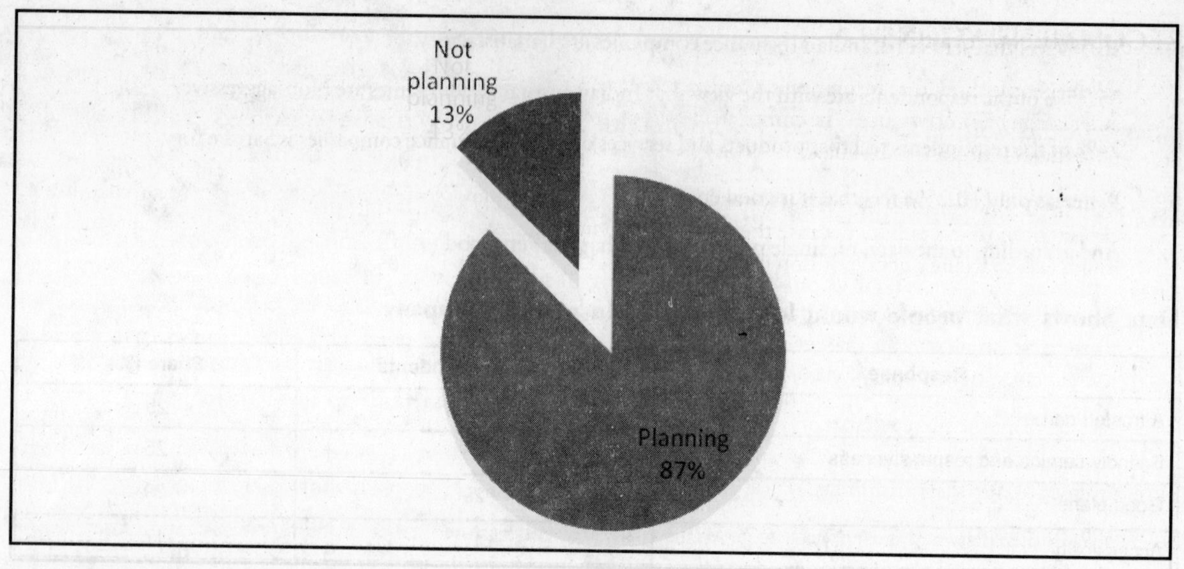

Interpretation

1. Only 12.5% of the customers contacted are not planning for new investments presently.
2. Whereas, 87.5% of the customers are still planning for new investments; this can be a great potential for Reliance Life Insurance to take them on their favor.

Data shows People Interested in Going for Insurance if a Service Provider Away from the city offers better Service & Products

Response	No. of Respondents	Share (%)
Yes	43	43
No	44	44
Uncertain	13	13
Total	100	100

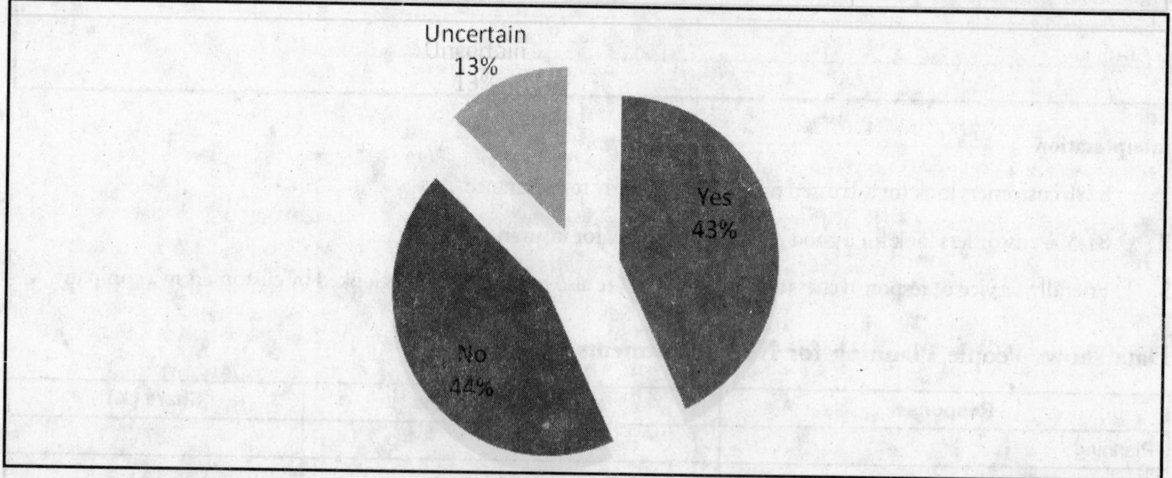

Interpretation

1. The interested customers, i.e., 43% are ready to go for insurance even away from a city if services and products are worthwhile, which again is a good prospect (potential) for Reliance Life Insurance to take them on their favor.

RECOMMENDATIONS

1. As the people think that insurance is a tool to protect their family and a tax saving device. They are aware of the fact and realizing its importance. The company should try to expand and build up its infrastructure because there is a large potential for insurance in India.

2. Company should come up with its branch in Chennai. With the objective and goals to meet the demands and expectations of the public. Because the entrance of private players will increase the competition and it would be a tough task to secure a good position in market.

3. Since HDFC Standard Life Insurance Company Ltd. is leading with several companies' policies it should be easy for them to penetrate into the market and secure a good position if they pay greater attention to the service part provided to their customer and thereby forming a long and trusted relationship.

4. As seen from the survey that at present 70% of the customers are having insurance policy out of which 87.5% of the customer are planning for new investments. So it can be a good potential for the company and they should make an attempt to trap these customers.

5. 43% of the customers is even ready to go for insurance if a service provider away from their home is providing it. But intend they should provide good products and services. The company should try to convince these customers and get them in its favor.

CONCLUSION

Our exhaustive research in the field of Life Insurance threw up some interesting trends which can be seen in the above analysis. A general impression that we gathered during data collection was the immense awareness and knowledge among people about various companies and their insurance products. People are beginning to look beyond LIC for their insurance needs and are willing to trust private players with their hard earned money.

People in general have been impressioned by the marketing and advertising campaigns of insurance companies. A high penetration of print, radio and television ad campaigns over the years is beginning to have its impact now.

Another heartening trend was in terms of people viewing insurance as a tax saving and investment instrument as much as a protective one. A very high number of respondents have opted for insurance for such purposes and it shows how insurance companies have been successful to attract public money in recent times.

The general satisfaction levels among public with regards to policy and agents still require improvement. But therein lies the oppurtunity for a relative newcomer like HDFC Standard Life Insurance Company Ltd. LIC has never been known for prompt service or customer-oriented methods and HDFC Standard Life can build on these factors.

MODEL QUESTION PAPERS

MARKETING RESEARCH

September, 2007

Time: 3 Hours **Max. Marks: 100**

Answer All Questions

PART – A (10 × 2 = 20 marks)

1. Write short notes on the following at one place only:

(a) Marketing Information System (MIS)

(b) Utility

(c) Sample Plan

(d) Regression

(e) Structured Questions

(f) ANOVA

(g) Hypothesis

(h) Report Presentation

(i) Research Design

(j) Markov Model

PART – B (5 × 16 = 80 marks)

2. (a) Why is it necessary to estimate the value and cost of information before conducting research?

Or

(b) Differentiate primary sources of data from secondary sources. What are projective techniques?

3. (a) What is meant by data processing? Explain the steps involved in data processing.

Or

(b) Explain the difference between problem situation models and choice criteria models.

4. (a) Explain the types of measurement scales. What are the criteria for a good scale?

Or

(b) Explain the sources and methods of gathering marketing information.

5. (a) An automobile company gives the following information about age groups and the liking for a particular model of car that it plans to launch.

Persons	Below 25	25 – 50	Above 50
Who liked the car	45	30	25
Who disliked the car	55	20	25

On the basis of the above data, can it be concluded that the model appeal is independent of the age group? Use 0.05 significance level.

Or

(b) Two salesmen, A and B are employed by a company. Recently, it has conducted a sample survey yielding the following data:

	Salesman A	Salesman B
No. of sales	20	22
Average sales (Rs.)	800	780
Standard deviation (Rs.)	70	60

Is there any significant difference between average sales of two salesmen? a = 0.05 level of significance.

6. (a) What is Discriminant Analysis? Explain the various steps involved in its usage in marketing research.

Or

(b) Explain the significance of a research report and narrate the various steps involved in writing such a report.

MARKETING RESEARCH

June, 2006

Time: 3 Hours | Max. Marks: 100

Answer All Questions

PART – A (10 × 2 = 20 marks)

1. Explain the following briefly, at one place only:
   (a) Hypothesis
   (b) EVPI
   (c) Simulation
   (d) Dendogram
   (e) Response Bias
   (f) Surrogate information error
   (g) Interval scale
   (h) Validity
   (i) Factorial design
   (j) Projective techniques

PART – B (5 × 16 = 80 marks)

2. (a) What is Marketing Information System? What are its components?

   Or

   (b) Discuss the cost and value of information and explain how EVPI is arrived at.

3. (a) What are the different choice criterion models? Explain with examples.

   Or

   (b) What are the sources and methods of gathering marketing information?

4. (a) Explain the major differences between 'Rating' and 'Rating' scales. Which is a better scale measurement technique for collecting attitudinal data on salesforce performance of people who sell vacuum cleaner?

   Or

   (b) Illustrate the process of editing, coding and tabulation.

5. (a) Following is the data related to the ages of five randomly selected workers in three plants of a company. Find out whether there is a significant difference in the mean ages of the workers at three plants use α = .01.(ages)

Sl. No.	Plants		
	1	2	3
1	29	32	25
2	27	33	24
3	30	31	24
4	27	34	25
5	28	30	26

Or

(b) Following is the data given as ranks for the size of the stores and sales. Do bigger stores have greater sales? Sales size 62375147265413.

6. (a) What is Multi-dimensional Scaling? Discuss the purpose and limitations of Multi-dimensional Scaling methods.

Or

(b) What is the purpose of Discriminant analysis? How might it be used to solve a marketing problem or identify a marketing opportunity?

MARKETING RESEARCH

December, 2005

Time: 3 Hours **Max. Marks: 100**

Answer All Questions

PART – A (10 × 2 = 20 marks)

1. Explain the following briefly, at one place only:
   (a) Causal research
   (b) Hypothesis
   (c) EVPI
   (d) External validity
   (e) One shot study
   (f) Double barrel question
   (g) Cluster sampling
   (h) Staple scale
   (i) Confidence levels
   (j) Type – II Error

PART – B (5 × 16 = 80 marks)

2. (a) Discuss the need, importance, and utility of Marketing Decision Support System (MDSS).

Or

(b) Explain the basic differences among exploratory, causative, and conclusive experimental designs.

3. (a) Discuss the different methods of sampling.

Or

(b) Design a questionnaire to measure the attitude of market toward the "Ready to eat" packed food which is just heat and eat category, offered by a popular Indian company.

4. (a) What is measurement? What are the objectives of measurement?

Or

(b) What is a semantic differential scale? How do you construct it for measuring the brand profiles of toothpaste?

5. (a) A Random poll of 309 lunch customers is taken, resulting in the following observed values. Test whether the type of beverage ordered with lunch is independent of the age of the consumer? Use α = .01.

	Preferred Beverage		
	Coffee	**Tea**	**Soft drink**
21-34	26	95	18
Age (Years) 35-55	41	40	20
> 55	24	13	32

Or

(b) Use the Mann-Whitney U test at a = .01 to determine whether there is a significant difference between the populations represented by the two samples given here.

Sample 1	Sample 2
573	547
532	566
544	551
565	538
540	557
548	560
536	557
523	547

6. (a) What is Factor Analysis? What do you understand about factor loadings, commonalities, and varimax rotation?

Or

(b) Outline the components of the research report for executives.

MARKETING RESEARCH

January, 2005

Time: 3 Hours | Max. Marks: 100

Answer All Questions

PART – A (10 × 2 = 20 marks)

1. Explain the following briefly, at one place only:

(a) Marketing Intelligence
(b) Research Proposal and Research Plan
(c) Surrogate information
(d) Self Perception
(e) Non-response error
(f) Construct validity
(g) Ordinal scales
(h) McNemar Test
(i) Completely Randomised Design
(j) MDS

PART – B (5 × 16 = 80 marks)

2. (a) "The planning and conducting of a marketing research project is essentially an exercise in error management". Explain the statement in detail with practical examples.

Or

(b) Write a detailed note regarding the sources of marketing information. From the various sources you have mentioned which of them would be useful for a study to be conducted regarding mobile phones in Hyderabad and Secunderabad? Why?

3. (a) Distinguish between the following:

(i) Structured - Unstructured observation
(ii) Disguised - Undisguised observation
(iii) Direct - Indirect observation
(iv) Observation under normal setting - Laboratory setting

Or

(b) "Experimental research is better than descriptive research", do you agree with this statement? Present your opinion with suitable practical examples.

4. (a) How is the Thurstone equal-appearing interval scale constructed? What are the criteria on which the statements are selected? What are the limitations of this scale?

Or

(b) Enumerate the difficulties faced by the Researcher in Cross-tabulation Analysis. How is cross-tabulation superior to simple one-way tabulation? Can the complexities of cross-tabulation be overcome with the help of computers? How?

5. (a) Chic-Burgers has four outlets in twin-cities. The sales of chicken-burgers recorded by these four outlets during a particular period are given. Based on this data, you are required to state,

whether the four outlets are selling the same number of chicken burgers, at 0.1 significance level, using an appropriate statistical test. Sales given in units:

Weak No.	Outlet – A Sales	Outlet – B Sales	Outlet – C Sales	Outlet – D Sales
1	1076	1055	1014	1082
2	1124	998	1058	1024
3	954	1025	984	1054
4	1079	1195	1116	1125
5	1198	1186	1156	1115
6	987	1094	1184	1126
7	1016	994	1074	1052
8	1189	1127	1112	1084
9	1217	1114	1034	1089

Or

(b) The Chief Executive of Chan Marketing has collected the salary statistics of his junior sales executives earnings. The ECO had presented the observed and the expected frequencies as below:

Earnings in thousands of Rupees	Observed Frequency	Expected Frequency
25 - 30	28	22
31 - 36	54	44
37 - 42	60	74
43 - 48	70	80
49 - 54	52	46
55 - 60	34	36
61 - 66	22	18

At 0.10 level of significance, can the CEO conclude that "the distribution of sales force earnings in normal"?

6. (a) What is conjoint analysis? Explain the various steps to be followed in its usage in marketing research with an example.

Or

(b) What is cluster analysis? Demonstrate its usage for a practical problem that can be most effectively studied with cluster analysis.

MARKETING RESEARCH

August/September, 2004

Time: 3 Hours **Max. Marks: 100**

Answer All Questions

PART – A (10 × 2 = 20 marks)

1. Explain the following briefly, at one place only:

(a) Choice criterion models
(b) Components of a problem
(c) Simulation
(d) Cognitive Dissonance
(e) Response bias
(f) Predictive validity
(g) Interval scale
(h) Markov analysis
(i) Latin square design
(j) Conjoint analysis

PART – B (5 × 16 = 80 marks)

2. (a) Discuss the types of errors that the likely to affect Research designs with suitable examples. How do you deal with such errors?

Or

(b) Compare the contrast Descriptive and causal studies, highlighting the situations under which these studies are highly preferred?

3. (a) Explain the following types of questions, with atleast two examples for each one of them: (i) Open-ended questions, (ii) Dichotomous questions, (iii) Multiple-choice questions, (iv) Opinion-oriented questions.

Or

(b) Write a detailed note regarding the various sources of secondary data from the viewpoint of their relative costs and flexibility.

4. (a) What are three dominant factors considered in Semantic Differential scale? What factors are generally considered in formulating a suitable semantic differential scale?

Or

(b) Editing and coding are the significant tasks to be carried out before tabulation. How important are they? Explain them in detail with an example.

5. (a) A company selling tea wanted to sell more during the festive season. For this purpose during certain days of the season, free samples of tea were distributed through a popular chain of super markets. The following table shows the sales achieved when free samples were distributed and when they were not distributed.

Sales when free samples were distributed	Sales when free samples were not distributed
41	49
47	39
51	35
35	51
43	55
57	45
39	57
41	53
49	37
49	37
45	39
41	31
47	47
59	-

At 5% level of significance, using an appropriate statistical test you are required to state "Whether the distribution of free samples produced greater sales".

Or

(b) A brand manager wants to find whether his brand's share is evenly distributed across the country? To study this he had divided the country into four zones i.e., Northern, Western, Southern and Eastern zones and from each of these zones 250 consumers were selected and surveyed. The results are presented below:

Consumers	Northern Region	Western Region	Southern Region	Eastern Region	Total
Purchased the brand	100	137	113	125	475
Did not purchase the brand	150	113	137	125	525
Total	250	250	250	250	250

Use an appropriate statistical test to state whether the brand share is same in all the regions at 5% level of significance.

6. (a) What is factor analysis? When it used? What are its limitations?

Or

(b) Why and when should a researcher prefer to use multi-variate analyses over univariate or bivariate analyses? Explain with two relevant examples.

MARKETING RESEARCH

February/March, 2004

Time: 3 Hours **Max. Marks: 100**

Answer All Questions

PART – A (10 × 2 = 20 marks)

1. Explain the following briefly, at one place only:
   - (a) Exploratory research
   - (b) Problem situation model
   - (c) Selection error
   - (d) Nominal scale
   - (e) Simulation
   - (f) Causal studies
   - (g) Constant sun scale
   - (h) Reliability
   - (i) Construct validity
   - (j) Controlled experiments

PART – B (5 × 16 = 80 marks)

2. (a) Differentiate between Market Research and Marketing Research.

Or

(b) What errors are like to occur while preparing a research design? What steps do you take to minimize these errors?

3. (a) Explain panels as sources of marketing information.

Or

(b) What is a sample plan? What are its contents?

4. (a) What are the concepts of measurement and scaling? Explain the role of scaling in marketing research.

Or

(b) What is Thurstones' equal appearing intervals scale? What are the steps in constructing?

5. (a) Following is the data on brand loyalty of a product an occupational status of a sample of 230 respondents:

Occupational Status	Brand Loyalty			
	Highly Loyalty	Moderately Loyal	No Loyalty	Total
White collor	30	42	18	90
Blue collor	14	20	31	65
Retired	34	25	16	75
	78	87	65	230

Test whether there is any association between Occupational status and Brand loyalty at 0.05 level of significance.

Or

(b) The following are the number of persons reported to have seen an advertisement in different locations of two cities.

Hyderabad	40	70	80	40	45	24	65	72	35	
Bangalore	85	65	70	55	90	84	24	68	50	35

Conduct Manu-Whitney's 'U' test and say whether the responses are different in City A and City B at $\alpha = .05$.

6. (a) What is factor analysis? How can you sue factor analysis in data reduction?

Or

(b) Discuss the utility of Regression in Marketing Research.

MARKETING RESEARCH

September, 2003

Time: 3 Hours **Max. Marks: 100**

Answer All Questions

PART – A (10 × 2 = 20 marks)

1. Explain the following briefly, attempt all the bits at one place only:

(a) Casual research (b) Cost and value of information

(c) Hypothesis (d) Ordinal scale

(e) Interaction effect (f) Q-sort technique

(g) Correlation (h) Non-parametric tests

(i) Attitude scales (j) Reliability

PART – B (5 × 16 = 80 marks)

2. (a) What are the different designs of experiments? Discuss.

Or

(b) What is marketing information system? What are components? Explain.

3. (a) What precautions are necessary to be taken in designing a good questionnaire?

Or

(b) What are the errors that can occur gathering data from respondents? What steps do you take to minimize them?

4. (a) What are the concepts of measurement and scaling? Explain the importance of scaling in marketing research.

Or

(b) Develop a semantic differential scale to study the profile of popular brands of tooth paste.

5. (a) A company is interested to evaluating the sales effect of two different colours of the package of its power. The company selected 10 stores and split them into two groups of 5 stores each. One group of stores was stocked with red colour and other with green colour. The following data shown the sales in each store for the study period. The company wants to know whether there is any significant difference in sales effectiveness of the two packages at 5% level.

Sales by stores:

S.No.	Red Colour	Green Colour
1	6	16
2	8	18
3	10	20
4	12	22
5	14	24

Or

(b) What are parametric and non-parametric tests? Explain the utility and importance of non-parametric tests in marketing research.

6. (a) Discuss the salient features of discriminant analysis.

Or

(b) Take an example of your choice and explain how cluster analysis is used in dividing a group of people into clusters.

MARKETING RESEARCH

March/April, 2003

Time: 3 Hours **Max. Marks: 100**

Answer All Questions

PART – A (10 × 2 = 20 marks)

1. Explain the following briefly, attempt all the bits.
   (a) Sales forecasting (b) Exploratory research
   (c) Panel research (d) Pay-off table
   (e) Measurement (f) Cross-tabulation
   (g) Rank correlation (h) Qualitative analysis
   (i) Automatic interaction detection (j) MDS

PART – B (5 × 16 = 80 marks)

2. (a) Contrast Marketing Research and Marketing information system as a framework of gathering information for Marketing decision-making.

Or

(b) What purposes will a research design serve? How do you establish causal relationship between events?

3. (a) A grocer is faced with a problem of how many packets of milk (in hundreds) to be stocked for the next day to meet the demand. Assume that the unsold milk packet is worthless the other day. Cost price of the milk packet is ₹ 8 and is sold at ₹ 10. Historical records indicate the following demand distribution.

Number of milk Packets (in hundreds)	14	15	16	17
Number of days	15	30	35	20

Advise the grocer with optimal stocking decision using EMV criterion.

Or

(b) A confectioner sells confectionary items. Post data of demand per week (in hundred kilograms) with frequency is given below:

Demand per week	5	10	15	20	25
Frequency	11	8	21	6	4

Using the following random numbers, generate the demand for next 10 weeks. Also find the average demand per week. The random numbers are:

35 90 13 52 73 34 57 66

4. (a) How do you establish the validity and reliability of an attitude scale? Explain.

Or

(b) Discuss Thurstone and Likert's scaling techniques using marketing examples.

5. (a) Two groups of men and women are asked to rate the performance of a bank on a rating scale of 1 to 100. The ratings are given below:

Men	86	64	79	90	94	72	90	85	75	88
Women	75	83	80	81	78	84	88	61	67	92

Test whether the groups "men" and "women" differ in terms of their attitude on the bank's performance by using Mann-Whitney test at a = 5%.

Or

(b) Two suppliers A and B supply an item to a company. Supplier A claimed that he supplies 3% defectives less than his competitor B. To test this claim, the company selected 400 items from supplier A and found that 35 items are defective whereas 300 items from B gave rise to 25 defectives. What can be said about the claim of supplier A? Use a = 0.05.

6. (a) Discuss the purpose and principles of factor analysis and Discriminant analysis.

Or

(b) What are the elements to be kept in mind while preparing and presenting a research report? Explain how do you do it by using a marketing example.

MARKETING RESEARCH

October, 2002

Time: 3 Hours **Max. Marks: 100**

Answer All Questions

PART – A (10 × 2 = 20 marks)

1. Explain the following briefly. Attempt all the bits.

(a) MIS (b) Problems Situation Model
(c) Scaling (d) Signed Rank Test
(e) Least Squares Principle (f) Cost and value of information
(g) Sample Plan (h) Coding of data
(i) Type – I, Type – II errors (j) Conjoint analysis

PART – B (5 × 16 = 80 marks)

2. (a) Explain the significance and limitations of Marketing Research. What are the elements to be considered while marketing research design?

Or

(b) Explain some basic features in which experimental design differs from descriptive and from quasi-experimental designs.

3. (a) Discuss in detail, various sources and methods of gathering marketing information.

Or

(b) Design a structured questionnaire for a consumer durable goods whose sales have suddenly declined. Use all types of questioning tools.

4. (a) What is attitude? Give a detailed note on developing any one scale useful in measuring it.

Or

(b) Explain about editing, coding, and tabulation. What do you mean by cross-tabulation?

5. (a) A manufacturer of electric bulbs claims that his brand 'A' bulbs are superior to brand 'B' by giving an additional service of 15 hours. The brands are priced same. The following information is available.

Brand	Sample	Mean Life (hours)	deviation hours
A	12	170	14
B	10	164	20

Test for the validity of the claim (use $\alpha = 0.05$).

Or

(b) A market survey is made on three brands of breakfast foods X, Y and Z. the following transition behaviour is recorded. Brand just purchased. $\begin{matrix} & X & Y & Z \\ X & 0.7 & 0.2 & 0.1 \\ Y & 0.3 & 0.5 & 0.2 \\ Z & 0.3 & 0.3 & 0.4 \end{matrix}$ It is known that to initial composition of brands X, Y and Z are 30%, 20% and 50% respectively. What will be the customer compositions after two time periods? Also determine the equilibrium compositions.

6. (a) The following Product Good Moderate Poor tables shown the target sales (in units) fixed for eight sales persons and the sales realized by them:

Target sales:	80	44	58	40	32	72	27	51
Sales realized:	123	74	92	63	55	118	48	81

Fit least squares equations of the forms 'y' on 'x' and 'x' on 'y'. Also find the co-efficient of correlation.

Or

(b) Write a detailed note on various multivariate techniques useful in marketing research.

GLOSSARY

Action Research: The systematic enquiry designed to yield practical results capable of improving a specific aspect of practice and made public to enable scrutiny and testing.

After-Only with Control Group: An experimental design involving groups of respondents. Neither group is measured before the experiment. During the experiment, the control group is not subjected to the experimental variable. At the conclusion of the experiment, both groups are measured. The control group's measurement is deducted from the other group's measurement.

Aggregate: A group of persons that have certain traits or characteristics in common without necessarily having any direct social connection with one another. For example, "all female physicians" is an aggregate; so is "all European cities with populations over 20,000." Gross National Income is an aggregation of data about individual incomes.

Alternative Hypothesis: A competing hypothesis to the null. A statement of what a statistical hypothesis test is set up to establish. The test result is communicated by rejecting the null hypothesis in favor of the alternative hypothesis or not rejecting the null hypothesis. The test does not reach an acceptance or rejection of the alternative hypothesis.

Analysis of Variance (ANOVA): A statistical method establishing the existence of a difference between several sample means.

Applied Research: Research undertaken with the intention of applying the results to some specific problem, such as studying the effects of different methods of law enforcement on crime rates. One of the biggest differences between applied and basic research is that in applied work, the research questions are most often determined, not by researchers, but by policy makers or others who want help. Types of applied research include evaluation research and action research.

Area Samples: Samples which include geographic areas as part of the sample design.

Asynchronous Qualitative Research: The researcher and respondent are not required to interact during the study at the same time.

Asynchronous Research: The technique in which the respondents record their responses on their own time. The response is not prompted by a direct question or event.

Attitudinal Scaling: A two-dimensional technique in which the respondent determines the two most important characteristics of a product such as price and quality. The goal is to better understand the participants' feelings about the product or service. Research aimed at expanding knowledge rather than solving a specific, pragmatic problem.

Autocorrelation: The same variable is observed over time. The observations produce different values which are correlated.

Basic Research: Research conducted to gain knowledge as opposed to research aimed to solve specific problems.

Bayesian Statistics: Statistics which incorporate prior knowledge and accumulated experience into probability calculations.

Before and after with a Control Group: Random assignment of subjects to experimental and control groups with pre-measurement of both groups.

Before-after Design: Experiment where a measurement is taken from respondents before they receive the experimental treatment condition; the experimental treatment is then introduced, and the post-treatment measurement is taken.

Before-after with Control Design: Experiment that adds a control group to the basic before-after design; the control group is never exposed to the experimental treatment.

Between-group Variations: Between-group differences in scores for groups that were exposed to different treatments - represents "explained" variation.

Bias: Any influence that distorts the results of a research study. Extent to which, over repeated samples, the mean of the sampling distribution differs from the true mean. Bias is generally hard to quantify, but is likely to increase if the sampling frame is deficient and/or the response rate is low.

Biased Questions: Questions which are phrased or expressed in such a way that they influence the respondent's opinion. They may provide information which leads the respondent to consider the subject in a specific way. Bias may be introduced through verbal or facial expressions, body language, or by paraphrasing questions.

Biased Responses: An untrue statement of an opinion or attitude given by the respondent. This biased or untrue reporting can be conscious or unconscious.

Biased Sample: A sample that is not representative of the Universe of the targeted audience.

Bipolar Scale: A measuring tool spanning two negative points at opposite ends of the spectrum with an ideal situation placed in the middle. Examples include soft/hard, too spicy/too bland.

Bivariate Analysis: Pertaining to two variables only.

Bivariate Data Set: An experiment where units are subject to be tested on two different variables.

Bivariate Regression Analysis: A linear regression line created to determine the strength of the relationship of two variables, an independent and dependent variable.

Bivariate Techniques: Multiple statistical strategies to analyze how two variables relate to one another.

Box Plot: A visual tool used to graph the data and exposed outliers.

Brand Associations: Consumer opinions of brand that are generally exposed and analyzed by qualitative research.

Brand Equity: A company's level of awareness as well as consumer goodwill determined by consumer's views of company brand and/or products.

Brand Extension: The development of new products to be marketed under an existing brand name.

Brand Switching: A consumer that purchases multiple brands of a product. For example, a consumer that purchases Pepsi one week and Coke the next week.

Brand Value: The value which a brand would be given if represented on a company balance sheet.

Categorical Variable: A variable with discrete values (e.g., a person's gender or a person's marital status).

Causal Research: Research that attempts to explain the relationship between two variables (if A causes B to occur).

Causality: Relationship where a change in one variable produces a change in another variable. One variable affects, influences, or determines some other variables.

Central Limit Theorem: Theory that states a collection of a large number of sample means, the means will have a normal distribution regardless of the population used for the sample.

Central Tendency: A measure of the typicality or centrality of a set of scores; the three main measures of central tendency are mean, median and mode.

Central-Location Study: A study that takes place at a physical site that is convenient for all participants to access.

Centroid: Points on a map that indicate the center of the 260,000 block groups and enumeration districts that exist in the United States.

Chi-square Test Statistic: Measure of the goodness of fit between the numbers observed in the sample and the numbers we should have seen in the sample, given the null hypothesis is true.

Chi-square: A test of statistical significance which tests one measure of how well your model of expected distribution fits the observed distribution.

Cluster Analysis: A multivariate statistical classification technique for discovering whether the individuals of a population fall into different groups by making quantitative comparisons of multiple characteristics. The differences within any group should be less than the differences between groups. Often used for consumer segmentation and brand positioning.

Cluster Sampling: A probability sampling strategy involving successive sampling of units (or clusters); the units sampled progress from larger ones to smaller ones (e.g., health authority/health board, trust, senior managers).

Cluster: Describes a group of homes that are assumed to have similar demographic, social, and economic characteristics as one another within a neighborhood.

Coding: A procedure for transforming raw data into a standardized format for data analysis purposes. Coding qualitative data involves identifying recurrent words, concepts or themes. In positivist research, coding involves attaching numerical values to categories.

Coefficient of Determination: A statistics term used with regression. The coefficient represents the percentage that the independent variable explains in the dependent variable.

Cognition: A person's knowledge, opinions, beliefs and thoughts about the object.

Collinearity: A bias in statistical procedure due to the correlation of multiple independent variables that influence a single dependent variable. This makes it difficult to recognize which independent variable is really causing the change in the dependent variable.

Comparative Scaling (Non-metric Scaling): Scaling process in which the subject is asked to compare a set of stimulus objects directly with one another.

Concurrent Validity: Using past results to predict a current very similar project because of valid measurement techniques.

Conditional Probability: The probability of a given event when additional information about that event is known. For example, the probability of rolling one on the toss of a die when we are given the additional information that the roll landed on an odd number.

Confidence Interval: Range into which the true population value of the characteristic being measured will fall, assuming a given level of certainty.

Confidence Level: A probability that is used to determine, with confidence, that the true population value is represented in the statistical distribution.

Confounding Variable: A variable, other than the variable(s) under investigation, which is not controlled for and which may distort the results of experimental research.

Conjoint Analysis: A way to quantify consumer's values associated with different product attributes using multivariate techniques. Participants compare products to establish preferences and can then explain the importance of different attributes. Functional brands benefit more from conjoint analysis than do fashionable brands as the analysis relies on utility theory and consumer rationality. There are several conjoint analysis tools.

Constant Comparative Method: A procedure used during grounded theory research whereby newly gathered data are continually compared with previously collected data in order to refine the development of theoretical categories.

Constant Sum Scales: Scales asking participants to assign their individual values perceptions of certain attributes so that the sum of all attribute values equals a certain number of points (100 is a common number).

Constitutive Definition: A construct is defined by other constructs in the set and the relationship that occurs between the constructs. This helps in setting boundaries for constructs.

Construct: An idea that powers research, for example, hypotheses or concepts are considered constructs.

Construct Validity: Refers to the degree to which a research instrument measures a theoretical concept (or construct) under investigation.

Consumer: The ultimate user who purchases a product or service to satisfy their needs.

Consumer Drawings: Respondents draw what they are feeling or how they perceive an object.

Consumer Expenditure: The amount consumers spend on goods and services.

Consumer Expenditure Survey (CEX): Data gathered in an ongoing survey by the Bureau of Labor Statistics on the expenditures of consumers.

Consumer Orientation: Identification of and focus on the individuals or firms most likely to buy a product or service.

Consumer Price Index (CPI): Compares the current cost of purchasing a fixed set of goods and services with the cost of the same set at a specific base year. The resulting measures can be compared over time.

Consumer Unit: All related members of a particular household; a person living alone or sharing a household with others, who is financially independent; two or more persons living together who pool their incomes to make joint purchases.

Contact Interviewers: Interaction with a potential respondent to determine eligibility for participation.

Contamination: The inclusion of an individual or group of respondents in a test group who do not represent the population.

Content: Validity is similar to face validity except that the researcher deliberately targets individuals acknowledged to be experts in the topic area to give their opinions on the validity of the measure.

Content Analysis: A procedure for organizing narrative, qualitative data into emerging themes and concepts.

Continuous Rating Scale (Graphic Rating Scale): Procedure that instructs the respondent to assign a rating by placing a marker at the appropriate position on a line that best describes the object under study.

Continuous Variable: A quantitative variable that can assume an infinite number of values associated with the numbers on a line interval. Normally, continuous variables are the result of some measurement process. Grade point average is a continuous variable because it can assume any value between 0.0 and 4.0.

Control Group: In experimental research, a group that, for the sake of comparison, does not receive the treatment the experimenter is interested in. In a true experimental design, the control group is the group that does not receive the intervention or treatment under investigation. The scores on the dependent variable for the control and the experimental groups are used to evaluate the effect of the independent variable. In other experimental designs, this group may be referred to as the comparison group.

Controlling Variable: Researchers may control some variables in order to allow the research to focus on specific variables without being distorted by the impact of the excluded variables. A common way to control a variable is to be selective; e.g., gender is controlled by selecting as respondents only men or only women; age can be partially controlled by restricting a sample to one age range, rather than any age. See also Control group.

Convenience Sample: A non-random sample that is collected based on those units that are made easily available to the researchers. There are no quotas or qualifications necessary for sample selection in a convenience sample.

Convenience Sampling (also referred to as accidental sampling): A non-probability sampling strategy that uses the most easily accessible people (or objects) to participate in a study. Purposive/purposeful sampling: a non-probability sampling strategy in which the researcher selects participants who are considered to be typical of the wider population (sometimes referred to as judgmental sampling).

Convergent Validity: Understanding how constructs that should be related to one another actually are related to one another through measurement processes that prove the relationships.

Correlation: The extent to which two or more things are related ("co-related") to one another. The degree of association between two variables. A tendency for variation in one variable to be linked to variation in a second variable. This is usually expressed as a correlation coefficient.

Correlation Analysis: A statistical technique that helps in determining the strength of the relationship between variables.

Correlation Coefficient: A measure of the degree of relationship between two variables. A correlation coefficient lies between +1.0 (indicating a perfect positive relationship), through 0 (indicating no relationship between two variables) to -1.0 (a perfect negative relationship).

Covariation: A state that exists when two things – such as the price and the sales of a commodity – vary together. Measures of association are designed to capture the degree of covariation.

Credibility: With its connotations of 'truth', credibility can be compared with internal validity in positivist research. A study's credibility is said to be confirmed when the reader recognizes the situation described by a research study as closely related to their own experience (sometimes referred to as confirmability).

Criterion Variables: Variables in a study that the researchers are examining in an effort to understand the causes behind past performances as well as predicting future results can be called the dependent variable as well.

Criterion-related: validity requires the researcher to identify a relevant criterion or 'gold standard', which is itself reliable and valid, to provide an independent check of the new measure (i.e., to compare the results from a well-established and a new measuring instrument).

Cross Tabs Crossbreaks: Also called cross-tabulation and cross-partitions. A way of arranging data about categorical variables in a matrix so that relations can be more clearly seen. This is not to be confused with a factorial table, in which two or more variables are related to a third. While not all researchers make these distinctions in the terms, the concepts are quite distinct.

Cross Tabulation: A process used to analyze data that attempts to better understand the results of a survey by comparing the answers of one question to the way each respondent answered one or more questions on the rest of the survey. Cross-tab can generate statistical outputs from research tables.

Cross-sectional Study: Studies conducted at one point in time, a 'snapshot' of a social phenomenon – contrasted to longitudinal study.

Custom Marketing Research: Market research that is tailored to a specific client's needs.

Customer Relationship Management/Marketing (CRM): A method of identifying and creating a relationship with long-term customers through customer service techniques that track information about a given customer such as their activities and preferences. Customer feedback research is important intelligence for improved CRM.

Customer Satisfaction Research: Conducted research to better understand how satisfied customers are with particular products or services and the attributes of the product or service.

Data: A set of observations. Information collected by a researcher. (Data is the plural term; datum the singular). Data are often thought of as statistical or quantitative, but they may take many other forms as well, such as transcripts of interviews or videotapes of social interactions. Non-quantitative data such as transcripts or videotapes are often coded or translated into numbers to make them easier to analyze.

Database: A collection of data organized for rapid search and retrieval, usually by a computer; often a consolidation of many records previously stored separately.

Data Collection: The gathering of information (figures, words or responses) that describe some situation from which conclusions can be drawn. The gathering of information from administered questionnaires.

Data Entry: The organizing procedure that allows for the collection of data to be analyzed. The process involves recording, classifying, sorting, summarizing, calculating, disseminating and storing data.

Data Mining: Data mining is the ability to query large data sets. This requires advanced skills and is a promising solution.

Data Processing: Organization of data for the purpose of producing desired information; involves recording, classifying, sorting, summarizing, calculating, disseminating and storing data.

Data Set: A collection of related data items, such as answers given by respondents to all questions on a survey.

Data Warehouse: A data warehouse is a massive collection of essential business intelligence. The use of data warehouse is evolving to include operational and analytic data.

Deductive Reasoning: A logical process of developing specific predictions (hypotheses) from general principles. This type of reasoning moves from the general to the particular.

Delphi Technique: A long-term forecasting technique that allows for expert judgment without empirical data. There are three stages to this technique. First, experts are anonymously polled. Next, the results are distributed to the group of experts who are then individually polled again after seeing their colleague's opinions. The process is repeated until the group arrives at a general consensus about the issue at hand.

Demographics: Statistics that describe a population's objective or quantifiable characteristics. Examples of demographics include age, sex, birth and mortality rates, income, marital status, occupation, and household characteristics.

Dependability: Dependability of a study is evaluated if it meets the associated criterion of auditability. Auditability is achieved when a researcher provides a sufficiently clear account of the research process to allow others to follow the researcher's thinking and conclusions about the data and thus assess whether the findings are dependable.

Dependent Variable: A concept that's value changes as an independent variable changes. Statistics are used to explain the strength of the relationship between the two variables. Can also be called a criterion variable. For example, in a study to see if there is a relationship between students' drinking of alcoholic beverages and their grade point averages, the drinking behavior would be the presumed cause (independent variable); the grade point average would be the effect (dependent variable). In experimental research, the dependent variable is the variable presumed within the research hypothesis to depend on (be caused by) another variable (the independent variable); it is sometimes referred to as the outcome variable.

Depth Interview ("one-on-one"): Sessions in which free association and hidden sources of feelings are discussed, generally through a very loose, unstructured question guide, administered by a highly skilled interviewer. It attempts to uncover underlying motivations, prejudice, attitudes toward sensitive issues, etc.

Descriptive Function: Data that is collected to provide facts rather than causal or exploratory research.

Descriptive Statistics: Statistics that summarize a data set, e.g., mean, median, mode, standard deviation. Statistical methods used to describe or summarize data collected from a specific sample (e.g. mean, median, mode, range, standard deviation).

Design Control: A pre-experiment set-up designed to reduce or eliminate extraneous causal factors.

Dichotomous Questions: Questions that offer only two possible responses. An example would be yes or no question.

Directional Hypothesis (or One-tailed Hypothesis): A hypothesis that makes a specific prediction about the nature and direction of the relationship between the independent and dependent variables.

Discrete Variable: A quantitative variable that has a set amount of possibilities as opposed to continuous variables which have an infinite set. An example would be the number of individuals in a family.

Discriminant Analysis: A technique used to understand a set of independent variables and their ability to predict outcomes of dependent variables.

Discriminant Coefficient: The value that is placed in front of the independent variable and describes the level of affect that the variable carries.

Discriminant Score: A value that is assigned to an object which then determines which group the object will belong to.

Discriminant Validity: The idea that two constructs that are supposed to be different are in fact observed to be different.

Double Sampling: A sample that is pulled from an existing larger sample because of the inexpensive first sample. The sub-sample is then selected from the larger sample based on desired population characteristics.

Double-barrelled Questions: Questions in which two opinions are joined together.

Editing: A system of checking and verifying that questionnaires were properly completed and accurate to the respondent's best knowledge.

Emancipatory Research: Emancipatory research is conducted on and with people from marginalized groups/communities. It is led by a researcher or research team who is either an indigenous or external insider; is interpreted within intellectual frameworks of that group; and is conducted largely for the purpose of empowering members of that community and improving services for them. It also engages members of the community as co-constructors or validators of knowledge.

Error: In statistics, the difference between an observed score and a predicted or estimated score. Symbolized as e or E.

Ethnography: A research methodology associated with anthropology and sociology that systematically describes the culture of a group of people. The goal of ethnographic research is to understand the natives'/insiders' view of their own world (a broad ethnic view of the world).

Expected Value: A probability distribution's mean value. It represents that value that the sample is expected to take in the long run.

Experiment: A set of observations that are performed in an attempt to solve a question or problem.

Experimental Design: A contrived situation designed so as to permit the researcher to manipulate one or more independent variables whilst controlling all extraneous variables and measuring the resultant effect on a dependent variable.

Experimental Group: A group receiving some treatment in an experiment. Data collected about people in the experimental group are compared with data about people in a control group (who received no treatment) and/or another experimental group (who received a different treatment). In experimental research, the group of subjects who receive the experimental treatment or intervention under investigation.

Experimental Research: A research methodology used to establish cause-and-effect relationships between the independent and dependent variables by means of manipulation of variables, control and randomization. A true experiment involves the random allocation of participants to experimental and control groups, manipulation of the independent variable, and the introduction of a control group (for comparison purposes). Participants are assessed before and after the manipulation of the independent variable in order to assess its effect on the dependent variable (the outcome).

Exploratory Focus Groups: Qualitative research that brings concepts to a group of people so that they can address customer needs, concepts for new products or evaluate existing products.

Exploratory Research: The most basic level of research that is performed to clarify the exact problem at hand.

Exponential Smoothing: Simply data recorded by time intervals.

External Validity: The extent to which the findings of a study are relevant to subjects and settings beyond those in the study. Another term for generalizability.

Extraneous Variable: A variable that interferes with the relationship between the independent and dependent variables and which therefore needs to be controlled for in some way.

Face Validity: The extent to which a measuring instrument appears to others to be measuring what it claims to measure.

Factor: In analysis of variance, an independent variable, that is, a variable presumed to cause or influence another variable. In factor analysis, a cluster of related variables that are distinguishable components of a larger set of variables. A number by which another number is multiplied, as in the statement: real estate values increased by a factor of three, meaning they tripled.

Factor Analysis: A search performed by researchers through rating scales that allow another smaller set of factors or composite variables to emerge and can then identify underlying information.

Factor Loadings: The identified correlation taking place between the original variables and each factor score.

Feminist Research: Feminism is a conceptual tool for critiquing traditional sociological research with key concepts of empowerment of women, the equality of the research relationship and understanding the social constructions of gender. It can be understood in terms of values and epistemology more than techniques and methodology.

Focus Group Facility: A central location in which focus groups are held. Conference rooms are connected to observation rooms by a two-way mirror so that researchers can observe the respondent's words and actions. Facilities also offer services that might include focus group recruiting, food for participants, competitive product samples, and/or session videotaping.

Focus Group Interview: Interview in which the interviewer listens to a group of individuals, who belong to the appropriate target market, talk about an important marketing issue.

Focus Group Moderator: The trained professional that leads the focus group and is appointed by the client.

Focus Group: An interview conducted with a small group of people to explore their ideas on a particular topic. Are typically open ended and are used to gain a deeper understanding of respondents' attitudes and opinions. Typically involve between 6-10 people, and last for 1-2 hours. A key feature of group is that participants are able to interact with, and react to each other. In order to facilitate this group dynamic it is, therefore, important to ensure that participants do not know each other beforehand and that they are broadly 'compatible'.

Forced Itemised Test: Procedure in which a respondent indicates a response on a scale, even though he or she may have "no opinion" or "no knowledge" about the question.

Forecast: An estimate on future occurrences based on past performance data. Projections are often made about trends such as births, deaths, or migration or demographic characteristics as in population growth rates.

Frame Error: An inaccurate or incomplete sample frame that results in an error.

Frequency Distribution: A visual display of numerical values ranging from the lowest to the highest, showing the number of times (frequency) each value occurs.

Frequency: The numerical value assigned to how often an event occurs, sometimes within a given time period.

Fresh Participants: Recruits that are participating in a focus group for the first time or have not participated for several years.

F-Test: A statistical probability test measuring a calculated value's ability to occur due to chance.

Generalizability: The extent to which you can come to conclusions about one thing (often a population) based on information about another (often a sample). Gives an in-depth understanding of why people hold particular views, and how they make judgments, in a way that structured quantitative research cannot, but is not intended to be statistically reliable. Newer types of qualitative research attempt not just to understand but also to inform participants' views by actively supplying them with information which allows them to reach a more considered view.

Graphic Rating Scales: Graphic continuums anchored by two extremes presented to respondents for evaluation of a concept or object.

Hypothesis: A statement that predicts the relationship between variables (specifically the relationship between the independent and dependent variables). A hypothesis may be directional or non-directional.

Hypothesis: Test of Proportions: Test to determine whether the difference between proportions is greater than would be expected because of sampling error.

Independent Samples: Measurement of a variable in one population has no effect on the measurement of the variable in the other.

Independent Variable: The presumed cause in a study. Also a variable that can be used to predict the values of another variable. Compare dependent variable. Some authors use the term "independent variable" for experimental research only; for non-experimental research, they use predictor variable. The variable (or antecedent) that is assumed to cause or influence the dependent variable(s) or outcome. The independent variable is manipulated in experimental research to observe its effect on the dependent variable(s). It is sometimes referred to as the treatment variable.

Inductive Reasoning: A logical process of reasoning used to develop more general rules from specific observations; this type of reasoning moves from the specific to the more generalized.

Inferential Statistics: Statistics that allow a researcher to make inferences about whether relationships observed in a sample are likely to occur in the wider population from which that sample was drawn. Inferential statistics use logic and mathematical processes in order to test hypotheses relating to a specific population based on data gathered from a sample of the population of interest.

Informed Consent: The process of obtaining voluntary participation of individuals in research based on a full understanding of the possible benefits and risks. A person's voluntary agreement, based upon adequate knowledge and understanding of relevant information, to participate in research or to undergo a diagnostic therapeutic or preventive procedure.

Internal Secondary Data: Data available within the organisation, for example, accounting records, management decision support systems, and sales records.

Internal Validity: The extent to which the results of a study (usually an experiment) can be attributed to the treatments rather than a flaw in the research design; in other words, the degree to which one can draw valid conclusions about the causal effects of one variable on another.

Interrater Reliability (Interobserver Reliability): A measure of the consistency between the ratings/values assigned to an attribute that is being rated or observed; it is usually expressed as a percentage of agreement between two raters/observers or as a coefficient of agreement which may then be expressed as a probability. Usually employed by researchers using structured observation techniques.

Interval Data: Measurements that allow us to tell how far apart two or more objects are with respect to attributes and consequently to compare the difference between the numbers assigned. Because the interval data lack a natural or absolute origin, the absolute magnitude of the numbers cannot be compared.

Interval Estimates: Inferences regarding the probability that a population value will fall within a certain range.

Interval Scale: Ordinal scale with the additional property that the distance between observations is meaningful. An example would be the temperature.

Interval: Taking a given number of units equally selected over the full population of study. The nth number interval is derived by dividing the total number of units by the sample number desired.

Interview: A method of data collection involving an interviewer asking questions of another person (a respondent) either face-to-face or over the telephone.

Interviewer Error: Error that results from conscious or unconscious bias in the interviewer's interaction with the participant.

Itemised (Closed-ended) Questions: Format in which the respondent is provided with numbers and/or predetermined descriptions and is asked to select the one that best describes his or her feelings.

Itemised Rating Scaling: The respondent is provided with a scale having numbers and/or brief descriptions associated with each category and asked to select one of the limited number of categories, ordered in terms of scale position, that best describes the object under study.

Judgemental Data: Information generally based on perceptions or preference may give better indications of future patterns of consumption.

Judgemental Sampling: Studies in which respondents are selected because it is expected that they are representatives of the population of interest and/or meet the specific needs of the research study.

Jury of Expert Opinion: A method of forecasting based on combining the views of key executives.

Kolmogorov-Smirnov Test: This test determines if two data sets are significantly different. It answers the question if a sample originates from a population with a specific distribution.

Laboratory Experimental Environment: Research environment constructed solely for the experiment. The experiment has direct control over most, if not all, of the crucial factors that might possibly affect the experimental outcome.

Level of Significance: When using statistics, it is the probability that a Type I error will be made. A Type I error occurs when the relationship of two things is rejected when in all actuality it is true.

Lifestyle Research: Research conducted in order to explain behavior by means of consumer opinions, activities, hobbies, and attitudes. This analysis can be used along with psychographic research. (Studying responses to statements about one's own activities, interests, and opinions).

Lifestyle Selectivity: Consumer behaviors that can be attributed to a certain population segment's lifestyle. This includes interests, ownership, and hobbies.

Likert Scale: An attitude scale that measures the level to which the respondent "agrees" or "disagrees" with a given statement in regard to a particular product or service. The scale will give an odd number of choices with an equal amount of agreement/ disagreement choices on either side of a neutral option.

Literature Review: A literature review brings together individual reviews of papers, etc. It should weave together the individual reviews into an overview of the area. The aim is to convey an awareness of the current state of knowledge in the subject. It is commonly used to set the scene for introducing new research or a new perspective on the research.

Literature Search: A manual and/or electronic search of the literature to find out what research has been carried out in your area of enquiry.

Loaded Questions: Questions that suggest what the answer should be or indicate the researcher's position on the issue under study.

Loadings: Weightings that give the correlation of the attribute with respect to the dimension.

Logit Model: Binary model of regression analysis that utilizes an S-shaped curve. For each question, responses can only be one of two options, like yes or no; or zero or one.

Longitudinal Study: A study intended to describe a process occurring over time - multiple measurement points in time.

Mail Questionnaires: Surveys sent through the mail. Respondents complete the surveys and mail back to the research organization.

Mail Surveys: Data-collection method that involves sending out a fairly structured questionnaire to a sample of respondents.

Market Potential: Is measured by size of the market in dollars sales and the growth of the market.

Market Risk: Are markets characterized by instability of demand and uncertainty of supply can be very risky.

Market Scale: Potential and penetration are critical to achieving a large-scale operation both in terms of market share and sales volume.

Market Segmentation: Is the identification of a group of consumers who have needs or responses that are different from other consumers.

Marketing Research: An objective approach to finding solutions to problems in marketing. Involves qualitative and quantitative research and analysis of the findings to help marketers' best target and reach their audiences. The systematic gathering, recording, and analyzing of data about problems relating to the marketing of goods and services.

Marketing Strategy: A company's projected marketing campaign that identifies resources available as well as past and future marketing capabilities.

Markov Model: Process using matrices to find the probability of users in one brand category switching to a different brand the next time they buy in that category. Represents significant results and can now be measured by retail scanners.

Mean Square Error: Used in statistics when measuring total errors expected to be found in a sample estimate. It is calculated by taking the square root of the sum of the standard error squared and the bias squared.

Mean: An average found by summing all observations then dividing the sum by the number of observations.

Measure of Location: The specific location of a single quantity in a frequency distribution. For example, the mean is found in the middle of the frequency distribution.

Measurement Error: A difference between an expected measurement and the actual information that was measured.

Measurement Scale: Measurement of a phenomenon or property means assigning a number or category to represent it. The methods used to display and/or analyze numerical (quantitative) data will depend on the type of scale used to measure the variable(s). There are four scales of measurement: nominal, ordinal, interval or ratio. The data associated with each measurement scale are referred to as nominal data, ordinal data, interval data and ratio data respectively.

Measurement: Process of assigning numbers to objects to represent quantities of attributes.

Media Marketing Areas: Defines the television audiences thanks to sampling. Can be called ADI (Areas of Dominant Influence) or DMA (Designated Market Areas).

Median: A descriptive statistic used to measure central tendency. The median is the score/value that is exactly in the middle of a distribution (i.e. the value above which and below which 50% of the scores lie).

Meta-analysis: A statistical technique for combining and integrating the data derived from a number of experimental studies undertaken on a specific topic.

Methodology: The procedure used as a proven method that, when repeated, should yield the same result. Steps need to be recorded properly so that the procedure can be redone exactly.

Metric Scale: Metrics are determined by measurable variables that define progress. There are several categories of metrics, from weight measurements to sales measurements in a company. The intervals between metrics on a particular scale are significant ratios to be used when quantifying metrics.

Minimal Risk: The probability and magnitude of harm or discomfort anticipated in the research are not greater in and of themselves than those ordinarily encountered in daily life or during the performance of routine physical or psychological examinations or tests.

Mode: A descriptive statistic that is a measure of central tendency; it is the score/value that occurs most frequently in a distribution of scores.

Modeling: The formulation of mathematically-expressed variables to simulate a business decision environment. For example, a model could be formulated using demographics and a company's financial data to select new markets that have the same combination of factors that are present in currently successful markets.

Multicollinearity: Addressed when finding a linear relationship with multiple independent variables. This problem often occurs because of the difficulty in identifying and separating the independent variable that is influencing the dependent variable.

Multidimensional Scaling (MDS): Procedure to detect underlying dimensions that allow researchers to explain observed similarities or dissimilarities between investigated objects.

Multiple Choice Questions: Questions that offer more than two possible answer choices and require a respondent to choose from the listed options.

Multiple Regression Analysis: Statistical procedure identifying the relationship between two or more independent variables in an effort to identify patterns within the relationship.

Multiple Time-Series Design: A study that is conducted using a control group for a particular set of time (e.g., month), but is not continuously conducted, rather revisited within the span of the study's time set.

Multivariate Analysis: Any of several methods for examining multiple variables at the same time. Usage varies. (a) Stricter usage reserves the term for designs with two or more independent variables and two or more dependent variables. (b) More loosely, multivariate analysis applies to designs with more than one independent variable or more than one dependent variable or both. Whichever usage you prefer, either allows researchers to examine the relation between two variables while simultaneously controlling for the influence of other variables. Examples include path analysis, factor analysis, multiple regression analysis, MANOVA, LISREL, canonical correlations, and discriminant analysis.

Mutually Exclusive – orthogonal: Said of two events, conditions, or variables which cannot occur at the same time. For example, one cannot be both male and female, or both Protestant and Catholic. Thus, the categories male and female, or Catholic and Protestant are said to be mutually exclusive.

Narrative Data: Narrative or biographical approaches to research are primarily qualitative, and include gathering/using data in the form of diaries, stories and life histories.

Naturalistic Paradigm: This paradigm assumes that there are multiple interpretations of reality and that the goal of researchers working within this perspective is to understand how individuals construct their own reality within their social context.

Negative Correlation: A relationship between two variables where higher values on one variable tend to be associated with lower values on the second variable; sometimes referred to as an inverse relationship (e.g., age of non-vintage cars and their market value).

Nominal Data: Measurement in which the numbers assigned allow us to place an object in one and only one of a set of mutually exclusive and collectively exhaustive classes with no implied ordering.

Nominal Scale: The lowest level of measurement that involves assigning characteristics into categories which are mutually exclusive, but which lack any intrinsic order (e.g., classification by gender or by the color of a person's hair or eyes).

Non-comparative Scaling (Monadic Scaling): Scaling method whereby the respondent is asked to evaluate each object on a scale independently of the other objects being investigated.

Non-directional Hypothesis (or Two-tailed Hypothesis): A hypothesis that does not specify the nature and direction of the relationship between the independent and dependent variables.

Non-parametric Statistics: Statistical tests that can be used to analyze nominal or ordinal data; they involve fewer rigorous assumptions about the underlying distribution of variables.

Non-probability Samples: Form of sampling where there is no way of determining exactly what the chance is of selecting any particular element or sampling unit into the sample.

Non-random: Occurs when probability is not a good predictor of future results because some part of the experiment is weighted.

Non-response Bias: Resulting error identifying a systematic difference in those who do and do not respond to the measurement instrument.

Non-response Error: Error that occurs because not all of the respondents included in the sample respond; in other words, with non-response, the mean true value (on the variable of interest) of the sample respondents who do respond may be different from the entire sample's true mean value (on the variable of interest).

Non-sampling Error: Any errors or inaccuracies in a study not including those considered sampling errors. A few examples are leading by the interviewer and recording/data entry errors.

Non-significant Result: The result of a statistical test which indicates that the outcome of an experimental research study could have occurred through random variation (or chance) at a specified level of significance, rather than as a result of manipulation of the independent variable.

Normal Distribution: A bell-shaped distribution that is bisymmetric to the mean.

Null Hypothesis: A statement that there is no relationship between the independent and dependent variables and that any relationship observed is due to chance or fluctuations in sampling.

Observation Research: An experiment conducted without any direct interaction between the investigators and the respondents. Also known as a quasi-experiment.

Observation: A method of data collection in which data are gathered through visual observations.

Observational Methods: Observation of behaviour, directly or indirectly, by human or mechanical methods.

One-Group: Pre-test Post-test Design: A design developed before the experiment with measurements before and after the test to note the difference since no control group is used.

One-Shot Case Study: An experiment design developed before the study that only measures the post-test results and does not use a control group.

One-tailed Test: Used by a researcher when testing a directional (or one-tailed) hypothesis, this type of test of statistical significance uses only one tail of an underlying distribution of scores/values to determine significance.

One-way Frequency Table: A way of charting how often particular responses are used for each question on a survey.

Open-Ended Question: A survey question that allows the respondent an opportunity to write in the response that best answers the question for them. There are no options to choose from so the respondent must use.

Operational Definition: The procedures or operations used to observe or measure a specific concept. Operationalization is the process of translating specific research concepts into observable phenomena that are measurable.

Optical Character Reader (OCR): A computer program that is able to scan printed characters and translate those codes into electronic data.

Optical Scanner: A device that is able to read and electronically store data from questionnaires or barcodes.

Order Bias: Condition whereby brands receive different ratings depending on whether they were shown first, second, third, etc.

Ordinal Data: Measurement in which the response alternatives define an ordered sequence so that the choice listed first is less (greater) that the second, the second less (greater) than the third, and so forth. The numbers assigned do not reflect the magnitude of an attribute possessed by an object.

Ordinal Scale: These categories can be used to rank order a variable, but the intervals between categories are not equal or fixed (e.g. strongly agree, agree, neither agree nor disagree, disagree, strongly disagree; social class I professional, II semi-professional, IIIa non-manual, IIIb manual, IV semi-skilled, and V unskilled).

p Value: P is the symbol for the probability that is associated with the outcome of a test of the null hypothesis (i.e., it is the probability that an observed inferential statistic occurred through chance variation). If the p value is less than or equal to the stated significance level - often set at 5% ($p < 0.05$) or 1% ($p < 0.01$) - then the researcher concludes that the results are unlikely to have occurred by chance and are more likely to have occurred because of the manipulation of the independent variable; the results are said to be 'statistically significant'. If the p value is greater than the significance level, the researcher concludes that the results are likely to have occurred by chance variation, and the results are said to be 'non-significant'.

Paired Comparison Designs: Tests where a consumer directly compares two products.

Paired Comparison Scale: Scale that presents the respondent with two objects at a time and asks the respondent to select one of the two according to some criterion.

Paired Comparison: An evaluation of two products that are given values based on set criteria as means of comparing the two items.

Panel: A group of respondents that participate in multiple surveys over an extensive period of time. Respondents willing participate with the market research project in return for some compensation. Specialty panels can be created for specific samples (e.g., doctors, IT professionals, youth), or for specialist research and product testing. Traditionally, panels are used for a wider range of projects, including general and consumer research. There are massive panels and databases of people available for research.

Paradigm: Kuhn defines a paradigm in two ways: first as the entire constellation of beliefs, values and techniques shared by a scientific community; and secondly as the procedures used to solve specific problems and take theories to their logical conclusion. Kuhn also suggests that paradigms function as maps or guides, dictating the kinds of problem/issue which are important to address, the kinds of theories or explanations that are regarded as acceptable, and the kinds of procedure that are used to tackle particular problems.

Parameter: A characteristic of a population (e.g. the mean age of all nurses studying the MSc in Nursing by distance learning with the RCN Institute).

Parametric Statistics: A type of inferential statistic that involves the estimation of at least one parameter. Such tests require either interval or ratio data and involve a number of assumptions about the variables under investigation including the fact that the variable is normally distributed.

Part Worths: An amount determined by respondents regarding value or utility that is associated with product/service attributes at different levels.

Participant: A person that has agreed to be involved in a survey, focus group, or study. Can also be referred to as a subject, unit, experimental unit, unit of analysis, or respondent.

Pearson's Correlation Coefficient: Most commonly used method to determine the strength associated with a set of variables.

Perceptual Mapping: Mathematical Analysis of Perception and Preference (MAPP). A technique used to chart a consumer's perceptions and preferences regarding a particular product with a visual aid, like a graph or map.

Pilot Study: Where research is conducted in advance of the actual study to assess the logistics of the study (i.e., the sample, methodology, question wording etc.). The aim is to highlight any areas of weakness which can then be eradicated in the actual study.

Point Estimator: Computed numerical value that serves as an estimate of the true parameter before data is collected.

Population: A group of persons that one wishes to describe or about which one wishes to generalize. To generalize about a population, one often studies a sample that is meant to be representative of the population. Also called "universe." The entire set of persons that have at least one common characteristic of interest to the researcher. The sample is selected from the population.

Positive Correlation: A relationship between two variables where higher values on one variable tend to be associated with higher values on the second variable (e.g., physical activity level and pulse rate).

Positivism: This paradigm assumes that human behavior is determined by external stimuli and that it is possible to use the principles and methods traditionally employed by the natural scientist to observe and measure social phenomena.

Pre-Coding: This occurs before the interviewing process. Computer codes are created and added to the questionnaire in order to accelerate the data processing of the respondent's answers.

Predictive Research: Predictive research is concerned with identifying indicators of future behavior or demand in a population on the basis of the current behaviour and demands of a sample. Predictive techniques use a number of statistical approaches.

Predictive Validity: The accuracy of forecasting with a particular measurement scale whose success is monitored to determine whether it will be a good predictor in the future.

Predictor Variables: Factors that are considered in determining future success of a marketing campaign. Examples of these independent variables are demographics and attitudes of the target market.

Pre-experimental Design: A research design that is set and does not have control over extraneous factors.

Pre-test: An evaluation of a questionnaire prior to its distribution. The survey can be sent to a small sample to ensure that questions are comprehended correctly and that responses are clear.

Primary Data: Data that is gathered to solve a particular problem as opposed to secondary data which is previously gathered and would need to be located to solve a problem.

Primary Research: Research conducted in search of new data to solve a marketing information discrepancy.

Primary Sampling Units: The geographic units that will be covered by a survey.

Probability (or density) Function: Identifies the probabilities of each of the possible values to be achieved. Generally comes in the form of a table or an equation. It is also referred to as a probability distribution.

Probability of a Simple Event: The numerical value representing the likelihood of an event occurring. The value will be between one and zero, with one occurring every time and zero never occurring. The sum of all probabilities associated with a sample must equal one.

Probability Sampling (Random Sampling): This type of sampling results in every sampling unit in a finite population having a calculable and non-zero probability of being selected in the sample. This means that the chance of a unit being included in a sample can be calculated.

Probability Sampling Designs: Samples drawn in such a way that each member of the population has a known, non-zero chance of being selected.

Project Proposal: A written description of the key research design that defines the proposed study.

Projective Techniques: A class of techniques which presume that respondents cannot or will not communicate their feelings and beliefs directly; provides a structured question format in which respondents can respond indirectly by projecting their own feelings and beliefs into the situation while they interpret the behaviour of others.

Psychographics: The "why" of consumer research to attempt to explain why consumers behave the way that they do. Research is conducted by observing and analyzing personality traits and values. Very closely related to lifestyle research.

Purposive Sampling: This process is the selection of a particular sample on purpose. Popular with qualitative research, the variables to which the sample is drawn up are analytically and theoretically linked to the research questions.

Q-sort Scale: Rank order procedure in which objects are sorted into piles based on similarity with respect to some criterion.

Q-sorting: A ranking process using card sorts.

Qualitative Data: Information gathered in narrative (non-numeric) form (e.g., a transcript of an unstructured interview).

Qualitative Research Methods: Techniques involving relatively large numbers of respondents, which are designed to generate information that can be projected to the whole population.

Qualitative Research: When referring to variables, "qualitative" is another term for categorical or nominal. When speaking of kinds of research, "qualitative" refers to studies of subjects that are hard to quantify, such as art history. Qualitative research tends to be a residual category for almost any kind of non-quantitative research.

Qualitative Variable: A result that cannot be quantified but rather belongs to a category or classification. Marital status, sex, and occupation are examples.

Qualitative: Research conducted that cannot be quantified or analyzed quantitatively. Qualitative data requires subjective analysis as it is not collected empirically. Focus groups, interviews, and open-ended questions are all forms of qualitative research.

Quantitative Data: Information gathered in numeric form.

Quantitative Research: Research performed in search of empirical evaluations explaining consumer attitudes, behavior, and/or performance. Conducted to forecast numerical measurements of product acceptance and consumer purchase intents.

Quantitative Variable: Variables that already exist as numbers or variables that are continuous or discreet. Age, weight, and income are all examples.

Quartiles: The four quarters in an observation distribution that each identify 25% of the observations.

Quasi-experiment: A type of research design for conducting studies in field or real-life situations where the researcher may be able to manipulate some independent variables but cannot randomly assign subjects to control experimental groups. The procedures of quasi-experimentation were developed mainly in the context of evaluation research projects. For example, you cannot cut off someone's unemployment benefits to see how well he or she could get along without them or to see whether an alternative job-training program would be more effective for some unemployed persons. But you could try to find volunteers for the new program. You could compare the results for the volunteer group (experimental group) with those of people in the regular program (control group). The study is quasi-experimental because you were unable to assign subjects at random to treatment and control groups.

Query: A search function within a database designed to find the answer to a question.

Questionnaire: A group of carefully worded questions that, with consumer responses, would aid researchers in achieving necessary data to fulfill research objectives. Or A group of written questions to which subjects respond. Some restrict the use of the term "questionnaire" to written responses.

Quota Sampling: Design that involves selecting specific numbers of respondents who possess certain characteristics known, or presumed, to affect the subject of the research study.

Random Digit Dialing (RDD): A computer based form of telephone sampling that pulls telephone numbers at random whether they be listed or not listed to provide a representative survey sample.

Random Error: Unexpected errors that occur in a measuring process to skew the data in a way that could not be recreated.

Random Sampling Error: Error caused when the selected sample is an imperfect representation of the overall population; therefore, the true mean value for the particular sample of respondents (on the variable of interest) differs from the true mean value for the overall population (on the variable of interest).

Random Sampling: A process of selecting a sample whereby each member of the population has an equal chance of being included.

Random Variable: A dependent variable that is evaluated by an outcome when that outcome has an equal probability of occurrence. An example would be either the "heads" or "tails" of a coin toss, where the outcome becomes the random variable.

Randomization: Within an experiment, randomization is the process of choosing subjects at random to be part of all groups to include all characteristics in each group.

Randomized Controlled Trial (RCT): In a RCT, participants are randomly assigned either to an intervention group (e.g., a drug treatment) or to a control group (e.g., a placebo treatment). Both groups are followed up over a specified period of time and the effects of the intervention on specific outcomes (dependent variables) defined at the outset are analyzed (e.g., serum cholesterol levels, death rates, remission rates).

Range: A measure of variability indicating the difference between the highest and lowest values in a distribution of scores.

Rank-order Scale: Scale in which respondents are presented with several objects simultaneously and requested to "order" or "rank" them.

Ratio Data: Measurements that have the same properties as interval scales, but which also have a natural or absolute origin.

Ratio Scale: A response scale for a survey or questionnaire that categorizes responses ranking them from smallest to largest and has a consistent range between each of the category choices. This scale is for variables that have a definitive zero as in age, weight, and height. An example of a ratio scale would be, "What height group do you belong to," with options "[<5'] [5'-5'6"] [5'7"-6'] [6'<] and so on.

Ratio: A measurement that explains one number or object in relation to another number or object.

References: In the context of a research report, a reference is a formal system for drawing attention to a literature source, usually published, both in the report itself (for instance, when you want to identify the source of a quotation) and in the bibliography or reading list at the end of the report.

Regression Analysis: A statistical technique that compares a dependent variable to an independent variable(s) in order to identify a relationship between the two or more variables.

Regression Coefficients: Values associated with the strength of a relationship and how one variable effects another between independent and dependent variables.

Regression to the Mean: An observation throughout an experiment when the respondents tend to progressively move toward the mean average of the behavior.

Rejection Region: A set of values that land outside of an acceptable range of the t-statistic. This leads to rejecting the null hypothesis.

Related Samples: Multiple samples taken from the same sample group where each sample from a particular participant influences later samples taken from that same participant.

Reliability: Reliability is concerned with the consistency and dependability of a measuring instrument, i.e., it is an indication of the degree to which it gives the same answers over time, across similar groups and irrespective of who administers it. A reliable measuring instrument will always give the same result on different occasions assuming that what is being measured has not changed during the intervening period. The consistency or stability of a measure or test from one use to the next. When repeated measurements of the same thing give identical or very similar results, the measure is said to be reliable. A number of techniques can be used to ensure the reliability of a standardized measuring instrument such as an attitude questionnaire, personality test or pressure sore risk calculator. These include test-retest, split-half and alternate forms. There are also statistical tests that can be used to assess reliability such as Cronbach Alpha and the Spearmanrho correlation coefficient test.

Replicability/Replication: As the name suggests, replication is the process of repeating a study undertaken by someone else, in the sense of using the same methodology. Commonly the location and research subjects will be different, though sometimes studies return to the same group of subjects after a period of time has passed, e.g., with child development studies. A good research report always includes enough information on the methods used to enable someone else to carryout a replication.

Representative Sample: A representative sample is one which has been selected in such a way that, as far as can be ascertained, the main characteristics of the sample match those of the parent population; i.e., the population from which the sample has been drawn.

Research Design: An overall plan of action to be followed during an experiment to be sure that the objectives are met. Often, the specific procedures to solve problems are included in the research design.

Research Methodology: Different approaches to systematic inquiry developed within a particular paradigm with associated epistemological assumptions (e.g., experimental research, grounded theory, and ethno methodology). Specific procedures used to gather and analyze research data.

Research Methods: This is how the research is being conducted. The research method is found in the research report. This allows for research replication.

Research Process: Steps involved in carrying out the research.

Research Proposal: This describes the design, schedule and budget for conducting a research project.

Research Question: A clear statement in the form of a question of the specific issue that a researcher wishes to answer in order to address a research problem. A research problem is an issue that lends itself to systematic investigation through research.

Research Specifications: These are the design characteristics of the proposed research.

Respondent Fatigue: During a lengthy research project, respondents can lose interest sometimes providing invalid responses.

Respondent: This is the individual that provides data to be collected during the research process. Also referred to as a unit, unit of analysis, participant, experimental unit, or subject.

Response Bias: An error in given answers to an interviewer's questions due to misinterpretation by the participant, or the participant responding in such a way that they believe the interviewer wishes them to answer as opposed to their true feelings. Therefore, response bias can occur both deliberately and unintentionally.

Response Error: Error that occurs because respondents (who do respond) may give inaccurate answers, or a respondent's answers may be misrecorded.

Response Rate: The proportion of those originally drawn at random from the population who actually participate in a survey. This indicates whether the data collected accurately reflects the views of the population interviewed. Response rate can also assess whether weighting or other methods might improve the quality of the data.

Sample Distribution: A measurement of the responses given from a single sample organized by frequency.

Sample Population: The description of the characteristics that define a particular population from which a sample is taken.

Sample Size: Number of sample units to be included in the sample.

Sample Space: A set including all possible outcomes for a particular experiment.

Sample Two-stage Cluster Sampling: Design in which the clusters at the first stage are selected by SRS; at the second stage, the sampling units are selected probabilistically by SRS from each sample cluster so that with clusters of equal size the same fraction of sampling units is drawn from each sample cluster.

Sample: A group of subjects selected from a larger group in the hope that studying this smaller group (the sample) will reveal important things about the larger group.

Sampling Bias: Distortion that occurs when a sample is not representative of the population from which it was drawn.

Sampling Error: The fluctuation in the value of a statistic from different samples drawn from the same population.

Sampling Frame: An explicit list of individuals or households that are eligible for inclusion in the sample.

Sampling Interval: Computed by taking n/N together with r, the first chosen element to be included in the sample, determines which elements will be included in the sample.

Sampling Unit: Those units that qualify to be sampled and are available during the sampling process to be selected.

Sampling Variable: Variable that represents the characteristic of the population that we wish to estimate.

Sampling: Distribution of the Proportion: A normally distributed graph showing combined proportion frequencies from many samples within a single population.

Sampling: Distribution of the Sample Means: A normally distributed graph showing combined mean frequencies from many samples within a single population.

Sampling: Distribution of the Sample Statistic: A probability distribution displaying probabilities of all possible variables that might occur with repeated sampling.

Sampling: The process of selecting a sub-group of a population to represent the entire population. There are several different types of sampling, including:

Scale Transformation: Procedures for transforming data by one of a number of simple arithmetic operations to make comparisons across respondents and/or scale items.

Scale: A group of related measures of a variable. The items in a scale are arranged in some order of intensity or importance. A scale differs from an index in that the items in an index need not be in a particular order, and each item usually has the same weight or importance.

Scaled-Response Questions: Select answer choices that are offered to contain the intensity of the attitude of the participant toward the object being measured.

Secondary Data: Data that have been collected for another project and have already been published. Sources can be in-house or external.

Secondary Research: The analysis of research that had been collected at an earlier time (for reasons unrelated to the current project) that can be applied to a study in progress.

Segmentation: Separating the population into subsets by common attributes. Age, income, product preference are just a few attributes.

Selection Bias: A bias that is present when choosing between the test group and the control group due to logical differences in the units.

Selection Error: An error that occurs in sampling when the researcher is pursuing sampling procedures that are either improper or incomplete.

Selective Perception: The act of a listener or reader choosing to filter out or not pay attention to stimuli either consciously or unconsciously.

Selective Research: The process researchers go through to determine which, of many alternatives, they will choose to study.

Semantic Differential Scale: Semantic scale utilising bi-polar adjectives as end points.

Semantic Differential: A scale that compares competitors by recognizing how each competitor ranks with a pair of words or phrases. The score or average measurement determines the correlation between a word and the object being tested. Similar to Likert Scale.

Sentence Completion: Projective technique whereby respondents are asked to complete a number of incomplete sentences with the first word or phrase that comes to mind.

Significance Level: Established at the outset by a researcher when using statistical analysis to test a hypothesis (e.g., 0.05 level or 0.01 significance level). A significance level of 0.05 indicates the probability that an observed difference or relationship would be found by chance only 5 times out of every 100 (1 out of every 100 for a significance level of 0.01). It indicates the risk of the researcher making a Type I error (i.e., an error that occurs when a researcher rejects the null hypothesis when it is true and concludes that a statistically significant relationship/difference exists when it does not).

Significant Difference: In a statistical test, it must be proven that the results found are strong enough to prove that the hypothesis needs to be rejected or fails to be rejected. Variance in confidence levels change the strength of the difference needed to be substantial.

Simple One-stage Cluster Sampling: One-step design in which the first stage clusters all sampling units are selected by SRS, and within each selected cluster all sampling units are chosen.

Simple Random Sampling: Design guaranteeing that every sample of a given size as well as every individual in the target population has an equal chance of being selected.

Single-stage Cluster Sample: One step design where, once the sample of clusters is selected, every sampling unit within each of the selected clusters is included in the sample.

Skewed: A weighted distribution that is not symmetrical which results in having one tail longer than the other on a frequency curve. The skew is titled after the longest tail, for example, if the right side had the longest tail, it would be called skewed right.

Snowball Design: Sample formed by having each respondent, after being interviewed, identify others who belong to the target population of interest.

Snowball Samples: An additional convenience sample pulled from referrals that were given by current participants.

Snowball Sampling: A non-probability sampling strategy whereby referrals from earlier participants are used to gather the required number of participants.

Spearman Rank-order Correlation: A method of analysis for ordinal data and correlation relationships.

Split-half Technique: A method used to check measuring instruments where half of the data is computed and is then correlated against the other half of data. A correlation coefficient of 9 would ensure an acceptable level of reliability in measurement.

Split-halves: Scale items split in terms of odd and even-numbered Hems or randomly.

Standard Deviation: A measure of dispersion that is found mathematically by the positive square root of the average squared difference between the mean and the sample or population values.

Standard Error(s): Indication of the reliability of an estimate of a population parameter; it is computed by dividing the standard deviation of the sample estimate by the square root of the sample size.

Standard Normal Distribution: A distribution curve that is centered on the mean which is equal to zero and the standard deviation is one.

Stapel Scale: A scale ranging from -5 to +5 that asks respondents to choose how well a given word (characteristic) describes a product or service and whether that strength portrays a positive or negative image.

Statistic: An estimate of a parameter calculated from a set of data gathered from a sample.

Statistical Analysis: Most statistical analysis is based on the principle of gathering data from a sample of individuals and using those data to make inferences about the wider population from which the sample was drawn.

Statistical Control: An adjustment to an equation to prevent confounded variables from adjusting the dependent variable's value within each treatment condition.

Statistical Inference: A procedure using the laws of probability to infer the attributes of a population based on information gathered from a sample.

Statistical Significance: A term used to indicate whether the results of an analysis of data drawn from a sample are unlikely to have been cause by chanced at a specified level of probability (usually 0.05 or 0.01).

Statistical Test: Measures of significance applied to collected data using a probability sample. This determines if the null hypothesis might be rejected and there is a degree of reliable difference between the two data sets.

Statistics: Practice of collecting, organizing, describing, and analyzing data to draw conclusions from the data to apply to a cause.

Store Audits: Studies that monitor performance in the marketplace among dollar and unit sales/share, distribution/out of stock, inventory, price, promotional.

Stratified Random Sampling: A stratified random sample is one obtained by separating the population into non-overlapping groups, called strata and then selecting a simple random sample from each stratum. It is used either to increase precision or to boost sample numbers within some sectors of the population.

Stratified Sampling: Design that involves partitioning the entire population of elements into sub-population, called strata, and then selecting elements separately from each sub-population.

Structured Interview: The interviewer asks the respondents the same questions using an interview schedule – a formal instrument that specifies the precise wording and ordering of all the questions to be asked of each respondent.

Structured Observation: A research study in which the observer records what they are witnessing. Can be done by filling out a questionnaire form or counting the occurrences of a certain activity.

Subjects: A term most often used in positivist research to describe those who participate in research and provide the data.

Survey: A research design in which a sample of subjects is drawn from a population and studied (usually interviewed) to make inferences about the population. This design is often contrasted with the true experiment in which subjects are randomly assigned to conditions or treatments.

Survey Research: A method of research to collect participant responses on facts, opinions, and attitudes through questionnaires.

Syndicated Research Services: Market research suppliers who collect data on a regular basis with standardised procedures. The data are sold to different clients.

Systematic Sampling: A probability sampling strategy involving the selection of participants randomly drawn from a population at fixed intervals (e.g., every 20th name from a sampling frame).

Systematic Sources of Error: Denoted by X, component made up of stable characteristics that affect the observed scale score in the same way each time the test is administered.

Target Population: A population with specific characteristics that researchers are studying.

T-distribution: A frequency distribution used with small samples that does not peak as high as a normal distribution.

Telephone Surveys: Survey that involves phoning a sample of respondents drawn from an eligible population and asking them a series of questions.

Telescoping: Condition that occurs when a respondent either compresses time or remembers an event as occurring more recently than it actually occurred.

Test Markets: A system that allows the marketing manager to evaluate the proposed national marketing program in a smaller, less expensive situation with a view to determining whether the potential profit opportunity from rolling out the new product or line extension outweighs the potential risks.

Test-retest Reliability: Consistency in test results when using the same instrument under nearly the same conditions for each test.

Tests of Significance: A mathematical test to determine if the findings in an experiment were due to influences of one or multiple variables on a dependent variable or merely by chance.

Thematic Apperception Test (TAT): Projective technique presenting respondents with a series of pictures or cartoons in which consumers and products are the primary topic of attention.

Theme: A recurring issue that emerges during the analysis of qualitative data.

Theoretical Framework: The conceptual underpinning of a research study which may be based on theory or a specific conceptual model (in which case it may be referred to as the conceptual framework).

Theoretical Notes: Notes about the observer's interpretation of observed activities found in field notes.

Theoretical Sampling: The selection of individuals within a naturalistic research study, based on emerging findings as the study progresses to ensure that key issues are adequately represented.

Theory: In its most general sense a theory describes or explains something. Often it is the answer to 'what', 'when', 'how' or 'why' questions.

Third Person/Role Playing: Projective technique that represents respondents with a verbal or visual situation and asks them to relate the feelings and beliefs of a third person to the situation, rather than to directly express their own feelings and beliefs about the situation. This is one of a series of four texts on marketing and agribusiness prepared by an FAO project for use in universities and colleges teaching agricultural marketing, agri-business and business studies. This text, marketing research and information systems, reviews the role of marketing research and the techniques used to undertake market research, including questionnaire design and sampling and writing of a research report. The principal components of a marketing information system and the use of marketing research information in decision-making are discussed.

Top-down Approach: Process of breaking down clusters or, at the beginning, all respondents belong to one segment, and then respondents are partitioned into two segments, then three segments, and so on until each respondent occupies his or her own segment.

Tracking: System for measuring the key sales components of customer awareness and trail and repeat purchases.

Trade-off Procedure: Technique where the respondent is asked to consider two attributes at a time – to rank the various combinations of each pair of attribute descriptions from a most preferred to least preferred.

Transferability: Equivalent to external validity in positivist research (it may also be referred to as applicability). A study is said to be transferable if the findings 'fit' contexts beyond the immediate study situation. In order to transfer the findings elsewhere, readers need sufficient information to be able to assess the extent to which a specific research setting is similar to other settings.

Treatment: In experiments, a treatment is what researchers do to the subjects in the experimental group, but not to those in the control group. A treatment is thus an independent variable.

Triangle Designs: Tests where a respondent is given two samples of one product and one sample of another and asked to identify the one that differs.

Triangulation: This term is used in a research context to describe the use of a variety of data sources or methods to examine a specific phenomenon either simultaneously or sequentially in order to produce a more accurate account of the phenomenon under investigation.

Trustworthiness: A term used to describe whether naturalistic research has been conducted in such a way that it gives the reader confidence in the findings. It can be assessed using the following criteria:

T-test: A statistically hypothesis test that is based on a single mean when the sample size is not large enough to use the Z-test. 'Twice as' large as another measure on the same scale (e.g. degrees Centigrade).

Two-tail Hypothesis Test: Test used when the alternative hypothesis is non-directional – the region of rejection is in both tails of the distribution.

Type I Error (A Error): Rejecting a null hypothesis when it should not have been rejected because it is true.

Type II Error (B Error): Accepting a null hypothesis when it should have been rejected because it is false.

Unbiased Estimator: The mean of the sample distribution and estimate distribution are equal.

Unbiased Samples: This is a way of limiting the sampling error as a result of randomness only by deriving the samples from an unbiased source.

Unidimensional Scaling: This process measures only one single attribute of an object or respondent.

Univariate Data Set: A data set in which one measurement (variable) has been made on each respondent.

Univariate: Analysis studying the distribution of cases of one variable only, for example, studying the ages of welfare recipients but not considering their gender, ethnicity, and so on.

Universe: The set of all the units from which a sample is drawn. Also called the population.

Unstructured Interview: The researcher asks open-ended questions which give the respondent considerable freedom to talk freely on the topic and to influence the direction of the interview since there is no predetermined plan about the specific information to be gathered from those being interviewed.

Unstructured Observation: The researcher uses direct observation to record behaviors as they occur, with no preconceived ideas of what will be seen; there is no predetermined plan about what will be observed.

Unstructured Question: This is a question that does not provoke or influence the answer of the respondent in any way.

Validation: A survey integrity safeguard where the respondent is contacted to confirm their survey responses.

Validity: In research terms, validity refers to the accuracy and truth of the data and findings that are produced. It refers to the concepts that are being investigated; the people or objects that are being studied; the methods by which data are collected; and the findings that are produced – a term to describe a measurement instrument or test that measures what it is supposed to measure; the extent to which a measure is free of systematic error. For example, a bathroom scale provides a reliable measure cannot give a valid measure of height. There are several different types of validity.

Variable: An attribute or characteristics of a person or an object that takes on different values (i.e., that varies) within the population under investigation (e.g., age, weight, pulse rate). Any characteristic or attribute of persons, objects, or events that can take on different numerical values. Any factor which may be relevant to a research study. In a survey, for example, you may choose to analyze data by the age and gender of respondents. 'Age' and 'Gender' are variables. See also Standard Variables, Dependent/Independent variables, and Controlling variables.

Variance: Variance measures the dispersion of a variable about its mean. The formula for calculating variance is the sum of the difference between the observed value and the mean value divided by the sample size.

Word Association: Projective technique whereby respondents are presented with a list of words, one at a time, and asked to indicate what word comes immediately to mind.

Z-Test: A statistical test used in inference determining if the difference between a sample mean and the population mean is large enough to be statistically significant. Z-Test reliability requires knowing the population mean, population standard deviation and there must be a simple random sample.

BIBLIOGRAPHY

1. Aaker, Kumar Day A., (2003), *Marketing Research*, Eighth Edition, John Wiley, USA.
2. Association for Survey Computing: http://www.asc.org.uk/.
3. Beit-Hallahmi B. & Argyle, M. (1997), *The Psychology of Religious Behaviour, Belief and Experience*, London: Routledge.
4. Beri G.C., *Marketing Research*, Third Edition, Tata Mcgraw Hill, New Delhi.
5. Bynner, J. and Stribley, K.M. (eds.) (1978), *Social Research: Principles and Procedures*.
6. Carl Mc Daniel and Roger Gates, (2006), *Marketing Research Essentials*, Fifth Edition, Wiley, USA.
7. Castro, E. (2000), *HTML for the World Wide Web*, Peachpit Press.
8. Conover, W. J. (1998), *Practical Nonparametric Statistics*, New York: John Wiley & Sons, Inc.
9. Coombs, C.H. (1953), *Theory and Methods of Social Measurement*, in Research Methods in the Behavioral Sciences, eds.
10. Crawford, I.M. (1990), *Marketing Research Centre for Agricultural Marketing Training in Eastern and Southern Africa*, Harare, Zimbabwe.
11. David.Luck & Ronald S.Rubin (1997), *Marketing Research*, Seventh Edition, Prentice Hall of India, New Delhi.
12. De Vaus, D.A. (1990), *Surveys in Social Research*, Unwin Hyman.
13. Dillon W. R., Madden, T.S. and Firtle, N.H. (1994), *Marketing Research in a Marketing Environment*, 3rd edition, Irwin.
14. Dipak Kumar Bhattacharyya (2006), *Research Methodology*, Excel Books, New Delhi.
15. Donald R. Cooper and Pamela S. Schindler, (2007), *Business research methods*, 9th edition, Tata McGraw Hill Publishing Company Ltd., New Delhi.
16. Fichter, J.H. (1952), The profile of Catholics religious life, *American Journal of Sociology*.
17. Foddy, W. (1994), *Constructing Questions for Interviews and Questionnaires*, Cambridge University Press.
18. Fowler, F.J., (1993), Jr. *Survey Research Methods* (2nd ed.), Thousand Oaks, CA: Sage Publications, Inc.
19. Gallup, G.H. (1980), *Index to International Public Opinion*, Westport, CT: Greenwood Press.
20. Gerard, D. (1985), *Religious Attitudes and Values*. In M. Abrams, D. Gerard, and N. Timms (Eds), Values and Social Change in Britain. London: MacMillan.
21. Goel. B.S. (2000), *Marketing Research*, Pragati Prakashan, Meerut.
22. Gupta P.K. Questionnaire Design and Surveys Sampling: http://obelia.jde.aca.mmu.ac.uk/ resdesgn/arsham/opre330Surveys.htm.
23. Gupta S.C., and Kapoor. V.K., (1997), *Fundamentals of Mathematical Statistics*, Sultan Chand and Sons, Delhi, 9th Edition.
24. Gupta S.P. and Gupta M.P., (2001), *Business Statistics*, Sultan Chand & Sons, New Delhi.
25. Gupta, S.C., (2004), *Fundamentals of Statistics*, Himalayan Publishing House, New Delhi.
26. Harper W. Boyd, Jr., Ralph Westfall, Stanley F. Stasch, (1996), *Marketing Research Text and Cases*, Seventh Edition, Irwin Publications, USA.

27. Hettmansperger, T. P., and J. W. McKean. Robust (1998), *Nonparametric Statistical Methods.*

28. Hollander, M., and D. Wolfe (1999), *Nonparametric Statistical Methods,* New York: John Wiley & Sons, Inc.

29. Howell, DC. (1997), *Psychology for statistics.* Duxbury Press.

30. Kothari, C.R., *Research Methodology–Methods and Techniques,* Wiley Eastern Limited, New Delhi.

31. Krishnaswami O.R. and Ranganatham M., (2006), *Methodology of Research in Social Sciences,* Himalaya Publishing House, Mumbai.

32. Kumar, V., Aaker, D.A. and Day, G.S. (1999), *Essentials of Marketing Research,* New York: John Wiley & Sons, Inc.

33. LaPage, W.F. (1994). "Using Panels for Travel and Tourism Research," Ch. 40 in Ritchie and Goeldner; Zikmund, W.G. (1997), *Exploring Marketing Research,* 6th edition. Orlando: The Dryden Press.

34. Lapage, W.F., Ch. 40 in Ritchie and Goeldner; Kumar, V., Aaker, D.A. and Day, G.S. (1999), *Essentials of Marketing Research,* New York: John Wiley & Sons, Inc.

35. Levin, I. Richard and Rubin S. David (2000), *Statistics for Management,* P H I, New Delhi.

36. Longman/ Open University Press.

37. Mishra M.N, (2003), *Modern Marketing Research,* Himalaya Publishing House, Mumbai.

38. Moeller, G.H. & Shafer, E.L., (1994), Ch. 39 in Ritchie and Goeldner, and Taylor, R.E. & Judd, L.L. "Delphi Forecasting" in Witt, S.F. & Moutinho, L. *Tourism Marketing and Management Handbook.* London: Prentice Hall.

39. Murray R. Spiegel and Larry J. Stephens, (1999), *Statistics- Schaum's Outlines,* Third edition, McGraw-Hill International Editions.

40. Murthy SN, Bhojanna U (2008), *Business Research Methods,* 2nd Edition, Excel Books, New Delhi.

41. Naresh K. Malhotra, (2004), *Marketing Research,* Pearson Education, New Delhi.

42. Oppenheim, A.N. (1968), *Questionnaire Design and Attitude Measurement,* Heinemann.

43. Pamela L. Alreck, Robert B. Settle, (2004), *The Survey Research Handbook,* 3rd edition, McGraw Hill, New Delhi.

44. Parasuraman A., Dhruv Grewal and Krishnan R., (2005), *Marketing Research,* First Indian Adaptation, Biztantra, New Delhi.

45. Paul E. Green, Donald S. Tull, Gerald Albaum, (1996) *Research for Marketing Decisions,* Fifth Edition, Prentice Hall, New Delhi.

46. Payne, S.L. (1951), *The Art of Asking Questions.* Princeton, NJ: Princeton University Press.

47. Pestonjee D.M.(2003), *Second handbook of psychological and social instruments,* Concept Publishing Company, New Delhi.

48. Ramanuj Majumdar, (1996), *Marketing Research,* New Age International, New Delhi.

49. Randles, R.H., and D. Wolfe (1991), *Introduction to the Theory of Nonparametric Statistics,* Krieger Publishing.

50. Research Methods Knowledge Base http://trochim.human.cornell.edu/KB/contents.htm.

51. Richard Levin Statistics for Management Statsoft Electronic Textbook http://www.statsoft.com/textbook/ stathome.html

52. Ritchie, J.R.B., E.L., (Ch. 42 in Ritchie and Goeldner).

53. Sancheti, D.C., and Kapoor, V.K. , *Business Statistics,* New Delhi.

54. Schuman, H. and Presser, S. (1981), *Questions and Answers in Attitude Surveys: Experiments in Question Form, Wording, and Context,* New York: Academic Press.

55. Sharma D.D. (1997), *Marketing Research Principles, Applications & Cases,* Sultan Chand & Sons, New Delhi.

56. Sharp, J.A. and Howard, K. (1998) *The Management of a Student Research Project*, Gower.

57. Siegel, S., and Castellan, N.J. (1988). *Nonparametric Statistics for the Behavioral Sciences,* (2ndEd.). New York, NY: McGraw-Hill.

58. Source: Dilip Roy and Goutam Saha Changes in Women's Dress Preference: An In-depth study based on Life style and Age, *South Asian Journal of Management,* Vol.14, Issue No.2, April-June 2007.

59. Stewart, D.W. and Shamdasani, P.N. (1990), *Focus Groups: Theorgy and Practice.* Newbury Park: Sage Publications.

60. Sudman, S. and Bradburn, N. (1982), *Asking Questions: A Practical Guide to Questionnaire Design.* San Francisco, CA: Jossey-Bass Inc.

61. Suja R. Nair, *Marketing Research,* Himalaya Publishing House, Mumbai, 2003.

62. Sumathi S. and Saravanavel P., (2005), *Marketing Research & Consumer Behaviour*, Vikas Publications, New Delhi.

63. Summary of Survey Analysis Software: http://www.fas.harvard.edu/~stats/ survey-soft/survey-soft.html.

64. The World-Wide Web Virtual Library:Statistics http://www.stat.ufl.edu/vlib/ statistics.html.

65. Thurstone, L.L., (1927), *A Law of Comparative Judgment*, Psychological Review.

66. William M.K. Trochim, (2003), *Research Methods*, Biztantra, New Delhi.

67. Yeaman, P. A. (1987), *Prophetic Voices: Differences between Men and Women.* Review of Religious Research.

68. Zikmund, W.G. (1997), *Exploring Marketing Research,* 6th edition. Orlando: The Dryden Press.

References of MR books

69. Aaker, Kumar and Daj, *Marketing Research,* 7th edition, John Wiley, 2005.

70. *Business Research Methods,* Alan Bryman and Emma Bell, 2e/Oxford/2007.

71. Churchill, *Marketing Research: Methodological Foundations,* Cengage Learning, 2007.

72. David. J. Luck and Donald. S. Rubin, *Marketing Research*, 7th edition, PHI, 2007.

73. Donald, R. Cooper and Pamila, S. Schindler, *Marketing Research Concept & Cases*, TMH, 2006.

74. G. C. Beri, *Marketing Research*, TMH, 2008.

75. Naresh K. Malhotra, *Marketing Research – An Applied Orientation*, PHI, 2007.

76. Parasuraman, Dhruv Grewal and R. Krishnan, *Marketing Research,* Biztantra, 2007.

77. S. Shajahan, *Marketing Reasearch Concepts & Practices in India,* Macmillan, 2004.

78. Zikmund, *Essentials of Marketing Research*, Cengage Learning, 2007.

INDEX